A LITERATURE
OF SPORTS

A LITERATURE OF SPORTS

Tom Dodge
Mountain View College

D. C. HEATH AND COMPANY
Lexington, Massachusetts   Toronto

Cover photograph:
Scala / Editorial Photocolor Archives, Inc. Museo delle Terme, Rome.

Published simultaneously in Canada.

Printed in the United States of America.

International Standard Book Number: 0-669-02744-8

Library of Congress Catalog Card Number: 79-88128

ACKNOWLEDGMENTS

George Abbe. "The Passer" reprinted from *Collected Poems, 1932–1961* by George Abbe, William L. Bauhan, Publisher, 1961. Reprinted by permission of the publisher.

Betty Adcock. "The Sixth Day" reprinted by permission of Louisiana State University Press from *Walking Out* by Betty Adcock; copyright © 1975 by Betty Adcock.

Samuel Allen. "To Satch" reprinted by permission of the author.

Anacreon. "The Thracian Filly" from *A Generation of Leaves, Greek Lyrics of Love and Death* translated by Tom Dodge, Texas Portfolio Press © 1977. Reprinted with permission.

Jon Anderson. "The Parachutist" from *Death & Friends* by Jon Anderson. Copyright © 1970 by Jon Anderson. Reprinted by permission of the author.

Reginald Arkell. "A Public Nuisance" from *Playing the Game* by Reginald Arkell. Reprinted by permission of Barrie & Jenkins. Originally published by Herbert Jenkins Ltd.

Richard Armour. "Fish Story" from *Light Armour* by Richard Armour. Copyright © 1954 by Richard Armour. "Good Sportsmanship" from *Nights With Armour* by Richard Armour. Copyright © 1958 by Richard Armour. Both are used with permission of McGraw-Hill Book Company.

W. H. Auden. "Hunting Season" copyright © 1955 by W. H. Auden. Reprinted from *Collected Poems*, by W. H. Auden, by permission of Random House, Inc.

William D. Barney. "Nearly Everybody Loves Harvey Martin," "The Rasslers," "A Post Card Out of Panama," "Caught in the Pocket" used with permission of William D. Barney. Copyright © William D. Barney, 1979.

Donald Barthelme. "The Wound" from *Amateurs* by Donald Barthelme. Copyright © 1973, 1976 by Donald Barthelme. Reprinted with the permission of Farrar, Straus & Giroux, Inc. "The Wound" appeared originally in *The New Yorker*.

John Berryman. "The Ball Poem" from *Short Poems* by John Berryman. Copyright 1948 by John Berryman. Copyright renewed © 1976 by Kate Berryman. Reprinted with the permission of Farrar, Straus & Giroux, Inc.

John Betjeman. "Seaside Golf" and "A Subaltern's Love Song" from *John Betjeman's Collected Poems* by John Betjeman. Reprinted by permission of John Murray (Publishers) Ltd.

Morris Bishop. "Settling Some Old Football Scores" excerpted from the book *A Bowl of Bishop* by Morris Bishop. Copyright © 1954 by Morris Bishop. Originally published in *The New Yorker*. Reprinted by permission of The Dial Press.

Edmund Blunden. "Winter: East Anglia" from *Poems of Many Years* by Edmund Blunden. Reprinted by permission of A. D. Peters and Co., Ltd.

Philip Booth. "Elegy for a Diver" and "Fisherman" from *Letter from a Distant Land* by Philip Booth. Copyright © 1953, 1957 by Philip Booth. All rights reserved. Reprinted by permission of Viking Penguin Inc. "First Lesson" from *Margins* by Philip Booth. Copyright © 1957 by Philip Booth. All rights reserved. Reprinted by permission of Viking Penguin Inc.

Thomas Boslooper and Marcia Hayes. "The Feminine Physique," copyright © 1973 by Thomas Boslooper and Marcia Hayes, from the book *The Femininity Game*. Reprinted with permission of Stein and Day Publishers.

Milton Bracker. "Where, O Where?" © 1962 by The New York Times Company. Reprinted by permission.

Gwendolyn Brooks. "Old Tennis Player" from *Selected Poems* by Gwendolyn Brooks. Copyright © 1963 by Gwendolyn Brooks Blakely. Reprinted by permission of Harper & Row, Publishers, Inc.

John Bruce. "The Pike" by John Bruce is reprinted by permission of the author.

William Cullen Bryant. "The Hunter of the Prairies" from *The Poetical Works of William Cullen Bryant*, Parke Godwin, ed., (1883). New York: Russell & Russell, 1967.

Callimachus. "The One Who Runs Away" from *A Generation of Leaves, Greek Lyrics of Love and Death* translated by Tom Dodge, Texas Portfolio Press © 1977. Reprinted with permission.

Fred Chappell. "Spitballer" from *The World Between the Eyes* by Fred Chappell; copyright © 1971 by Fred Chappell. Reprinted by permission of Louisiana State University Press.

John Ciardi. "Polo Match" from *Person to Person* by John Ciardi. Copyright 1964 by Rutgers, The State University. Reprinted by permission of the author.

Tom Clark. "Baseball" © 1978 by Tom Clark. "Baseball and Classicism," "The Ty Cobb Story," "To Bert Campaneris," "And You Are There," "The X of the Unknown" all © 1979 by Tom Clark and used with his permission.

Richard Connell. "The Most Dangerous

Game" by Richard Connell, copyright, 1924, by Richard Connell. Copyright renewed, 1952, by Louis Fox Connell. Reprinted by permission of Brandt & Brandt Literary Agents, Inc.

J. V. Cunningham. "The Chase" reprinted from *The Collected Poems and Epigrams of J. V. Cunningham*, © 1971 by J. V. Cunningham. Reprinted by permission of The Swallow Press, Chicago.

Babette Deutsch. "Morning Workout" from *New Poems by American Poets*, edited by Rolfe Humphries; copyright 1957 by Ballantine Books. "A Bull" from *The Collected Poems of Babette Deutsch;* copyright © 1969 by Babette Deutsch. Both selections used by permission of the author.

R. P. Dexter. "Shadow Dirge" reprinted by permission of the author.

James Dickey. "The Lifeguard," "Listening to the Foxhounds," "The Summons," "Winter Trout," "For the Last Wolverine," "The Bee" copyright © 1960, 1961, 1964, 1966 by James Dickey. Reprinted from *Poems 1957–1967* by permission of Wesleyan University Press. "The Lifeguard" and "Listening to the Foxhounds" first appeared in *The New Yorker*. "In the Pocket." copyright © 1970 by James Dickey, and "Looking for the Buckhead Boys," copyright © 1967 by The Atlantic Monthly Co., both from *The Eye-Beaters, Blood, Victory, Madness, Buckhead and Mercy* by James Dickey. Reprinted by permission of Doubleday & Company, Inc. "For the Death of Vince Lombardi" by James Dickey, from *Esquire* (September, 1971). Reprinted by permission of *Esquire* magazine. Copyright © 1971 Esquire, Inc.

Conrad Diekmann. "Winter Trees" reprinted by permission from *Sports Illustrated*, January 5, 1959; © 1959 Time Inc.

Alan Dugan. "On Hurricane Jackson" from *Poems* by Alan Dugan. Copyright © 1961 by Yale University Press, New Haven, Conn. Reprinted by permission of the author.

Stephen Dunn. "Day and Night Handball" reprinted by permission of The University of Massachusetts Press from *Looking for Holes in the Ceiling* (1974) by Stephen Dunn; "Day and Night Handball" copyright © 1973 by Three Rivers Press.

Richard Eberhart. "Spring Mountain Climb" and "Ball Game" from *Collected Poems 1930–1976* by Richard Eberhart. Copyright © Richard Eberhart 1976. Reprinted by permission of Oxford University Press, Inc. and Chatto & Windus Ltd.

Edward Field. "The Sleeper" from *Stand Up Friend With Me* by Edward Field. Copyright © 1963 by Edward Field. Reprinted by permission of Grove Press, Inc.

R. A. D. Ford. "Revenge of the Hunted" by R. A. D. Ford from *Modern Canadian Verse*, A. J. M. Smith, ed. Reprinted by permission of R. A. D. Ford.

Eldon Ray Fox. "The Bumper Sticker on His Pickup Said, 'I'm a Lover, I'm a Fighter, I'm a Wild Bull Rider,'" reprinted by permission of the author.

Robert Francis. "The Base Stealer," "Swimmer," "Catch," "Pitcher," "High Diver," "Two Wrestlers" reprinted from *The Orb Weaver* by permission of Wesleyan University Press. Copyright © 1948, 1950, 1953, 1959 by Robert Francis. "Watching Gymnasts," "Diver," "Skier," "That Dark Other Mountain" reprinted by permission of Robert Francis and The University of Massachusetts Press from *Collected Poems 1936–1976*. Copyright 1936, 1964, 1961, 1959, 1944, 1972 by Robert Francis. "Skier" originally appeared in *Transatlantic Review*.

Robert Frost. "The Rabbit-Hunter" from *The Poetry of Robert Frost* edited by Edward Connery Lathem. Copyright 1942 by Robert Frost. Copyright © 1969 by Holt, Rinehart and Winston. Copyright © 1970 by Lesley Frost Ballantine. Reprinted by permission of Holt, Rinehart and Winston, Publishers.

Walker Gibson. "Athletes" and "Billiards" from *The Reckless Spenders* by Walker Gibson, © 1954 by Walker Gibson. Reprinted by permission of Indiana University Press.

Gary Gildner. "First Practice" reprinted from *First Practice* by Gary Gildner by permission of the University of Pittsburgh Press. Copyright © 1969 by the University of Pittsburgh Press.

Louise Glück. "The Racer's Widow" reprinted by permission; © 1967 by Louise Glück. Originally appeared in *The New Yorker*.

Paul Goodman. "Don Larsen's Perfect Game" copyright © 1967 by Paul Goodman. "Surfers at Santa Cruz" copyright © 1966 by Paul Goodman. Both reprinted from *Collected Poems*, by Paul Goodman, edited by Taylor Stoehr, by permission of Random House, Inc.

Peter S. Greenberg. "Wild in the Stands" from *New Times*, November 11, 1977. Reprinted by permission of *New Times*.

Daniel Halpern. "The Hunt" from *Travelling on Credit* by Daniel Halpern. Copyright © 1970 by Daniel Halpern. All rights reserved. Reprinted by permission of Viking Penguin Inc.

St. John Emile Clavering Hankin. "De Gustibus" reprinted courtesy of *Punch*.

William Harrison. From *Roller Ball Murder* (1974) by William Harrison: "Roller Ball Murder" and "Nirvana, Götterdämmerung and the Shot Put," both copyright © 1973 by William Harrison. Reprinted by permission of William Morrow & Company.

Robert Hayden. "The Diver" is reprinted from *Angle of Ascent, New and Selected Poems,* by Robert Hayden, with the permission of Liveright Publishing Corporation. Copyright © 1975, 1972, 1970, 1966 by Robert Hayden.

Ernest Hemingway. "My Old Man" reprinted by permission of Charles Scribner's Sons from *In Our Time* by Ernest Hemingway, copyright 1925 by Charles Scribner's Sons.

William Heyen. "The Stadium" from *Depth of Field* by William Heyen. Copyright © 1970 by William Heyen. Reprinted by permission of Louisiana State University Press.

David Hilton. "The Poet Tries to Turn in His Jock" reprinted by permission of the author.

Paul Hoch. "Coliseums and Gladiators" from *Rip Off the Big Game* by Paul Hoch. Copyright © 1972 by Paul Hoch. Reprinted by permission of Doubleday & Company, Inc.

Jerome Holtzman. "Jimmy Cannon" from *No Cheering in the Press Box* recorded and edited by Jerome Holtzman. Copyright © 1973, 1974 by Jerome Holtzman. Reprinted by permission of Holt, Rinehart and Winston, Publishers.

Homer. Excerpts from *The Iliad of Homer* and *The Odyssey of Homer,* translated by Ennis Rees. Copyright © 1963 by Ennis Rees, copyright © 1977 by The Bobbs-Merrill Co., Inc. Reprinted by permission of the publisher.

A. E. Housman. "Is my team ploughing," "To an Athlete Dying Young," "Twice a week the winter thorough" from "A Shropshire Lad" — Authorised Edition — from *The Collected Poems of A. E. Housman.* Copyright 1939, 1940, © 1965 by Holt, Rinehart and Winston. Copyright © 1967, 1968 by Robert E. Symons. Reprinted by permission of Holt, Rinehart and Winston, Publishers, The Society of Authors as the literary representative of the Estate of A. E. Housman, and Jonathan Cape Ltd., publishers of A. E. Housman's *Collected Poems.*

Barbara Howes. "Out Fishing," "Landscape, Deer Season," "In Autumn," © 1959, 1966 by Barbara Howes. Reprinted from *A Private Signal: Poems New and Selected,* by permission of Wesleyan University Press.

Rolfe Humphries. "Polo Grounds" from *Collected Poems of Rolfe Humphries.* Copyright © 1956 by Indiana University Press. Reprinted by permission of the publisher. Originally appeared in *The New Yorker.*

Randall Jarrell. "Say Goodbye to Big Daddy" from *The Complete Poems* by Randall Jarrell. Copyright © 1966, 1969 by Mrs. Randall Jarrell. Reprinted with the permission of Farrar, Straus & Giroux, Inc.

Don Johnson. "Ripper Collins' Legacy" reprinted by permission of the author.

Nancy Jones. "Running Blind" from *Swallowing the Poison* (Summer, 1978), I:1. Reprinted by permission of the author.

Donald Justice. "Here in Katmandu" from *The Summer Anniversaries* by Donald Justice. Copyright © 1956 by Donald Justice. Originally appeared in *Poetry.* Reprinted by permission of Wesleyan University Press.

Maxine Kumin. "400-Meter Freestyle" reprinted by permission of Curtis Brown, Ltd. Copyright © 1961 by Maxine Kumin. "Morning Swim" from *The Privilege* by Maxine Kumin. Copyright © 1962 by Maxine W. Kumin. Reprinted by permission of Harper & Row, Publishers, Inc.

Mabel M. Kuykendall. "The Baseball Pitcher" reprinted by permission of the author.

Ring Lardner. "Champion" reprinted by permission of Charles Scribner's Sons from *Round Up* by Ring Lardner, copyright 1929 by Charles Scribner's Sons. "A Caddy's Diary" reprinted by permission of Charles Scribner's Sons from *How To Write Short Stories* by Ring Lardner. Copyright 1924 by Charles Scribner's Sons.

Richmond Lattimore. "Sky Diving" and "Game Resumed" reprinted from *Poems From Three Decades* by Richmond Lattimore. Reprinted by permission of the author. "Game Resumed" originally appeared in *The New Yorker.*

Laurence Lieberman. "My Father Dreams of Baseball" reprinted with permission of Macmillan Publishing Co., Inc. from *The Unblinding* by Laurence Lieberman. Copyright © 1963, 1968 by Laurence Lieberman. Originally appeared in *The Atlantic Monthly.*

Lou Lipsitz. "To a Fighter Killed in the Ring" from *Cold Water* by Lou Lipsitz. Copyright © 1963 by Lou Lipsitz. Reprinted by permission of Wesleyan University Press.

Robert Lipsyte. Excerpts copyright © 1975 by Robert Lipsyte. Reprinted by permission of TIMES BOOKS, a division of Quadrangle/The New York Times Book Co., Inc. from *SportsWorld* by Robert Lipsyte.

Jack London. "A Piece of Steak" and "The White Hope" reprinted by permission of The Estate of Irving Shepard.

John Masefield. "Partridges" reprinted with permission of Macmillan Publishing Co., Inc. from *Poems* by John Masefield. Copyright 1936 by John Masefield, renewed 1964 by John Masefield.

David McCord. "The Sportsman" from *The*

Old Bateau and Other Poems by David McCord, by permission of Little, Brown and Co. Copyright 1941, 1950, 1951, 1952, 1953 by David McCord.

Roger McGough. "40——Love" from *After the Merrymaking* by Roger McGough. Copyright © 1971 by Roger McGough. Reprinted by permission of Hope Leresche & Sayle.

J. A. R. McKellar. "Football Field: Evening" reprinted from *Collected Poems of J. A. R. McKellar* by permission of Angus & Roberson Publishers.

Larry McMurtry. "It's Always We Rambled: An Essay on Rodeo," copyright © 1972, 1974 by Larry McMurtry. First published in *New York* and reprinted by permission of Larry McMurtry.

Peter Meinke. "Byron vs. DiMaggio" from *The Night Train and the Golden Bird,* copyright © 1977 by Peter Meinke; "To an Athlete Turned Poet" reprinted by permission of the author.

Eve Merriam. "Cheers" copyright © 1964 by Eve Merriam from *It Doesn't Always Have to Rhyme.* Used by permission of Atheneum Publishers.

Edna St. Vincent Millay. "Huntsman, What Quarry?" from *Collected Poems,* Harper & Row. Copyright 1939, 1967 by Edna St. Vincent Millay and Norma Millay Ellis.

Marianne Moore. "Baseball and Writing" from *The Complete Poems of Marianne Moore.* Copyright © 1961 by Marianne Moore. Originally appeared in *The New Yorker.* All rights reserved. Reprinted by permission of Viking Penguin Inc.

W. R. Moses. "Little-League Baseball Fan" from *Identities* by W. R. Moses. Copyright © 1962 by W. R. Moses. Reprinted by permission of Wesleyan University Press.

Michael Murphy. "Golf's Hidden But Accessible Meaning" from *Golf in the Kingdom* by Michael Murphy. Copyright © 1972 by Michael Murphy. All rights reserved. Reprinted by permission of Viking Penguin Inc.

Ogden Nash. "Confessions of a Born Spectator" from *The Face is Familiar* by Ogden Nash. Copyright 1937 by Ogden Nash. Originally appeared in *The New Yorker.* "Who Taught Caddies to Count? or A Burnt Golfer Fears the Child" copyright 1947 by Ogden Nash, and "The Hunter" copyright 1949 by Ogden Nash both from *Verses from 1929 On and Versus* by Ogden Nash. All selections reprinted by permission of Little, Brown and Co.

Bink Noll. "The Picador Bit" from *The Center of the Circle,* © 1962 by Bink Noll. Reprinted by permission of Harcourt Brace Jovanovich, Inc.

Elder Olson. "Ice-Skaters" from *Collected Poems* by Elder Olson, University of Chicago Press. Copyright © 1963 by the University of Chicago. Reprinted by permission of Elder Olson. Originally appeared in *Poetry.*

Ovid. "Atalanta" from *Metamorphoses,* translated by Rolfe Humphries, © 1955 by Indiana University Press. Reprinted by permission. "Entellus" reprinted by permission of Charles Scribner's Sons from *The Aeneid of Virgil,* translated by Rolfe Humphries. Copyright 1951 Charles Scribner's Sons.

Kenneth Patchen. "The Origin of Baseball" from *Collected Poems* by Kenneth Patchen. Copyright 1942 by New Directions Publishing Corporation. Reprinted by permission of New Directions.

Donald Petersen. "The Ballad of Dead Yankees" from *The Spectral Boy* by Donald Petersen. Copyright © 1958 by Donald Petersen. Reprinted by permission of Wesleyan University Press.

Paul Petrie. "The Old Pro's Lament" from *Under the Hill of Night* by Paul Petrie. Copyright © 1969 by Vanderbilt University Press, Nashville, Tennessee. Originally appeared in *The New Yorker.*

Ezra Pound. "For E. McC." from *Personae* by Ezra Pound. Copyright 1926 by Erza Pound. Reprinted by permission of New Directions.

Max Rafferty. "Interscholastic Athletics: The Gathering Storm" reprinted by permission of Max Rafferty.

Mary Renault. "The Athenian Runner" from *The Last of the Wine* by Mary Renault. Copyright © 1956 by Mary Renault. Reprinted by permission of Pantheon Books, a Division of Random House, Inc., and Curtis Brown Ltd.

Adrienne Rich. "Phantasia for Elvira Shatayev" is reprinted from *The Dream of a Common Language,* Poems, 1974–1977, by Adrienne Rich, by permission of W. W. Norton & Company, Inc. Copyright © 1978 by W. W. Norton & Company, Inc.

Edwin Arlington Robinson. "A Mighty Runner" reprinted with permission of Macmillan Publishing Co., Inc. from *Collected Poems* by Edwin Arlington Robinson. Copyright 1915 by Edwin Arlington Robinson, renewed 1943 by Ruth Nivison.

Alan Ross. "Stanley Matthews" from *Poems 1942–67* by Alan Ross. Reprinted by permission of Eyre & Spottiswoode (Publishers) Ltd.

Damon Runyon. "Undertaker Song" and "Bred for Battle," © King Features Syndicate, Inc. 1964.

Irwin Shaw. "The Eighty-Yard Run" reprinted by permission of the author and the author's agent, Irving Paul Lazar, Literary Agent.

Wilfrid Sheed. "Muhammad Ali — King of the Picture Gods" from *Muhammad Ali* by Wilfrid Sheed. Copyright © 1975 by Wilfrid Sheed and Alskog, Inc. Reprinted by permission of Alskog, Inc.

Alan Sillitoe. "The Match" and "The Loneliness of the Long-Distance Runner" from *The Loneliness of the Long-Distance Runner*, by Alan Sillitoe. Copyright © 1959 by Alan Sillitoe. Reprinted by permission of Alfred A. Knopf, Inc.

Dave Smith. "Night Fishing for Blues" reprinted from *Shenandoah: The Washington and Lee University Review* with the permission of the Editor. Copyright © 1975 by Washington and Lee University. "Running Back" reprinted by permission of *Quarterly West*. Copyright © 1978 by Dave Smith. "The Roundhouse Voices" from *Goshawk, Antelope* (University of Illinois Press). Reprinted by permission; © 1979 by Dave Smith. Originally appeared in *The New Yorker*. "Blues For Benny Kid Paret" reprinted from *Cumberland Station* (University of Illinois Press). Reprinted by permission; © 1977 by Dave Smith.

Jon Stallworthy. "First Blood" from *Out of Bounds* by Jon Stallworthy, © Oxford University Press 1963. Reprinted by permission of Oxford University Press.

Adrien Stoutenburg. "Sky Diver" from *Short History of the Fur Trade* by Adrien Stoutenburg. Copyright © 1968 by Adrien Stoutenburg. Reprinted by permission of Houghton Mifflin Company.

Dabney Stuart. "Ties" © 1966 by Dabney Stuart, "The Fisherman" © 1969 by Dabney Stuart; both are reprinted by permission of the author.

Al Stump. "Fight to Live" reprinted by permission of Al Stump. Originally appeared in *True*.

May Swenson. "Death Invited" copyright © 1962 by May Swenson, "Bronco Busting, Event #1" copyright © 1976 by May Swenson, "Watching the Jets Lose to Buffalo at Shea" all reprinted from *New & Selected Things Taking Place* by May Swenson, by permission of Little, Brown and Co. in association with the Atlantic Monthly Press. "Bronco Busting, Event #1" originally appeared in *The Atlantic*.

R. S. Thomas. "Alpine" from *Tares*. Reprinted by permission of Granada Publishing Limited.

Francis Thompson. "At Lord's" reprinted by permission of The Bodley Head Publishers.

James Thurber. "You Could Look It Up," copyright 1935 by James Thurber. Copyright © 1973 by Helen W. Thurber and Rosemary Thurber Sauers. From *The Middle-Aged Man on the Flying Trapeze*, published by Harper & Row. Originally printed in *The Saturday Evening Post*.

Dennis Trudell. "The Jump Shooter" copyright © 1967 by Dennis Trudell. Originally appeared in *The Fiddlehead*. Reprinted by permission of the author.

John R. Tunis. "The Great Sports Myth" from *$port$, Heroics and Hysterics* by John R. Tunis. Copyright 1928 by John R. Tunis.

John Updike. "Ex-Basketball Player" copyright © 1957 by John Updike. Originally appeared in *The New Yorker*. "Tao in the Yankee Stadium Bleachers" copyright © 1956 by John Updike. Originally appeared in *The New Yorker*. "Superman" copyright © 1955 by John Updike. All selections reprinted from *The Carpentered Hen and Other Tame Creatures* by John Updike, and reprinted by permission of Harper & Row, Publishers, Inc. "Golfers" copyright © 1975 by John Updike. Reprinted from *Tossing and Turning,* by John Updike, by permission of Alfred A. Knopf, Inc.

Stephen Vincent. "Basketball" reprinted from *White Lights & Whale Hearts,* The Crossing Press, Trumansberg, New York, with the consent of the author and publisher. Copyright © 1971 by Stephen Vincent.

Andrei Voznesensky. "Soccer" from *Selected Poems of Andrei Voznesensky* reprinted by permission of Grove Press, Inc. Copyright © 1964 by Grove Press, Inc.

Robert Wallace. "The Double Play" © 1960 by Robert Wallace. "On the College Archery Range" and "After the Swimmer" © 1968 by Robert Wallace. "A Snapshot for Miss Bricka . . ." © 1961 by Robert Wallace. "Driving By" and "Swimmer in the Rain" © 1974 by Robert Wallace; both reprinted from *Swimmer in the Rain* (1979) by permission of Carnegie-Mellon University Press.

Robert Penn Warren. "Skiers" copyright © 1968 by Robert Penn Warren. "He Was Formidable" copyright © 1960 by Robert Penn Warren. Both are reprinted from *Selected Poems 1923–1975,* by Robert Penn Warren, by permission of Random House, Inc.

Neil Weiss. "The Aging Athlete" from *Changes of Garments* by Neil Weiss, © 1956 by Indiana University Press. Reprinted by permission.

Paul Weiss. "Women Athletes" from *Sport: A Philosophic Inquiry* by Paul Weiss. Copyright © 1969 by Southern Illinois University Press. Reprinted by permission of Southern Illinois University Press.

E. B. White. "The Decline of Sport" from *The Second Tree from the Corner* by E. B.

White. Copyright 1947 by E. B. White. Originally appeared in *The New Yorker*.

John Williams. "The Skaters" copyright 1963 by John Williams. Reprinted by permission of the author.

William Carlos Williams. "The Yachts" and "At the Ball Game" from *Collected Earlier Poems* by William Carlos Williams. Copyright 1938 by New Directions Publishing Corporation. Reprinted by permission of New Directions.

P. G. Wodehouse. "The Clicking of Cuthbert" reprinted by permission of the author and the author's agents, Scott Meredith Literary Agency, Inc., 845 Third Avenue, New York, New York 10022.

James Wright. "A Mad Fight Song for William S. Carpenter, 1966" from *Collected Poems* by James Wright. Copyright © 1971 by James Wright. Reprinted by permission of Wesleyan University Press.

Judith Wright. "Sports Field" reprinted from *Judith Wright: Collected Poems* 1942–1970 by permission of Angus & Robertson Publishers.

William Butler Yeats. "The Fisherman" reprinted with permission of Macmillan Publishing Co., Inc., M. B. Yeats, and Miss Anne Yeats from *Collected Poems* by William Butler Yeats. Copyright 1919 by Macmillan Publishing Co., Inc., renewed 1947 by Bertha Georgia Yeats. "At Galway Races" reprinted with permission of Macmillan Publishing Co., Inc., M. B. Yeats, and Miss Anne Yeats from *Collected Poems* by William Butler Yeats. Copyright 1912 by Macmillan Publishing Co., Inc., renewed 1940 by Bertha Georgia Yeats.

Andrew Young. "Climbing in Glencoe" from *Complete Poems* by Andrew Young, edited by Leonard Clark. Reprinted by permission of Martin Secker & Warburg Limited.

PREFACE

There is nothing new about sports as a subject for literature, but perhaps at no other time in history have they played such a prominent part in the lives of us all — a prominence due more than likely to television and to the leisure time afforded us by technology. As a result, students often come to college with an active interest in athletics of all kinds and enjoy reading sports-related selections when they can find them in their textbooks. In an attempt to accommodate that interest, I have gathered a substantial variety of readings that should satisfy students' natural appetites for reading about sports, and at the same time help them learn new things about themselves, others, and the world around them.

Included are writings ancient and contemporary, traditional and iconoclastic, concrete and abstract. Many selections, naturally, concern the major sports — boxing, football, baseball — but a number of them reflect a new interest in such sports as running, tennis, soccer, and skiing. The dramatic emergence of women as serious competitors in all areas of sport, apparent in much of the current sports literature, is also well represented.

The book is divided into three major sections: (1) Fiction; (2) Essays; and (3) Poetry. Each selection is followed by questions for discussion. Section introductions provide a framework for the selections. The fiction and poetry introductions are followed by brief surveys of relevant literary techniques and devices as an aid to reading. Appendixes include suggested writing topics, a glossary of literary terms, and a selected bibliography.

The selections within each section are organized according to the important themes that illuminate, through the central sports motif, the most significant periods of life: growing up, falling in love, growing old, and dying. The themes also testify to the exhilaration of life and the appreciation of beauty, both spiritual and earthly. And they underscore, also, the eternal human struggle against nature, against fellow humans, and against the self.

I am very grateful to Jo Marie Moore, my expert researcher, for helping me round up the poems in this book. Also, I wish to thank those responsible at Mountain View College and the Dallas County Community College District for providing me with a sabbatical leave to complete this book. A special thanks to my wife Brenda, who has endured this project like a good sport.

Tom Dodge

CONTENTS

ESSAYS   197

POETRY   329

THOSE WATCHING   398

MYSTERY, MYTH, SYMMETRY, SOURCE   412

EASY TARGETS, TO WIT: 438

MEANINGS QUESTIONED, AIMS IN DOUBT   445

IN PROFILE   502

FALLEN STARS   509

APPENDIXES   529

A LITERATURE
OF SPORTS

FICTION

Literature is older than writing. Artists originally composed their stories and sang or recited them to audiences, large and small, to the accompaniment of a lyre. Even stories as long as *The Iliad* were memorized and passed on to a new generation. It was a great and wonderful tradition, the sole purpose of which was to amuse, entertain, and distract from the ever-present miseries of life. In listening, the audiences may have learned something about themselves and others in the world around them. If a story was to be entertaining, it had to depict heroic figures whose lives involved them in goodly portions of action and romance. And it had to *sound* good. Even after the development of writing, silent reading did not become widespread until the invention of the printing press in the fifteenth century. So artists were extremely sensitive to sounds and rhythms (as the best ones are today). The author of *The Iliad* chose for his meter, the thundering dactyl (a long beat and two shorts), eighteen beats in every line. The beauty of its rolling cadences alone was enough to keep an audience alert, This emphasis on entertainment remained until the Middle Ages when literature, along with the other arts, was controlled by the somber scholastics who institutionalized it and shrouded it in mystery. The keys that unlocked the mystery were kept in the great universities of Europe, which were open only to the very elite.

Although institutional tradition is strong even today, it is changing more and more as time goes by. The once widespread notion that there is something mysterious about "literature," that it is something approaching "holy writ," and that professors are the clerics that interpret it, is out of keeping with the spirit of modern community colleges and of many colleges and universities. The only thing mysterious about literature is that it is conceived in the most uncharted regions of the human psyche. Yet it is quite possibly among the simplest of human achievements, springing as it does from a child-like world of "let's pretend" and often requiring the uninhibited abandon of a child to be appreciated. Some of the most enduring works of art have been favorites of children—*Alice in Wonderland, Gulliver's Travels, Huckleberry Finn, Robinson Crusoe, Grimm's Fairy Tales,* stories from the Old Testament, and Greek myths. "In the greatest books," says critic Lewis Mumford, "the words are for children and the meanings are for men."

In addition to reading for amusement, we also read to find out about ourselves and, unless we are forced to do so, we will not read a story that doesn't reflect ourselves as we think we are, or would like to be. The most interesting and amusing story is one about people like us.

The following stories are grouped according to their most outstanding themes. In "Roller Ball Murder" and "The Most Dangerous Game," the authors speculate on the inherent dangers in the search for more thrills and less meaning in sports. The next section includes stories that depict sports' unlimited capabilities to influence social behavior. Midge, the boxing champion in Ring Lardner's "Champion" is a totally irredeemable sociopath who gets to the top, not because he is a nice guy, but because he can hit harder and with less concern than anyone else. He never gets the retribution he deserves because, in Lardner's naturalistic view, "evil" and "good" are but arbitrary ideas in an indifferent cosmos. "The Match" displays the ways in which violent sports can stimulate spectators toward either violence or love, depending upon their own individual self-esteem.

Highlighting society's "insiders" and "outsiders" is the clever but hardhitting story, "The Clicking of Cuthbert," a satirical view of a love-sick golfer who thinks he has to become an "intellectual" to win his lover, a bonafide intellectual who wants to be a golfer, and a group of pseudo-intellectuals who haven't the slightest idea what they want. "A Caddy's Diary" is peopled with hypocrites of a similar stripe, and Lardner leaves no character untainted. Even the young caddy himself who has learned to emulate the corporate moguls who cheat on the links, clearly reveals a distorted sense of values and easily-compromised integrity. "The Loneliness of the Long-Distance Runner" is a shocking insight into the governing structure, as seen through the perceptive eyes of Colin Smith, the young inmate, whose observations would make Nietzsche beam with admiration.

In the section dealing with the trials of growing up are "Nirvana, Götterdämmerung and the Shot Put," a mythical tale of an athlete who discards the traditional notions of competition and success in favor of a mystical serenity derived simply from joyous participation; "The Athenian Runner" in which a young athlete discovers that the race is not necessarily to the swift, but sometimes to the rich; and "Lynx-Hunting," in which a young boy struggles with the conflicts between peer pressure and family allegiance.

The longest section treats the persistent question of what is to become of the aging athlete. Jack London's "A Piece of Steak" is the classic prototype for many succeeding stories, including Hemingway's "My Old Man" and Irwin Shaw's "The Eighty-Yard Run."

Finally, James Thurber's "You Could Look It Up" burlesques the traditional baseball yarn by depicting the hilarious exploits of an arrogant midget used by a Major League baseball team that conspicuously resembles the St. Louis Cardinals' "Gas House Gang" of the 1930s. Damon Runyon's "Undertaker Song" and "Bred for Battle" introduce modern readers to the lovable ne'er-do-wells of Runyon's romantic world of sports.

And Donald Barthelme's "The Wound" is a surrealistic story of a bullfighter who has been gored in the foot.

Reading Fiction

Fiction consists of incidents and ideas arranged in coherent sequence and told in language designed to convey the effect of their truths in an engaging manner. Students often ask whether a particular story is true, and a thoughtful teacher might reply that if they mean "factual," probably not, certainly not entirely; but if they are asking whether it successfully reveals an essence of life that adds another dimension to their understanding, or causes them to re-evaluate an existing conception, then that is another question entirely and one which they themselves will finally have to answer. There are few achievements in education more important than the first realization that truths are no less true when they are revealed through **symbol** than when related through fact. A fact has little significance until it is placed in a context of unifying ideas, concepts, and situations. Our obsession with facts, or literalness, is a direct result of our waning imaginations, precipitated perhaps by the continuing influence of science, a system based on solely empirical, observable evidence. In answer to those who insist that truth is to be found only in literal facts, poet David Jones says,

> I am told in the same evenness of voice with which they recount the day's activities, that in Day's Past, a real city fell at the sound of real trumpets and real shouts. And I tell them that I myself have seen real "walls" fall, with nothing but a brave whistle and a whimper for God's help.

The "walls" in this passage are not brick or concrete walls; they are mental barriers, no less real or forbidding just because they exist in the mind. Jones is using walls to symbolize the restraints placed on us and also those we place on ourselves. Christian Darling's eighty-yard touchdown run in "The Eighty-Yard Run" is a symbol of his athleticism, and his re-enactment years later of that moment of glory is a ritual (the acting-out of a symbol) that he must perform in order to pass into middle age. Truth. How unwillingly it yields, even to those who know how often it lies just beneath the surface.

The more levels on which a story may be read, the more artistic it is said to be. For example, "The Wound," Donald Barthelme's story about a bullfighter who has been gored in the foot, often appeals most to certain readers who have somehow managed to "unlearn" enough of civilization's "rules of perception" to appreciate the strange and the bizarre. Barthelme evidently assumes that ideas, as they are transmitted through language (which is a system of symbols that, among other functions, sets boundaries of perception), can take on almost limitless dimensions when these boundaries are ignored. In other words, we see the torero, not in the familiar setting (boundaries) of the bullring, but in his bedroom, surrounded by a group of the most bizarre guests imaginable—his mother, his mistress, a bishop, a Gypsy queen, a "famous aficionado," and various other odd people. All this is, of course, very strange to us at first because our brains allow us to "see" only what language permits. For example, trees are not really a combination of sounds nor configurations of black marks on a page. They are more than that, but that is our "concept" of them, which is based on the way they look, feel, smell, and sound when the wind rustles their leaves. That is the "acceptable" concept of trees. But what if one fine day we were to see them sprouting upside down from the clouds? If that possibility is interesting to you, then you will probably appreciate "The Wound."

Readers who are familiar with the basic techniques of fiction will better understand and appreciate the stories they read. One of the most traditional of these techniques is **plot,** the sequence of events within the narrative. Every story has a plot of some kind. It may be the most important aspect ("The Most Dangerous Game") or it may be insignificant, obscure, or subordinate to other techniques. In "The Match," the plot consists of a few hours of a man's life centered around his attendance at a football game. It is not the events themselves that are important but his attitude toward them. In "Nirvana, Götterdämmerung and the Shot Put," the almost mythical quality of the plot is subordinate to the religious nature of the **theme.** It is virtually impossible to define *theme* without oversimplifying, but it is easy to say what it is not: it is not a "moral" or "message." It comprises all the other elements; it is the controlling factor, its reason for being. In order for the plot and theme to develop there must be a **conflict,** an obstacle which must be faced and perhaps overcome in order for the character to undergo a change or awakening. Sometimes it takes the form of choices a character must make. In "The Loneliness of the Long-Distance Runner," Smith must decide whether his pride and integrity are more important than winning the race to please the governor. In the story within the story, he must decide between certain poverty and possible imprisonment if he turns to thievery. The story within this story is achieved through **flashback,** a technique of taking the reader back in time to a previous related event in the character's life. This technique brings the event into clearer focus by showing it to be a result of the earlier event, thereby shedding light on the character's present behavior.

The eyes through which we see the events of the story and the mind through which the ideas are filtered is called **point of view.** If a character within the story narrates the events, then it is said to be **first-person narration.** The narrator may be a prominent participant in the action ("My Old Man," "A Caddy's Diary," "The Athenian Runner," "The Loneliness of the Long-Distance Runner"), or merely a remote onlooker ("The Clicking of Cuthbert"). If the author tells the story in the third person, moving from the mind of one character to another and relating their thoughts, then the point of view is said to be **omniscient** ("The Match," "The Eighty-Yard Run"). This third-person point of view limited to but one person in a kind of "over-the-shoulder" account is called **limited omniscient.** The **objective** point of view is the telling of a story by a disinterested third person, without comment on either the actions, the dialogue, or the behavior or the attitudes of the characters ("The Wound"). An author sometimes feels obliged to use two or more points of view, or a **mix** ("The Most Dangerous Game").

Each method has its advantages and disadvantages. The first person is excellent for imparting a personal mood, an immediacy of action, as well as enabling the reader to view the events through the eyes of a character, events the reader may know more about than the character ("My Old Man"), thus providing an extra dimension to the story. The greatest disadvantage is that the author is limited to indirect comment through the narrator, so he must not attribute more perceptive powers and discrimination to this person than the characterization warrants. Furthermore, since the narrator can relate only what he knows, he must be present in every scene; and a less than skillful writer may rely too much on coincidence to provide the narrator with information that he should acquire naturally.

Because the omniscient point of view offers the greatest possibilities for range and scope, it is probably the most frequently used but, mishandled, it can disintegrate into a jumble of characters, attitudes, and events. The limited omniscient offers most of the advantages of the first-person narration and also allows the author to comment on the events and perceptions of the character over whose shoulder he is looking. Its disadvantage is, however, that the author cannot achieve the subtlety offered by the first person, nor the freedom of movement of the omniscient. Near the end of "The Most Dangerous Game," Connell finds it necessary to switch from the limited point of view of Rainsford to that of General Zaroff after Rainsford has disappeared into the sea, until he reappears later in Zaroff's bedroom.

Many authors depend more on **characterization** than on plot to enrich the story, finding it more natural to express thematic ideas through characters and their reactions to events and each other, as in the case of "My Old Man." An author may characterize directly through **exposition** by commenting omnisciently on the character's thoughts and behavior, or by allowing another character to do it. If another character does it, he may betray more about himself in the process than about the person he is describing. Good writers characterize by dramatizing, by showing the characters doing things. They do not tell the reader that a person is noble; they show him doing something noble. In fact, the author's selection of what the characters do and say can usually provide a richer insight than an entire chapter of exposition.

Authors often add an extra level of meaning to a story through the use of **symbol,** an extension of something material to something abstract, to a dimension where it becomes more than "just what it is." Although some damage has been done by zealous "interpreters" too eager to attach symbolic meaning to everything, it is also true that the best stories appeal to readers on the symbolic, as well as the literal, level. Louise's hat in "The Eighty-Yard Run" symbolizes for Christian the urbane, cosmopolitan life from which he feels so alienated. In addition, the names that authors select for characters sometimes hold symbolic meaning, names such as Christian Darling, for example, and Tom King ("A Piece of Steak").

Another device, frequently used to add depth to a story, is **irony,** which may take several forms. One form is *verbal irony,* a statement that suggests more or less than is actually said, the effect of which the reader usually understands, even though the character may not. For example, Dick, the young caddy who narrates Ring Lardner's "A Caddy's Diary," is too innocent to see the immorality suggested by what the rich country club golfers say, although the reader may see it quite clearly. When Charles Crane, the underpaid employee of Mr. Thomas' bank, steals $8000 and runs off with a "swell looking dame," Mr. Thomas, who is an unconscionable cheater and stroke-shaver, says that "what makes me sore is not only that he has proved himself dishonest but that he could . . . sell his soul for $8000 and a pretty face." The full impact of this verbal irony Lardner saves for the end when it becomes clear that by shaving golf strokes Mr. Thomas has sold his soul to win nine golf balls. And, worse yet, Dick himself, who kicks Mrs. Doan's ball out of the rough because she is pretty, has sold his soul for a smile. Another kind of irony, *dramatic irony,* consists of a tragic reversal of affairs from what the characters expect. In "My Old Man" the way in which Butler seeks to regain his youth brings about his death.

Satire is a technique through which an author makes a serious statement in the guise of humor or ridicule. In so doing, the author is attempting to effect a reform by showing a person, idea, or thing in its most absurd light. The ladies of Wood Hills in "The Clicking of Cuthbert" are shown to be not intellectuals at all but empty-headed social climbers who use "culture" to distinguish themselves from those they consider to be beneath them in status.

One of the most difficult elements for an author to control is the dramatization of **emotion.** The boy's desperate statement at the end of "My Old Man"—"Seems like when they get started they don't leave a guy nothing" —is a perfect example of what David Hume meant when he said that "fine writing consists of sentiments which are natural without being obvious." A less sensible writer might have tried to wring the incident of every drop of false emotion by having the boy throw himself across the body of his father, weeping and beating his breast, as the cruel headmaster comes and drags him off to the orphanage. Emotion carried too far is called **pathos** or **sentimentality,** a mawkish style, capitalizing on evil stepmothers, crippled children, mistreated animals, bullies, separated twins, and martyrs—all cheap contrivances designed to pump artificial emotion into a circumstance that doesn't warrant it.

Another important element is **dialogue,** the conversation exchanged between two or more characters. Nothing can so weaken a story as trite, pompous, irrelevant, didactic, or bombastic dialogue, while nothing can so enrich one as witty or poignant exchanges. Every line should either move the plot or add to the characterization. A story should not contain one extraneous line, nor should a character utter a line that is out of keeping with his characterization. Dialogue should, of course, reflect a character's experience and education. Smith, the narrator of "The Loneliness of the Long-Distance Runner," uses poor grammar, relying heavily on vulgarity and slang, but it would be ludicrous to have an uneducated Cockney boy speak with the erudition of Rainsford, the highly educated man of the world in "The Most Dangerous Game." A good story may contain an abundance of dialogue ("The Clicking of Cuthbert"), or almost none at all ("A Piece of Steak"), depending on the author's intentions and, perhaps, his ability to write it well.

The most pervading single element of a story is its **tone** or **mood.** This is generally defined as the writer's attitude toward his subject but, since it consists essentially of a feeling, it is easier to illustrate by an example. "The Most Dangerous Game" begins with:

> "Off there to the right—somewhere—is a large island," said Whitney. "It's rather a mystery—"

Descriptions like, "dank tropical night," "God-forsaken place"; and the liberal use of words like "dread," "superstition," "fear," "cannibals," "devil," "danger," and so on, abound in the first two pages. This mood of mystery and eerie suspense is a hint of things to follow, a mood which intensifies as the story unfolds.

A final technique is **imagery,** "word pictures" that represent sense experience. Mary Renault, in "The Athenian Runner," conveys how it *feels* to stand atop the mountain overlooking ancient Corinth:

> It was quiet, so that one could hear the bees in the asphodel, the little clappers of the mountain goats, and a shepherd piping. Beyond the walls were great spaces of blue air . . .

In "The Eighty-Yard Run," Irwin Shaw's description of Christian Darling getting dressed after a hard workout creates a feeling for those who have never experienced it that is second only to the actual incident, and re-creates it for every athlete who knows it well but has never seen it so expressed:

> He dressed slowly, the softness of his shirt and the soft warmth of his wool socks and his flannel trousers a reward against his skin after the harsh pressure

of the shoulder harness and thigh and hip pads. He drank three glasses of cold water, the liquid reaching down coldly inside of him, soothing the harsh dry places in his throat and belly left by the sweat and running and shouting of practice.

Imagery, like all the other literary techniques, can be overdone. In fact it is not unusual for otherwise good writers to overload their prose with fragrances of all kinds, soft rain, rustling leaves, cool breezes, and sunshine. You will find few, if any, such weaknesses in the following stories. On the contrary, they are masterfully crafted and contain many or all of these techniques in their most beautiful and natural forms. Reading them with these elements in mind will pay off greatly in both understanding and pleasure.

THE QUEST FOR
THE ULTIMATE THRILL

I hear of games in Manila, now, or in Barcelona with no time limits, men bashing each other until there are no more runners left, no way of scoring points.

—**William Harrison**

WILLIAM HARRISON

Roller Ball Murder

The game, the game: here we go again. All glory to it, all things I am and own because of Roller Ball Murder.

Our team stands in a row, twenty of us in salute as the corporation hymn is played by the band. We view the hardwood oval track which offers us the bumps and rewards of mayhem: fifty yards long, thirty yards across the ends, high banked, and at the top of the walls the cannons which fire those frenzied twenty-pound balls—similar to bowling balls, made of ebonite—at velocities over three hundred miles an hour. The balls careen around the track, eventually slowing and falling with diminishing centrifugal force, and as they go to ground or strike a player another volley fires. Here we are, our team: ten roller skaters, five motor-bike riders, five runners (or clubbers). As the hymn plays, we stand erect and tough; eighty thousand sit watching in the stands and another two billion view-ers around the world inspect the set of our jaws on multivision.

The runners, those bastards, slip into their heavy leather gloves and shoulder their lacrosselike paddles—with which they either catch the whizzing balls or bash the rest of us. The bikers ride high on the walls (beware, mates, that's where the cannon shots are too hot to handle) and swoop down to help the runners at opportune times. The skaters, those of us with the juice for it, protest: we clog the way, try to keep the runners from passing us and scoring points, and become the fodder in the brawl. So two teams of us, forty in all, go skating and running and biking around the track while the big balls are fired in the same direction as we move—always coming up behind us to scatter and maim us—and the object of the game, fans, as if you didn't know, is for the runners to pass all

9

skaters on the opposing team, field a ball, and pass it to a biker for one point. Those bikers, by the way, may give the runners a lift—in which case those of us on skates have our hands full overturning 175cc motorbikes.

No rest periods, no substitute players. If you lose a man, your team plays short.

Today I turn my best side to the cameras. I'm Jonathan E, none other, and nobody passes me on the track. I'm the core of the Houston team and for the two hours of play—no rules, no penalties once the first cannon fires—I'll level any bastard runner who raises a paddle at me.

We move: immediately there are pileups of bikes, skaters, referees, and runners, all tangled and punching and scrambling when one of the balls zooms around the corner and belts us. I pick up momentum and heave an opposing skater into the infield at center ring; I'm brute speed today, driving, pushing up on the track, dodging a ball, hurtling downward beyond those bastard runners. Two runners do hand-to-hand combat and one gets his helmet knocked off in a blow which tears away half his face; the victor stands there too long admiring his work and gets wiped out by a biker who swoops down and flattens him. The crowd screams and I know the cameramen have it on an isolated shot and that viewers in Melbourne, Berlin, Rio, and L.A. are heaving with excitement in their easy chairs.

When an hour is gone I'm still wheeling along, naturally, though we have four team members out with broken parts, one rookie maybe dead, two bikes demolished. The other team, good old London, is worse off.

One of their motorbikes roars out of control, takes a hit from one of the balls, and bursts into flame. Wild cheering.

Cruising up next to their famous Jackie Magee, I time my punch. He turns in my direction, exposes the ugly snarl inside his helmet, and I take him out of action. In that tiniest instant, I feel his teeth and bone give way and the crowd screams approval. We have them now, we really have them, we do, and the score ends 7–2.

The years pass and the rules alter—always in favor of a greater crowd-pleasing carnage. I've been at this more than fifteen years, amazing, with only broken arms and collarbones to slow me down, and I'm not as spry as ever, but meaner—and no rookie, no matter how much in shape, can learn this slaughter unless he comes out and takes me on in the real thing.

But the rules. I hear of games in Manila, now, or in Barcelona with no time limits, men bashing each other until there are no more runners left, no way of scoring points. That's the coming thing. I hear of Roller Ball Murder played with mixed teams, men and women, wearing tear-away jerseys which add a little tit and vulnerable exposure to the action. Everything will happen. They'll change the rules until we skate on a slick of blood, we all know that.

Before this century began, before the Great Asian war of the 1990's, before the corporations replaced nationalism and the corporate police forces supplanted the world's armies, in the last days of American football and the World Cup in Europe, I was a tough young rookie who knew all the rewards of this game.

Women: I had them all—even, pity, a good marriage once. I had so much money after my first trophies that I could buy houses and land and lakes beyond the huge cities where only the executive class was allowed. My photo, then, as now, was on the covers of magazines, so that my name and the name of the sport were one, and I was Jonathan E, no other, a survivor and much more in the bloodiest sport.

At the beginning I played for Oil Conglomerates, then those corporations became known as ENERGY; I've always played for the team here in Houston, they've given me everything.

"How're you feeling?" Mr. Bartholemew asks me. He's taking the head of ENERGY, one of the most powerful men in the world, and he talks to me like I'm his son.

"Feeling mean," I answer, so that he smiles.

He tells me they want to do a special on multivision about my career, lots of shots on the side screens showing my greatest plays, and the story of my life, how ENERGY takes in such orphans, gives them work and protection, and makes careers possible.

"Really feel mean, eh?" Mr. Bartholemew asks again, and I answer the same, not telling him all that's inside me because he would possibly misunderstand; not telling him that I'm tired of the long season, that I'm lonely and miss my wife, that I yearn for high, lost, important thoughts, and that maybe, just maybe, I've got a deep rupture in the soul.

An old buddy, Jim Cletus, comes by the ranch for the weekend. Mackie, my present girl, takes our dinners out of the freezer and turns the rays on them; not so domestic, that Mackie, but she has enormous breasts and a waist smaller than my thigh.

Cletus works as a judge now. At every game there are two referees—clowns, whose job it is to see nothing amiss—and the judge who records the points scored. Cletus is also on the International Rules Committee and tells me they are still considering several changes.

"A penalty for being lapped by your own team, for one thing," he tells us. "A damned simple penalty, too: they'll take off your helmet."

Mackie, bless her bosom, makes an O with her lips.

Cletus, once a runner for Toronto, fills up my oversized furniture and rests his hands on his bad knees.

"What else?" I ask him. "Or can you tell me?"

"Oh, just financial things. More bonuses for superior attacks. Bigger bonuses for being named World All-Star—which ought to be good news for you again. And, yeah, talk of reducing the two-month off-season. The viewers want more."

After dinner Cletus walks around the ranch with me. We trudge up the path of a hillside and the Texas countryside stretches before us. Pavilions of clouds.

"Did you ever think about death in your playing days?" I ask, knowing I'm a bit too pensive for old Clete.

"Never in the game itself," he answers proudly. "Off the track—yeah, sometimes I never thought about anything else."

We pause and take a good long look at the horizon.

"There's another thing going in the Rules Committee," he finally admits. "They're considering dropping the time limit—at least, god help us, Johnny, the suggestion has come up officially."

I like a place with rolling hills. Another of my houses is near Lyons in France, the hills similar to these although more lush, and I take my evening strolls there over an ancient battleground. The cities are too much, so large and uninhabitable that one has to have a business passport to enter such immensities as New York.

"Naturally I'm holding out for the time limit," Cletus goes on. "I've played, so I know a man's limits. Sometimes in that committee, Johnny, I feel like I'm the last moral man on earth sitting there and insisting that there should be a few rules."

The statistical nuances of Roller Ball Murder entertain the multitudes as much as any other aspect of the game. The greatest number of points scored in a single game: 81. The highest velocity of a ball when actually caught by a runner: 176 mph. Highest number of players put out of action in a single game by a single skater: 13—world's record by yours truly. Most deaths in a single contest: 9—Rome vs. Chicago, December 4, 2012.

The giant lighted boards circling above the track monitor our pace, record each separate fact of the slaughter, and we have millions of fans—strange, it always seemed to me—who never look directly at the action, but just study those statistics.

A multivision survey established this.

Before going to the stadium in Paris for our evening game, I stroll under the archways and along the Seine.

Some of the French fans call to me, waving and talking to my bodyguards as well, so I become oddly conscious of myself, conscious of my size and clothes and the way I walk. A curious moment.

I'm six-foot three inches and weigh 255 pounds. My neck is 18½ inches. Fingers like a pianist. I wear my conservative pinstriped jump suit and the famous flat Spanish hat. I am 34 years old now, and when I grow old, I think, I'll look a lot like the poet Robert Graves.

The most powerful men in the world are the executives. They run the major corporations which fix prices, wages, and the general economy, and we all know they're crooked, that they have almost unlimited power and money, but I have considerable power and money myself and I'm still anxious. What can I possibly want, I ask myself, except, possibly, more knowledge?

I consider recent history—which is virtually all anyone remembers—and how the corporate wars ended, so that we settled into the Six Majors: ENERGY, TRANSPORT, FOOD, HOUSING, SERVICES, and LUXURY. Sometimes I forget who runs what—for instance, now that the universities are operated by the Majors (and provide the farm system for Roller Ball Murder), which Major runs them? SERVICES or LUXURY? Music is one of our biggest industries, but I can't remember who administers it. Narcotic research is now under FOOD, I know, though it used to be under LUXURY.

Anyway, I think I'll ask Mr. Bartholemew about knowledge. He's a man with a big view of the world, with values, with memory. My team flings itself into the void while his team harnesses the sun, taps the sea, finds new alloys, and is clearly just a hell of a lot more serious.

✿   ✿   ✿

The Mexico City game has a new wrinkle: they've changed the shape of the ball on us.

Cletus didn't even warn me—perhaps he couldn't—but here we are playing with a ball not quite round, its center of gravity altered, so that it rumbles around the track in irregular patterns.

This particular game is bad enough because the bikers down here are getting wise to me; for years, since my reputation was established, bikers have always tried to take me out of a game early. But early in the game I'm wary and strong and I'll always gladly take on a biker—even since they put shields on the motor-bikes so that we can't grab the handlebars. Now, though, these bastards know I'm getting older—still mean, but slowing down, as the sports pages say about me—so they let me bash it out with the skaters and runners for as long as possible before sending the bikers after me. Knock out Jonathan E, they say, and you've beaten Houston; and that's right enough, but they haven't done it yet.

The fans down here, all low-class FOOD workers mostly, boil over as I manage to keep my cool—and the oblong ball, zigzagging around at lurching speeds, hopping two feet off the track at times, knocks out virtually their whole team. Finally, some of us catch their last runner/clubber and beat him to a pulp, so that's it: no runners, no points. Those dumb FOOD workers file out of the stadium while we show off and score a few fancy and uncontested points. The score 37—4. I feel wonderful, like pure brute speed.

Mackie is gone—her mouth no longer makes an O around my villa or ranch— and in her place is the new one, Daphne. My Daphne is tall and English and likes photos—always wants to pose for me. Sometimes we get out our boxes of old pictures (mine as a player, mostly, and hers as a model) and look at ourselves, and it occurs to me that the photos spread out on the rug are the real us, our public and performing true selves, and the two of us here in the sitting room, Gaelic gray winter outside our window, aren't too real at all.

"Look at the muscles in your back!" Daphne says in amazement as she studies a shot of me at the California beach—and it's as though she never before noticed.

After the photos, I stroll out beyond the garden. The brown waving grass of the fields reminds me of Ella, my only wife, and of her soft long hair which made a tent over my face when we kissed.

I lecture to the ENERGY-sponsored rookie camp and tell them they can't possibly comprehend anything until they're out on the track getting belted.

My talk tonight concerns how to stop a biker who wants to run you down. "You can throw a shoulder right into the shield," I begin. "And that way it's you or him."

The rookies look at me as though I'm crazy.

"Or you can hit the deck, cover yourself, tense up, and let the bastard flip over your body," I go on, counting on my fingers for them and doing my best not to laugh. "Or you can feint, sidestep up hill, and kick him off the track—which takes some practice and timing."

None of them knows what to say. We're sitting in the infield grass, the track lighted, the stands empty, and their faces are filled with stupid awe. "Or if a biker comes at you with good speed and balance," I continue, "then naturally let the bastard by—even if he carries a runner. That runner, remember, has to dismount and field one of the new odd-shaped balls which isn't easy—and you can usually catch up."

The rookies begin to get a smug look on their faces when a biker bears down on me in the demonstration period.

Brute speed. I jump to one side, dodge the shield, grab the bastard's arm and separate him from his machine in one movement. The bike skids away. The poor biker's shoulder is out of socket.

"Oh yeah," I say, getting back to my feet. "I forgot about that move."

Toward midseason when I see Mr. Bartholemew again he has been deposed as the chief executive at ENERGY. He is still very important, but lacks some of the old certainty; his mood is reflective, so that I decide to take this opportunity to talk about what's bothering me.

We lunch in Houston Tower, viewing an expanse of city. A nice Beef Wellington and Burgundy. Daphne sits there like a stone, probably imagining that she's in a movie.

"Knowledge, ah, I see," Mr. Bartholemew replies in response to my topic. "What're you interested in, Jonathan? History? The arts?"

"Can I be personal with you?"

This makes him slightly uncomfortable. "Sure, naturally," he answers easily, and although Mr. Bartholemew isn't especially one to inspire confession I decide to blunder along.

"I began in the university," I remind him. "That was—let's see—more than seventeen years ago. In those days we still had books and I read some, quite a few, because I thought I might make an executive."

"Jonathan, believe me, I can guess what you're going to say," Mr. Bartholemew sighs, sipping the Burgundy and glancing at Daphne. "I'm one of the few with real regrets about what happened to the books. Everything is still on tapes, but it just isn't the same, is it? Nowadays only the computer specialists read the tapes and we're right back in the Middle Ages when only the monks could read the Latin script."

"Exactly," I answer, letting my beef go cold.

"Would you like me to assign you a specialist?"

"No, that's not exactly it."

"We have the great film libraries: you could get a permit to see anything you want. The Renaissance. Greek philosophers. I saw a nice summary film on the life and thought of Plato once."

"All I know," I say with hesitation, "is Roller Ball Murder."

"You don't want out of the game?" he asks warily.

"No, not at all. It's just that I want—god, Mr. Bartholemew, I don't know how to say it: I want *more*."

He offers a blank look.

"But not things in the world," I add. "More for *me*."

He heaves a great sigh, leans back, and allows the steward to refill his glass. Curiously, I know that he understands; he is a man of sixty, enormously wealthy, powerful in our most powerful executive class, and behind his eyes is the deep, weary, undeniable comprehension of the life he has lived.

"Knowledge," he tells me, "either converts to power or it converts to melancholy. Which could you possibly want, Jonathan? You *have* power. You have status and skill and the whole masculine dream many of us would like to have. And in Roller Ball Murder there's no room for melancholy, is there? In the game the mind exists for the body, to make a harmony of havoc, right? Do you want to change that? Do you want the mind to exist for itself alone? I don't think you actually want that, do you?"

"I really don't know," I admit.

"I'll get you some permits, Jonathan. You can see video films, learn something about reading tapes, if you want."

"I don't think I really *have* any power," I say, still groping.

"Oh, come on. What do *you* say about that?" he asks, turning to Daphne.

"He definitely has power," she answers with a wan smile.

Somehow the conversation drifts away from me; Daphne, on cue, like the good spy for the corporation she probably is, begins feeding Mr. Bartholemew lines and soon, oddly enough, we're discussing my upcoming game with Stockholm.

A hollow space begins to grow inside me, as though fire is eating out a hole. The conversation concerns the end of the season, the All-Star Game, records being set this year, but my disappointment—in what, exactly, I don't even know —begins to sicken me.

Mr. Bartholemew eventually asks what's wrong.

"The food," I answer. "Usually I have great digestion, but maybe not today."

In the locker room the dreary late-season pall takes us. We hardly speak among ourselves, now, and like soldiers or gladiators sensing what lies ahead, we move around in these sickening surgical odors of the locker room.

Our last training and instruction this year concerns the delivery of deathblows to opposing players; no time now for the tolerant shoving and bumping of yesteryear. I consider that I possess two good weapons: because of my unusually good balance on skates, I can often shatter my opponent's knee with a kick; also, I have a good backhand blow to the ribs and heart, if, wheeling along side by side with some bastard, he raises an arm against me. If the new rules change removes a player's helmet, of course, that's death; as it is right now (there are rumors, rumors every day about what new version of RBM we'll have next) you go for the windpipe, the ribs or heart, the diaphragm, or anyplace you don't break your hand.

Our instructors are a pair of giddy Oriental gentlemen who have all sorts of anatomical solutions for us and show drawings of the human figure with nerve centers painted in pink.

"What you do is this," says Moonpie, in parody of these two. Moonpie is a fine skater in his fourth season and fancies himself an old-fashioned drawling Texan. "What you do is hit 'em on the jawbone and drive it up into their ganglia."

"Their *what?*" I ask, giving Moonpie a grin.

"Their goddamned *ganglia*. Bunch of nerves right here underneath the ear. Drive their jawbones into that mess of nerves and it'll ring their bells sure."

Daphne is gone now, too, and in this interim before another companion arrives, courtesy of all my friends and employers at ENERGY, Ella floats back into my dreams and daylight fantasies.

I was a corporation child, some executive's bastard boy, I always preferred to think, brought up in the Galveston section of the city. A big kid, naturally, athletic and strong—and this, according to my theory, gave me healthy mental genes, too, because I take it now that strong in body is strong in mind: a man with brute speed surely also has the capacity to mull over his life. Anyway, I married at age fifteen while I worked on the docks for Oil Conglomerates. Ella was a secretary, slim with long brown hair, and we managed to get permits to both marry and enter the university together. Her fellowship was in General Electronics—she was clever, give her that—and mine was in Roller Ball Murder. She fed me well that first year, so I put on thirty hard pounds and at night she soothed my bruises (was she a spy, too, I've sometimes wondered, whose job it was to prime the bull for the charge?) and perhaps it was because she was my first woman ever, eighteen years old, lovely, that I've never properly forgotten.

She left me for an executive, just packed up and went to Europe with him. Six years ago I saw them at a sports banquet where I was presented an award: there they were, smiling and being nice, and I asked them only one question, just one, "You two ever had children?" It gave me odd satisfaction that they had applied for a permit, but had been denied.

Ella, love: one does consider: did you beef me up and break my heart in some great design of corporate society?

There I was, whatever, angry and hurt. Beyond repair, I thought at the time. And the hand which stroked Ella soon dropped all the foes of Houston.

I take sad stock of myself in this quiet period before another woman arrives; I'm smart enough, I know that: I had to be to survive. Yet, I seem to know nothing—and can feel the hollow spaces in my own heart. Like one of those computer specialists, I have my own brutal technical know-how; I know what today means, what tomorrow likely holds, but maybe it's because the books are gone—Mr. Bartholemew was right, it's a shame they're transformed—that I feel so vacant. If I didn't remember my Ella—this I realize—I wouldn't even *want* to remember because it's love I'm recollecting as well as those old university days.

Recollect, sure: I read quite a few books that year with Ella and afterward, too, before turning professional in the game. Apart from all the volumes about how to get along in business, I read the history of the kings of England, that

pillars of wisdom book by T. E. Lawrence, all the forlorn novels, some Rousseau, a bio of Thomas Jefferson, and other odd bits. On tapes now, all that, whirring away in a cool basement someplace.

The rules crumble once more.

At the Tokyo game, we discover that there will be three oblong balls in play
at all times.

Some of our most experienced players are afraid to go out on the track. Then,
after they're coaxed and threatened and finally consent to join the flow, they
fake injury whenever they can and sprawl in the infield like rabbits. As for me, I
play with greater abandon than ever and give the crowd its money's worth. The
Tokyo skaters are either peering over their shoulders looking for approaching
balls when I smash them, or, poor devils, they're looking for me when a ball takes
them out of action.

One little bastard with a broken back flaps around for a moment like a fish,
then shudders and dies.

Balls jump at us as though they have brains.

But fate carries me, as I somehow know it will; I'm a force field, a destroyer.
I kick a biker into the path of a ball going at least two hundred miles an hour. I
swerve around a pileup of bikes and skaters, ride high on the track, zoom down,
and find a runner/clubber who panics and misses with a roundhouse swing of
his paddle; without much ado, I belt him out of play with the almost certain
knowledge—I've felt it before—that he's dead before he hits the infield.

One ball flips out of play soon after being fired from the cannon, jumps the
railing, sails high, and plows into the spectators. Beautiful.

I take a hit from a ball, one of the three or four times I've ever been belted.
The ball is riding low on the track when it catches me and I sprawl like a baby.
One bastard runner comes after me, but one of our bikers chases him off. Then
one of their skaters glides by and takes a shot at me, but I dig him in the groin
and discourage him, too.

Down and hurting, I see Moonpie killed. They take off his helmet, working
slowly—it's like slow motion and I'm writhing and cursing and unable to help—
and open his mouth on the toe of some bastard skater's boot. Then they kick
the back of his head and knock out all his teeth—which rattle downhill on the
track. Then kick again and stomp: his brains this time. He drawls a last groaning
good-bye while the cameras record it.

And later I'm up, pushing along once more, feeling bad, but knowing everyone else feels the same; I have that last surge of energy, the one I always get
when I'm going good, and near the closing gun I manage a nice move: grabbing
one of their runners with a headlock, I skate him off to limbo, bashing his face
with my free fist, picking up speed until he drags behind like a dropped flag,
and disposing of him in front of a ball which carries him off in a comic flop.
Oh, god, god.

Before the All-Star Game, Cletus comes to me with the news I expect: this
one will be a no-time-limit extravaganza in New York, every multivision set in
the world tuned in. The bikes will be more high-powered, four oblong balls will

be in play simultaneously, and the referees will blow the whistle on any sluggish player and remove his helmet as a penalty.

Cletus is apologetic.

"With those rules, no worry," I tell him. "It'll go no more than an hour and we'll all be dead."

We're at the Houston ranch on a Saturday afternoon, riding around in my electrocart viewing the Santa Gertrudis stock. This is probably the ultimate spectacle of my wealth: my own beef cattle in a day when only a few special members of the executive class have any meat to eat with the exception of mass-produced fish. Cletus is so impressed with my cattle that he keeps going on this afternoon and seems so pathetic to me, a judge who doesn't judge, the pawn of a committee, another feeble hulk of an old RBM player.

"You owe me a favor, Clete," I tell him.

"Anything," he answers, not looking me in the eyes.

I turn the cart up a lane beside my rustic rail fence, an archway of oak trees overhead and the early spring bluebonnets and daffodils sending up fragrances from the nearby fields. Far back in my thoughts is the awareness that I can't possibly last and that I'd like to be buried out here—burial is seldom allowed anymore, everyone just incinerated and scattered—to become the mulch of flowers.

"I want you to bring Ella to me," I tell him. "After all these years, yeah: that's what I want. You arrange it and don't give me any excuses, okay?"

We meet at the villa near Lyons in early June, only a week before the All-Star Game in New York, and I think she immediately reads something in my eyes which helps her to love me again. Of course I love her: I realize, seeing her, that I have only a vague recollection of being alive at all, and that was a long time ago, in another century of the heart when I had no identity except my name, when I was a simple dock worker, before I ever saw all the world's places or moved in the rumbling nightmares of Roller Ball Murder.

She kisses my fingers. "Oh," she says softly, and her face is filled with true wonder, "what's happened to you, Johnny?"

A few soft days. When our bodies aren't entwined in lovemaking, we try to remember and tell each other everything: the way we used to hold hands, how we fretted about receiving a marriage permit, how the books looked on our shelves in the old apartment in River Oaks. We strain, at times, trying to recollect the impossible; it's true that history is really gone, that we have no families or touchstones, that our short personal lives alone judge us, and I want to hear about her husband, the places they've lived, the furniture in her house, anything. I tell her, in turn, about all the women, about Mr. Bartholemew and Jim Cletus, about the ranch in the hills outside Houston.

Come to me, Ella. If I can remember us, I can recollect meaning and time.

It would be nice, I think, once, to imagine that she was taken away from me by some malevolent force in this awful age, but I know the truth of that: she went away, simply, because I wasn't enough back then, because those were the days before I yearned for anything, when I was beginning to live to play the game. But no matter. For a few days she sits on my bed and I touch her skin like a blind man groping back over the years.

On our last morning together she comes out in her traveling suit with her hair pulled up underneath a fur cap. The softness has faded from her voice and she smiles with efficiency, as if she has just come back to the practical world; I recall, briefly, this scene played out a thousand years ago when she explained that she was going away with her executive.

She plays like a biker, I decide; she rides up there high above the turmoil, decides when to swoop down, and makes a clean kill.

"Good-bye, Ella," I say, and she turns her head slightly away from my kiss so that I touch her fur cap with my lips.

"I'm glad I came," she says politely. "Good luck, Johnny."

New York is frenzied with what is about to happen.

The crowds throng into Energy Plaza, swarm the ticket offices at the stadium, and wherever I go people are reaching for my hands, pushing my bodyguards away, trying to touch my sleeve as though I'm some ancient religious figure, a seer or prophet.

Before the game begins I stand with my team as the corporation hymns are played. I'm brute speed today, I tell myself, trying to rev myself up; yet, adream in my thoughts, I'm a bit unconvinced.

A chorus of voices joins the band now as the music swells.

The game, the game, all glory to it, the music rings, and I can feel my lips move with the words, singing.

Considerations

1. "Roller Ball Murder" is Harrison's imaginary sport of the future. List and explain the forces that have contributed to its development.
2. Like all other good futuristic fiction, this story says more about the present than the future. Judging from the story, discuss the author's concerns about present attitudes and developments that may possibly lead to such a society as reflected in this story. (See "Wild in the Stands.")
3. Exactly how is a society reflected in its taste in sports? Discuss the society reflected in "Roller Ball Murder." What does our own taste in sports say about us? What is our equivalent of the Energy Bowl?
4. Judging from Harrison's description of "Roller Ball Murder," which present-day sport does it most resemble? Is it a combination of several? What element do they have in common?
5. Discuss Roller Ball's connection with religion in the eyes of the fans. Include in your discussion an assessment of the following statement by Jonathan E:

    ". . . wherever I go people are reaching for my hands, pushing my bodyguards away, trying to touch my sleeve as though I'm some ancient religious figure, a seer or prophet."

6. Discuss the following passage from the story:

    Before this century began, the great Asian war of the 1990's, before the corporations replaced nationalism and the corporate police forces supplanted the world's armies. . . .

7. Discuss Jonathan E's ambivalence (look up this word) toward the sport.
8. Why is it necessary for a narrator to be more complex than the other characters around him? Discuss Jonathan E's complexity. Look up "ambiguity."
9. What is symbolized by Jonathan E's wife? By books?
10. If you have seen the movie, *Roller Ball*, compare and contrast it with the story. Does the movie contain the social criticism of the story?
11. What part did the media play in the development of this sport? Cite examples from the story to show the author's attitude toward the media. What do you think is the author's attitude toward the fans? Support your answer.
12. *Brave New World*, *1984*, and *Fahrenheit 451* are other examples of futuristic fiction that predict similar nightmares. Can you list others?

RICHARD CONNELL

The Most Dangerous Game

"Off there to the right—somewhere—is a large island," said Whitney. "It's rather a mystery—"

"What island is it?" Rainsford asked.

"The old charts call it 'Ship-Trap Island,'" Whitney replied. "A suggestive name, isn't it? Sailors have a curious dread of the place. I don't know why. Some superstition—"

"Can't see it," remarked Rainsford, trying to peer through the dank tropical night that was palpable as it pressed its thick warm blackness in upon the yacht.

"You've good eyes," said Whitney, with a laugh, "and I've seen you pick off a moose moving in the brown fall bush at four hundred yards, but even you can't see four miles or so through a moonless Caribbean night."

"Nor four yards," admitted Rainsford. "Ugh! It's like moist black velvet."

"It will be light in Rio," promised Whitney. "We should make it in a few days. I hope the jaguar guns have come from Purdey's. We should have some good hunting up the Amazon. Great sport, hunting."

"The best sport in the world," agreed Rainsford.

"For the hunter," amended Whitney. "Not for the jaguar."

"Don't talk rot, Whitney," said Rainsford. "You're a big-game hunter, not a philosopher. Who cares how a jaguar feels?"

"Perhaps the jaguar does," observed Whitney.

"Bah! They've no understanding."

"Even so. I rather think they understand one thing—fear. The fear of pain and the fear of death."

"Nonsense," laughed Rainsford. "This hot weather is making you soft, Whitney. Be a realist. The world is made up of two classes—the hunters and the huntees. Luckily, you and I are hunters. Do you think we've passed that island yet?"

"I can't tell in the dark. I hope so."

"Why?" asked Rainsford.

"The place has a reputation—a bad one."

"Cannibals?" suggested Rainsford.

"Hardly. Even cannibals wouldn't live in such a God-forsaken place. But it's gotten into sailor lore, somehow. Didn't you notice that the crew's nerves seemed a bit jumpy to-day?"

"They were a bit strange, now you mention it. Even Captain Nielsen—"

"Yes, even that tough-minded old Swede, who'd go up to the devil himself and ask him for a light. Those fishy blue eyes held a look I never saw there before. All I could get out of him was: 'This place has an evil name among sea-faring men, sir.' Then he said to me, very gravely: 'Don't you feel anything?'—as if the air about us was actually poisonous. Now, you mustn't laugh when I tell you this—I did feel something like a sudden chill.

"There was no breeze. The sea was as flat as a plate-glass window. We were drawing near the island then. What I felt was a—a mental chill; a sort of sudden dread."

"Pure imagination," said Rainsford. "One superstitious sailor can taint the whole ship's company with his fear."

"Maybe. But sometimes I think sailors have an extra sense that tells them when they are in danger. Sometimes I think evil is a tangible thing—with wave lengths, just as sound and light have. An evil place can, so to speak, broadcast vibrations of evil. Anyhow, I'm glad we're getting out of this zone. Well, I think I'll turn in now, Rainsford."

"I'm not sleepy," said Rainsford. "I'm going to smoke another pipe up on the after deck."

"Good night, then, Rainsford. See you at breakfast."

"Right. Good night, Whitney."

There was no sound in the night as Rainsford sat there, but the muffled throb of the engine that drove the yacht swiftly through the darkness, and the swish and ripple of the wash of the propeller.

Rainsford, reclining in a steamer chair, indolently puffed on his favorite brier. The sensuous drowsiness of the night was on him. "It's so dark," he thought, "that I could sleep without closing my eyes; the night would be my eyelids—"

An abrupt sound startled him. Off to the right he heard it, and his ears, expert in such matters, could not be mistaken. Again he heard the sound, and again. Somewhere, off in the blackness, some one had fired a gun three times.

Rainsford sprang up and moved quickly to the rail, mystified. He strained his eyes in the direction from which the reports had come, but it was like trying to see through a blanket. He leaped upon the rail and balanced himself there, to get greater elevation; his pipe, striking a rope, was knocked from his mouth. He lunged for it; a short, hoarse cry came from his lips as he realized he had reached too far and had lost his balance. The cry was pinched off short as the blood-warm waters of the Caribbean Sea closed over his head.

He struggled up to the surface and tried to cry out, but the wash from the speeding yacht slapped him in the face and the salt water in his open mouth made him gag and strangle. Desperately he struck out with strong strokes after the receding lights of the yacht, but he stopped before he had swum fifty feet. A certain cool-headedness had come to him; it was not the first time he had been in a tight place. There was a chance that his cries could be heard by some one aboard the yacht, but that chance was slender, and grew more slender as the yacht raced on. He wrestled himself out of his clothes, and shouted with all his power. The lights of the yacht became faint and ever-vanishing fireflies; then they were blotted out entirely by the night.

Rainsford remembered the shots. They had come from the right, and doggedly he swam in that direction, swimming with slow, deliberate strokes, conserving his strength. For a seemingly endless time he fought the sea. He began to count his strokes; he could do possibly a hundred more and then—

Rainsford heard a sound. It came out of the darkness, a high screaming sound, the sound of an animal in an extremity of anguish and terror.

He did not recognize the animal that made the sound; he did not try to; with fresh vitality he swam toward the sound. He heard it again; then it was cut short by another noise, crisp, staccato.

"Pistol shot," muttered Rainsford, swimming on.

Ten minutes of determined effort brought another sound to his ears—the most welcome he had ever heard—the muttering and growling of the sea breaking on a rocky shore. He was almost on the rocks before he saw them; on a night less calm he would have been shattered against them. With his remaining strength he dragged himself from the swirling waters. Jagged crags appeared to jut into the opaqueness, he forced himself upward, hand over hand. Gasping, his hands raw, he reached a flat place at the top. Dense jungle came down to the very edge of the cliffs. What perils that tangle of trees and underbrush might hold for him did not concern Rainsford just then. All he knew was that he was safe from his enemy, the sea, and that utter weariness was on him. He flung himself down at the jungle edge and tumbled headlong into the deepest sleep of his life.

When he opened his eyes he knew from the position of the sun that it was late in the afternoon. Sleep had given him new vigor; a sharp hunger was picking at him. He looked about him, almost cheerfully.

"Where there are pistol shots, there are men. Where there are men, there is food," he thought. But what kind of men, he wondered, in so forbidding a place? An unbroken front of snarled and ragged jungle fringed the shore.

He saw no sign of a trail through the closely knit web of weeds and trees; it was easier to go along the shore, and Rainsford floundered along by the water. Not far from where he had landed, he stopped.

Some wounded thing, by the evidence a large animal, had thrashed about in the underbrush; the jungle weeds were crushed down and the moss was lacerated; one patch of weeds was stained crimson. A small, glattering object not far away caught Rainsford's eye and he picked it up. It was an empty cartridge.

"A twenty-two," he remarked. "That's odd. It must have been a fairly large animal too. The hunter had his nerve with him to tackle it with a light gun. It's clear that the brute put up a fight. I suppose the first three shots I heard was when the hunter flushed his quarry and wounded it. The last shot was when he trailed it here and finished it."

He examined the ground closely and found what he had hoped to find—the print of hunting boots. They pointed along the cliff in the direction he had been going. Eagerly he hurried along, now slipping on a rotten log or a loose stone, but making headway; night was beginning to settle down on the island.

Bleak darkness was blacking out the sea and jungle when Rainsford sighted the lights. He came upon them as he turned a crook in the coast line, and his first thought was that he had come upon a village, for there were many lights. But as he forged along he saw to his great astonishment that all the lights were in one enormous building—a lofty structure with pointed towers plunging upward into the gloom. His eyes made out the shadowy outlines of a palatial château; it was set on a high bluff, and on three sides of it cliffs dived down to where the sea licked greedy lips in the shadows.

"Mirage," thought Rainsford. But it was no mirage, he found, when he opened the tall spiked iron gate. The stone steps were real enough; the massive door with a leering gargoyle for a knocker was real enough; yet about it all hung an air of unreality.

He lifted the knocker, and it creaked up stiffly, as if it had never before been used. He let it fall, and it startled him with its booming loudness. He thought he heard steps within; the door remained closed. Again Rainsford lifted the heavy knocker, and let it fall. The door opened then, opened as suddenly as if it were on a spring, and Rainsford stood blinking in the river of glaring gold light that poured out. The first thing Rainsford's eyes discerned was the largest man Rainsford had ever seen—a gigantic creature, solidly made and black-bearded to the waist. In his hand the man held a long-barreled revolver, and he was pointing it straight at Rainsford's heart.

Out of the snarl of beard two small eyes regarded Rainsford.

"Don't be alarmed," said Rainsford, with a smile which he hoped was disarming. "I'm no robber. I fell off a yacht. My name is Sanger Rainsford of New York City."

The menacing look in the eyes did not change. The revolver pointed as rigidly as if the giant were a statue. He gave no sign that he understood Rainsford's words, or that he had even heard them. He was dressed in uniform, a black uniform trimmed with gray astrakhan.

"I'm Sanger Rainsford of New York," Rainsford began again. "I fell off a yacht. I am hungry."

The man's only answer was to raise with his thumb the hammer of his revolver. Then Rainsford saw the man's free hand go to his forehead in a military salute, and he saw him click his heels together and stand at attention. Another man was coming down the broad marble steps, an erect, slender man in evening clothes. He advanced to Rainsford and held out his hand.

In a cultivated voice marked by a slight accent that gave it added precision and deliberateness, he said: "It is a very great pleasure and honor to welcome Mr. Sanger Rainsford, the celebrated hunter, to my home."

Automatically Rainsford shook the man's hand.

"I've read your book about hunting snow leopards in Tibet, you see," explained the man. "I am General Zaroff."

Rainsford's first impression was that the man was singularly handsome; his second was that there was an original, almost bizarre quality about the general's face. He was a tall man past middle age, for his hair was a vivid white; but his thick eyebrows and pointed military mustache were as black as the night from which Rainsford had come. His eyes, too, were black and very bright. He had high cheek bones, a sharp-cut nose, a spare, dark face, the face of a man used to giving orders, the face of an aristocrat. Turning to the giant in uniform, the general made a sign. The giant put away his pistol, saluted, withdrew.

"Ivan is an incredibly strong fellow," remarked the general, "but he has the misfortune to be deaf and dumb. A simple fellow, but, I'm afraid, like all his race, a bit of a savage."

"Is he Russian?"

"He is a Cossack," said the general, and his smile showed red lips and pointed teeth. "So am I."

"Come," he said, "we shouldn't be chatting here. We can talk later. Now you want clothes, food, rest. You shall have them. This is a most restful spot."

Ivan had reappeared, and the general spoke to him with lips that moved but gave forth no sound.

"Follow Ivan, if you please, Mr. Rainsford," said the general. "I was about to have my dinner when you came. I'll wait for you. You'll find that my clothes will fit you, I think."

It was to a huge, beam-ceilinged bedroom with a canopied bed big enough for six men that Rainsford followed the silent giant. Ivan laid out an evening suit, and Rainsford, as he put it on, noticed that it came from a London tailor who ordinarily cut and sewed for none below the rank of duke.

The dining room to which Ivan conducted him was in many ways remarkable. There was a medieval magnificence abut it; it suggested a baronial hall of feudal times with its oaken panels, its high ceiling, its vast refectory table where two-score men could sit down to eat. About the hall were the mounted heads of many animals—lions, tigers, elephants, moose, bears; larger or more perfect specimens Rainsford had never seen. At the great table the general was sitting, alone.

"You'll have a cocktail, Mr. Rainsford," he suggested. The cocktail was surpassingly good; and Rainsford noted, the table appointments were of the finest—the linen, the crystal, the silver, the china.

They were eating *borsch*, the rich, red soup with whipped cream so dear to Russian palates. Half apologetically General Zaroff said; "We do our best to preserve the amenities of civilization here. Please forgive any lapses. We are well off the beaten track, you know. Do you think the champagne has suffered from its long ocean trip?"

"Not in the least," declared Rainsford. He was finding the general a most thoughtful and affable host, a true cosmopolite. But there was one small trait of the general's that made Rainsford uncomfortable. Whenever he looked up from his plate he found the general studying him, appraising him narrowly.

"Perhaps," said General Zaroff, "you were surprised that I recognized your name. You see, I read all books on hunting published in English, French, and Russian. I have but one passion in my life, Mr. Rainsford, and it is the hunt."

"You have some wonderful heads here," said Rainsford as he ate a particularly well cooked filet mignon. "That Cape buffalo is the largest I ever saw."

"Oh, that fellow. Yes, he was a monster."

"Did he charge you?"

"Hurled me against a tree," said the general. "Fractured my skull. But I got the brute."

"I've always thought," said Rainsford, "that the Cape buffalo is the most dangerous of all big game."

For a moment the general did not reply; he was smiling his curious red-lipped smile. Then he said slowly: "No. You are wrong, sir. The Cape buffalo is not the most dangerous big game." He sipped his wine. "Here in my preserve on this island," he said in the same slow tone, "I hunt more dangerous game."

Rainsford expressed his surprise. "Is there big game on this island?"

The general nodded. "The biggest."

"Really?"

"Oh, it isn't here naturally, of course. I have to stock the island."

"What have you imported, general?" Rainsford asked. "Tigers?"

The general smiled. "No," he said. "Hunting tigers ceased to interest me some years ago. I exhausted their possibilities, you see. No thrill left in tigers, no real danger. I live for danger, Mr. Rainsford."

The general took from his pocket a gold cigaret case and offered his guest a long black cigaret with a silver tip; it was perfumed and gave off a smell like incense.

"We will have some capital hunting, you and I," said the general. "I shall be most glad to have your society."

"But what game—" began Rainsford.

"I'll tell you," said the general. "You will be amused, I know. I think I may say, in all modesty, that I have done a rare thing. I have invented a new sensation. May I pour you another glass of port, Mr. Rainsford?"

"Thank you, general."

The general filled both glasses, and said: "God makes some men poets. Some He makes kings, some beggars. Me He made a hunter. My hand was made for the trigger, my father said. He was a very rich man with a quarter of a million acres in the Crimea, and he was an ardent sportsman. When I was only five years old he gave me a little gun, specially made in Moscow for me, to shoot sparrows with. When I shot some of his prize turkeys with it, he did not punish me; he complimented me on my marksmanship. I killed my first bear in the Caucasus when I was ten. My whole life has been one prolonged hunt. I went into the army—it was expected of noblemen's sons—and for a time commanded a division of Cossack cavalry, but my real interest was always the hunt. I have hunted every kind of game in every land. It would be impossible for me to tell you how many animals I have killed."

The general puffed at his cigaret.

"After the debacle in Russia I left the country, for it was imprudent for an officer of the Czar to stay there. Many noble Russians lost everything. I, luckily, had invested heavily in American securities, so I shall never have to open a tea room in Monte Carlo or drive a taxi in Paris. Naturally, I continued to hunt— grizzlies in your Rockies, crocodiles in the Ganges, rhinoceroses in East Africa. It was in Africa that the Cape buffalo hit me and laid me up for six months. As soon as I recovered I started for the Amazon to hunt jaguars, for I had heard they were unusually cunning. They weren't." The Cossack sighed. "They were no match at all for a hunter with his wits about him, and a high-powered rifle. I was bitterly disappointed. I was lying in my tent with a splitting headache one night when a terrible thought pushed its way into my mind. Hunting was beginning to bore me! And hunting, remember, had been my life. I have heard that in America business men often go to pieces when they give up the business that has been their life."

"Yes, that's so," said Rainsford.

The general smiled. "I had no wish to go to pieces," he said. "I must do something. Now, mine is an analytical mind, Mr. Rainsford. Doubtless that is why I enjoy the problems of the chase."

"No doubt, General Zaroff."

"So," continued the general, "I asked myself why the hunt no longer fascinated me. You are much younger than I am, Mr. Rainsford, and have not hunted as much, but you perhaps can guess the answer."

"What was it?"

"Simply this: hunting had ceased to be what you call 'a sporting proposition.' It had become too easy. I always got my quarry. Always. There is no greater bore than perfection."

The general lit a fresh cigaret.

"No animal had a chance with me any more. That is no boast; it is a mathematical certainty. The animal had nothing but his legs and his instinct. Instinct is no match for reason. When I thought of this it was a tragic moment for me, I can tell you."

Rainsford leaned across the table, absorbed in what his host was saying.

"It came to me as an inspiration what I must do," the general went on.

"And that was?"

The general smiled the quiet smile of one who has faced an obstacle and surmounted it with success. "I had to invent a new animal to hunt," he said.

"A new animal? You're joking."

"Not at all," said the general. "I never joke about hunting. I needed a new animal. I found one. So I bought this island, built this house, and here I do my hunting. The island is perfect for my purposes—there are jungles with a maze of trails in them, hills, swamps—"

"But the animal, General Zaroff?"

"Oh," said the general, "it supplies me with the most exciting hunting in the world. No other hunting compares with it for an instant. Every day I hunt, and I never grow bored now, for I have a quarry with which I can match my wits."

Rainsford's bewilderment showed in his face.

"I wanted the ideal animal to hunt," explained the general. "So I said: 'What are the attributes of an ideal quarry?' And the answer was, of course: 'It must have courage, cunning, and, above all, it must be able to reason.' "

"But no animal can reason," objected Rainsford.

"My dear fellow," said the general, "there is one that can."

"But you can't mean—" gasped Rainsford.

"And why not?"

"I can't believe you are serious, General Zaroff. This is a grisly joke."

"Why should I not be serious? I am speaking of hunting."

"Hunting? Good God, General Zaroff, what you speak of is murder."

The general laughed with entire good nature. He regarded Rainsford quizzically. "I refuse to believe that so modern and civilized a young man as you seem to be harbors romantic ideas about the value of human life. Surely your experiences in the war—"

"Did not make me condone cold-blooded murder," finished Rainsford stiffly.

Laughter shook the general. "How extraordinarily droll you are!" he said. "One does not expect nowadays to find a young man of the educated class, even in America, with such a naïve, and, if I may say so, mid-Victorian point of view. It's like finding a snuff-box in a limousine. Ah, well, doubtless you had Puritan ancestors. So many Americans appear to have had. I'll wager you'll forget your notions when you go hunting with me. You've a genuine new thrill in store for you, Mr. Rainsford."

"Thank you, I'm a hunter, not a murderer."

"Dear me," said the general, quite unruffled, "again that unpleasant word. But I think I can show you that your scruples are quite ill founded."

"Yes?"

"Life is for the strong, to be lived by the strong, and, if need be, taken by the strong. The weak of the world were put here to give the strong pleasure. I am strong. Why should I not use my gift? If I wish to hunt, why should I not? I hunt the scum of the earth—sailors from tramp ships—lascars, blacks, Chinese, whites, mongrels—a thorobred horse or hound is worth more than a score of them."

"But they are men," said Rainsford hotly.

"Precisely," said the general. "That is why I use them. It gives me pleasure. They can reason, after a fashion. So they are dangerous."

"But where do you get them?"

The general's left eyelid fluttered down in a wink. "This island is called Ship-Trap," he answered. "Sometimes an angry god of the high seas sends them to me. Sometimes, when Providence is not so kind, I help Providence a bit. Come to the window with me."

Rainsford went to the window and looked out toward the sea.

"Watch! Out there!" exclaimed the general, pointing into the night. Rainsford's eyes saw only blackness, and then, as the general pressed a button, far out to sea Rainsford saw the flash of lights.

The general chuckled. "They indicate a channel," he said, "where there's none: giant rocks with razor edges crouch like a sea monster with wide-open jaws. They can crush a ship as easily as I crush this nut." He dropped a walnut on the hardwood floor and brought his heel grinding down on it. "Oh, yes," he said, casually, as if in answer to a question, "I have electricity. We try to be civilized here."

"Civilized? And you shoot down men?"

A trace of anger was in the general's black eyes, but it was there for but a second, and he said, in his most pleasant manner: "Dear me, what a righteous young man you are! I assure you I do not do the thing you suggest. That would be barbarous. I treat these visitors with every consideration. They get plenty of good food and exercise. They get into splendid physical condition. You shall see for yourself to-morrow."

"What do you mean?"

"We'll visit my training school," smiled the general. "It's in the cellar. I have about a dozen pupils down there now. They're from the Spanish bark San Lucar that had the bad luck to go on the rocks out there. A very inferior lot, I regret to say. Poor specimens and more accustomed to the deck than to the jungle."

He raised his hand, and Ivan, who served as waiter, brought thick Turkish coffee. Rainsford, with an effort, held his tongue in check.

"It's a game, you see," pursued the general blandly. "I suggest to one of them that we go hunting. I give him a supply of food and an excellent hunting knife. I give him three hours' start. I am to follow, armed only with a pistol of the smallest caliber and range. If my quarry eludes me for three whole days, he wins the game. If I find him"—the general smiled—"he loses."

"Suppose he refuses to be hunted?"

"Oh," said the general, "I give him his option, of course. He need not play that game if he doesn't wish to. If he does not wish to hunt, I turn him over to Ivan. Ivan once had the honor of serving as official knouter to the Great White Czar, and he has his own ideas of sport. Invariably, Mr. Rainsford, invariably they choose the hunt."

"And if they win?"

The smile on the general's face widened. "To date I have not lost," he said.

Then he added, hastily: "I don't wish you to think me a braggart, Mr. Rainsford. Many of them afford only the most elementary sort of problem. Occasionally I strike a tartar. One almost did win. I eventually had to use the dogs."

"The dogs?"

"This way, please. I'll show you."

The general steered Rainsford to a window. The lights from the windows sent a flickering illumination that made grotesque patterns on the courtyard below, and Rainsford could see moving about there a dozen or so huge black shapes; as they turned toward him, their eyes glittered greenly.

"A rather good lot, I think," observed the general. "They are let out at seven every night. If anyone should try to get into my house—or out of it—something extremely regrettable would occur to him." He hummed a snatch of song from the Folies Bergère.

"And now," said the general, "I want to show you my new collection of heads. Will you come with me to the library?"

"I hope," said Rainsford, "that you will excuse me to-night, General Zaroff. I'm really not feeling at all well."

"Ah, indeed?" the general inquired solicitously. "Well, I suppose that's only natural, after your long swim. You need a good, restful night's sleep. To-morrow you'll feel like a new man, I'll wager. Then we'll hunt, eh? I've one rather promising prospect—"

Rainsford was hurrying from the room.

"Sorry you can't go with me to-night," called the general. "I expect rather fair sport—a big, strong black. He looks resourceful—Well, good night, Mr. Rainsford; I hope you have a good night's rest."

The bed was good, and the pajamas of the softest silk, and he was tired in every fiber of his being, but nevertheless Rainsford could not quiet his brain with the opiate of sleep. He lay, eyes wide open. Once he thought he heard stealthy steps in the corridor outside his room. He sought to throw open the door; it would not open. He went to the window and looked out. His room was high up in one of the towers. The lights of the château were out now, and it was dark and silent, but there was a fragment of sallow moon, and by its wan light he could see, dimly, the courtyard; there, weaving in and out in the pattern of shadow, were black, noiseless forms; the hounds heard him at the window and looked up, expectantly, with their green eyes. Rainsford went back to the bed and lay down. By many methods he tried to put himself to sleep. He had achieved a doze when, just as morning began to come, he heard, far off in the jungle, the faint report of a pistol.

General Zaroff did not appear until luncheon. He was dressed faultlessly in the tweeds of a country squire. He was solicitous about the state of Rainsford's health.

"As for me," sighed the general, "I do not feel so well. I am worried, Mr. Rainsford. Last night I detected traces of my old complaint."

To Rainsford's questioning glance the general said: "Ennui. Boredom."

Then, taking a second helping of Crêpes Suzette, the general explained: "The hunting was not good last night. The fellow lost his head. He made a straight trail that offered no problems at all. That's the trouble with these sailors; they have dull brains to begin with, and they do not know how to get about in the woods. They do excessively stupid and obvious things. It's most annoying. Will you have another glass of Chablis, Mr. Rainsford?"

"General," said Rainsford firmly, "I wish to leave this island at once."

The general raised his thickets of eyebrows; he seemed hurt. "But, my dear fellow," the general protested, "you've only just come. You've had no hunting—"

"I wish to go to-day," said Rainsford. He saw the dead black eyes of the general on him, studying him. General Zaroff's face suddenly brightened.

He filled Rainsford's glass with venerable Chablis from a dusty bottle.

"To-night," said the general, "we will hunt—you and I."

Rainsford shook his head. "No, general," he said. "I will not hunt."

The general shrugged his shoulders and delicately ate a hothouse grape. "As you wish, my friend," he said. "The choice rests entirely with you. But may I not venture to suggest that you will find my idea of sport more diverting than Ivan's?"

He nodded toward the corner to where the giant stood, scowling, his thick arms crossed on his hogshead of chest.

"You don't mean—" cried Rainsford.

"My dear fellow," said the general, "have I not told you I always mean what I say about hunting? This is really an inspiration. I drink to a foeman worthy of my steel—at last."

The general raised his glass, but Rainsford sat staring at him.

"You'll find this game worth playing," the general said enthusiastically. "Your brain against mine. Your woodcraft against mine. Your strength and stamina against mine. Outdoor chess! And the stake is not without value, eh?"

"And if I win—" began Rainsford huskily.

"I'll cheerfully acknowledge myself defeated if I do not find you by midnight of the third day," said General Zaroff. "My sloop will place you on the mainland near a town."

The general read what Rainsford was thinking.

"Oh, you can trust me," said the Cossack. "I will give you my word as a gentleman and a sportsman. Of course you, in turn, must agree to say nothing of your visit here."

"I'll agree to nothing of the kind," said Rainsford.

"Oh," said the general, "in that case—But why discuss that now? Three days hence we can discuss it over a bottle of Veuve Cliquot, unless—"

The general sipped his wine.

Then a businesslike air animated him. "Ivan," he said to Rainsford "will supply you with hunting clothes, food, a knife. I suggest you wear moccasins; they leave a poorer trail. I suggest too that you avoid the big swamp in the southeast corner of the island. We call it Death Swamp. There's quicksand there. One foolish fellow tried it. The deplorable part of it was that Lazarus followed him. You can imagine my feelings, Mr. Rainsford. I loved Lazarus; he was the finest hound in my pack. Well, I must beg you to excuse me now. I always take a siesta after lunch. You'll hardly have time for a nap, I fear. You'll want to start, no doubt. I shall not follow till dusk. Hunting at night is so much more exciting than by day, don't you think? Au revoir, Mr. Rainsford, au revoir."

General Zaroff, with a deep, courtly bow, strolled from the room.

From another door came Ivan. Under one arm he carried khaki hunting clothes, a haversack of food, a leather sheath containing a long-bladed hunting knife; his right hand rested on a cocked revolver thrust in the crimson sash about his waist. . . .

Rainsford had fought his way through the bush for two hours. "I must keep my nerve. I must keep my nerve," he said through tight teeth.

He had not been entirely clear-headed when the château gates snapped shut behind him. His whole idea at first was to put distance between himself and General Zaroff, and, to this end, he had plunged along, spurred on by the sharp rowels of something very like panic. Now he had got a grip on himself, had stopped, and was taking stock of himself and the situation.

He saw that straight flight was futile; inevitably it would bring him face to face with the sea. He was in a picture with a frame of water, and his operations, clearly, must take place within that frame.

"I'll give him a trail to follow," muttered Rainsford, and he struck off from the rude paths he had been following into the trackless wilderness. He executed a series of intricate loops; he doubled on his trail again and again, recalling all the lore of the fox hunt, and all the dodges of the fox. Night found him leg-weary, with hands and face lashed by the branches, on a thickly wooded ridge. He knew it would be insane to blunder on through the dark, even if he had the strength. His need for rest was imperative and he thought: "I have played the fox, now I must play the cat of the fable." A big tree with a thick trunk and outspread branches was nearby, and, taking care to leave not the slightest mark, he climbed up into the crotch, and stretching out on one of the broad limbs, after a fashion, rested. Rest brought him new confidence and almost a feeling of se-curity. Even so zealous a hunter as General Zaroff could not trace him there, he told himself; only the devil himself could follow that complicated trail through the jungle after dark. But, perhaps, the general was a devil—

An apprehensive night crawled slowly by like a wounded snake, and sleep did not visit Rainsford, altho the silence of a dead world was on the jungle. Toward morning when a dingy gray was varnishing the sky, the cry of some startled bird focused Rainsford's attention in that direction. Something was com-ing through the bush, coming slowly, carefully, coming by the same winding way Rainsford had come. He flattened himself down on the limb, and through a screen of leaves almost as thick as tapestry, he watched. The thing that was approaching was a man.

It was General Zaroff. He made his way along with his eyes fixed in utmost concentration on the ground before him. He paused, almost beneath the tree, dropped to his knees and studied the ground. Rainsford's impulse was to hurl himself down like a panther, but he saw that the general's right hand held some-thing metallic—a small automatic pistol.

The hunter shook his head several times, as if he were puzzled. Then he straightened up and took from his case one of his black cigarets; its pungent incense-like smoke floated up to Rainsford's nostrils.

Rainsford held his breath. The general's eyes had left the ground and were traveling inch by inch up the tree. Rainsford froze there, every muscle tensed for a spring. But the sharp eyes of the hunter stopped before they reached the limb where Rainsford lay; a smile spread over his brown face. Very deliberately he blew a smoke ring into the air; then he turned his back on the tree and walked carelessly away, back along the trail he had come. The swish of the underbrush against his hunting boots grew fainter and fainter.

The pent-up air burst hotly from Rainsford's lungs. His first thought made him feel sick and numb. The general could follow a trail through the woods at night; he could follow an extremely difficult trail; he must have uncanny powers; only by the merest chance had the Cossack failed to see his quarry.

Rainsford's second thought was even more terrible. It sent a shudder of cold horror through his whole being. Why had the general smiled? Why had he turned back?

Rainsford did not want to believe what his reason told him was true, but the truth was as evident as the sun that had by now pushed through the morning mists. The general was playing with him! The general was saving him for an-other day's sport! The Cossack was the cat; he was the mouse. Then it was that Rainsford knew the full meaning of terror.

"I will not lose my nerve. I will not."

He slid down from the tree, and struck off again into the woods. His face was set and he forced the machinery of his mind to function. Three hundred yards from his hiding place he stopped where a huge dead tree leaned precariously on a smaller, living one. Throwing off his sack of food, Rainsford took his knife from its sheath and began to work with all his energy.

The job was finished at last, and he threw himself down behind a fallen log a hundred feet away. He did not have to wait long. The cat was coming again to play with the mouse.

Following the trail with the sureness of a bloodhound, came General Zaroff. Nothing escaped those searching black eyes, no crushed blade of grass, no bent twig, no mark, no matter how faint, in the moss. So intent was the Cossack on his stalking that he was upon the thing Rainsford had made before he saw it. His foot touched the protruding bough that was the trigger. Even as he touched it, the general sensed his danger and leaped back with the agility of an ape. But he was not quite quick enough; the dead tree, delicately adjusted to rest on the cut living one, crashed down and struck the general a glancing blow on the shoulder as it fell; but for his alertness he must have been smashed beneath it. He staggered, but he did not fall; nor did he drop his revolver. He stood there, rubbing his injured shoulder, and Rainsford, with fear again gripping his heart, heard the general's mocking laugh ring through the jungle.

"Rainsford," called the general, "if you are within sound of my voice, as I suppose you are, let me congratulate you. Not many men know how to make a Malay man-catcher. Luckily, for me, I too have hunted in Malacca. You are proving interesting, Mr. Rainsford. I am going now to have my wound dressed; it's only a slight one. But I shall be back. I shall be back."

When the general, nursing his bruised shoulder, had gone, Rainsford took up his flight again. It was flight now, a desperate, hopeless flight, that carried him on for some hours. Dusk came, then darkness, and still he pressed on. The ground grew softer under his moccasins; the vegetation grew ranker, denser; insects bit him savagely. Then, as he stepped forward, his foot sank into the ooze. He tried to wrench it back, but the muck sucked viciously at his foot as if it were a giant leech. With a violent effort, he tore his foot loose. He knew where he was now. Death Swamp and its quicksand.

His hands were tight closed as if his nerve were something tangible that some one in the darkness was trying to tear from his grip. The softness of the earth had given him an idea. He stepped back from the quicksand a dozen feet or so and, like some huge prehistoric beaver, he began to dig.

Rainsford had dug himself in in France when a second's delay meant death. That had been a placid pastime compared to his digging now. The pit grew deeper; when it was above his shoulders, he climbed out and from some hard saplings cut stakes and sharpened them to a fine point. These stakes he planted in the bottom of the pit with the points sticking up. With flying fingers he wove a rough carpet of weeds and branches and with it he covered the mouth of the pit. Then, wet with sweat and aching with tiredness, he crouched behind the stump of a lightning-charred tree.

He knew his pursuer was coming; he heard the padding sound of feet on the soft earth, and the night breeze brought him the perfume of the general's cigaret. It seemed to Rainsford that the general was coming with unusual swiftness; he was not feeling his way along, foot by foot. Rainsford, crouching there, could not see the general, nor could he see the pit. He lived a year in a minute. Then he felt an impulse to cry aloud with joy, for he heard the sharp crackle of the breaking branches as the cover of the pit gave way; he heard the sharp scream of pain as the pointed stakes found their mark. He leaped up from his place of concealment. Then he cowered back. Three feet from the pit a man was standing, with an electric torch in his hand.

"You've done well, Rainsford," the voice of the general called. "Your Burmese tiger pit has claimed one of my best dogs. Again you score. I think, Mr. Rainsford, I'll see what you can do against my whole pack. I'm going home for a rest now. Thank you for a most amusing evening."

At daybreak Rainsford, lying near the swamp, was awakened by a sound that made him know that he had new things to learn about fear. It was a distant sound, faint and wavering, but he knew it. It was the baying of a pack of hounds.

Rainsford knew he could do one of two things. He could stay where he was and wait. That was suicide. He could flee. That was postponing the inevitable. For a moment he stood there, thinking. An idea that held a wild chance came to him, and, tightening his belt, he headed away from the swamp.

The baying of the hounds drew nearer, then still nearer, nearer, ever nearer. On a ridge Rainsford climbed a tree. Down a watercourse, not a quarter of a mile away, he could see the bush moving. Straining his eyes, he saw the lean figure of General Zaroff; just ahead of him Rainsford made out another figure whose wide shoulders surged through the tall jungle weeds; it was the giant Ivan, and he seemed pulled forward by unseen force; Rainsford knew that Ivan must be holding the pack in leash.

They would be on him any minute now. His mind worked frantically. He thought of a native trick he had learned in Uganda. He slid down the tree. He caught hold of a springy young sapling and to it he fastened his hunting knife, with the blade pointing down the trail; with a bit of wild grapevine he tied back the sapling. Then he ran for his life. The hounds raised their voices as they hit the fresh scent. Rainsford knew now how an animal at bay feels.

He had to stop to get his breath. The baying of the hounds stopped abruptly, and Rainsford's heart stopped too. They must have reached the knife.

He shinnied excitedly up a tree and looked back. His pursuers had stopped. But the hope that was in Rainsford's brain when he climbed died, for he saw in the shallow valley that General Zaroff was still on his feet. But Ivan was not. The knife, driven by the recoil of the springing tree, had not wholly failed.

Rainsford had hardly tumbled to the ground when the pack took up the cry again.

"Nerve, nerve, nerve!" he panted, as he dashed along. A blue gap showed between the trees dead ahead. Ever nearer drew the hounds. Rainsford forced himself on toward that gap. He reached it. It was the shore of the sea. Across a cove he could see the gloomy gray stone of the château. Twenty feet below him the sea rumbled and hissed. Rainsford hesitated. He heard the hounds. Then he leaped far out into the sea. . . .

When the general and his pack reached the place by the sea, the Cossack stopped. For some minutes he stood regarding the blue-green expanse of water. He shrugged his shoulders. Then he sat down, took a drink of brandy from a silver flask, lit a perfumed cigaret, and hummed a bit from "Madame Butterfly."

General Zaroff had an exceedingly good dinner in his great paneled dining hall that evening. With it he had a bottle of Pol Roger and half a bottle of Chambertin. Two slight annoyances kept him from perfect enjoyment. One was the thought that it would be difficult to replace Ivan; the other was that his quarry had escaped him; of course the American hadn't played the game—so thought the general as he tasted his after-dinner liqueur, In his library he read, to soothe himself, from the works of Marcus Aurelius. At ten he went up to his bedroom. He was deliciously tired, he said to himself, as he locked himself in. There was a little moonlight, so, before turning on his light, he went to the window and looked down at the courtyard. He could see the great hounds, and he called: "Better luck another time," to them. Then he switched on the light.

A man, who had been hiding in the curtains of the bed, was standing there.

"Rainsford!" screamed the general. "How in God's name did you get here?"

"Swam," said Rainsford. "I found it quicker than walking through the jungle."

The general sucked in his breath and smiled. "I congratulate you," he said. "You have won the game."

Rainsford did not smile. "I am still a beast at bay," he said, in a low, hoarse voice. "Get ready, General Zaroff."

The general made one of his deepest bows. "I see," he said. "Splendid! One of us is to furnish a repast for the hounds. The other will sleep in this very excellent bed. On guard, Rainsford. . . ."

He had never slept in a better bed, Rainsford decided.

Considerations

1. In this story, why has General Zaroff's love for hunting developed into such an insane obsession?
2. What does the general mean when he says, ". . . There is no greater bore than perfection"?
3. In the discussion between Rainsford and General Zaroff on the subject of murder, what does the general imply when he says, "Surely your experiences in the war—"?
4. Although Connell carefully avoids any direct comment on "morality" in this story, why is that subject nevertheless an important element?
5. Exactly how does Rainsford's attitude toward murder seem to change by the end of the story? Does he display feelings of guilt or remorse? Do you think he will now replace Zaroff as the hunter in this "most dangerous game"? If so, what would such a decision suggest about human nature?
6. Discuss the author's use of coincidence in this story? Does he use it convincingly or does he overdo it? Support your answer.

PSYCHOLOGICAL REALISM
Sports as Agent of
Social Deviance

Midge Kelly scored his first knockout when he was seventeen. The knockee was his brother Connie, three years his junior and a cripple.

—**Ring Lardner**

RING LARDNER

Champion

Midge Kelly scored his first knockout when he was seventeen. The knockee was his brother Connie, three years his junior and a cripple. The purse was a half dollar given to the younger Kelly by a lady whose electric had just missed bumping his soul from his frail little body.

Connie did not know Midge was in the house, else he never would have risked laying the prize on the arm of the least comfortable chair in the room, the better to observe its shining beauty. As Midge entered from the kitchen, the crippled boy covered the coin with his hand, but the movement lacked the speed required to escape his brother's quick eye.

"Watcha got there?" demanded Midge.

"Nothin'," said Connie.

"Your're a one legged liar!" said Midge.

He strode over to his brother's chair and grasped the hand that concealed the coin.

"Let loose!" he ordered.

Connie began to cry.

"Let loose and shut up your noise," said the elder, and jerked his brother's hand from the chair arm.

35

The coin fell onto the bare floor. Midge pounced on it. His weak mouth widened in a triumphant smile.

"Nothin', huh?" he said. "All right, if it's nothin' you don't want it."

"Give that back," sobbed the younger.

"I'll give you a red nose, you little sneak! Where'd you steal it?"

"I didn't steal it. It's mine. A lady give it to me after she pretty near hit me with a car."

"It's a crime she missed you," said Midge.

Midge started for the front door. The cripple picked up his crutch, rose from his chair with difficulty, and, still sobbing, came toward Midge. The latter heard him and stopped.

"You better stay where you're at," he said.

"I want my money," cried the boy.

"I know what you want," said Midge.

Doubling up the fist that held the half dollar, he landed with all his strength on his brother's mouth. Connie fell to the floor with a thud, the crutch tumbling on top of him. Midge stood beside the prostrate form.

"Is that enough?" he said. "Or do you want this, too?"

And he kicked him in the crippled leg.

"I guess that'll hold you," he said.

There was no response from the boy on the floor. Midge looked at him a moment, then at the coin in his hand, and then went out into the street, whistling.

An hour later, when Mrs. Kelly came home from her day's work at Faulkner's Steam Laundry, she found Connie on the floor, moaning. Dropping on her knees beside him, she called him by name a score of times. Then she got up and, pale as a ghost, dashed from the house. Dr. Ryan left the Kelly abode about dusk and walked toward Halsted Street. Mrs. Dorgan spied him as he passed her gate.

"Who's sick, Doctor?" she called.

"Poor little Connie," he replied. "He had a bad fall."

"How did it happen?"

"I can't say for sure, Margaret, but I'd almost bet he was knocked down."

"Knocked down!" exclaimed Mrs. Dorgan.

"Why, who—?"

"Have you seen the other one lately?"

"Michael? No, not since mornin'. You can't be thinkin'—"

"I wouldn't put it past him, Margaret," said the doctor gravely. "The lad's mouth is swollen and cut, and his poor, skinny little leg is bruised. He surely didn't do it to himself and I think Helen suspects the other one."

"Lord save us!" said Mrs. Dorgan. "I'll run over and see if I can help."

"That's a good woman," said Doctor Ryan, and went on down the street.

Near midnight, when Midge came home, his mother was sitting at Connie's bedside. She did not look up.

"Well," said Midge, "what's the matter?"

She remained silent. Midge repeated his question.

"Michael, you know what's the matter," she said at length.

"I don't know nothin'," said Midge.

"Don't lie to me, Michael. What did you do to your brother?"

"Nothin'."

"You hit him."

"Well, then, I hit him. What of it? It ain't the first time."

Her lips pressed tightly together, her face like chalk, Ellen Kelly rose from her chair and made straight for him. Midge backed against the door.

"Lay off'n me, Ma. I don't want to fight no woman."

Still she came on breathing heavily.

"Stop where you're at, Ma," he warned.

There was a brief struggle and Midge's mother lay on the floor before him.

"You ain't hurt, Ma. You're lucky I didn't land good. And I told you to lay off'n me."

"God forgive you, Michael!"

Midge found Hap Collins in the showdown game at the Royal.

"Come on out a minute," he said.

Hap followed him out on the walk.

"I'm leavin' town for a w'ile," said Midge.

"What for?"

"Well, we had a little run-in up to the house. The kid stole a half buck off'n me, and when I went after it he cracked me with his crutch. So I nailed him. And the old lady came at me with a chair and I took it off'n her and she fell down."

"How is Connie hurt?"

"Not bad."

"What are you runnin' away for?"

"Who the hell said I was runnin' away? I'm sick and tired o' gettin' picked on; that's all. So I'm leavin' for a w'ile and I want a piece o' money."

"I ain't only got six bits," said Happy.

"You're in bad shape, ain't you? Well, come through with it."

Happy came through.

"You oughtn't to hit the kid," he said.

"I ain't astin' you who can I hit," snarled Midge. "You try to put somethin' over on me and you'll get the same dose. I'm goin' now."

"Go as far as you like," said Happy, but not until he was sure that Kelly was out of hearing.

Early the following morning, Midge boarded a train for Milwaukee. He had no ticket, but no one knew the difference. The conductor remained in the caboose.

On a night six months later, Midge hurried out of the "stage door" of the Star Boxing Club and made for Duane's saloon, two blocks away. In his pocket were twelve dollars, his reward for having battered up one Demon Dempsey through the six rounds of the first preliminary.

It was Midge's first professional engagement in the manly art. Also it was the first time in weeks that he had earned twelve dollars.

On the way to Duane's he had to pass Niemann's. He pulled his cap over his eyes and increased his pace until he had gone by. Inside Niemann's stood a trusting bartender, who for ten days had staked Midge to drinks and allowed him to ravage the lunch on a promise to come in and settle the moment he was paid for the "prelim."

Midge strode into Duane's and aroused the napping bartender by slapping a silver dollar on the festive board.

"Gimme a shot," said Midge.

The shooting continued until the wind-up at the Star was over and part of the fight crowd joined Midge in front of Duane's bar. A youth in the early twenties, standing next to young Kelly, finally summoned sufficient courage to address him.

"Wasn't you in the first bout?" he ventured.

"Yeh," Midge replied.

"My name's Hersch," said the other.

Midge received the startling information in silence.

"I don't want to butt in," continued Mr. Hersch, "but I'd like to buy you a drink."

"All right," said Midge, "but don't overstrain yourself."

Mr. Hersch laughed uproariously and beckoned to the bartender.

"You certainly gave that wop a trimmin' tonight," said the buyer of the drink, when they had been served. "I thought you'd kill him."

"I would if I hadn't let up," Midge replied. "I'll kill 'em all."

"You got the wallop all right," the other said admiringly.

"Have I got the wallop?" said Midge. "Say, I can kick like a mule. Did you notice them muscles in my shoulders?"

"Notice 'em? I couldn't help from noticin' 'em," said Hersch. "I says to the fella settin' alongside o' me, I says: 'Look at them shoulders! No wonder he can hit,' I says to him."

"Just let me land and it's good-by, baby," said Midge. "I'll kill 'em all."

The oral manslaughter continued until Duane's closed for the night. At parting, Midge and his new friend shook hands and arranged for a meeting the following evening.

For nearly a week the two were together almost constantly. It was Hersch's pleasant role to listen to Midge's modest revelations concerning himself, and to buy every time Midge's glass was empty. But there came an evening when Hersch regretfully announced that he must go home to supper.

"I got a date for eight bells," he confided. "I could stick till then, only I must clean up and put on the Sunday clo'es, 'cause she's the prettiest little thing in Milwaukee."

"Can't you fix it for two?" asked Midge.

"I don't know who to get," Hersch replied. "Wait, though. I got a sister and if she ain't busy, it'll be O.K. She's no bum for looks herself."

So it came about that Midge and Emma Hersch and Emma's brother and the prettiest little thing in Milwaukee foregathered at Wall's and danced half the night away. And Midge and Emma danced every dance together, for though every little onestep seemed to induce a new thirst of its own, Lou Hersch stayed too sober to dance with his own sister.

The next day, penniless at last in spite of his phenomenal ability to make someone else settle, Midge Kelly sought out Doc Hammond, matchmaker for the Star, and asked to be booked for the next show.

"I could put you on with Tracy for the next bout," said Doc.

"What's they in it?" asked Midge.

"Twenty if you cop," Doc told him.

"Have a heart," protested Midge. "Didn't I look good the other night?"

"You looked all right. But you aren't Freddie Welsh yet by a consid-'able margin."

"I ain't scared of Freddie Welsh or none of 'em," said Midge.

"Well, we don't pay our boxers by the size of their chests," Doc said. "I'm offerin' you this Tracy bout. Take it or leave it."

"All right; I'm on," said Midge, and he passed a pleasant afternoon at Duane's on the strength of his booking.

Young Tracy's manager came to Midge the night before the show.

"How do you feel about this go?" he asked.

"Me?" said Midge, "I feel all right. What do you mean, how do I feel?"

"I mean," said Tracy's manager, "that we're mighty anxious to win, 'cause the boy's got a chanct in Philly if he cops this one."

"What's your proposition?" asked Midge.

"Fifty bucks," said Tracy's manager.

"What do you think I am, a crook? Me lay down for fifty bucks. Not me!"

"Seventy-five, then," said Tracy's manager.

The market closed on eighty and the details were agreed on in short order. And the next night Midge was stopped in the second round by a terrific slap on the forearm.

This time Midge passed up both Niemann's and Duane's, having a sizable account at each place, and sought his refreshment at Stein's farther down the street.

When the profits of his deal with Tracy were gone, he learned, by first-hand information from Doc Hammond and the matchmakers at other "clubs," that he was no longer desired for even the cheapest of preliminaries. There was no danger of his starving or dying of thirst while Emma and Lou Hersch lived. But he made up his mind, four months after his defeat by Young Tracy, that Milwaukee was not the ideal place for him to live.

"I can lick the best of 'em," he reasoned, "but there ain't no more chanct for me here. I can maybe go east and get on somewheres. And besides——"

But just after Midge had purchased a ticket to Chicago with the money he had "borrowed" from Emma Hersch "to buy shoes," a heavy hand was laid on his shoulders and he turned to face two strangers.

"Where are you goin', Kelly?" inquired the owner of the heavy hand.

"Nowheres," said Midge. "What the hell do you care?"

The other stranger spoke:

"Kelly, I'm employed by Emma Hersch's mother to see that you do right by her. And we want you to stay here till you've done it."

"You won't get nothin' but the worst of it, monkeying with me," said Midge.

Nevertheless he did not depart for Chicago that night. Two days later, Emma Hersch became Mrs. Kelly, and the gift of the groom, when once they were alone, was a crushing blow on the bride's pale cheek.

Next morning, Midge left Milwaukee as he had entered it—by fast freight.

"They's no use kiddin' ourself any more," said Tommy Haley. "He might get down to thirty-seven in a pinch, but if he done below that a mouse could stop him. He's a welter; that's what he is and he knows it as well as I do. He's growed like a weed in the last six mont's. I told him, I says, 'If you don't quit growin' they won't be nobody for you to box, only Willard and them.' He says, 'Well, I wouldn't run away from Willard if I weighed twenty pounds more.'"

"He must hate himself," said Tommy's brother.

"I never seen a good one that didn't," said Tommy. "And Midge is a good one; don't make no mistake about that. I wisht we could of got Welsh before the kid growed so big. But it's too late now. I won't make no holler, though, if we can match him up with the Dutchman."

"Who do you mean?"

"Young Goetz, the welter champ. We mightn't not get so much dough for the bout itself, but it'd roll in afterward. What a drawin' card we'd be, 'cause the people pays their money to see the fella with the wallop, and that's Midge. And we'd keep the title just as long as Midge could make the weight."

"Can't you land no match with Goetz?"

"Sure, 'cause he needs the money. But I've went careful with the kid so far and look at the results I got! So what's the use of takin a chanct? The kid's comin' every minute and Goetz is goin' back faster'n big Johnson did. I think we could lick him now; I'd bet my life on it. But six mont's from now they won't be no risk. He'll of licked hisself before that time. Then all as we'll have to do is sign up with him and wait for the referee to stop it. But Midge is so crazy to get at him now that I can't hardly hold him back."

The brothers Haley were lunching in a Boston hotel. Dan had come down from Holyoke to visit with Tommy and to watch the latter's protégé go twelve rounds, or less, with Bud Cross. The bout promised little in the way of a contest, for Midge had twice stopped the Baltimore youth and Bud's reputation for gameness was all that had earned him the date. The fans were willing to pay the price to see Midge's hay-making left, but they wanted to see it used on an opponent who would not jump out of the ring the first time he felt its crushing force. Bud Cross was such an opponent, and his willingness to stop boxing-gloves with his eyes, ears, nose and throat had long enabled him to escape the horrors of honest labor. A game boy was Bud, and he showed it in his battered, swollen, discolored face.

"I should think," said Dan Haley, "that the kid'd do whatever you tell him after all you done for him."

"Well," said Tommy, "he's took my dope pretty straight so far, but he's so sure of hisself that he can't see no reason for waitin'. He'll do what I say, though; he'd be a sucker not to."

"You got a contrac' with him?"

"No, I don't need no contrac'. He knows it was me that drug him out o' the gutter and he ain't goin' to turn me down now, when he's got the dough and bound to get more. Where'd he of been at if I hadn't listened to him when he first come to me? That's pretty near two years ago now, but it seems like last week. I was settin' in the s'loon acrost from the Pleasant Club in Philly, waitin' for McCann to count the dough and come over, when this little bum blowed in and tried to stand the house off for a drink. They told him nothin' doin' and to beat it out o' there, and then he seen me and come over to where I was settin' and ast me wasn't I a boxin' man and I told him who I was. Then he ast me for money to buy a shot and I told him to set down and I'd buy it for him.

"Then we got talkin' things over and he told me his name and told me about fightin' a couple o' prelims out to Milwaukee. So I says, 'Well, boy, I don't know how good or how rotten you are, but you won't never get nowheres trainin' on that stuff.' So he says he'd cut it out if he could get on in a bout and I says I would give him a chanct if he played square with me and didn't touch no more to drink. So we shook hands and I took him up to the hotel with me and give him a bath and the next day I bought him some clo'es. And I staked him to eats and sleeps for over six weeks. He had a hard time breakin' away from the polish, but finally I thought he was fit and I give him his chanct. He went on with Smiley Sayer and stopped him so quick that Smiley thought sure he was poisoned.

"Well, you know what he's did since. The only beatin' in his record was by Tracy in Milwaukee before I got hold of him, and he's licked Tracy three times in the last year.

"I've gave him all the best of it in a money way and he's got seven thousand bucks in cold storage. How's that for a kid that was in the gutter two years ago? And he'd have still more yet if he wasn't so nuts over clo'es and got to stop at the good hotels and so forth."

"Where's his home at?"

"Well, he ain't really got no home. He came from Chicago and his mother canned him out o' the house for bein' no good. She give him a raw deal, I guess, and he says he won't have nothin' to do with her unless she comes to him first. She's got a pile o' money, he says, so he ain't worryin' about her."

The gentleman under discussion entered the café and swaggered to Tommy's table, while the whole room turned to look.

Midge was the picture of health despite a slightly colored eye and an ear that seemed to have no opening. But perhaps it was not his healthiness that drew all eyes. His diamond horse-shoe tie pin, his purple cross-striped shirt, his orange shoes and his light blue suit fairly screamed for attention.

"Where you been?" he asked Tommy. "I been lookin' all over for you."

"Set down," said his manager.

"No time," said Midge. "I'm goin' down to the w'arf and see 'em unload the fish."

"Shake hands with my brother Dan," said Tommy.

Midge shook hands with the Holyoke Haley.

"If you're Tommy's brother, you're O.K. with me," said Midge, and the brothers beamed with pleasure.

Dan moistened his lips and murmured an embarrassed reply, but it was lost on the young gladiator.

"Leave me take twenty," Midge was saying. "I prob'ly won't need it, but I don't like to be caught short."

Tommy parted with a twenty dollar bill and recorded the transaction in a small black book the insurance company had given him for Christmas.

"But," he said, "it won't cost you no twenty to look at them fish. Want me to go along?"

"No," said Midge hastily. "You and your brother here prob'ly got a lot to say to each other."

"Well," said Tommy, "don't take no bad money and don't get lost. And you better be back at four o'clock and lay down a w'ile."

"I don't need no rest to beat this guy," said Midge. "He'll do enough layin' down for the both of us."

And laughing even more than the jest called for, he strode out through the fire of admiring and startled glances.

The corner of Boylston and Tremont was the nearest Midge got to the wharf, but the lady awaiting him was doubtless a more dazzling sight than the catch of the luckiest Massachusetts fisherman. She could talk, too—probably better than the fish.

"O you Kid!" she said, flashing a few silver teeth among the gold. "O you fighting man!"

Midge smiled up at her.

"We'll go somewheres and get a drink," he said. "One won't hurt."

In New Orleans, five months after he had rearranged the map of Bud Cross for the third time, Midge finished training for his championship bout with the Dutchman.

Back in his hotel after the final workout, Midge stopped to chat with some of the boys from up north, who had made the long trip to see a champion dethroned, for the result of this bout was so nearly a foregone conclusion that even the experts had guessed it.

Tommy Haley secured the key and the mail and ascended to the Kelly suite. He was bathing when Midge came in, half an hour later.

"Any mail?" asked Midge.

"There on the bed," replied Tommy from the tub.

Midge picked up the stack of letters and postcards and glanced them over. From the pile he sorted out three letters and laid them on the table. The rest he tossed into the waste-basket. Then he picked up the three and sat for a few moments holding them, while his eyes gazed off into space. At length he looked again at the three unopened letters in his hand; then he put one in his pocket and tossed the other two at the basket. They missed their target and fell on the floor.

"Hell!" said Midge, and stooping over picked them up.

He opened one postmarked Milwaukee and read:

DEAR HUSBAND:

I have wrote to you so manny times and got no anser and I dont know if you ever got them, so I am writing again in the hopes you will get this letter and anser. I dont like to bother you with my trubles and I would not only for the baby and I am not asking you should write to me but only send a little money and I am not asking for myself but the baby has not been well a day sence last Aug. and the dr. told me she cant live much longer unless I give her better food and thats impossible the ways things are. Lou has not been working for a year and what I make dont hardley pay for the rent. I am not asking for you to give me any money, but only you should send what I loaned when convenient and I think it amts. to about $36.00. Please try and send that amt. and it will help me, but if you cant send the whole amt. try and send me something.

Your wife,
EMMA.

Midge tore the letter into a hundred pieces and scattered them over the floor.

"Money, money, money!" he said. "They must think I'm made o' money. I s'pose the old woman's after it too."

He opened his mother's letter:

dear Michael Connie wonted me to rite and say you must beet the dutchman and he is sur you wil and wonted me to say we wont you to rite and tell us about it, but I guess you haven't no time to rite or we herd from you long beffore this but I wish you would rite jest a line or 2 boy becaus it wuld be better for Connie then a barl of medisin. It wuld help me to keep things going if you send me money now and then when you can spair it but if you cant send no money try and fine time to rite a letter onley a few lines and it will please Connie, jest think boy he hasent got out of bed in over 3 yrs. Conie says good luck.

Your Mother,
ELLEN F. KELLY.

"I thought so," said Midge. "They're all alike."

The third letter was from New York. It read:

Hon:—This is the last letter you will get from me before your champ, but I will send you a telegram Saturday, but I can't say as much in a telegram as in a letter and I am writeing this to let you know I am thinking of you and praying for good luck.

Lick him good hon and don't wait no longer than you have to and don't forget to wire me as soon as its over. Give him that little old left of yours on the nose hon and don't be afraid of spoiling his good looks because he couldn't be no homlier than he is. But don't let him spoil my baby's pretty face. You won't will you hon.

Well hon I would give anything to be there and see it, but I guess you love Haley better than me or you wouldn't let him keep me away. But when your champ hon we can do as we please and tell Haley to go to the devil.

Well hon I well send you a telegram Saturday and I almost fogot to tell you I will need some more money, a couple hundred say and you will have to wire it to me as soon as you get this. You will won't you hon.

I will send you a telegram Saturday and remember hon I am pulling for you. Well good-by sweetheart and good luck.

GRACE.

"They're all alike," said Midge. "Money, money, money."

Tommy Haley, shining from his ablutions, came in from the adjoining room.

"Thought you'd be layin' down," he said.

"I'm going to," said Midge, unbuttoning his orange shoes.

"I'll call you at six and you can eat up here without no bugs to pester you. I got to go down and give them birds their tickets."

"Did you hear from Goldberg?" asked Midge.

"Didn't I tell you? Sure; fifteen weeks at five hundred, if we win. And we can get a guarantee o' twelve thousand, with privileges either in New York or Milwaukee."

"Who with?"

"Anybody that'll stand up in front of you. You don't care who it is, do you?"

"Not me. I'll make 'em all look like a monkey."

"Well you better lay down aw'ile."

"Oh, say, wire two hundred to Grace for me, will you? Right away; the New York address."

"Two hundred! You just sent her three hundred last Sunday."

"Well, what the hell do you care?"

"All right, all right. Don't get sore about it. Anything else?"

"That's all," said Midge, and dropped onto the bed.

"And I want the deed done before I come back," said Grace as she rose from the table. "You won't fall down on me, will you, hon?"

"Leave it to me," said Midge. "And don't spend no more than you have to."

Grace smiled a farewell and left the café. Midge continued to sip his coffee and read his paper.

They were in Chicago and they were in the middle of Midge's first week in vaudeville. He had come straight north to reap the rewards of his glorious victory over the broken down Dutchman. A fortnight had been spent in learning his act, which consisted of a gymnastic exhibition and a ten minutes' monologue on the various excellences of Midge Kelly. And now he was twice daily turning 'em away from the Madison Theater.

His breakfast over and his paper read, Midge sauntered into the lobby and asked for his key. He then beckoned to a bell-boy, who had been hoping for that very honor.

"Find Haley, Tommy Haley," said Midge. "Tell him to come up to my room."

"Yes, sir, Mr. Kelly," said the boy, and proceeded to break all his former records for diligence.

Midge was looking out of his seventh-story window when Tommy answered the summons.

"What'll it be?" inquired his manager.

There was a pause before Midge replied.

"Haley," he said, "twenty-five per cent's a whole lot o' money."

"I guess I got it comin', ain't I?" said Tommy.

"I don't see how you figger it. I don't see where you're worth it to me."

"Well," said Tommy, "I didn't expect nothin' like this. I thought you was satisfied with the bargain. I don't want to beat nobody out o' nothin', but I don't see where you could have got anybody else that would of did all I done for you."

"Sure, that's all right," said the champion. "You done a lot for me in Philly. And you got good money for it, didn't you?"

"I ain't makin' no holler. Still and all, the big money's still ahead of us yet.

And if it hadn't of been for me, you wouldn't of never got within grabbin' distance."

"Oh, I guess I could of went along all right," said Midge. "Who was it that hung that left on the Dutchman's jaw, me or you?"

"Yes, but you wouldn't been in the ring with the Dutchman if it wasn't for how I handled you."

"Well, this won't get us nowheres. The idear is that you ain't worth no twenty-five per cent now and it don't make no diff'rence what come off a year or two ago."

"Don't it?" said Tommy. "I'd say it made a whole lot of difference."

"Well, I say it don't and I guess that settles it."

"Look here, Midge," Tommy said, "I thought I was fair with you, but if you don't thing so, I'm willin' to hear what you think is fair. I don't want nobody callin' me a Sherlock. Let's go down to business and sign up a contrac'. What's your figger?"

"I ain't namin' no figger," Midge replied. "I'm sayin' that twenty-five's too much. Now what are you willin' to take?"

"How about twenty?"

"Twenty's too much," said Kelly.

"What ain't too much?" asked Tommy.

"Well, Haley, I might as well give it to you straight. They ain't nothin' that ain't too much."

"You mean you don't want me at no figger?"

"That's the idear."

There was a minute's silence. Then Tommy Haley walked toward the door.

"Midge," he said, in a choking voice, "you're makin' a big mistake, boy. You can't throw down your best friends and get away with it. That damn woman will ruin you."

Midge sprang from his seat.

"You shut your mouth!" he stormed. "Get out o' here before they have to carry you out. You been spongin' off o' me long enough. Say one more word about the girl or about anything else and you'll get what the Dutchman got. Now get out!"

And Tommy Haley, having a very vivid memory of the Dutchman's face as he fell, got out.

Grace came in later, dropped her numerous bundles on the lounge and perched herself on the arm of Midge's chair.

"Well?" she said.

"Well," said Midge, "I got rid of him."

"Good boy!" said Grace. "And now I think you might give me that twenty-five per cent."

"Besides the seventy-five you're already gettin'?" said Midge.

"Don't be no grouch, hon. You don't look pretty when you're grouchy."

"It ain't my business to look pretty," Midge replied.

"Wait till you see how I look with the stuff I bought this mornin'!"

Midge glanced at the bundles on the lounge.

"There's Haley's twenty-five per cent," he said, "and then some."

The champion did not remain long without a manager. Haley's successor was none other than Jerome Harris, who saw in Midge a better meal ticket than his popular-priced musical show had been.

The contract, giving Mr. Harris twenty-five per cent of Midge's earnings, was signed in Detroit the week after Tommy Haley had heard his dismissal read. It had taken Midge just six days to learn that a popular actor cannot get on without the ministrations of a man who thinks, talks and means business. At first Grace objected to the new member of the firm, but when Mr. Harris had demanded and secured from the vaudeville people a one-hundred dollar increase in Midge's weekly stipend, she was convinced that the champion had acted for the best.

"You and my missus will have some great old times," Harris told Grace. "I'd of wired her to join us here, only I seen the Kid's bookin' takes us to Milwaukee next week, and that's where she is."

But when they were introduced in the Milwaukee hotel, Grace admitted to herself that her feeling for Mrs. Harris could hardly be called love at first sight. Midge, on the contrary, gave his new manager's wife the many times over and seemed loath to end the feast of his eyes.

"Some doll," he said to Grace when they were alone.

"Doll is right," the lady replied, "and sawdust where her brains ought to be."

"I'm li'ble to steal that baby," said Midge, and he smiled as he noted the effect of his words on his audience's face.

On Tuesday of the Milwaukee week the champion successfully defended his title in a bout that the newspapers never reported. Midge was alone in his room that morning when a visitor entered without knocking. The visitor was Lou Hersch.

Midge turned white at sight of him.

"What do you want?" he demanded.

"I guess you know," said Lou Hersch. "Your wife's starvin' to death and your baby's starvin' to death and I'm starvin' to death. And you're dirty with money."

"Listen," said Midge, "if it wasn't for you, I wouldn't never saw your sister. And, if you ain't man enough to hold a job, what's that to me? The best thing you can do is keep away from me."

"You give me a piece o' money and I'll go."

Midge's reply to the ultimatum was a straight right to his brother-in-law's narrow chest.

"Take that home to your sister."

And after Lou Hersch picked himself up and slunk away, Midge thought: "It's lucky I didn't give him my left or I'd of croaked him. And if I'd hit him in the stomach, I'd of broke his spine."

There was a party after each evening performance during the Milwaukee engagement. The wine flowed freely and Midge had more of it than Tommy Haley ever would have permitted him. Mr. Harris offered no objection, which was possibly just as well for his own physical comfort.

In the dancing between drinks, Midge had his new manager's wife for a partner as often as Grace. The latter's face as she floundered round in the arms of the portly Harris, belied her frequent protestations that she was having the time of her life.

Several times that week, Midge thought Grace was on the point of starting the quarrel he hoped to have. But it was not until Friday night that she accommodated. He and Mrs. Harris had disappeared after the matinee and when Grace saw him again at the close of the night show, she came to the point at once.

"What are you tryin' to pull off?" she demanded.

"It's none o' your business, is it?" said Midge.

"You bet it's my business; mine and Harris's. You cut it short or you'll find out."

"Listen," said Midge, "have you got a mortgage on me or somethin'? You talk like we was married."

"We're goin' to be, too. And to-morrow's as good a time as any."

"Just about," Midge said. "You got as much chanct o' marryin' me to-morrow as the next day or next year and that ain't no chanct at all."

"We'll find out," said Grace.

"You're the one that's got somethin' to find out."

"What do you mean?"

"I mean I'm married already."

"You lie!"

"You think so, do you? Well, s'pose you go to this here address and get acquainted with my missus."

Midge scrawled a number on a piece of paper and handed it to her. She stared at it unseeingly.

"Well," said Midge, "I ain't kiddin' you. You go there and ask for Mrs. Michael Kelly, and if you don't find her, I'll marry you to-morrow before breakfast."

Still Grace stared at the scrap of paper. To Midge it seemed an age before she spoke again.

"You lied to me all this w'ile."

"You never ast me was I married. What's more, what the hell diff'rence did it make to you? You got a split, didn't you? Better'n fifty-fifty."

He started away.

"Where you goin'?"

"I'm goin' to meet Harris and his wife."

"I'm goin' with you. You're not goin' to shake me now."

"Yes, I am, too," said Midge quietly. "When I leave town tomorrow night, you're going to stay here. And if I see where you're goin' to make a fuss, I'll put you in a hospital where they'll keep you quiet. You can get your stuff to-morrow mornin' and I'll slip you a hundred bucks. And then I don't want to see no more o' you. And don't try and tag along now or I'll have to add another K. O. to the old record."

When Grace returned to the hotel that night, she discovered that Midge and the Harrises had moved to another. And when Midge left town the following night, he was again without a manager, and Mr. Harris was without a wife.

Three days prior to Midge Kelly's ten-round bout when Young Milton in New York City, the sporting editor of *The News* assigned Joe Morgan to write two or three thousand words about the champion to run with a picture lay-out for Sunday.

Joe Morgan dropped in at Midge's training quarters Friday afternoon. Midge, he learned, was doing road work, but Midge's manager, Wallie Adams, stood ready and willing to supply reams of dope about the greatest fighter of the age.

"Let's hear what you've got," said Joe, "and then I'll try to fix up something."

So Wallie stepped on the accelerator of his imagination and shot away.

"Just a kid; that's all he is; a regular boy. Get what I mean? Don't know the meanin' o' bad habits. Never tasted liquor in his life and would prob'ly get sick if he smelled it. Clean livin' put him up where he's at. Get what I mean? And modest and unassumin' as a school girl. He's so quiet you wouldn't never know he was round. And he'd go to jail before he'd talk about himself.

"No job at all to get him in shape, 'cause he's always that way. The only trouble we have with him is gettin' him to light into these poor bums they match him up with. He's scared he'll hurt somebody. Get what I mean? He's tickled to death over this match with Milton, 'cause everybody says Milton can stand the gaff. Midge'll maybe be able to cut loose a little this time. But the last two bouts he had, the guys hadn't no business in the ring with him, and he was holdin' back all the w'ile for the fear he'd kill somebody. Get what I mean?"

"Is he married?" inquired Joe.

"Say, you'd think he was married to hear him rave about them kiddies he's got. His fam'ly's up in Canada to their summer home and Midge is wild to get up there with 'em. He thinks more o' that wife and them kiddies than all the money in the world. Get what I mean?"

"How many children has he?"

"I don't know, four or five, I guess. All boys and every one of 'em a dead ringer for their dad."

"Is his father living?"

"No, the old man died when he was a kid. But he's got a grand old mother and a kid brother out in Chi. They're the first one he thinks about after a match, them and his wife and kiddies. And he don't forget to send the old woman a thousand bucks after every bout. He's goin' to buy her a new home as soon as they pay him off for this match."

"How about his brother? Is he going to tackle the game?"

"Sure, and Midge says he'll be a champion before he's twenty years old. They're a fightin' fam'ly and all of 'em honest and straight as a die. Get what I mean? A fella that I can't tell you his name come to Midge in Milwaukee onct and wanted him to throw a fight and Midge give him such a trimmin' in the street that he couldn't go on that night. That's the kind he is. Get what I mean?"

Joe Morgan hung around the camp until Midge and his trainers returned.

"One o' the boys from *The News*" said Wallie by way of introduction. "I been givin' him your fam'ly hist'ry."

"Did he give you good dope?" he inquired.

"He's some historian," said Joe.

"Don't call me no names," said Wallie smiling. "Call us up if they's anything more you want. And keep your eyes on us Monday night. Get what I mean?"

The story in Sunday's *News* was read by thousands of lovers of the manly art. It was well written and full of human interest. Its slight inaccuracies went unchallenged, though three readers, besides Wallie Adams and Midge Kelly, saw and recognized them. The three were Grace, Tommy Haley and Jerome Harris and the comments they made were not for publication.

Neither the Mrs. Kelly in Chicago nor the Mrs. Kelly in Milwaukee knew that there was such a paper as the New York *News*. And even if they had known of it and that it contained two columns of reading matter about Midge, neither mother nor wife could have bought it. For *The News* on Sunday is a nickel a copy.

Joe Morgan could have written more accurately, no doubt, if instead of Wallie Adams, he had interviewed Ellen Kelly and Connie Kelly and Emma Kelly and Lou Hersch and Grace and Jerome Harris and Tommy Haley and Hap Collins and two or three Milwaukee bartenders.

But a story built on their evidence would never have passed the sporting editor.

"Suppose you can prove it," that gentleman would have said, "It wouldn't get us anything but abuse to print it. The people don't want to see him knocked. He's champion."

Considerations

1. Would you consider this story an indictment of boxing? Could Midge just as easily have been another kind of athlete, or a person of notoriety in any field?
2. Perhaps you have heard that good always triumphs over evil in the end, and that people like Midge will "get theirs" eventually. Judging from this story, is there reason to believe that Lardner thought otherwise?
3. Perhaps the main point of the story lies in its very last segment. What is Lardner suggesting about our "heroes" and about the media that provide the public with its information about them? And what is he implying about those of us who believe everything we are told by the media about these figures? And, again, could Midge be representative of such figures of all fields? Give examples.
4. Lardner is known for his witty (often caustic) understatement. For example, his description of the girl as "a more dazzling sight than the catch of the luckiest Massachusetts fisherman. She could talk, too—probably better than the fish." Cite other examples.
5. Midge is described as having a "weak mouth." Is this inconsistent with his other characteristics, or perhaps an example of Lardner's keen insight into human nature? Explain.
6. "Champion" is something of a parody of the more usual sentimental sports stories, written by Grantland Rice, Paul Gallico, and others of the "Gee Whiz!" school. Which kind is more popular with sports fans? Can you think of any sportswriters or commentators whose unsentimental views may have made them unpopular with fans?
7. Ring Lardner is known as a realist. Perhaps you would call him a pessimist. Other writers with a similar view of the world are Mark Twain, Ambrose Bierce, A. E. Housman, and Euripides. Can you list others?

ALAN SILLITOE

The Match

Bristol City had played Notts County and won. Right from the kick-off Lennox had somehow known that Notts was going to lose, not through any prophetic knowledge of each home-player's performance, but because he himself, a spectator, hadn't been feeling in top form. One-track pessimism had made him godly enough to inform his mechanic friend Fred Iremonger who stood by his side: "I knew they'd bleddy-well lose, all the time."

Towards the end of the match, when Bristol scored their winning goal, the players could only just be seen, and the ball was a roll of mist being kicked about the field. Advertising boards above the stands, telling of pork-pies, ales, whisky, cigarettes and other delights of Saturday night, faded with the afternoon visibility.

They stood in the one-and-threes, Lennox trying to fix his eyes on the ball, to follow each one of its erratic well-kicked movements, but after ten minutes going from blurred player to player he gave it up and turned to look at the spectators massed in the rising stands that reached out in a wide arc on either side and joined dimly way out over the pitch. This proving equally futile he rubbed a clenched hand into his weak eyes and squeezed them tight, as if pain would give them more strength. Useless. All it produced was a mass of grey squares dancing before his open lids, so that when they cleared his sight was no better than before. Such an affliction made him appear more phlegmatic at a football match than Fred and most of the others round about, who spun rattles, waved hats and scarves, opened their throats wide to each fresh vaccillation in the game.

During his temporary blindness the Notts' forwards were pecking and weaving around the Bristol goal and a bright slam from one of them gave rise to a false alarm, an indecisive rolling of cheers roofed in by a grey heavy sky. "What's up?" Lennox asked Fred. "Who scored? Anybody?"

Fred was a younger man, recently married, done up in his Saturday afternoon best of sports coat, gaberdine trousers and rain-mac, dark hair sleeked back with oil. "Not in a month of Sundays," he laughed, "but they had a bleddy good try, I'll tell you that."

By the time Lennox had focused his eyes once more on the players the battle had moved to Notts' goal and Bristol were about to score. He saw a player running down the field, hearing in his imagination the thud of boots on damp introdden turf. A knot of adversaries dribbled out in a line and straggled behind him at a trot. Suddenly the man with the ball spurted forward, was seen to be clear of everyone as if, in a second of time that hadn't existed to any spectator or other player, he'd been catapulted into a hallowed untouchable area before the goal posts. Lennox's heart stopped beating. He peered between two oaken unmovable shoulders that, he thought with anger, had swayed in front purposely to stop him seeing. The renegade centre-forward from the opposing side was seen, like a puppet worked by someone above the low clouds, to bring his leg back, lunge out heavily with his booted foot. "No," Lennox had time to say. "Get on to him you dozy sods. Don't let him get it in."

From being an animal pacing within the prescribed area of his defended posts, the goalkeeper turned into a leaping ape, arms and legs outstretched, then became a mere stick that swung into a curve—and missed the ball as it sped to one side and lost itself in folds of net behind him.

The lull in the general noise seemed like silence for the mass of people packed about the field. Everyone had settled it in his mind that the match, as bad as it was, would be a draw, but now it was clear that Notts, the home team, had lost. A great roar of disappointment and joy, from the thirty thousand spectators who had expected a miracle from their own stars at the last moment, ran up the packed embankments, overflowing into streets outside where groups of people, startled at the sudden noise of an erupting mob, speculated as to which team had scored.

Fred was laughing wildly, jumping up and down, bellowing something between a cheer and a shout of hilarious anger, as if out to get his money's worth on the principle that an adverse goal was better than no goal at all. "Would you believe it?" he called at Lennox. "Would you believe it? Ninety-five thousand quid gone up like Scotch mist!"

Hardly knowing what he was doing Lennox pulled out a cigarette, lit it. "It's no good," he cursed, "they've lost. They should have walked away with the game"—adding under his breath that he must get some glasses in order to see things better. His sight was now so bad that the line of each eye crossed and converged some distance in front of him. At the cinema he was forced down to the front row, and he was never the first to recognize a pal on the street. And it spelt ruination for any football match. He could remember being able to pinpoint each player's face, and distinguish every spectator around the field, yet he still persuaded himself that he had no need of glasses and that somehow his sight would begin to improve. A more barbed occurrence connected with such eyes was that people were beginning to call him Cock-eye. At the garage where he worked the men sat down to tea-break the other day, and because he wasn't in the room one of them said: "Where's owd Cock-eye? 'Is tea'll get cold."

"What hard lines," Fred shouted, as if no one yet knew about the goal. "Would you believe it?" The cheering and booing were beginning to die down.

"That goalie's a bloody fool," Lennox swore, cap pulled low over his forehead. "He couldn't even catch a bleeding cold."

"It was dead lucky," Fred put in reluctantly, "they deserved it, I suppose"—simmering down now, the full force of the tragedy seeping through even to his newly wedded body and soul. "Christ, I should have stayed at home with my missis. I'd a bin warm there, I know that much. I might even have cut myself a chunk of hearthrug pie if I'd have asked her right!"

The laugh and wink were intended for Lennox, who was still in the backwater of his personal defeat. "I suppose that's all you think on these days," he said wryly.

"'Appen I do, but I don't get all that much of it, I can tell you." It was obvious though that he got enough to keep him in good spirits at a cold and disappointing football match.

"Well," Lennox pronounced, "all that'll alter in a bit. You can bet on that."

"Not if I know it," Fred said with a broad smile. "And I reckon it's better after a bad match than if I didn't come to one."

"You never said a truer word about bad," Lennox said. He bit his lip with anger. "Bloody team. They'd even lose at blow football." A woman behind, swathed in a thick woolen scarf coloured white and black like the Notts players, who had been screaming herself hoarse in support of the home team all the afternoon was almost in tears at the adverse goal. "Foul! Foul! Get the dirty lot off the field. Send 'em back to Bristol where they came from. Foul! Foul I tell yer."

People all around were stamping feet dead from the cold, having for more than an hour staved off its encroachment into their limbs by the hope of at least one home-team win before Christmas. Lennox could hardly feel his, hadn't the will to help them back to life, especially in face of an added force to the bitter wind, and a goal that had been given away so easily. Movement on the pitch was now desultory, for there were only ten minutes of play left to go. The two teams knotted up towards one goal, then spread out around an invisible ball, and moved down the field again, back to the other with no decisive result. It seemed that both teams had accepted the present score to be the final state of the game, as though all effort had deserted their limbs and lungs.

"They're done for," Lennox observed to Fred. People began leaving the ground, making a way between those who were determined to see the game out to its bitter end. Right up to the dull warbling blast of the final whistle the hard core of optimists hoped for a miraculous revival in the worn-out players.

"I'm ready when yo' are," Fred said.

"Suits me." He threw his cigarette-end to the floor and, with a grimace of disappointment and disgust, made his way up the steps. At the highest point he turned a last glance over the field, saw two players running and the rest standing around in deepening mist—nothing doing—so went on down towards the barriers. When they were on the road a great cheer rose behind, as a whistle blew the signal for a mass rush to follow.

Lamps were already lit along the road, and bus queues grew quickly in semi-darkness. Fastening up his mac Lennox hurried across the road. Fred lagged behind, dodged a trolley-bus that sloped up to the pavement edge like a man-eating monster and carried off a crowd of people to the city-centre with blue lights flickering from overhead wires. "Well," Lennox said when they came close, "after that little lot I only hope the wife's got summat nice for my tea."

"I can think of more than that to hope for," Fred said. "I'm not one to grumble about my grub."

"'Course," Lennox sneered, "you're living on love. If you had Kit-E-Kat shoved in front of you you'd say it was a good dinner." They turned off by the recruiting centre into the heart of the Meadows, an ageing suburb of black houses and small factories. "That's what yo' think," Fred retorted, slightly offended yet too full of hope to really mind. "I'm just not one to grumble a lot about my snap, that's all."

"It wouldn't be any good if you was," Lennox rejoined, "but the grub's rotten these days, that's the trouble. Either frozen, or in tins. Nowt natural. The bread's enough to choke yer." And so was the fog: weighed down by frost it lingered and thickened, causing Fred to pull up his rain-mac collar. A man who came level with them on the same side called out derisively: "Did you ever see such a game?"

"Never in all my born days," Fred replied.

"It's always the same though," Lennox was glad to comment, "the best players are never on the field. I don't know what they pay 'em for."

The man laughed at this sound logic. "They'll 'appen get 'em on nex' wik. That'll show 'em."

"Let's hope so," Lennox called out as the man was lost in the fog. "It ain't a bad team," he added to Fred. But that wasn't what he was thinking. He remembered how he had been up before the gaffer yesterday at the garage for clouting the mash-lad who had called him Cock-eye in front of the office-girl, and the manager said that if it happened again he would get his cards. And now he wasn't sure that he wouldn't ask for them anyway. He'd never lack a job, he told himself, knowing his own worth and the sureness of his instinct when dissecting piston from cylinder, camshaft and connecting-rod and searching among a thousand-and-one possible faults before setting an engine bursting once more with life. A small boy called from the doorway of a house: "What's the score, mate?"

"They lost, two-one," he said curtly, and heard a loud clear-sounding door-slam as the boy ran in with the news. He walked with hands in pockets, and a cigarette at the corner of his mouth so that ash occasionally fell on to his mac. The smell of fish-and-chips came from a well-lit shop, making him feel hungry.

"No pictures for me tonight," Fred was saying. "I know the best place in weather like this." The Meadows were hollow with the clatter of boots behind them, the muttering of voices hot in discussion about the lost match. Groups gathered at each corner, arguing and teasing any girl that passed, lighted gas-lamps a weakening ally in the fog. Lennox turned into an entry, where the cold damp smell of backyards mingled with that of dustbins. They pushed open gates to their separate houses.

"So long. See you tomorrow at the pub maybe."

"Not tomorrow," Fred answered, already at his back door. "I'll have a job on mending my bike. I'm going to gi' it a coat of enamel and fix in some new brake blocks. I nearly got flattened by a bus the other day when they didn't work."

The gate-latch clattered. "All right then," Lennox said, "see you soon"—opening the back door and going into his house.

He walked through the small living-room without speaking, took off his mac in the parlour. "You should mek a fire in there," he said, coming out. "It smells musty. No wonder the clo'es go to pieces inside six months." His wife sat by the fire knitting from two balls of electric-blue wool in her lap. She was forty, the same age as Lennox, but gone to a plainness and discontented fat, while he had stayed thin and wiry from the same reason. Three children, the eldest a girl of fourteen, were at the table finishing tea.

Mrs. Lennox went on knitting. "I was going to make one today but I didn't have time."

"Iris can mek one," Lennox said, sitting down at the table.

The girl looked up. "I haven't finished my tea yet, our dad." The wheedling tone of her voice made him angry. "Finish it later," he said with a threatening look. "The fire needs making now, so come on, look sharp and get some coal from the cellar."

She didn't move, sat there with the obstinacy of the young spoiled by a mother. Lennox stood up. "Don't let me have to tell you again." Tears came into her eyes. "Go on," he shouted. "Do as you're told." He ignored his wife's plea to stop picking on her and lifted his hand to settle her with a blow.

"All right, I'm going, Look"—she got up and went to the cellar door. So he sat down again, his eyes roaming over the well-set table before him, holding his hands tightly clenched beneath the cloth. "What's for tea, then?"

His wife looked up again from her knitting. "There's two kippers in the oven."

He did not move, sat morosely fingering a knife and fork, "Well?" he demanded. "Do I have to wait all night for a bit o' summat t'eat?"

Quietly she took a plate from the oven and put it before him. Two brown kippers lay steaming across it. "One of these days," he said, pulling a long strip of white flesh from the bone, "we'll have a change."

"That's the best I can do," she said, her deliberate patience no way to stop his grumbling—though she didn't know what else would. And the fact that he detected it made things worse.

"I'm sure it is," he retorted. The coal bucket clattered from the parlour where the girl was making a fire. Slowly, he picked his kippers to pieces without eating any. The other two children sat on the sofa watching him, not daring to talk. On one side of his plate he laid bones; on the other, flesh. When the cat rubbed against his leg he dropped pieces of fish for it on to the lino, and when he considered that it had eaten enough he kicked it away with such force that its head knocked against the sideboard. It leapt on to a chair and began to lick itself, looking at him with green surprised eyes.

He gave one of the boys sixpence to fetch a *Football Guardian*. "And be quick about it," he called after him. He pushed his plate away, and nodded towards the mauled kippers. "I don't want this. You'd better send somebody out for some pastries. And mash some fresh tea," he added as an afterthought, "that pot's stewed."

He had gone too far. Why did he make Saturday afternoon such hell on earth? Anger throbbed violently in her temples. Through the furious beating of her heart she cried out: "If you want some pastries you'll fetch 'em yourself. And you'll mash your own tea as well."

"When a man goes to work all week he wants some tea," he said, glaring at her. Nodding at the boy: "Send him out for some cakes."

The boy had already stood up. "Don't go. Sit down," she said to him. "Get 'em yourself," she retorted to her husband. "The tea I've already put on the table's good enough for anybody. There's nowt wrong wi' it at all, and then you carry on like this. I suppose they lost at the match, because I can't think of any other reason why you should have such a long face."

He was shocked by such a sustained tirade, stood up to subdue her. "You what?" he shouted. "What do you think you're on wi'?"

Her face turned a deep pink. "You heard," she called back. "A few home truths might do you a bit of good."

He picked up the plate of fish and, with exaggerated deliberation, threw it to the floor. "There," he roared. "That's what you can do with your bleeding tea."

"You're a lunatic," she screamed. "You're mental."

He hit her once, twice, three times across the head, and knocked her to the ground. The little boy wailed, and his sister came running in from the parlour. . . .

Fred and his young wife in the house next door heard a commotion through the thin walls. They caught the cadence of voices and shifting chairs, but didn't really think anything amiss until the shriller climax was reached. "Would you believe it?" Ruby said, slipping off Fred's knee and straightening her skirt. "Just because Notts have lost again. I'm glad yo' aren't like that."

Ruby was nineteen, plump like a pear not round like a pudding, already pregnant though they'd only been married a month. Fred held her back by the waist. "I'm not so daft as to let owt like that bother me."

She wrenched herself free. "It's a good job you're not; because if you was I'd bosh you one."

Fred sat by the fire with a bemused, Cheshire-cat grin on his face while Ruby was in the scullery getting them something to eat. The noise in the next house had died down. After a slamming of doors and much walking to and fro outside Lennox's wife had taken the children, and left him for the last time.

Considerations

1. In this story, a spectator's reaction to a game of European football is the focal point of Sillitoe's comment on a particularly unfortunate attitude that many people hold towards sports. They are commonly called "fans." Look up the exact meaning of this word. Do you know any "fans"? (See "Wild in the Stands.")
2. Explain how sports can become an extension of one's life. In this story, we see the reactions of two neighbors to Notts County's loss. Why are they different?
3. Freud's research into psychoses indicates that violence is sensually stimulating to see and can result in either constructive or destructive behavior in the viewer, depending on the psychological stability of the viewer. Discuss this story from such a viewpoint.
4. An understanding of this story may shed light on the current debate as to whether watching violence (or any other activity, for that matter) causes the viewer to imitate what he sees; or whether, as others hold, that it promotes a catharsis—a healthy release of pent-up feelings of aggression. What do the reactions of the two spectators seem to indicate? Give specific examples.
5. List the specific examples that suggest that violence is sensually stimulating.
6. From what point of view is "The Match" told? If the author had chosen the first-person narrative from Fred's point of view, how would the story have been different? Give specific examples.

SOCIETY'S INS AND OUTS
Cultural Hypocrisy

*And there are thousands of them, all over the poxeaten
country, in shops, offices, railway stations, cars, houses,
pubs—In-law blokes like you and them, all on the watch
for Out-law blokes like me and us—and waiting to 'phone
for the coppers as soon as we make a false move.*

—Alan Sillitoe

P. G. WODEHOUSE

The Clicking of Cuthbert

The young man came into the smoking-room of the club-house, and flung his
bag with a clatter on the floor. He sank moodily into an arm-chair and pressed
the bell.

"Waiter!"

"Sir?"

The young man pointed at the bag with every evidence of distaste.

"You may have these clubs," he said. "Take them away. If you don't want
them yourself, give them to one of the caddies."

Across the room the Oldest Member gazed at him with a grave sadness through
the smoke of his pipe. His eye was deep and dreamy—the eye of a man who, as
the poet says, has seen Golf steadily and seen it whole.

"You are giving up golf?" he said.

He was not altogether unprepared for such an attitude on the young man's
part: for from his eyrie on the terrace above the ninth green he had observed
him start out on the afternoon's round and had seen him lose a couple of balls
in the lake at the second hole after taking seven strokes at the first.

"Yes!" cried the young man fiercely. "For ever, dammit! Footling game!
Blanked infernal fat-headed silly ass of a game! Nothing but a waste of time."

The Sage winced.

"Don't say that, my boy."

"But I do say it. What earthly good is golf? Life is stern and life is earnest. We live in a practical age. All round us we see foreign competition making itself unpleasant. And we spend our time playing golf! What do we get out of it? Is golf any *use?* That's what I'm asking you. Can you name me a single case where devotion to this pestilential pastime has done a man any practical good?"

The Sage smiled gently.

"I could name a thousand."

"One will do."

"I will select," said the Sage, "from the innumerable memories that rush to my mind, the story of Cuthbert Banks."

"Never heard of him."

"Be of good cheer," said the Oldest Member. "You are going to hear of him now."

It was in the picturesque little settlement of Wood Hills (said the Oldest Member) that the incidents occurred which I am about to relate. Even if you have never been in Wood Hills, that suburban paradise is probably familiar to you by name. Situated at a convenient distance from the city, it combines in a notable manner the advantages of town life with the pleasant surroundings and healthful air of the country. Its inhabitants live in commodious houses, standing in their own grounds, and enjoy so many luxuries—such as gravel soil, main drainage, electric light, telephone, baths (h. and c.), and company's own water, that you might be pardoned for imagining life to be so ideal for them that no possible improvement could be added to their lot. Mrs. Willoughby Smethurst was under no such delusion. What Wood Hills needed to make it perfect, she realized, was Culture. Material comforts are all very well, but, if the *summum bonum* is to be achieved, the Soul also demands a look in, and it was Mrs. Smethurst's unfaltering resolve that never while she had her strength should the Soul be handed the loser's end. It was her intention to make Wood Hills a centre of all that was most cultivated and refined, and, golly! how she had succeeded. Under her presidency the Wood Hills Literary and Debating Society had tripled its membership.

But there is always a fly in the ointment, a caterpillar in the salad. The local golf club, an institution to which Mrs. Smethurst strongly objected, had also tripled its membership; and the division of the community into two rival camps, the Golfers and the Cultured, had become more marked than ever. This division, always acute, had attained now to the dimensions of a Schism. The rival sects treated one another with a cold hostility.

Unfortunate episodes came to widen the breach. Mrs. Smethurst's house adjoined the links, standing to the right of the fourth tee: and, as the Literary Society was in the habit of entertaining visiting lecturers, many a golfer had foozled his drive owing to sudden loud outbursts of applause coinciding with his downswing. And not long before this story opens a sliced ball, whizzing in at the open window, had come within an ace of incapacitating Raymond Parslow Devine, the rising young novelist (who rose at that moment a clear foot and a half) from any further exercise of his art. Two inches, indeed, to the right and Raymond must inevitably have handed in his dinner-pail.

To make matters worse, a ring at the front-door bell followed almost immediately, and the maid ushered in a young man of pleasing appearance in a sweater and baggy knickerbockers who apologetically but firmly insisted on playing his ball where it lay, and, what with the shock of the lecturer's narrow escape and the spectacle of the intruder standing on the table and working away with a niblick, the afternoon's session had to be classed as a complete frost. Mr. Devine's determination, from which no argument could swerve him, to deliver the rest of his lecture in the coal-cellar gave the meeting a jolt from which it never recovered.

I have dwelt upon this incident, because it was the means of introducing Cuthbert Banks to Mrs. Smethurst's niece, Adeline. As Cuthbert, for it was he who had so nearly reduced the muster-roll of rising novelists by one, hopped down from the table after his stroke, he was suddenly aware that a beautiful girl was looking at him intently. As a matter of fact, everyone in the room was looking at him intently, none more so than Raymond Parsloe Devine, but none of the others were beautiful girls. Long as the members of Wood Hills Literary Society were on brain, they were short on looks, and, to Cuthbert's excited eye, Adeline Smethurst stood out like a jewel in a pile of coke.

He had never seen her before, for she had only arrived at her aunt's house on the previous day, but he was perfectly certain that life, even when lived in the midst of gravel soil, main drainage, and company's own water, was going to be a pretty poor affair if he did not see her again. Yes, Cuthbert was in love: and it is interesting to record, as showing the effect of the tender emotion on a man's game that twenty minutes after he had met Adeline he did the short eleventh in one, and as near as a toucher got a three on the four-hundred-yard twelfth.

I will skip lightly over the intermediate stages of Cuthbert's courtship and come to the moment when—at the annual ball in aid of the local Cottage Hospital, the only occasion during the year on which the lion, so to speak, lay down with the lamb, and the Golfers and the Cultured met on terms of easy comradeship, their differences temporarily laid aside—he proposed to Adeline and was badly stymied.

That fair, soulful girl could not see him with a spy-glass.

"Mr. Banks," she said, "I will speak frankly."

"Charge right ahead," assented Cuthbert.

"Deeply sensible as I am of——"

"I know. Of the honour and the compliment and all that. But, passing lightly over all that guff, what seems to be the trouble? I love you to distraction——"

"Love is not everything."

"You're wrong," said Cuthbert earnestly. "You're right off it. Love——" And he was about to dilate on the theme when she interrupted him.

"I am a girl of ambition."

"And very nice, too," said Cuthbert.

"I am a girl of ambition," repeated Adeline, "and I realize that the fulfilment of my ambitions must come through my husband. I am very ordinary myself——"

"What!" cried Cuthbert. "You ordinary? Why, you are a pearl among women, the queen of your sex. You can't have been looking in a glass lately. You stand alone. Simply alone. You make the rest look like battered repaints."

"Well," said Adeline, softening a trifle, "I believe I am fairly good-looking——"

"Anybody who was content to call you fairly good-looking would describe the Taj Mahal as a pretty nifty tomb."

"But that is not the point. What I mean is, if I marry a nonentity I shall be a nonentity myself for ever. And I would sooner die than be a nonentity."

"And, if I follow your reasoning, you think that that lets *me* out?"

"Well, really, Mr. Banks, *have* you done anything, or are you likely ever to do anything worth while?"

Cuthbert hesitated.

"It's true," he said, "I didn't finish in the first ten in the Open, and I was knocked out in the semi-final of the Amateur, but I won the French Open last year."

"The—what?"

"The French Open Championship. Golf, you know."

"Golf! You waste all your time playing golf. I admire a man who is more spiritual, more intellectual."

A pang of jealousy rent Cuthbert's bosom.

"Like What's-his-name Devine?" he said, sullenly.

"Mr. Devine," replied Adeline, blushing faintly, "is going to be a great man. Already he has achieved much. The critics say that he is more Russian than any other young English writer."

"And is that good?"

"Of course it's good."

"I should have thought the wheeze would be to be more English than any other young English writer."

"Nonsense! Who wants an English writer to be English? You've got to be Russian or Spanish or something to be a real success. The mantle of the great Russians has descended on Mr. Devine."

"From what I've heard of Russians, I should hate to have that happen to *me*."

"There is no danger of that," said Adeline scornfully.

"Oh! Well, let me tell you that there is a lot more in me than you think."

"That might easily be so."

"You think I'm not spiritual and intellectual," said Cuthbert, deeply moved. "Very well. Tomorrow I join the Literary Society."

Even as he spoke the words his leg was itching to kick himself for being such a chump, but the sudden expression of pleasure on Adeline's face soothed him; and he went home that night with the feeling that he had taken on something rather attractive. It was only in the cold grey light of the morning that he realized what he had let himself in for .

I do not know if you have had any experience of suburban literary societies, but the one that flourished under the eye of Mrs. Willoughby Smethurst at Wood Hills was rather more so than the average. With my feeble powers of narrative, I cannot hope to make clear to you all that Cuthbert Banks endured in the next few weeks. And, even if I could, I doubt if I should do so. It is all very well to excite pity and terror, as Aristotle recommends, but there are limits.

In the ancient Greek tragedies it was an ironclad rule that the real rough stuff should take place off-stage, and I shall follow this admirable principle. It will suffice if I say merely that J. Cuthbert Banks had a thin time. After attending eleven debates and fourteen lectures on *vers libre* Poetry, the Seventeenth-Century Essayists, the Neo-Scandinavian Movement in Portuguese Literature, and other subjects of a similar nature, he grew so enfeebled that, on the rare occasions when he had time for a visit to the links, he had to take a full iron for his mashie shots.

It was not simply the oppressive nature of the debates and lectures that sapped his vitality. What really got right in amongst him was the torture of seeing Adeline's adoration of Raymond Parsloe Devine. The man seemed to have made the deepest possible impression upon her plastic emotions. When he spoke, she leaned forward with parted lips and looked at him. When he was not speaking—which was seldom—she leaned back and looked at him. And when he happened to take the next seat to her, she leaned sideways and looked at him. One glance at Mr. Devine would have been more than enough for Cuthbert; but Adeline found him a spectacle that never palled. She could not have gazed at him with a more rapturous intensity if she had been a small child and he a saucer of ice-cream. All this Cuthbert had to witness while still endeavouring to retain the possession of his faculties sufficiently to enable him to duck and back away if somebody suddenly asked him what he thought of the sombre realism of Vladimir Brusiloff. It is little wonder that he tossed in bed, picking at the coverlet, through sleepless nights, and had to have all his waistcoats taken in three inches to keep them from sagging.

This Vladimir Brusiloff to whom I have referred was the famous Russian novelist, and, owing to the fact of his being in the country on a lecturing tour at the moment, there had been something of a boom in his works. The Wood Hills Literary Society had been studying them for weeks, and never since his first entrance into intellectual circles had Cuthbert Banks come nearer to throwing in the towel. Vladimir specialized in grey studies of hopeless misery, where nothing happened till page three hundred and eighty, when the moujik decided to commit suicide. It was tough going for a man whose deepest reading hitherto had been Vardon on the Push-Shot, and there can be no greater proof of the magic of love than the fact that Cuthbert stuck it without a cry. But the strain was terrible and I am inclined to think that he must have cracked, had it not been for the daily reports in the papers of the internecine strife which was proceeding so briskly in Russia. Cuthbert was an optimist at heart, and it seemed to him that, at the rate at which the inhabitants of that interesting country were murdering one another, the supply of Russian novelists must eventually give out.

One morning, as he tottered down the road for the short walk which was now almost the only exercise to which he was equal, Cuthbert met Adeline. A spasm of anguish flitted through all his nerve-centres as he saw that she was accompanied by Raymond Parsloe Devine.

"Good morning, Mr. Banks," said Adeline.

"Good morning," said Cuthbert hollowly.

"Such good news about Vladimir Brusiloff."

"Dead?" said Cuthbert, with a touch of hope.

"Dead? Of course not. Why should he be? No, Aunt Emily met his manager after his lecture at Queen's Hall yesterday, and he has promised that Mr. Brusiloff shall come to her next Wednesday reception.

"Oh, ah!" said Cuthbert, dully.

"I don't know how she managed it. I think she must have told him that Mr. Devine would be there to meet him."

"But you said he was coming," argued Cuthbert.

"I shall be very glad," said Raymond Devine, "of the opportunity of meeting Brusiloff."

"I'm sure," said Adeline, "he will be very glad of the opportunity of meeting you."

"Possibly," said Mr. Devine. "Possibly. Competent critics have said that my work closely resembles that of the great Russian Masters."

"Your psychology is so deep."

"Yes, yes."

"And your atmosphere."

"Quite."

Cuthbert in a perfect agony of spirit prepared to withdraw from this love-feast. The sun was shining brightly, but the world was black to him. Birds sang in the tree-tops, but he did not hear them. He might have been a moujik for all the pleasure he found in life.

"You will be there, Mr. Banks?" said Adeline, as he turned away.

"Oh, all right," said Cuthbert.

When Cuthbert had entered the drawing-room on the following Wednesday and had taken his usual place in a distant corner where, while able to feast his gaze on Adeline, he had a sporting chance of being overlooked or mistaken for a piece of furniture, he perceived the great Russian thinker seated in the midst of a circle of admiring females. Raymond Parsloe Devine had not yet arrived.

His first glance at the novelist surprised Cuthbert. Doubtless with the best motives, Vladimir Brusiloff had permitted his face to become almost entirely concealed behind a dense zareba of hair, but his eyes were visible through the undergrowth, and it seemed to Cuthbert that there was an expression in them not unlike that of a cat in a strange backyard surrounded by small boys. The man looked forlorn and hopeless, and Cuthbert wondered whether he had had bad news from home.

This was not the case. The latest news which Vladimir Brusiloff had had from Russia had been particularly cheering. Three of his principal creditors had perished in the last massacre of the *bourgeoisie*, and a man whom he owed for five years for a samovar and a pair of overshoes had fled the country, and had not been heard of since. It was not bad news from home that was depressing Vladimir. What was wrong with him was the fact that this was the eighty-second suburban literary reception he had been compelled to attend since he had landed in the country on his lecturing tour, and he was sick to death of it. When his agent had first suggested the trip, he had signed on the dotted line without an instant's hesitation. Worked out in roubles, the fees offered had seemed just about right. But now, as he peered through the brushwood at the faces round him, and realized that eight out of ten of those present had manuscripts of some sort concealed on their persons, and were only waiting for an opportunity to whip them out and start reading, he wished that he had stayed at his quiet home in Nijni-Novgorod, where the worst thing that could happen to a fellow was a brace of bombs coming in through the window and mixing themselves up with his breakfast egg.

At this point in his meditations he was aware that his hostess was looming up before him with a pale young man in horn-rimmed spectacles at her side. There was in Mrs. Smethurst's demeanour something of the unction of the master-of-ceremonies at the big fight who introduces the earnest gentleman who wishes to challenge the winner.

"Oh, Mr. Brusiloff," said Mrs. Smethurst, "I do so want you to meet Mr. Raymond Parsloe Devine, whose work I expect you know. He is one of the younger novelists."

The distinguished visitor peered in a wary and defensive manner through the shrubbery, but did not speak. Inwardly he was thinking how exactly like Mr. Devine was to the eighty-one other younger novelists to whom he had been introduced at various hamlets throughout the country. Raymond Parsloe Devine bowed courteously, while Cuthbert, wedged into his corner, glowered at him.

"The critics," said Mr. Devine, "have been kind enough to say that my poor efforts contain a good deal of the Russian spirit. I owe much to the great Russians. I have been greatly influenced by Sovietski."

Down in the forest something stirred. It was Vladimir Brusiloff's mouth opening, as he prepared to speak. He was not a man who prattled readily, especially in a foreign tongue. He gave the impression that each word was excavated from his interior by some up-to-date process of mining. He glared bleakly at Mr. Devine, and allowed three words to drop out of him.

"Sovietski no good!"

He paused for a moment, set the machinery working again, and delivered five more at the pithead.

"I spit me of Sovietski!"

There was a painful sensation. The lot of a popular idol is in many ways an enviable one, but it has the drawback of uncertainty. Here today and gone tomorrow. Until this moment Raymond Parsloe Devine's stock had stood at something considerably over par in Wood Hills intellectual circles, but now there was a rapid slump. Hitherto he had been greatly admired for being influenced by Sovietski, but it appeared now that this was not a good thing to be. It was evidently a rotten thing to be. The law could not touch you for being influenced by Sovietski, but there is an ethical as well as a legal code, and this it was obvious that Raymond Parsloe Devine had transgressed. Women drew away from him slightly, holding their skirts. Men looked at him censoriously. Adeline Smethurst started violently, and dropped a tea-cup. And Cuthbert Banks, doing his popular imitation of a sardine in his corner, felt for the first time that life held something of sunshine.

Raymond Parsloe Devine was plainly shaken, but he made an adroit attempt to recover his lost prestige.

"When I say I have been influenced by Sovietski, I mean, of course, that I was once under his spell. A young writer commits many follies. I have long since passed through that phase. The false glamour of Sovietski has ceased to dazzle me. I now belong whole-heartedly to the school of Nastikoff."

There was a reaction. People nodded at one another sympathetically. After all, we cannot expect old heads on young shoulders, and a lapse at the outset of one's career should not be held against one who has eventually seen the light.

"Nastikoff no good," said Vladimir Brusiloff, coldly. He paused, listening to the machinery.

"Nastikoff worse than Sovietski."

He paused again.

"I spit me of Nastikoff!" he said.

This time there was no doubt about it. The bottom had dropped out of the market, and Raymond Parsloe Devine Preferred were down in the cellar with no takers. It was clear to the entire assembled company that they had been all wrong about Raymond Parsloe Devine. They had allowed him to play on their innocence and sell them a pup. They had taken him at his own valuation, and had been cheated into admiring him as a man who amounted to something, and all the while he had belonged to the school of Nastikoff. You never can tell. Mrs. Smethurst's guests were well-bred, and there was consequently no violent demonstration, but you could see by their faces what they felt. Those nearest Raymond Parsloe jostled to get further away. Mrs. Smethurst eyed him stonily through a raised lorgnette. One or two low hisses were heard, and over at the other end of the room somebody opened the window in a marked manner.

Raymond Parsloe Devine hesitated for a moment, then, realizing his situation, turned and slunk to the door. There was an audible sigh of relief as it closed behind him.

Vladimir Brusiloff proceeded to sum up.

"No novelists any good except me. Sovietski—yah! Nastikoff—bah! I spit me of zem all. No novelists anywhere any good except me. P. G. Wodehouse and Tolstoi not bad. Not good, but not bad. No novelists any good except me."

And, having uttered this dictum, he removed a slab of cake from a near-by plate, steered it through the jungle, and began to champ.

It is too much to say that there was a dead silence. There could never be that in any room in which Vladimir Brusiloff was eating cake. But certainly what you might call the general chit-chat was pretty well down and out. Nobody liked to be the first to speak. The members of the Wood Hills Literary Society looked at one another timidly. Cuthbert, for his part, gazed at Adeline; and Adeline gazed into space. It was plain that the girl was deeply stirred. Her eyes were opened wide, a faint flush crimsoned her cheeks, and her breath was coming quickly.

Adeline's mind was in a whirl. She felt as if she had been walking gaily along a pleasant path and had stopped suddenly on the very brink of a precipice. It would be idle to deny that Raymond Parsloe Devine had attracted her extraordinarily. She had taken him at his own valuation as an extremely hot potato, and her hero-worship had gradually been turning into love. And now her hero had been shown to have feet of clay. It was hard, I consider, on Raymond Parsloe Devine, but that is how it goes in this world. You get a following as a celebrity, and then you run up against another bigger celebrity and your admirers desert you. One could moralize on this at considerable length, but better not, perhaps. Enough to say that the glamour of Raymond Devine ceased abruptly in that moment for Adeline, and her most coherent thought at this juncture was the resolve, as soon as she got up to her room, to burn the three signed photographs he had sent her and to give the autographed presentation set of his books to the grocer's boy.

Mrs. Smethurst, meanwhile, having rallied somewhat, was endeavouring to set the feast of reason and flow of soul going again.

"And how do you like England, Mr. Brusiloff?" she asked.

The celebrity paused in the act of lowering another segment of cake.

"Dam good," he replied, cordially.

"I suppose you have travelled all over the country by this time?"

"You said it," agreed the Thinker.

"Have you met many of our great public men?"

"Yais—Yais—Quite a few of the nibs—Lloyid Gorge, I meet him. But——"
Beneath the matting a discontented expression came into his face, and his voice took on a peevish note. "But I not meet your *real* great men—your Arbmishel, your Arreevadon—I not meet them. That's what gives me the pipovitch. Have *you* ever met Arbmishel and Arreevadon?"

A strained, anguished look came into Mrs. Smethurst's face and was reflected in the faces of the other members of the circle. The eminent Russian had sprung two entirely new ones on them, and they felt that their ignorance was about to be exposed. What would Vladimir Brusiloff think of the Wood Hills Literary Society? The reputation of the Wood Hills Literary Society was at stake, trembling in the balance, and coming up for the third time. In dumb agony Mrs. Smethurst rolled her eyes about the room searching for someone capable of coming to the rescue. She drew blank.

And then, from a distant corner, there sounded a deprecating cough, and those nearest Cuthbert Banks saw that he had stopped twisting his right foot round his left ankle and his left foot round his right ankle and was sitting up with a light of almost human intelligence in his eyes.

"Er——" said Cuthbert, blushing as every eye in the room seemed to fix itself on him, "I think he means Abe Mitchell and Harry Vardon."

"Abe Mitchell and Harry Vardon?" repeated Mrs. Smethurst, blankly. "I never heard of——"

"Yais! Yais! Most! Very!" shouted Vladimir Brusiloff, enthusiastically. "Arbmishel and Arreevadon. You know them, yes, what, no, perhaps?"

"I've played with Abe Mitchell often, and I was partnered with Harry Vardon in last year's Open."

The great Russian uttered a cry that shook the chandelier.

"You play in ze Open? Why," he demanded reproachfully of Mrs. Smethurst, "was I not been introduced to this young man who play in opens?"

"Well, really," faltered Mrs. Smethurst. "Well, the fact is, Mr. Brusiloff——"

She broke off. She was unequal to the task of explaining, without hurting anyone's feelings, that she had always regarded Cuthbert as a piece of cheese and a blot on the landscape.

"Introduct me!" thundered the Celebrity.

"Why, certainly, certainly, of course. This is Mr.——." She looked appealingly at Cuthbert.

"Banks," prompted Cuthbert.

"Banks!" cried Vladimir Brusiloff. "Not Cootaboot Banks?"

"*Is* your name Cootaboot?" asked Mrs. Smethurst, faintly.

"Well, it's Cuthbert."

"Yais! Yais! Cootaboot!" There was a rush and swirl, as the effervescent Muscovite burst his way through the throng and rushed to where Cuthbert sat. He stood for a moment eyeing him excitedly, then, stooping swiftly, kissed him on both cheeks before Cuthbert could get his guard up. "My dear young man, I saw you win ze French Open. Great! Great! Grand! Superb! Hot stuff, and you can say I said so! Will you permit one who is but eighteen at Nijni-Novgorod to salute you once more?"

And he kissed Cuthbert again. Then, brushing aside one or two intellectuals who were in the way, he dragged up a chair and sat down.

"You are a great man!" he said.

"Oh, no," said Cuthbert modestly.

"Yais! Great. Most! Very! The way you lay your approach-putts dead from anywhere!"

"Oh, I don't know."

Mr. Brusiloff drew his chair closer.

"Let me tell you one vairy funny story about putting. It was one day I play at Nijni-Novgorod with the pro. against Lenin and Trotsky, and Trotsky had a two-inch putt for the hole. But, just as he addresses the ball, someone in the crowd he tries to assassinate Lenin with a rewolwer—you know that is our great national sport, trying to assassinate Lenin with rewolwers—and the bang puts Trotsky off his stroke and he goes five yards past the hole, and then Lenin, who is rather shaken, you understand, he misses again himself, and we win the hole and match and I clean up three hundred and ninety-six thousand roubles, or fifteen shillings in your money. Some gameovitch! And now let me tell you one other vairy funny story——"

Desultory conversation had begun in murmurs over the rest of the room, as the Wood Hills intellectuals politely endeavoured to conceal the fact that they realized that they were about as much out of it at this re-union of twin souls as cats at a dog-show. From time to time they started as Vladimir Brusiloff's laugh boomed out. Perhaps it was a consolation to them to know that he was enjoying himself.

As for Adeline, how shall I describe her emotions? She was stunned. Before her very eyes the stone which the builders had rejected had become the main thing, the hundred-to-one shot had walked away with the race. A rush of tender admiration for Cuthbert Banks flooded her heart. She saw that she had been all wrong. Cuthbert, whom she had always treated with a patronizing superiority, was really a man to be looked up to and worshipped. A deep, dreamy sigh shook Adeline's fragile form.

Half an hour later Vladimir and Cuthbert Banks rose.

"Goot-a-bye, Mrs. Smet-thirst," said the Celebrity. "Zank you for a most charming visit. My friend Cootaboot and me we go now to shoot a few holes. You will lend me clobs, friend Cootaboot?"

"Any you want."

"The niblicksky is what I use most. Goot-a-bye, Mrs. Smet-thirst."

They were moving to the door, when Cuthbert felt a light touch on his arm. Adeline was looking up at him tenderly.

"May I come, too, and walk round with you?"

Cuthbert's bosom heaved.

"Oh," he said, with a tremor in his voice, "that you would walk round with me for life!"

Her eyes met his.

"Perhaps," she whispered, softly, "it could be arranged."

"And so" (concluded the Oldest Member), "you see that golf can be of the greatest practical assistance to a man in Life's struggle. Raymond Parsloe Devine, who was no player, had to move out of the neighborhood immediately, and is now, I believe, writing scenarios out in California for the Flicker Film Company. Adeline is married to Cuthbert, and it was only his earnest pleading which prevented her from having their eldest son christened Abe Mitchell Ribbed-Faced Mashie Banks, for she is now as keen a devotee of the great game as her husband. Those who know them say that theirs is a union so devoted, so——"

The Sage broke off abruptly, for the young man had rushed to the door and out into the passage. Through the open door he could hear him crying passionately to the waiter to bring back his clubs.

Considerations

1. On the surface, this is a simple story about a young golfer, disillusioned with the game, who is brought back to it because of an inspirational anecdote told to him by the old Sage of Golfdom. But explain why it may be a bit deeper than that. What is a satire?
2. Explain how the following are targets of Wodehouse's satire:
   (a) The Wood Hills Literary and Debating Society
   (b) Raymond Parsloe Devine, the "rising" novelist
   (c) Mrs. Smethurst
   (d) The suburb of Wood Hills
   (e) Russian novelists
   (f) "Culture" in Wood Hills
   (g) P. G. Wodehouse
3. What is the point of the bizarre incident with the Russian novelist at the Wood Hills Literary Society? Why is "a little learning a dangerous thing"? Explain why Brusiloff takes an immediate liking to Cuthbert.
4. What are pseudo-intellectuals? Why would someone who fits this particular characterization tend to exalt an "image" of someone like Brusiloff but disapprove of him personally, and especially disapprove of someone of no "importance," like Cuthbert, although he has very much in common with Brusiloff?

5. Discuss the speed and ease with which the Society members, Adeline included, abandon poor Devine once he has been exposed as being an ordinary person.

6. Is Wodehouse implying that intellectual pretense is a symptom of vaunting ambition? Discuss this possibility in terms of Adeline's behavior.

7. Are we to believe that Cuthbert is a lucky boy to have married Adeline? If so, what are we to think of Mr. Wodehouse's taste in women?

8. Discuss the implications of the following statements from the story:

   (a) Long as the members of Wood Hills Literary Society were on brain, they were short on looks. . . .

   (b) "I am a girl of ambition," repeated Adeline, "and I realize that the fulfilment of my ambitions must come through my husband."

   (c) You get a following as a celebrity, and then you run up against another celebrity and your admirers desert you.

RING LARDNER

A Caddy's Diary

Wed. Apr. 12.

I am 16 of age and am a caddy at the Pleasant View Golf Club but only temporary as I expect to soon land a job some wheres as asst pro as my game is good enough now to be a pro but to young looking. My pal Joe Bean also says I have not got enough swell head to make a good pro but suppose that will come in time, Joe is a wise cracker.

But first will put down how I come to be writeing this diary, we have got a member name Mr Colby who writes articles in the newspapers and I hope for his sakes that he is a better writer than he plays golf but any way I cadded for him a good many times last yr and today he was out for the first time this yr and I cadded for him and we got talking about this in that and something was mentioned in regards to the golf articles by Alex Laird that comes out every Sun in the paper Mr Colby writes his articles for so I asked Mr Colby did he know how much Laird got paid for the articles and he said he did not know but supposed that Laird had to split 50-50 with who ever wrote the articles for him. So I said don't he write the articles himself and Mr Colby said why no he guessed not. Laird may be a master mind in regards to golf he said, but that is no sign he can write about it as very few men can write decent let alone a pro. Writeing is a nag.

How do you learn it I asked him.

Well he said read what other people writes and study them and write things yourself, and maybe you will get on to the nag and maybe you wont.

Well Mr Colby I said do you think I could get on to it?

Why he said smileing I did not know that was your ambition to be a writer.

Not exactly was my reply, but I am going to be a golf pro myself and maybe some day I will get good enough so as the papers will want I should write them articles and if I can learn to write them myself why I will not have to hire another writer and split with them.

Well said Mr Colby smileing you have certainly got the right temperament for a pro, they are all big hearted fellows.

But listen Mr Colby I said if I want to learn it would not do me no good to copy down what other writers have wrote, what I would have to do would be write things out of my own head.

That is true said Mr. Colby.

Well I said what could I write about?

Well said Mr Colby why don't you keep a diary and every night after your supper set down and write what happened that day and write who you cadded for and what they done only leave me out of it. And you can write down what people say and what you think and etc., it will be the best kind of practice for you, and once in a wile you can bring me your writeings and I will tell you the truth if they are good or rotten.

So that is how I come to be writeing this diary is so as I can get some practice writeing and maybe if I keep at it long enough I can get on to the nag.

Friday, Apr. 14.

We been haveing Apr. showers for a couple days and nobody out on the course so they has been nothing happen that I could write down in my diary but dont want to leave it go to long or will never learn the trick so will try and write a few lines about a caddys life and some of our members and etc.

Well I and Joe Bean is the 2 oldest caddys in the club and I been cadding now for 5 yrs and quit school 3 yrs ago tho my mother did not like it for me to quit but my father said he can read and write and figure so what is the use in keeping him there any longer as greek and latin dont get you no credit at the grocer, so they lied about my age to the trunce officer and I been cadding every yr from March till Nov and the rest of the winter I work around Heismans store in the village.

Dureing the time I am cadding I genally always manage to play at least 9 holes a day myself on wk days and some times 18 and am never more than 2 or 3 over par figures on our course but it is a cinch.

I played the engineers course 1 day last summer in 75 which is some golf and some of our members who has been playing 20 yrs would give their right eye to play as good as myself.

I used to play around with our pro Jack Andrews till I got so as I could beat him pretty near every time we played and now he wont play with me no more, he is not a very good player for a pro but they claim he is a good teacher. Personly I think golf teachers is a joke tho I am glad people is suckers enough to fall for it as I expect to make my liveing that way. We have got a member Mr. Dunham who must of took 500 lessons in the past 3 yrs and when he starts to shoot he trys to remember all the junk Andrews has learned him and he gets dizzy and they is no telling where the ball will go and about the safest place to stand when he is shooting is between he and the hole.

I dont beleive the club pays Andrews much salary but of course he makes pretty fair money giveing lessons but his best graft is a 3 some which he plays 2 and 3 times a wk with Mr Perdue and Mr Lewis and he gives Mr Lewis a stroke a hole and they genally break some wheres near even but Mr Perdue made a 83 one time so he thinks that is his game so he insists on playing Jack even, well they always play for $5.00 a hole and Andrews makes $20.00 to $30.00 per round and if he wanted to cut loose and play his best he could make $50.00 to $60.00 per round but a couple of wallops like that and Mr Perdue might get cured so Jack figures a small stedy income is safer.

I have got a pal name Joe Bean and we pal around together as he is about my age and he says some comical things and some times will wisper some thing comical to me wile we are cadding and it is all I can do to help from laughing out loud, that is one of the first things a caddy has got to learn is never laugh out loud only when a member makes a joke. How ever on the days when theys ladies on the course I dont get a chance to caddy with Joe because for some reason another the woman folks dont like Joe to caddy for them wile on the other hand they are always after me tho I am no Othello for looks or do I seek their flavors, in fact it is just the opp and I try to keep in the back ground when the fair sex appears on the seen as cadding for ladies means you will get just so much money and no more as theys no chance of them loosning up. As Joe says the rule against tipping is the only rule the woman folks keeps.

Theys one lady how ever who I like to caddy for as she looks like Lillian Gish and it is a pleasure to just look at her and I would caddy for her for nothing tho it is hard to keep your eye on the ball when you are cadding for this lady, her name is Mrs Doane.

Sat. Apr. 15.

This was a long day and I am pretty well wore out but must not get behind in my writeing practice. I and Joe carried all day for Mr Thomas and Mr Blake. Mr Thomas is the vice president of one of the big banks down town and he always slips you a $1.00 extra per round but beleive me you earn it cadding for Mr Thomas, there is just 16 clubs in his bag includeing 5 wood clubs tho he has not used the wood in 3 yrs but says he has got to have them along in case his irons goes wrong on him. I dont know how bad his irons will have to get before he will think they have went wrong on him but personly if I made some of the tee shots he made today I would certainly consider some kind of change of weppons.

Mr Thomas is one of the kind of players that when it has took him more than 6 shots to get on the green he will turn to you and say how many have I had caddy and then you are suppose to pretend like you was thinking a minute and then say 4, then he will say to the man he is playing with well I did not know if I had shot 4 or 5 but the caddy says it is 4. You see in this way it is not him that is cheating but the caddy but he makes it up to the caddy afterwards with a $1.00 tip.

Mr Blake gives Mr Thomas a stroke a hole and they play a $10.00 nassua and neither one of them wins much money from the other one but even if they did why $10.00 is chickens food to men like they. But the way they crab and squak about different things you would think their last $1.00 was at stake. Mr Thomas started out this A.M. with a 8 and a 7 and of course that spoilt the day for him and me to. Theys lots of men that if they dont make a good score on the first 2 holes they will founder all the rest of the way around and raze H with their caddy and if I was laying out a golf course I would make the first 2 holes so darn easy that you could not help from getting a 4 or better on them and in that way everybody would start off good natured and it would be a few holes at least before they begun to turn sour.

Mr. Thomas was beat both in the A.M. and P.M. in spite of my help as Mr. Blake is a pretty fair counter himself and I heard him say he got a 88 in the P.M. which is about a 94 but any way it was good enough to win. Mr Blakes regular game is about a 90 takeing his own figures and he is one of these cocky guys that takes his own game serious and snears at men that cant break 100 and if you was to ask him if he had ever been over 100 himself he would say not since the first yr he begun to play. Well I have watched a lot of those guys like he and I will tell you how they keep from going over 100 namely by doing just what he done this A.M. when he come to the 13th hole. Well he missed his tee shot and dubbed along and finely he got in a trap on his 4th shot and I seen him take 6 wallops in the trap and when he had took the 6th one his ball was worse off then when he started so he picked it up and marked a X down on his score card. Well if he had of played out the hole why the best he could of got was a 11 by holeing his next niblick shot but he would of probly got about a 20 which would of made him around 108 as he admitted taking a 88 for the other 17 holes. But I bet if you was to ask him what score he had made he would say O I was terrible and I picked up on one hole but if I had played them all out I guess I would of had about a 92.

These is the kind of men that laughs themselfs horse when they hear of some dub takeing 10 strokes for a hole but if they was made to play out every hole and mark down their real score their card would be decorated with many a big casino.

Well as I say I had a hard day and was pretty sore along towards the finish but still I had to laugh at Joe Bean on the 15th hole which is a par 3 and you can get there with a fair drive and personly I am genally hole high with a midiron, but Mr Thomas topped his tee shot and dubbed a couple with his mashie and was still quiet a ways off the green and he stood studying the situation a minute and said to Mr Blake well I wonder what I better take here. So Joe Bean was standing by me and he said under his breath take my advice and quit you old rascal.

Mon. Apr. 17.

Yesterday was Sun and I was to wore out last night to write as I cadded 45 holes. I cadded for Mr Colby in the A.M. and Mr Langley in the P.M.

Mr Thomas thinks golf is wrong on the sabath tho as Joe Bean says it is wrong any day the way he plays it.

This A. M. they was nobody on the course and I played 18 holes by myself and had a 5 for a 76 on the 18th hole but the wind got a hold of my drive and it went out of bounds. This P. M. they was 3 of us had a game of rummy started but Miss Rennie and Mrs Thomas come out to play and asked for me to caddy for them, they are both terrible.

Mrs Thomas is Mr Thomas wife and she is big and fat and shakes like jell and she always says she plays golf just to make her skinny and she dont care how rotten she plays as long as she is getting the exercise, well maybe so but when we find her ball in a bad lie she aint never sure it is hers till she picks it up and smells it and when she puts it back beleive me she dont cram it down no gopher hole.

Miss Rennie is a good looker and young and they say she is engaged to Chas Crane, he is one of our members and is the best player in the club and dont cheat hardly at all and he has got a job in the bank where Mr Thomas is the vice president. Well I have cadded for Miss Rennie when she was playing with Mr Crane and I have cadded for her when she was playing alone or with another lady and I often think if Mr Crane could hear her talk when he was not around he would not be so stuck on her. You would be surprised at some of the words that falls from those fare lips.

Well the 2 ladies played for 2 bits a hole and Miss Rennie was haveing a terrible time wile Mrs Thomas was shot with luck on the greens and sunk 3 or 4 putts that was murder. Well Miss Rennie used some expressions which was best not repeated but towards the last the luck changed around and it was Miss Rennie that was sinking the long ones and when they got to the 18th tee Mrs Thomas was only 1 up.

Well we had started pretty late and when we left the 17th green Miss Rennie made the remark that we would have to hurry to get the last hole played, well it was her honor and she got the best drive she made all day about 120 yds down the fair way. Well Mrs Thomas got nervous and looked up and missed her ball a ft and then done the same thing right over and when she finely hit it she only knocked it about 20 yds and this made her lay 3. Well her 4th went wild and lit over in the rough in the apple trees. It was a cinch Miss Rennie would win the hole unless she dropped dead.

Well we all went over to hunt for Mrs Thomas ball but we would of been lucky to find it even in day light but now you could not hardly see under the trees, so Miss Rennie said drop another ball and we will not count no penalty. Well it is some job any time to make a woman give up hunting for a lost ball and all the more so when it is going to cost her 2 bits to play the hole out so there we stayed for at lease 10 minutes till it was so dark we could not see each other let alone a lost ball and finely Mrs Thomas said well it looks like we could not finish, how do we stand? Just like she did not know how they stood.

You had me one down up to this hole said Miss Rennie.

Well that is finishing pretty close said Mrs. Thomas.

I will have to give Miss Rennie credit that what ever word she thought of for this occasion she did not say it out loud but when she was paying me she said

I might of give you a quarter tip only I have to give Mrs Thomas a quarter she dont deserve so you dont get it.

Fat chance I would of had any way.

Thurs. Apr. 20.

Well we have been haveing some more bad weather but today the weather was all right but that was the only thing that was all right. This P. M. I cadded double for Mr Thomas and Chas Crane the club champion who is stuck on Miss Rennie. It was a 4 some with he and Mr Thomas against Mr Blake and Jack Andrews the pro, they was only playing best ball so it was really just a match between Mr Crane and Jack Andrews and Mr Crane win by 1 up. Joe Bean cadded for Jack and Mr Blake. Mr Thomas was terrible and I put in a swell P. M. lugging that heavy bag of his besides Mr Cranes bag.

Mr Thomas did not go off the course as much as usual but he kept hitting behind the ball and he run me ragged replaceing his divots but still I had to laugh when we was playing the 4th hole which you have to drive over a ravine and every time Mr Thomas misses his tee shot on this hole why he makes a squak about the ravine and says it ought not to be there and etc.

Today he had a terrible time getting over it and afterwards he said to Jack Andrews this is a joke hole and ought to be changed. So Joe Bean wispered to me that if Mr Thomas kept on playing like he was the whole course would be changed.

Then a little wile later when we come to the long 9th hole Mr Thomas got a fair tee shot but then he whiffed twice missing the ball by a ft and the 3d time he hit it but it only went a little ways and Joe Bean said that is 3 trys and no gain, he will have to punt.

But I must write down about my tough luck, well we finely got through the 18 holes and Mr Thomas reached down in his pocket for the money to pay me and he genally pays for Mr Crane to when they play together as Mr Crane is just a employ in the bank and dont have much money but this time all Mr Thomas had was a $20.00 bill so he said to Mr Crane I guess you will have to pay the boy Charley so Charley dug down and got the money to pay me and he paid just what it was and not a dime over, where if Mr Thomas had of had the change I would of got a $1.00 extra at lease and maybe I was not sore and Joe Bean to because of course Andrews never gives you nothing and Mr Blake dont tip his caddy unless he wins.

They are a fine bunch of tight wads said Joe and I said well Crane is all right only he just has not got no money.

He aint all right no more than the rest of them said Joe.

Well at lease he dont cheat on his score I said.

And you know why that is said Joe, neither does Jack Andrews cheat on his score but that is because they play to good. Players like Crane and Andrews that goes around in 80 or better cant cheat on their score because they make the most of the holes in around 4 strokes and the 4 strokes includes their tee shot and a couple of putts which everybody is right there to watch them when they make them and count them right along with them. So if they make a 4 and claim a 3 why people would just laugh in their face and say how did the ball get from the fair way on to the green, did it fly? But the boys that takes 7 and 8 strokes to a hole can shave their score and you know they are shaveing it but you have to let them get away with it because you cant prove nothing. But that is one of the penaltys for being a good player, you cant cheat.

To hear Joe tell it pretty near everybody are born crooks, well maybe he is right.

Wed. Apr. 26.

Today Mrs Doane was out for the first time this yr and asked for me to caddy for her and you bet I was on the job. Well how are you Dick she said, she always calls me by name. She asked me what had I been doing all winter and was I glad to see her and etc.

She said she had been down south all winter and played golf pretty near every day and would I watch her and notice how much she had improved.

Well to tell the truth she was no better than last yr and wont never be no better and I guess she is just to pretty to be a golf player but of course when she asked me did I think her game was improved I had to reply yes indeed as I would not hurt her feelings and she laughed like my reply pleased her. She played with Mr and Mrs Carter and I carried the 2 ladies bags wile Joe Bean cadded for Mr Carter. Mrs Carter is a ugly dame with things on her face and it must make Mr Carter feel sore when he looks at Mrs Doane to think he married Mrs Carter but I suppose they could not all marry the same one and besides Mrs Doane would not be a sucker enough to marry a man like he who drinks all the time and is pretty near always stood, tho Mr Doane who she did marry aint such a H of a man himself tho dirty with money.

They all gave me the laugh on the 3d hole when Mrs Doane was makeing her 2d shot and the ball was in the fair way but laid kind of bad and she just ticked it and then she asked me if winter rules was in force and I said yes so we teed her ball up so as she could get a good shot at it and they gave me the laugh for saying winter rules was in force.

You have got the caddys bribed Mr Carter said to her.

But she just smiled and put her hand on my sholder and said Dick is my pal. That is enough of a bribe to just have her touch you and I would caddy all day for her and never ask for a cent only to have her smile at me and call me her pal.

Sat. Apr. 29

Today they had the first club tournament of the yr and they have a monthly tournament every month and today was the first one, it is a handicap tournament and everybody plays in it and they have prizes for low net score and low gross score and etc. I cadded for Mr Thomas today and will tell what happened.

They played a 4 some and besides Mr Thomas we had Mr Blake and Mr Carter and Mr Dunham. Mr Dunham is the worst man player in the club and the other men would not play with him a specialy on a Saturday only him and Mr Blake is partners together in business. Mr Dunham has got the highest handicap in the club which is 50 but it would have to be 150 for him to win a prize. Mr Blake and Mr Carter has got a handicap of about 15 a piece I think and Mr Thomas is 30, the first prize for the low net score for the day was a dozen golf balls and the second low score a ½ dozen golf balls and etc.

Well we had a great battle and Mr Colby ought to been along to write it up or some good writer. Mr Carter and Mr Dunham played partners against Mr Thomas and Mr Blake which ment that Mr Carter was playing Thomas and Blakes best ball, well Mr Dunham took the honor and the first ball he hit went strate off to the right and over the fence outside of the grounds, well he done the same thing 3 times. Well when he finely did hit one in the course why Mr Carter said why not let us not count them 3 first shots of Mr Dunham as they was just practice. Like H we wont count them said Mr Thomas we must count every shot and keep our scores correct for the tournament.

All right said Mr. Carter.

Well we got down to the green and Mr Dunham had about 11 and Mr Carter sunk a long putt for a par 5, Mr Blake all ready had 5 strokes and so did Mr Thomas and when Mr Carter sunk his putt why Mr Thomas picked his ball up and said Carter wins the hole and I and Blake will take 6s. Like H you will said Mr Carter, this is a tournament and we must play every hole out and keep our scores correct. So Mr Dunham putted and went down in 13 and Mr Blake got a 6 and Mr Thomas missed 2 easy putts and took a 8 and maybe he was not boiling.

Well it was still their honor and Mr Dunham had one of his dizzy spells on the 2d tee and he missed the ball twice before he hit it and then Mr Carter drove the green which is only a mid-iron shot and then Mr Thomas stepped up and missed the ball just like Mr Dunham. He was wild and yelled at Mr Dunham no man could play golf playing with a man like you, you would spoil anybodys game.

Your game was all ready spoiled said Mr Dunham, it turned sour on the 1st green.

You would turn anybody sour said Mr Thomas.

Well Mr Thomas finely took a 8 for the hole which is a par 3 and it certainly looked bad for him winning a prize when he started out with 2 8s, and he and Mr Dunham had another terrible time on No 3 and wile they was messing things up a 2 some come up behind us and hollered fore and we left them go through tho it was Mr Clayton and Mr Joyce and as Joe Bean said they was probly dissapointed when we left them go through as they are the kind that feels like the day is lost if they cant write to some committee and preffer charges.

Well Mr Thomas got a 7 on the 3d and he said well it is no wonder I am off of my game today as I was up ½ the night with my teeth.

Well said Mr Carter if I had your money why on the night before a big tournament like this I would hire somebody else to set up with my teeth.

Well I wished I could remember all that was said and done but any way Mr Thomas kept getting sore and sore and we got to the 7th tee and he had not made a decent tee shot all day so Mr Blake said to him why dont you try the wood as you cant do no worse?

By Geo I believe I will said Mr Thomas and took his driver out of the bag which he had not used it for 3 yrs.

Well he swang and zowie away went the ball pretty near 8 inches distants wile the head of the club broke off clean and saled 50 yds down the course. Well I have got a hold on myself so as I dont never laugh out loud and I beleive the other men was scarred to laugh or he would of killed them so we all stood there in silents waiting for what would happen.

Well without saying a word he come to where I was standing and took his other 4 wood clubs out of the bag and took them to a tree which stands a little ways from the tee box and one by one he swang them with all his strength against the trunk of the tree and smashed them to H and gone, all right gentlemen that is over he said.

Well to cut it short Mr Thomas score for the first 9 was a even 60 and then we started out on the 2d 9 and you would not think it was the same man playing, on the first 3 holes he made 2 4s and a 5 and beat Mr Carter even and followed up with a 6 and a 5 and that is how he kept going up to the 17th hole.

What has got in to you Thomas said Mr Carter.

Nothing said Mr Thomas only I broke my hoodoo when I broke them 5 wood clubs.

Yes I said to myself and if you had broke them 5 wood clubs 3 yrs ago I would not of broke my back lugging them around.

Well we come to the 18th tee and Mr Thomas had a 39 which give him a 99 for 17 holes, well everybody drove off and as we was following along why Mr Klabor come walking down the course from the club house on his way to the 17th green to join some friends and Mr Thomas asked him what had he made and he said he had turned in a 93 but his handicap is only 12 so that give him a 81.

That wont get me no wheres he said as Charley Crane made a 75.

Well said Mr Thomas I can tie Crane for low net if I get a 6 on this hole.

Well it come his turn to make his 2d and zowie he hit the ball pretty good but they was a hook on it and away she went in to the woods on the left, the ball laid in behind a tree so as they was only one thing to do and that was waste a shot getting it back on the fair so that is what Mr Thomas done and it took him 2 more to reach the green.

How many have you had Thomas said Mr Carter when we was all on the green.

Let me see said Mr Thomas and then turned to me, how many have I had caddy?

I dont know I said.

Well it is either 4 or 5 said Mr Thomas.

I think it is 5 said Mr Carter.

I think it is 4 said Mr Thomas and turned to me again and said how many have I had caddy?

So I said 4.

Well said Mr Thomas personly I was not sure myself but my caddy says 4 and I guess he is right.

Well the other men looked at each other and I and Joe Bean looked at each other but Mr Thomas went ahead and putted and was down in 2 putts.

Well he said I certainly come to life on them last 9 holes.

So he turned in his score as 105 and with his handicap of 30 why that give him a net of 75 which was the same as Mr Crane so instead of Mr Crane getting 1 dozen golf balls and Mr Thomas getting ½ a dozen golf balls why they will split the 1st and 2d prize makeing 9 golf balls a piece.

Tues. May 2.

This was the first ladies day of the season and even Joe Bean had to carry for the fair sex. We cadded for a 4 some which was Miss Rennie and Mrs Thomas against Mrs Doane and Mrs Carter. I guess if they had of kept their score right the total for the 4 of them would of ran well over a 1000.

Our course has a great many trees and they seemed to have a traction for our 4 ladies today and we was in amongst the trees more than we was on the fair way.

Well said Joe Bean theys one thing about cadding for these dames, it keeps you out of the hot sun.

And another time he said he felt like a boy scout studing wood craft.

These dames is always up against a stump he said.

And another time he said that it was not fair to charge these dames regular ladies dues in the club as they hardly ever used the course.

Well it seems like they was a party in the village last night and of course the ladies was talking about it and Mrs Doane said what a lovely dress Miss Rennie wore to the party and Miss Rennie said she did not care for the dress herself.

Well said Mrs Doane if you want to get rid of it just hand it over to me.

I wont give it to you said Miss Rennie but I will sell it to you at ½ what it cost me and it was a bargain at that as it only cost me a $100.00 and I will sell it to you for $50.00.

I have not got $50.00 just now to spend said Mrs Doane and besides I dont know would it fit me.

Sure it would fit you said Miss Rennie, you and I are exactly the same size and figure, I tell you what I will do with you I will play you golf for it and if you beat me you can have the gown for nothing and if I beat you why you will give me $50.00 for it.

All right but if I loose you may have to wait for your money said Mrs. Doane.

So this was on the 4th hole and they started from there to play for the dress and they was both terrible and worse then usual on acct of being nervous as this was the biggest stakes they had either of them ever played for tho the Doanes has got a bbl of money and $50.00 is chickens food.

Well we was on the 16th hole and Mrs Doane was 1 up and Miss Rennie sliced her tee shot off in the rough and Mrs Doane landed in some rough over on the left so they was clear across the course from each other. Well I and Mrs

Doane went over to her ball and as luck would have it it had come to rest in a kind of a groove where a good player could not hardly make a good shot of it let alone Mrs Doane. Well Mrs Thomas was out in the middle of the course for once in her life and the other 2 ladies was over on the right side and Joe Bean with them so they was nobody near Mrs Doane and I.

Do I have to play it from there she said. I guess you do was my reply.

Why Dick have you went back on me she said and give me one of her looks.

Well I looked to see if the others was looking and then I kind of give the ball a shove with my toe and it come out of the groove and laid where she could get a swipe at it.

This was the 16th hole and Mrs Doane win it by 11 strokes to 10 and that made her 2 up and 2 to go. Miss Rennie win the 17th but they both took a 10 for the 18th and that give Mrs Doane the match.

Well I wont never have a chance to see her in Miss Rennies dress but if I did I aint sure that I would like it on her.

Fri. May 5.

Well I never thought we would have so much excitement in the club and so much to write down in my diary but I guess I better get busy writeing it down as here it is Friday and it was Wed. A. M. when the excitement broke loose and I was getting ready to play around when Harry Lear the caddy master come running out with the paper in his hand and showed it to me on the first page.

It told how Chas Crane our club champion had went south with $8000 which he had stole out of Mr Thomas bank and a swell looking dame that was a stenographer in the bank had elloped with him and they had her picture in the paper and I will say she is a pip but who would of thought a nice quiet young man like Mr Crane was going to prove himself a gay Romeo and a specialy as he was engaged to Miss Rennie tho she now says she broke their engagement a month ago but any way the whole affair has certainly give everybody something to talk about and one of the caddys Lou Crowell busted Fat Brunner in the nose because Fat claimed to of been the last one that cadded for Crane. Lou was really the last one and cadded for him last Sunday which was the last time Crane was at the club.

Well everybody was thinking how sore Mr Thomas would be and they would better not mention the affair around him and etc. but who should show up to play yesterday but Mr Thomas himself and he played with Mr Blake and all they talked about the whole P. M. was Crane and what he had pulled.

Well Thomas said Mr Blake I am curious to know if the thing come as a surprise to you or if you ever had a hunch that he was libel to do a thing like this.

Well Blake said Mr Thomas I will admit that the whole thing come as a complete surprise to me as Crane was all most like my son you might say and I was going to see that he got along all right and that is what makes me sore is not only that he has proved himself dishonest but that he could be such a sucker as to give up a bright future for a sum of money like $8000 and a doll face girl that cant be no good or she would not of let him do it. When you think how young he was and the carreer he might of had why it certainly seems like he sold his soul pretty cheap.

That is what Mr Thomas had to say or at least part of it as I cant remember a ½ of all he said but any way this P. M. I cadded for Mrs Thomas and Mrs Doane and that is all they talked about to, and Mrs Thomas talked along the same lines like her husband and said she had always thought Crane was to smart a young man to pull a thing like that and ruin his whole future.

He was getting $4000 a yr said Mrs Thomas and everybody liked him and said he was bound to get ahead so that is what makes it such a silly thing for him to of done, sell his soul for $8000 and a pretty face.

Yes indeed said Mrs Doane.

Well all the time I was listening to Mr Thomas and Mr Blake and Mrs Thomas and Mrs Doane why I was thinking about something which I wanted to say to them but it would of ment me looseing my job so I kept it to myself but I sprung it on my pal Joe Bean on the way home tonight.

Joe I said what do these people mean when they talk about Crane selling his soul?

Why you know what they mean said Joe, they mean that a person that does something dishonest for a bunch of money or a gal or any kind of a reward why the person that does it is selling his soul.

All right I said and it dont make no differents does it if the reward is big or little?

Why no said Joe only the bigger it is the less of a sucker the person is that goes after it.

Well I said here is Mr Thomas who is vice president of a big bank and worth a bbl of money and it is just a few days ago when he lied about his golf score in order so as he would win 9 golf balls instead of a ½ a dozen.

Sure said Joe.

And how about his wife Mrs Thomas I said, who plays for 2 bits a hole and when her ball dont lie good why she picks it up and pretends to look at it to see if it is hers and then puts it back in a good lie where she can sock it.

And how about my friend Mrs Doane that made me move her ball out of a rut to help her beat Miss Rennie out of a party dress.

Well said Joe what of it?

Well I said it seems to me like these people have got a lot of nerve to pan Mr Crane and call him a sucker for doing what he done, it seems to me like $8000 and a swell dame is a pretty fair reward compared with what some of these other people sells their soul for, and I would like to tell them about it.

Well said Joe go ahead and tell them but maybe they will tell you something right back.

What will they tell me?

Well said Joe they might tell you this, that when Mr Thomas asks you how many shots he has had and you say 4 when you know he has had 5, why you are selling your soul for a $1.00 tip. And when you move Mrs Doanes ball out of a rut and give it a good lie, what are you selling your soul for? Just a smile.

O keep your mouth shut I said to him.

I am going to said Joe and would advice you to do the same.

Considerations

1. The most readily apparent characteristics of this story are its format and its use of sub-literate language. Explain how the boy's use of the language greatly enhances the story. How does Lardner justify using the diary?
2. Ring Lardner is known for his caustic wit. Cite examples or how he uses it to convey an attitude toward his characters, women for example.
3. Discuss hypocrisy as a theme in this story. Which character is least hypocritical? Why?
4. "A Caddy's Diary" raises a fundamental question: Who has the right to judge? Does it answer the question satisfactorily?
5. Is this story a more effective attack on hypocrisy than a sermon would be? Why or why not? Would someone like Mr. Thomas see himself reflected in such a story?
6. Discuss the way in which Lardner uses golf as a metaphor.
7. Another question raised in the story is, Which is worse: to sell your soul for $8000, or for three golf balls? Or for a smile? Discuss the philosophical implications of these questions.
8. Which characters does the author seem to like least? Support your answer.
9. The last two lines constitute a devastating indictment of human nature. Do you agree or disagree with Joe Bean's (Lardner's) advice?
10. Lardner was the forerunner of the "Aw Nuts!" school of sportswriters, at least thirty years ahead of his contemporaries (aside from Damon Runyon) who were writing the "Gee Whiz!" stories. List some sportswriters and commentators of each school among today's crop. Which are more popular with fans? (For a boxing story by Lardner, read "Champion.")

ALAN SILLITOE

The Loneliness of the Long-Distance Runner

I

As soon as I got to Borstal they made me a long-distance cross-country runner. I suppose they thought I was just the build for it because I was long and skinny for my age (and still am) and in any case I didn't mind it much, to tell you the truth, because running had always been made much of in our family, especially running away from the police. I've always been a good runner, quick and with a big stride as well, the only trouble being that no matter how fast I run, and I did a very fair lick even though I do say so myself, it didn't stop me getting caught by the cops after that bakery job.

You might think it a bit rare, having long-distance cross-country runners in Borstal, thinking that the first thing a long-distance runner would do when they set him loose at them fields and woods would be to run as far away from the place as he could get on a bellyful of Borstal slumgullion—but you're wrong, and I'll tell you why. The first thing is that them bastards over us aren't as daft as they most of the time look, and for another thing I am not so daft as I would look if I tried to make a break for it on my long-distance running, because to abscond and then get caught is nothing but a mug's game, and I'm not falling for it. Cunning is what counts in this life, and even that you've got to use in the slyest way you can; I'm telling you straight: they're cunning, and I'm cunning. If only 'them' and 'us' had the same ideas we'd get on like a house on fire, and they don't see eye to eye with us and we don't see eye to eye with them, so that's how it stands and how it will always stand. The one fact is that all of us are cunning, and because of this there's no love lost between us. So the thing is that they know I won't try to get away from them: they sit there like spiders in that crumbly manor house, perched like jumped-up jackdaws on the roof, watching out over the drives and fields like German generals from the tops of tanks. And even when I jog-trot on behind a wood and they can't see me anymore they know my sweeping-brush head will bob along that hedge-top in an hour's time and that I'll report to the bloke on the gate. Because when on a raw and frosty morning I get up at five o'clock and stand shivering my belly off on the stone floor and all the rest still have another hour to snooze before the bells go, I slink downstairs through all the corridors to the big outside door with a permit running-card in my fist, I feel like the first and last man on the world, both at once, if you can believe what I'm trying to say. I feel like the first man because I've hardly got a stitch on and am sent against the frozen fields in a shimmy and shorts—even the first poor bastard dropped on to the earth in midwinter knew how to make a suit of leaves, or how to skin a pterodactyl for a topcoat. But there I am, frozen stiff, with nothing to get me warm except a couple of hours' long-distance running before breakfast, not even a slice of bread-and-sheepdip. They're training me up fine for the big sports day when all the pig-faced snotty-nosed dukes and ladies—who can't add two and two together and would mess themselves like loonies if they didn't have slavies to beck-and-call—come and make speeches to us about sports being just the thing to get us leading an honest life and keep our itching finger-ends off them shop locks and safe handles and hairgrips to open gas meters. They give us a bit of blue ribbon and a cup for a prize after we've shagged ourselves out running or jumping, like race horses, only we don't get so well looked-after as race horses, that's the only thing.

So there I am, standing in the doorway in shimmy and shorts, not even a dry crust in my guts, looking out at frosty flowers on the ground. I suppose you think this is enough to make me cry? Not likely. Just because I feel like the first bloke in the world wouldn't make me bawl. It makes me feel fifty times better than when I'm cooped up in that dormitory with three hundred others. No, it's sometimes when I stand there feeling like the *last* man in the world that I don't feel so good. I feel like the last man in the world because I think that all those three hundred sleepers behind me are dead. They sleep so well I think that every scruffy head's kicked the bucket in the night and I'm the only one left, and when I look out into the bushes and frozen ponds I have the feeling that it's going to get colder and colder until everything I can see, meaning my red arms as well, is going to be covered with a thousand miles of ice, all the earth, right up to the sky and over every bit of land and sea. So I try to kick this feeling and act like I'm the first man on earth. And that makes me feel good, so as soon as I'm steamed up enough to get this feeling in me, I take a flying leap out of the doorway, and off I trot.

I'm in Essex. It's supposed to be a good Borstal, at least that's what the governor said to me when I got here from Nottingham. "We want to trust you while you are in this establishment," he said, smoothing out his newspaper with lily-white workless hands, while I read the big words upside down: *Daily Telegraph.* "If you play ball with us, we'll play ball with you." (Honest to God, you'd have thought it was going to be one long tennis match.) "We want hard honest work and we want good athletics," he said as well. "And if you give us both these things you can be sure we'll do right by you and send you back into the world an honest man." Well, I could have died laughing, especially when straight after this I hear the barking sergeant-major's voice calling me and two others to attention and marching us off like we was Grenadier Guards. And when the governor kept saying how 'we' wanted you to do this, and 'we' wanted you to do that, I kept looking round for the other blokes, wondering how many of them there was. Of course, I knew there were thousands of them, but as far as I knew only one was in the room. And there *are* thousands of them, all over the pox-eaten country, in shops, offices, railway stations, cars, houses, pubs—In-law blokes like you and them, all on the watch for Out-law blokes like me and us— and waiting to 'phone for the coppers as soon as we make a false move. And it'll always be there, I'll tell you that now, because I haven't finished making all my false moves yet, and I dare say I won't until I kick the bucket. If the In-laws are hoping to stop me making false moves they're wasting their time. They might as well stand me up against a wall and let fly with a dozen rifles. That's the only way they'll stop me, and a few million others. Because I've been doing a lot of thinking since coming here. They can spy on us all day to see if we're pulling our puddings and if we're working good or doing our "athletics" but they can't make an X-ray of our guts to find out what we're telling ourselves. I've been asking myself all sorts of questions, and thinking about my life up to now. And I like doing all this. It's a treat. It passes the time away and don't make Borstal seem half so bad as the boys in our street used to say it was. And this long-distance running lark is the best of all, because it makes me think so good that I learn things even better than when I'm on my bed at night. And apart from that, what with thinking so much while I'm running I'm getting to be one of the best runners in the Borstal. I can go my five miles round better than anybody else I know.

So as soon as I tell myself I'm the first man ever to be dropped into the world, and as soon as I take that first flying leap out into the frosty grass of an early morning when even birds haven't the heart to whistle, I get to thinking, and that's what I like. I go my rounds in a dream, turning at lane or footpath corners without knowing I'm turning, leaping brooks without knowing they're there, and shouting good morning to the early cow-milker without seeing him. It's a treat, being a long-distance runner, out in the world by yourself with not a soul to make you bad-tempered or tell you what to do or that there's a shop to break and enter a bit back from the next street. Sometimes I think that I've never been so free as during that couple of hours when I'm trotting up the path out of the gates and turning by that bare-faced, big-bellied oak tree at the lane end. Everything's dead, but good, because it's dead before coming alive, not dead after being alive. That's how I look at it. Mind you, I often feel frozen stiff at first. I can't feel my hands or feet or flesh at all, like a ghost who wouldn't know the earth was under him if he didn't see it now and again through the mist. But even though some people would call this frost-pain suffering if they wrote about it to their mams in a letter, I don't, because I know that in half an hour I'm going to be warm, that by the time I get to the main road and am turning on to the wheatfield footpath by the bus stop I'm going to feel as hot as a potbellied stove and as happy as a dog with a tin tail.

It's a good life, I'm saying to myself, if you don't give in to coppers and Borstal-bosses and the rest of them bastard-faced In-laws. Trot-trot-trot. Puff-puff-puff. Slap-slap-slap go my feet on the hard soil. Swish-swish-swish as my arms and side catch the bare branches of a bush. For I'm seventeen now, and when they let me out of this—if I don't make a break and see that things turn out otherwise—they'll try to get me in the army, and what's the difference between the army and this place I'm in now? They can't kid me, the bastards. I've seen the barracks near where I live, and if there weren't swaddies on guard outside with rifles you wouldn't know the difference between their high walls and the place I'm in now. Even though the swaddies come out at odd times a week for a pint of ale, so what? Don't I come out three mornings a week on my long-distance running, which is fifty times better than boozing. When they first said that I was to do my long-distance running without a guard pedalling beside me on a bike I couldn't believe it; but they called it a progressive and modern place, though they can't kid me because I know it's just like any other Borstal, going by the stories I've heard, except that they let me trot about like this. Borstal's Borstal no matter what they do; but anyway I moaned about it being a bit thick sending me out so early to run five miles on an empty stomach, until they talked me round to thinking it wasn't so bad—which I knew all the time—until they called me a good sport and patted me on the back when I said I'd do it and that I'd try to win them the Borstal Blue Ribbon Prize Cup For Long-Distance Cross Country Running (All England). And now the governor talks to me when he comes on his rounds, almost as he'd talk to his prize race horse, if he had one.

"All right, Smith?" he asks.

"Yes, sir," I answer.

He flicks his grey moustache: "How's the running coming along?"

"I've set myself to trot round the grounds after dinner just to keep my hand in, sir," I tell him.

The pot-bellied pop-eyed bastard gets pleased at this: "Good show. I know you'll get us that cup," he says.

And I swear under my breath: "Like boggery, I will." No, I won't get them that cup, even though the stupid tash-twitching bastard has all his hopes in me. Because what does his barmy hope mean? I ask myself. Trot-trot-trot, slap-slap-slap, over the stream and into the wood where it's almost dark and frosty-dew twigs sting my legs. It don't mean a bloody thing to me, only to him, and it means as much to him as it would mean to me if I picked up the racing paper and put my bet on a hoss I didn't know, had never seen, and didn't care a sod if I ever did see. That's what it means to him. And I'll lose that race, because I'm not a race horse at all, and I'll let him know it when I'm about to get out— if I don't sling my hook even before the race. By Christ I will. I'm a human being and I've got thoughts and secrets and bloody life inside me that he doesn't know is there, and he'll never know what's there because he's stupid. I suppose you'll laugh at this, me saying the governor's a stupid bastard when I know hardly how to write and he can read and write and add-up like a professor. But what I say is true right enough. He's stupid, and I'm not, because I can see further into the likes of him than he can see into the likes of me. Admitted, we're both cunning, but I'm more cunning and I'll win in the end even if I die in gaol at eighty-two, because I'll have more fun and fire out of my life than he'll ever get out of his. He's read a thousand books I suppose, and for all I know he might even have writtten a few, but I know for a dead cert, as sure as I'm sitting here, that what I'm scribbling down is worth a million to what he could ever scribble down. I don't care what anybody says, but that's the truth and can't be denied. I know when he talks to me and I look into his army mug that I'm alive and he's dead. He's as dead as a doornail. If he ran ten yards he'd drop dead. If he got ten yards into what goes on in my guts he'd drop dead as well— with surprise. At the moment it's dead blokes like him as have the whip-hand over blokes like me, and I'm almost dead sure it'll always be like that, but even so, by Christ, I'd rather be like I am—always on the run and breaking into shops for a packet of fags and a jar of jam—than have the whip-hand over somebody else and be dead from the toenails up. Maybe as soon as you get the whip-hand over somebody you do go dead. By God, to say that last sentence has needed a few hundred miles of long-distance running. I could no more have said that at first than I could have took a million-pound note from my back pocket. But it's true, you know, now I think of it again, and has always been true, and always will be true, and I'm surer of it every time I see the governor open that door and say Good-morning lads.

As I run and see my smoky breath going out into the air as if I had ten cigars stuck in different parts of my body I think more on the little speech the governor made when I first came. Honesty. Be honest. I laughed so much one morning I went ten minutes down in my timing because I had to stop and get rid of the stitch in my side. The governor was so worried when I got back late that he sent me to the doctor's for an X-ray and heart check. Be honest. It's like saying: Be dead, like me, and then you'll have no more pain of leaving your nice slummy house for Borstal or prison. Be honest and settle down in a cosy six pounds a week job. Well, even with all this long-distance running I haven't yet been able to decide what he means by this, although I'm just about beginning to—and I don't like what it means. Because after all my thinking I found that it adds up to something that can't be true about me, being born and brought up as I was. Because another thing people like the governor will never understand is that I *am* honest, that I've never been anything else but honest, and that I'll always be honest. Sounds funny. But it's true because I know what honest means according to me and he only knows what it means according to him. I think my honesty is the only sort in the world, and he thinks his is the only sort in the world as well. That's why this dirty great walled-up and fenced-up manor house in the middle of nowhere has been used to coop-up blokes like me. And if I had the whip-hand I wouldn't even bother to build a place like this to put all the cops, governors, posh whores, penpushers, army officers, Members of Parliament in; no, I'd stick them up against a wall and let them have it, like they'd have done with blokes like us years ago, that is, if they'd ever known what it means to be honest, which they don't and never will so help me God Almighty.

I was nearly eighteen months in Borstal before I thought about getting out. I can't tell you much about what it was like there because I haven't got the hang of describing buildings or saying how many crumby chairs and slatted windows make a room. Neither can I do much complaining, because to tell you the truth I didn't suffer in Borstal at all. I gave the same answer a pal of mine gave when someone asked him how much he hated it in the army. "I didn't hate it," he said. "They fed me, gave me a suit, and pocket-money, which was a bloody sight more than I ever got before, unless I worked myself to death for it, and most of the time they wouldn't let me work but sent me to the dole office twice a week." Well, that's more or less what I say. Borstal didn't hurt me in that respect, so since I've got no complaints I don't have to describe what they gave us to eat, what the dorms were like, or how they treated us. But in another way Borstal does something to me. No, it doesn't get my back up, because it's always been up, right from when I was born. What it does do is show me what they've been trying to frighten me with. They're got other things as well, like prison and, in the end, the rope. It's like me rushing up to thump a man and snatch the coat off his back when, suddenly, I pull up because he whips out a knife and lifts it to stick me like a pig if I come too close. That knife is Borstal, clink, the rope. But once you've seen the knife you learn a bit of unarmed combat. You have to, because you'll never get that sort of knife in your own hands, and this unarmed combat doesn't amount to much. Still, there it is, and you keep on rushing up to this man, knife or not, hoping to get one of your hands on his wrist and the other on his elbow both at the same time, and press back until he drops the knife.

You see, by sending me to Borstal they've shown me the knife, and from now on I know something I didn't know before: that it's war between me and them. I always knew this, naturally, because I was in Remand Homes as well and the boys there told me a lot about their brothers in Borstal, but it was only touch and go then, like kittens, like boxing-gloves, like dobbie. But now that they've shown me the knife, whether I ever pinch another thing in my life again or not, I know who my enemies are and what war is. They can drop all the atom bombs they like for all I care: I'll never call it war and wear a soldier's uniform, because I'm in a different sort of war, that they think is child's play. The war they think is war is suicide, and those that go and get killed in war should be put in clink for attempted suicide because that's the feeling in blokes' minds when they rush to join up or let themselves be called up. I know, because I've thought how good it would be sometimes to do myself in and the easiest way to do it, it occurred to me, was to hope for a big war so's I could join up and get killed. But I got past that when I knew I already was in a war of my own, that I was born into one, that I grew up hearing the sound of 'old soldiers' who'd been over the top at Dartmoor, half-killed at Lincoln, trapped in no-man's-land at Borstal, that sounded louder than any Jerry bombs. Government wars aren't my wars; they've got nowt to do with me, because my own war's all that I'll ever be bothered about. I remember when I was fourteen and I went into the country with three of my cousins, all about the same age, who later went to different Borstals, and then to different regiments, from which they soon deserted, and then to different gaols where they still are as far as I know. But anyway, we were all kids then, and wanted to go out to the woods for a change, to get away from the roads of stinking hot tar one summer. We climbed over fences and went through fields, scrumping a few sour apples on our way, until we saw the wood about a mile off. Up Collier's Pad we heard another lot of kids talking in high-school voices behind a hedge. We crept up on them and peeped through the brambles, and saw they were eating a picnic, a real posh spread out of baskets and flasks and towels. There must have been about seven of them, lads and girls sent out by their mams and dads for the afternoon. So we went on our bellies through the hedge like crocodiles and surrounded them, and then dashed into the middle, scattering the fire and batting their tabs and snatching up all there was to eat, then running off over Cherry Orchard fields into the wood, with a man chasing us who'd come up while we were ransacking their picnic. We got away all right, and had a good feed into the bargain, because we'd been clambed to death and couldn't wait long enough to get our chops ripping into them thin lettuce and ham sandwiches and creamy cakes.

Well, I'll always feel during every bit of my life like those daft kids should have felt before we broke them up. But they never dreamed that what happened was going to happen, just like the governor of this Borstal who spouts to us about honesty and all that wappy stuff don't know a bloody thing, while I know every minute of my life that a big boot is always likely to smash any nice picnic I might be barmy and dishonest enough to make for myself. I admit that there've been times when I've thought of telling the governor all this so as to put him on his guard, but when I've got as close as seeing him I've changed my mind, thinking to let him either find out for himself or go through the same mill as I've gone through. I'm not hard-hearted (in fact I've helped a few blokes in my time with the odd quid, lie, fag, or shelter from the rain when they've been on the run) but I'm boggered if I'm going to risk being put in the cells just for trying to give the governor a bit of advice he don't deserve. If my heart's soft I know the sort of people I'm going to save it for. And any advice I'd give the governor wouldn't do him the least bit of good; it'd only trip him up sooner than if he wasn't told at all, which I suppose is what I want to happen. But for the time being I'll let things go on as they are, which is something else I've learned in the last year or two. (It's a good job I can only think of these things as fast as I can write with this stub of pencil that's clutched in my paw, otherwise I'd have dropped the whole thing weeks ago.)

By the time I'm half-way through my morning course, when after a frost-bitten dawn I can see a phlegmy bit of sunlight hanging from the bare twigs of beech and sycamore, and when I've measured my half-way mark by the short-cut scrimmage down the steep bush-covered bank and into the sunken lane, when still there's not a soul in sight and not a sound except the neighing of a piebald foal in a cottage stable that I can't see, I get to thinking the deepest and daftest of all. The governor would have a fit if he could see me sliding down the bank because I could break my neck or ankle, but I can't not do it because it's the only risk I take and the only excitement I ever get, flying flat-out like one of them pterodactyls from the "Lost World" I once heard on the wireless, crazy like a cut-balled cockerel, scratching myself to bits and almost letting myself go but not quite. It's the most wonderful minute because there's not one thought or word or picture of anything in my head while I'm going down. I'm empty, as empty as I was before I was born, and I don't let myself go, I suppose, because whatever it is that's farthest down inside me don't want me to die or hurt myself bad. And it's daft to think deep, you know, because it gets you nowhere, though deep is what I am when I've passed this half-way mark because the long-distance run of an early morning makes me think that every run like this is a life—a little life, I know—but a life as full of misery and happiness and things happening as you can ever get really around yourself—and I remember that after a lot of these runs I thought that it didn't need much know-how to tell how a life was going to end once it had got well started. But as usual I was wrong, caught first by the cops and then by my own bad brain, I could never trust myself to fly scot-free over these traps, was always tripped up sooner or later no matter how many I got over to the good without even knowing it. Looking back I suppose them big trees put their branches to their snouts and gave each other the wink, and there I was whizzing down the bank and not seeing a bloody thing.

II

I don't say to myself: "You shouldn't have done the job and then you'd have stayed away from Borstal"; no, what I ram into my runner-brain is that my luck had no right to scram just when I was on my way to making the coppers think I hadn't done the job after all. The time was autumn and the night foggy enough to set me and my mate Mike roaming the streets when we should have been rooted in front of the telly or stuck into a plush posh seat at the pictures, but I was restless after six weeks away from any sort of work, and well you might ask me why I'd been bone-idle for so long because normally I sweated my thin guts out on a milling-machine with the rest of them, but you see, my dad died from cancer of the throat, and mam collected a cool five hundred in insurance and benefits from the factory where he'd worked, "for your bereavement," they said, or words like that.

Now I believe, and my mam must have thought the same, that a wad of crisp blue-black fivers ain't a sight of good to a living soul unless they're flying out of your hand into some shopkeeper's till, and the shopkeeper is passing you tip-top things in exchange over the counter, so as soon as she got the money, mam took me and my five brothers and sisters out to town and got us dolled-up in new clothes. Then she ordered a twenty-one-inch telly, a new carpet because the old one was covered with blood from dad's dying and wouldn't wash out, and took a taxi home with bags of grub and a new fur coat. And do you know—you wain't believe me when I tell you—she'd still near three hundred left in her bulging handbag the next day, so how could any of us go to work after that? Poor old dad, he didn't get a look in, and he was the one who'd done the suffering and dying for such a lot of lolly.

Night after night we sat in front of the telly with a ham sandwich in one hand, a bar of chocolate in the other, and a bottle of lemonade between our boots, while mam was with some fancy-man upstairs on the new bed she'd ordered, and I'd never known a family as happy as ours was in that couple of months when we'd got all the money we needed. And when the dough ran out I didn't think about anything much, but just roamed the streets—looking for another job, I told mam—hoping I suppose to get my hands on another five hundred nicker so's the nice life we'd got used to could go on and on for ever. Because it's surprising how quick you can get used to a different life. To begin with, the adverts on the telly had shown us how much more there was in the world to buy than we'd ever dreamed of when we'd looked into shop windows but hadn't seen all there was to see because we didn't have the money to buy it with any- way. And the telly made all these things seem twenty times better than we'd ever thought they were. Even adverts at the cinema were cool and tame, be- cause now we were seeing them in private at home. We used to cock our noses up at things in shops that didn't move, but suddenly we saw their real value because they jumped and glittered around the screen and had some pasty-faced tart going head over heels to get her nail-polished grabbers on to them or her lipstick lips over them, not like the crumby adverts you saw on posters or in newspapers as dead as doornails; these were flickering around loose, half-open packets and tins, making you think that all you had to do was finish opening them before they were yours, like seeing an unlocked safe through a shop win- dow with the man gone away for a cup of tea without thinking to guard his lolly. The films they showed were good as well, in that way, because we couldn't get our eyes unglued from the cops chasing the robbers who had satchel-bags crammed with cash and looked like getting away to spend it—until the last moment. I always hoped they would end up free to blow the lot, and could never stop wanting to put my hand out, smash into the screen (it only looked a bit of rag-screen like at the pictures) and get the copper in a half-nelson so's he'd stop following the bloke with the money-bags. Even when he'd knocked off a couple of bank clerks I hoped he wouldn't get nabbed. In fact then I wished more than ever he wouldn't because it meant the hot-chair if he did, I wouldn't wish that on anybody no matter what they'd done, because I'd read in a book where the hot-chair worn't a quick death at all, but that you just sat there scorching to death until you were dead. And it was when these cops were chas- ing the crooks that we played some good tricks with the telly, because when one of them opened his big gob to spout about getting their man I'd turn the sound down and see his mouth move like a goldfish or mackerel or a minnow mimick- ing what they were supposed to be acting—it was so funny the whole family nearly went into fits on the brand-new carpet that hadn't yet found its way to the bedroom. It was the best of all though when we did it to some Tory telling us about how good his government was going to be if we kept on voting for them—their slack chops rolling, opening and bumbling, hands lifting to twitch moustaches and touching their buttonholes to make sure the flower hadn't wilted, so that you could see they didn't mean a word they said, especially with not a murmur coming out because we'd cut off the sound. When the governor of the Borstal first talked to me I was reminded of those times so much that I nearly killed myself trying not to laugh. Yes, we played so many good stunts on the box of tricks that mam used to call us the Telly Boys, we got so clever at it.

My pal Mike got let off with probation because it was his first job—anyway the first they ever knew about—and because they said he would never have done it if it hadn't been for me talking him into it. They said I was a menace to honest lads like Mike—hands in his pockets so that they looked stone-empty, head bent forward as if looking for half-crowns to fill 'em with, a ripped jersey and his hair falling into his eyes so that he could go up to women and ask them for a shilling because he was hungry—and that I was the brains behind the job, the guiding light when it came to making up anybody's mind, but I swear to God I worn't owt like that because really I ain't got no more brains than a gnat after hiding the money in the place I did. And I—being cranky like I am—got sent to Borstal because to tell you the honest truth I'd been to Remand Homes before—though that's another story and I suppose if ever I tell it it'll be just as boring as this one is. I was glad though that Mike got away with it, and I only hope he always will, not like silly bastard me.

So on this foggy night we tore ourselves away from the telly and slammed the front door behind us, setting off up our wide street like slow tugs on a river that'd broken their hooters, for we didn't know where the housefronts began what with the perishing cold mist all around. I was snatched to death without an overcoat: mam had forgotten to buy me one in the scrummage of shopping, and by the time I thought to remind her of it the dough was gone. So we whistled "The Teddy Boys Picnic" to keep us warm, and I told myself that I'd get a coat soon if it was the last thing I did. Mike said he thought the same about himself, adding that he'd also get some brand-new glasses with gold rims, to wear instead of the wire frames they'd given him at the school clinic years ago. He didn't twig it was foggy at first and cleaned his glasses every time I pulled him back from a lamp-post or car, but when he saw the lights on Alfreton Road looking like octopus eyes he put them in his pocket and didn't wear them again until we did the job. We hadn't got two ha-pennies between us, and though we weren't hungry we wished we'd got a bob or two when we passed the fish and chip shops because the delicious sniffs of salt and vinegar and frying fat made our mouths water. I don't mind telling you we walked the town from one end to the other and if our eyes worn't glued to the ground looking for lost wallets and watches they was swivelling around house windows and shop doors in case we saw something easy and worth nipping into.

Neither of us said as much as this to each other, but I know for a fact that that was what we was thinking. What I don't know—and as sure as I sit here I know I'll never know—is which of us was the first bastard to latch his peepers on to that baker's backyard. Oh yes, it's all right me telling myself it was me, but the truth is that I've never known whether it was Mike or not, because I do know that I didn't see the open window until he stabbed me in the ribs and pointed it out. "See it?" he said.

"Yes," I told him, "so let's get cracking."

"But what about the wall though?" he whispered, looking a bit closer.

"On your shoulders," I chipped in.

His eyes were already up there: "Will you be able to reach?" It was the only time he ever showed any life.

"Leave it to me," I said, ever-ready. "I can reach anywhere from your ham-hock shoulders."

Mike was a nipper compared to me, but underneath the scruffy draught-board jersey he wore were muscles as hard as iron, and you wouldn't think to see him walking down the street with glasses on and hands in pockets that he'd harm a fly, but I never liked to get on the wrong side of him in a fight because he's the sort that don't say a word for weeks on end—sits plugged in front of the telly, or reads a cowboy book, or just sleeps—when suddenly BIFF—half kills somebody for almost nothing at all, such as beating him in a race for the last Football Post on a Saturday night, pushing in before him at a bus stop, or bumping into him when he was day-dreaming about Dolly-on-the-Tub next door. I saw him set on a bloke once for no more than fixing him in a funny way with his eyes, and it turned out that the bloke was cockeyed but nobody knew it because he'd just that day come to live in our street. At other times none of these things would matter a bit, and I suppose the only reason why I was pals with him was because I didn't say much from one month's end to another either.

He put his hands up in the air like he was being covered with a Gatling-Gun, and moved to the wall like he was going to be mowed down, and I climbed up him like he was a stile or step-ladder, and there he stood, the palms of his up-shot maulers flat and turned out so's I could step on 'em like they was the ad-justable jackspanner under a car, not a sound of a breath nor the shiver of a flinch coming from him. I lost no time in any case, took my coat from between my teeth, chucked it up to the glass-topped wall (where the glass worn't too sharp because the jags had been worn down by years of accidental stones) and was sitting astraddle before I knew where I was. Then down the other side, with my legs rammed up into my throat when I hit the ground, the crack coming about as hard as when you fall after a high parachute drop, that one of my mates told me was like jumping off a twelve-foot wall, which this must have been. Then I picked up my bits and pieces and opened the gate for Mike, who was still grinning and full of life because the hardest part of the job was already done. "I came, I broke, I entered," like that clever-dick Borstal song.

I didn't think about anything at all, as usual, because I never do when I'm busy, when I'm draining pipes, looting sacks, yaling locks, lifting latches, forcing my bony hands and lanky legs into making something move, hardly feeling my lungs going in-whiff and out-whaff, not realizing whether my mouth is clamped tight or gaping, whether I'm hungry, itching from scabies, or whether my flies are open and flashing dirty words like muck and spit into the late-night final fog. And when I don't know anything about all this then how can I honest-to-God say I think of anything at such times? When I'm wondering what's the best way to get a window open or how to force a door, how can I be thinking or have anything on my mind? That's what the four-eyed white-smocked bloke with the note-book couldn't understand when he asked me questions for days and days after I got to Borstal; and I couldn't explain it to him then like I'm writing it down now; and even if I'd been able to maybe he still wouldn't have caught on because I don't know whether I can understand it myself even at this moment, though I'm doing my best you can bet.

So before I knew where I was I was inside the baker's office watching Mike picking up that cash box after he'd struck a match to see where it was, wearing a tailor-made fifty-shilling grin on his square crew-cut nut as his paws closed over the box like he'd squash it to nothing.

"Out," he suddenly said, shaking it so's it rattled. "Let's scram."

"Maybe there's some more," I said, pulling half a dozen drawers out of a rollertop desk.

"No," he said, like he'd already been twenty years in the game, "this is the lot," patting his tin box, "this is it."

I pulled out another few drawers, full of bills, books and letters. "How do you know, you loony sod?"

He barged past me like a bull at a gate. "Because I do."

Right or wrong, we'd both got to stick together and do the same thing. I looked at an ever-loving babe of a brand-new typewriter, but knew it was too traceable, so blew it a kiss, and went out after him. "Hang on," I said, pulling the door to, "we're in no hurry."

"Not much we aren't," he says over his shoulder.

"We've got months to splash the lolly," I whispered as we crossed the yard, "only don't let that gate creak too much or you'll have the narks tuning-in."

"You think I'm barmy?" he said, creaking the gate so that the whole street heard.

I don't know about Mike, but now I started to think of how we'd get back safe through the streets with that money-box up my jumper. Because he'd clapped it into my hand as soon as we'd got to the main road, which might have meant that he'd started thinking as well, which only goes to show how you don't know what's in anybody else's mind unless you think about things yourself. But as far as my thinking went at that moment it wasn't up to much, only a bit of fright that wouldn't budge not even with a hot blow-lamp, about what we'd say if a copper asked us where we were off to with that hump in my guts.

"What is it?" he'd ask, and I'd say: "A growth." "What do you mean, a growth, my lad?" he'd say back, narky light. I'd cough and cluch myself like I was in the most tripe-twisting pain in the world, and screw my eyes up like I was on my way to the hospital, and Mike would take my arm like he was the best pal I'd got. "Cancer," I'd manage to say to Narker, which would make his slow punch-drunk brain suspect a thing or two. "A lad of your age?" So I'd groan again, and hope to make him feel a real bully of a bastard, which would be impossible, but anyway: "It's in the family. Dad died of it last month, and I'll die of it next month by the feel of it." "What, did he have it in the guts?" "No, in the throat. But it's got me in the stomach." Groan and cough. "Well, you shouldn't be out like this if you've got cancer, you should be in the hospital." I'd get ratty now: "That's where I'm trying to go if only you'd let me and stop asking so many questions. Aren't I, Mike?" Grunt from Mike as he unslung his cosh. Then just in time the copper would tell us to get on our way, kind and considerate all of a sudden, saying that the outpatient department of the hospital closes at twelve, so hadn't he better call us a taxi? He would if we liked, he says, and he'd pay for it as well. But we tell him not to bother, that he's a good bloke even if he is a copper, that we know a short cut anyway. Then just as we're turning a corner he gets it into his big batchy head that we're going the opposite way to the hospital, and calls us back. So we'd start to run. . . if you can call all that thinking.

Up in my room Mike rips open that money-box with a hammer and chisel, and before we know where we are we've got seventy-eight pound fifteen and fourpence ha'penny *each* lying all over my bed like tea spread out on Christmas Day: cake and trifle, salad and sandwiches, jam tarts and bars of chocolate: all shared and shared alike between Mike and me because we believed in equal work and equal pay, just like the comrades my dad was in until he couldn't do a stroke anymore and had no breath left to argue with. I thought how good it was that blokes like that poor baker didn't stash all his cash in one of the big marble-fronted banks that take up every corner of the town, how lucky for us that he didn't trust them no matter how many millions of tons of concrete or how many iron bars and boxes they were made of, or how many coppers kept their blue pop-eyed peepers glued on to them, how smashing it was that he believed in money-boxes when so many shopkeepers thought it old-fashioned and tried to be modern by using a bank, which wouldn't give a couple of sincere, honest, hardworking, conscientious blokes like Mike and me a chance.

Now you'd think, and I'd think, and anybody with a bit of imagination would think, that we'd done as clean a job as could ever be done, that, with the baker's shop being at least a mile from where we lived, and with not a soul having seen us, and what with the fog and the fact that we weren't more than five minutes in the place, that the coppers should never have been able to trace us. But then, you'd be wrong. I'd be wrong, and everybody else would be wrong, no matter how much imagination was diced out between us.

Even so, Mike and I didn't splash the money about, because that would have made people think straightaway that we'd latched on to something that didn't belong to us. Which wouldn't do at all, because even in a street like ours there are people who love to do a good turn for the coppers, though I never know why they do. Some people are so mean-gutted that even if they've only got tuppence more than you and they think you're the sort that would take it if you have half the chance, they'd get you put inside if they saw you ripping lead out of a lavatory, even if it weren't their lavatory—just to keep their tuppence out of your reach. And so we didn't do anything to let on about how rich we were, nothing like going down town and coming back dressed in brand-new Teddy boy suits and carrying a set of skiffle-drums like another pal of ours who'd done a factory office about six months before. No, we took the odd bobs and pennies out and folded the notes into bundles and stuffed them up the drainpipe outside the door in the backyard. "Nobody'll ever think of looking for it here," I said to Mike. "We'll keep it doggo for a week or two, then take a few quid a week out till it's all gone. We might be thieving bastards, but we're not green."

Some days later a plain-clothes dick knocked at the door. And asked for me.

I was still in bed, at eleven o'clock, and had to unroll myself from the comfortable black sheets when I heard mam calling me. "A man to see you," she said. "Hurry up, or he'll be gone."

I could hear her keeping him at the back door, nattering about how fine it had been but how it looked like rain since early this morning—and he didn't answer her except to snap out a snotty yes or no. I scrambled into my trousers and wondered why he'd come—knowing it was a copper because "a man to see you" always meant just that in our house—and if I'd had any idea that one had gone to Mike's house as well at the same time I'd have twigged it to be because of that hundred and fifty quid's worth of paper stuffed up the dainpipe outside the back door about ten inches away from that plain-clothed copper's boot, where mam still talked to him thinking she was doing me a favour, and I wishing to God she'd ask him in, though on second thoughts realizing that that would seem more suspicious than keeping him outside, because they know we hate their guts and smell a rat if they think we're trying to be nice to them. Mam wasn't born yesterday, I thought, thumping my way down the creaking stairs.

I'd seen him before: Borstal Bernard in nicky-hat, Remand Home Ronald in rowing-boat boots, Probation Pete in a pit-prop mackintosh, three-months clink in collar and tie (all this out of a Borstal skiffle-ballad that my new mate made up, and I'd tell you it in full but it doesn't belong in this story), a 'tec, who'd never had as much in his pocket as that drainpipe had up its jackses. He was like Hitler in the face, right down to the paint-brush tash, except that being six-foot tall made him seem worse. But I straightened my shoulders to look into his illiterate blue eyes—like I always do with any copper.

Then he started asking me questions, and my mother from behind said: "He's never left that television set for the last three months, so you've got nowt on him, mate. You might as well look for somebody else, because you're wasting the rates you get out of my rent and the income-tax that comes out of my pay-packet standing there like that"—which was a laugh because she'd never paid either to my knowledge, and never would, I hoped.

"Well, you know where Papplewick Street is, don't you?" the copper asked me, taking no notice of mam.

"Ain't it off Alfreton Road?" I asked him back, helpful and bright.

"You know there's a baker's half-way down on the left-hand side, don't you?"

"Ain't it next door to a pub, then?" I wanted to know.

He answered me sharp: "No, it bloody well ain't." Coppers always lose their tempers as quick as this, and more often than not they gain nothing by it. "Then I don't know it," I told him, saved by the bell.

He slid his big boot round and round on the doorstep. "Where were you last Friday night?" Back in the ring, but this was worse than a boxing match.

I didn't like him trying to accuse me of something he wasn't sure I'd done. "Was I at the baker's you mentioned? Or in the pub next door?"

"You'll get five years in Borstal if you don't give me a straight answer," he said, unbuttoning his mac even though it was cold where he was standing.

"I was glued to the telly, like mam says," I swore blind. But he went on and on with his loony questions: "Have you got a television?"

The things he asked wouldn't have taken in a kid of two, and what else could I say to the last one except: "Has the aerial fell down? Or would you like to come in and see it?"

He was liking me even less for saying that. "We know you weren't listening to the television set last Friday, and so do you, don't you?"

"'P'raps not, but I was *looking* at it, because sometimes we turn the sound down for a bit of fun." I could hear mam laughing from the kitchen, and I hoped Mike's mam was doing the same if the cops had gone to him as well.

"We know you weren't in the house," he said, starting up again, cranking himself with the handle. They always say 'We' 'We', never 'I' 'I'—as if they feel braver and righter knowing there's a lot of them against only one.

"I've got witnesses," I said to him. "Mam for one. Her fancy-man, for two. Ain't that enough? I can get you a dozen more, or thirteen altogether, if it was a baker's that got robbed."

"I don't want no lies," he said, not catching on about the baker's dozen. Where do they scrape cops up from anyway? "All I want is to get from you where you put that money."

Don't get mad, I kept saying to myself, don't get mad—hearing mam setting out cups and saucers and putting the pan on the stove for bacon. I stood back and waved him inside like I was a butler. "Come and search the house. If you've got a warrant."

"Listen, my lad," he said, like the dirty bullying jumped-up bastard he was, "I don't want too much of your lip, because if we get you down to the Guildhall you'll get a few bruises and black-eyes for your trouble." And I knew he wasn't kidding either, because I'd heard about all them sort of tricks. I hoped one day though that him and all his pals would be the ones to get the black-eyes and kicks; you never knew. It might come sooner than anybody thinks, like in Hungary. "Tell me where the money is, and I'll get you off with probation."

"What money?" I asked him, because I'd heard that one before as well.

"You know what money."

"Do I look as though I'd know owt about money?" I said, pushing my fist through a hole in my shirt.

"The money that was pinched, that you know all about," he said. "You can't trick me, so it's no use trying."

"Was it three-and-eightpence ha'penny?" I asked.

"You thieving young bastard. We'll teach you to steal money that doesn't belong to you."

I turned my head around: "Mam," I called out, "get my lawyer on the blower, will you?"

"Clever, aren't you?" he said in a very unfriendly way, "but we won't rest until we clear all this up."

"Look," I pleaded, as if about to sob my socks off because he'd got me wrong, "it's all very well us talking like this, it's like a game almost, but I wish you'd tell me what it's all about, because honest-to-God I've just got out of bed and here you are at the door talking about me having pinched a lot of money, money that I don't know anything about."

He swung around now as if he'd trapped me, though I couldn't see why he might think so. "Who said anything about money? I didn't. What made you bring money into this little talk we're having?"

"It's you," I answered, thinking he was going barmy and about to start foaming at the chops, "you've got money on the brain, like all policemen. Baker's shops as well."

He screwed his face up. "I want an answer from you: where's that money?"

But I was getting fed-up with all this. "I'll do a deal."

Judging by his flash-bulb face he thought he was suddenly on to a good thing. "What sort of a deal?"

So I told him: "I'll give you all the money I've got, one and four-pence ha'-penny, if you stop this third-degree and let me go in and get my breakfast. Honest, I'm clambed to death. I ain't had a bite since yesterday. Can't you hear my guts rollin'?"

His jaw dropped, but on he went, pumping me for another half hour. A routine check-up, as they say on the pictures. But I knew I was winning on points.

Then he left, but came back in the afternoon to search the house. He didn't find a thing, not a French farthing. He asked me questions again and I didn't tell him anything except lies, lies, because I can go on doing that forever without batting an eyelid. He'd got nothing on me and we both of us knew it, otherwise I'd have been down at the Guildhall in no time, but he kept on keeping on because I'd been in a Remand Home for a high-wall job before; and Mike was put through the same mill because all the local cops knew he was my best pal.

When it got dark me and Mike were in our parlour with a low light on and the telly off, Mike taking it easy in the rocking chair and me slouched out on the settee, both of us puffing a packet of Woods. With the door bolted and curtains drawn we talked about the dough we'd crammed up the drainpipe. Mike thought we should take it out and both of us do a bunk to Skegness or Cleethorpes for a good time in the arcades, living like lords in a boarding house near the pier, then at least we'd both have had a big beano before getting sent down.

"Listen, you daft bleeder," I said, "we aren't going to get caught at all, *and* we'll have a good time, later." We were so clever we didn't even go out to the pictures, though we wanted to.

In the morning old Hitler-face questioned me again, with one of his pals this time, and the next day they came, trying as hard as they could to get something out of me, but I didn't budge an inch. I know I'm showing off when I say this, but in me he'd met his match, and I'd never give in to questions no matter how long it was kept up. They searched the house a couple of times as well, which made me think they thought they really had something to go by, but I know now that they hadn't, and that it was all buckshee speculation. They turned the house upside down and inside out like an old sock, went from top to bottom and front to back but naturally didn't find a thing. The copper even poked his face up the front-room chimney (that hadn't been used or swept for years) and came down looking like Al Jolson so that he had to swill himself clean at the scullery sink. They kept tapping and pottering around the big aspidistra plant that grandma had left to mam, lifting it up from the table to look under the cloth, putting it aside so's they could move the table and get at the boards under the rug—but the big headed stupid ignorant bastards never once thought of emptying the soil out of the plant pot, where they'd have found the crumpled-up money-box that we'd buried the night we did the job. I suppose it's still there, now I think about it, and I suppose mam wonders now and again why the plant don't prosper like it used to—as if it could with a fistful of thick black tin wrapped around its guts.

The last time he knocked at our door was one wet morning at five minutes to nine and I was sleep-logged in my crumby bed as usual. Mam had gone to work that day so I shouted for him to hold on a bit, and then went down to see who it was. There he stood, six-feet tall and sopping wet, and for the first time in my life I did a spiteful thing I'll never forgive myself for: I didn't ask him to come in out of the rain, because I wanted him to get double pneumonia and die. I suppose he could have pushed by me and come in if he'd wanted, but maybe he'd got used to asking questions on the doorstep and didn't want to be put off by changing his ground even though it was raining. Not that I don't like being spiteful because of any barmy principle I've got, but this bit of spite, as it turned out, did me no good at all. I should have treated him as a brother I hadn't seen for twenty years and dragged him in for a cup of tea and a fag, told him about the picture I hadn't seen the night before, asked him how his wife was after her operation and whether they'd shaved her moustache off to make it, and then sent him happy and satisfied out by the front door. But no, I thought, let's see what he's got to say for himself now.

He stood a little to one side of the door, either because it was less wet there, or because he wanted to see me from a different angle, perhaps having found it monotonous to watch a bloke's face always telling lies from the same side. "You've been identified," he said, twitching raindrops from his tash. "A woman saw you and your mate yesterday and she swears blind you are the same chaps she saw going into that bakery."

I was dead sure he was still bluffing, because Mike and I hadn't even seen each other the day before, but I looked worried. "She's a menace then to innocent people, whoever she is, because the only bakery I've been in lately is the one up our street to get some cut-bread on tick for mam."

He didn't bite on this. "So now I want to know where the money is"—as if I hadn't answered him at all.

"I think mam took it to work this morning to get herself some tea in the canteen." Rain was splashing down so hard I thought he'd get washed away if he didn't come inside. But I wasn't much bothered, and went on: "I remember I put it in the telly-vase last night—it was my only one-and-three and I was saving it for a packet of tips this morning—and I nearly had a jibbering black fit just now when I saw it had gone. I was reckoning on it for getting me through today because I don't think life's worth living without a fag, do you?"

I was getting into my stride and began to feel good, twigging that this would be my last pack of lies, and that if I kept it up for long enough this time I'd have the bastards beat: Mike and me would be off to the coast in a few weeks time having the fun of our lives, playing at penny football and latching on to a couple of tarts that would give us all they were good for. "And this weather's no good for picking-up fag-ends in the street," I said, "because they'd be sopping wet.

Course, I know you could dry 'em out near the fire, but it don't taste the same you know, all said and done. Rainwater does summat to 'em that don't bear thinkin' about: it turns 'em back into hoss-tods without the taste though."

I began to wonder, at the back of my brainless eyes, why old copper-lugs didn't pull me up sharp and say he hadn't got time to listen to all this, but he wasn't looking at me anymore, and all my thoughts about Skegness went bursting to smithereens in my sludgy loaf. I could have dropped into the earth when I saw what he'd fixed his eyes on.

He was looking at *it*, an ever-loving fiver, and I could only jabber: "The one thing is to have some real fags because new hoss-tods is always better than stuff that's been rained on and dried, and I know how you feel about not being able to find money because one-and-three's one-and-three in anybody's pocket, and naturally if I see it knocking around I'll get you on the blower tomorrow straight-away and tell you where you can find it."

I thought I'd go down in a fit: three green-backs as well had been washed down by the water, and more were following, lying flat at first after their fall, then getting tilted at the corners by wind and rainspots as if they were alive and wanted to get back into the dry snug drain-pipe out of the terrible weather, and you can't imagine how I wished they'd be able to. Old Hitler-face didn't know what to make of it but just kept staring down and down, and I thought I'd better keep on talking, though I knew it wasn't much good now.

"It's a fact, I know, that money's hard to come by and half-crowns don't get found on bus seats or in dustbins, and I didn't see any in bed last night because I'd 'ave known about it, wouldn't I? You can't sleep with things like that in the bed because they're too hard, and anyway at first they're . . ." It took Hitler-boy a long time to catch on; they were beginning to spread over the yard a bit, reinforced by the third colour of a ten-bob note, before his hand clamped itself on to my shoulder.

III

The pop-eyed potbellied governor said to a pop-eyed potbellied Member of Parliament who sat next to his pop-eyed potbellied whore of a wife that I was his only hope for getting the Borstal Blue Ribbon Prize Cup For Long-Distance Cross-Country Running (all England), which I was, and it set me laughing to myself inside, and I didn't say a word to any potbellied pop-eyed bastard that might give them real hope, though I knew the governor anyway took my quiet-ness to mean he'd got that cup already stuck on the bookshelf in his office among the few other mildewed trophies.

"He might take up running in a sort of professional way when he gets out," and it wasn't until he'd said this and I'd heard it with my own flap-tabs that I realized it might be possible to do such a thing, run for money, trot for wages on piece work at a bob a puff rising bit by bit to a guinea a gasp and retiring through old age at thirty-two because of lace-curtain lungs, a football heart, and legs like varicose beanstalks. But I'd have a wife and car and get my grinning long-distance clock in the papers and have a smashing secretary to answer piles of letters sent by tarts who'd mob me when they saw who I was as I pushed my way into Woolworth's for a packet of razor blades and a cup of tea. It was something to think about all right, and sure enough the governor knew he'd got me when he said, turning to me as if I would at any rate have to be consulted about it all: "How does this matter strike you, then, Smith, my lad?"

A line of potbellied pop-eyes gleamed at me and a row of goldfish mouths opened and wiggled gold teeth at me, so I gave them the answer they wanted because I'd hold my trump card until later. "It'd suit me fine, sir," I said.

"Good lad. Good show. Right spirit. Splendid."

"Well," the governor said, "get that cup for us today and I'll do all I can for you. I'll get you trained so that you whack every man in the Free World." And I had a picture in my brain of me running and beating everybody in the world, leaving them all behind until only I was trot-trotting across a big wide moor alone, doing a marvellous speed as I ripped between boulders and reed-clumps, when suddenly: CRACK! CRACK!—bullets that can go faster than any man running, coming from a copper's rifle planted in a tree, winged me and split my gizzard in spite of my perfect running, and down I fell.

The potbellies expected me to say something else. "Thank you, sir," I said.

Told to go, I trotted down the pavilion steps, out on to the field because the big cross-country was about to begin and the two entries from Gunthorpe had fixed themselves early at the starting line and were ready to move off like white kangaroos. The sports ground looked a treat: with big tea-tents all round and flags flying and seats for families—empty because no mam or dad had known what opening day meant—and boys still running heats for the hundred yards, and lords and ladies walking from stall to stall, and the Borstal Boys Brass Band in blue uniforms; and up on the stands the brown jackets of Hucknall as well as our own grey blazers, and then the Gunthorpe lot with shirt sleeves rolled. The blue sky was full of sunshine and it couldn't have been a better day, and all of the big show was like something out of Ivanhoe that we'd seen on the pictures a few days before.

"Come on, Smith," Roach the sports master called to me, "we don't want you to be late for the big race, eh? Although I dare say you'd catch them up if you were." The others cat-called and grunted at this, but I took no notice and placed myself between Gunthorpe and one of the Aylesham trusties, dropped on my knees and plucked a few grass blades to suck on the way round. So the big race it was, for them, watching from the grandstand under a fluttering Union Jack, a race for the governor, that he had been waiting for, and I hoped he and all the rest of his pop-eyed gang were busy placing big bets on me, hundred to one to win, all the money they had in their pockets, all the wages they were going to get for the next five years, and the more they placed the happier I'd be. Because here was a dead cert going to die on the big name they'd built for him, going to go down dying with laughter whether it choked him or not. My knees felt the cool soil pressing into them, and out of my eye's corner I saw Roach lift his hand. The Gunthorpe boy twitched before the signal was given; somebody cheered too soon; Medway bent forward; then the gun went, and I was away.

We went once around the field and then along a half-mile drive of elms, being cheered all the way, and I seemed to feel I was in the lead as we went out by the gate and into the lane, though I wasn't interested enough to find out. The five-mile course was marked by splashes of whitewash gleaming on gateposts and trunks and stiles and stones, and a boy with a waterbottle and bandage-box stood every half-mile waiting for those that dropped out or fainted. Over the first stile, without trying, I was still nearly in the lead but one; and if any of you want tips about running, never be in a hurry, and never let any of the other runners know you are in a hurry even if you are. You can always overtake on long-distance running without letting the others smell the hurry in you; and when you've used your craft like this to reach the two or three up front then you can do a big dash later that puts everybody ele's hurry in the shade because you've not had to make haste up till then. I ran to a steady jog-trot rhythm, and soon it was so smooth that I forgot I was running, and I was hardly able to know that my legs were lifting and falling and my arms going in and out, and my lungs didn't seem to working at all, and my heart stopped that wicked thumping I always get at the beginning of a run. Because you see I never race at all; I just run, and somehow I know that if I forget I'm racing and only jog-trot along until I don't know I'm running I always win the race. For when my eyes recognize that I'm getting near the end of the course—by seeing a stile or cottage corner—I put on a spurt, and such a fast big spurt it is because I feel that up till then I haven't been running and that I've used up no energy at all. And I've been able to do this because I've been thinking; and I wonder if I'm the only one in the running business with this system of forgetting that I'm running because I'm too busy thinking; and I wonder if any of the other lads are on the same lark, though I know for a fact that they aren't. Off like the wind along the cobbled footpath and rutted lane, smoother than the flat grass track on the field and better for thinking because it's not too smooth, and I was in my element that afternoon knowing that nobody could beat me at running but intending to beat myself before the day was over. For when the governor talked to me of being honest when I first came in he didn't know what the word meant or he wouldn't have had me here in this race, trotting along in shimmy and shorts and sunshine. He'd have had me where I'd have had him if I'd been in his place: in a quarry breaking rocks until he broke his back. At least old Hitler-face the plain-clothes dick was honester than the governor, because he at any rate had had it in for me and I for him, and when my case was coming up in court a copper knocked at our front door at four o'clock in the morning and got my mother out of bed when she was paralytic tired, reminding her she had to be in court at dead on half past nine. It was the finest bit of spite I've ever heard of, but I would call it honest, the same as my mam's words were honest when she really told that copper what she thought of him and called him all the dirty names she's ever heard of, which took her half an hour and woke the terrace up.

I trotted on along the edge of a field bordered by the sunken lane, smelling green grass and honeysuckle, and I felt as though I came from a long line of whippets trained to run on two legs, only I couldn't see a toy rabbit in front and there wasn't a collier's cosh behind to make me keep up the pace. I passed the Gunthorpe runner whose shimmy was already black with sweat and I could just see the corner of the fenced-up copse in front where the only man I had to pass to win the race was going all out to gain the half-way mark. Then he turned into a tongue of trees and bushes where I couldn't see him anymore, and I couldn't see anybody, and I knew what the loneliness of the long-distance runner running across country felt like, realizing that as far as I was concerned this feeling was the only honesty and realness there was in the world and I knowing it would be no different ever, no matter what I felt at odd times, and no matter what anybody else tried to tell me. The runner behind me must have been a long way off because it was so quiet, and there was even less noise and movement than there had been at five o'clock of a frosty winter morning. It was hard to understand, and all I knew was that you had to run, run, run, without knowing why you were running, but on you went through fields you didn't understand and into woods that made you afraid, over hills without knowing you'd been up and down, and shooting across streams that would have cut the heart out of you had you fallen into them. And the winning post was no end to it, even though crowds might be cheering you in, because on you had to go before you got your breath back, and the only time you stopped really was when you tripped over a tree trunk and broke your neck or fell into a disused well and stayed dead in the darkness forever. So I thought: they aren't going to get me on this racing lark, this running and trying to win, this jog-trotting for a bit of blue ribbon, because it's not the way to go on at all, though they swear blind that it is. You should think about nobody and go your own way, not on a course marked out for you by people holding mugs of water and bottles of iodine in case you fall and cut yourself so that they can pick you up—even if you want to stay where you are— and get you moving again.

On I went, out of the wood, passing the man leading without knowing I was going to do so. Flip-flap, flip flap, jog-trot, jog-trot, crunchslap-crunchslap, across the middle of a broad field agrain, rhythmically running in my greyhound effortless fashion, knowing I had won the race though it wasn't half over, won it if I wanted it, could go on for ten or fifteen or twenty miles if I had to and drop dead at the finish of it, which would be the same, in the end, as living an honest life like the governor wanted me to. It amounted to: win the race and be honest, and on trot-trotting I went, having the time of my life, loving my progress because it did me good and set me thinking which by now I liked to do, but not caring at all when I remembered that I had to win this race as well as run it. One of the two, I had to win the race or run it, and I knew I could do both because my legs had carried me well in front—now coming to the short cut down the bramble bank and over the sunken road—and would carry me further because they seemed made of electric cable and easily alive to keep on slapping at those ruts and roots, but I'm not going to win because the only way I'd see I came in first would be if winning meant that I was going to escape the coppers after doing the biggest bank job of my life, but winning means the exact opposite, no matter how they try to kill or kid me, means running right into their white-gloved wall-barred hands and grinning mugs and staying there for the rest of my natural long life of stone-breaking anyway, but stone-breaking in the way I want to do it and not in the way they tell me.

Another honest thought that comes is that I could swing left at the next hedge of the field, and under its cover beat my slow retreat away from the sports ground winning post. I could do three or six or a dozen miles across the turf like this and cut a few main roads behind me so's they'd never know which one I'd taken; and maybe on the last one when it got dark I could thumb a lorry-lift and get a free ride north with somebody who might not give me away. But no, I said I wasn't daft didn't I? I won't pull out with only six months left, and besides there's nothing I want to dodge and run away from; I only want a bit of my own back on the In-laws and Potbellies by letting them sit up there on their big posh seats and watch me lose this race, though as sure as God made me I know that when I do lose I'll get the dirtiest crap and kitchen jobs in the months to go before my time is up. I won't be worth a threpp'ny-bit to anybody here, which will be all the thanks I get for being honest in the only way I know. For when the governor told me to be honest it was meant to be in his way not mine, and if I kept on being honest in the way he wanted and won my race for him he'd see I got the cushiest six months still left to run; but in my own way, well, it's not allowed, and if I find a way of doing it such as I've got now then I'll get what-for in every mean trick he can set his mind to. And if you look at it in my way, who can blame him? For this is war—and ain't I said so?—and when I hit him in the only place he knows he'll be sure to get his own back on me for not collaring that cup when his heart's been set for ages on seeing himself standing up at the end of the afternoon to clap me on the back as I take the cup from Lord Earwig or some such chinless wonder with a name like that. And so I'll hit him where it hurts a lot, and he'll do all he can to get his own back, tit for tat, though I'll enjoy it most because I'm hitting first, and because I planned it longer. I don't know why I think these thoughts are better than any I've ever had, but I do, and I don't care why. I suppose it took me a long time to get going on all this because I've had no time and peace in all my bandit life, and now my thoughts are coming pat and the only trouble is I often can't stop, even when my brain feels as if it's got cramp, frostbite and creeping paralysis all rolled into one and I have to give it a rest by slap-dashing down through the brambles of the sunken lane. And all this is another uppercut I'm getting in first at people like the governor, to show how—if I can—his races are never won even though some bloke always comes unknowingly in first, how in the end the governor is going to be doomed while blokes like me will take the pickings of his roasted bones and dance like maniacs around his Borstal's ruins. And so this story's like the race and once again I won't bring off a winner to suit the governor; no, I'm being honest like he told me to, without him knowing what he means, though I don't suppose he'll ever come in with a story of his own, even if he reads this one of mine and knows who I'm talking about.

I've just come up out of the sunken lane, kneed and elbowed, thumped and bramble-scratched, and the race is two-thirds over, and a voice is going like a wireless in my mind saying that when you've had enough of feeling good like the first man on earth of a frosty morning and you've known how it is to be taken bad like the last man on earth on a summer's afternoon, then you get at last to being like the only man on earth and don't give a bogger about either good or bad, but just trot on with your slippers slapping the good dry soil that at least would never do you a bad turn. Now the words are like coming from a crystal-set that's broken down, and something's happening inside the shell-case of my guts that bothers me and I don't know why or what to blame it on, a grinding near my ticker as though a bag of rusty screws is loose inside me and I shake them up every time I trot forward. Now and again I break my rhythm to feel my left shoulder-blade by swinging a right hand across my chest as if to rub the knife away that has somehow got stuck there. But I know it's nothing to bother about, that more likely it's caused by too much thinking that now and again I take for worry. For sometimes I'm the greatest worrier in the world I think (as you twigged I'll bet from me having got this story out) which is funny anyway because my mam don't know the meaning of the word so I don't take after her; though dad had a hard time of worry all his life up to when he filled his bedroom with hot blood and kicked the bucket that morning when nobody was in the house. I'll never forget it, straight I won't, because I was the one that found him and I often wished I hadn't. Back from a session on the fruit-machines at the fish-and-chip shop, jingling my three-lemon loot to a nail-dead house, as soon as I got in I knew something was wrong, stood leaning my head against the cold mirror above the mantelpiece trying not to open my eyes and see my stone-cold clock—because I knew I'd gone as white as a piece of chalk since coming in as if I'd been got at by a Dracula-vampire and even my penny-pocket winnings kept quiet on purpose.

Gunthorpe nearly caught me up. Birds were singing from the briar hedge, and a couple of thrushies flew like lightning into some thorny bushes. Corn had grown high in the next field and would be cut down soon with scythes and mowers; but I never wanted to notice much while running in case it put me off my stroke, so by the haystack I decided to leave it all behind and put on such a spurt, in spite of nails in my guts, that before long I'd left both Gunthorpe and the birds a good way off; I wasn't far now from going into that last mile and a half like a knife through margarine, but the quietness I suddenly trotted into between two pickets was like opening my eyes underwater and looking at the pebbles on a stream bottom, reminding me again of going back that morning to the house in which my old man had croaked, which is funny because I hadn't thought about it at all since it happened and even then I didn't brood much on it. I wonder why? I suppose that since I started to think on these long-distance runs I'm liable to have anything crop up and pester at my tripes and innards, and now that I see my bloody dad behind each grass-blade in my barmy runner-brain I'm not so sure I like to think and that it's such a good thing after all. I choke my phlegm and keep on running anyway and curse the Borstal-builders and their athletics—flappity-flap, slop-slop, crunchslap-crunchslap-crunchslap— who've maybe got their own back on me from the bright beginning by sliding magic-lantern slides into my head that never stood a chance before. Only if I take whatever comes like this in my runner's stride can I keep on keeping on like my old self and beat them back; and now I've thought on this far I know I'll win, in the crunchslap end. So anyway after a bit I went upstairs one step at a time not thinking anything about how I should find dad and what I'd do when I did. But now I'm making up for it by going over the rotten life mam led him ever since I can remember, knocking-on with different men even when he was alive and fit and she not caring whether he knew it or not, and most of the time he wasn't so blind as she thought and cursed and roared and threatened to punch her tab, and I had to stand up to stop him even though I knew she deserved it. What a life for all of us. Well, I'm not grumbling, because if I did I might just as well win this bleeding race, which I'm not going to do, though if I don't lose speed I'll win it before I know where I am, and then where would I be?

Now I can hear the sportsground noise and music as I head back for the flags and the lead-in drive, the fresh new feel of underfoot gravel going against the iron muscles of my legs. I'm nowhere near puffed despite that bag of nails that rattles as much as ever, and I can still give a big last leap like gale-force wind if I want to, but everything is under control and I know now that there ain't another long-distance cross-country running runner in England to touch my speed and style. Our doddering bastard of a governor, our half-dead gangrened gaffer is hollow like an empty petrol drum, and he wants me and my running life to give him glory, to put in him blood and throbbing veins he never had, wants his potbellied pals to be his witnesses as I gasp and stagger up to his winning post so's he can say: "My Borstal gets that cup, you see. I win my bet, because it pays to be honest and try to gain the prizes I offer to my lads, and they know it, have known it all along. They'll always be honest now, because I made them so." And his pals will think: "He trains his lads to live right, after all; he deserves a medal but we'll get him made a Sir"—and at this very moment as the birds come back to whistling I can tell myself I'll never care a sod what any of the chinless spineless In-laws think or say. They've seen me and they're cheering now and loudspeakers set around the field like elephant's ears are spreading out the big news that I'm well in the lead, and can't do anything else but stay there. But I'm still thinking of the Out-law death my dad died, telling the doctors to scat from the house when they wanted him to finish up in hospital (like a bleeding guinea-pig, he raved at them). He got up in bed to throw them out and even followed them down the stairs in his shirt though he was no more than skin and stick. They tried to tell him he'd want some drugs but he didn't fall for it, and only took the pain-killer that mam and I got from a herb seller in the next street. It's not till now that I know what guts he had, and when I went into the room that morning he was lying on his stomach with the clothes thrown back, looking like a skinned rabbit, his grey head resting just on the edge of the bed, and on the floor must have been all the blood he'd had in his body, right from his toenails up, for nearly all of the lino and carpet was covered in it, thin and pink.

And down the drive I went, carrying a heart blocked up like Boulder Dam across my arteries, the nail-bag clamped down tighter and tighter as though in a woodwork vice, yet with my feet like birdwings and arms like talons ready to fly across the field except that I didn't want to give anybody that much of a show, or win the race by accident. I smell the hot dry day now as I run towards the end, passing a mountain-heap of grass emptied from cans hooked on to the fronts of lawnmowers pushed by my pals; I rip a piece of tree-bark with my fingers and stuff it in my mouth, chewing wood and dust and maybe maggots as I run until I'm nearly sick, yet swallowing what I can of it just the same because a little birdie whistled to me that I've got to go on living for at least a bloody sight longer yet but that for six months I'm not going to smell that grass or taste that dusty bark or trot this lovely path. I hate to have to say this but something bloody-well made me cry, and crying is a thing I haven't bloody-well done since I was a kid of two or three. Because I'm slowing down now for Gunthorpe to catch me up, and I'm doing it in a place just where the drive turns into the sportsfield—where they can see what I'm doing, especially the governor and his gang from the grandstand, and I'm going so slow I'm almost marking time. Those on the nearest seats haven't caught on yet to what's happening and are still cheering like mad ready for when I make that mark, and I keep on wondering when the bleeding hell Gunthorpe behind me is going to nip by on to the field because I can't hold this up all day, and I think Oh Christ it's just my rotten luck that Gunthorpe's dropped out and that I'll be here for half an hour before the next bloke comes up, but even so, I say, I won't budge, I won't go for that last hundred yards if I have to sit down cross-legged on the grass and have the governor and his chinless wonders pick me up and carry me there, which is against their rules so you can bet they'd never do it because they're not clever enough to break the rules—like I would be in their place—even though they are their own. No, I'll show him what honesty means if it's the last thing I do, though I'm sure he'll never understand because if he and all them like him did it'd mean they'd be on my side which is impossible. By God I'll stick this out like my dad stuck out his pain and kicked them doctors down the stairs: if he had guts for that then I've got guts for this and here I stay waiting for Gunthorpe or Aylesham to bash that turf and go right slap-up against that bit of clothes-line stretched across the winning post. As for me, the only time I'll hit that clothes-line will be when I'm dead and a comfortable coffin's been got ready on the other side. Until then I'm a long-distance runner, crossing country all on my own no matter how bad it feels.

The Essex boys were shouting themselves blue in the face telling me to get a move on, waving their arms, standing up and making as if to run at that rope themselves because they were only a few yards to the side of it. You cranky lot, I thought, stuck at that winning post, and yet I knew they didn't mean what they were shouting, were really on my side and always would be, not able to keep their maulers to themselves, in and out of copshops and clink. And there they were now having the time of their lives letting themselves go in cheering me which made the governor think they were heart and soul on his side when he wouldn't have thought any such thing if he'd had a grain of sense. And I could hear the lords and ladies now from the grandstand, and could see them standing up to wave me in: "Run!" they were shouting in their posh voices. "Run!" But I was deaf, daft and blind, and stood where I was, still tasting the bark in my mouth and still blubbing like a baby, blubbing now out of gladness that I'd got them beat at last.

Because I heard a roar and saw the Gunthorpe gang throwing their coats up in the air and I felt the pat-pat of feet on the drive behind me getting closer and closer and suddenly a smell of sweat and a pair of lungs on their last gasp passed me by and went swinging on towards that rope, all shagged out and rocking from side to side, grunting like a Zulu that didn't know any better, like the ghost of me at ninety when I'm heading for that fat upholstered coffin. I could have cheered him myself: "Go on, go on, get cracking. Knot yourself up on that piece of tape." But he was already there, and so I went on, trot-trotting after him until I got to the rope, and collapsed, with a murderous sounding roar going up through my ears while I was still on the wrong side of it.

It's about time to stop; though don't think I'm not still running, because I am, one way or another. The governor at Borstal proved me right; he didn't respect my honesty at all; not that I expected him to, or tried to explain it to him, but if he's supposed to be educated then he should have more or less twigged it. He got his own back right enough, or thought he did, because he had me carting dustbins about every morning from the big full-working kitchen to the garden-bottoms where I had to empty them, and in the afternoon I spread out slops over spuds and carrots growing in the allotments. In the evenings I scrubbed floors, miles and miles of them. But it wasn't a bad life for six months, which was another thing he could never understand and would have made it grimmer if he could, and it was worth it when I look back on it, considering all the thinking I did, and the fact that the boys caught on to me losing the race on purpose and never had enough good words to say about me, or curses to throw out (to themselves) at the governor.

The work didn't break me; if anything it made me stronger in many ways, and the governor knew, when I left, that his spite had got him nowhere. For since leaving Borstal they tried to get me in the army, but I didn't pass the medical and I'll tell you why. No sooner was I out, after that final run and six-months hard, than I went down with pleurisy, which means as far as I'm concerned that I lost the governor's race all right, and won my own twice over, because I know for certain that if I hadn't raced my race I wouldn't have got this pleurisy, which keeps me out of khaki but doesn't stop me doing the sort of work my itchy fingers want to do.

I'm out now and the heat's switched on again, but the rats haven't got me for the last thing I pulled. I counted six hundred and twenty-eight pounds and am still living off it because I did the job all on my own, and after it I had the peace to write all this, and it'll be money enough to keep me going until I finish my plans for doing an even bigger snatch, something up my sleeve I wouldn't tell to a living soul. I worked out my systems and hiding-places while pushing scrubbing-brushes around them Borstal floors, planned my outward life of innocence and honest work, yet at the same time grew perfect in the razor-edges of my craft for what I knew I had to do once free; and what I'll do again if netted by the poaching coppers.

In the meantime (as they say in one or two books I've read since, useless though because all of them ended on a winning post and didn't teach me a thing) I'm going to give this story to a pal of mine and tell him that if I do get captured again by the coppers he can try and get it put into a book or something, because I'd like to see the governor's face when he reads it, if he does, which I don't suppose he will; even if he did read it though I don't think he'd know what it was all about. And if I don't get caught the bloke I give this story to will never give me away; he's lived on our terrace for as long as I can remember, and he's my pal. That I do know.

Considerations

1. One of the advantages of the first-person narrative is that the reader is afforded the opportunity to make judgments that the narrator himself may be unable or

unwilling to make. Describe Smith, the narrator, according to the things he says about himself and then according to your *interpretation* of those statements.

2. Discuss the various ways this story could be told. List the ways it would be different, told from the point of view of the governor.

3. How does Smith characterize the reader? Is this a mere justification of his predicament, or would you agree with it?

4. This is more than just a story about a boy who discovers a hidden talent while in prison; it is a severe commentary on political systems, systems of which the governor is a symbol. Consider Smith's assessment of the governor and what he represents, discussing as many of the implications as you can:

> At the moment it's dead blokes like him as have the whip-hand over blokes like me, and I'm almost dead sure it'll always be like that, but even so, by Christ I'd rather be like I am—always on the run and breaking into shops for a packet of fags and a jar of jam—than have the whip-hand over somebody else and be dead from the toenails up. Maybe as soon as you get the whip-hand over somebody you do go dead.

5. Discuss his statement about real honesty:

> And if I had the whip-hand I wouldn't even bother to build a place like this to put all the cops, governors, posh whores, penpushers, army officers, Members of Parliament in; no, I'd stick them up against a wall and let them have it, like they'd have done with blokes like us years ago, that is, if they'd ever known what it is to be honest, which they don't and never will so help me God Almighty.

6. What does he mean when he says that he has "a war of my own, that I was born into one"?

7. He says that every run is "a little life." Explain the implications of this statement. In this context, what are the implications of the title?

8. It is often said that money doesn't bring happiness (Howard Hughes, it is said, is a good example), and it is the theme of countless books. But is it the theme of this one? How do Smith and his family get along while they have his father's insurance money? Is it a significant point that he doesn't rob the bakery during this period?

9. Summarize his poignant comments about the "telly" and its "adverts." Why is this a problem of growing concern among intelligent people in our own country?

10. Smith is obviously an excellent athlete, but why doesn't he think like the ordinary "jock"? Is having the "right attitude" necessary to become a champion athlete? What is the "right attitude"? Is it a state of mind defined by people like the governor? For what purpose?

11. If this story were adapted for television, exactly how might it be changed to appeal to the widest possible audience?

12. Why does Smith allow someone else to win the race? What answer do you think he would have for Vince Lombardi's famous definition of winning as not "everything," but "the only thing"?

13. The vernacular is the language of the common people. Discuss the imaginative use of it in this story. Make a list of Smith's especially expressive statements.

THE RITES OF PASSAGE
Forming Identity
Through Sports

Then he pulled trigger. To him there was a frightful roar, his cheek and his shoulder took a stunning blow, his face felt a hot flush of fire, and, opening his two eyes, he found that he was still alive. He was not too dazed to instantly adopt a becoming egotism. It had been the first shot of his life.

—Stephen Crane

WILLIAM HARRISON

Nirvana, Götterdämmerung
and the Shot Put

Toby Grogan, like all shot-putters everywhere, was crazy from the beginning. Most of his mammoth life he stood in that small circle, stared transfixed into distant space, pressed an iron ball to his cheek, talked to it, stooped, wheeled, and heaved with all his strength.

He knew it was stupid, but he did little else.

He became a mutterer after his college days, talking to inanimate objects much in the way that he spoke to his iron ball. Also, his back ached. Doorknobs sometimes came off in his hands, too, and he broke chairs when he sat in them. Once in Lafayette, Indiana, he was trying to make love to a willing fan of track and field events, but the bed collapsed and in his ensuing fury he smashed holes in the motel walls with his fists so that Coach Fain had to pay for damages. Grogan spent years going to track meets, back and forth across the country in the cramped seats of buses and planes to the Kansas Relays, the Olympic Trials, the AAU Championships, or the Madison Square Garden Indoor Games. His weight stayed at an even 322 pounds, but sometimes his brain threatened to explode on him. Problems everywhere: too embarrassed to eat all that he craved in a single restaurant, he often wasted hours taking a meal at two or three establishments; his sponsor, the Greater Chicago Athletic Club, nagged him to return the barbells he carried around the country in his suitcases; and for seven years he kept putting the shot around 70 feet—never quite up to the world's record of 71 feet, 5½ inches. His life, like furniture, kept caving in on him and he turned into a mystic.

"A what?" Coach Fain asked him.

"I read this magazine article on the plane coming back from Denver," Toby explained. "This article about Zen concentration. I began practicing. I began talking to my ball about it."

Abraham Fain was a darkly handsome man who resembled Gregory Peck, but who rejected that image to behave like a worried, nervous, midget track coach—the sort who wore his baseball cap backwards, paced, and continually clapped his hands. His Chicago team—once famous, but needing recruits—consisted of Toby Grogan, a vaulter, two sprinters, and a broad-jumping black who wanted to be listed in all the programs as The Leopard.

"I realize you got problems," Coach Fain observed, trying to restrain himself. "You got that lousy vertebra. You got social problems in restaurants. Also, a mild case of athlete's foot, too many letters from your mama, and sexual desires: I know it all. But I told you, please: put nothing in your head prior to Munich. Remember I especially said keep away from new women or books of any sort."

"This was just a magazine article. It said that in the back of the brain there's this pink fogbank. You climb inside it, so there's no possible chance of outside interference."

Coach Fain rolled his eyes.

The workouts were at Soldier's Field and the Chicago sky was a comforting cobalt blue. Home ground, the Athletic Club just a few blocks away. Workmen, as always, tapped and sawed from someplace behind the stands and from the distant trees and walkways of the surrounding park Toby could hear the voices of birds and children. He tromped over to his familiar ring, fixed the wooden block in place, and hefted his ball. As he kicked his feet, loosening up, Coach Fain's dowdy family, the wife and six plump girls, entered at the far end of the stadium. Toby sighed, thinking how Abe suffered their visits during Chicago practice sessions, and considered the benefits of the somewhat lonely nomadic life. Then he slipped out of his warm-up pants and tried to conjure up a pink fogbank.

"Ball," he whispered, "I'm the big cannon that's going to fire you out of pink smoke today." He then addressed his toes, feet, legs, biceps, forearms, and fingertips by way of urging them, as usual, to do their separate and fluid parts in the effort.

He fought for a mind clear of Coach Fain's loud wife and daughters and all the sounds and distractions of the stadium and nearby park and he struggled against all brute desires and psychic fancies. He didn't even think of food. And for once even his lifelong ambition to heave the iron ball a record distance faded in his gathering concentration. He was beyond ambition and he glimpsed a rolling curtain of fog, stared into it, and took his stance. Down, crouched low, then up, whirling, springing forward, crying, "AAaaaahhmm!" He knew it was one hell of a shot as it came off his fingers.

Eighty feet flat. He measured it twice, three times. Since this was his first and only effort, there was no mistaking that lone indentation out in the dirt where the chalk lines curved and beckoned. He retrieved his ball, walked around that little crater another time, and once more measured its distance back to the circle before strolling over to the coach.

Coach Fain, who was finally disposing of his family with a rigid smile, agreed to stroll across the football field to check Toby's claim. He took two measurements himself and when he had confirmed the accuracy of the metal tape his eyes narrowed and he said, "Okay, Big Tobe, give it another try, huh?"

Toby set himself in the circle, waited, briefly dreamed of the pink fog, and let go again.

"Sixty-six feet, four inches!" Coach Fain called back with a smirk. Then he turned away to watch The Leopard take aim on a nearby sandpit.

Toby went back to his circle holding the ball shoulder-high, He supposed he hadn't allowed the power, the full rapture of the fog, to accumulate properly, so while Coach Fain yelled and the others panted around the track Toby set himself again. A full trance this time: he felt his nerve ends humming, heard voices, watched the fog roll toward him once again. The ball arched into a high orbit beyond his grunt and cry.

Just over eighty feet. He stretched the metal tape to that impossible length once, twice, then, satisfied, he quit for the day.

The room where Toby stayed that spring before the Munich Olympics bore all the tokens of his life. A somewhat narrow mirror on the closet door reflected less than half his full girth while his meager wardrobe peered out from the closet itself: worn seersucker slacks, blue blazer with the shield of the CCAC on the pocket, his English tweed suit (never properly large enough across the back), the fat shoes, and all his sweat clothes. Beneath these, the suitcases stood ready. Near his bed were the barbells and footlocker, its lid thrown open to expose a few pictures glued inside: an old news photo of Randy Matson and last April's Playmate, among others. Beside the portable television set on his bedside table was the packet of letters from his mother in Des Moines, each letter with its plea—entreating him to go into the ministry, to testify against drug abuse like all the other athletes were doing, to come home and farm with his deadbeat father, to marry. The letters gave him indigestion or worse—either heartburn or heartsickness, he once told Coach Fain. The remainder of his room was decorated with loving cups, statuettes, engraved plates and awards topped with gold-plated athletic figurines pointing into space. When traveling, Toby kept the trophies in his footlocker.

That spring in his one-room Chicago apartment he viewed as much of himself as his mirror allowed. He saw a giant, heavy in the heart. Twenty-nine years old now and he had always been a shot-putter. Not that he wanted it especially —though he dreamt, sure, of world records and medals—he just *was* a shot-putter, nothing else. Now he came so close to the mirror that his breath steamed the word which he spoke almost like a kiss. "Mystic," he whispered. Every day he came and scrutinized himself and pronounced that word, and in the nights, bulging with anticipation he really didn't understand, he tossed in his sleep as the bed moaned beneath him. He didn't know why those magnificent throws came only in private. But a great moment, he assumed was upon him.

Then everybody went to Munich. Coach Fain, his new Olympic coaches on the American squad, The Leopard, the proud and the mighty.

A festive city: the river flashing with summer, all the girls, the pageantry, the Hofbräuhaus decked with pennants. From the very beginning a sense of pleasant destiny came over him and Toby enjoyed himself. Heedless of the curfew posted on the bulletin board at the Olympic compound, he walked along the Maximilianstrasse as if he owned it, mixing with the beer drinkers. And, a curiosity: the Germans, admiring his girth and capacity in the taverns, followed him around. Stout knight, they toasted him. *Mammut.* Some of them—particularly a large blond girl named Karin with heavy breasts bumping beneath her sweat shirt—waited for him outside the Olympic Village in the afternoons after practice, eager to accompany him on his nightly rounds. Or a crowd gathered at the fence in the mornings, peering into the shadows of the new domed stadium, too far away to judge the distance of his efforts, but wondering even then why he seemed to save himself for moments alone, why, alone, his coaches occupied elsewhere, he set himself in a forlorn and deeply melancholy trance, then, coming up, bellowing, erupted with his most magnificent shots.

It was his deep solitude—they presumed it was old-fashioned melancholy because, being German, they *understood* melancholy—which touched them. Also, he performed with an iron ball and they, well, *liked* iron, as they tried to explain to him; there was something definitely medieval about it. But, also, he was just a good fellow, right? They watched him quaff twenty-six liters of beer at the Bräuhallen one night. And he accepted their praise and appreciation, but more: he began to feel strangely at home, at terms with himself and these people and the brooding land and city that lay around the sleek architecture of the new Olympic compound. He talked to his ball about this, pressing it to his cheek and saying, "This crowd likes big things. They want what I want, too: something large and important. That's why they're out there in the mornings looking through the fence." The Olympics, after all: a moment perilous, awful, nearly occult in its majesty.

The week of warm-ups made him a celebrity. A newspaper carried his photo as he posed in the Goetheplatz, a somewhat dreamy expression on his wide face. His admirers multiplied, following him into a shop where he bought a souvenir, an enameled beer stein, for his mother. In the rousing oom-pahing of the Hofbräuhaus he shyly consented to kiss the busty blonde in the sweat shirt and everyone roared approval. They hadn't even seen him throw, for he waved them back to seek the winning rapture of the pink fog on his own, but this didn't matter. *Süss Ungeheuer,* they called him. The Happy Iron Man. Our Toby. They viewed him from a distance as he strode out into the stadium infield, waving coaches away, disdaining measurements. They understood. He was moody, they said, and this was only a sign that his power simmered inside him.

Coach Fain told Toby, "You're not just your usual neurotic self, baby. You're out of it." But when he insisted on measuring a couple of Toby's throws, Toby waved him away.

"Leave me alone, Abe," he said, giving the coach an even stare.

"Allow him a little temperament," Abe finally told the other coaches on the American squad. "Maybe he's got seventy feet in him on a good day." Abe Fain kept his distance, then, and the night after the opening processional he even joined the shot-putter and the entourage for the nightly rounds. "Live and let live," he told Toby. "And, besides, the wife and daughters are back home and you've got some fantastic fräuleins at your elbow, right?"

Karin, the blonde in the sweat shirt, seemed pleased enough with Toby's coach and she and Abe held hands, sang, drank beers, and discussed the phenomenon. "He said a curious thing to me the other night," she confided in Abe.

"What, baby?" he asked earnestly. "Tell the old coach."

"He said he thought—well, this is odd. He felt he had been here before. Long ago, you see. In another life. Did he mention this to you?"

"Never, baby, because I got rules. No books, No women either—but be realistic about that, I say—so especially no books or kooky new ideas. Get what I mean?"

"What muscles," Karin sighed, looking down the table where Toby had agreed to simultaneously arm wrestle two of his admirers.

The night grew rowdy. In high good humor Toby paraded among the tables, one thick arm raised in salute as they chanted, *"Mammut! Mammut!"* Karin, dazed and large and lovely, led the marchers who fell in behind him. Someone pulled the American pennant off the wall and waved it.

The field events initiated the Olympics—as if such promethean heaves and tosses were less important than the later and climactic track events. A shirt-sleeved crowd—Toby's boisterous followers included—gathered early beneath the cool dome of the stadium. The Russian shot-putter was huge, his legs like oaks, and the Turk was big, too, but Toby seemed to dwarf them all; impervious, he stood apart. His expectant admirers called to him, to each other, to the confused Russian, who had been kept from either reading the newspapers or drinking beer. Names were announced on the loudspeaker. Vasily Nikolaivich. Saul Deeter. Jacques Brol. Toby Grogan. Cheers and whistles at the mention of his name.

Except for Toby all the shot-putters gathered close to the circle, standing around or jogging in place or bending to touch their toes. Toby drifted beyond the track, however, and spoke to his ball until an official, a little Austrian all dapper in his Olympic cap and sports coat, ran over and instructed Toby to conform. But Toby demurred. The official wagged a finger up into Toby's face, Toby stood his ground, and the admirers in the stands took this as a sign of exciting things to come and applauded lightly. The Austrian went back and fussed with an American coach, but as the event opened Toby still wasn't in the group.

Alone, a distant gaze in his eyes, Toby took a practice shot; the ball went out in a mighty arch, bringing a gasp from the crowd. It made an ugly hole in the artificial turf where it was clearly not supposed to fall. The little Austrian came back, then, pointing at the crater in the artificial turf and shouting, and from the distant vantage point of the stands he seemed pathetic and funny to Toby's admirers. They slapped their legs.

The loudspeaker then announced Toby's name, but he stayed across the track, unmoving, while a second and third official joined the argument.

Tucking the ball underneath his chin, he mused and spoke to it. He speculated if he somehow might be reincarnated, if once, hundreds of years ago, perhaps, he might have been something, say, as inanimate as a cannon; or a knight, heavier still in a coat of armor and chain mail; or even an actual mammoth, one of those solitary beasts who roamed the Alps and European low-lands, mythic in size, lumbering along, leaving only a few bones and footprints as it shuffled toward its extinction.

"Mr. Grogan," called the voice from the loudspeaker. "Report for your first effort or forfeit the try." This was repeated in four other languages.

Abe Fain was now with the officials, arguing and gesturing with them in the shadow of Toby's frame as if he weren't there. And Toby mostly wasn't. He was considering that first practice shot. It must have traveled eighty-five feet, he knew, and he wondered where such moments came from, why he could never do such things for the record books, only for his own final knowledge. And while they shouted around him he set himself for another attempt, bending, clearing his head again, dreaming the awesome fog, then letting go. This time Abe Fain caught a sidelong glimpse of the distance, made a quick calculation, and started toward Toby. But they were both consumed in official wrath. Another hole in the artificial turf.

"Here you are not supposed to be!" the red-faced and trembling Austrian spat at Toby. "In der proper place only! There! Throwing in der sand!"

"One more minute and you are disqualified in your first attempt, Mr. Grogan," the voice on the loudspeaker remarked in five languages.

"Big Tobe, baby!" Abe shouted, pushing through the crowd.

Next, two policemen appeared. Following the Austrian's frenzied orders, they proceeded to give Toby harsh instructions, pointing with their nightsticks. Then one of them placed a hand on Toby's arm and found himself whisked up and thrown—not unlike a wrinkled black javelin—until he landed, crash helmet first, in the cinders of the track several feet from the dispute. The second police-man raised his stick, came forward, but was jumped and pummeled by Karin; others followed her from the stands, all the beer drinkers and admirers. Police whistles everywhere. A roar of dismay from those still in their seats and expect-ing a sporting event. Following this, the announcement that Mr. Grogan is dis-qualified in the first round, but may have his second and third attempts later. As Karin wrestled the nightstick from the downed policeman, Toby strolled over and picked up his ball. Abe, busy explaining his athlete's temperament to the judges, was clubbed from behind with a low hurdle and fell forward, his base-ball cap knocked off. The Austrian was attacked by a flügelhorn. As always, someone thought to have the band play a national anthem, but it was no music anyone recognized so the mayhem continued.

Toby, disdainful of all such distraction, then made what might have been his single greatest heave: he put the ball over the wire fence—the same his admirers had clutched to watch him from afar—and out of the stadium area. Dumbstruck, those left in the crowd broke into applause, but he was gone, stalking off after his ball, which had bounced on a cement runway and rolled downhill beyond everyone's sight. Atop the fence, waving and beckoning, The Leopard called Toby's followers and they streamed out, shoving aside anyone who tried to halt them.

Abe stood up, his nose bleeding, and watched them go.

For a time after that the newspapers charted Toby's travels.

Shuffling across the high meadows and valleys he put the shot, heaving it out ahead, retrieving it, tossing it again, striding after it in a strange journey. When he came close to villages the people came out and watched, giving him and his friends cheese and country wine. The girl and others stayed with him for weeks, then she went back to her job, others dispersed, and still others came to join the trek. An odd band: wandering in a herky-jerky movement all over the continent, into Switzerland, over near Grenoble, then back into Italy, into Yugoslavia. At last he was alone, his followers gone, arching that iron ball into the thin mountain air, mostly staying up in the high country away from the cities, pausing, crouching, putting the shot from his deep trance, passing on. By the time winter arrived the newspapers no longer concerned themselves with him and—as all such stories go—he was never seen again.

Considerations

1. In the very last sentence, this story is compared with "other stories." Exactly what type story is it?
2. Would another appropriate title be "Zen and the Art of Putting the Shot"? What part does Zen play in the story?
3. Describe Coach Fain. Is he a fair representation of athletic coaches? Why doesn't he encourage Toby's eccentricity?
4. Does the fact that Toby is "beyond ambition" have anything to do with his eighty-foot heaves? Support your answer.
5. Ambition and competition are generally considered worthy traits in sports. Give examples to show that this story suggests otherwise.
6. Explain what is suggested in the following passage:
   > Beside the portable television set on his bedside table was the packet of letters from his mother in Des Moines, each letter with its plea—entreating him to go into the ministry, to testify against drug abuse like all the other athletes were doing, to come home and farm with his deadbeat father, to marry.
7. Exactly what does this story imply about the general attitude toward sports?

MARY RENAULT

The Athenian Runner

On the day appointed, we assembled at Piraeus: the priests and important citizens who were to lead the procession; two trainers; and the athletes, men and boys. The lad Aristokles greeted me on the dock with his old-fashioned courtliness. His nickname had stuck; boys, trainers and everyone called him Plato now. He took it cheerfully, and I soon got in the way of it like the rest.

The City sent us to Corinth in the State galley *Paralos*. This was my first acquaintance with men I was to know much better afterwards; but it is remarkable how quickly you notice the difference in a ship where the whole crew are free citizens, rowers and all. A place on the *Paralos* was the most honourable open to any man who could not afford the panoply of a hoplite, which is the reason in many cases why a man takes to the sea. But their necessity had become their choice. They were great democrats and stood no nonsense from anyone; and one or two of the passengers, who were oligarch-minded, complained of their insolence. For myself, after weeks of palaestra small-talk I could have listened to them by the hour. I confess I cannot see why a sailor should not take as much pride in himself as a soldier or even an athlete. No one can say it is a base employment, like that of a man cramped indoors at a work-bench, which spoils the body and confines the soul.

Autolykos was a favourite with them, as with everyone else. I have heard superior people say he had no more mind than a fine bull, and I don't pretend he would have shone in a disputation; but he was modest in success, a good fellow and a thorough gentleman. Once when Lysis was praising him to me, I said, "I can't think how you pankratiasts manage in the contest. A runner only needs to leave his rivals behind; but in a day or two, if you and Autolykos are drawn in the same heat, you will be buffeting each other about the ears, flinging each other down, kicking and twisting and throttling; doing each other as much harm, short of biting and gouging, as two men can without weapons in their hands. Don't you mind it?" He laughed and said, "One doesn't go out to do a man harm, only to make him give in. I can tell you, Autolykos in action is no object for tenderness."

We were having supper at the time at a tavern in Salamis, where the wind being contrary we had put in for the night. Autolykos was there too, treating the pilot. I said to Lysis, "He's grown very heavy this last year. It has almost spoiled his looks. I've never seen a man eat as much as he does."—"He's only following his training-diet; in fact, according to that he ought to eat even more, two pounds of meat a day."—"Meat every day! I should think it would make one slower than an ox."—"Well, there is something in weight too, and the City trainers are rather divided on it, so they let us go on as we did with our trainers before. I agree with mine that the pankration was founded to be the test of a man, and the right weight for a man is the weight for a pankratiast."

The inn lamp had been lit; and all Salamis, it seemed, had gathered outside on the harbour front to watch us eating, word having got round of who we were. Seeing them stare, I looked at Lysis with a stranger's eyes, which I had almost forgotten how to do. I thought that Theseus, setting forth in his flower of strength to wrestle at the Isthmus, could have looked no better. His mantle being open, the lamplight showed the beautiful hard sheen of his body, like oiled beechwood, and the smooth curve of muscle and sinew. His neck and shoulders, though firm as rock, had not thickened; he moved them as lightly as a racehorse. It was plain that the people outside were betting on his victory, and envying my place beside him. Yet he thought in his modesty that they were looking at me.

Next day we sighted the port of Isthmia, and, standing against the sky, the round-topped mountain where the Corinthian citadel is. As the haze lifted, one could see the walls twined like a fillet about its brows. On the very summit I saw a small temple shining, and asked Lysis if he knew what it was. He said, "That must be the shrine of Aphrodite, to whom the Girls of the Goddess belong."

"Do they live there?" I asked him. It seemed beautiful to me that Aphrodite should keep her girls like doves in a tall pine-tree, not lightly to be won; I pictured them waking in the dawn, and clothing their rosy limbs against the brisk air of morning, and going down to the mountain spring; girls like milk, like honey or like dark wine, presents to the Cyprian from every land under the sun. "No," he said, smiling as he watched my face, "the shrine's for people like you, who like love on top of a mountain. The girls are in the City precinct, or the Goddess wouldn't grow very rich. But never mind; after the Games we'll go to both. The girls at night; daybreak for the mountain. We'll watch them make the morning sacrifice to Helios as he rises from the sea."

I agreed, thinking all this very fitting for men who have been contending for glory before a god. In my mind I saw the girl of my choice, opening her arms by the light of a little lamp, her shining hair heavy on the pillow.

Round about us people were watching the coast grow nearer, and talking, as men in strict training will, of the pleasures of Corinth, exchanging the names of bath-houses and brothels, and of the famous hetairas from Laïs down. Seeing the lad Plato near by, looking as usual rather serious, I clapped him on the shoulder and said, "Well, my friend, what do *you* want to do in Corinth?" He looked round at me and answered, without so much as a pause for thought. "To drink from the Fountain of Peirene."

"From Peirene?" I said staring. "The spring of Pegasos? You're not intending to set up as a poet, are you?" He gave me a straight look, to see if I was laughing at him (I had remarked already that he was no fool) and having satisfied himself, said, "Yes, I hope so." I looked at his heavy brows and solid frame. His face had a distinction which just kept one from calling him ugly; it occurred to me that as a man he might even become impressive. So I asked him with proper gravity whether he composed already. He said he had written a number of epigrams and elegies, and had almost completed a tragedy, upon Hippolytos. Then he dropped his voice, partly with a boy's shyness, but partly, it seemed, with the discretion of a man. "I was thinking, Alexias, if you and Lysis should both be crowned at the Games, what a subject for an ode!"—"You young fool!" I said, half laughing and half angry with him. "It's a proverb for bad luck, to make the triumph-song before the contest. No more of your odes, in Apollo's name!"

But now nearing the port we saw between the pines the great temple of Poseidon, and around it the gymnasiums and palaestras, the stadium and the hippodrome. The Council of the Games met us very courteously when we landed, read us the rules, and saw we were shown our lodgings and the athletes' mess. All the dressing-places and the baths were much finer than at home; marble everywhere, and every water-spout made of wrought bronze. The place was full already of competitors who had arrived before us. When I got out on the practice-track, I found youths from every city in the Aegean, and as far as Ephesos.

The practice itself was quite properly conducted. But I did not care for the way that all kinds of idlers were allowed to crowd in: hucksters selling luck-charms and unguents, touts from the brothels, and gamblers who laid their odds on us as noisily as if we had been horses. It was hard to keep one's mind on what one was about; but when I was used to it all, and had time to study the form of the other youths, I did not think there were more than two or three from whom I had much to fear. One of these was a Spartan, called Eumastas, to whom I spoke out of curiosity; I had never conversed with one, unless it is conversation to shout the paean at one another. His behaviour on the track was excellent, but his manners were rather uncouth; having never been outside Lakonia before even for war, he felt unsure of himself in this large concourse, and thought to cover it by standing on his dignity. I fancy he envied me my battle-scars; for he showed me the stripes on his back, where he had been flogged before Artemis Orthia, according to their custom. He had been the victor, he told me, in the contest, having held out the longest; the runner-up, he said, had died. I was at a loss for a proper reply, but congratulated him. There seemed no harm in him, beyond some dullness of wit.

I liked much less a youth from Corinth, one Tisander. His chances were a good deal fancied, by himself even more than the rest; and finding a newcomer talked of as a threat to him, he showed his pique with an openness as laughable as unseemly. I made a sprint or two, and left him to his conjectures.

Lysis, when we met, told me the crowds had been worse in the palaestra than at the stadium; for the Corinthians are devoted to wrestling and the pankration. I did not ask after his rivals' form; for naturally no pankratiast practises the all-in-fight just before the Games, for fear of getting an injury. He was rather quiet; but before I could ask him why, it was put out of my mind by the din about us. We had intended to walk over the Isthmus to Corinth. It seemed, however, that not only Corinth had come to us, but most of Hellas and all of Ionia. The throngs at the Panathenaia were nothing to this. Every shop-keeper in Corinth had set up a stall here; there were whole streets of them, selling not only oil-flasks and ribbons and strigils, and such things as you find at any Games, but all the costly luxuries of the City: bronze images and mirrors, helmets studded with silver and gold, silks you could see through, jewels and toys. The rich hetairas in clouds of perfume were walking with their slaves, pricing others' merchandise and showing their own. Mountebanks were swallowing swords and serpents, tossing torches in the air, or leaping into circles of knives; dancers and mimes and musicians were quarrelling for pitches. I thought I should never be tired of walking up and down; every moment there was something new. We visited the temple, in whose porch a crowd of sophists was debating, and saw, within, the great gold and ivory Poseidon, who almost touched the roof. Then we walked back through the shops again. My eye began to be caught by things: a silver-mounted sword, a gold necklace which seemed made for my mother, and a beautiful painted wine-cup with the exploits of Theseus, which was just the kind of keepsake I had always wished to offer Lysis. I found I was thinking for the first time about the hundred drachmas the City gives to an Isthmian victor, and of what they would buy.

Next morning I went seriously to work; for we were within three days of the

Games. In any strange gymnasium one will drift into someone's company more than the rest, scraping each other's backs or sluicing each other in the wash-room, and this happened with me and Eumastas; from curiosity at first, and from our both disliking Tisander, and thereafter I can't tell why. I had never known anyone so dour, nor he, it was plain, anyone so talkative; yet when I got tired of talking for two, in his curt way he would contrive to start me off again. Once when we were resting he asked me if all Athenians had smooth legs like mine; he thought it was natural, and I had to explain to him the uses of a barber. He was a lank youth, with the leather look all Spartans have from rough living, and a shock head; he was just starting to grow his hair long, at the age when we cut it off. I even made one attempt to tell him about Sokrates; but he said any-one would soon be run out of Sparta who taught the boys to answer back.

I feared Eumastas as my greatest rival in staying-power; Tisander in a sprint; and Nikomedes of Kos because he was variable, the kind who may take sudden fire during the race. My mind was running on all this towards the end of the second morning, when the flute-player came in to time the jumping. As I was waiting in line to take my turn, I saw a man beckoning me from the side. One might have taken him for an ill-bred suitor; but, knowing those, I saw that this was some other thing. So I went over, and asked him what he wanted.

He said he was a trainer, and was studying the Athenian methods, having been out of the way of it because of the war; and he asked me a few questions. I thought them not much to the purpose, and soon began doubting that he was what he claimed. When he asked me what I thought of my own chances, I put him down as a common gamester, and answering with some trite proverb would have gone away. But he detained me, and began running on about young Ti-sander, his birth and wealth, and his family's devotion to him, till I made sure I was listening to some besotted lover. Suddenly he dropped his voice, and fixed his eyes on mine. "The lad's father told me, only today, that it would be worth five hundred drachmas to him to watch his son win."

It may be that we are born remembering evil, as well as good; or I don't know how I understood him so quickly. I had been practising the long jump with the hand-weights, and had them still in my hands. I felt my right begin to come up of itself, and saw the man flinch backward. Yet even in his fright there was some calculation. It came to my mind that if I struck him down, I should be taken up for brawling in the sacred precinct, and could not run. I said, "You ditch-born son of a slave and a whore, tell your master to meet me after the truce. I will show him then what is the price of an Athenian."

He was a man nearly as old as my father would have been; yet he took this from me, with a silly smile. "Don't be a foolish boy. Nikomedes has agreed, and Eumastas: but if you won't come in, then the deal is off; you may be beaten by any of them, without being an obol to the good. I shall be in this same place at noon. Think it over."

I threw at him a filthy phrase that boys were using just then, and left him. The flute was still piping away. You must have seen in battle a hurt man get up, not yet feeling it and thinking he can go on; so I went straight back into the line and took my turn, and was surprised when I made the worst leap ever seen, I should think, upon that ground. Once was enough of that, and I withdrew. I could see neither what to do, nor, indeed, the use of doing anything. All the world I knew seemed to give, like rotten fruit, under my hand.

In the line of jumpers I could pick out the tall back of Eumastas, by the pink shiny scars on his brown skin. If anyone had told me I considered him a friend, I should have stared and laughed; yet now a bitter sickness filled me. I remembered what one always hears of the Spartans, that never being allowed to see money at home, when they meet it they are sooner corrupted than anyone. You may well ask why I should be tender for the honour of someone who next year might be killing me, or burning my farm. Yet I thought, "I will go to him, and tell him of this. Then, if he has agreed to take the bribe, he will merely deny it. But if he has been offered it and refused, he will agree to come with me and report it to the Council of the Games. Thus I shall be sure of him; and Tisander will be whipped, and scratched from the race. But wait. In a place where men buy their rivals out, slander may be commoner still, being much cheaper. If we report and are disbelieved, the dirt will stick to us forever. And if Eumastas with this in mind refuses to go with me, I have no witness; nor shall I ever know whether he was bribed or not. No; let me run a good race, and keep my own hands clean; what is it to me how clean the others are?"

With this I felt quieter, and firmer in mind; till it seemed that the voice of the Corinthian whispered in my ear, "Clever lad! You guessed I lied to you when I said the others would call off their deal if you refused. I told you that lest you should grasp the chance of an easy win. Well, you were too quick for me. Eumastas is bribed, and Nikomedes; now you have only Tisander to beat. Go in, and get your crown?"

I walked away from the gymnasium, not regarding where I went. It seemed there was no way I could turn with perfect honour, and that I should never be clean again. In my trouble, my feet had carried me of themselves to the gate of the men's palaestra. I thought, "He will know what I should do," and already my heart was lighter; till it paused, and said to me, "Is that what you call friendship, Alexias? The Games are almost on us; for a man fighting the pankration, his own troubles are enough."

He came out rather before the usual time. I did not ask how it had gone with him that day, in case he should return my question. He was quiet, which I was glad of, having little to say myself; but after we had walked a short way, he said, "It's fine and clear, and the wind is cool. Shall we climb the mountain?"

I was rather surpised; for it was unlike him, having fixed a time for anything, to change it at a whim. I was afraid he had noticed my low spirits; but indeed I was glad of this diversion. The noonday heat was over, and the tower-wreathed head of Acrocorinth looked golden against the tender sky of spring. As we climbed, the other hills grew tall around us, Corinth shone below, and the blue sea spread wide. When we were just below the walls, I said that perhaps the Corinthians would bar us from their citadel, being their enemies but for the sacred truce. But the man in the gatehouse spoke civilly, chatted about the Games and let us in.

There is still a good way to climb on Acrocorinth after you have passed the walls. Being so high, the place is not thronged like our own High City; it was quiet, so that one could hear the bees in the asphodel, the little clappers of the mountain goats, and a shepherd piping. Beyond the walls were great spaces of blue air; for the citadel stands on high cliffs, like a roof on the columns of a temple.

The sacred way wound up between shrines, and holy springs. There was one sanctuary built of grey stone, which we entered. After the bright sunlight it seemed very dark; in the midst, where the god should stand, was a curtain of purple. A priest in a dark-red robe came out and said, "Strangers, come no nearer. This is the temple of Necessity and Force; and the image of this god is not to be looked upon." I would have gone at once, for the place disquieted me; but Lysis paused and said, "Is it permitted to make an offering?" The priest answered, "No. This god accepts only the appointed sacrifice." Lysis said, "Be it so, then," and to me, "Let us go." After this he was silent so long that I asked if anything troubled him. He smiled, and shook his head, and pointed forward; for now we had reached the crown of Acrocorinth, and stepping on small heath and mountain flowers, saw before us the shrine.

The image of Aphrodite there is armed with shield and spear; yet I never knew a place so full of peace. The temple is delicate and small, with a terrace from which the slopes fall gently; the walls and towers seem far below; the mountains round about hang like veils of grey and purple, and the two seas stretch away, all silken in the light. I thought of the day when Lysis and I had heard Sokrates and gone up to the High City; it seemed that the memory had been already here awaiting us, as if the place were a dwelling of such things.

After a while Lysis pointed downward and said, "Look how small it is." I looked, and saw the precinct of the Games, the temple, and the fair-booths round it, smaller than children's toys of painted clay. My soul felt light and free, and washed from the taint of the morning. Lysis laid his hand on my shoulder; it seemed to me that doubt or trouble could never assail us again. We stood looking down; I traced the long wall of the Isthmus, cutting the south of Hellas from the north. Lysis drew in his breath; I think then he would have spoken; but something had caught my eye; and I called out, "Lysis, look there! There are ships moving on the land!"

I pointed. There was a track drawn across the Isthmus, as thin to our eyes as the scratch of a child's stick. Along it the ships were creeping, with movement scarcely to be seen. Around each prow was a swarm as fine as dust, of seamen and hauliers dragging on the ropes, or going before with rollers. We counted four on the shipway, and eight in the Gulf of Corinth, waiting their turn. They were moving from the western to the eastern sea.

I turned to Lysis. He looked as he did before a battle, and did not see me. I caught at his arm, asking what it was. He said, "I have heard of the shipway; that is nothing. But the ships are too many." On this I understood. "You mean they're Spartan ships, slipping through to the Aegean behind our backs?"—"Revolt in the Islands somewhere, and the Spartans supporting it. I thought Alkibiades had been quiet too long."

"We must go down," I said, "and tell the delegates." The snake which had slept all winter was putting forth its head. Yet this seemed small, compared with the grief I felt that we must go down from the mountain. I said to Lysis, "We will come here again together, after the Games." He did not answer, but pointed eastward. The light came slanting from the west, and was very clear. I said, "I can see even as far as Salamis; there is the ridge of her hills, with the dip in the middle."—"Yes," he said. "Can you see beyond?" I narrowed my eyes. Beyond the dip something shone like a chip of crystal in the sun. "It is the High City, Lysis. It is the Temple of the Maiden." He nodded, but did not speak, only stood looking, like a man sealing what he sees upon his mind.

It was dark when we got down into Isthmia, but we went straight to the harbour and hailed the *Paralos*. Most of the crew were enjoying themselves in Corinth; but Agios the pilot was there, a stocky man, red-faced and white-haired, who offered us wine beneath the cresset burning on the poop. When he had heard, he whistled between his teeth. "So," he said, "that's what is coming into Kenchreai." He told us that he and his mate, walking by the shore, had seen the harbour there filling with ships; but before they could get near, some guards had turned them away. "Spartan guards," he said. "I've not seen the Corinthians taking trouble to keep this quiet."—"No," said Lysis, "or why are we Athenians here at all? It's their right to ask us and ours to come, both cities founded the Games together; yet it's a strange time to offer us the sacred truce, with this work on hand."

Agios said, "They've always been our rivals in trade; to see us poor would suit them well; but never tell me they'd welcome a Spartan Hellas. Pretty toys; pleasure; luxury; it's more than their life, it's their living. It may well be that they're trimming now, with things as they are. I'll see the men go about Corinth with their ears open. One thing at a time; you lads should be going to bed, with the Games so soon."

On the way back we met Autolykos, taking his training-walk after supper. He hailed Lysis, asking what he had been doing to miss it. "I'm turning in," Lysis said, "we climbed Acrocorinth this afternoon." Autolykos raised his brows at us; he looked quite shocked, but he only bade us goodnight and walked on.

Next morning I woke a little stiff from the climb; so I spent an hour with the masseur, and after that only did the exercises to music, to loosen up and keep fresh for tomorrow; for the foot-race opens the Games. I was civil to Eumastas when we met. Once I caught him looking at me; but if I had grown more taciturn, it was not for a Spartan to notice it.

Besides all this, the Cretan athletes had arrived, the last of everyone, having been held up by a storm. Considering their fame as runners, I had more than Eumastas to think about. Sure enough, warming-up on the track I found a lithe swarthy youth who, I could tell at a glance, might well be the master of us all. The news flew through the Stadium that he had run at Olympia, and had come in second. Though anxious on my own account, I could not keep from laughing when I thought, "Tisander won't sleep tonight."

I woke to the sound that is like no other, the noise of the Stadium when the benches and the slopes are filling. People must have started arriving long before the first light. Already you could pick out the "Houp!" of the jugglers and acrobats, the hawkers crying ribbons and cakes and myrtle, the call of the water-sellers, bookmakers giving the odds, the sudden shouts of people squabbling for a place; and through it all the buzz of talk, like bees in an old temple. It is the sound that tightens one's belly, and makes one shiver behind the neck.

I got up, and ran to the water-conduit outside. Someone overtook me; it was Eumastas; he picked up the pitcher and sluiced me down. He always threw the water hard in one great drench, trying to make one gasp. I rinsed him in turn, and watched it trickle down his scars. Suddenly I felt compelled, and said, "I'm running to win, Eumastas." He stared and said in his abrupt way, "How not?" His face never showed surprise, nor anything he felt. I did not know if he spoke in innocence, or discretion, or deceit. Not from that day have I ever known.

At the march-in, the Athenians were cheered as much as the Spartans. The people were there to enjoy themselves, and forget the war. I sat with Lysis, watching the boys' races. The Athenians did quite well, but did not win anything. There was a break; the tumblers and flute-players came out; then suddenly all round the Stadium the ephebes were getting up. Lysis laid his hand on my knee and smiled. I made a little sign which was a secret between us, and got up with the rest. Next moment, as it seemed, I was standing beside the Cretan youth, feeling with my toes the grooves of the starting-stone, and hearing the umpire call for the second time, "Runners! Feet to the lines!"

It was one of those fresh spring days that make one feel at first one could run forever, and tempt beginners to crowd on pace as they never would at a summer Games. I let these people pass me; but when Eumastas went ahead it was another thing. It was hard to look at his striped back and not spurt after it. "Know yourself, Alexias," I thought, "and look to what you know." Tisander too was using discretion. We were almost neck and neck.

After those of no account, the first runner to fail was Nikodemes. I had seen yesterday that he had lost his hopes beforehand to the Cretan. For him that was reason enough.

Tisander, gaining a little, moved sideways. I thought he was going to foul me; it would have disqualified him, and I need have watched my thoughts no longer. But he changed his mind. Then there was a diversion, when some nobody put on a sprint and got in front. All this time I had known the Cretan was just behind me, because I never saw him when I turned the post. Now, smoothly as a wolf, he shot forward, and straight on into the lead. It was halfway up in the sixth lap. "Alexias," I thought, "it is time to run."

After that I thought with my breath and my legs. At the starting-turn I passed Eumastas. I was sure he would challenge my lead; but no, he was finished. He had gone ahead too soon,—like the green boys. That left Tisander and the Cretan. At the start I had seen that Tisander was wearing a horse's tooth round his neck as a charm, and had despised him for it; but as a runner he was not at all to be despised. He knew himself, and would not be flurried. Before us was the Cretan, running smoothly, well in hand. We turned into the last lap. People who had been quiet before began to shout, and those who had been shouting to roar. Suddenly over it all I heard Lysis yell, "Come on, Alexias!" It was the voice he used in battle, for the paean; it carried like a trumpet-call. Just as if something were lifting me, I felt my spirit overflow and fill my flesh. Soon after the turning-post I left Tisander behind me; and the Cretan I overtook halfway down. I glanced at his face; he looked surprised. We ran level for a while; but little by little he fell back out of my sight.

The crowd had pressed right up to the finishing-post, and I ran into the midst of it. It parted for me at first, then closed round. My head was ringing, and the noise made it spin; a great spear seemed to transfix my breast, so that I clutched at it with both my hands. While myrtle-sprays fell on my shoulders and struck me in the face, I fought for my next breath against the thrust of the spear. Then there was an arm stretched out to make space for me, and shelter me from the press. I leaned back against Lysis' shoulder, and the weight of the spear grew less. In a little while I could distinguish the people about me and even speak to them. To Lysis I had not spoken, nor he to me. I turned round for him to tie the ribbons on, and we looked at each other. His white mantle, which he had put on clean that morning for the sacrifice to Poseidon, was smothered all over the front with oil and dust. He looked so filthy that I laughed; but he said softly in my ear that he would put it away and keep it as it was. I thought, "I could die now, for surely the gods can have no greater joy for me"; and then I said in my heart, "Olympia next."

When the Athenian delegates had congratulated me, Lysis took me away to get clean and to rest before watching the stade-race. He got me some cooled wine and water, and some honey-cakes, knowing I was always mad for sweet things after a race; and we lay down under a pine-tree just above the Stadium. One or two friends came up with ribbons they had bought for me, and tied them on, and stayed to chat. Somebody said, "Young Tisander was lucky at the end, to get the second place."—"Tisander?" I said. "He came in third; the Cretan was second." Lysis said laughing, "Well, no one sees less of a race than the winner." The other man said, "You took the heart out of the Cretan when you passed him; there was no fight left in him after that."—"I thought he was better-winded than Tisander," I said. "Careful," said Lysis, taking hold of the wine-jar; "you nearly spilt it; your hand's not steady yet."

I bent and scooped a little pit in the pine-needles, to hold the jar. The ribbons they had tied round my head fell about my face, but I did not push them aside. I remembered seeing the Cretan sprint ahead, and thinking, "There goes victory, the real victory of the gods." He had looked so proud on the practice-track, as sure of himself as a man could be; and he had come so late. Yet after all, he had been at Isthmia overnight. I recalled the surprise in his face when I drew level. I had supposed he was astonished to find anyone there his match.

I find in the archives that the men's long-race was won by someone from Rhodes, and the stade by a Theban. All I remember of these events is that I shouted loudly; I would not have it said that I cared for no victory but my own.

Next day were the boxing and hurling events; then came the day of the wrestling. The weather held bright and clear. Quite early the Athenians had a victory; for young Plato won the contest for boys. He fought some very good, scientific bouts, using his head as well as his broad shoulders, and was well cheered. Lysis praised him highly. I could see how this pleased the boy; when his eyes lit up under their heavy brows, he had even a kind of beauty. Before he went, he wished Lysis luck in his own event. "Lysis," I said after, "how well do you and this Aristokles know each other? You smiled so seriously into each other's eyes, that I'm still wondering whether to be jealous."—"Don't be a fool," he said laughing. "You know that's always his way; what about yourself?" Yet

I had really felt, for a moment, that they were sharing some thought unknown to me.

In the Frontier Guard the boys had a phrase, "As cool as Lysis." He played up to his legend, as any good officer will. He could deceive even me; but not every time. I always knew he was on edge when he was very still. The herald called the pankratiasts; he made our sign to me; I watched him out of sight into the dressing-room, and waited till the heats were drawn. He was in the third bout, matched against Autolykos. "If he wins that," I thought, "then nothing can keep the crown from him." I jumped up from my seat, for I had made my plan; and I ran up the sacred steps to the great temple. There I took from my bosom a gift I had bought for the god at one of the shops outside. It was a little horse made of fine bronze, with mane and tail silvered, and a bridle of gold. I bought incense, and went up to the altar. Always I am awed in the presence of Poseidon, so old a god, who holds the earthquake and the sea-storm in his hand. But horses are dear to him, and this was the best one I could find. I gave it to the priest for him, and saw it offered, and made my prayer.

Although they hold the contests just before the temple, when I got back to my place the first bout was over, and the athletes had gone in. The crowd seemed excited by the fight, and I was sorry to have missed it, in case Lysis should meet the winner later on. The second bout, however, was not very remarkable; a Mantinean won it, a lumbering fellow, who got a body-hold that Lysis would never have given him time for. Then the herald called, "Autolykos son of Lykon; Lysis son of Demokrates; both of Athens."

It was Autolykos after all who held my eye. "What has become of his beauty?" I thought. When he was dressed one looked at his pleasant face, and did not see how much his body had coarsened. No sculptor would have looked at him for a model now. The crowd cheered them in; one could tell, as one commonly can, that they were cheering Autolykos for what they had heard of him, and Lysis for what they saw. He stood like a bronze of Polykleitos; you could not fault him anywhere; whereas Autolykos looked burly, like a village strong-man who lifts a bull-calf for a bet. But I was not fool enough to underrate him. He was still very fast for all his bulk, and knew every trick in the game. While they were exchanging the standing buffets, I could see the weight his had behind them; and I prayed that when they went down Lysis would fall on top.

Yet for all my fears, within the time it takes to run five stades I was cheering myself hoarse with joy. I fought my way through the crowd and ran to Lysis. He was not very much the worse for the bout. He had got a thick ear, and some bruises, and he was rubbing his left wrist where Autolykos had got a grip and nearly broken it, trying to twist him round for a flying mare. But on the whole he was in very good shape. I walked in with him and we went to see Autolykos, whom Lysis had had to help to his feet after the decision. He had torn one of the big muscles in his back, and it was that which had finished him. He was in a good deal of pain, and it was years since he had yielded the crown to anyone; but he took Lysis' hand and congratulated him on a good win, like the gentleman he always was. "I deserve this," he said, "for listening to too much advice in training. You had more sense, Lysis. Bring in the parsley, and good luck to you."

I had lost my place; but Plato made room for me by heaving everyone sideways. He was the strongest boy at his age that I remember. During the other heats I saw no one who seemed to me the match of Autolykos. Then it was time for the semi-finals. There were eight contestants, so no one had drawn a bye. The herald called out, "Lysis son of Demokrates, of Athens. Sostratos son of Eupolos, of Argos." The name was unknown to me. I guessed this must be the winner of the first bout, which I had missed while in the temple. Then they came out, and I saw the man.

At first I could not trust my eyes; the more because I recognised him. Two or three times, indeed, I had seen this monstrous creature, going about the fair. I had not doubted he was some travelling mountebank, whose act consisted of raising boulders or bending iron bars; so I had been struck by his air of absurd conceit. Once Lysis had been beside me, and I pointed out the man, laughing, and saying, "What a hideous fellow! What can he be, and who does he think he is?" Lysis had answered, "He's no beauty, is he?" and spoken of something else. Now here he stood, a mountain of gross flesh, great muscles like twisted oakwood gnarling his body and arms; a neck like a bull's; his legs, though they were thick and knotty, seemed bowed by the weight of his ungainly trunk. Why do I go on describing a sight with which everyone has grown familiar? Today even at Olympia they appear without shame, and afterwards some sculptor has to turn out a portrait that people can see in the sacred Altis without disgust.

It must seem to you now that we were simple in those days. For at the sight of a man too heavy to leap or run, who would fall dead if he had to make a forced march in armour, and whom no horse could carry, we thought we were looking at someone worse than a slave, since he had chosen his own condition. We waited to see him run out of the company of free Hellenes, and cheered Lysis on to do it. He stood by this ugly hulk like the image of victory: hero against monster, Theseus with the Beast.

Then the fight began; the voices altered; and I woke from my dream.

I had not seen Sostratos' first bout; but the crowd had, and got used sooner than I did to seeing Lysis duck away from a buffet. No one booed him, and one or two people cheered. When he landed one himself they went wild. But you could see it was like punching a rock. The man's great arms were like flying boulders; one caught Lysis' cheek, only glancing, and at once the blood began to flow. And now, as if the news had been brought to me for the first time, I thought, "This creature too is a pankratiast."

Lysis was the first to close. He grabbed Sostratos' arm as it was striking, and the hand grew limp in his strong grip. I knew what came next; a quick twist and then the heave, a cross-buttock. I saw him begin it; and could tell the very moment when he knew he could not get this ton of flesh high enough for a throw. Then Sostratos reached for a neck-hold; if Lysis had not been as quick as a cat, he would never have got away. The crowd cheered him for escaping, as if he had scored. By now he had measured the enemy's speed, and he began to take those risks that the faster man can take with the slower; except that here the risks were doubled. He ran in head first; I heard the monster grunt; before he could seize Lysis' head he had slid free and got a body-hold. Then he hooked his leg behind Sostratos' knee, and they went over together. The thud was like a block of stone falling.

The crowd cheered. But I saw that as they fell Sostratos had rolled over on Lysis' arm. He lay like a man trapped by a landslide. Sostratos was starting to come over on him; but Lysis got a knee up in time. He was still pinned by the arm. I got to my feet and shouted for him. I tried to make it carry, though I don't suppose he could hear me above the noise. He thrust his flat hand into Sostratos' great pig-face and pushed the head back and got his arm free. It was scraped and bloody, but he could still use it. He twisted round like a flash; they struggled together on the ground, hitting and grappling. Always it was Lysis who had the speed. But speed in the pankration is only a man's defence. It is strength that wins.

Someone was punching me on the knee. I found it was Eumastas the Spartan, attracting my notice. He never wasted words. When I glanced round he said, "Is the man your lover?"—"Which one?" I asked; I had no time for him just then. He said. "The man." I nodded, without turning again. I could feel him watching me; waiting to approve of me, if I could see Lysis mauled with a wooden face. I could have killed him where he sat.

Just then Lysis came uppermost for a moment. His hair was matted with dusty blood; blood covered his face like a mask, and streaked his body. He rose, then seemed to fall backward, and the crowd groaned. But as Sostratos rushed upon him, he threw up his foot and swung the man right over so that he crashed to the earth instead. The noise was so great I could hardly hear myself cheer. But there was something new in it. I had not noticed it at first, but it was growing. In those days, the pankration was a contest for fighting men. I suppose there had always been a few slave-minded ones who had got another sort of pleasure from it; but they had known enough to keep it to themselves. Now, like ghosts who get strength from drinking blood, they came out into the light and one heard their voice.

As Sostratos went over him, Lysis had gripped his ankle and held on. He was twisting the foot, trying to make Sostratos give in. Sostratos managed at last to kick him off with the other foot, and I saw the great mass coming down on him again. But Lysis slipped from under, grabbing an arm as he went; next moment he was on Sostratos' back, legs locked round his middle, and as fine a stranglehold on his neck as I ever saw. Sostratos' free arm was all he had to hold up on; Lysis had pinned the other. All around people were on their feet; young Plato, whose every existence I had forgotten, was digging his fingers into my arm. The fight looked as good as won.

Then I saw Sostratos begin to rise. With the weight of a strong man on his back, and half-throttled, still the huge creature heaved up on his knees. I heard the blood-bay from the faces I had not seen. "Let go, Lysis!" I shouted. "Let go!" But I suppose his strength was nearly done, and he knew it was now or never. He set his teeth and squeezed his arm round Sostratos' bull-throat. And Sostratos upreared backward, and fell on him like a tree. There was a great silence; then the blood-voices cheered.

All I could see of Lysis at first was his arm and hand. It lay, palm up, in the dust; then I saw it feel for a purchase. Sostratos turned over. I saw for the first time in his wide face his little eyes; not the eyes of a boar in rage, but cold, like a usurer's. Lysis began to struggle up on his arm. I waited to see him lift his hand to the umpire. It may be he was too angry to give in; but I think he was only too dazed to know where he was. At all events, Sostratos hurled him back on the ground so that you could hear the blow of his head meeting it. Even after that I thought I saw them move; but the umpire brought down his forked rod, and stopped the fight.

I jumped to my feet. Plato was holding me by the arm, saying something; I shook the boy off and climbed through the crowd, while people I had trodden on shouted and cursed me. I ran to the dressing-room, and got there while they were still carrying him in. They took him through to a little room at the back, where there was a pallet on the floor, and a water-tap shaped like a lion's mouth, running into a basin. Outside, the next bout had begun. I could hear the cheering.

The man in charge said to me, "Are you a friend of his?"—"Yes," I said. "Is he dead?" I could not see life or breath in him. "No; he is stunned, and I daresay some of his ribs are broken. But he may die. Is his father here?"—"We're Athenians," I said. "Are you a doctor? Tell me what to do."—"Nothing," said the man, "but keep him quiet if he wakes with his wits astray. Give him water if he asks for it, but no wine." Then he looked up from Lysis and seemed to see me for the first time, and said, "He fought a fine pankration; but I wonder what made him enter, at his weight." He went then to watch the fight outside, and we were left alone.

He was breathing, but very slowly, and so lightly that I could hardly hear. One side of his face was bruised all over; his nose had been bleeding and his scalp was cut. His forehead was split over the eyebrow; I could see he would never lose the scar. I drew down the old blanket they had thrown over him; his body was so battered and grimed that I could not tell what might be broken. I took a towel that was hanging on the wall, and washed from him the black blood, the oil and dust, as far as I could reach; I was afraid to turn him over. I talked to him, and called his name aloud; but he did not stir. Then I saw I ought not to have washed him; for the water was cold from the spring, and the place was made of stone; his flesh under my hands grew as cold as marble, and his mouth looked blue. I thought he would die as I watched him. Someone's clothes were lying in a corner; I heaped those on him, but he still felt cold, so I added my own, and came in beside him.

As I held him, trying to put some life in him, and cold myself with fear, I thought of the long patrols with the Guard, in the winter mountains, when even the wolves in their caves had been warm together, and he had lain alone. "You gave me courage in battle," I thought; "when I was unhorsed, you saved me and took a wound. After so much toil, who would not have looked for honey from the rock? Yet you offered it to heaven; there was only blood for you, and the salt-tasting sea. What is justice, if the gods are not just? They have been taken your crown away from you, and set it on a beast."

His mouth felt cold to mine; he neither opened his eyes, nor spoke, nor moved. I said in my heart, "Too late I am here within your cloak, I who never of my own will would have denied you anything. Time and death and change are unforgiving, and love lost in the time of youth never returns again."

Someone was coming, so I got up. The light was darkened in the doorway. I saw that what filled it was Sostratos. He said, "How is he?" It was strange to hear human speech coming out of him, instead of a boar's grunt. I was glad to see Lysis' marks on him. "He is alive," I said. The man came near, stared, and went away. I lay down with Lysis again. Bitterness filled my heart. I remembered his statue at school, done before I knew him; and thought how from a boy he had run and jumped, thrown the disk and javelin, swum and wrestled, and ridden on manoeuvre; how I myself had toiled, swinging the pick and throwing the weight, to balance my shoulders with my legs; how young Plato had run in armour; how all of us had sacrificed in the gymnasium to Apollo, the lord of measure and of harmony. This man had sold grace and swiftness, and the honour of a soldier in the field, not caring at all to be beautiful in the eyes of the gods, but only caring to be crowned. And yet to him the victory had been given.

The fight was over outside. The crowd was chattering, and someone was playing a double flute. Lysis moved, and groaned. He felt a little warmer. Presently he tried to sit up, and was sick. As I finished cleaning up, the doctor came in again. He pinched Lysis' arm, and seeing him flinch a little said, "Good. But keep him still, for men who have been stunned sometimes die if they exert themselves soon after." When he had gone, Lysis started to toss about, and to talk nonsense. He thought he was on a battlefield with a spear in his side, and ordered me not to touch it, but to fetch Alexias, who would draw it out. I was at my wit's end, remembering the doctor's words. While I was trying to lay him down, Sostratos came in again, and asked how he was. I answered shortly, but thought a little better of the man for his concern.

Soon afterwards the shouting began again outside; the final was on. It seemed hardly to have begun before it was over. I thought Sostratos must have finished his antagonist with a buffet; what had really happened was that this man, having seen Lysis carried off, had gone down on the ground almost at once, and given the bout away. I heard the herald announce the victor. The cheers were rather half-hearted; there had been neither a good fight nor any blood, so no one was pleased.

The crowd dispersed; outside in the dressing-room people chatted and laughed. Presently the man whose clothes I had put on Lysis came in to get them. It was getting cooler, but I dared not leave him to look for more, and hoped someone would come in. At last voices approached; Sostratos stood in the doorway, speaking to someone over his shoulder. The ribbons tied on him made him look like a bull going to sacrifice. As he paused, I heard the man who had been in for his clothes say, "Come, be easy, Sostratos; I went in just now and heard him talking. He will do till after the Games, and it makes no difference then." I had forgotten that, except in Sparta, to kill in the pankration disqualifies the victor.

I sat looking at Lysis; then I heard someone behind me. Sostratos had come in after all. He peered into Lysis' face, then asked me again how he was. I did not trust myself to answer. He began looking at me instead; suddenly he assumed fine manners, which sat on him like a violet-wreath upon a swine. "Why so downcast, beautiful youth? Fortune rules the Games. Will you spend the time of your triumph moping here, like one in prison? Come away, and meet some of the other winners. It is time you and I knew each other better."

There is a certain gesture of refusal which everyone knows, but no gentleman employs. I wished however to be explicit. "You have got your crown," I said to him. "Go and play with that."

As he was going, I heard Lysis say, "Alexias." He sounded angry with me. I don't know how much he had understood. I bent down and said, "Here I am; what is it?" But his eyes grew dull again. He looked very weary. The cold of evening came on; but I was afraid that if I went for more clothes he would try to stand. It would soon be dark. Tears stirred in me like sickness; but I dared not weep, lest he should hear.

By now the dressing-room outside had emptied; a footstep sounded loud in it. Young Plato came in quietly, and stood looking down. While we were watching the fight he had been wearing his ribbons; but they were gone now. I said, "Can you find me a cloak, Plato? Lysis is cold."—"You look cold yourself," he said. After a short time he came back with two shepherds' blankets; I laid them over Lysis, and put my clothes on. Plato watched in silence; then he said, "They have given the crown to Sostratos."—"Yes?" said I. "And the war's over in Troy; what else is new?"—"This is new to me. What does Sostratos think he has got? What good? What pleasure? What did he want?"—"I don't know, Plato. You might as well ask why the gods allow it."—"The gods? he said; raising his heavy brows and drawing them down again, just as he does today. "What use would it be for the gods to do anything, if it's not enough that they are? Have you had any supper? I brought you something to eat." I felt warmer for the food. When he had gone, I saw that both the blankets were new; I think he must have bought them himself in the market.

At nightfall, they carried Lysis to the precinct of Asklepios; next day he could speak sensibly and take food, though because of his broken ribs it hurt him to move. He did not talk much, and I let him rest. I wanted to stay with him, but he said I must watch the chariot-races; it seemed to fret him, so I went. They were held with great splendour, to the glory of horse-loving Poseidon, who had not been moved by my horse of bronze. I understood that this was the great day of the Games, which every Corinthian came to see, and that no one was thinking about the long-race or the pankration.

When I got back, Lysis seemed stronger. He said he was going to get up next day, to see me crowned. This was too much for me, and I told him the story of the long-race. He listened quietly, frowning a little, rather in thought than in anger or surprise. "Don't brood on it," he said. "You ran a fine race; and very likely no one was bribed at all. Any fool could have picked you out as the fastest, and would have made sure of you before throwing money away on the others. I was watching the Cretan, and he looked spent to me."—"Perhaps. But now I shall never know it."—"Why think of it then? We must take the world as we find it, Alexias." Then he said again, "But you ran a fine race. You had them all in your hand."

Next morning was the procession to the temple; and the winners were crowned before Poseidon. There was a great deal of music and ceremony, much more than at home. The priests of the precinct would not let Lysis get up. I went back to him afterwards, and he made me show him my crown. I had had enough of their parsley garnishing; but when I threw it in a corner he told me sharply not to play the fool, but to go out and celebrate in Corinth with the others.

It was evening. The sun was shining on the mountain with its wreath of walls. He must have known that if he waited till after the Games, he would never climb it. "What should I do in Corinth?" I said. But he became impatient, and then angry, and said I should be talked of if I stayed away. Then I knew what troubled him, that they might say he had kept me back from the revels out of envy; so I said I would go.

There is a great deal of coloured marble in Corinth, and much bronze, some of it gilded; they burn perfume in the shop doorways; the tavern where we drank had a talking bird in a cage outside, that whistled and said "Come in". I was with the runners and the boxers; then some of the wrestlers arrived. I got drunk as quickly as I could; and for a little while Corinth looked quite gay to me. We walked through the streets singing, and bought garlands to wear; then we went into a bath-house, but it turned out to be a respectable one, and we were asked to leave. Someone had got pushed in the plunge-bath, and walked dripping water; one or two flute-girls, who had been picked up on the way, played us along. We came to a tall porch of slender columns, ornamented with doves and garlands; someone said, "Here's where we're going, to the Girls of Aphrodite. Come on." When I would not go in, he tried to drag me, and I struck him in the face. Then someone else, whom the wine had made genial, stopped the fight, and said we would all go to Kallisto's house instead. It had a fountain in the courtyard, of a girl holding her breast, which spouted water. Kallisto made us welcome, and a boy and girl acted the mime of Dionysos and Ariadne, while we drank more wine. A little later five or six of the wrestlers calling for music jumped up to dance the kordax, and started throwing off their clothes. They called to me to join them, but I was past dancing even if I would. One of the girls lay down with me, and presently took me away. When I woke she made a great tale of my performance, as they do with young men to make them pay well. I can't even recall whether I did anything or not.

Two days later we went back to Athens. Lysis could not sit a horse, his bones not having knit, and had to be carried to the ship on a litter. The passage was rough, and he was in pain all the way. Agios the pilot came to see us, and said it was Chios the Spartan ships were making for; he had employed his time in Corinth better than I. So we made haste back, to bring this news to the City.

That is all I have to relate of the Isthmian festival, the first of the ninety-second Olympiad. Since Theseus founded the Games to honour his father Poseidon, they had been held every second year in the same place, before the same god; and if you ask me why this year's Games should have brought forth something different from those before them, I cannot tell.

Considerations

1. The Isthmian Games of this story were held at Corinth during a truce in the war between Athens and Sparta in the fifth century B.C. Do you know the name of the war? Do you consider it odd to call a truce during a war to hold sporting events

between the two warring principals? Does it point up the importance of the games, or the unimportance of the war? Is war the ultimate game? Explain.

2. Some of the characters in this story are historical figures. Can you name one?

3. Pope's famous lines,

> A little learning is a dangerous thing;
>
> Drink deep or taste not the Pierian Spring,

refer to the fountain from which Plato, the young wrestler, wished to drink. From your knowledge of literary history, would you say he drank deep?

4. The main conflict in this story centers around the bribe offered to Alexias. Why is he upset to hear that the Cretan runner finished third?

5. Discuss the importance of religious ritual in the games. List some examples of the importance of religious ritual in sports today.

6. What is the exact relationship between Alexias and Lysis? From your understanding of the story, would you say that such a relationship was common among Greek athletes? Why are they less common among modern athletes? Or are they?

7. What is the point of view in this story? What clues indicate the narrator is now much older than he was when the events occurred?

8. Discuss the character of Alexias. Does Renault give him too much sophistication for a boy of his years, and an athlete, at that? Do modern athletes write their own autobiographies?

STEPHEN CRANE

Lynx-Hunting

Jimmie lounged about the dining room and watched his mother with large, serious eyes. Suddenly he said, "Ma—now—can I borrow pa's gun?"

She was overcome with the feminine horror which is able to mistake preliminary words for the full accomplishment of the dread thing. "Why, Jimmie!" she cried. "Of al-l wonders! Your father's gun! No indeed you can't!"

He was fairly well crushed, but he managed to mutter, sullenly, "Well, Willie Dalzel, he's got a gun." In reality his heart had previously been beating with such tumult—he had himself been so impressed with the daring and sin of his request—that he was glad that all was over now, and his mother could do very little further harm to his sensibilities. He had been influenced into the venture by the larger boys.

"Huh!" the Dalzel urchin had said; "your father's got a gun, hasn't he? Well, why don't you bring that?"

Puffing himself, Jimmie had replied, "Well, I can, if I want to." It was a black lie, but really the Dalzel boy was too outrageous with his eternal bill-posting about the gun which a beaming uncle had entrusted to him. Its possession made him superior in manfulness to most boys in the neighborhood—or at least they enviously conceded him such position—but he was so overbearing, and stuffed the fact of his treasure so relentlessly down their throats, that on this occasion the miserable Jimmie had lied as naturally as most animals swim.

Willie Dalzel had not been checkmated, for he had instantly retorted, "Why don't you get it, then?"

"Well, I can, if I want to."

"Well, get it, then!"

"Well, I can, if I want to."

Thereupon Jimmie had paced away with great airs of surety as far as the door of his home, where his manner changed to one of tremulous misgivings as it came upon him to address his mother in the dining room. There had happened that which had happened.

When Jimmie returned to his two distinguished companions he was blown out with a singular pomposity. He spoke these noble words: "Oh, well, I guess I don't want to take the gun out today."

They had been watching him with gleaming ferret eyes, and they detected his falsity at once. They challenged him with shouted gibes, but it was not in the rules for the conduct of boys that one should admit anything whatsoever, and so Jimmie, backed into an ethical corner, lied as stupidly, as desperately, as hopelessly as ever lone savage fights when surrounded at last in his jungle.

Such accusations were never known to come to any point, for the reason that the number and kind of denials always equaled or exceeded the number of accusations, and no boy was ever brought really to book for these misdeeds.

In the end they went off together, Willie Dalzel with his gun being a trifle in advance and discoursing upon his various works. They passed along a maple-lined avenue, a highway common to boys bound for that free land of hills and woods in which they lived in some part their romance of the moment, whether it was of Indians, miners, smugglers, soldiers, or outlaws. The paths were their paths, and much was known to them of the secrets of the dark green hemlock thickets, the wastes of sweet fern and huckleberry, the cliffs of gaunt bluestone with the sumach burning red at their feet. Each boy had, I am sure, a conviction that some day the wilderness was to give forth to him a marvelous secret. They felt that the hills and the forest knew much, and they heard a voice of it in the silence. It was vague, thrilling, fearful, and altogether fabulous. The grown folk seemed to regard these wastes merely as so much distance between one place and another place, or as a rabbit-cover, or as a district to be judged according to the value of the timber; but to the boys it spoke some great inspiring word, which they knew even as those who pace the shore know the enigmatic speech of the surf. In the meantime they lived there, in season, lives of ringing adventure—by dint of imagination.

The boys left the avenue, skirted hastily through some private grounds, climbed a fence, and entered the thickets. It happened that at school the previous day Willie Dalzel had been forced to read and acquire in some part a solemn description of a lynx. The meager information thrust upon him had caused him grimaces of suffering, but now he said, suddenly, "I'm goin' to shoot a lynx."

The other boys admired this statement, but they were silent for a time. Finally Jimmie said, meekly, "What's a lynx?" He had endured his ignorance as long as he was able.

The Dalzel boy mocked him. "Why, don't you know what a lynx is? A lynx?

Why, a lynx is a animal somethin' like a cat, an' it's got great big green eyes, and it sits on the limb of a tree an' jus' glares at you. It's a pretty bad animal, I tell you. Why, when I—"

"Huh!" said the third boy. "Where'd you ever see a lynx?"

"Oh, I've seen 'em—plenty of 'em. I bet you'd be scared if you seen one once."

Jimmie and the other boy each demanded, "How do you know I would?"

They penetrated deeper into the wood. The climbed a rocky zigzag path which led them at times where with their hands they could almost touch the tops of giant pines. The gray cliffs sprang sheer toward the sky. Willie Dalzel babbled about his impossible lynx, and they stalked the mountain-side like chamois-hunters, although no noise of bird or beast broke the stillness of the hills. Below them Whilomville was spread out somewhat like the cheap green-and-black lithograph of the time— "A Bird's-eye View of Whilomville, N.Y."

In the end the boys reached the top of the mountain and scouted off among wild and desolate ridges. They were burning with the desire to slay large animals. They thought continually of elephants, lions, tigers, crocodiles. They discoursed upon their immaculate conduct in case such monsters confronted them, and they all lied carefully about their courage.

The breeze was heavy with the smell of sweet fern. The pins and hemlocks sighed as they waved their branches. In the hollows the leaves of the laurels were lacquered where the sunlight found them. No matter the weather, it would be impossible to long continue an expedition of this kind without a fire, and presently they built one, snapping down for fuel the brittle under branches of the pines. About this fire they were willed to conduct a sort of play, the Dalzel boy taking the part of a bandit chief, and the other boys being his trusty lieutenants. They stalked to and fro, long-strided, stern yet devil-may-care, three terrible little figures.

Jimmie had an uncle who made game of him whenever he caught him in this kind of play, and often this uncle quoted derisively the following classic: "Once aboard the lugger, Bill, and the girl is mine. Now to burn the château and destroy all evidence of our crime. But, hark 'e, Bill, no wiolence." Wheeling abruptly, he addressed these dramatic words to his comrades. They were impressed; they decided at once to be smugglers, and in the most ribald fashion they talked about carrying off young women.

At last they continued their march through the woods. The smuggling *motif* was now grafted fantastically upon the original lynx idea, which Willie Dalzel refused to abandon at any price.

Once they came upon an innocent bird which happened to be looking another way at the time. After a great deal of maneuvering and big words, Willie Dalzel reared his fowling piece and blew this poor thing into a mere rag of wet feathers, of which he was proud.

Afterward the other big boy had a turn at another bird. Then it was plainly Jimmie's chance. The two others had, of course, some thought of cheating him out of his chance, but of a truth he was timid to explode such a thunderous weapon, and as soon as they detected this fear they simply overbore him, and made it clearly understood that if he refused to shoot he would lose his caste, his scalp-lock, his girdle, his honor.

They had reached the old death-colored snake-fence which marked the limits of the upper pasture of the Fleming farm. Under some hickory trees the path ran parallel to the fence. Behold! a small priestly chipmunk came to a rail and, folding his hands on his abdomen, addressed them in his own tongue. It was Jimmie's shot. Adjured by the others, he took the gun. His face was stiff with apprehension. The Dalzel boy was giving forth fine words. "Go ahead. Aw, don't be afraid. It's nothin' to do. Why, I've done it a million times. Don't shut both your eyes, now. Jus' keep one open and shut the other one. He'll get away if you don't watch out. Now you're all right. Why don't you let 'er go? Go ahead."

Jimmie, with his legs braced apart, was in the center of the path. His back was greatly bent, owing to the mechanics of supporting the heavy gun. His companions were screeching in the rear. There was a wait.

Then he pulled trigger. To him there was a frightful roar, his cheek and his shoulder took a stunning blow, his face felt a hot flush of fire, and, opening his two eyes, he found that he was still alive. He was not too dazed to instantly adopt a becoming egotism. It had been the first shot of his life.

But directly after the well-mannered celebration of this victory a certain cow, which had been grazing in the line of fire, was seen to break wildly across the pasture, bellowing and bucking. The three smugglers and lynx-hunters looked at each other out of blanched faces. Jimmie had hit the cow. The first evidence of his comprehension of this fact was in the celerity with which he returned the discharged gun to Willie Dalzel.

They turned to flee. The land was black, as if it had been overshadowed suddenly with thick storm-clouds, and even as they fled in their horror a gigantic Swedish farm hand came from the heavens and fell upon them, shrieking in eerie triumph. In a twinkle they were clouted prostrate. The Swede was elate and ferocious in a foreign and fulsome way. He continued to beat them and yell.

From the ground they raised their dismal appeal. "Oh, please, mister, we didn't do it! He did it! I didn't do it! We didn't do it! We didn't mean to do it! Oh, please, mister!"

In these moments of childish terror little lads go half blind, and it is possible that few moments of their after life made them suffer as they did when the Swede flung them over the fence and marched them toward the farmhouse. They begged like cowards on the scaffold, and each one was for himself. "Oh, please let me go, mister! I didn't do it, mister! He did it! Oh, p-l-ease let me go, mister!"

The boyish view belongs to boys alone, and if this tall and knotted laborer was needlessly without charity, none of the three lads questioned it. Usually when they were punished they decided that they deserved it, and the more they were punished the more they were convinced they were criminals of a most subterranean type. As to the hitting of the cow being a pure accident, and therefore not of necessity a criminal matter, such reading never entered their heads. When things happened and they were caught, they commonly paid dire consequences, and they were accustomed to measure the probabilities of woe utterly by the damage done, and not in any way by the culpability. The shooting of the cow was plainly heinous, and undoubtedly their dungeons would be knee-deep in water.

"He did it, mister!" This was a general outcry. Jimmie used it as often as did the others. As for them, it is certain that they had no direct thought of betraying their comrade for their own salvation. They thought themselves guilty because they were caught; when boys were not caught they might possibly be innocent. But captured boys were guilty. When they cried out that Jimmie was the culprit, it was principally a simple expression of terror.

Old Henry Fleming, the owner of the farm, strode across the pasture toward them. He had in his hand a most cruel whip. The whip he flourished. At his approach the boys suffered the agonies of the fire regions. And yet anybody with half an eye could see that the whip in his hand was a mere accident, and that he was a kind old man—when he cared.

When he had come near he spoke crisply. "What you boys ben doin' to my cow?" The tone had deep threat in it. They all answered by saying that none of them had shot the cow. Their denials were tearful and clamorous, and they crawled knee by knee. The vision of it was like three martyrs being dragged toward the stake. Old Fleming stood there, grim, tight-lipped. After a time he said, "Which boy done it?"

There was some confusion, and then Jimmie spake. "I done it, mister."

Fleming looked at him. Then he asked, "Well, what did you shoot 'er fer?"

Jimmie thought, hesitated, decided, faltered, and then formulated this: "I thought she was a lynx."

Old Fleming and his Swede at once lay down in the grass and laughed themselves helpless.

September, 1899

Considerations

1. Look up the meaning of "rites of passage" and point out the importance of this idea in this story. What is the chief symbol of manhood in this story?
2. "Lynx-Hunting" displays Crane's talents as a humorist, but discuss the very serious questions that lie just beneath the surface. Consider the following passage in your answer:

    The grown folk seemed to regard these wastes merely as so much distance between one place and another place, or as a rabbit-cover, or as a district to be judged according to the value of the timber; but to the boys it spoke some great inspiring word, which they knew even as those who pace the shore know the enigmatic speech of the surf.

3. What philosophical idea is suggested by the incident in which Willie Dalzel shoots the bird? Is insensitivity to pain and death in someone or something else an inherited characteristic? Is sensitivity learned?
4. Naturalism is the idea that developed in the late nineteenth century as a result of Darwin's books and others, that morality does not exist in nature but was conceived by man as a means of survival. In Crane's more famous stories, such as "The Open Boat" and "The Blue Hotel," this idea is much more obvious, but can you nevertheless point out some examples of this idea in this story?
5. Cite examples indicating that Crane thinks man is by nature an imaginative creature. If this is true, what happens to our imaginations in the process of maturing? Do schools as a rule foster imagination in children?
6. One of Crane's more illustrious contemporaries was Mark Twain, the author of *Tom Sawyer*, a book which Crane most certainly read as a child. Read the chapter dealing with Tom and his friends on Jackson's Island and compare it with this story.

THE AGING ATHLETE

He had never heard that a man's life was the life of his arteries, but well he knew the meaning of those big, up-standing veins. His heart had pumped too much blood through them at top pressure. They no longer did the work.

—Jack London

JACK LONDON

A Piece of Steak

With the last morsel of bread Tom King wiped his plate clean of the last particle of flour gravy and chewed the resulting mouthful in a slow and meditative way. When he arose from the table, he was oppressed by the feeling that he was distinctly hungry. Yet he alone had eaten. The two children in the other room had been sent early to bed in order that in sleep they might forget they had gone supperless. His wife had touched nothing, and had sat silently and watched him with solicitous eyes. She was a thin, worn woman of the working class, though signs of an earlier prettiness were not wanting in her face. The flour for the gravy she had borrowed from the neighbor across the hall. The last two ha'pennies had gone to buy the bread.

He sat down by the window on a rickety chair that protested under his weight, and quite mechanically he put his pipe in his mouth and dipped into the side pocket of his coat. The absence of any tobacco made him aware of his action, and with a scowl for his forgetfulness he put the pipe away. His movements were slow, almost hulking, as though he were burdened by the heavy weight of his muscles. He was a solid-bodied, stolid-looking man, and his appearance did not suffer from being overprepossessing. His rough clothes were old and slouchy. The uppers of his shoes were too weak to carry the heavy resoling that was itself of no recent date. And his cotton shirt, a cheap, two-shilling affair, showed a frayed collar and ineradicable paint stains.

But it was Tom King's face that advertised him unmistakably for what he was. It was the face of a typical prize fighter; of one who had put in long years of service in the squared ring and, by that means, developed and emphasized all the marks of the fighting beast. It was distinctly a lowering countenance, and, that no feature of it might escape notice, it was clean-shaven. The lips were shapeless and constituted a mouth harsh to excess, that was like a gash in his face. The jaw was aggressive, brutal, heavy. The eyes, slow of movement and heavy-lidded, were almost expressionless under the shaggy, indrawn brows. Sheer animal that he was, the eyes were the most animallike feature about him. They were sleepy, lionlike—the eyes of a fighting animal. The forehead slanted quickly back to the hair, which, clipped close, showed every bump of a villainous-looking head. A nose, twice broken and molded variously by count-less blows, and a cauliflower ear, permanently swollen and distorted to twice its size, completed his adornment, while the beard, fresh-shaven as it was, sprouted in the skin and gave the face a blue-black stain.

Altogether, it was the face of a man to be afraid of in a dark alley or lonely place. And yet Tom King was not a criminal, nor had he ever done anything criminal. Outside of brawls, common to his walk in life, he had harmed no one. Nor had he ever been known to pick a quarrel. He was a professional, and all the fighting brutishness of him was reserved for his professional appearances. Outside the ring he was slow-going, easy-natured, and, in his younger days, when money was flush, too openhanded for his own good. He bore no grudges and had few enemies. Fighting was a business with him. In the ring he struck to hurt, struck to maim, struck to destroy; but there was no animus in it. It was a plain business proposition. Audiences assembled and paid for the spectacle of men knocking each other out. The winner took the big end of the purse. When Tom King faced the Woolloomoolloo Gouger, twenty years before, he knew that the Gouger's jaw was only four months healed after having been broken in a Newcastle bout. And he had played for that jaw and broken it again in the ninth round, not because he bore the Gouger any ill will, but because that was the surest way to put the Gouger out and win the big end of the purse. Nor had the Gouger borne him any ill will for it. It was the game, and both knew the game and played it.

Tom King had never been a talker, and he sat by the window, morosely silent, staring at his hands. The veins stood out on the backs of the hands, large and swollen; and the knuckles, smashed and battered and malformed, testified to the use to which they had been put. He had never heard that a man's life was the life of his arteries, but well he knew the meaning of those big, upstanding veins. His heart had pumped too much blood through them at top pressure. They no longer did the work. He had stretched the elasticity out of them, and with their distention had passed his endurance. He tired easily now. No longer could he do a fast twenty rounds, hammer and tongs, fight, fight, fight, from gong to gong, with fierce rally on top of fierce rally, beaten to the ropes and in turn beating his opponent to the ropes, and rallying fiercest and fastest of all in that last, twentieth round, with the house on its feet and yelling, himself rushing, striking, ducking, raining showers of blows upon showers of blows and receiving showers of blows in return, and all the time the heart faithfully pumping the surging blood through the adequate veins. The veins, swollen at the time, had always shrunk down again, though not quite—each time, imperceptibly at first, re-maining just a trifle larger than before. He stared at them and at his battered knuckles, and, for the moment, caught a vision of the youthful excellence of those hands before the first knuckle had been smashed on the head of Benny Jones, otherwise known as the Welsh Terror.

The impression of his hunger came back on him.

"Blimey, but couldn't I go a piece of steak!" he muttered aloud, clenching his huge fists and spitting out a smothered oath.

"I tried both Burke's an' Sawley's," his wife said half apologetically.

"An' they wouldn't?" he demanded.

"Not a ha'penny. Burke said——" She faltered.

"G'wan! Wot'd he say?"

"As how 'e was thinkin' Sandel 'ud do ye tonight, an' as how yer score was comfortable big as it was."

Tom King grunted but did not reply. He was busy thinking of the bull terrier he had kept in his younger days to which he had fed steaks without end. Burke would have given him credit for a thousand steaks—then. But times had changed. Tom King was getting old; and old men, fighting before second-rate clubs, couldn't expect to run bills of any size with the tradesmen.

He had got up in the morning with a longing for a piece of steak, and the longing had not abated. He had not had a fair training for this fight. It was a drought year in Australia, times were hard, and even the most irregular work was difficult to find. He had had no sparring partner, and his food had not been of the best nor always sufficient. He had done a few days' navvy work when he could get it, and he had run around the Domain in the early mornings to get his legs in shape. But it was hard, training without a partner and with a wife and two kiddies that must be fed. Credit with the tradesmen had undergone very slight expansion when he was matched with Sandel. The secretary of the Gayety Club had advanced him three pounds—the loser's end of the purse—and beyond that had refused to go. Now and again he had managed to borrow a few shillings from old pals, who would have lent more only that it was a drought year and they were hard put themselves. No—and there was no use in disguising the fact—his training had not been satisfactory. He should have had better food and no worries. Besides, when a man is forty, it is harder to get into condition than when he is twenty.

"What time is it, Lizzie?" he asked.

His wife went across the hall to inquire, and came back.

"Quarter before eight."

"They'll be startin' the first bout in a few minutes," he said. "Only a tryout. Then there's a four-round spar 'tween Dealer Wells an' Gridley, an' a ten-round go 'tween Starlight an' some sailor bloke. I don't come on for over an hour."

At the end of another silent ten minutes he rose to his feet.

"Truth is, Lizzie, I ain't had proper trainin'."

He reached for his hat and started for the door. He did not offer to kiss her—he never did on going out—but on this night she dared to kiss him, throwing her arms around him and compelling him to bend down to her face. She looked quite small against the massive bulk of the man.

"Good luck, Tom," she said. "You gotter do 'im."

"Ay, I gotter do 'im," he repeated. "That's all there is to it. I jus' gotter do 'im."

He laughed with an attempt at heartiness, while she pressed more closely against him. Across her shoulders he looked around the bare room. It was all he had in the world, with the rent overdue, and her and the kiddies. And he was leaving it to go out into the night to get meat for his mate and cubs—not like a modern workingman going to his machine grind, but in the old, primitive, royal, animal way, by fighting for it.

"I gotter do 'im," he repeated, this time a hint of desperation in his voice. "If it's a win, it's thirty quid—an' I can pay all that's owin', with a lump o' money left over. If it's a lose, I get naught—not even a penny for me to ride home on the tram. The secretary's give all that's comin' from a loser's end. Good-by, old woman. I'll come straight home if it's a win."

"An' I'll be waitin' up," she called to him along the hall.

It was full two miles to the Gayety, and as he walked along he remembered how in his palmy days—he had once been the heavyweight champion of New South Wales—he would have ridden in a cab to the fight, and how, most likely, some heavy backer would have paid for the cab and ridden with him. There were Tommy Burns and that Yankee, Jack Johnson—they rode about in motor-cars. And he walked! And, as any man knew, a hard two miles was not the best preliminary to a fight. He was an old un, and the world did not wag well with old uns. He was good for nothing now except navvy work, and his broken nose and swollen ear were against him even in that. He found himself wishing that he had learned a trade. It would have been better in the long run. But no one had told him, and he knew, deep down in his heart, that he would not have listened if they had. It had been so easy. Big money—sharp, glorious fights—periods of rest and loafing in between—a following of eager flatterers, the slaps on the back, the shakes of the hand, the toffs glad to buy him a drink for the privilege of five minutes' talk—and the glory of it, the yelling houses, the whirl-wind finish, the referee's "King wins!" and his name in the sporting columns next day.

Those had been times! But he realized now, in his slow, ruminating way, that it was the old uns he had been putting away. He was Youth, rising; and they were Age, sinking. No wonder it had been easy—they with their swollen veins and battered knuckles and weary in the bones of them from the long battles they had already fought. He remembered the time he put out old Stowsher Bill, at Rush-Cutters Bay, in the eighteenth round, and how old Bill had cried after-ward in the dressing room like a baby. Perhaps old Bill's rent had been overdue. Perhaps he'd had at home a missus an' a couple of kiddies. And perhaps Bill, that very day of the fight, had had a hungering for a piece of steak. Bill had fought game and taken incredible punishment. He could see now, after he had gone through the mill himself, that Stowsher Bill had fought for a bigger stake, that night twenty years ago, than had young Tom King, who had fought for glory and easy money. No wonder Stowsher Bill had cried afterward in the dressing room.

Well, a man had only so many fights in him, to begin with. It was the iron law of the game. One man might have a hundred hard fights in him, another man only twenty; each, according to the make of him and the quality of his fiber, had a definite number, and when he had fought them he was done. Yes, he had had more fights in him than most of them, and he had had far more than his share of the hard, grueling fights—the kind that worked the heart and lungs to bursting, that took the elastic out of the arteries and made hard knots of muscle out of youth's sleek suppleness, that wore out nerve and stamina and made brain and bones weary from excess of effort and endurance overwrought. Yes, he had done better than all of them. There was none of his old fighting partners left. He was the last of the old guard. He had seen them all finished, and he had had a hand in finishing some of them.

They had tried him out against the old uns, and one after another he had put them away—laughing when, like old Stowsher Bill, they cried in the dressing room. And now he was an old un, and they tried out the youngsters on him. There was that bloke Sandel. He had come over from New Zealand with a record behind him. But nobody in Australia knew anything about him, so they put him up against old Tom King. If Sandel made a showing, he would be given better men to fight, with bigger purses to win; so it was to be depended upon that he would put up a fierce battle. He had everything to win by it—money and glory and career; and Tom King was the grizzled old chopping block that guarded the highway to fame and fortune. And he had nothing to win except thirty quid, to pay to the landlord and the tradesmen. And as Tom King thus ruminated, there came to his stolid vision the form of youth, glorious youth, rising exultant and invincible, supple of muscle and silken of skin, with heart and lungs that had never been tired and torn and that laughed at limitation of effort. Yes, youth was the nemesis. It destroyed the old uns and recked not that, in so doing, it destroyed itself. It enlarged its arteries and smashed its knuckles, and was in turn destroyed by youth. For youth was ever youthful. It was only age that grew old.

At Castlereagh Street he turned to the left, and three blocks along came to the Gayety. A crowd of young larrikins hanging outside the door made respectful way for him, and he heard one say to another: "That's 'im! That's Tom King!"

Inside, on the way to his dressing room, he encountered the secretary, a keen-eyed, shrewd-faced young man, who shook his hand.

"How are you feelin', Tom?" he asked.

"Fit as a fiddle," King answered, though he knew that he lied, and that if he had a quid he would give it right there for a good piece of steak.

When he emerged from the dressing room, his seconds behind him, and came down the aisle to the squared ring in the center of the hall, a burst of greeting and applause went up from the waiting crowd. He acknowledged salutations right and left, though few of the faces did he know. Most of them were the faces of kiddies unborn when he was winning his first laurels in the squared ring. He leaped lightly to the raised platform and ducked through the ropes to his corner, where he sat down on a folding stool. Jack Ball, the referee, came over and shook his hand. Ball was a broken-down pugilist who for over ten years had not entered the ring as a principal. King was glad that he had him for referee. They were both old uns. If he should rough it with Sandel a bit beyond the rules, he knew Ball could be depended upon to pass it by.

Aspiring young heavyweights, one after another, were climbing into the ring and being presented to the audience by the referee. Also he issued their challenges for them.

"Young Pronto," Bill announced, "from North Sydney, challenges the winner for fifty pounds side bet."

The audience applauded, and applauded again as Sandel himself sprang through the ropes and sat down in his corner. Tom King looked across the ring at him curiously, for in a few minutes they would be locked together in merciless combat, each trying with all the force of him to knock the other into unconsciousness. But little could he see, for Sandel, like himself, had trousers and sweater on over his ring costume. His face was strongly handsome, crowned with a curly mop of yellow hair, while his thick, muscular neck hinted at bodily magnificence.

Young Pronto went to one corner and then the other, shaking hands with the principals and dropping down out of the ring. The challenges went on. Ever youth climbed through the ropes—youth unknown but insatiable, crying out to mankind that with strength and skill it would match issues with the winner. A few years before, in his own heyday of invincibleness, Tom King would have been amused and bored by these preliminaries. But now he sat fascinated, unable to shake the vision of youth from his eyes. Always were these youngsters rising up in the boxing game, springing through the ropes and shouting their defiance; and always were the old uns going down before them. They climbed to success over the bodies of the old uns. And ever they came, more and more youngsters—youth unquenchable and irresistible—and ever they put the old uns away, themselves becoming old uns and traveling the same downward path, while behind them, ever pressing on them, was youth eternal—the new babies, grown lusty and dragging their elders down, with behind them more babies to the end of time—youth that must have its will and that will never die.

King glanced over to the press box and nodded to Morgan, of the *Sportsman*, and Corbett, of the *Referee*. Then he held out his hands, while Sid Sullivan and Charley Bates, his seconds, slipped on his gloves and laced them tight, closely watched by one of Sandel's seconds, who first examined critically the tapes on King's knuckles. A second of his own was in Sandel's corner, performing a like office. Sandel's trousers were pulled off, and as he stood up his sweater was skinned off over his head. And Tom King, looking, saw youth incarnate, deep-chested, heavy-thewed, with muscles that slipped and slid like live things under the white satin skin. The whole body was acrawl with life, and Tom King knew that it was a life that had never oozed its freshness out through the aching pores during the long fights wherein youth paid its toll and departed not quite so young as when it entered.

The two men advanced to meet each other, and as the gong sounded and the seconds clattered out of the ring with the folding stools, they shook hands and instantly took their fighting attitudes. And instantly, like a mechanism of steel and springs balanced on a hair trigger, Sandel was in and out and in again, landing a left to the eyes, a right to the ribs, ducking a counter, dancing lightly away and dancing menacingly back again. He was swift and clever. It was a dazzling exhibition. The house yelled its approbation. But King was not dazzled. He had fought too many fights and too many youngsters. He knew the blows for what they were—too quick and too deft to be dangerous. Evidently Sandel was going to rush things from the start. It was to be expected. It was the way of youth, expending its splendor and excellence in wild insurgence and furious onslaught, overwhelming opposition with its own unlimited glory of strength and desire.

Sandel was in and out, here, there, and everywhere, light-footed and eager-hearted, a living wonder of white flesh and stinging muscle that wove itself into a dazzling fabric of attack, slipping and leaping like a flying shuttle from action to action through a thousand actions, all of them centered upon the destruction of Tom King, who stood between him and fortune. And Tom King patiently endured. He knew his business, and he knew youth now that youth was no longer his. There was nothing to do till the other lost some of his steam, was his thought, and he grinned to himself as he deliberately ducked so as to receive a heavy blow on the top of his head. It was a wicked thing to do, yet eminently fair according to the rules of the boxing game. A man was supposed to take care of his own knuckles, and if he insisted on hitting an opponent on the top of the head he did so at his own peril. King could have ducked lower and left the blow whiz harmlessly past, but he remembered his own early fights and how he smashed his first knuckle on the head of the Welsh Terror. He was but playing the game. That duck had accounted for one of Sandel's knuckles. Not that Sandel would mind it now. He would go on, superbly regardless, hitting as hard as ever throughout the fight. But later on, when the long ring battles had begun to tell, he would regret that knuckle and look back and remember how he smashed it on Tom King's head.

The first round was all Sandel's, and he had the house yelling with the rapidity of his whirlwind rushes. He overwhelmed King with avalanches of punches, and King did nothing. He never struck once, contenting himself with covering up, blocking and ducking and clinching to avoid punishment. He occasionally feinted, shook his head when the weight of a punch landed, and moved stolidly about, never leaping or springing or wasting an ounce of strength. Sandel must foam the froth of youth away before discreet age could dare to retaliate. All King's movements were slow and methodical, and his heavy-lidded, slow-moving eyes gave him the appearance of being half asleep or dazed. Yet they were eyes that saw everything, that had been trained to see everything through all his twenty years and odd in the ring. They were eyes that did not blink or waver before an impending blow, but that coolly saw and measured distance.

Seated in his corner for the minute's rest at the end of the round, he lay back with outstretched legs, his arms resting on the right angle of the ropes, his chest and abdomen heaving frankly and deeply as he gulped down the air driven by the towels of his seconds. He listened with closed eyes to the voices of the house, "Why don't yeh fight, Tom?" many were crying. "Yeh ain't afraid of 'im, are yeh?"

"Muscle-bound," he heard a man on a front seat comment. "He can't move quicker. Two to one on Sandel, in quids."

The gong struck and the two men advanced from their corners. Sandel came forward fully three quarters of the distance, eager to begin again; but King was content to advance the shorter distance. It was in line with his policy of econ-omy. He had not been well-trained, and he had not had enough to eat, and every step counted. Besides, he had already walked two miles to the ringside. It was a repetition of the first round, with Sandel attacking like a whirlwind and with the audience indignantly demanding why King did not fight. Beyond feinting and several slowly delivered and ineffectual blows he did nothing save block and stall and clinch. Sandel wanted to make the pace fast, while King, out of his wisdom, refused to accommodate him. He grinned with a certain wistful pathos in his ring-battered countenance, and went on cherishing his strength with the jealousy of which only age is capable. Sandel was youth, and he threw his strength away with the munificent abandon of youth. To King belonged the ring generalship, the wisdom bred of long, aching fights. He watched with cool eyes and head, moving slowly and waiting for Sandel's froth to foam away. To the majority of the onlookers it seemed as though King was hopelessly outclassed, and they voiced their opinion in offers of three to one on Sandel. But there were wise ones, a few, who knew King of old time, and who covered what they considered easy money.

The third round began as usual, one-sided, with Sandel doing all the leading and delivering all the punishment. A half minute had passed when Sandel, overconfident, left an opening. King's eyes and right arm flashed in the same instant. It was his first real blow—a hook, with the twisted arch of the arm to make it rigid, and with all the weight of the half-pivoted body behind it. It was like a sleepy-seeming lion suddenly thrusting out a lightning paw. Sandel, caught on the side of the jaw, was felled like a bullock. The audience gasped and murmured awe-stricken applause. The man was not muscle-bound, after all, and he could drive a blow like a trip hammer.

Sandel was shaken. He rolled over and attempted to rise, but the sharp yells from his seconds to take the count restrained him. He knelt on one knee, ready to rise, and waited, while the referee stood over him, counting the seconds loudly in his ear. At the ninth he rose in fighting attitude, and Tom King, facing him, knew regret that the blow had not been an inch nearer the point of the jaw. That would have been a knockout, and he could have carried the thirty quid home to the missus and the kiddies.

The round continued to the end of its three minutes, Sandel for the first time respectful of his opponent and King slow of movement and sleepy-eyed as ever. As the round neared its close, King, warned of the fact by sight of the seconds crouching outside ready for the spring in through the ropes, worked the fight around to his own corner. And when the gong struck, he sat down immediately on the waiting stool, while Sandel had to walk all the way across the diagonal of the square to his own corner. It was a little thing, but it was the sum of little things that counted. Sandel was compelled to walk that many more steps, to give up that much energy, and to lose a part of the precious minute of rest. At the beginning of every round King loafed slowly out from his corner, forcing his opponent to advance the greater distance. The end of every round found the fight maneuvered by King into his own corner so that he could immediately sit down.

Two more rounds went by, in which King was parsimonious of effort and Sandel prodigal. The latter's attempt to force a fast pace made King uncomfortable, for a fair percentage of the multitudinous blows showered upon him went home. Yet King persisted in his dogged slowness, despite the crying of the young hotheads for him to go in and fight. Again, in the sixth round, Sandel was careless, again Tom King's fearful right flashed out to the jaw, and again Sandel took the nine seconds' count.

By the seventh round Sandel's pink of condition was gone, and he settled down to what he knew was to be the hardest fight in his experience. Tom King was an old un, but a better old un than he had ever encountered—an old un who never lost his head, who was remarkably able at defense, whose blows had the impact of a knotted club, and who had a knockout in either hand. Nevertheless, Tom King dared not hit often. He never forgot his battered knuckles, and knew that every hit must count if the knuckles were to last out the fight. As he sat in his corner, glancing across at his opponent, the thought came to him that the sum of his wisdom and Sandel's youth would constitute a world's champion heavyweight. But that was the trouble. Sandel would never become a world champion. He lacked the wisdom, and the only way for him to get it was to buy it with youth; and when wisdom was his, youth would have been spent in buying it.

King took every advantage he knew. He never missed an opportunity to clinch, and in effecting most of the clinches his shoulder drove stiffly into the other's ribs. In the philosophy of the ring a shoulder was as good as a punch so far as damage was concerned, and a great deal better so far as concerned expenditure of effort. Also in the clinches King rested his weight on his opponent, and was loath to let go. This compelled the interference of the referee, who tore them apart, always assisted by Sandel, who had not yet learned to rest. He could not refrain from using those glorious flying arms and writhing muscles of his, and when the other rushed into a clinch, striking shoulder against ribs, and with head resting under Sandel's left arm, Sandel almost invariably swung his right behind his own back and into the projecting face. It was a clever stroke, much admired by the audience, but it was not dangerous, and was, therefore, just that much wasted strength. But Sandel was tireless and unaware of limitations, and King grinned and doggedly endured.

Sandel developed a fierce right to the body, which made it appear that King was taking an enormous amount of punishment, and it was only the old ringsters who appreciated the deft touch of King's left glove to the other's biceps just before the impact of the blow. It was true, the blow landed each time; but each time it was robbed of its power by that touch on the biceps. In the ninth round, three times inside a minute, King's right hooked its twisted arch to the jaw; and three times Sandel's body, heavy as it was, was leveled to the mat. Each time he took the nine seconds allowed him and rose to his feet, shaken and jarred, but still strong. He had lost much of his speed, and he wasted less effort. He was fighting grimly; but he continued to draw upon his chief asset, which was youth. King's chief asset was experience. As his vitality had dimmed and his vigor abated, he had replaced them with cunning, with wisdom born of the long fights and with a careful shepherding of strength. Not alone had he learned never to make a superfluous movement, but he had learned how to seduce an opponent into throwing his strength away. Again and again, by feint of foot and hand and body, he continued to inveigle Sandel into leaping back, ducking, or countering. King rested, but he never permitted Sandel to rest. It was the strategy of age.

Early in the tenth round King began stopping the other's rushes with straight lefts to the face, and Sandel, grown wary, responded by drawing the left, then by ducking it and delivering his right in a swinging hook to the side of the head. It was too high up to be vitally effective; but when first it landed King knew the old familiar descent of the black veil of unconsciousness across his mind. For the instant, or for the slightest fraction of an instant, rather, he ceased. In the one moment he saw his opponent ducking out of his field of vision and the background of white, watching faces; in the next moment he again saw his opponent and the background of faces. It was as if he had slept for a time and just opened his eyes again, and yet the interval of unconsciousness was so microscopically short that there had been no time for him to fall. The audience saw him totter and his knees give, and then saw him recover and tuck his chin deeper into the shelter of his left shoulder.

Several times Sandel repeated the blow, keeping King partially dazed, and then the latter worked out his defense, which was also a counter. Feinting with his left, he took a half step backward, at the same time uppercutting with the whole strength of his right. So accurately was it timed that it landed squarely on Sandel's face in the full, downward sweep of the duck, and Sandel lifted in the air and curled backward, striking the mat on his head and shoulders. Twice King achieved this, then turned loose and hammered his opponent to the ropes. He gave Sandel no chance to rest or to set himself, but smashed blow in upon blow till the house rose to its feet and the air was filled with an unbroken roar of applause. But Sandel's strength and endurance were superb, and he continued to stay on his feet. A knockout seemed certain, and a captain of police, appalled at the dreadful punishment, arose by the ringside to stop the fight. The gong struck for the end of the round and Sandel staggered to his corner, protesting to the captain that he was sound and strong. To prove it, he threw two back air-springs, and the police captain gave in.

Tom King, leaning back in his corner and breathing hard, was disappointed. If the fight had been stopped, the referee, perforce, would have rendered him the decision and the purse would have been his. Unlike Sandel, he was not fighting for glory or career, but for thirty quid. And now Sandel would recuperate in the minute of rest.

Youth will be served—this saying flashed into King's mind, and he remembered the first time he had heard it, the night when he had put away Stowsher Bill. The toff who had bought him a drink after the fight and patted him on the shoulder had used those words. Youth will be served! The toff was right. And on that night in the long ago he had been youth. Tonight youth sat in the opposite corner. As for himself, he had been fighting for half an hour now, and he was an old man. Had he fought like Sandel, he would not have lasted fifteen minutes. But the point was that he did not recuperate. Those upstanding arteries and that sorely tried heart would not enable him to gather strength in the intervals between the rounds. And he had not had sufficient strength in him to begin with. His legs were heavy under him and beginning to cramp. He should not have walked those two miles to the fight. And there was the steak which he had got up longing for that morning. A great and terrible hatred rose up in him for the butchers who had refused him credit. It was hard for an old man to go into a fight without enough to eat. And a piece of steak was such a little thing, a few pennies at best; yet it meant thirty quid to him.

With the gong that opened the eleventh round Sandel rushed, making a show of freshness which he did not really possess. King knew it for what it was—a bluff as old as the game itself. He clinched to save himself, then, going free, allowed Sandel to get set. This was what King desired. He feinted with his left, drew the answering duck and swinging upward hook, then made the half step backward, delivered the uppercut full to the face and crumpled Sandel over to the mat. After that he never let him rest, receiving punishment himself, but inflicting far more, smashing Sandel to the ropes, hooking and driving all manner of blows into him, tearing away from his clinches or punching him out of attempted clinches, and ever when Sandel would have fallen, catching him with one uplifting hand and with the other immediately smashing him into the ropes where he could not fall.

The house by this time had gone mad, and it was his house, nearly every voice yelling: "Go it, Tom!" "Get 'im! Get 'im!" "You've got 'im, Tom! You've got 'im!" It was to be a whirlwind finish, and that was what a ringside audience paid to see.

And Tom King, who for half an hour had conserved his strength, now expended it prodigally in the one great effort he knew he had in him. It was his one chance—now or not at all. His strength was waning fast, and his hope was that before the last of it ebbed out of him he would have beaten his opponent down for the count. And as he continued to strike and force, coolly estimating the weight of his blows and the quality of the damage wrought, he realized how hard a man Sandel was to knock out. Stamina and endurance were his to an extreme degree, and they were the virgin stamina and endurance of youth. Sandel was certainly a coming man. He had it in him. Only out of such rugged fiber were successful fighters fashioned.

Sandel was reeling and staggering, but Tom King's legs were cramping and his knuckles going back on him. Yet he steeled himself to strike the fierce blows, every one of which brought anguish to his tortured hands. Though now he was receiving practically no punishment, he was weakening as rapidly as the other. His blows went home, but there was no longer the weight behind them, and each blow was the result of a severe effort of will. His legs were like lead, and they dragged visibly under him; while Sandel's backers, cheered by this symptom, began calling encouragement to their man.

King was spurred to a burst of effort. He delivered two blows in succession— a left, a trifle too high, to the solar plexus, and a right cross to the jaw. They were not heavy blows, yet so weak and dazed was Sandel that he went down and lay quivering. The referee stood over him, shouting the count of the fatal seconds in his ear. If before the tenth second was called he did not rise, the fight was lost. The house stood in hushed silence. King rested on trembling legs. A mortal dizziness was upon him, and before his eyes the sea of faces sagged and swayed, while to his ears, as from a remote distance, came the count of the referee. Yet he looked upon the fight as his. It was impossible that a man so punished could rise.

Only youth could rise, and Sandel rose. At the fourth second he rolled over on his face and groped blindly for the ropes. By the seventh second he had dragged himself to his knee, where he rested, his head rolling groggily on his shoulders. As the referee cried "Nine!" Sandel stood upright, in proper stalling position, his left arm wrapped about his face, his right wrapped about his stomach. Thus were his vital points guarded, while he lurched forward toward King in the hope of effecting a clinch and gaining more time.

At the instant Sandel arose, King was at him, but the two blows he delivered were muffled on the stalled arms. The next moment Sandel was in the clinch and holding on desperately while the referee strove to drag the two men apart. King helped to force himself free. He knew the rapidity with which youth recovered, and he knew that Sandel was his if he could prevent that recovery. One stiff punch would do it. Sandel was his, indubitably his. He had outgeneraled him, outfought him, outpointed him. Sandel reeled out of the clinch, balanced on the hairline between defeat or survival. One good blow would topple him over and down and out. And Tom King, in a flash of bitterness, remembered the piece of steak and wished that he had it then behind that necessary punch he must deliver. He nerved himself for the blow, but it was not heavy enough nor swift enough. Sandel swayed but did not fall, staggering back to the ropes and holding on. King staggered after him, and, with a pang like that of dissolution, delivered another blow. But his body had deserted him. All that was left of him was a fighting intelligence that was dimmed and clouded from exhaustion. The blow that was aimed for the jaw struck no higher than the shoulder. He had willed the blow higher, but the tired muscles had not been able to obey. And, from the impact of the blow, Tom King himself reeled back and nearly fell. Once again he strove. This time his punch missed altogether, and from absolute weakness he fell against Sandel and clinched, holding on to him to save himself from sinking to the floor.

King did not attempt to free himself. He had shot his bolt. He was gone. And youth had been served. Even in the clinch he could feel Sandel growing stronger against him. When the referee thrust them apart, there, before his eyes, he saw youth recuperate. From instant to instant Sandel grew stronger. His punches, weak and futile at first, became stiff and accurate. Tom King's bleared eyes saw the gloved fist driving at his jaw, and he willed to guard it by interposing his arm. He saw the danger, willed the act; but the arm was too heavy. It seemed burdened with a hundredweight of lead. It would not lift itself, and he strove to lift it with his soul. Then the gloved fist landed home. He experienced a sharp snap that was like an electric spark, and simultaneously the veil of blackness enveloped him.

When he opened his eyes again he was in his corner, and he heard the yelling of the audience like the roar of the surf at Bondi Beach. A wet sponge was being pressed against the base of his brain, and Sid Sullivan was blowing cold water in a refreshing spray over his face and chest. His gloves had already been removed, and Sandel, bending over him, was shaking his hand. He bore no ill will toward the man who had put him out, and he returned the grip with a heartiness that made his battered knuckles protest. Then Sandel stepped to the center of the ring and the audience hushed its pandemonium to hear him accept young Pronto's challenge and offer to increase the side bet to one hundred pounds.

King looked on apathetically while his seconds mopped the streaming water from him, dried his face, and prepared him to leave the ring. He felt hungry. It was not the ordinary, gnawing kind, but a great faintness, a palpitation at the pit of the stomach that communicated itself to all his body. He remembered back into the fight to the moment when he had Sandel swaying and tottering on the hair-line balance of defeat. Ah, that piece of steak would have done it! He had lacked just that for the decisive blow, and he had lost. It was all because of the piece of steak.

His seconds were half supporting him as they helped him through the ropes. He tore free from them, ducked through the ropes unaided, and leaped heavily to the floor, following on their heels as they forced a passage for him down the crowded center aisle. Leaving the dressing room for the street, in the entrance to the hall, some young fellow spoke to him.

"W'y didn't yuh go in an' get 'im when yuh 'ad 'im?" the young fellow asked.

"Aw, go to hell!" said Tom King, and passed down the steps to the sidewalk.

The doors of the public house at the corner were swinging wide, and he saw the lights and the smiling barmaids, heard the many voices discussing the fight and the prosperous chink of money on the bar. Somebody called to him to have a drink. He hesitated perceptibly, then refused and went on his way.

He had not a copper in his pocket, and the two-mile walk home seemed very long. He was certainly getting old. Crossing the Domain he sat down suddenly on a bench, unnerved by the thought of the missus sitting up for him, waiting to learn the outcome of the fight. That was harder than any knockout, and it seemed almost impossible to face.

He felt weak and sore, and the pain of his smashed knuckles warned him that, even if he could find a job at navvy work, it would be a week before he could grip a pick handle or a shovel. The hunger palpitation at the pit of the stomach was sickening. His wretchedness overwhelmed him, and into his eyes came an unwonted moisture. He covered his face with his hands, and, as he cried, he remembered Stowsher Bill and how he had served him that night in the long ago. Poor old Stowsher Bill! He could understand now why Bill had cried in the dressing room.

Considerations

1. It is said that all boxing stories owe a debt to this one, as it was the first to use the boxing ring as a metaphor of life. Exactly what kind of life does London portray in this story? Support your answer.
2. Perhaps no other American writer has displayed such an ambivalent attitude toward his subjects as Jack London. He seems to have embraced both the Darwinian idea of "survival of the fittest" and the Marxian idea of socialism. From this story, cite examples of this dual allegiance.
3. Many later writers have addressed the sad question, What is to be done with the worn-out athlete? (See "The Eighty-Yard Run" and "My Old Man.") Does London offer any answer? If the ring is a metaphor for life, then what hope does he offer?
4. Explain how the idea of the young knocking off the old compares with this process among animals, such as deer, goats, sheep, and horses. How does London reconcile this cold fact of nature with his obvious sympathy for Tom and his family?

5. Like Ambrose Bierce and John Steinbeck, among others, London was acutely conscious of man's animal qualities. Point out the instances in which Tom King is compared with an animal.
6. Would you say that London had more than a layman's familiarity with boxing? (See "The White Hope.")
7. Few great boxers have known when to quit. Gene Tunney was one who did. Joe Louis was one, among many others, who did not. Keeping in mind the mythology that surrounds great champions, explain why the idea of retiring in one's prime, or better still, dying, is the ideal.

ERNEST HEMINGWAY

My Old Man

I guess looking at it, now, my old man was cut out for a fat guy, one of those regular little roly fat guys you see around, but he sure never got that way, except a little toward the last, and then it wasn't his fault, he was riding over the jumps only and he could afford to carry plenty of weight then. I remember the way he'd pull on a rubber shirt over a couple of jerseys and a big sweat shirt over that, and get me to run with him in the forenoon in the hot sun. He'd have, maybe, taken a trial trip with one of Razzo's skins early in the morning after just getting in from Torino at four o'clock in the morning and beating it out to the stables in a cab and then with the dew all over everything and the sun just starting to get going, I'd help him pull off his boots and he'd get into a pair of sneakers and all these sweaters and we'd start out.

"Come on, kid," he'd say, stepping up and down on his toes in front of the jock's dressing room, "let's get moving."

Then we'd start off jogging around the infield once, maybe, with him ahead, running nice, and then turn out the gate and along one of those roads with all the trees along both sides of them that run out from San Siro. I'd go ahead of him when we hit the road and I could run pretty good and I'd look around and he'd be jogging easy just behind me and after a little while I'd look around again and he'd begun to sweat. Sweating heavy and he'd just be dogging it along with his eyes on my back, but when he'd catch me looking at him he'd grin and say, "Sweating plenty?" When my old man grinned, nobody could help but grin too. We'd keep right on running out toward the mountains and then my old man would yell, "Hey, Joe!" and I'd look back and he'd be sitting under a tree with a towel he'd had around his waist wrapped around his neck.

I'd come back and sit down beside him and he'd pull a rope out of his pocket and start skipping rope out in the sun with the sweat pouring off his face and him skipping rope out in the white dust with the rope going cloppetty, cloppetty, clop, clop, clop, and the sun hotter, and him working harder up and down a patch of the road. Say, it was a treat to see my old man skip rope, too. He could whirr it fast or lop it slow and fancy. Say, you ought to have seen wops look at us sometimes, when they'd come by, going into town walking along with big white steers hauling the cart. They sure looked as though they thought the old man was nuts. He'd start the rope whirring till they'd stop dead still and watch him, then give the steers a cluck and a poke with the goad and get going again.

When I'd sit watching him working out in the hot sun I sure felt fond of him. He sure was fun and he done his work so hard and he'd finish up with a regular whirring that'd drive the sweat out on his face like water and then sling the rope at the tree and come over and sit down with me and lean back against the tree with the towel and a sweater wrapped around his neck.

"Sure is hell keeping it down, Joe," he'd say and lean back and shut his eyes and breathe long and deep, "it ain't like when you're a kid." Then he'd get up and before he started to cool we'd jog along back to the stables. That's the way it was keeping down to weight. He was worried all the time. Most jocks can just about ride off all they want to. A jock loses about a kilo every time he rides, but my old man was sort of dried out and he couldn't keep down his kilos without all that running.

I remember once at San Siro, Regoli, a little wop, that was riding for Buzoni, came out across the paddock going to the bar for something cool; and flicking his boots with his whip, after he'd just weighed in and my old man had just weighed in too, and came out with the saddle under his arm looking red-faced and tired and too big for his silks and he stood there looking at young Regoli standing up to the outdoors bar, cool and kid-looking, and I said, "What's the matter, Dad?" cause I thought maybe Regoli had bumped him or something and he just looked at Regoli and said, "Oh, to hell with it," and went on to the dressing room.

Well, it would have been all right, maybe, if we'd stayed in Milan and ridden at Milan and Torino, 'cause if there ever were any easy courses, it's those two. "Pianola, Joe," my old man said when he dismounted in the winning stall after what the wops thought was a hell of a steeplechase. I asked him once. "This course rides itself. It's the pace you're going at, that makes riding the jumps dangerous, Joe. We ain't going any pace here, and they ain't really bad jumps either. But it's the pace always—not the jumps—that makes the trouble."

San Siro was the swellest course I'd ever seen but the old man said it was a dog's life. Going back and forth between Mirafiore and San Siro and riding just about every day in the week with a train ride every other night.

I was nuts about the horses, too. There's something about it, when they come out and go up the track to the post. Sort of dancy and tight looking with the jock keeping a tight hold on them and maybe easing off a little and letting them run a little going up. Then once they were at the barrier it got me worse than anything. Especially at San Siro with that big green infield and the mountains way off and the fat wop starter with his big whip and the jocks fiddling them around and then the barrier snapping up and that bell going off and them all getting off in a bunch and then commencing to string out. You know the way a bunch of skins gets off. If you're up in the stand with a pair of glasses all you see is them plunging off and then that bell goes off and it seems like it rings for a thousand years and then they come sweeping round the turn. There wasn't ever anything like it for me.

But my old man said one day, in the dressing room, when he was getting into his street clothes, "None of these things are horses, Joe. They'd kill that bunch of skates for their hides and hoofs up at Paris." That was the day he'd won the Premio Commercio with Lantorna shooting her out of the field the last hundred meters like pulling a cork out of a bottle.

It was right after the Premio Commercio that we pulled out and left Italy. My old man and Holbrook and a fat wop in a straw hat that kept wiping his face with a handkerchief were having an argument at a table in the Galleria. They were all talking French and the two of them was after my old man about something. Finally he didn't say anything any more but just sat there and looked at Holbrook, and the two of them kept after him, first one talking and then the other, and the fat wop always butting in on Holbrook.

"You go out and buy me a *Sportsman*, will you, Joe?" my old man said, and handed me a couple of soldi without looking away from Holbrook.

So I went out of the Galleria and walked over to in front of the Scala and bought a paper, and came back and stood a little way away because I didn't want to butt in and my old man was sitting back in his chair looking down at his coffee and fooling with a spoon and Holbrook and the big wop were standing and the big wop was wiping his face and shaking his head. And I came up and my old man acted just as though the two of them weren't standing there and said, "Want an ice, Joe?" Holbrook looked down at my old man and said slow and careful, "You son of a bitch," and he and the fat wop went out through the tables.

My old man sat there and sort of smiled at me, but his face was white and he looked sick as hell and I was scared and felt sick inside because I knew something had happened and I didn't see how anybody could call my old man a son of a bitch, and get away with it. My old man opened up the *Sportsman* and studied the handicaps for a while and then he said, "You got to take a lot of things in this world, Joe." And three days later we left Milan for good on the Turin train for Paris, after an auction sale out in front of Turner's stables of everything we couldn't get into a trunk and a suit case.

We got into Paris early in the morning in a long, dirty station the old man told me was the Gare de Lyon. Paris was an awful big town after Milan. Seems like in Milan everybody is going somewhere and all the trams run somewhere and there ain't any sort of a mix-up, but Paris is all balled up and they never do straighten it out. I got to like it, though, part of it, anyway, and say, it's got the best race courses in the world. Seems as though that were the thing that keeps it all going and about the only thing you can figure on is that every day the buses will be going out to whatever track they're running at, going right out through everything to the track. I never really got to know Paris well, because I just came in about once or twice a week with the old man from Maisons and he always sat at the Café de la Paix on the Opera side with the rest of the gang from Maisons and I guess that's one of the busiest parts of the town. But, say, it is funny that a big town like Paris wouldn't have a Galleria, isn't it?

Well, we went out to live at Maisons-Lafitte, where just about everybody lives except the gang at Chantilly, with a Mrs. Meyers that runs a boarding house. Maisons is about the swellest place to live I've ever seen in all my life.

The town ain't so much, but there's a lake and a swell forest that we used to go off bumming in all day, a couple of us kids, and my old man made me a sling shot and we got a lot of things with it but the best one was a magpie. Young Dick Atkinson shot a rabbit with it one day and we put it under a tree and were all sitting around and Dick had some cigarettes and all of a sudden the rabbit jumped up and beat it into the brush and we chased it but couldn't find it. Gee, we had fun at Maisons. Mrs. Meyers used to give me lunch in the morning and I'd be gone all day. I learned to talk French quick. It's an easy language.

As soon as we got to Maisons, my old man wrote to Milan for his license and he was pretty worried till it came. He used to sit around the Café de Paris in Maisons with the gang, there were lots of guys he'd known when he rode up at Paris, before the war, lived at Maisons, and there's a lot of time to sit around because the work around a racing stable, for the jocks, that is, is all cleaned up by nine o'clock in the morning. They take the first bunch of skins out to gallop them at 5:30 in the morning and they work the second lot at 8 o'clock. That means getting up early all right and going to bed early, too. If a jock's riding for somebody too, he can't go boozing around because the trainer always has an eye on him if he's a kid and if he ain't a kid he's always got an eye on himself. So mostly if a jock ain't working he sits around the Café de Paris with the gang and they can all sit around about two or three hours in front of some drink like a vermouth and seltz and they talk and tell stories and shoot pool and it's sort of like a club or the Galleria in Milan. Only it ain't like the Galleria because there everybody is going by all the time and there's everybody around at the tables.

Well, my old man got his license all right. They sent it through to him without a word and he rode a couple of times. Amiens, up country and that sort of thing, but he didn't seem to get any engagement. Everybody liked him and whenever I'd come into the Café in the forenoon I'd find somebody drinking with him because my old man wasn't tight like most of these jockeys that have got the first dollar they made riding at the World's Fair in St. Louis in nineteen ought four. That's what my old man would say when he'd kid George Burns. But it seemed like everybody steered clear of giving my old man any mounts.

We went out to wherever they were running every day with the car from Maisons and that was the most fun of all. I was glad when the horses came back from Deauville and the summer. Even though it meant no more bumming in the woods, 'cause then we'd ride to Enghien or Tremblay or St. Cloud and watch them from the trainers' and jockeys' stand. I sure learned about racing from going out with that gang and the fun of it was going every day.

I remember once out at St. Cloud. It was a big two hundred thousand franc race with seven entries and Kzar a big favorite. I went around to the paddock to see the horses with my old man and you never saw such horses. This Kzar is a great big yellow horse that looks like just nothing but run. I never saw such a horse. He was being led around the paddocks with his head down and when he went by me I felt all hollow inside he was so beautiful. There never was such a wonderful, lean, running built horse. And he went around the paddock putting his feet just so and quiet and careful and moving easy like he knew just what he had to do and not jerking and standing up on his legs and getting wild eyed like you see these selling platers with a shot of dope in them. The crowd was so thick I couldn't see him again except just his legs going by and some yellow and my old man started out through the crowd and I followed him over to the jock's dressing room back in the trees and there was a big crowd around there, too, but the man at the door in a derby nodded to my old man and we got in and everybody was sitting around and getting dressed and pulling shirts over their heads and pulling boots on and it all smelled hot and sweaty and linimenty and outside was the crowd looking in.

The old man went over and sat down beside George Gardner that was getting into his pants and said, "What's the dope, George?" just in an ordinary tone of voice 'cause there ain't any use him feeling around because George either can tell him or he can't tell him.

"He won't win," George says very low, leaning over and buttoning the bottoms of his breeches.

"Who will?" my old man says, leaning over close so nobody can hear.

"Kircubbin," George says, "and if he does, save me a couple of tickets."

My old man says something in a regular voice to George and George says, "Don't ever bet on anything I tell you," kidding like, and we beat it out and through all the crowd that was looking in, over to the 100 franc mutuel machine. But I knew something big was up because George is Kzar's jockey. On the way he gets one of the yellow odds-sheets with the starting prices on and Kzar is only paying 5 for 10, Cefisidote is next at 3 to 1 and fifth down the list this Kircubbin at 8 to 1. My old man bets five thousand on Kircubbin to win and puts on a thousand to place and we went around back of the grandstand to go up the stairs and get a place to watch the race.

We were jammed in tight and first a man in a long coat with a gray tall hat and a whip folded up in his hand came out and then one after another the horses, with the jocks up and a stable boy holding the bridle on each side and walking along, followed the old guy. That big yellow horse Kzar came first. He didn't look so big when you first looked at him until you saw the length of his legs and the whole way he's built and the way he moves. Gosh, I never saw such a horse. George Gardner was riding him and they moved along slow, back of the old guy in the gray tall hat that walked along like he was a ring master in a circus. Back of Kzar, moving along smooth and yellow in the sun, was a good looking black with a nice head with Tommy Archibald riding him; and after the black was a string of five more horses all moving along slow in a procession past the grandstand and the pesage. My old man said the black was Kircubbin and I took a good look at him and he was a nice-looking horse, all right, but nothing like Kzar.

Everybody cheered Kzar when he went by and he sure was one swell-looking horse. The procession of them went around on the other side past the pelouse and then back up to the near end of the course and the circus master had the stable boys turn them loose one after another so they could gallop by the stands on their way up to the post and let everybody have a good look at them. They weren't at the post hardly any time at all when the gong started and you could see them way off across the infield all in a bunch starting on the first swing like a lot of little toy horses. I was watching them through the glasses and Kzar was running well back, with one of the bays making the pace. They swept down and around and came pounding past and Kzar was way back when they passed us and this Kircubbin horse in front and going smooth. Gee, it's awful when they go by you and then you have to watch them go farther away and get smaller and smaller and then all bunched up on the turns and then come around towards into the stretch and you feel like swearing and goddamming worse and worse. Finally they made the last turn and came into the straightaway with this Kircubbin horse way out in front. Everybody was looking funny and saying "Kzar" in sort of a sick way and them pounding nearer down the stretch, and then something came out of the pack right into my glasses like a horse-headed yellow streak and everybody began to yell "Kzar" as though they were crazy. Kzar came on faster than I'd ever seen anything in my life and pulled up on Kircubbin that was going fast as any black horse could go with the jock flogging hell out of him with the gad and they were right dead neck and neck for a second but Kzar seemed going about twice as fast with those great jumps and that head out—but it was while they were neck and neck that they passed the winning post and when the numbers went up in the slots the first one was 2 and that meant that Kircubbin had won.

I felt all trembly and funny inside, and then we were all jammed in with the people going downstairs to stand in front of the board where they'd post what Kircubbin paid. Honest, watching the race I'd forgot how much my old man had bet on Kircubbin. I'd wanted Kzar to win so damned bad. But now it was all over it was swell to know we had the winner.

"Wasn't it a swell race, Dad?" I said to him.

He looked at me sort of funny with his derby on the back of his head. "George Gardner's a swell jockey, all right," he said. "It sure took a great jock to keep that Kzar horse from winning."

Of course I knew it was funny all the time. But my old man saying that right out like that sure took the kick all out of it for me and I didn't get the real kick back again ever, even when they posted the numbers upon the board and the bell rang to pay off and we saw that Kircubbin paid 67.50 for 10. All round people were saying, "Poor Kzar! Poor Kzar!" And I thought, I wish I were a jockey and could have rode him instead of that son of a bitch. And that was funny, thinking of George Gardner as a son of a bitch because I'd always liked him and besides he'd given us the winner, but I guess that's what he is, all right.

My old man had a big lot of money after that race and he took to coming into Paris oftener. If they raced at Tremblay he'd have them drop him in town on their way back to Maisons and he and I'd sit out in front of the Café de la Paix and watch the people go by. It's funny sitting there. There's streams of people going by and all sorts of guys come up and want to sell you things, and I loved to sit there with my old man. That was when we'd have the most fun. Guys would come by selling funny rabbits that jumped if you squeezed a bulb and they'd come up to us and my old man would kid with them. He could talk French just like English and all those kind of guys knew him 'cause you can always tell a jockey—and then we always sat at the same table and they got used to seeing us there. There were guys selling matrimonial papers and girls selling rubber eggs that when you squeezed them a rooster came out of them and one old wormy-looking guy that went by with post-cards of Paris, showing them to everybody, and, of course, nobody ever bought any, and then he would come back and show the under side of the pack and they would all be smutty post-cards and lots of people would dig down and buy them.

Gee, I remember the funny people that used to go by. Girls around supper time looking for somebody to take them out to eat and they'd speak to my old man and he'd make some joke at them in French and they'd pat me on the head and go on. Once there was an American woman sitting with her kid daughter at the next table to us and they were both eating ices and I kept looking at the girl and she was awfully good looking and I smiled at her and she smiled at me but that was all that ever came of it because I looked for her mother and her every day and I made up ways that I was going to speak to her and I wondered if I got to know her if her mother would let me take her out to Auteuil or Tremblay but I never saw either of them again. Anyway, I guess it wouldn't have been any good, anyway, because looking back on it I remember the way I thought out would be best to speak to her was to say, "Pardon me, but perhaps I can give you a winner at Enghien today?" and, after all, maybe she would have thought I was a tout instead of really trying to give her a winner.

We'd sit at the Café de la Paix, my old man and me, and we had a big drag with the waiter because my old man drank whisky and it cost five francs, and that meant a good tip when the saucers were counted up. My old man was drinking more than I'd ever seen him, but he wasn't riding at all now and besides he said that whisky kept his weight down. But I noticed he was putting it on, all right, just the same. He'd busted away from his old gang out at Maisons and seemed to like just sitting around on the boulevard with me. But he was dropping money every day at the track. He'd feel sort of doleful after the last race, if he'd lost on the day, until we'd get to our table and he'd have his first whisky and then he'd be fine.

He'd be reading the *Paris-Sport* and he'd look over at me and say, "Where's your girl, Joe?" to kid me on account I had told him about the girl that day at the next table. And I'd get red, but I liked being kidded about her. It gave me a good feeling. "Keep your eye peeled for her, Joe," he'd say, "she'll be back."

He'd ask me questions about things and some of the things I'd say he'd laugh. And then he'd get started talking about things. About riding down in Egypt, or at St. Moritz on the ice before my mother died, and about during the war when they had regular races down in the south of France without any purses, or betting or crowd or anything just to keep the breed up. Regular races with the jocks riding hell out of the horses. Gee, I could listen to my old man talk by the hour, especially when he'd had a couple or so of drinks. He'd tell me about when he was a boy in Kentucky and going coon hunting, and the old days in the States before everything went on the bum there. And he'd say, "Joe, when we've got a decent stake, you're going back there to the States and go to school."

"What've I got to go back there to go to school for when everything's on the bum there?" I'd ask him.

"That's different," he'd say and get the waiter over and pay the pile of saucers and we'd get a taxi to the Gare St. Lazare and get on the train out to Maisons.

One day at Auteuil, after a selling steeplechase, my old man bought in the winner for 30,000 francs. He had to bid a little to get him but the stable let the horse go finally and my old man had his permit and his colors in a week. Gee, I felt proud when my old man was an owner. He fixed it up for stable space with Charles Drake and cut out coming in to Paris, and started his running and sweating out again, and him and I were the whole stable gang. Our horse's name was Gilford, he was Irish bred and a nice, sweet jumper. My old man figured that training him and riding him, himself, he was a good investment. I was proud of everything and I thought Gilford was as good a horse as Kzar. He was a good, solid jumper, a bay, with plenty of speed on the flat, if you asked him for it, and he was a nice-looking horse, too.

Gee, I was fond of him. The first time he started with my old man up, he finished third in a 2500 meter hurdle race and when my old man got off him, all sweating and happy in the place stall, and went in to weigh, I felt as proud of him as though it was the first race he'd ever placed in. You see, when a guy ain't been riding for a long time, you can't make yourself really believe that he has ever rode. The whole thing was different now, 'cause down in Milan, even big races never seemed to make any difference to my old man, if he won he wasn't ever excited or anything, and now it was so I couldn't hardly sleep the night before a race and I knew my old man was excited, too, even if he didn't show it. Riding for yourself makes an awful difference.

Second time Gilford and my old man started, was a rainy Sunday at Auteuil, in the Prix du Marat, a 4500 meter steeplechase. As soon as he'd gone out I beat it up in the stand with the new glasses my old man had bought for me to watch them. They started way over at the far end of the course and there was some trouble at the barrier. Something with goggle blinders on was making a great fuss and rearing around and busted the barrier once, but I could see my old man in our black jacket, with a white cross and a black cap, sitting up on Gilford, and patting him with his hand. Then they were off in a jump and out of sight behind the trees and the gong going for dear life and the pari-mutuel wickets rattling down. Gosh, I was so excited, I was afraid to look at them, but I fixed the glasses on the place where they would come out back of the trees and then out they came with the old black jacket going third and they all sailing over the jump like birds. Then they went out of sight again and then they came pounding out and down the hill and all going nice and sweet and easy and taking the fence smooth in a bunch, and moving away from us all solid. Looked as though you could walk across on their backs they were all so bunched and going so smooth. Then they bellied over the big double Bullfinch and something came down. I couldn't see who it was, but in a minute the horse was up and galloping free and the field, all bunched still, sweeping around the long left turn into the straightaway. They jumped the stone wall and came jammed down the stretch toward the big water-jump right in front of the stands. I saw them coming and hollered at my old man as he went by, and he was leading by about a length and riding way out, and light as a monkey, and they were racing for the water-jump. They took off over the big hedge of the water-jump in a pack and then there was a crash, and two horses pulled sideways out off it, and kept on going, and three others were piled up. I couldn't see my old man anywhere. One horse kneed himself up and the jock had hold of the bridle and mounted and went slamming on after the place money. The other horse was up and away by himself, jerking his head and galloping with the bridle rein hanging and the jock staggered over to one side of the track against the fence. Then Gilford rolled over to one side off my old man and got up and started to run on three legs with his front off hoof dangling and there was my old man laying there on the grass flat out with his face up and blood all over the side of his head. I ran down the stand and bumped into a jam of people and got to the rail and a cop grabbed me and held me and two big stretcher-bearers were going out after my old man and around on the other side of the course I saw three horses, strung way out, coming out of the trees and taking the jump.

My old man was dead when they brought him in and while a doctor was listening to his heart with a thing plugged in his ears, I heard a shot up the track that meant they'd killed Gilford. I lay down beside my old man, when they carried the stretcher into the hospital room, and hung onto the stretcher and cried and cried, and he looked so white and gone and so awfully dead, and I couldn't help feeling that if my old man was dead maybe they didn't need to have shot Gilford. His hoof might have got well. I don't know. I loved my old man so much.

Then a couple of guys came in and one of them patted me on the back and then went over and looked at my old man and then pulled a sheet off the cot and spread it over him; and the other was telephoning in French for them to send the ambulance to take him out to Maisons. And I couldn't stop crying, crying and choking, sort of, and George Gardner came in and sat down beside me on the floor and put his arm around me and says, "Come on, Joe, old boy. Get up and we'll go out and wait for the ambulance."

George and I went out to the gate and I was trying to stop bawling and George wiped off my face with his handkerchief and we were standing back a little ways while the crowd was going out of the gate and a couple of guys stopped near us while we were waiting for the crowd to get through the gate and one of them was counting a bunch of mutuel tickets and he said, "Well, Butler got his, all right."

The other guy said, "I don't give a good goddam if he did, the crook. He had it coming to him on the stuff he's pulled."

"I'll say he had," said the other guy, and tore the bunch of tickets in two.

And George Gardner looked at me to see if I'd heard and I had all right and he said, "Don't you listen to what those bums said, Joe. Your old man was one swell guy."

But I don't know. Seems like when they get started they don't leave a guy nothing.

Considerations

1. In the sport of horseracing, so much attention is placed on the horses that the jockeys are often not given their due as athletes. Cite examples from this story that show horseracing to be a highly vigorous sport.
2. Hemingway avoided stating the obvious, a talent he cultivated, he said, by studying the Impressionists' paintings in the Louvre. Look up a definition of Impressionism and explain how this story may have been influenced by this movement.

3. By his choice of narrator, how is Hemingway able to tell much of the story by implication? Cite examples.
4. Why does Butler, the boy's father, stand and stare at Regoli, the young jockey, in the bar after the race? Is it a symptom of the aging-athlete syndrome? If so, what are some of the other symptoms he displays? Do you know of any real-life athletes who may be undergoing such a "mid-life crisis"?
5. What is the subject of the argument between Butler, Holbrook and the "fat wop in a straw hat"? Does it have any connection with the Premio Commercio and their leaving Milan in a rush? Does the narrator know the answers?
6. In Paris, why does Butler worry until his license arrives?
7. Try to explain the psychological reasons for Butler buying the racehorse. Why was such a venture doomed from the start? Do athletes past their prime make themselves look foolish trying to make "comebacks"? Why do they do it?
8. What is meant by the spectator's statement after Butler's death: "He had it coming to him on the stuff he's pulled"?
9. What are the implications of the boy's last statement?

IRWIN SHAW

The Eighty-Yard Run

The pass was high and wide and he jumped for it, feeling it slap flatly against his hands, as he shook his hips to throw off the halfback who was diving at him. The center floated by, his hands desperately brushing Darling's knee as Darling picked his feet up high and delicately ran over a blocker and an opposing linesman in a jumble on the ground near the scrimmage line. He had ten yards in the clear and picked up speed, breathing easily, feeling his thigh pads rising and falling against his legs, listening to the sound of cleats behind him, pulling away from them, watching the other backs heading him off toward the sideline, the whole picture, the men closing in on him, the blockers fighting for position, the ground he had to cross, all suddenly clear in his head, for the first time in his life not a meaningless confusion of men, sounds, speed. He smiled a little to himself as he ran, holding the ball lightly in front of him with his two hands, his knees pumping high, his hips twisting in the almost girlish run of a back in a broken field. The first halfback came at him and he fed him his leg, then swung at the last moment, took the shock of the man's shoulder without breaking stride, ran right through him, his cleats biting securely into the turf. There was only the safety man now, coming warily at him, his arms crooked, hands spread. Darling tucked the ball in, spurted at him, driving hard, hurling himself along, all two hundred pounds bunched into controlled attack. He was sure he was going to get past the safety man. Without thought, his arms and legs working beautifully together, he headed right for the safety man, stiff-armed him, feeling blood spurt instantaneously from the man's nose onto his hand, seeing his face go awry, head turned, mouth pulled to one side. He pivoted away, keeping the arm locked, dropping the safety man as he ran easily toward the goal line, with the drumming of cleats diminishing behind him.

How long ago? It was autumn then, and the ground was getting hard because the nights were cold and leaves from the maples around the stadium blew across the practice fields in gusts of wind, and the girls were beginning to put polo coats over their sweaters when they came to watch practice in the afternoon. . . . Fifteen years. Darling walked slowly over the same ground in the spring twilight, in his neat shoes, a man of thirty-five dressed in a double-breasted suit, ten pounds heavier in the fifteen years, but not fat, with the years between 1925 and 1940 showing in his face.

The coach was smiling quietly to himself and the assistant coaches were looking at each other with pleasure the way they always did when one of the second stringers suddenly did something fine, bringing credit to them, making their $2,000 a year a tiny bit more secure.

Darling trotted back, smiling, breathing deeply but easily, feeling wonderful, not tired, though this was the tail end of practice and he'd run eighty yards. The sweat poured off his face and soaked his jersey and he liked the feeling, the warm moistness lubricating his skin like oil. Off in a corner of the field some players were punting and the smack of leather against the ball came pleasantly through the afternoon air. The freshmen were running signals on the next field and the quarterback's sharp voice, the pound of the eleven pairs of cleats, the "Dig, now *dig!*" of the coaches, the laughter of the players all somehow made him feel happy as he trotted back to midfield, listening to the applause and shouts of the students along the sidelines, knowing that after that run the coach would have to start him Saturday against Illinois.

Fifteen years, Darling thought, remembering the shower after the workout, the hot water steaming off his skin and the deep soapsuds and all the young voices singing with the water streaming down and towels going and managers running in and out and the sharp sweet smell of oil of wintergreen and everybody clapping him on the back as he dressed and Packard, the captain, who took being captain very seriously, coming over to him and shaking his hand and saying, "Darling, you're going to go places in the next two years."

The assistant manager fussed over him, wiping a cut on his leg with alcohol and iodine, the little sting making him realize suddenly how fresh and whole and solid his body felt. The manager slapped a piece of adhesive tape over the cut, and Darling noticed the sharp clean white of the tape against the ruddiness of the skin, fresh from the shower.

He dressed slowly, the softness of his shirt and the soft warmth of his wool socks and his flannel trousers a reward against his skin after the harsh pressure of the shoulder harness and thigh and hip pads. He drank three glasses of cold water, the liquid reaching down coldly inside of him, soothing the harsh dry places in his throat and belly left by the sweat and running and shouting of practice.

Fifteen years.

The sun had gone down and the sky was green behind the stadium and he laughed quietly to himself as he looked at the stadium, rearing above the trees, and knew that on Saturday when the 70,000 voices roared as the team came running out onto the field, part of that enormous salute would be for him. He walked slowly, listening to the gravel crunch satisfactorily under his shoes in the still twilight, feeling his clothes swing lightly against his skin, breathing the thin evening air, feeling the wind more softly in his damp hair, wonderfully cool behind his ears and at the nape of his neck.

Louise was waiting for him at the road, in her car. The top was down and he noticed all over again, as he always did when he saw her, how pretty she was, the rough blonde hair and the large, inquiring eyes and the bright mouth, smiling now.

She threw the door open. "Were you good today?" she asked.

"Pretty good," he said. He climbed in, sank luxuriously into the soft leather, stretched his legs far out. He smiled, thinking of the eighty yards. "Pretty damn good."

She looked at him seriously for a moment, then scrambled around, like a little girl, kneeling on the seat next to him, grabbed him, her hands along his ears, and kissed him as he sprawled, head back, on the seat cushion. She let go of him, but kept her head close to his, over his. Darling reached up slowly and rubbed the back of his hand against her cheek, lit softly by a street lamp a hundred feet away. They looked at each other, smiling.

Louise drove down to the lake and they sat there silently, watching the moon rise behind the hills on the other side. Finally he reached over, pulled her gently to him, kissed her. Her lips grew soft, her body sank into his, tears formed slowly in her eyes. He knew, for the first time, that he could do whatever he wanted with her.

"Tonight," he said. "I'll call for you at seven-thirty. Can you get out?"

She looked at him. She was smiling, but the tears were still full in her eyes. "All right," she said. "I'll get out. How about you? Won't the coach raise hell?"

Darling grinned. "I got the coach in the palm of my hand," he said. "Can you wait till seven-thirty?"

She grinned back at him. "No," she said.

They kissed and she started the car and they went back to town for dinner. He sang on the way home.

Christian Darling, thirty-five years old, sat on the frail spring grass, greener now than it ever would be again on the practice field, looked thoughtfully up at the stadium, a deserted ruin in the twilight. He had started on the first team that Saturday and every Saturday after that for the next two years, but it had never been as satisfactory as it should have been. He never had broken away, the longest run he'd ever made was thirty-five yards, and that in a game that was already won, and then that kid had come up from the third team, Diederich, a blank-faced German kid from Wisconsin, who ran like a bull, ripping lines to pieces Saturday after Saturday, plowing through, never getting hurt, never changing his expression, scoring more points, gaining more ground than all the rest of the team put together, making everybody's All-American, carrying the ball three times out of four, keeping everybody else out of the headlines. Darling was a good blocker and he spent his Saturday afternoons working on the big Swedes and Polacks who played tackle and end for Michigan, Illinois, Purdue, hurling into huge pile-ups, bobbing his head wildly to elude the great raw hands swinging like meat-cleavers at him as he went charging in to open up holes for Diederich coming through like a locomotive behind him. Still, it wasn't so bad. Everybody liked him and he did his job and he was pointed out on the campus and boys always felt important when they introduced their girls to him at their proms, and Louise loved him and watched him faithfully in the games, even in the mud, when your own mother wouldn't know you, and drove him around in her car keeping the top down because she was proud of him and wanted to show everybody that she was Christian Darling's girl. She bought him crazy presents because her father was rich, watches, pipes, humidors, an icebox for beer for his room, curtains, wallets, a fifty-dollar dictionary.

"You'll spend every cent your old man owns," Darling protested once when she showed up at his rooms with seven different packages in her arms and tossed them onto the couch.

"Kiss me," Louise said, "and shut up."

"Do you want to break your poor old man?"

"I don't mind. I want to buy you presents."

"Why?"

"It makes me feel good. Kiss me. I don't know why. Did you know that you're an important figure?"

"Yes," Darling said gravely.

"When I was waiting for you at the library yesterday two girls saw you coming and one of them said to the other, 'That's Christian Darling. He's an important figure.'"

"You're a liar."

"I'm in love with an important figure."

"Still, why the hell did you have to give me a forty-pound dictionary?"

"I wanted to make sure," Louise said, "that you had a token of my esteem. I want to smother you in tokens of my esteem."

Fifteen years ago.

They'd married when they got out of college. There'd been other women for him, but all casual and secret, more for curiosity's sake, and vanity, women who'd thrown themselves at him and flattered him, a pretty mother at a summer camp for boys, and old girl from his home town who'd suddenly blossomed into a coquette, a friend of Louise's who had dogged him grimly for six months and had taken advantage of the two weeks that Louise went home when her mother died. Perhaps Louise had known, but she'd kept quiet, loving him completely, filling his rooms with presents, religiously watching him battling with the big Swedes and Polacks on the line of scrimmage on Saturday afternoons, making plans for marrying him and living with him in New York and going with him there to the night clubs, the theaters, the good restaurants, being proud of him in advance, tall, white-teethed, smiling, large, yet moving lightly, with an athlete's grace, dressed in evening clothes, approvingly eyed by magnificently dressed and famous women in theater lobbies, with Louise adoringly at his side.

Her father, who manufactured inks, set up a New York office for Darling to manage and presented him with three hundred accounts, and they lived on Beekman Place with a view of the river with fifteen thousand dollars a year

between them, because everybody was buying everything in those days, including ink. They saw all the shows and went to all the speakeasies and spent their
fifteen thousand dollars a year and in the afternoons Louise went to the art galleries and the matinees of the more serious plays that Darling didn't like to sit
through and Darling slept with a girl who danced in the chorus of *Rosalie* and
with the wife of a man who owned three copper mines. Darling played squash
three times a week and remained as solid as a stone barn and Louise never took
her eyes off him when they were in the same room together, watching him with
a secret, miser's smile, with a trick of coming over to him in the middle of a
crowded room and saying gravely, in a low voice, "You're the handsomest man
I've ever seen in my whole life. Want a drink?"

Nineteen twenty-nine came to Darling and to his wife and father-in-law, the
maker of inks, just as it came to everyone else. The father-in-law waited until
1933 and then blew his brains out and when Darling went to Chicago to see what
the books of the firm looked like he found out all that was left were debts and
three or four gallons of unbought ink.

"Please, Christian," Louise said, sitting in their neat Beekman Place apartment, with a view of the river and prints of paintings by Dufy and Braque and
Picasso on the wall, "please, why do you want to start drinking at two o'clock in
the afternoon?"

"I have nothing else to do," Darling said, putting down his glass, emptied of
its fourth drink. "Please pass the whisky."

Louise filled his glass. "Come take a walk with me," she said. "We'll walk
along the river."

"I don't want to walk along the river," Darling said, squinting intensely at the
prints of paintings by Dufy, Braque and Picasso.

"We'll walk along Fifth Avenue."

"I don't want to walk along Fifth Avenue."

"Maybe," Louise said gently, "you'd like to come with me to some art galleries.
There's an exhibition by a man named Klee. . . ."

"I don't want to go to any art galleries. I want to sit here and drink Scotch
whisky," Darling said. "Who the hell hung these goddam pictures up on the
wall?"

"I did," Louise said.

"I hate them."

"I'll take them down," Louise said.

"Leave them there. It gives me something to do in the afternoon. I can hate
them." Darling took a long swallow. "Is that the way people paint these days?"

"Yes, Christian. Please don't drink any more."

"Do you like painting like that?"

"Yes, dear."

"Really?"

"Really."

Darling looked carefully at the prints once more. "Little Louise Tucker. The
middle-western beauty. I like pictures with horses in them. Why should you
like pictures like that?"

"I just happen to have gone to a lot of galleries in the last few years . . ."

"Is that what you do in the afternoon?"

"That's what I do in the afternoon," Louise said.

"I drink in the afternoon."

Louise kissed him lightly on the top of his head as he sat there squinting at the pictures on the wall, the glass of whisky held firmly in his hand. She put on her coat and went out without saying another word. When she came back in the early evening, she had a job on a woman's fashion magazine.

They moved downtown and Louise went out to work every morning and Darling sat home and drank and Louise paid the bills as they came up. She made believe she was going to quit work as soon as Darling found a job, even though she was taking over more responsibility day by day at the magazine, interviewing authors, picking painters for the illustrations and covers, getting actresses to pose for pictures, going out for drinks with the right people, making a thousand new friends whom she loyally introduced to Darling.

"I don't like your hat," Darling said, once, when she came in in the evening and kissed him, her breath rich with Martinis.

"What's the matter with my hat, Baby?" she asked, running her fingers through his hair. "Everybody says it's very smart."

"It's too damned smart," he said. "It's not for you. It's for a rich, sophisticated woman of thirty-five with admirers."

Louise laughed. "I'm practicing to be a rich, sophisticated woman of thirty-five with admirers," she said. He stared soberly at her. "Now, don't look so grim, Baby. It's still the same simple little wife under the hat." She took the hat off, threw it into a corner, sat on his lap. "See? Homebody Number One."

"Your breath could run a train," Darling said, not wanting to be mean, but talking out of boredom, and sudden shock at seeing his wife curiously a stranger in a new hat, with a new expression in her eyes under the little brim, secret, confident, knowing.

Louise tucked her head under his chin so he couldn't smell her breath. "I had to take an author out for cocktails," she said. "He's a boy from the Ozark Mountains and he drinks like a fish. He's a Communist."

"What the hell is a Communist from the Ozarks doing writing for a woman's fashion magazine?"

Louise chuckled. "The magazine business is getting all mixed up these days. The publishers want to have a foot in every camp. And anyway, you can't find an author under seventy these days who isn't a Communist."

"I don't think I like you to associate with all those people, Louise," Darling said. "Drinking with them."

"He's a very nice, gentle boy," Louise said. "He reads Ernest Dowson."

"Who's Ernest Dowson?"

Louise patted his arm, stood up, fixed her hair. "He's an English poet."

Darling felt that somehow he had disappointed her. "Am I supposed to know who Ernest Dowson is?"

"No, dear. I'd better go in and take a bath."

After she had gone, Darling went over to the corner where the hat was lying and picked it up. It was nothing, a scrap of straw, a red flower, a veil, meaningless on his big hand, but on his wife's head a signal of something . . . big city,

smart and knowing women drinking and dining with men other than their husbands, conversation about things a normal man wouldn't know much about,
Frenchmen who painted as though they used their elbows instead of brushes,
composers who wrote whole symphonies without a single melody in them,
writers who knew all about politics and women who knew all about writers, the
movement of the proletariat, Marx, somehow mixed up with five-dollar dinners
and the best looking women in America and fairies who made them laugh and
half-sentences immediately understood and secretly hilarious and wives who
called their husbands "Baby." He put the hat down, a scrap of straw and a red
flower, and a little veil. He drank some whisky straight and went into the bath-
room where his wife was lying deep in her bath, singing to herself and smiling
from time to time like a little girl, paddling the water gently with her hands,
sending up a slight spicy fragrance from the bath salts she used.

He stood over her, looking down at her. She smiled up at him, her eyes half
closed, her body pink and shimmering in the warm, scented water. All over
again, with all the old suddenness, he was hit deep inside him with the knowledge of how beautiful she was, how much he needed her.

"I came in here," he said, "to tell you I wish you wouldn't call me 'Baby.'"

She looked up at him from the bath, her eyes quickly full of sorrow, half-
understanding what he meant. He knelt and put his arms around her, his sleeves
plunged heedlessly in the water, his shirt and jacket soaking wet as he clutched
her wordlessly, holding her crazily tight, crushing her breath from her, kissing
her desperately, searchingly, regretfully.

He got jobs after that, selling real estate and automobiles, but somehow, although he had a desk with his name on a wooden wedge on it, and he went to
the office religiously at nine each morning, he never managed to sell anything
and he never made any money.

Louise was made assistant editor, and the house was always full of strange
men and women who talked fast and got angry on abstract subjects like mural
painting, novelists, labor unions. Negro short-story writers drank Louise's liquor,
and a lot of Jews, and big solemn men with scarred faces and knotted hands
who talked slowly but clearly about picket lines and battles with guns and
leadpipe at mine-shaft-heads and in front of factory gates. And Louise moved
among them all, confidently, knowing what they were talking about, with opinions that they listened to and argued about just as though she were a man. She
knew everybody, condescended to no one, devoured books that Darling had
never heard of, walked along the streets of the city, excited, at home, soaking in
all the million tides of New York without fear, with constant wonder.

Her friends liked Darling and sometimes he found a man who wanted to get
off in the corner and talk about the new boy who played fullback for Princeton,
and the decline of the double wing-back, or even the state of the stock market,
but for the most part he sat on the edge of things, solid and quiet in the high
storm of words. "The dialectics of the situation . . . The theater has been given
over to expert jugglers . . . Picasso? What man has a right to paint old bones and
collect ten thousand dollars for them? . . . I stand firmly behind Trotsky . . . Poe
was the last American critic. When he died they put lilies on the grave of American criticism. I don't say this because they panned my last book, but . . ."

Once in a while he caught Louise looking soberly and consideringly at him through the cigarette smoke and the noise and he avoided her eyes and found an excuse to get up and go into the kitchen for more ice or to open another bottle.

"Come on," Cathal Flaherty was saying, standing at the door with a girl, "you've got to come down and see this. It's down on Fourteenth Street, in the old Civic Repertory, and you can only see it on Sunday nights and I guarantee you'll come out of the theater singing." Flaherty was a big young Irishman with a broken nose who was the lawyer for a longshoreman's union, and he had been hanging around the house for six months on and off, roaring and shutting everybody else up when he got in an argument. "It's a new play, *Waiting for Lefty;* it's about taxi-drivers."

"Odets," the girl with Flaherty said. "It's by a guy named Odets."

"I never heard of him," Darling said.

"He's a new one," the girl said.

"It's like watching a bombardment," Flaherty said. "I saw it last Sunday night. You've got to see it."

"Come on, Baby," Louise said to Darling, excitement in her eyes already. "We've been sitting in the Sunday *Times* all day, this'll be a great change."

"I see enough taxi-drivers every day," Darling said, not because he meant that, but because he didn't like to be around Flaherty, who said things that made Louise laugh a lot and whose judgment she accepted on almost every subject. "Let's go to the movies."

"You've never seen anything like this before," Flaherty said. "He wrote this play with a baseball bat."

"Come on," Louise coaxed, "I bet it's wonderful."

"He has long hair," the girl with Flaherty said. "Odets. I met him at a party. He's an actor. He didn't say a goddam thing all night."

"I don't feel like going down to Fourteenth Street," Darling said, wishing Flaherty and his girl would get out. "It's gloomy."

"Oh, hell!" Louise said loudly. She looked coolly at Darling, as though she'd just been introduced to him and was making up her mind about him, and not very favorably. He saw her looking at him, knowing there was something new and dangerous in her face and he wanted to say something, but Flaherty was there and his damned girl, and anyway, he didn't know what to say.

"I'm going," Louise said, getting her coat. "I don't think Fourteenth Street is gloomy."

"I'm telling you," Flaherty was saying, helping her on with her coat, "it's the Battle of Gettysburg, in Brooklynese."

"Nobody could get a word out of him," Flaherty's girl was saying as they went through the door. "He just sat there all night."

The door closed. Louise hadn't said good night to him. Darling walked around the room four times, then sprawled out on the sofa, on top of the Sunday *Times.* He lay there for five minutes looking at the ceiling, thinking of Flaherty walking down the street talking in that booming voice, between the girls, holding their arms.

Louise had looked wonderful. She'd washed her hair in the afternoon and it had been very soft and light and clung close to her head as she stood there angrily putting her coat on. Louise was getting prettier every year, partly because she knew by now how pretty she was, and made the most of it.

"Nuts," Darling said, standing up. "Oh, nuts."

He put on his coat and went down to the nearest bar and had five drinks off by himself in a corner before his money ran out.

The years since then had been foggy and downhill. Louise had been nice to him, and in a way, loving and kind, and they'd fought only once, when he said he was going to vote for Landon. ("Oh, Christ," she'd said, "doesn't *anything* happen inside your head? Don't you read the papers? The penniless Republican!") She'd been sorry later and apologized for hurting him, but apologized as she might to a child. He'd tried hard, had gone grimly to the art galleries, the concert halls, the bookshops, trying to gain on the trail of his wife, but it was no use. He was bored, and none of what he saw or heard or dutifully read made much sense to him and finally he gave it up. He had thought, many nights as he ate dinner alone, knowing that Louise would come home late and drop silently into bed without explanation, of getting a divorce, but he knew the loneliness, the hopelessness, of not seeing her again would be too much to take. So he was good, completely devoted, ready at all times to go any place with her, do anything she wanted. He even got a small job, in a broker's office and paid his own way, bought his own liquor.

Then he'd been offered the job of going from college to college as a tailor's representative. "We want a man," Mr. Rosenberg had said, "who as soon as you look at him, you say, 'There's a university man.'" Rosenberg had looked approvingly at Darling's broad shoulders and well-kept waist, at his carefully brushed hair and his honest, wrinkleless face. "Frankly, Mr. Darling, I am willing to make you a proposition. I have inquired about you, you are favorably known on your old campus. I understand you were in the backfield with Alfred Diederich."

Darling nodded. "Whatever happened to him?"

"He is walking around in a cast for seven years now. An iron brace. He played professional football and they broke his neck for him."

Darling smiled. That, at least, had turned out well.

"Our suits are an easy product to sell, Mr. Darling," Rosenberg said. "We have a handsome, custom-made garment. What has Brooks Brothers got that we haven't got? A name. No more."

"I can make fifty-sixty dollars a week," Darling said to Louise that night. "And expenses. I can save some money and then come back to New York and really get started here."

"Yes, Baby," Louise said.

"As it is," Darling said carefully, "I can make it back here once a month, and holidays and the summer. We can see each other often."

"Yes, Baby." He looked at her face, lovelier now at thirty-five than it had ever been before, but fogged over now as it had been for five years with a kind of patient, kindly, remote boredom.

"What do you say?" he asked. "Should I take it?" Deep within him he hoped fiercely, longingly, for her to say, "No, Baby, you stay right here," but she said, as he knew she'd say, "I think you'd better take it."

He nodded. He had to get up and stand with his back to her, looking out the window, because there were things plain on his face that she had never seen in the fifteen years she'd known him. "Fifty dollars is a lot of money," he said. "I never thought I'd ever see fifty dollars again." He laughed. Louise laughed, too.

Christian Darling sat on the frail green grass of the practice field. The shadow of the stadium had reached out and covered him. In the distance the lights of the university shone a little mistily in the light haze of evening. Fifteen years. Flaherty even now was calling for his wife, buying her a drink, filling whatever bar they were in with that voice of his and that easy laugh. Darling half-closed his eyes, almost saw the boy fifteen years ago reach for the pass, slip the half-back, go skittering lightly down the field, his knees high and fast and graceful, smiling to himself because he knew he was going to get past the safety man. That was the high point, Darling thought, fifteen years ago, on an autumn afternoon, twenty years old and far from death, with the air coming easily into his lungs, and a deep feeling inside him that he could do anything, knock over anybody, outrun whatever had to be outrun. And the shower after and the three glasses of water and the cool night air on his damp head and Louise sitting hatless in the open car with a smile and the first kiss she ever really meant. The high point, an eighty-yard run in the practice, and a girl's kiss and everything after that a decline. Darling laughed. He had practiced the wrong thing, perhaps. He hadn't practiced for 1929 and New York City and a girl who would turn into a woman. Somewhere, he thought, there must have been a point where she moved up to me, was even with me for a moment, when I could have held her hand, if I'd known, held tight, gone with her. Well, he'd never known. Here he was on a playing field that was fifteen years away and his wife was in another city having dinner with another and better man, speaking with him a different, new language, a language nobody had ever taught him.

Darling stood up, smiled a little, because if he didn't smile he knew the tears would come. He looked around him. This was the spot. O'Connor's pass had come sliding out just to here . . . the high point. Darling put up his hands, felt all over again the flat slap of the ball. He shook his hips to throw off the halfback, cut back inside the center, picked his knees high as he ran gracefully over two men jumbled on the ground at the line of scrimmage, ran easily, gaining speed, for ten yards, holding the ball lightly in his two hands, swung away from the halfback diving at him, ran, swinging his hips in the almost girlish manner of a back in a broken field, tore into the safety man, his shoes drumming heavily on the turf, stiff-armed, elbow locked, pivoted, raced lightly and exultantly for the goal line.

It was only after he had sped over the goal line and slowed to a trot that he saw the boy and girl sitting together on the turf, looking at him wonderingly.

He stopped short, dropping his arms. "I . . ." he said, gasping a little, though his condition was fine and the run hadn't winded him. "I—once I played here."

The boy and the girl said nothing. Darling laughed embarrassedly, looked

hard at them sitting there, close to each other, shrugged, turned and went toward his hotel, the sweat breaking out on his face and running down into his
collar.

Considerations

1. The uselessness of the former star athlete is the theme of many American stories.
   How is Christian Darling's situation perhaps an even sadder one?
2. Discuss the characterization of Darling, considering the following passage in your
   discussion: "The high point, an eighty-yard run in the practice, and a girl's kiss
   and everything after that a decline."
3. How is it ironical that the high point occurred in *practice?*
4. Discuss the significance of his name. Why does he object to being called "Baby"
   by Louise? How do "pet names" characterize people? Do they imply dominance
   in the person applying the name?
5. List examples of Darling's emotional immaturity. Do athletes, especially star
   athletes, generally experience difficulty in maturing normally? If so, why?
6. Does Christian Darling seem educated enough to hold a college degree? Is Shaw
   implying that there is a lack of emphasis on learning in college, especially for
   athletes?
7. Discuss the shift of dominance in his marriage with Louise. Consider the following
   quotation in your discussion: "He had practiced the wrong thing, perhaps. He
   hadn't practiced for 1929 and New York City and a girl who would turn into a
   woman." Exactly why do athletes, especially star athletes, have difficulty adjusting
   to the real world after their athletic careers are over?
8. Why doesn't he like Louise's hat? What does it symbolize?
9. Is the event of Darling's recreation of his run a happy, or sad, one? Critics have
   discussed this event in terms of Darling's atempt to be "reborn." Can you explain
   why such may be the case? What does "rebirth" symbolize?
10. What is Shaw's attitude toward Darling? Louise? What about Flaherty? Do you
    attach any significance to the fact that he doesn't even bother to give a name to
    Flaherty's "girl"?
11. Discuss the structure of the story, especially Shaw's handling of time. Are the
    flashbacks effective? Support your answer.
12. If the story were told from the first-person point of view, which character's view-
    point would be most appropriate. Point out the disadvantages of such a choice.
13. What usually becomes of former athletes today? What about the majority who are
    not particularly articulate?

MYTH AND FANTASY
Lovable Bums and
Sports Kooks

"Right this way, folks!" he yells. "Come on in and see the greatest collection of freaks in the world! See the armless pitchers, see the eyeless batters, see the infielders with five thumbs!"

—James Thurber

JAMES THURBER

You Could Look It Up

It all begun when we dropped down to C'lumbus, Ohio, from Pittsburgh to play a exhibition game on our way out to St. Louis. It was gettin' on into September, and though we'd been leadin' the league by six, seven games most of the season, we was now in first place by a margin you could 'a' got it into the eye of a thimble, bein' only a half a game ahead of St. Louis. Our slump had given the boys the leapin' jumps, and they was like a bunch a old ladies at a lawn fete with a thunderstorm comin' up, runnin' around snarlin' at each other, eatin' bad and sleepin' worse, and battin' for a team average of maybe .186. Half the time nobody'd speak to nobody else, without it was to bawl 'em out.

Squawks Magrew was managin' the boys at the time, and he was darn near crazy. They called him "Squawks" 'cause when things was goin' bad he lost his voice, or perty near lost it, and squealed at you like a little girl you stepped on her doll or somethin'. He yelled at everybody and wouldn't listen to nobody, without maybe it was me. I'd been trainin' the boys for ten year, and he'd take more lip from me than from anybody else. He knowed I was smarter'n him, anyways, like you're goin' to hear.

This was thirty, thirty-one year ago; you could look it up, 'cause it was the same year C'lumbus decided to call itself the Arch City, on account of a lot of iron arches with electric-light bulbs into 'em which stretched acrost High Street.

Thomas Albert Edison sent 'em a telegram, and they was speeches and maybe even President Taft opened the celebration by pushin' a button. It was a great week for the Buckeye capital, which was why they got us out there for this exhibition game.

Well, we just lose a double-header to Pittsburgh, 11 to 5 and 7 to 3, so we snarled all the way to C'lumbus. where we put up at the Chittaden Hotel, still snarlin'. Everybody was tetchy, and when Billy Klinger took a sock at Whitey Cott at breakfast, Whitey throwed marmalade all over his face.

"Blind each other, whatta I care?" says Magrew. "You can't see nothin' anyways."

C'lumbus win the exhibition game, 3 to 2, whilst Magrew set in the dugout, mutterin' and cursin' like a fourteen-year-old Scotty. He bad-mouthed every-body on the ball club and he bad-mouthed everybody offa the ball club, includin' the Wright brothers, who, he claimed, had yet to build a airship big enough for any of our boys to hit with a ball bat.

"I wisht I was dead," he says to me. "I wisht I was in heaven with the angels."

I told him to pull hisself together, 'cause he was drivin' the boys crazy, the way he was goin' on, sulkin' and bad-mouthin' and whinin'. I was older'n he was and smarter'n he was, and he knowed it. I was ten times smarter'n he was about this Pearl du Monville, first time I ever laid eyes on the little guy, which was one of the saddest days of my ife.

Now, most people name of Pearl is girls, but this Pearl du Monville was a man, if you could call a fella a man who was only thirty-four, thirty-fives inches high. Pearl du Monville was a midget. He was part French and part Hungarian, and maybe even part Bulgarian or somethin'. I can see him now, a sneer on his little pushed-in pan, swingin' a bamboo cane and smokin' a big cigar. He had a gray suit with a big black check into it, and he had a gray felt hat with one of them rainbow-colored hatbands onto it, like the young fellas wore in them days. He talked like he was talkin' into a tin can, but he didn't have no foreign accent. He might a been fifteen or he might a been a hundred, you couldn't tell. Pearl du Monville.

After the game with C'lumbus, Magrew headed straight for the Chittaden bar—the train for St. Louis wasn't goin' for three, four hours—and there he set, drinkin' rye and talkin' to this bartender.

"How I pity me, brother," Magrew was tellin' this bartender. "How I pity me." That was alwuz his favorite tune. So he was settin' there, tellin' this bar-tender how heartbreakin' it was to be manager of a bunch of blindfolded circus clowns, when up pops this Pearl du Monville outa nowheres.

It give Magrew the leapin' jumps. He thought at first maybe the D.T.'s had come back on him; he claimed he'd had 'em once, and little guys had popped up all around him, wearin' red, white and blue hats.

"Go on, now!" Magrew yells. "Get away from me!"

But the midget clumb up on a chair acrost the table from Magrew and says, "I seen that game today, Junior, and you ain't got no ball club. What you got there, Junior," he says, "is a side show."

"Whatta ya mean, 'Junior'?" says Magrew, touchin' the little guy to satisfy hisself he was real.

"Don't pay him no attention, mister," says the bartender. "Pearl calls everybody 'Junior,' 'cause it alwuz turns out he's a year older'n anybody else."

"Yeh?" says Magrew. "How old is he?"

"How old are you, Junior?" says the midget.

"Who, me? I'm fifty-three," says Magrew.

"Well, I'm fifty-four," says the midget.

Magrew grins and asts him what he'll have, and that was the beginnin' of their beautiful friendship, if you don't care what you say.

Pearl du Monville stood up on his chair and waved his cane around and pretended like he was ballyhooin' for a circus. "Right this way, folks!" he yells. "Come on in and see the greatest collection of freaks in the world! See the armless pitchers, see the eyeless batters, see the infielders with five thumbs!" and on and on like that, feedin' Magrew gall and handin' him a laugh at the same time, you might say.

You could hear him and Pearl du Monville hootin' and hollerin' and singin' way up to the fourth floor of the Chittaden, where the boys was packin' up. When it come time to go to the station, you can imagine how disgusted we was when we crowded into the doorway of that bar and seen them two singin' and goin' on.

"Well, well, well," says Magrew, lookin' up and spottin' us. "Look who's here. . . . Clowns, this is Pearl du Monville, a monseer of the old, old school. . . . Don't shake hands with 'em, Pearl, 'cause their fingers is made of chalk and would bust right off in your paws," he says, and he starts guffawin' and Pearl starts titterin' and we stand there givin' 'em the iron eye, it bein' the lowest ebb a ball-club manager'd got hisself down to since the national pastime was started.

Then the midget begun givin' us the ballyhoo. "Come on in!" he says, wavin' his cane. "See the legless base runners, see the outfielders with the butter fingers, see the southpaw with the arm of a little chee-ild!"

Then him and Magrew begun to hoop and holler and nudge each other till you'd of thought this little guy was the funniest guy than even Charlie Chaplin. The fellas filed outa the bar without a word and went on up to the Union Depot, leavin' me to handle Magrew and his new-found crony.

Well, I got 'em outa there finely. I had to take the little guy along, 'cause Magrew had a holt onto him like a vise and I couldn't pry him loose.

"He's comin' along as masket," says Magrew, holdin' the midget in the crouch of his arm like a football. And come along he did, hollerin' and protestin' and beatin' at Magrew with his little fists.

"Cut it out, will ya, Junior?" the little guy kept whinin'. "Come on, leave a man loose, will ya, Junior?"

But Junior kept a holt onto him and begun yellin', "See the guys with the glass arm, see the guys with the cast-iron brains, see the fielders with the feet on their wrists!"

So it goes, right through the whole Union Depot, with people starin' and catcallin', and he don't put the midget down till he gets him through the gates.

"How'm I goin' to go along without no toothbrush?" the midget asts. "What'm I goin' to do without no other suit?" he says.

"Doc here," says Magrew, meanin' me—"doc here will look after you like you was his own son, won't you, doc?"

I give him the iron eye, and he finely got on the train and prob'ly went to sleep with his clothes on.

This left me alone with the midget. "Lookit," I says to him. "Why don't you go on home now? Come mornin', Magrew'll forget all about you. He'll prob'ly think you was somethin' he seen in a nightmare maybe. And he ain't goin' to laugh so easy in the mornin', neither," I says. "So why don't you go on home?"

"Nix," he says to me. "Skiddoo," he says, "twenty-three for you," and he tosses his cane up into the vestibule of the coach and clam'ers on up after it like a cat. So that's the way Pearl du Monville come to go to St. Louis with the ball club.

I seen 'em first at breakfast the next day, settin' opposite each other; the midget playin' "Turkey in the Straw" on a harmonium and Magrew starin' at his eggs and bacon like they was a uncooked bird with its feathers still on.

"Remember where you found this?" I says, jerkin' my thumb at the midget. "Or maybe you think they come with breakfast on these trains," I says, bein' a good hand at turnin' a sharp remark in them days.

The midget puts down the harmonium and turns on me. "Sneeze," he says; "your brains is dusty." Then he snaps a couple drops of water at me from a tumbler. "Drown," he says, tryin' to make his voice deep.

Now, both of them cracks is Civil War cracks, but you'd of thought they was brand new and the funniest than any crack Magrew'd ever heard in his whole life. He started hoopin' and hollerin', and the midget started hoopin' and hollerin', so I walked on away and set down with Bugs Courtney and Hank Metters, payin' no attention to this weak-minded Damon and Phidias acrost the aisle.

Well, sir, the first game with St. Louis was rained out, and there we was facin' a double-header next day. Like maybe I told you, we lose the last three double-headers we play, makin' maybe twenty-five errors in the six games, which is all right for the intimates of a school for the blind, but is disgraceful for the world's champions. It was too wet to go to the zoo, and Magrew wouldn't let us go to the movies, 'cause they flickered so bad in them days. So we just set around, stewin' and frettin'.

One of the newspaper boys come over to take a picture of Billy Klinger and Whitey Cott shakin' hands—this reporter'd heard about the fight—and whilst they was standin' there, toe to toe, shakin' hands, Billy give a back lunge and a jerk, and throwed Whitey over his shoulder into a corner of the room, like a sack a salt. Whitey come back at him with a chair, and Bethlehem broke loose in that there room. The camera was tromped to pieces like a berry basket. When we finely got 'em pulled apart, I heard a laugh, and there was Magrew and the midget standin' in the door and given' us the iron eye.

"Wrasslers," says Magrew, cold-like, "that's what I got for a ball club, Mr. Du Monville, wrasslers—and not very good wrasslers at that, you ast me."

"A man can't be good at everythin'," says Pearl, "but he oughta be good at somethin'."

This sets Magrew gaffawin' again, and away they go, the midget taggin' along by his side like a hound dog and handin' him a fast line of so-called comic cracks.

When we went out to face that battlin' St. Louis club in a double-header the next afternoon, the boys was jumpy as tin toys with keys in their back. We lose the first game, 7 to 2, and are trailin', 4 to 0, when the second game ain't but ten minutes old. Magrew set there like a stone statue, speakin' to nobody. Then, in their half a the fourth, somebody singled to center and knocked in two more runs for St. Louis.

That made Magrew squawk. "I wisht one thing," he says. "I wisht I was manager of a old ladies' sewin' circus 'stead of a ball club."

"You are, Junior, you are," says a familyer and disagreeable voice.

It was that Pearl du Monville again, poppin' up outa nowheres, swingin' his bamboo cane and smokin' a cigar that's three sizes too big for his face. By this time we'd finely got the other side out, and Hank Metters slithered a bat acrost the ground, and the midget had to jump to keep both his ankles from bein' broke.

I thought Magrew'd bust a blood vessel. "You hurt Pearl and I'll break your neck!" he yelled.

Hank muttered somethin' and went on up to the plate and struck out.

We managed to get a couple runs acrost in our half a the sixth, but they come back with three more in their half a the seventh, and this was too much for Magrew.

"Come on, Pearl," he says. "We're gettin' outa here."

"Where you think you're goin'?" I ast him.

"To the lawyer's again," he says cryptly.

"I didn't know you'd been to the lawyer's once, yet," I says.

"Which that goes to show how much you don't know," he says.

With that, they was gone, and I didn't see 'em the rest of the day, nor know what they was up to, which was a God's blessin'. We lose the nightcap, 9 to 3, and that puts us into second place plenty, and as low in our mind as a ball club can get.

The next day was a horrible day, like anybody that lived through it can tell you. Practice was just over and the St. Louis club was takin' the field, when I hears this strange sound from the stands. It sounds like the nervous whickerin' a horse gives when he smells somethin' funny on the wind. It was the fans ketchin' sight of Pearl du Monville, like you have prob'ly guessed. The midget had popped up onto the field all dressed up in a minacher club uniform, sox, cap, little letters sewed onto his chest, and all. He was swingin' a kid's bat and the only thing kept him from lookin' like a real ballplayer seen through the wrong end of a microscope was this cigar he was smokin'.

Bugs Courtney reached over and jerked it outa his mouth and throwed it away. "You're wearin' that suit on the playin' field," he says to him, severe as a judge. "You go insultin' it and I'll take you out to the zoo and feed you to the bears."

Pearl just blowed some smoke at him which he still has in his mouth.

Whilst Whitey was foulin' off four or five prior to strikin' out, I went on over to Magrew. "If I was as comic as you," I says, "I'd laugh myself to death," I says, "Is that any way to treat the uniform, makin' a mockery out of it?"

"It might surprise you to know I ain't makin' no mockery outa the uniform," says Magrew. "Pearl du Monville here has been made a bone-of-fida member of this so-called ball club. I fixed it up with the front office by long-distance phone."

"Yeh?" I says. "I can just hear Mr. Dillworth or Bart Jenkins agreein' to hire a midget for the ball club. I can just hear 'em." Mr. Dillworth was the owner of the club and Bart Jenkins was the secretary, and they never stood for no monkey business. "May I be so bold as to inquire," I says, "just what you told 'em?"

"I told 'em," he says, "I wanted to sign up a guy they ain't no pitcher in the league can strike him out."

"Uh-huh," I says, "and did you tell 'em what size of a man he is?"

"Never mind about that," he says. "I got papers on me, made out legal and proper, constitutin' one Pearl du Monville a bone-of-fida member of this former ball club. Maybe that'll shame them big babies into gettin' in there and swingin', knowin' I can replace any one of 'em with a midget, if I have a mind to. A St. Louis lawyer I seen twice tells me it's all legal and proper."

"A St. Louis lawyer would," I says, "seein' nothin' could make him happier than havin' you makin' a mockery outa this one-time baseball outfit," I says.

Well, sir, it'll all be there in the papers of thirty, thirty-one year ago, and you could look it up. The game went along without no scorin' for seven innings, and since they ain't nothin' much to watch but guys poppin' up or strikin' out, the fans pay most of their attention to the goin's-on of Pearl du Monville. He's out there in front a the dugout, turnin' hand-springs, balancin' his bat on his chin, walkin' a imaginary line, and so on. The fans clapped and laughed at him, and he ate it up.

So it went up to the last a the eighth, nothin' to nothin', not more'n seven, eight hits all told, and no errors on neither side. Our pitcher gets the first two men out easy in the eighth. Then up come a fella name of Porter or Billings, or some such name, and he lammed one up against the tobacco sign for three bases. The next guy up slapped the first ball out into left for a base hit, and in come the fella from third for the only run of the ball game so far. The crowd yelled, the look a death come onto Magrew's face again, and even the midget quit his tom-foolin'. Their next man fouled out back a third, and we come up for our last bats like a bunch a schoolgirls steppin' into a pool of cold water. I was lower in my mind than I'd been since the day in Nineteen-four when Chesbro throwed the wild pitch in the ninth inning with a man on third and lost the pennant for the Highlanders. I knowed something just as bad was goin' to happen, which shows I'm a clairvoyun, or was then.

When Gordy Mills hit out to second, I just closed my eyes. I opened 'em up again to see Dutch Muller standin' on second, dustin' off his pants, him havin' got his first hit in maybe twenty times to the plate. Next up was Harry Loesing, battin' for our pitcher, and he got a base on balls, walkin' on a fourth one you could a combed your hair with.

Then up come Whitey Cott, our lead-off man. He crotches down in what was prob'ly the most fearsome stanch in organized ball, but all he can do is pop out to short. That brung up Billy Klinger, with two down and a man on first and second. Billy took a cut at one you could a knocked a plug hat offa this here

Carnera with it, but then he gets sense enough to wait 'em out, and finely he walks, too, fillin' the bases.

Yes, sir, there you are; the tyin' run on third and the winnin' run on second, first a the ninth, two men down, and Hank Metters comin' to the bat. Hank was built like a Pope-Hartford and he couldn't run no faster'n President Taft, but he had five home runs to his credit for the season, and that wasn't bad in them days. Hank was still hittin' better anybody else on the ball club, and it was mighty heartenin' seein' him stridin' up towards the plate. But he never got there.

"Wait a minute!" yells Magrew, jumpin' to his feet. "I'm sendin' in a pinch hitter!" he yells.

You could a heard a bomb drop. When a ball-club manager says he's sendin' in a pinch hitter for the best batter on the club, you know and I know and everybody knows he's lost his holt.

"They're goin' to be sendin' the funny wagon for you, if you don't watch out," I says, grabbin' a holt of his arm.

But he pulled away and run out towards the plate yellin', "Du Monville battin' for Metters!"

All the fellas begun squawlin' at once, except Hank, and he just stood there starin' at Magrew like he'd gone crazy and was clamin' to be Ty Cobb's grandma or somethin' Their pitcher stood out there with his hands on his hips and a disagreeable look on his face, and the plate umpire told Magrew to go on and get a batter up. Magrew told him again Du Monville was battin' for Metters, and the St. Louis manager finely got the idea. It brung him outa his dugout, howlin' and bawlin' like he'd lost a female dog and her seven pups.

Magrew pushed the midget towards the plate and he says to him, he says, "Just stand up there and hold that bat on your shoulder. They ain't a man in the world can throw three strikes in there 'fore he throws four balls!" he says.

"I get it, Junior!" says the midget. "He'll walk me and force in the tyin' run!" And he starts on up to the plate as cocky as if he was Willie Keeler.

I don't need to tell you Bethlehem broke loose on that there ball field. The fans got onto their hind legs yellin' and whistlin', and everybody on the field begun wavin' their arms and hollerin' and shovin'. The plate umpire stalked over to Magrew like a traffic cop, waggin' his jaw and pointin' his finger, and the St. Louis manager kept yellin' like his house was on fire. When Pearl got up to the plate and stood there, the pitcher slammed his glove down onto the ground and started stompin' on it, and they ain't nobody can blame him. He's just walked two normal-sized human bein's, and now here's a guy up to the plate they ain't more'n twenty inches between his knees and his shoulders.

The plate umpire called in the field umpire, and they talked a while, like a couple doctors seein' the bucolic plague or somethin' for the first time. Then the plate umpire come over to Magrew with his arms folded acrost his chest, and he told him to go on and get a batter up, or he'd forfeit the game to St. Louis. He pulled out his watch, but somebody batted it outa his hand in the scufflin', and I thought there'd be a free-for-all, with everybody yellin' and shovin' except Pearl du Monville, who stood up at the plate with his little bat on his shoulder, not movin' a muscle.

Then Magrew played his ace. I seen him pull some papers outa his pocket and show 'em to the plate umpire. The umpire begun lookin' at 'em like they was bills for somethin' he not only never bought it, he never even heard of it. The other umpire studied 'em like they was a death warren, and all this time the St. Louis manager and the fans and the players is yellin' and hollerin'.

Well, sir, they fought about him bein' a midget and they fought about him usin' a kid's bat, and they fought about where'd he been all season. They was eight or nine rule books brung out and everybody was thumbin' through 'em, tryin' to find out what it says about midgets, but it don't say nothin' about midgets, 'cause this was somethin' never'd come up in the history of the game before, and nobody'd ever dreamed about it, even when they has nightmares. Maybe you can't send no midgets in to bat nowadays, 'cause the old game's changed a lot, mostly for the worst, but you could then, it turned out.

The plate umpire finely decided the contrack papers was all legal and proper, like Magrew said, so he waved the St. Louis players back to their places and he pointed his finger at their manager and told him to quit hollerin' and get on back in the dugout. The manager says the game is percedin' under protest, and the umpire bawls, "Play ball!" over 'n' above the yellin' and booin', him havin' a voice like a hog-caller.

The St. Louis pitcher picked up his glove and beat at it with his fist six or eight times, and then got set on the mound and studied the situation. The fans realized he was really goin' to pitch to the midget, and they went crazy, hoopin' and hollerin' louder'n ever, and throwin' pop bottles and hats and cushions down onto the field. It took five, ten minutes to get the fans quieted down again, whilst our fellas that was on base set down on the bags and waited. And Pearl du Monville kept standin' up there with the bat on his shoulder, like he'd been told to.

So the pitcher starts studyin' the setup again, and you got to admit it was the strangest setup in a ball game since the players cut off their beards and begun wearin' gloves. I wisht I could call the pitcher's name—it wasn't Barney Pelty nor Nig Jack Powell nor Harry Howell. He was a big right-hander, but I can't call his name. You could look it up. Even in a crotchin' position, the ketcher towers over the midget like the Washington Monument.

The plate umpire tries standin' on his tiptoes, then he tries crotchin' down, and he finely gets hisself into a stanch nobody'd ever seen on a ball field before, kinda squattin' down on his hanches.

Well, the pitcher is sore as a old buggy horse in fly time. He slams in the first pitch, hard and wild, and maybe two foot higher'n the midget's head.

"Ball one!" hollers the umpire over 'n' above the racket, 'cause everybody is yellin' worsten ever.

The ketcher goes on out towards the mound and talks to the pitcher and hands him the ball. This time the big right-hander tried a undershoot, and it comes in a little closer, maybe no higher'n a foot, foot and a half above Pearl's head. It would a been a strike with a human bein' in there, but the umpire's got to call it, and he does.

"Ball two!" he bellers.

The ketcher walks on out to the mound again, and the whole infield comes over and gives advice to the pitcher about what they'd do in a case like this, with two balls and no strikes on a batter that oughta be in a bottle of alcohol 'stead of up there at the plate in a big-league game between the teams that is fightin' for first place.

For the third pitch, the pitcher stands there flat-footed and tosses up the ball like he's playin' ketch with a little girl.

Pearl stands there motionless as a hitchin' post and the ball comes in big and slow and high—high for Pearl, that is, it bein' about on a level with his eyes, or a little higher'n a grown man's knees.

They ain't nothin' else for the umpire to do, so he calls, "Ball three!"

Everybody is onto their feet, hoopin' and hollerin', as the pitcher sets to throw ball four. The St. Louis manager is makin' signs and faces like he was a contorturer, and the infield is givin' the pitcher some more advice about what to do this time. Our boys who was on base stick right onto the bag, runnin' no risk of bein' nipped for the last out.

Well, the pitcher decides to give him a toss again, seein' he come closer with that than with a fast ball. They ain't nobody ever seen a slower ball throwed. It come in big as a balloon and slower'n any ball ever throwed before in the major leagues. It come right in over the plate in front of Pearl's chest, lookin' prob'ly big as a full moon to Pearl. They ain't never been a minute like the minute that followed since the United States was founded by the Pilgrim grandfathers.

Pearl du Monville took a cut at that ball, and he hit it! Magrew give a groan like a poleaved steer as the ball rolls out in front a the plate into fair territory.

"Fair ball!" yells the umpire, and the midget starts runnin' for first, still carryin' that little bat, and makin' maybe ninety foot an hour. Bethlehem breaks loose on that ball field and in them stands. They ain't never been nothin' like it since creation was begun.

The ball's rollin' slow, on down towards third, goin' maybe eight, ten, foot. The infield comes in fast and our boys break from their bases like hares in a brush fire. Everybody is standin' up, yellin' and hollerin', and Magrew is tearin' his hair outa his head, and the midget is scamperin' for first with all the speed of one of them little dashhounds carryin' a satchel in his mouth.

The ketcher gets to the ball first, but he boots it on out past the pitcher's box, the pitcher fallin' on his face tryin' to stop it, the shortstop sprawlin' after it full length and zaggin' it on over towards the second baseman, whilst Muller is scorin' with the tyin' run and Loesing is roundin' third with the winnin' run. Ty Cobb could a made a three-bagger outa that bunt, with everybody fallin' over theirself tryin' to pick the ball up. But Pearl is still maybe fifteen, twenty feet from the bag, toddlin' like a baby and yeepin' like a trapped rabbit, when the second baseman finely gets a holt of that ball and slams it over to first. The first baseman ketches it and stomps on the bag, the base umpire waves Pearl out, and there goes your old ball game, the craziest ball game ever played in the history of the organized world.

Their players start runnin' in, and then I see Magrew. He starts after Pearl, runnin' faster'n any man ever run before. Pearl sees him comin' and runs behind the base umpire's legs and gets a holt onto 'em. Magrew comes up, pantin' and roarin', and him and the midget plays ring-around-a-rosy with the umpire, who keeps shovin' at Magrew with one hand and tryin' to slap the midget loose from his legs with the other.

Finely Magrew ketches the midget, who is still yeepin' like a stuck sheep. He gets holt of that little guy by both his ankles and starts whirlin' him round and round his head like Magrew was a hammer thrower and Pearl was the hammer. Nobody can stop him without gettin' their head knocked off, so everybody just stands there and yells. Then Magrew lets the midget fly. He flies on out towards second, high and fast, like a human home run, headed for the soap sign in center field.

Their shortstop tries to get to him, but he can't make it, and I knowed the little fella was goin' to bust to pieces like a dollar watch on a asphalt street when he hit the ground. But it so happens their center fielder is just crossin' second, and he starts runnin' back, tryin' to get under the midget, who had took to spiralin' like a football 'stead of turnin' head over foot, which give him more speed and more distance.

I know you never seen a midget ketched, and you prob'ly never even seen one throwed. To ketch a midget that's been throwed by a heavy-muscled man and is flyin' through the air, you got to run under him and with him and pull your hands and arms back and down when you ketch him, to break the compact of his body, or you'll bust him in two like a matchstick. I seen Bill Lange and Willie Keeler and Tris Speaker make some wonderful ketches in my day, but I never seen nothin' like that center fielder. He goes back and back and still further back and he pulls that midget down outa the air like he was liftin' a sleepin' baby from a cradle. They wasn't a bruise onto him, only his face was the color of cat's meat and he ain't got no air in his chest. In his excitement, the base umpire, who was runnin' back with the center fielder when he ketched Pearl, yells, "Out!" and that give hysteries to the Bethlehem which was ragin' like Niagry on that ball field.

Everybody was hoopin' and hollerin' and yellin' and runnin', with the fans swarmin' onto the field, and the cops tryin' to keep order, and some guys laughin' and some of the women fans cryin', and six or eight of us holdin' onto Magrew to keep him from gettin' at that midget and finishin' him off. Some of the fans picks up the St. Louis pitcher and the center fielder, and starts carryin' 'em around on their shoulders, and they was the craziest goin's-on knowed to the history of organized ball on this side of the 'Lantic Ocean.

I seen Pearl du Monville strugglin' in the arms of a lady fan with a ample bosom, who was laughin' and cryin' at the same time, and him beatin' at her with his little fists and bawlin' and yellin'. He clawed his way loose finely and disappeared in the forest of legs which made that ball field like it was Coney Island on a hot summer's day.

That was the last I ever seen of Pearl du Monville. I never seen hide nor hair of him from that day to this, and neither did nobody else. He just vanished into the thin of the air, as the fella says. He was ketched for the final out of the ball game and that was the end of him, just like it was the end of the ball game, you might say, and also the end of our losin' streak, like I'm goin' to tell you.

That night we piled onto a train for Chicago, but we wasn't snarlin' and snappin' any more. No sir, the ice was finely broke and a new spirit come into that ball club. The old zip come back with the disappearance of Pearl du Monville out back a second base. We got to laughin' and talkin' and kiddin' together, and 'fore long Magrew was laughin' with us. He got a human look onto his pan again, and he quit whinin' and complainin' and wishtin' he was in heaven with the angels.

Well, sir, we wiped up that Chicago series, winnin' all four games, and makin' seventeen hits in one of 'em. Funny thing was, St. Louis was so shook up by that last game with us, they never did hit their stride again. Their center fielder took to misjudgin' everything that come his way, and the rest a the fellas followed suit, the way a club'll do when one guy blows up.

'Fore we left Chicago, I and some of the fellas went out and bought a pair of them little baby shoes, which we had 'em golded over and give 'em to Magrew for a souvenir, and he took it all in good spirit. Whitey Cott and Billy Klinger made up and was fast friends again, and we hit our home lot like a ton of dynamite and they was nothin' could stop us from then on.

I don't recollect things as clear as I did thirty, forty, years ago. I can't read no fine print no more, and the only person I got to check with on the golden days of the national pastime, as the fella says, is my friend, old Milt Kline, over in Springfield, and his mind ain't as strong as it once was.

He gets Rube Waddell mixed up with Rube Marquad, for one thing, and anybody does that oughta be put away where he won't bother nobody. So I can't tell you the exact margin we win the pennant by. Maybe it was two and a half games, or maybe it was three and a half. But it'll all be there in the newspapers and record books of thirty, thirty-one year ago and, like I was sayin', you could look it up.

Considerations

1. Discuss the point of view in this story. How would it have been different told by Squawks Magrew? Or by Pearl? Support your answer.
2. Baseball, perhaps more than any other sport, seems to attract colorful characters, such as those in this story. The Old "Gas House Gang" of the St. Louis Cardinals in the thirties is a good example in real life. Can you name others?
3. This story, written in 1941, deals with the idea of a baseball manager signing a midget to serve as a pinch hitter. On August 19, 1951, fiction became fact in the American League, making James Thurber something of a clairvoyant. Find out the details of this event and compare it with the one in this story.
4. Explain the following references in this story:
   (a) Pope-Hartford
   (b) Ty Cobb (See "'Fight to Live")
   (c) Bill Lange
   (d) Tris Speaker
   (e) Willie Keeler
   (f) Rube Waddell

DAMON   RUNYON
Undertaker Song

Now this story I am going to tell you is about the game of football, a very healthy pastime for the young, and a great character builder from all I hear, but to get around to this game of football I am compelled to bring in some most obnoxious characters, beginning with a guy by the name of Joey Perhaps, and all I can conscientiously say about Joey is you can have him.

It is a matter of maybe four years since I see this Joey Perhaps until I notice him on a train going to Boston, Mass., one Friday afternoon. He is sitting across from me in the dining-car, where I am enjoying a small portion of baked beans and brown bread, and he looks over to me once, but he does not rap to me.

There is no doubt but what Joey Perhaps is bad company, because the last I hear of him he is hollering copper on a guy by the name of Jack Ortega, and as a result of Joey Perhaps hollering copper, this Jack Ortega is taken to the city of Ossining, N.Y., and placed in an electric chair, and given a very, very, very severe shock in the seat of his pants.

It is something about plugging a most legitimate business guy in the city of Rochester, N.Y., when Joey Perhaps and Jack Ortega are engaged together in a little enterprise to shake the guy down, but the details of this transaction are dull, sordid, and quite uninteresting, except that Joey Perhaps turns state's evidence and announces that Jack Ortega fires the shot which cools the legitimate guy off, for which service he is rewarded with only a small stretch.

I must say for Joey Perhaps that he looks good, and he is very well dressed, but then Joey is always particular about clothes, and he is quite a handy guy with the dolls in his day and, to tell the truth, many citizens along Broadway are by no means displeased when Joey is placed in the state institution, because they are generally pretty uneasy about their dolls when he is around.

Naturally, I am wondering why Joey Perhaps is on this train going to Boston, Mass., but for all I know maybe he is wondering the same thing about me, although personally I am making no secret about it. The idea is I am en route to Boston, Mass., to see a contest of skill and science that is to take place there this very Friday night between a party by the name of Lefty Ledoux and another party by the name of Mickey McCoy, who are very prominent middleweights.

Now ordinarily I will not go around the corner to see a contest of skill and science between Lefty Ledoux and Mickey McCoy, or anybody else, as far as that is concerned, unless they are using blackjacks and promise to hurt each other, but I am the guest on this trip of a party by the name of Meyer Marmalade, and I will go anywhere to see anything if I am a guest.

This Meyer Marmalade is really a most superior character, who is called Meyer Marmalade because nobody can ever think of his last name, which is something like Marmaladowski, and he is known far and wide for the way he likes to make bets on any sporting proposition, such as baseball, or horse races, or ice hockey, or contests of skill and science, and especially contests of skill and science.

So he wishes to be present at this contest in Boston, Mass., between Lefty Ledoux and Mickey McCoy to have a nice wager on McCoy, as he has reliable information that McCoy's manager, a party by the name of Koons, has both judges and the referee in the satchel.

If there is one thing Meyer Marmalade dearly loves, it is to have a bet on a contest of skill and science of this nature, and so he is going to Boston, Mass. But Meyer Marmalade is such a guy as loathes and despises traveling all alone, so when he offers to pay my expenses if I will go along to keep him company, naturally I am pleased to accept, as I have nothing on of importance at the moment and, in fact, I do not have anything on of importance for the past ten years.

I warn Meyer Marmalade in advance that if he is looking to take anything off of anybody in Boston, Mass., he may as well remain at home, because everybody knows that statistics show that the percentage of anything being taken off of the citizens of Boston, Mass., is less per capita than anywhere else in the United States, especially when it comes to contests of skill and science, but Meyer Marmalade says this is the first time they ever had two judges and a referee running against the statistics, and he is very confident.

Well, by and by I go from the dining-car back to my seat in another car, where Meyer Marmalade is sitting reading a detective magazine, and I speak of seeing Joey Perhaps to him. But Meyer Marmalade does not seem greatly interested, although he says to me like this:

"Joey Perhaps, eh?" he says. "A wrong gee. A dead wrong gee. He must just get out. I run into the late Jack Ortega's brother, young Ollie, in Mindy's restaurant last week," Meyer Marmalade says, "and when we happen to get to talking of wrong gees, naturally Joey Perhaps' name comes up, and Ollie remarks he understands Joey Perhaps is about due out, and that he will be pleased to see him some day. Personally," Meyer Marmalade says, "I do not care for any part of Joey Perhaps at any price."

Now our car is loaded with guys and dolls who are going to Boston, Mass., to witness a large football game between the Harvards and the Yales at Cambridge, Mass., the next day, and the reason I know this is because they are talking of nothing else.

So this is where the football starts getting into this story.

One old guy that I figured must be a Harvard from the way he talks seems to have a party all his own, and he is getting so much attention from one and all in the party that I figure he must be a guy of some importance, because they laugh heartily at his remarks, and although I listen very carefully to everything he says he does not sound so very humorous to me.

He is a heavy-set guy with a bald head and a deep voice, and anybody can see that he is such a guy as is accustomed to plenty of authority. I am wondering out loud to Meyer Marmalade who the guy can be, and Meyer Marmalade states as follows:

"Why," he says, "he is nobody but Mr. Phillips Randolph, who makes the automobiles. He is the sixth richest guy in this country," Meyer says, "or maybe it is the seventh. Anyway, he is pretty well up with the front runners. I spot his monicker on his suitcase, and then I ask the porter, to make sure. It is a great honor for us to be traveling with Mr. Phillips Randolph," Meyer says, "because of him being such a public benefactor and having so much dough, especially having so much dough."

Well, naturally everybody knows who Mr. Phillips Randolph is, and I am surprised that I do not recognize his face myself from seeing it so often in the newspapers alongside the latest model automobile his factory turns out, and I am as much pleasured up as Meyer Marmalade over being in the same car with Mr. Phillips Randolph.

He seems to be a good-natured old guy, at that, and he is having a grand time, what with talking, and laughing, and taking a dram now and then out of a bottle, and when old Crip McGonnigle comes gimping through the car selling his football souvenirs, such as red and blue feathers, and little badges and pennants, and one thing and another, as Crip is doing around the large football games since Hickory Slim is a two-year-old, Mr. Phillips Randolph stops him and buys all of Crip's red feathers, which have a little white H on them to show they are for the Harvards.

Then Mr. Phillips Randolph distributes the feathers around among his party, and the guys and dolls stick them in their hats, or pin them on their coats, but he has quite a number of feathers left over, and about this time who comes through the car but Joey Perhaps, and Mr. Phillips Randolph steps out in the aisle and stops Joey and politely offers him a red feather, and speaks as follows:

"Will you honor us by wearing our colors?"

Well, of course Mr. Phillips Randolph is only full of good spirits, and means no harm whatever, and the guys and dolls in his party laugh heartily as if they consider his action very funny, but maybe because they laugh, and maybe because he is just naturally a hostile guy, Joey Perhaps knocks Mr. Phillips Randolph's hand down, and says like this:

"Get out of my way," Joey says. "Are you trying to make a sucker out of somebody?"

Personally, I always claim that Joey Perhaps has a right to reject the red feather, because for all I know he may prefer a blue feather, which means the Yales, but what I say is he does not need to be so impolite to an old guy such as Mr. Phillips Randolph, although of course Joey has no way of knowing at this time about Mr. Phillips Randolph having so much dough.

Anyway, Mr. Phillips Randolph stands staring at Joey as if he is greatly startled, and the chances are he is, at that, for the chances are nobody ever speaks to him in such a manner in all his life, and Joey Perhaps also stands there a minute staring back at Mr. Phillips Randolph, and finally Joey speaks as follows:

"Take a good peek," Joey Perhaps says. "Maybe you will remember me if you ever see me again."

"Yes," Mr. Phillips Randolph says, very quiet. "Maybe I will. They say I have a good memory for faces. I beg your pardon for stopping you, sir. It is all in fun, but I am sorry," he says.

Then Joey Perhaps goes on, and he does not seem to notice Meyer Marmalade and me sitting there in the car, and Mr. Phillips Randolph sits down, and his face is redder than somewhat, and all the joy is gone out of him, and out of his party, too. Personally, I am very sorry Joey Perhaps comes along, because I figure Mr. Phillips Randolph will give me one of his spare feathers, and I will consider it a wonderful keepsake.

But now there is not much more talking, and no laughing whatever in Mr. Phillips Randolph's party, and he just sits there as if he is thinking, and for all I know he may be thinking that that there ought to be a law against a guy speaking so disrespectfully to a guy with all his dough as Joey Perhaps speaks to him.

Well, the contest of skill and science between Lefty Ledoux and Mickey McCoy turns out to be something of a disappointment, and in fact, it is a stinkeroo, because there is little skill and no science whatever in it, and by the fourth round the customers are scuffling their feet, and saying throw these bums out, and making other derogatory remarks and furthermore it seems that this Koons does not have either one of the judges, or even as much as the referee, in the satchel, and Ledoux gets the duke by unanimous vote of the officials.

So Meyer Marmalade is out a couple of C's, which is all he can wager at the ringside, because it seems that nobody in Boston, Mass., cares a cuss about who wins the contest, and Meyer is much disgusted with life, and so am I, and we go back to the Copley Plaza Hotel, where we are stopping, and sit down in the lobby to meditate on the injustice of everything.

Well, the lobby is a scene of gayety, as it seems there are a number of football dinners and dances going on in the hotel, and guys and dolls in evening clothes are all around and about, and the dolls are so young and beautiful that I got to thinking that this is not such a bad old world, after all, and even Meyer Marmalade begins taking notice.

All of a sudden, a very, very beautiful young doll who is about 40 per cent in and 60 per cent out of an evening gown walks right up to us sitting there, and holds out her hand to me, and speaks as follows:

"Do you remember me?"

Naturally, I do not remember her, but naturally I am not going to admit it, because it is never my policy to discourage any doll who wishes to strike up an acquaintance with me, which is what I figure this doll is trying to do; then I see that she is nobody but Doria Logan, one of the prettiest dolls that ever hits Broadway, and about the same time Meyer Marmalade also recognizes her.

Doria changes no little since last I see her, which is quite some time back, but there is no doubt the change is for the better, because she is once a very rattle-headed young doll, and now she seems older, and quieter, and even prettier than ever. Naturally, Meyer Marmalade and I are glad to see her looking so well, and we ask her how are tricks, and what is the good word, and all this and that, and finally Doria Logan states to us as follows:

"I am in great trouble," Doria says. "I am in terrible trouble, and you are the first ones I see that I can talk to about it."

Well, at this, Meyer Marmalade begins to tuck in somewhat, because he figures it is the old lug coming up, and Meyer Marmalade is not such as guy as will go for the lug from a doll unless he gets something more than a story. But I can see Doria Logan is in great earnest.

"Do you remember Joey Perhaps?" she says.

"A wrong gee," Meyer Marmalade says. "A dead wrong gee."

"I not only remember Joey Perhaps," I say, "but I see him on the train today."

"Yes," Doria says, "he is here in town. He hunts me up only a few hours ago. He is here to do me great harm. He is here to finish ruining my life."

"A wrong gee," Meyer Marmalade puts in again. "Always a 100 per cent wrong gee."

Then Doria Logan gets us to go with her to a quiet corner of the lobby, and she tells us a strange story, as follows, and also to wit:

It seems that she is once tangled up with Joey Perhaps, which is something I never know before, and neither does Meyer Marmalade, and, in fact, the news shocks us quite some. It is back in the days when she is just about sixteen and is in the chorus of Earl Carroll's Vanities, and I remember well what a standout she is for looks, to be sure.

Naturally, at sixteen, Doria is quite a chump doll, and does not know which way is south, or what time it is, which is the way all dolls at sixteen are bound to be, and she has no idea what a wrong gee Joey Perhaps is, as he is goodlooking and young, and seems very romantic, and is always speaking of love and one thing and another.

Well, the upshot of it all is the upshot of thousands of other cases since chump dolls commence coming to Broadway, and the first thing she knows, Doria Logan finds herself mixed up with a very bad character, and does not know what to do about it.

By and by, Joey Perhaps commences mistreating her no little, and finally he tries to use her in some nefarious schemes of his, and of course everybody along Broadway knows that most of Joey's schemes are especially nefarious, because Joey is on the shake almost since infancy.

Well, one day Doria says to herself that if this is love, she has all she can stand, and she hauls off and runs away from Joey Perhaps. She goes back to her people, who live in the city of Cambridge, Mass., which is the same place where the Harvards have their college, and she goes there because she does not know of any other place to go.

It seems that Doria's people are poor, and Doria goes to a business school and learns to be a stenographer, and she is working for a guy in the real estate dodge by the name of Poopnoodle, and doing all right for herself, and in the meantime she hears that Joey Perhaps gets sent away, so she figures her troubles are all over as far as he is concerned.

Now Doria Logan goes along quietly through life, working for Mr. Poopnoodle, and never thinking of love, or anything of a similar nature, when she meets up with a young guy who is one of the Harvards, and who is maybe twenty-one years old, and is quite a football player, and where Doria meets up with this guy is in a drug store over a banana split.

Well, the young Harvard takes quite a fancy to Doria and, in fact, he is practically on fire about her, but by this time Doria is going on twenty, and is no longer a chump doll, and she has no wish to get tangled up in love again.

In fact, whenever she thinks of Joey Perhaps, Doria takes to hating guys in general, but somehow she cannot seem to get up a real good hate on the young Harvard, because, to hear her tell it, he is handsome, and noble, and has wonderful ideas.

Now as time goes on, Doria finds she is growing pale, and is losing her appetite, and cannot sleep, and this worries her no little, as she is always a first-class feeder, and finally she comes to the conclusion that what ails her is that she is in love with the young Harvard, and can scarcely live without him, so she admits as much to him one night when the moon is shining on the Charles River, and everything is a dead cold setup for love.

Well, naturally, after a little offhand guzzling, which is quite permissible under the circumstances, the young guy wishes her to name the happy day, and Doria has half a notion to make it the following Monday, this being Sunday night, but then she gets to thinking about her past with Joey Perhaps, and all, and she figures it will be bilking the young Harvard to marry him unless she has a small talk with him first about Joey, because she is well aware that many young guys may have some objection to wedding a doll with a skeleton in her closet, and especially a skeleton such as Joey Perhaps.

But she is so happy she does not wish to run the chance of spoiling everything by these narrations right away, so she keeps her trap closed about Joey, although she promises to marry the young Harvard when he gets out of college, which will be the following year, if he still insists, because Doria figures that by then she will be able to break the news to him about Joey very gradually, and gently, and especially gently.

Anyway, Doria says she is bound and determined to tell him before the wedding, even if he takes the wind on her as a consequence, and personally I claim this is very considerate of Doria, because many dolls never tell before the wedding, or even after. So Doria and the young Harvard are engaged, and great happiness prevails, when, all of a sudden, in pops Joey Perhaps.

It seems that Joey learns of Doria's engagement as soon as he gets out of the state institution, and he hastens to Boston, Mass., with an inside coat pocket packed with letters that Doria writes him long ago, and also a lot of pictures they have taken together, as young guys and dolls are bound to do, and while there is nothing much out of line about these letters and pictures, put them all together they spell a terrible pain in the neck to Doria at this particular time.

"A wrong gee," Meyer Marmalade says. "But," he says, "he is only going back to his old shakedown dodge, so all you have to do is to buy him off."

Well, at this, Doria Logan laughs one of these little short dry laughs that go "hah," and says like this:

"Of course he is looking to get bought off, but," she says, "where will I get any money to buy him off? I do not have a dime of my own, and Joey is talking large figures, because he knows my fiancé's papa has plenty. He wishes me to go to my fiancé and make him get the money off his papa, or he threatens to personally deliver the letters and pictures to my fiancé's papa.

"You can see the predicament I am in," Doria says, "and you can see what my fiancé's papa will think of me if he learns I am once mixed up with a blackmailer such as Joey Perhaps.

"Besides," Doria says, "it is something besides money with Joey Perhaps, and I am not so sure he will not doublecross me even if I can pay him his price. Joey Perhaps is very angry at me, I think," she says, "if he can spoil my happiness, it will mean more to him than money."

Well, Doria states that all she can think of when she is talking to Joey Perhaps is to stall for time, and she tells Joey that, no matter what, she cannot see her fiancé until after the large football game between the Harvards and the Yales as he has to do a little football playing for the Harvards,, and Joey asks her if she is going to see the game, and naturally she is.

And then Joey says he thinks he will look up a ticket speculator, and buy a ticket and attend the game himself, as he is very fond of football, and where will she be sitting, as he hopes and trusts he will be able to see something of her during the game, and this statement alarms Doria Logan no little, for who is she going with but her fiancé's papa, and a party of his friends, and she feels that there is no telling what Joey Perhaps may be up to.

She explains to Joey that she does not know exactly where she will be sitting, except that it will be on the Harvards' side of the field, but Joey is anxious for more details than this.

"In fact," Doria says, "he is most insistent, and he stands at my elbow while I call up Mr. Randolph at this very hotel, and he tells me the exact location of our seats. Then Joey says he will endeavor to get a seat as close to me as possible, and he goes away."

"What Mr. Randolph?" Meyer says. "Which Mr. Randolph?" he says. "You do not mean Mr. Phillips Randolph, by any chance, do you?"

"Why, to be sure," Doria says. "Do you know him?"

Naturally, from now on Meyer Marmalade gazes at Doria Logan with deep respect, and so do I, although by now she is crying a little, and I am by no means in favor of crying dolls. But while she is crying, Meyer Marmalade seems to be doing some more thinking, and finally he speaks as follows:

"Kindly see if you can recall these locations you speak of."

So here is where the football game comes in once more.

Only I regret to state that personally I do not witness this game, and the reason I do not witness it is because nobody wakes me up the next day in time for me to witness it, and the way I look at it, this is all for the best, as I am scarcely a football enthusiast.

So from now on the story belongs to Meyer Marmalade, and I will tell it to you as Meyer tells it to me.

It is a most exciting game (Meyer says). The place is full of people, and there are bands playing, and much cheering, and more lovely dolls than you can shake a stick at, although I do not believe there are any lovelier present than Doria Logan.

It is a good thing she remembers the seat locations, otherwise I will never find her, but there she is surrounded by some very nice-looking people, including Mr. Phillips Randolph, and there I am two rows back of Mr. Phillips Randolph, and the ticket spec I get my seat off of says he cannot understand why everybody wishes to sit near Mr. Phillips Randolph to-day when there are other seats just as good, and maybe better, on the Harvards' side.

So I judge he has other calls similar to mine for this location, and a sweet price he gets for it, too, and I judge that maybe at least one call is from Joey Perhaps, as I see Joey a couple of rows on back up of where I am sitting, but off to my left on an aisle, while I am almost in a direct line with Mr. Phillips Randolph.

To show you that Joey is such a guy as attracts attention, Mr. Phillips Randolph stands up a few minutes before the game starts, peering around and about to see who is present that he knows, and all of a sudden his eyes fall on Joey Perhaps, and then Mr. Phillips Randolph proves he has a good memory for faces, to be sure, for he states as follows:

"Why," he says, "there is the chap who rebuffs me so churlishly on the train when I offer him our colors. Yes," he says, "I am sure it is the same chap."

Well, what happens in the football game is much pulling and hauling this way and that, and to and fro, between the Harvards and the Yales without a tally right down to the last five minutes of play, and then all of a sudden the Yales shove the football down to within about three-eighths of an inch of the Harvards' goal line.

At this moment quite some excitement prevails. Then the next thing anybody knows, the Yales outshove the Harvards, and now the game is over, and Mr. Phillips Randolph gets up out of his seat, and I hear Mr. Phillips Randolph say like this:

"Well," he says, "the score is not so bad as it might be, and it is a wonderful game, and," he says, "we seem to make one convert to our cause, anyway, for see who is wearing our colors."

And with this he points to Joey Perhaps, who is still sitting down, with people stepping around him and over him, and he is still smiling a little smile, and Mr. Phillips Randolph seems greatly pleased to see that Joey Perhaps has a big, broad crimson ribbon where he once wears his white silk muffler.

But the chances are Mr. Phillips Randolph will be greatly surprised if he knows that the crimson ribbon across Joey's bosom comes of Ollie Ortega planting a short knife in Joey's throat, or do I forget to mention before that Ollie Ortega is among those present?

I send for Ollie after I leave you last night, figuring he may love to see a nice football game. He arrives by plane this morning, and I am not wrong in my figuring. Ollie thinks the game is swell.

Well, personally, I will never forget this game, it is so exciting. Just after the tally comes off, all of a sudden, from the Yales in the stand across the field from the Harvards, comes a long-drawn-out wail that sounds so mournful it makes me feel very sad, to be sure. It starts off something like Oh-oh-oh-oh-oh, with all the Yales Oh-oh-oh-oh-oh-ing at once, and I ask a guy next to me what it is all about.

"Why," the guy says, "it is the Yales' 'Undertaker Song.' They always sing it when they have the other guy licked. I am an old Yale myself, and I will now personally sing this song for you."

And with this the guy throws back his head, and opens his mouth wide and lets out a yowl like a wolf calling to its mate.

Well, I stop the guy, and tell him it is a very lovely song, to be sure, and quite appropriate all the way around, and then I hasten away from the football game without getting a chance to say good-by to Doria, although afterwards I mail her the package of letters and pictures that Ollie gets out of Joey Perhaps' inside coat pocket during the confusion that prevails when the Yales make their tally, and I hope and trust that she will think the crimson streaks across the package are just a little touch of color in honor of the Harvards.

But the greatest thing about the football game (Meyer Marmalade says) is I win two C's off of one of the Harvards sitting near me, so I am now practically even on my tip.

Considerations

1. Explain the irony, or double meaning, of the title.
2. Why does Mr. Phillips Randolph suddenly become more lovable in the narrator's eyes when the narrator finds out who he is? Do most people curry up to the rich because, as psychologists say, of the survival instinct? If not, why?
3. If you have read *The Godfather* or seen the film, discuss the difference in the way the mobsters are characterized by Runyon. Consider the murder of Joey Perhaps in your discussion.
4. Describe the narrator in this story. Why do you think Runyon chooses to have him miss the football game and have him report the events, including the death of Joey Perhaps, through the eyes of Meyer Marmalade?
5. Do you detect a bit of ridicule in Meyer Marmalade's (Runyon's) description of the football game as "much pulling and hauling this way and that, and to and fro, between the Harvards and the Yales. . . ."? Do you consider the assessment absurd, or fairly astute?
6. Can you list any modern sportswriters who may have been influenced by Damon Runyon?

DAMON RUNYON

Bred for Battle

One night a guy by the name of Bill Corum, who is one of these sport scribes, gives me a Chinee for a fight at Madison Square Garden, a Chinee being a ducket with holes punched in it like old-fashioned Chink money, to show that it is a free ducket, and the reason I am explaining to you how I get this ducket is because I do not wish anybody to think I am ever simple enough to pay out my own potatoes for a ducket to a fight, even if I have any potatoes.

Personally, I will not give you a bad two-bit piece to see a fight anywhere, because the way I look at it, half the time the guys who are supposed to do the fighting go in there and put on the old do-se-do, and I consider this a great fraud upon the public, and I do not believe in encouraging dishonesty.

But of course I never refuse a Chinee to such events, because the way I figure it, what can I lose except my time, and my time is not worth more than a bob a week the way things are. So on the night in question I am standing in the lobby of the Garden with many other citizens, and I am trying to find out if there is any skullduggery doing in connection with the fight, because any time there is any skullduggery doing I love to know it, as it is something worth knowing in case a guy wishes to get a small wager down.

Well, while I am standing there, somebody comes up behind me and hits me an awful belt on the back, knocking my wind plumb out of me, and making me very indignant indeed. As soon as I get a little of my wind back again, I turn around figuring to put a large blast on the guy who slaps me, but who is it but a guy by the name of Spider McCoy, who is known far and wide as a manager of fighters.

Well, of course I do not put the blast on Spider McCoy, because he is an old friend of mine, and furthermore, Spider McCoy is such a guy as is apt to let a left hook go at anybody who puts the blast on him, and I do not believe in getting in trouble, especially with good left-hookers.

So I say hello to Spider, and am willing to let it go at that, but Spider seems glad to see me, and says to me like this:

"Well, well, well, well, well!" Spider says.

"Well," I say to Spider McCoy, "how many wells does it take to make a river?"

"One, if it is big enough," Spider says, so I can see he knows the answer all right. "Listen," he says, "I just think up the greatest proposition I ever think of in my whole life, and who knows but what I can interest you in same."

"Well, Spider," I say, "I do not care to hear any propositions at this time, because it may be a long story, and I wish to step inside and see the impending battle. Anyway," I say, "if it is a proposition involving financial support, I wish to state that I do not have any resources whatever at this time."

"Never mind the battle inside," Spider says. "It is nothing but a tank job, anyway. And as for financial support," Spider says, "this does not require more than a pound note, tops, and I know you have a pound note because I know you put the bite on Overcoat Obie for this amount not an hour ago. Listen," Spider McCoy says, "I know where I can place my hands on the greatest heavyweight prospect in the world to-day, and all I need is the price of car-fare to where he is."

Well, off and on, I know Spider McCoy twenty years, and in all this time I never know him when he is not looking for the greatest heavyweight prospect in the world. And as long as Spider knows I have the pound note, I know there is no use trying to play the duck for him, so I stand there wondering who the stool pigeon can be who informs him of my financial status.

"Listen," Spider says, "I just discover that I am all out of line in the way I am looking for heavyweight prospects in the past. I am always looking for nothing but plenty of size," he says. "Where I make my mistake is not looking for blood lines. Professor D just smartens me up," Spider says.

Well, when he mentions the name of Professor D, I commence taking a little interest, because it is well known to one and all that Professor D is one of the smartest old guys in the world. He is once a professor in a college out in Ohio, but quits this dodge to handicap the horses, and he is a first-rate handicapper, at that. But besides knowing how to handicap the horses, Professor D knows many other things, and is highly respected in all walks of life, especially on Broadway.

"Now then," Spider says, "Professor D calls my attention this afternoon to the fact that when a guy is looking for a race horse, he does not take just any horse that comes along, but he find out if the horse's papa is able to run in his day, and if the horse's mamma can get out of her own way when she is young. Professor D shows me how a guy looks for speed in a horse's breeding away back to its great-great-great-great-grandpa and grandmamma," Spider McCoy says.

"Well," I say, "anybody knows this without asking Professor D. In fact," I say, "you even look up a horse's parents to see if they can mud before betting on a plug to win in heavy going."

"All right," Spider says, "I know all this myself, but I never think much about it before Professor D mentions it. Professor D says if a guy is looking for a hunting dog he does not pick a Pekingese pooch, but he gets a dog that is bred to hunt from away back yonder, and if he is after a game chicken he does not take a Plymouth Rock out of the back yard.

"So then," Spider says, "Professor D wishes to know why, when I am looking for a fighter, I do not look for one who comes of fighting stock. Professor D wishes to know," Spider says, "why I do not look for some guy who is bred to fight, and when I think this over, I can see the professor is right.

"And then all of a sudden," Spider says, "I get the largest idea I ever have in all my life. Do you remember a guy I have about twenty years back by the name of Shamus Mulrooney, the Fighting Harp?" Spider says. "A big, rough, tough heavyweight out of Newark?"

"Yes," I say, "I remember Shamus very well indeed. The last time I see him is the night Pounder Pat O'Shea almost murders him in the old Garden," I say. "I never see a guy with more ticker than Shamus, unless maybe it is Pat."

"Yes," Spider says, "Shamus has plenty of ticker. He is about through the night of the fight you speak of, otherwise Pat will never lay a glove on him. It is not long after this fight that Shamus packs in and goes back to bricklaying in Newark, and it is also about this same time," Spider says, "that he marries Pat O'Shea's sister, Bridget.

"Well, now," Spider says, "I remember they have a boy who must be around nineteen years old now, and if ever a buy is bred to fight it is a boy by Shamus Mulrooney out of Bridget O'Shea, because," Spider says, "Bridget herself can lick half the heavyweights I see around nowadays if she is half as good as she is the last time I see her. So now you have my wonderful idea. We will go to Newark and get this boy and make him heavyweight champion of the world."

"What you state is very interesting indeed, Spider," I say. "But," I say, "how do you know this boy is a heavyweight?"

"Why," Spider says, "how can he be anything else but a heavyweight, what with his papa as big as a house, and his mamma weighing maybe a hundred and seventy pounds in her step-ins? Although of course," Spider says, "I never see Bridget weigh in in such manner.

"But," Spider says, "even if she does carry more weight than I will personally care to spot a doll, Bridget is by no means a pelican when she marries Shamus. In fact," he says, "she is pretty good-looking. I remember their wedding well, because it comes out that Bridget is in love with some other guy at the time, and this guy comes to see the nuptials, and Shamus runs him all the way from Newark to Elizabeth, figuring to break a couple of legs for the guy if he catches him.

But," Spider says, "the guy is too speedy for Shamus, who never has much foot anyway."

Well, all that Spider says appeals to me as a very sound business proposition, so the upshot of it is. I give him my pound note to finance his trip to Newark.

Then I do not see Spider McCoy again for a week, but one day he calls me up and tells me to hurry over to the Pioneer gymnasium to see the next heavyweight champion of the world, Thunderbolt Mulrooney.

I am personally somewhat disappointed when I see Thunderbolt Mulrooney, and especially when I find out his first name is Raymond and not Thunderbolt at all, because I am expecting to see a big, fierce guy with red hair and a chest like a barrel, such as Shamus Muldooney has when he is in his prime. But who do I see but a tall, pale looking young guy with blond hair and thin legs.

Furthermore, he has pale blue eyes, and a far-away look in them, and he speaks in a low voice, which is nothing like the voice of Shamus Mulrooney. But Spider seems satisfied with Thunderbolt, and when I tell him Thunderbolt does not look to me like the next heavyweight champion of the world, Spider says like this:

"Why," he says, "the guy is nothing but a baby, and you must give him time to fill out. He may grow to be bigger than his papa. But you know," Spider says, getting indignant as he thinks about it, "Bridget Mulrooney does not wish to let this guy be the next heavyweight champion of the world. In fact," Spider says, "she kicks up an awful row when I go to get him, and Shamus finally has to speak to her severely. Shamus says he does not know if I can ever make a fighter of this guy because Bridget coddles him until he is nothing but a mushhead, and Shamus says he is sick and tired of seeing the guy sitting around the house doing nothing but reading and playing the zither."

"Does he play the zither yet?" I asked Spider McCoy.

"No," Spider says, "I do not allow my fighters to play zithers. I figure it softens them up. This guy does not play at present. He seems to be in a daze most of the time, but of course everything is new to him. He is bound to come out okay, because," Spider says, "he is certainly bred right. I find out from Shamus that all the Mulrooneys are great fighters back in the old country," Spider says, "and furthermore he tells me Bridget's mother once licks four Newark cops who try to stop her from pasting her old man, so," Spider says, "this lad is just naturally steaming with fighting blood."

Well, I drop around to the Pioneer once or twice a week after this, and Spider McCoy is certainly working hard with Thunderbolt Mulrooney. Furthermore, the guy seems to be improving right along, and gets so he can box fairly well and punch the bag, and all this and that, but he always has that far-away look in his eyes, and personally I do not care for fighters with far-away looks.

Finally one day Spider calls me up and tells me he has Thunderbolt Mulrooney matched in a four-round preliminary bout at the St. Nick with a guy by the name of Bubbles Browning, who is fighting almost as far back as the first battle of Bull Run, so I can see Spider is being very careful in matching Thunderbolt. In fact, I congratulate Spider on his carefulness.

"Well," Spider says, "I am taking this match just to give Thunderbolt the feel of the ring. I am taking Bubbles because he is an old friend of mine, and very deserving, and furthermore," Spider says, "he gives me his word he will not hit Thunderbolt very hard and will become unconscious the instant Thunderbolt hits him. You know," Spider says, "you must encourage a young heavyweight, and there is nothing that encourages one so much as knocking somebody unconscious."

Now of course it is nothing for Bubbles to promise not to hit anybody very hard because even when he is a young guy, Bubbles cannot punch his way out of a paper bag, but I am glad to learn that he also promises to become unconscious very soon, as naturally I am greatly interested in Thunderbolt's career, what with owning a piece of him, and having an investment of one pound in him already.

So the night of the fight, I am at the St. Nick very early, and many other citizens are there ahead of me, because by this time Spider McCoy gets plenty of publicity for Thunderbolt by telling the boxing scribes about his wonderful fighting blood lines, and everybody wishes to see a guy who is bred for battle, like Thunderbolt.

I take a guest with me to the fight by the name of Harry the Horse, who comes from Brooklyn, and as I am anxious to help Spider McCoy all I can, as well as to protect my investment in Thunderbolt, I request Harry to call on Bubbles Browning in his dressing room and remind him of his promise about hitting Thunderbolt.

Harry the Horse does this for me, and furthermore he shows Bubbles a large revolver and tells Bubbles that he will be compelled to shoot his ears off if Bubbles forgets his promise, but Bubbles says all this is most unnecessary, as his eyesight is so bad he cannot see to hit anybody, anyway.

Well, I know a party who is a friend of the guy who is going to referee the preliminary bouts, and I am looking for this party to get him to tell the referee to disqualify Bubbles in case it looks as if he is forgetting his promise and is liable to hit Thunderbolt, but before I can locate the party, they are announcing the opening bout, and there is Thunderbolt in the ring looking very far away indeed, with Spider McCoy behind him.

It seems to me I never see a guy who is so pale all over as Thunderbolt Mulrooney, but Spider looks down at me and tips me a large wink, so I can see that everything is as right as rain, especially when Harry the Horse makes motions at Bubbles Browning like a guy firing a large revolver at somebody, and Bubbles smiles, and also winks.

Well, when the bell rings, Spider gives Thunderbolt a shove toward the center, and Thunderbolt comes out with his hands up, but looking more far away than somewhat, and something tells me that Thunderbolt by no means feels the killer instinct such as I love to see in fighters. In fact, something tells me that Thunderbolt is not feeling enthusiastic about this proposition in any way, shape, manner, or form.

Old Bubbles almost falls over his own feet coming out of his corner, and he starts bouncing around making passes at Thunderbolt, and waiting for Thunderbolt to hit him so he can become unconscious. Naturally, Bubbles does not wish to become unconscious without getting hit, as this may look suspicious to the public.

Well, instead of hitting Bubbles, what does Thunderbolt Mulrooney do but turn around and walk over to a neutral corner, and lean over the ropes with his face in his gloves, and burst out crying. Naturally, this is a most surprising incident to one and all, and especially to Bubbles Browning.

The referee walks over to Thunderbolt Mulrooney and tries to turn him around, but Thunderbolt keeps his face in his gloves and sobs so loud that the referee is deeply touched and starts sobbing with him. Between sobs he asks Thunderbolt if he wishes to continue the fight, and Thunderbolt shakes his head, although as a matter of fact no fight whatever starts so far, so the referee declares Bubbles Browning the winner, which is a terrible surprise to Bubbles.

Then the referee puts his arm around Thunderbolt and leads him over to Spider McCoy, who is standing in his corner with a very strange expression on his face. Personally, I consider the entire spectacle so revolting that I go out into the air, and stand around awhile expecting to hear any minute that Spider McCoy is in the hands of the gendarmes on a charge of mayhem.

But it seems that nothing happens, and when Spider finally comes out of the St. Nick, he is only looking sorrowful because he just hears that the promoter declines to pay him the fifty bobs he is supposed to receive for Thunderbolt's services, the promoter claiming that Thunderbolt renders no service.

"Well," Spider says, "I fear this is not the next heavyweight champion of the world after all. There is nothing in Professor D's idea about blood lines as far as fighters are concerned, although," he says, "it may work out all right with horses and dogs, and one thing and another. I am greatly disappointed," Spider says, "but then I am always being disappointed in heavyweights. There is nothing we can do but take this guy back home, because," Spider says, "the last thing I promise Bridget Mulrooney is that I will personally return him to her in case I am not able to make him heavyweight champion, as she is afraid he will get lost if he tries to find his way home alone."

So the next day, Spider McCoy and I take Thunderbolt Mulrooney over to Newark and to his home, which turns out to be a nice little house in a side street with a yard all around and about, and Spider and I are just as well pleased that that old Shamus Mulrooney is absent when we arrive, because Spider says that Shamus is just such a guy as will be asking a lot of questions about the fifty bobbos that Thunderbolt does not get.

Well, when we reach the front door of the house, out comes a big, fine-looking doll with red cheeks, all excited, and she takes Thunderbolt in her arms and kisses him, so I know this is Bridget Mulrooney, and I can see she knows what happens, and in fact I afterwards learn that Thunderbolt telephones her the night before.

After a while she pushes Thunderbolt into the house and stands at the door as if she is guarding it against us entering to get him again, which of course is very unnecessary. And all this time Thunderbolt is sobbing no little, although by and by the sobs die away, and from somewhere in the house comes the sound of music I seem to recognize as the music of a zither.

Well, Bridget Mulrooney never says a word to us as she stands in the door, and Spider McCoy keeps staring at her in a way that I consider very rude indeed.

I am wondering if he is waiting for a receipt for Thunderbolt, but finally he speaks as follows:

"Bridget," Spider says, "I hope and trust that you will not consider me too fresh, but I wish to learn the name of the guy you are going around with just before you marry Shamus. I remember him well," Spider says, "but I cannot think of his name, and it bothers me not being able to think of names. He is a tall, skinny, stoop-shouldered guy," Spider says, "with a hollow chest and a soft voice, and he loves music."

Well, Bridget Mulrooney stands there in the doorway, staring back at Spider, and it seems to me that the red suddenly fades out of her cheeks, and just then we hear a lot of yelling, and around the corner of the house comes a bunch of six kids, who seem to be running from another kid.

This kid is not very big, and is maybe fifteen or sixteen years old, and he has red hair and many freckles, and he seems very mad at the other kids. In fact, when he catches up with them, he starts belting away at them with his fists, and before anybody can as much as say boo, he has three of them on the ground as flat as pancakes, while the others are yelling bloody murder.

Personally, I never see such wonderful punching by a kid, especially with his left hand, and Spider McCoy is also much impressed, and is watching the kid with great interest. Then Bridget Mulrooney runs out and grabs the freckle-faced kid with one hand and smacks him with the other hand and hauls him, squirming and kicking, over to Spider McCoy and says to Spider like this:

"Mr. McCoy," Bridget says, "this is my youngest son, Terence, and though he is not a heavyweight, and will never be a heavyweight, perhaps he will answer your purpose. Suppose you see his father about him sometime," she says, "and hoping you will learn to mind your own business, I wish you a very good day."

Then she takes the kid into the house under her arm and slams the door in our kissers, and there is nothing for us to do but walk away. And as we are walking away, all of a sudden Spider McCoy snaps his fingers as guys will do when they get an unexpected thought, and says like this:

"I remember the guy's name," he says. "It is Cedric Tilbury, and he is a floor-walker in Hamburgher's department store, and," Spider says, "how he can play the zither!"

I see in the papers the other day where Jimmy Johnston, the match maker at the Garden, matches Tearing Terry Mulrooney, the new sensation of the light-weight division, to fight for the championship, but it seems from what Spider McCoy tells me that my investment with him does not cover any fighters in his stable except maybe heavyweights.

And it also seems that Spider McCoy is not monkeying with heavyweights since he gets Tearing Terry.

Considerations

1. Damon Runyon is famous for his lighthearted stories about lovable con-men, prostitutes, bookies, pimps, thieves, and murderers. What literary term do we use to describe a writer who views his materials so? Would you call such a style a weak-

ness? Can you think of a recent Nobel Prize winner who had a similar view of his material?

2. In this story Runyon pokes a lot of good-natured fun at boxing and its shady reputation. Why has this sport been traditionally most susceptible to bribery and other kinds of fixes?

3. Modern readers may sense something distasteful about the premise of this story. Discuss the title's macabre implications (of which Runyon was almost certainly unaware, since the story was written in the early thirties).

4. Discuss Runyon's unique style of writing in the present tense. How does such a style enhance the story?

5. What is the role of Harry the Horse in the story? What would you say is his "occupation"?

DONALD BARTHELME

The Wound

He sits up again. He makes a wild grab for his mother's hair. The hair of his mother! But she neatly avoids him. The cook enters with the roast beef. The mother of the torero tastes the sauce, which is presented separately, in a silver dish. She makes a face. The torero, ignoring the roast beef, takes the silver dish from his mother and sips from it, meanwhile maintaining intense eye contact with his mistress. The torero's mistress hands the camera to the torero's mother and reaches for the silver dish. "What is all this nonsense with the dish?" asks the famous aficionado who is sitting by the bedside. The torero offers the aficionado a slice of beef, carved from the roast with a sword, of which there are perhaps a dozen on the bed. "These fellows with their swords, they think they're so fine," says one of the *imbéciles* to another, quietly. The second *imbécil* says, "We would all think ourselves fine if we could. But we can't. Something prevents us."

The torero looks with irritation in the direction of the *imbéciles*. His mistress takes the 8-mm. movie camera from his mother and begins to film something outside the window. The torero has been gored in the foot. He is, in addition, surrounded by *imbéciles, idiotas,* and *bobos*. He shifts uncomfortably in his bed. Several swords fall on the floor. A telegram is delivered. The mistress of the torero puts down the camera and removes her shirt. The mother of the torero looks angrily at the *imbéciles*. The famous aficionado reads the telegram aloud. The telegram suggests the torero is a clown and a *cucaracha* for allowing himself to be gored in the foot, thus both insulting the noble profession of which he is such a poor representative and irrevocably ruining the telegram sender's Sunday afternoon, and that, furthermore, the telegram sender is even now on his way to the Church of Our Lady of the Several Sorrows to pray *against* the torero, whose future, he cordially hopes, is a thing of the past. The torero's head flops forward into the cupped hands of an adjacent *bobo*.

The mother of the torero turns on the television set, where the goring of the foot of the torero is being shown first at normal speed, then in exquisite slow motion. The torero's head remains in the cupped hands of the *bobo*. "My foot!" he shouts. Someone turns off the television. The beautiful breasts of the torero's mistress are appreciated by the aficionado, who is also an aficionado of breasts. The *imbéciles* and *idiots* are afraid to look. So they do not. One *idiota* says to another *idiota*, "I would greatly like some of that roast beef." "But it has not been offered to us," his companion replies, "because we are so insignificant." "But no one else is eating it," the first says. "It simply sits there, on the plate." They regard the attractive roast of beef.

The torero's mother picks up the movie camera that his mistress has relinquished and begins filming the torero's foot, playing with the zoom lens. The torero, head still in the hands of the *bobo*, reaches into a drawer in the bedside table and removes from a box there a Cuban cigar of the first quality. Two *bobos* and an *imbécil* rush to light it for him, bumping into each other in the process. "Lysol," says the mother of the torero. "I forgot the application of the Lysol." She puts down the camera and looks around for the Lysol bottle. But the cook has taken it away. The mother of the torero leaves the room, in search of the Lysol bottle. He, the torero, lifts his head and follows her exit. More pain?

His mother reenters the room carrying a bottle of Lysol. The torero places his bandaged foot under a pillow, and both hands, fingers spread wide, on top of the pillow. His mother unscrews the top of the bottle of Lysol. The Bishop of Valencia enters with attendants. The Bishop is a heavy man with his head cocked permanently to the left—the result of years of hearing confessions in a confessional whose right-hand box was said to be inhabited by vipers. The torero's mistress hastily puts on her shirt. The *imbéciles* and *idiotas* retire into the walls. The Bishop extends his hand. The torero kisses the Bishop's ring. The famous aficionado does likewise. The Bishop asks if he may inspect the wound. The torero takes his foot out from under the pillow. The torero's mother unwraps the bandage. There is the foot, swollen almost twice normal size. In the center of the foot, the wound, surrounded by angry flesh. The Bishop shakes his head, closes his eyes, raises his head (on the diagonal), and murmurs a short prayer. Then he opens his eyes and looks about him for a chair. An *idiota* rushes forward with a chair. The Bishop seats himself by the bedside. The torero offers the Bishop some cold roast beef. The Bishop begins to talk about his psychoanalysis: "I am a different man now," the Bishop says. "Gloomier, duller, more fearful. In the name of the Holy Ghost, you would not believe what I see under the bed, in the middle of the night." The Bishop laughs heartily. The torero joins him. The torero's mistress is filming the Bishop. "I was happier with my whiskey," the Bishop says, laughing even harder. The laughter of the Bishop threatens the chair he is sitting in. One *bobo* says to another *bobo*, "The privileged classes can afford psychoanalysis and whiskey. Whereas all we get is sermons and sour wine. This is manifestly unfair. I protest, silently." "It is because we are no good," the second *bobo* says. "It is because we are nothings."

The torero opens a bottle of Chivas Regal. He offers a shot to the Bishop, who graciously accepts, and then pours one for himself. The torero's mother edges toward the bottle of Chivas Regal. The torero's mistress films his mother's surreptitious approach. The Bishop and the torero discuss whiskey and psychoanalysis. The torero's mother has a hand on the neck of the bottle. The torero makes a sudden wild grab for her hair. The hair of his mother! He misses and she scuttles off into a corner of the room, clutching the bottle. The torero picks a killing sword, an *estoque,* from the half dozen still on the bed. The Queen of the Gypsies enters.

The Queen hurries to the torero, little tufts of dried grass falling from her robes as she crosses the room. "Unwrap the wound!" she cries. "The wound, the wound, the wound!" The torero recoils. The Bishop sits severely. His attendants stir and whisper. The torero's mother takes a swig from the Chivas Regal bottle. The famous aficionado crosses himself. The torero's mistress looks down through her half-open blouse at her breasts. The torero quickly reaches into the drawer of the bedside table and removes the cigar box. He takes from the cigar box the ears and tail of a bull he killed, with excellence and emotion, long ago. He spreads them out on the bedcovers, offering them to the Queen. The ears resemble bloody wallets, the tail the hair of some long-dead saint, robbed from a reliquary. "No," the Queen says. She grasps the torero's foot and begins to unwrap the bandages. The torero grimaces but submits. The Queen withdraws from her belt a sharp knife. The torero's mistress picks up a violin and begins to play an air by Valdéz. The Queen whacks off a huge portion of roast beef, which she stuffs into her mouth while bent over the wound—gazing deeply into it, savoring it. Everyone shrinks—the torero, his mother, his mistress, the Bishop, the aficionado, the *imbéciles, idiotas,* and *bobos.* An ecstasy of shrinking. The Queen says, "I want this wound. *This one.* It is mine. Come, pick him up." Everyone present takes a handful of the torero and lifts him high above their heads (he is screaming). But the doorway is suddenly blocked by the figure of an immense black bull. The bull begins to ring, like a telephone.

Considerations

1. Why does this story seem strange to us? (See critical remarks in "Reading Fiction.") Is it stranger than, say, *Alice in Wonderland* or, for that matter, the Book of Revelation in the Bible? Explain.
2. There are several objects of Barthelme's ridicule in the story, such as television viewers' interest in seeing slow-motion replays of exciting sports events. List and discuss others.
3. What is a "famous aficionado"? Whoever it might represent, he is the target of a good deal of ridicule. Who was the most famous of all aficionados of the bullfight?
4. What is the meaning of the bull at the end, which "begins to ring, like a telephone"? Is Barthelme at last giving his torero, and his readers, a "bullring"?

ESSAYS

Although essays are to be found throughout Ancient Greek literature and the Bible, and in the writings of St. Augustine and Thomas Aquinas, the form is often associated with Montaigne, the great literary genius of sixteenth-century France. It was he who coined the word *essais*, "tests," and elevated this method of writing into an art. Nowadays, however, essays are often referred to simply as "non-fiction," whether they be biography, sermon, review, or speech. Some of the following selections are essays only in the latter sense; for example, "Wild in the Stands," is an excellent piece of journalistic reporting; "Interscholastic Athletics: The Gathering Storm" is a speech to an athletic convention. Others—such as "Women Athletes" by Paul Weiss and "It's Always We Rambled: An Essay on Rodeo" by Larry McMurtry—demonstrate the more traditional essay form.

Leslie Fiedler, one of today's most classical essayists, critic, and author of *Love and Death in the American Novel*, has attributed the elevation of the essay to an art form to the dissolution of the Monarchy and the corresponding shift of importance to the Individual. The great epics and tragic dramas were written in tribute to kings and the elite societies they represented. Only in the Renaissance, when the Monarchy and the Church were in upheaval and the Individual gaining in importance, could such a modest and unpretentious literary form flourish.

Perhaps the essay reached its peak in the eighteenth century with the writings of Hume, Diderot, Voltaire, and Rousseau, and their revolutionary admirers in America—Jefferson and Paine. Today the essay is still widely used, but the current obsession with facts may, if continued, diminish the importance of the essayist who, as critic-essayist Joseph Wood Krutch has said, "deals with personal experiences, opinions, tastes, notions, and prejudices." The essayist operates in the realm of values and, as Krutch goes on to say, "Value judgments cannot be based on facts alone—and that's a fact." In addition to the essays by Weiss and McMurtry, other selections in this book that rely heavily on "personal experiences, opinions, tastes, notions, and prejudices" are "Designated Heroes, Ranking Gods, All-Star Holy Persons" by Robert Lipsyte; "Coliseums and Gladiators" by Paul Hoch; and "Interscholastic Athletics: The Gathering Storm" by Max Rafferty.

The sports essay, as a special form, is relatively new. The ancients certainly considered sports a suitable subject but, despite the fact that Pindar wrote many an Olympian ode, he can hardly be called a sportswriter. The genre developed in the nineteenth century with refined writers like Pierce

Egan, whose *Boxiana* contributed almost singularly to the re-establishment of boxing as a legitimate (and legal) sport, so that a century later Jack London could further explore it in America as an appropriate subject for both fiction and non-fiction, such as in "The White Hope."

Reading these early sportswriters, one quickly realizes that sport was representative of life, as it is today; but, unlike today, there was little emphasis on individual athletes, statistics, and records. The finest examples of that early tradition in sportswriting can be found today in the essays of E. B. White ("The Decline of Sport") and McMurtry.

An altogether unique development in sports is the recent emergence of women, whose new determination to be taken seriously in strenuous physical events has cast more than a little doubt on the credibility of Weiss's assessment of them as "fractional men." This new female pride is reflected in selections by Lipsyte, and by Boslooper and Hayes who, in "The Feminine Physique," take issue with Weiss and what they consider to be his antifeminist theories.

Another controversy, dealing with whether sports is "only a game" or "more than a game," constitutes the major portion of the largest section— *The Four Horsemen of the Western World: Religion, War, Government, and Sports.* Critics like Hoch warn of the dangers of the all-powerful ruling bodies of modern sports organizations. Rafferty, on the other hand, defends this disciplinary tradition as a vital force in the perpetuation of family and religion.

The essays comprising *Light from the East* represent a spiritual approach to sports not ordinarily seen in the sports pages of newspapers and magazines. George Leonard suggests that sports should promote harmony in our lives, emphasizing that sports is a dance and the ultimate athlete a dancer. Michael Murphy's fictional Shivas Irons is a mystic who points out the cosmic symbolism of golf.

Loyal Renegades contains profiles of three of the most colorful and outspoken figures in sports. Wilfrid Sheed speculates on the future of three-time heavyweight champion, Muhammad Ali, with amazing accuracy, as recent events have shown ("Muhammad Ali—King of the Picture Gods"). In an informal essay ("A Self-Interview"), Jimmy Cannon reminisces about his life, literature, and his association with some of the greatest sports figures in history. And, finally, what must be one of the most bizarre sports stories ever written ("Fight to Live"), Al Stump details the almost unbelievable antics of Ty Cobb—in his seventies and literally infuriated by by the pain of cancer—as he stays alive by feeding on his own bitterness and hatred.

THE IRREVERENCE
OF HUMOR

"Bobby Joe," his father yelled, "crack somebody *out there.*
You just standin' around."

—Larry King

E. B. WHITE

The Decline of Sport

In the third decade of the supersonic age, sport gripped the nation in an ever tightening grip. The horse tracks, the ball parks, the fight rings, the gridirons, all drew crowds in steadily increasing numbers. Every time a game was played, an attendance record was broken. Usually some other sort of record was broken, too—such as the record for the number of consecutive doubles hit by left-handed batters in a Series game, or some such thing as that. Records fell like ripe apples on a windy day. Customs and manners changed, and the five-day business week was reduced to four days, then to three, to give everyone a better chance to memorize the scores.

Not only did sport proliferate but the demands it made on the spectator became greater. Nobody was content to take in one event at a time, and thanks to the magic of radio and television nobody had to. A Yale alumnus, class of 1962, returning to the Bowl with 197,000 others to see the Yale-Cornell football game would take along his pocket radio and pick up the Yankee Stadium, so that while his eye might be following a fumble on the Cornell twenty-two-yard line, his ear would be following a man going down to second in the top of the fifth, seventy miles away. High in the blue sky above the Bowl, skywriters would be at work writing the scores of other major and minor sporting contests, weaving an interminable record of victory and defeat, and using the new high-visibility pink news-smoke perfected by Pepsi-Cola engineers. And in the frames of the giant video sets, just behind the goal posts, this same alumnus could watch Dejected win the Futurity before a record-breaking crowd of 349,872 at Belmont, each of whom was tuned to the Yale Bowl and following the World Series game

199

in the video and searching the sky for further news of events either under way or just completed. The effect of this vast cyclorama of sport was to divide the spectator's attention, oversubtilize his appreciation, and deaden his passion. As the fourth supersonic decade was ushered in, the picture changed and sport began to wane.

A good many factors contributed to the decline of sport. Substitutions in football had increased to such an extent that there were very few fans in the United States capable of holding the players in mind during play. Each play that was called saw two entirely new elevens lined up, and the players whose names and faces you had familiarized yourself with in the first period were seldom seen or heard of again. The spectacle became as diffuse as the main concourse in Grand Central at the commuting hour.

Express motor highways leading to the parks and stadia had become so wide, so unobstructed, so devoid of all life except automobiles and trees that sport fans had got into the habit of traveling enormous distances to attend events. The normal driving speed had been stepped up to ninety-five miles an hour, and the distance between cars had been decreased to fifteen feet. This put an extraordinary strain on the sport lover's nervous system, and he arrived home from a Saturday game, after a road trip of three hundred and fifty miles, glassy-eyed, dazed, and spent. He hadn't really had any relaxation and he had failed to see Czlika (who had gone in for Trusky) take the pass from Bkeeo (who had gone in for Bjallo) in the third period, because at that moment a youngster named Lavagetto had been put in to pinch-hit for Art Gurlack in the bottom of the ninth with the tying run on second, and the skywriter who was attempting to write "Princeton 0—Lafayette 43" had banked the wrong way, muffed the "3," and distracted everyone's attention from the fact that Lavagetto had been whiffed.

Cheering, of course, lost its stimulating effect on players, because cheers were no longer associated necessarily with the immediate scene but might as easily apply to something that was happening somewhere else. This was enough to infuriate even the steadiest performer. A football star, hearing the stands break into a roar before the ball was snapped, would realize that their minds were not on him and would become dispirited and grumpy. Two or three of the big coaches worried so about this that they considered equipping all players with tiny ear sets, so that they, too, could keep abreast of other sporting events while playing, but the idea was abandoned as impractical, and the coaches put it aside in tickler files, to bring up again later.

I think the event that marked the turning point in sport and started it downhill was the Midwest's classic Dust Bowl game of 1975, when Eastern Reserve's great right end, Ed Pistachio, was shot by a spectator. This man, the one who did the shooting, was seated well down in the stands near the forty-yard line on a bleak October afternoon and was so saturated with sport and with the disappointments of sport that he had clearly become deranged. With a minute and fifteen seconds to play and the score tied, the Eastern Reserve quarterback had whipped a long pass over Army's heads into Pistachio's waiting arms. There was no other player anywhere near him, and all Pistachio had to do was catch the ball and run it across the line. He dropped it. At exactly this moment, the spectator—a man named Homer T. Parkinson, of 35 Edgemere Drive, Toledo, O.—suffered at least three other major disappointments in the realm of sport. His horse, Hiccough, on which he had a five-hundred-dollar bet, fell while getting away from the starting gate at Pimlico and broke its leg (clearly visible in the video); his favorite shortshop, Lucky Frimstitch, struck out and let three men die on base in the final game of the Series (to which Parkinson was tuned); and the Governor Dummer soccer team, on which Parkinson's youngest son played goalie, lost to Kent, 4-3, as recorded in the sky overhead. Before anyone could stop him, he drew a gun and drilled Pistachio, before 954,000 persons, the largest crowd that had ever attended a football game and the *second* largest crowd that had ever assembled for any sporting event in any month except July.

This tragedy, by itself, wouldn't have caused sport to decline, I suppose, but it set in motion a chain of other tragedies, the cumulative effect of which was terrific. Almost as soon as the shot was fired, the news flash was picked up by one of the skywriters directly above the field. He glanced down to see whether he could spot the trouble below, and in doing so failed to see another skywriter approaching. The two planes collided and fell, wings locked, leaving a confusing trail of smoke, which some observers tried to interpret as a late sports score. The planes struck in the middle of the nearby eastbound coast-to-coast Sunlight Parkway, and a motorist driving a convertible coupé stopped so short, to avoid hitting them, that he was bumped from behind. The pile-up of cars that ensued involved 1,482 vehicles, a record for eastbound parkways. A total of more than three thousand persons lost their lives in the highway accident, including the two pilots, and when panic broke out in the stadium, it cost another 872 in dead and injured. News of the disaster spread quicky to other sports arenas, and started other panics among the crowds trying to get to the exits, where they could buy a paper and study a list of the dead. All in all, the afternoon of sport cost 20,003 lives, a record. And nobody had much to show for it except one small Midwestern boy who hung around the smoking wrecks of the planes, captured some aero news-smoke in a milk bottle, and took it home as a souvenir.

From that day on, sport waned. Through long, noncompetitive Saturday afternoons, the stadia slumbered. Even the parkways fell into disuse as motorists rediscovered the charms of old, twisty roads that led through main streets and past barnyards, with their mild congestions and pleasant smells.

Considerations

1. This essay was written in 1947. Discuss White's talent for prediction.
2. What is the purpose of this essay? Is it a successful essay? Why or why not?
3. White never offers an explanation why people gave up their lives to sport. What is your explanation? Are we near such a point now? Support your answer.
4. Is this essay more or less effective than it would have been written in a straightforward expository style? Why or why not?

LARRY KING

Getting 'em Ready
for Darrell

The day was miserably cold and wet for mid-October, the wind cutting down from the north with a keen blade. A ghostly mist blew in about midnight. By daylight the Texas desert air knew a coastal chill, clammy and bone-numbing. Soon Midland's flat paved streets flowed like shallow rivers.

Seventh and eighth graders of the city's three junior high schools on awakening may have groaned into the weather's wet face, but they pulled on their football jerseys in compliance with a tradition requiring them to set themselves apart as gladiators each Thursday, which is Game Day. They would wear the jerseys in their classrooms.

Three hundred strong, ranging in age from twelve to fourteen years, they comprised the dozen junior high football teams—four to a school, two to a grade —that play blood-and-thunder eight-game schedules with provisions for the more successful to play through to a city championship. Each team practices from two to two and one-half hours per day, except on game days; no homework is assigned to football players the night before a game.

A blond twelve year old named Bradley, who weighed all of 107 pounds and limped on a swollen left knee, was having a more modest thought than of the city championship. "Maybe we can score on a wet field," he said. "We haven't done so good on a dry one." His team, the San Jacinto Seventh Grade Blues, had not known the dignity or solace of a touchdown in four previous outings. Their frustrated coach, a chunky, red-faced young man only recently out of college, had promised to run two laps around the football field for each touchdown his Blues scored against the unbeaten Trinity Orange. This prospect made Bradley grin. "You gonna play on that bad knee?" Bradley's visiting father asked. "I played on it last week," he shrugged.

There were perhaps a dozen shivering spectators behind each bench—mostly parents—when the Blues kicked off to Trinity at 3:30 p.m. Bradley, who had started all four previous games, was chagrined to find himself benched. "Maybe the coach is protecting your knee," his father suggested.

But Bradley believed he had been benched because he had missed two practice sessions that week, due to the death of his grandfather.

Trinity marched through the Blues for four consecutive first downs, most of the damage done by a ponderous fullback who, though slow, had enough strength and size to run over the smaller defensive kids. Even so, his performance did not satisfy his coach. "Come on, Don," he shouted from the Orange sideline. "Duck that shoulder and *go!* You're just falling forward out there!"

Meanwhile, the Blues' coach exhorted his collapsing defense: "Get mean out there! Come on, pop 'em! Bobby Joe, dammit, I'm gonna come out there and *kick* you if you let that ole fat boy run over you again!" Bobby Joe, who may have weighed all of a hundred pounds, sneaked a timid glance at the sideline.

"You look like a *girl*, Bobby Joe," a man in boots and a western hat shouted through his cupped hands. "I'm his father," he said to a glaring visitor, as if that mitigated the circumstance.

Trinity fumbled five yards away from a certain touchdown, losing the ball. The Blues jumped and yelled in celebration, while over on the Trinity side the Orange coach tore his rain-wet hair and shouted toward the sullen heavens. "Start runnin', coach," a skinny Blue said, picking up his helmet. "We're gonna score." "Way to *talk*, Donny!" an assistant coach said, slapping the youngster's rump as he ran on the field.

But scoreless San Jacinto could not move the ball. Backs, attempting double and multiple handoffs, ran into each other and fell. Orange linemen poured through to overwhelm the quarterback before he could pass. "We gonna have us some blocking practice at half time if you guys don't knock somebody down," the Blue coach screamed. As if in defiance, the Blue line next permitted several Orange linemen to roar through and block a punt near their own goal line. "Blocking practice at the half!" the Blue coach screamed, his face contorted. "I mean it, now. You dadgummed guys didn't touch a man!" The Orange in four plays plunged for a touchdown, then ran in the two-point conversion for an 8-0 lead.

"I told you guys to get in a goal-line defense, Mike!" the Blue coach raved. "Dammit, *always* get in a goal-line defense inside the ten."

"I thought we was *in* a goal-line defense," Mike alibied, his teeth chattering in the cold. He turned to a teammate: "Gene, wasn't we in a goal-line defense?" Gene was bent over, his head between his legs, arms hugging his ribs. "Somebody kicked me in the belly," he answered. The Blue coach missed this drama. He was up at the fifty-yard line, shooing off a concerned mother attempting to wrap the substitutes in blankets she had brought from a station wagon. "They won't be cold if they'll *hit* somebody," the coach shouted.

"Same ole thing," Bradley muttered from the bench as his team prepared to receive the kickoff. He had been inserted into the game long enough to know the indignity of having the touchdown scored over his left tackle position. "I had 'em," he said, "but then I slipped in the mud." Nobody said anything, for Bradley had clearly been driven out of the play like a dump truck.

Midway in the second quarter Bradley redeemed himself, fighting off two blockers to dump a ball carrier who had gotten outside the defensive end. He ended up at the bottom of a considerable pile and rose dragging his right foot, hopping back into position while grimacing at the sidelines as if in hope of relief. The coach did not see him, however, for he was busy chastising the offending end: "Paul, dammit, don't give him the outside! Protect your territory!" "Bobby Joe," his father yelled, "*crack* somebody out there. You just standin' around." Bradley played the remainder of the half, limping more on the injured ankle than on the swollen knee. Rain was coming down in windblown and near-freezing torrents when the young teams ran to their respective buses for half-time inspirations.

Four or five fathers shivered near the fifty-yard line, asses turned to the wind, smoking and talking of the 41–9 crusher applied to Oklahoma by the University of Texas. "They sure looked good," one of them said. "I think ole Darrell Royal's got his best team."

A mother in red slacks, her coat collar turned up and her nose red, approached the men. "I think it's just terrible to play those little fellers in weather like this," she said. The men chuckled indulgently. "Well," one of them said, "we got to git 'em ready for Darrell." The men laughed.

A balding, portly man in a mackinaw puffed up. "How's Jerry doing?" he inquired. "Well," one of the men hedged, "none of our boys lookin' *too* good. Especially on offense." "I went to see my other boy play the first half," the newcomer said. "His bunch was ahead 19–0. They looked great. 'Course, they're eighth graders."

When the teams returned to the field the newcomer grabbed his son, a thick-legged little back. "Jerry," he said, "son, you got to get tough. Leland's lookin' tough. His team's ahead 19–0."

"We got to *hurt* some people," a stubby little towhead with the complexion of a small girl said. "We got to *kill* us some people." The men laughed.

Bradley, soaking wet like all his teammates, was dispirited. What had the coach said to the Blues at half time? "He said we're better than they are and that we can beat 'em." The disapproving mother had returned with her blankets. Having wrapped up the bench warmers, she approached Bradley, who shrugged warmth off with a grunt: "I'm starting." An assistant coach, moving in to confiscate the coddling blankets, thought better of it when the mother stood her ground. "Damnfool *men*," she muttered, glaring.

The Blues drove sixty yards in the third period, their best-sustained drive of the season, inspiring their coach to whoop and holler like a delegate to the Democratic National Convention. "Way to *go*, Jerry!" the portly father shouted on play after play as he ran up and down. "Get outta them blankets!" the assistant coach yelled at the bench warmers as soon as the corrupting mother had fled to her station wagon. "If you don't think about being cold you won't *be* cold." Ten yards short of a touchdown three Blue backs collided behind the line in attempting a tricky double reverse, fumbling the ball and losing it in the process. The coach threw his red baseball cap in the mud and stomped it some.

"Coach," the visiting father said, "don't you think your offense is pretty complicated for a bunch of kids? I mean, why not have simple plays they can execute?"

The harassed coach cast a suspicious glance at the visitor. "We teach 'em the same basic system they'll need in high school," he snapped, turning away.

Trinity's Orange picked up a couple of first downs and then fumbled the ball back. The Blues, trembling in a new opportunity, came to the line of scrimmage a man short of the required eleven. The coach grabbed Bradley and thrust him into the game at right guard. Four plays later, failing to pick up a first down, the Blue offense trooped off the field. Water ran down their young faces. Two little girls in short cheerleaders' skirts gave them soggy rah-rahs from beneath a tent of blankets, their voices thin and self-conscious.

"Coach," Bradley said, "I don't know the plays for guard."

"You *don't?* Well, why not? Didn't you study the playbook?"

"Yeah, but you never *played* me at guard before. I'm a tackle."

"Oh," the coach said. "Well . . . Bobby *Joe*, dern you, *hit* somebody!"

"Way to *go*, Jerry!" the portly father shouted, breathing heavily as he kept pace with the action, jogging up and down the sideline. He turned to a bystander, puffing and beaming: "Jerry's not the ballplayer Leland is. 'Course, Leland's an eighth grader."

The visiting father touched the wet arm of his downcast son. "Bradley," he said, "you're standing up on defense before you charge. That gives the blocking linemen a better angle on you. Go in low. If your first charge is forward instead of up, you'll have so much power the laws of physics will guarantee your penetration."

"*Wow!*" one of the teenybopper cheerleaders said. "The laws of physics! Outta sight!" Her legs were blue in the cold.

"Way to *go*, Jerry!"

On his next defensive opportunity, Bradley charged in low and powerfully, his penetration carrying him so deep into the Orange backfield that he overran the ball carrier—who immediately shot through the vacated territory for a twenty-yard gain. Bradley stood back at the fifty-yard line, hands on hips, shaking his head in disgust and staring coldly at the visiting father, who suddenly studied his shoes.

San Jacinto's scoreless Blues got off a final fourth-quarter drive, aided by two unnecessary roughness penalties against the Orange. "Coach," one of the bench warmers sang out, "they're playing dirty."

"Let 'em play dirty," Jerry's father responded. "We'll take that fifteen yards every *time*, baby."

But balls were dropped and young feet slid in the mud, and in the end the Blue drive ended ignominiously. San Jacinto's Blues were fighting off another Orange advance when the game ended. They lost again, 0–8; their coach was safe from running laps.

"We gonna work in the blocking pits next week," he promised his young charges as they ran through the rain to their bus.

Bradley, showered and dressed in street clothes, limped slowly to his visiting father's car. His right shoe was unlaced because of the swollen ankle; by nightfall it would show dark blue around the shinbone with bright red welts running along the heel base.

"I'm sorry I didn't do better," Bradley said. "I got confused. You yelled one thing at me and the coach yelled another. *You* said charge hard and *he* said just stay there and plug up the hole."

"Well," the visiting father said lamely, "I'm sorry I yelled anything at you." There had been too much yelling. "Can't you get heat treatment for that ankle? Or at least some supporting tape?"

"Naw," Bradley said. "They don't give us those things until high school."

They drove along in the rain, the windows steaming over. They passed Robert E. Lee High School, where a squad of perhaps sixty young men drilled in the rain, padless, tuning up for their Friday-night game against Abilene. Thousands would drive the two hundred miles east, some of them drunk or drinking. Probably at least one would hit another car or a telephone pole.

"I may not play in high school," Bradley blurted. "I may not even play next year. The eighth-grade coach came scouting around last week, and he asked me some questions and I told him I might not even *play* next year." His blond hair was wet, his creamy young face was red. He looked angry and haggard and somehow old.

"Way to *go*, Bradley," his visiting father said.

Texas Observer
NOVEMBER 1970

Afterword

A love-hate relationship with football may rest deep in the family genes. My son came to me shortly after "Getting 'em Ready for Darrell" had appeared in the *Texas Observer* to indicate—with a bit of bashful toe digging—that he might try football for one more year. Why? "Well," he said with an abashed grin, "I kinda liked the publicity." He was on the verge of quitting a second time when the article was reprinted in *Chris Schenkel's Football Sportscene*—inspiring him to consider himself a national, rather than a regional, celebrity. He now has given up the game, however, and is in a private school where competitive sports are limited to swimming, sailing, and soccer. "I just got tired of football," he said recently. "Hell, I played seven years." Bradley King is fifteen.

Considerations

1. On the surface this essay is an objective report of a junior high school football game, but actually King is making a very serious point. Can you filter out his feelings and state his thesis in one sentence?
2. Could King have made his point more effectively by using a more direct method of exposition? Support your answer.
3. Discuss the following paragraph from the essay:

   "We got to *hurt* some people," a stubby little towhead with the complexion of a small girl said. "We got to *kill* us some people." The men laughed.

4. A gifted writer like King can speak volumes with one simple statement, such as his description of the young cheerleader: "Her legs were blue in the cold." Point out other examples.
5. This essay has serious implications. Discuss what you consider to be the most significant. Is football the only sport to be considered in such a light? What about baseball?

THE FOUR HORSEMEN OF THE WESTERN WORLD: RELIGION, WAR, GOVERNMENT, AND SPORTS

[The] intellectual vials of wrath are constantly over-flowing onto the hapless head of the athlete because of his hopeless Philistinism and his alleged inability to communicate with his peers save in monosyllabic grunts. Yet the halls of Congress and the board rooms of giant industrial complexes are alike populated by a striking number of ex-athletes who seem to have no difficulty whatever in communicating.

—Max Rafferty

JOHN R. TUNIS

The Great Sports Myth

"Suppose that while the motor pants,
We miss the nightingale?"

—E. V. Lucas

I

I have an English friend who, some thirty years ago, was champion of a little golf club situated on the Sussex Downs between Hove and Worthing. During the Boer War, in which he served as a subaltern, he lost his left arm, which incapacitated him for golf. With zeal he turned to tennis, developed a good game and in a few years became, despite his handicap, one of the best players in the local club. When the World War arrived he somehow wangled a commission for himself and, leading a battalion into action on the Somme, lost his right leg. My last meeting with him took place several winters ago at a British Lawn

Tennis and Croquet Club on the French Riviera. He had learned croquet and was by then a low-handicap player, pressing the club champion closely.

That man, I submit, is a sportsman. He knows the thrill of real sport, of playing, not for championships, for titles, for cash, for publicity, for medals, for applause, but simply for the love of playing. Everyone knows this thrill who has felt a golf ball soar from his club and watched it bound down the middle of the course, two hundred and fifty yards ahead; who has finished a long, tense rally at tennis with a passing shot that cuts the sideline and leaves a helpless adversary shaking his head in admiration at the net; who has followed two Airedales jumping and leaping through country uplands on a mellow, crisp afternoon in fall. A long cross-country walk with a dog, three close sets of tennis, a foursome on a day when the course is uncrowded and the sun shines high above—this is sport, real sport, the expression of the sporting spirit at its best. On these occasions one tastes the full flavor of the game, one finds that complete and satisfying relaxation of mind and body which to the work-weary brain is such perfect solace. In this informal and unorganized sport one finds not only the game, but the player at his best. Umpires? Referees? Officials? The need of them does not exist. Implicitly one trusts one's opponent because one trusts oneself; impossible to question the score, impossible to hesitate as to whether a shot did or did not touch the line. All that is finest in sport can be found—is found—in such friendly encounters upon golf links and tennis courts.

But of late years a strange and curious fiction appears to have grown up regarding sport, whereby the effects of such friendly sport are improperly attributed to those highly organized athletic competitions that take place each year from January to December.

Let us grant that sport between individuals is a working laboratory for the building of character. Let us admit freely that the health of nations is being improved by friendly outdoor games. By all means let us give thanks and sing praises for the opportunities afforded by such sports to get out into the open air and freshen ourselves for the burdens of life that grow daily more exhausting. But let us not confound the precious informality of individual sport with the huge, widely advertised sporting contests with which we are being inundated from year's end to year's end.

This fiction I call the Great Sports Myth. It is a fiction sustained and built up by the large class of people now financially interested in sport. There are the newsgatherers and the sports functionaries for the daily press; in their very natural efforts to glorify their trade, they have preached unceasingly the notion that all the values to be found in informal athletic games are present as well in the huge, organized, sporting spectacles. There is the paid instructor, the football or baseball or track coach, the trainer or association head who, after all, can hardly be blamed if he attempts to depict his efforts as a cross between those of a religious revivalist and of a social service uplifter. These gentry—the newsgatherer, and the new professional sports uplifter—tell us that competitive sport, as well as informal, unorganized sport, is health-giving, character-building, brain-making. They imply, more or less directly, that its exponents are heroes, possessed of none but the highest moral qualities; tempered and steeled in the great, white heat of competition; purified and made holy by their devotion to intercollegiate and international sport. Thanks to them—and to others not entirely disinterested—there has grown up in the public mind an exaggerated and sentimental notion of the moral value of great, competitive, sport spectacles.

The sports writers are required to regard the whole sporting panorama with an almost religious seriousness. It is their job; their bread and butter. Hardly one dares publicly to question the sanctity of organized competitive athletics. One who should dare to suggest that our idols of the sporting world have feet of clay might find himself in serious trouble when next he went out upon a story. If he intimates that this or that sport has become a vast and complicated business, he will get short shift should he ever visit its Association headquarters. What more natural, therefore, than that everyone so employed should further embroider that delightful fiction, the Great Sports Myth? Hence the annual appeal to rally to the defense of the Davis Cup is as solemn as if our national life hung in the balance. And the amount of space given by the press to the college football system is proof of the hold the Great Sports Myth has upon us. On the evening before the Harvard-Yale game at Cambridge, even as sedate a newspaper as the Boston *Transcript* devotes no less than four pages to the conflict; special writers, sporting writers, feature writers, editors, and their more humble confreres, treat the morrow's match as earnestly and sententiously as they do the forecasts of a Presidential election upon Election Eve.

II

The manner in which the American public is fostered and fed upon the Great Sports Myth is not only amazing; for anyone who gets an opportunity to peek behind the scenes it is one of the most disconcerting signs of the times. For the sporting heroes of the nation are its gods. From day to day, from month to month, from year to year, we are deluged with a torrent of words about these Galahads of sport; the amateur football players of the colleges, and the "shamateur" golf or tennis players, who often take a hand in exalting their own personalities through the medium of the press. In the winter months we are treated to columns of "dope" about these supermen, of chatter and gossip about their every movement. In early spring the star of sport moves eastward; for six weeks we are regaled, via the Atlantic cables, with the feats of Mr. Tilden, Mr. Hagen, Miss Wills, or Mrs. Mallory, in the great French and British tennis and golf championships. By July the travelers are back again in their native haunts—not infrequently with hard words to say about conditions and competitors across the sea—and then the deluge of sporting bunk begins in earnest. The channel swimmers are busy explaining why channels are so broad and trainers so thick. In August come the big aquatic events, the yachting and motor boat races; in early September, the matches for the Davis Cup. Almost every fall we have a "major league" prize fight. October brings colds, coal bills, and the World's Series, with its front page cavortings of Home-run Kings and Strike-out Emperors. And as the sporting year draws to an end in late November, the nation goes completely daft over intercollegiate football. Except for the imposing lists of All-American teams—composed by gentlemen who have perhaps seen in action some three hundred of the thirty thousand football players of the United States—we have a rest in December. And we need it!

Man has always, I suppose, been a hero worshiper. Doubtless he always will be. We Americans do not seem to take to religious prophets. We have no Queen Marie, nor even a Mussolini, to raise upon a pedestal. Consequently we turn hopefully to the world of sports. There we find the material to satisfy our lust for hero worship; there we discover the true gods of the nation. Messrs. Hagen, Tunney, Tilden, Jones, Ruth, Cohen, Dempsey—these become the idols of America's masculine population, young and old. And why not? After all, we ask ourselves, are they not athletes? Have they not been cleansed (and so sanctified) in the great white heat of competition, upon the links or the gridiron, the court or the diamond? That competitive sport—any kind of competitive sport from squash tennis to prize fighting—makes for nobility of character, such is the first commandment of the American sporting public. This, in fact, is the foundation of the Great Sports Myth.

III

Yet, in plain truth, highly organized competitive sports are not character-building; on the contrary, after a good deal of assistance at and some competition in them, I am convinced that the reverse is true. So far are they from building character that, in my opinion, continuous and excessive participation in competitive sports tends to destroy it. Under the terrific stress of striving for victory, victory, victory, all sorts of unpleasant traits are brought out and strengthened. Too frequently the player's worst side is magnified; his self-control is broken down much more than it is built up. I know this is heresy. I realize that the contrary is preached from every side. (Most fervently, however, the preachers are sports writers, football coaches, or others who have some other direct and personal interest in the furtherance of the Great Sports Myth.) I am aware that the participants in American sports are all supposed to be little short of demigods. Yet if football, for instance, is the noble, elevating and character-building sport it is supposed to be why, I wonder, is it necessary to station an umpire, a field judge, a head linesman, and half a dozen assistants to follow the play at a distance of a few yards and to watch zealously every one of the twenty-two contestants in order that no heads and no rules may be simultaneously broken?

"NERVE TENSED STALWARTS KEYED UP FOR SUPREME EFFORT OF SEASON."

So ran the headline of a pre-game football story in a big New York daily last fall. Anyone who has seen the average athletic contest at close range will testify to the accuracy of this characterization. Instead of being in sound mental and physical condition when they go out on the links, the gridiron, or the river, our gods are actually in a state of nerves which often leads them to do things otherwise incomprehensible. The plain truth is that the intensive strain of modern competition and the glare of publicity created by the press, the movies, and the radio, wear down and destroy the nerve tissue of the average competitor. How else can one explain the petulant outburst and the no less petulant actions of Mr. Walter Hagen on his return from his trip to England after having failed to win their golfing title some years ago? Or the performances of Mr. Tilden upon the court? Off the court, Mr. Tilden, as his friends will testify, is a charming and urbane gentleman. Once he gets into combat, however, he becomes, in his zest for victory—a zest that every champion in competitive sport must have or perish—something totally unlike his normal self. He will turn and glare at any linesman who dares give a decision against his judgment; before the thousands in the stands he will demand the removal of the offender; he will request "lets" at crucial moments, object when new balls are thrown out, in short do things he would never do were he not so intensely concentrated on winning.

Nor would it be just to Mr. Tilden to single him out for criticism. Those who saw the Davis Cup Challenge Round in 1914, will remember the childish behavior of the man who is considered by many the greatest tennis player of all time, Mr. Norman Everard Brookes. After the third set of his match with Mr. R. N. Williams (which was won by the American, 10-8) the crowd, anticipating a victory for the United States, rose—as was but natural—in loud and vociferous cheering. Mr. Brookes promptly clapped his hands to his ears and kept them there as long as the cheering went on.

Anyone who has spent a winter in the south of France during the reign of the late Queen of French tennis, Mademoiselle Suzanne Lenglen, will testify to her strenuous efforts to avoid defeat by remaining out of tournaments in which she seemed likely to be beaten. In 1926, during the visit of Miss Helen Wills to the Riviera, her attempts to avoid the American were so amusing that a famous Parisian daily ran an article entitled, "Tennis ou Cache-Cache?" (Tennis or Hide and Seek?) This, mind you, is not the conduct of youngsters new to competitive sport; it is the conduct of champions and super-champions. Concentrating as they must to win, they hardly know what they are doing or saying. For the time being, they become self-hypnotized. Follow them around the sport circle from week to week, and from year to year, and you will, I am sure, lose any illusion you may have about the uplifting effect of present-day competitive sport.

The popular belief is that sport teaches self-control, that it shows us how to accept not only victory but defeat with a graceful and sincere smile. If you are a believer in the Great Sports Myth, I wish you might visit the locker-rooms and dressing-quarters of our clubhouses and athletic buildings and mingle with our champions before and after their contests.

"He beat the gun, that's why he copped."

"I was interfered with in the last quarter, on that forward pass, or I'd have scored a touchdown."

"I'll beat that big stiff or burst a blood vessel."

"That decision in the third set cost me the match—sure the ball was on the line, I saw it."

"This man Smith has always been against us; we'll have to see he doesn't get a chance to referee any of the 'varsity games again."

These—with embellishments unprintable—are the sort of things you hear on the inside at every big sporting contest. You may, perhaps, imagine this to be an exaggeration. Get someone who has umpired a match between Mr. Tilden and Mr. Richards to tell you how they addressed each other as they shook hands across the net after a tense, five-set battle! It is no accident that Mr. Robert T.

Jones is almost the only champion in any branch of sport who is genuinely popular with those who play against him and, therefore, see him under the stress of modern competition. The strain at the top is too great for most men.

Curiously enough, although the majority of our sporting heroes are magnified and worshiped, Mr. Jones seems to have had something less than the breaks from the gentry of the sporting press. This doubtless came about because these devotees of the Great Sports Myth have created a charming fable about Mr. Jones which exactly fitted into their ideas about the character-building benefits of competitive sport. Mr. Jones as a youngster, they aver, was a perfectly terrible chap. When he first took up golf he threw his clubs about. He broke them up whenever he missed a six-foot putt. He swore. He cursed. Really, he was a perfectly terrible fellow! But behold the influence of the game! Now a more charming young sportsman it would be hard to find. Due, of course, the inference is, to the soul-saving and character-forming effects of sport.

A lovely fiction. But untrue. Yet I have never seen this untruth refuted in an American newspaper; to do so would tend to destroy the Great Sports Myth. However, to an English reporter, about a year ago in London, Mr. Jones vouchsafed the following:

"I've read newspaper comments in which I am told that I not only won the British championship at St. Andrews but conquered myself as well. What is it all about? Have I ever been a bunch of fireworks? I played my first championship when I was fourteen years old, and I am twenty-five now. In all that time I have made a fool of myself only twice, once at the Red Cross tournament in Boston in 1915, when I was fifteen years old, and once at the British open championship at St. Andrews when I was nineteen. Is that being worse than anyone else? Chick Evans can throw a club away in the midst of a championship and nobody minds. Why pick on me?

"The only break I ever made at home was in Boston ten years ago. I've played right along since then. Where's the sense of throwing Boston at me now? Of course it's nice to have people say nice things about you, but honestly, when New York papers make me out such a glowing example of moral discipline I don't know what to make of it."

Poor Mr. Jones. Of all our athletic stars, he is most surely the one who deserves a fair break and yet, thanks to the obsession of sporting writers and their devotion to the Great Sports Myth, he has received a bad one. There is a moral in this for those who have the time and patience to discover it.

IV

Yet another tenet of the Great Sports Myth is the time-worn belief that international competition in sport strengthens the bonds between nations and between individuals. It usually does nothing of the sort! Surely, if football players from two of the largest universities in the United States indulge in fisticuffs before eighty thousand spectators in their big test of the season, there is little chance for a general kissing-match at an international sporting reunion such as the Olympic games!

When these games approach and one hears the usual platitudes about the great good they do in international relations and the benefits they confer upon humanity at large, I am minded of a small paragraph which was culled from the *Auto,* the great Parisian sporting newspaper. Translated exactly, it reads:

"M. Moneton, the referee of the match between the Racing Club de Calais and the Stade Roubaisienne, thanks the members of the Racing Club de Calais team for saving his life directly after the match."

Not every sporting contest ends in a free fight as this one presumably did, but there is far more hard feeling generated by sport than is usually admitted by the adherents of the Great Sports Myth. When the Irish rugby team played France last winter, the crowd got out of hand, broke down the barriers, swarmed onto the field and rushed for the referee, the captain of a Scottish team twenty-five years ago. He managed to escape to the dressing-room whence, as the mob stood outside howling for his blood, he was eventually escorted from the grounds under police protection.

You never hear much about such things? Certainly not. The sporting writers do not dwell upon them for very obvious reasons. The sort of thing they prefer to play up can be illustrated by an article which appeared several years ago in the *Princeton Alumni Weekly* entitled, "The Sublimation of War." The writer's argument was to the effect that if all nations were "sport loving and dominated by the true instincts of sport," war would be completely eradicated. The Sublimation of War! We had a taste of it several months later when the break came between Harvard and Princeton.

Dignified in front-page headlines by the sonorous title, "SEVERANCE OF ATH-LETIC RELATIONS," this episode reflected credit upon neither of the universities nor upon their followers. According to the tenets of the Great Sports Myth, Princeton and Harvard undergraduates should have been loyal friends and good fellows both on the field and in the stands. Such, as the saying goes, was not the case. Trouble began early in 1922 when one after another of the best Harvard players were taken from the gridiron in the Princeton game with various injuries which removed them from the "sublimating" effects of sport for the rest of the season. Murmurs of rough play were heard at Cambridge; they continued, these murmurs, during the next few years, in increasing volume, as Princeton went on defeating Harvard by overwhelming scores. The climax was reached in the season of 1926 when, the day before the game, the Harvard *Lampoon* appeared with a disgraceful attack upon Princeton and her supporters. The game which followed was a sorry spectacle; hisses and groans arose from both sides of the field and, in their comments during the following week, even the most ardent devotees of the Great Sports Myth, in writing for the press, agreed that such an affair was neither stimulating nor worth repeating. After the game the undergraduates of the two universities regarded one another much as did Germans and Americans in 1918. With all the solemnity of a nation rupturing diplomatic relations with a powerful neighbor, Princeton "broke with Harvard," as the newspapers screamed in headlines from their front pages.

Recriminations, insinuations, rhetorical attacks and counterattacks ensued; the press carried columns and pages of the effect of this break upon the world of sport—and not a soul who commented on the fracas appeared to see the amusing side of the whole affair. Sport, the healer of relationships between na-tions; sport, the promoter of good feeling and good comradeship; sport, that brings forth all that is best and noblest in human nature, was producing—what? Gouged noses, broken ankles, bad feeling, cursing, and reviling in the sanctity of dressing-rooms; coarse accusations and cheap humor in the publications of a great university. If sport cannot do better than this among the representatives of two of the principal American colleges, how can it be expected to unite Gaul and Teuton, Arab and Scandinavian, black man and white, as it is popularly supposed to do by those who prate glibly about peoples "dominated by the true instincts of sport."

Such breaks in relations between our universities, are not, it appears, uncommon in intercollegiate football. The facts are not generally known; but almost every large college in the country has, at some time in its history, broken with some great rival. Thus the Army and Navy broke between 1893 and 1899; now they are at it again. Harvard and Yale broke between 1894 and 1897. Pennsylvania and Lafayette broke between 1900 and 1903. Princeton and Harvard, after breaking between 1897 and 1912, broke again in 1926 until some future date unknown, thereby bidding fair to establish a National Intercollegiate Breaking record for all time. At the present moment the list of colleges which have broken relations with other colleges is a fairly large one; should it increase materially it would seem that our universities might have difficulty in completing their schedules. Thus Princeton, having broken with Pennsylvania years ago, has now broken with Harvard; the Army has broken with Syracuse; Columbia has broken with New York University; and the Navy has broken with the Army. These are some of the breaks publicly announced. Others are being kept under cover.

Now, if our highly organized sports taught us as much of mutual understanding, generosity, and forbearance as their advocates claim that they do, there might be some excuse for the elevation of sport into a kind of national religion. Yet why is it that the United States, by common acclaim the greatest sporting nation in the world, is so sensitive to criticism, so open to flattery? In point of fact, what the fetish of competitive sport inculcates in us most successfully is the desire to win. Not at any cost? Certainly not! There are far too many linesmen, referees, umpires, field judges, and minor officials to permit of that sort of thing. But our gods are all winners: it is Tunney, Hagen, Jones, Miss Wills, not Mrs. Mallory, Johnston, or Ouimet who are worshiped and glorified. It is the champion, not the way in which the championship is won or lost, that attracts the plaudits of the mob whose creed is the Great Sports Myth. The King can do no wrong. And the King (pro tem) is always the man at the top of the pile.

Moreover, by thus elevating our athletic heroes to peaks of prominence, by prying into their private lives, by following them incessantly in the columns of the daily press, by demanding of them victories and yet more victories, we force them to lose all sense of proportion—if indeed they ever had any. For it is a debatable question whether anyone with a sense of proportion—or a sense of humor, which comes to much the same thing—could so far lose himself in this sporting miasma as to become a champion. Judging by their remarks in public, one is forced to conclude that many, if not all, of our sporting gods are muscle bound between the ears!

Considerations

1. This essay was written in 1928 by one of the great sportswriters of that era. What does it seem to say to those who maintain that pointing out the weaknesses in athletics is a recent phenomenon, originated by the new journalists?
2. Summarize what Tunis calls "The Great Sports Myth."
3. List the "conspirators" in this great sports fiction. What does each have to gain in perpetuating this fiction?
4. "The sporting heroes of the nation are its gods," he says, and lists Mr. Tilden, Mr. Hagen, Miss Wills, and Mrs. Mallory. Will our "gods" be as unrecognizable 50 years from now?
5. What is the "foundation" of the Great Sports Myth? Is the same true today?
6. Does the "Myth" extend to the Olympic games? Explain.
7. What is Tunis's idea of a true sportsman?

MAX RAFFERTY

Interscholastic Athletics:
The Gathering Storm

There are two great national institutions which simply cannot tolerate either internal dissension or external interference: our armed forces, and our interscholastic sports program. Both are of necessity benevolent dictatorships because by their very nature they cannot be otherwise. A combat squad which has to sit down and poll its members before it reacts to an emergency has had it, and so has a football team which lets its opponents tell it whom to start in next Saturday's game.

Ridiculous, you say? Yet both these ridiculous things are happening, or threatening to happen. If you're up on the news at all, you're familiar with the problem the army and marines have been having in recent months with men who go on hunger strikes and who refuse to obey orders on the battlefield. You should be even more familiar with what's happening on the athletic field.

To pinpoint what I'm talking about, let's look at a couple of examples of how sports are being pressured and used to do things they were never intended to do at all.

First, let's look at the "Great Pumpkin," as his Oregon State players call coach Dee Andros. Andros is of Greek descent, like Spiro Agnew, and he's just as good at football coaching as Agnew is at pointing out the faults of the news media, which is pretty darned good. Unfortunately, Andros has a problem.

For 21 years, he's had an invariable rule that his gridiron gladiators look the part. His squads have always enjoyed sky-high morale, much of it due to the fact that the players are encouraged to regard the team as more important than the individual player, and the combined effort more valuable than the heroics of the loner. Long ago, the coach banned the freak out as an acceptable avocation for Oregon State footballers.

In other words: if you want to play for me, fellows, no girlish necklaces and cutesy medallions, no Iroquois scalplocks, no hairmattress beards, and no Fu Manchu moustaches. You can sport these execrable excrescences and still go to Oregon State, but you can't massage your egos thus publicly and still play football for Dee Andros. Period.

At least right up until last spring it was "period." The Battling Beavers of OSU won a lot more games than they lost, and what's far more important they managed to win them while looking like decent human beings instead of like fugitives from a Barnum and Bailey side show.

They were shaven, they were shorn, they wore men's clothing rather than feminine fripperies, and they actually looked as though they bathed once in a while. In short, the varsity players stood out like lighthouses alongside the campus activists, many of whom look and smell as though they had recently emerged from ten years' solitary confinement on Devil's Island.

And this last is undoubtedly what triggered Andros' current crisis.

It seems that some hulking lout on his squad decided to defy the team's personal appearance rules and to sprout a luxuriant thicket of facial foliage which viewed under his helmet and behind his face-guard made him virtually indistinguishable from a gorilla. The coach said: "Shave it off or shove off." The player refused and appealed to Oregon State's president on the grounds that his civil rights were being violated.

Instead of backing up his coach and telling the hairy one to get lost, the OSU prexy appointed a Commission on Human Rights to investigate the coach, thus firmly establishing the president's credentials as an even bigger ass than the exhibitionist player. The commission dutifully censured Andros for showing "insufficient sensitivity to the sacred right of adolescent showoffs to break coaching rules."

Kindly note at this juncture that nobody at Oregon State is compelled to play football. Note also that the coach's rules have been part of his winning formula for more than two decades, and are well-known to almost everyone in the state of Oregon. The alternative is laughably simple, and it's true on every campus and for every sport: if you don't like the rules, don't go out for the sport.

Now just where does the decision by the Human Rights Commission's driveling academicians leave Dee Andros? What's the future of a coach whose players now know he may be road-blocked and face-slapped by some ad hoc committee every time he tells them to do something they don't want to do?

I can't think of a better way to destroy a fine football team, can you? Or a fine coach, for that matter. But maybe that's the whole idea.

Up to now, I've never known that exquisite sensitivity to a player's pampered ego was one of the prerequisites for a good coach. I've always thought a coach's job was to make men out of wet-behind-the-ears boys.

Can you imagine the expression on gruff old Knute Rockne's face if some cap-and-gowned buffoon had called him "insufficiently sensitive"?

Second, along the same lines but with even more unsavory overtones, there's the recent case of Stanford University's foray into the unlovely field of religious persecution, with athletics playing the role of unwilling patsy. It seems that Stanford recently and scathingly severed athletic relations with Brigham Young

University because of one of the fundamental tenets of the Mormon faith: that the descendants of Canaan are ineligible by Old Testament mandate to hold the highest offices in the Church. Inasmuch as those descendants are held by long tradition to be black, Negroes are thus disqualified from taking their place as priests and bishops of the Mormon faith.

Result: not many Negroes are Mormons. Additional result: no black football players at BYU. So Stanford joins several other colleges in a kind of anti-Mormon Coalition which is boycotting the Utah school until it mends its allegedly wicked ways, and they are presently writing unctuous letters to each other congratulating themselves on their own virtue.

So far, so good. But let's carry the story one step further. The Coalition isn't trying merely to get Brigham Young to put Negroes on its football team. If that's all there were to it, you wouldn't be hearing a single squawk out of me, because I firmly believe that all education, and athletics in particular, should be completely integrated and conspicuously multiracial. Unlike some southern schools which the Coalition somehow didn't get around to denouncing, though, BYU is perfectly willing to do just that, has in fact featured black athletes on some of its past teams, and is currently looking for some more. No, what the Coalition is really demanding is something far, far, different. It's that the Church of the Latter Day Saints repudiate part of its established dogma, given to it a century and a half ago, according to its scriptures by divine revelation.

Now this is quite another matter. What on earth would you do if you were athletic director in a case of this kind? Brigham Young University, you see, is a Church school. Its policies must perforce reflect the teachings of that Church, and cannot contravene them. In effect, the Church *is* the school, and vice versa. So the Coalition isn't just demanding that a sister school simply change an athletic policy; it's conducting an organized boycott of a deeply held theological belief, and this sort of religious persecution in the final third of the twentieth century is absolutely intolerable.

It's as though the Coalition were to boycott an Episcopalian college because we Episcopalians don't permit females to be bishops, or to put pressure on a Jewish university because Judaism won't allow ham sandwich-munchers to become rabbis. I don't happen to agree at all that the color of a man's skin should keep him from becoming a priest, a bishop, or a pope, for that matter, in any church. But I don't happen to be a Mormon, and what the Mormons devoutly believe is simply none of my Episcopalian business. Neither is it the business of athletics in general, or the Coalition in particular.

So long as BYU keeps up its academic standards, behaves itself properly on the playing field, and opens its classrooms and its athletic teams alike to all who qualify for entrance regardless of color or race, it's as outrageous for the Coalition to use athletics to interfere with a church's right to practice its own faith as it was for the jolly jesters of the Third Reich to interfere with the German Jews' right to practice theirs. The BYU students, incidentally, have an impeccable record in regard to the criteria I've just listed, and what's more, stayed soberly in class last year while the Stanfordites were bloodily occupying administration buildings and raising hell generally.

Ah, well. Football is supposed to teach players sportsmanship, fellowship, and fair play. I'm sure BYU can find other schools beside those of the Coalition to supply this desired mixture, and which won't also expose its players to the added and unwelcome ingredient of religious intolerance.

My purpose in bringing these incidents before you tonight is simply to remind you of their increasing frequency. At San Jose, Wyoming, Washington, and a dozen other distracted colleges, players have challenged their coaches, walked out on their own teams, and boycotted their own schools, all in the name of some social, economic, or political grievance which the sport in question had never had anything to do with and with which it was never set up to cope.

As athletic directors, you're up against more than just a challenge to your authority or that of your coaches, a temporary road-block in the path of bigger and better athletic competition. What's facing you in the very near future is the possible elimination of school sports altogether, if only because sports as we know them cannot survive their transformation into a mere tool of various activist groups with their own non-athletic axes to grind.

It's ironical, in fact, that those who hate athletics the most are the ones currently trying to use athletics for their own ends. These, of course, are the "Let's-give-aid-and-comfort-to-the-Communists" agitators, the hairy, loud-mouthed freaks of both sexes who infest our campuses today like so many unbathed boll weevils. The activists and the pseudo-intellectuals have created a myth—a kind of anti-athlete cartoon caricature which I'd like to analyze briefly.

The stereotype is that of the muscle-bound and moronic athlete. Of late he has receipted for so many "avant garde" jokes that he has become a permanent cliché, like the college widow and the absent-minded professor. Yet when one puts the myth of the jug-headed, oafish muscle-man under the cold light of logical analysis, it doesn't hold up worth a nickel.

The beard-and-sandal set claims the athlete is stupid. Yet in every high school where I've ever worked the grade-point average of the varsity players was higher than that of the student body as a whole.

The lank-haired leaders of our campus revolutionists sneer at the varsity letterman for his allegedly juvenile enthusiasms and his willingness to die for dear old Rutgers. But they themselves are quite openly and ardently guilty of enthusiasms for such strange causes as raising bail money for Mario Savio and paying Joan Baez's taxes, and they seem ready to die at a moment's notice for a smile from Kosygin or even for the slightest relaxation of the built-in scowl on the face of Mao-Tse-Tung. By comparison, dying for Rutgers has its points.

Their intellectual vials of wrath are constantly overflowing onto the hapless head of the athlete because of his hopeless Philistinism and his alleged inability to communicate with his peers save in monosyllabic grunts. Yet the halls of Congress and the board rooms of giant industrial complexes are alike populated by a striking number of ex-athletes who seem to have no difficulty whatever in communicating. And the Philistine mentality of such former contenders on the playing fields as Douglas MacArthur, John F. Kennedy, and Justice Byron "Whizzer" White may be left safely for history to judge.

As another football season ends and another basketball season begins, I have to confess a lifelong fondness for the amateur athlete. Over the past thirty years, eight of which were spent as a high school coach and athletic director,

I've seen a remarkable number of athletes fighting and even dying for their country, and remarkably few of them ending up in jail or taking the Fifth Amendment before a Congressional investigating committee. They seem to be conspicuously absent, too, from Communist-inspired demonstrations and Filthy Speech Movements.

They are, in short, above-average, decent, reasonably patriotic Americans. Maybe that's why they're under increasing attack from the kooks, the crumbums, and Commies.

I'm not too worried about the outcome. The love of clean, competitive sports is too deeply imbedded in the American matrix, too much a part of the warp and woof of our free people, ever to surrender to the burning-eyed, bearded draft-card-burners who hate and envy the athlete because he is something they can never be—a *man*.

Our greatest soldier-statesman of the twentieth century once had this to say about athletics and the men who follow its rigorous and rewarding discipline: "Upon the fields of friendly strife are sown the seeds which, on other days, on other fields, will bear the seeds of victory."

As athletic directors, you have a decision to make. The college syndrome I have noted and documented in this brief talk is spreading into American high schools even as we meet together tonight. Your choice is simple: you can back up your coaches' authority to do with their teams what coaches have done for the last hundred years, or you can play a cowardly game of patty-cake with the activists and watch your sports program go down the drain with your own jobs going right along with it.

I didn't come here tonight to make you feel good, but rather to do two things: warn you, and promise to help. Little enough of idealism and faith and cheerful willingness to fight on steadfastly for the right remains to us Americans in these, the Sick Sixties. Interscholastic sports, rising surprisingly and increasingly above their age-old status as mere games, serve today as the staunch custodians of these treasured concepts out of our great past.

If you elect to cop out on all this and to let your teams be used for their own sinister purposes by those who are the enemies of all athletics, you will deserve exactly what you will get, and you will receive no sympathy from me. But if you decide to stand your ground and fight for the future of American sports against those who would destroy everything you've worked for all your lives, then indeed you will have formidable allies: my own Department; the vast majority of our state legislators; above all, the millions of Californians who love athletics and who believe with all their hearts that it symbolizes the clean, bright, fighting spirit which is America herself.

A tough job, this one which I am urging upon you? You bet. But you are tough men, or should be. These are rugged times, and we need rugged men to stand up to them. My own job, over the years, has not been exactly a bed of roses. All you and I can do is to lower our heads and do our level best, keeping the goals of our great profession constantly before our mind's eye, disregarding as best we can the barrage of the opposition, striving to keep our feet despite the shell holes and the booby traps, satisfied if the end of each day finds us a little closer to our hearts' desire.

When I grow tired, as I occasionally do—when I get discouraged, as once in a while happens—when the slings and arrows of our common enemies get to me, as they do now and then—there is one never-failing source of inspiration upon which I learned long ago to rely, and which always sends me back into the fray with renewed strength and a stout heart.

It's a very simple thing. I merely close my eyes and call up from the depths of memory my old teams—the myriad faces which have passed before me for so many years—the bright, fresh, questing faces of the kids with whom I lived and worked for so long. Those strong, eager boys, so willing to learn, so wrapped up in the joy of playing the game for the game's sake, the only way it ever should be played. I look back upon the long parade of faces, and in my mind I see the countless more whom in reality I will never get to see—the youngsters of California—your own teams—thronging in their untold thousands from the redwood country of the north to the great desert which lies along our southern border.

And suddenly it's all worth while. What men ever had more children than you and I to work for, to hope for, to live for? More than two million boys—the joy, the hope, the whole future of our state. It's a family worth fighting for.

I recommend it to you.

Considerations

1. Both Rafferty and Hoch (see "Coliseums and Gladiators") are critical of the state of modern athletics, but they disagree as to what is wrong. Read Hoch's essay and discuss their philosophical differences.
2. They were written in the sixties and each constitutes something of a warning. Which is the more realistic? Support your answer.
3. Thorstein Veblen pointed out in the nineteenth century that sports, religion, government, and war are four intertwined elements of a rich and powerful society. Can you cite examples of this phenomenon in Rafferty's speech?
4. Discuss the following statement:

   Your choice is simple: you can back up your coaches' authority to do with their teams what coaches have done for the last hundred years, or you can play a cowardly game of patty-cake with the activists and watch your sports program go down the drain with your jobs going right along with it.

5. Hoch uses documented sources in his essay, and Rafferty uses rhetoric (look up this word). Would Rafferty have been more effective had he used documented evidence to support his thesis? Support your answer.

PETER S. GREENBERG

Wild in the Stands

fan (fan), *n.*, enthusiastic devotee or follower: *a sports fan.* [short for FANATIC]

The game started at 9 p.m. last October 18, but the fans began drinking their dinners hours earlier, en route to Schaefer Stadium and in the parking lots outside the Foxboro, Massachusetts, sports complex. By game time, all the participants—the New England Patriots, the New York Jets, the ABC Monday Night Football crew and the crowd—were primed for action. There was plenty of it. While the Patriots were routing the Jets, 41–7, jubilant fans turned on each other, on the cops, and out onto the field. The game was interrupted half a dozen times as eleven rowdies, chased by security guards, tried out the Astro Turf. Twenty-one fans were arrested for disorderly conduct, eighteen were taken into protective custody for public intoxication, two were booked for throwing missiles, two for assault and battery and one for possession of a dangerous weapon. One fan stole another's wheelchair and was charged with larceny. Thirty spectators were taken to a hospital with cuts and bruises, one was stabbed and two died of heart attacks. Foxboro policeman Tom Blaisdell sustained a dislocated jaw and a concussion, and while a local sheriff was administering mouth-to-mouth resuscitation to a coronary victim in the stands, a drunken fan urinated on them both. "It was a tough game," said Foxboro police chief John Gaudett as he reviewed that night's blotter. "But I've seen even worse."

This year, it all started to build up again in the ninth inning of the second game of the World Series at Yankee Stadium.

It was a long, easy fly ball to center field on a beer-filled, capacity crowd night. Dodger outfielder Glenn Burke positioned himself for the catch. A dozen feet away, as right fielder Reggie Smith ran behind Burke to watch him make the final putout of the game, he was pasted in the head by a hard, red rubber ball hurled with malicious accuracy from the upper deck.

The ball popped Smith on the button of his cap, driving his head into his neck and knocked him to the ground. He was stunned and dizzy, but miraculously he made it back to the Los Angeles dugout. Forty minutes later, while his teammates were celebrating, Smith sat in front of his locker. He still had his uniform on, and he was mad. "I've got spasms in the back of my neck and pain in the back of my head," he told reporters. "Those people were throwing ice cubes, apples and frisbees. Nothing they do surprises me."

Life in the Dodger bullpen that evening had been at least as dangerous. "The fans above us were going crazy," reported Dodger catcher Johnny Oates. "I was standing out there and I felt something graze my ear. It turned out to be an empty fifth of whiskey. But they were throwing beer cans, smoke bombs, brandy bottles and everything else they could get their hands on."

For obvious reasons, many Dodgers couldn't wait to recross the Hudson River. As pitcher Mike Garman said, "We need three wins at home, so we don't have to come back here and see those animals."

Unfortunately, the Dodgers were not that lucky. For the sixth (and, as it turned out, final) Series game, everyone had to come back to the house that Ruth built. And they came prepared.

Instead of using one of the three main passenger terminals at Kennedy Airport, the Dodgers had their chartered plane land at a deserted hangar usually reserved for cargo. Yankee Stadium officials hired an additional 300 rent-a-cops to patrol the inside perimeter of the ballpark and New York's finest announced that a special contingent of 350 policemen would also be on hand.

But would they be ready for Rick? The 18-year-old college dropout had arrived two hours early for the night game. Near the left field foul pole, he was drinking his fourth beer with Bob, his underage friend from Connecticut.

"I've waited a long time for this game," Rick said, wiping some spilled brew from his dark blue nylon Yankee warm-up jacket. He started to laugh. "Those monuments," he boasted, pointing to the plaques honoring Gehrig, Higgins and Ruth, "they mean nothing to me. I'm just here to see it happen for myself and get down. And," he predicted with a sly, half-drunk grin, "it's gonna happen. They can't stop us."

Rick and Bob weren't alone. By game time the bleachers and upper decks were teeming with similar white middle-class types, a bizarre menagerie of *Clockwork Orange* and *Happy Days* escapees who had bought their tickets for one apparent goal: kick ass if we lose, and kick ass if we win.

Outside the stadium, and out of view of the ABC cameras, two dozen blue-and-white Dodge arrest vans, mounted police, communications trucks and ambulances anticipated the end of that championship season.

They didn't have to wait long. By the sixth inning, some twenty loyal locals had been forcibly escorted from the game for fighting, and another six had been busted for disorderly conduct.

Despite the activity, the playing field stayed deceptively clear of fans and debris. Until the eighth inning. You could almost feel it coming. With the Yankees ahead by a comfortable 8–3 margin, they started to move. The inside cement ramps leading from the upper decks were jammed with fans, clenching cans, sticks and amber glass missiles of Schlitz, Miller and Rheingold beer bottles. They were scrambling as though on some demented Strategic Air Command mission, to take their self-appointed positions as close to the field as possible.

As if in a predictable and poorly choreographed opera, the rent-a-cops took up positions near the third base rain tarpaulin and by the photographers' box just off first. The electronic scoreboard, which all evening had exhorted the fans to "CHARGE!" after each Yankee hit, now lit up with a different message:

LET'S SHOW OUR GUESTS THAT NEW YORK FANS ARE NOT ONLY THE GREATEST IN THE WORLD BUT THE MOST CONSIDERATE AS WE WELCOME THE DODGERS INTO OUR HOME . . .

The announcement wasn't even met with the expected chorus of Bronx jeers. It was ignored. Rick was right. It was about to happen. Out in right field, Reggie Jackson was beginning to realize how the other Reggie felt. Jackson had hit three home runs that night, was voted the MVP award, but in the top of the ninth it suddenly didn't matter. He wasn't as much a hero as he was a target.

> HOWARD COSELL: Now a fan ran out. A fan ran out to hug Reggie Jackson. Reggie personally escorts him back into the stands. Still another, doing the same thing. Reggie shakes his hand.
> P.A. SYSTEM: Ladies and gentlemen, no one is to go on the field at the end of the game.
> COSELL: Do you hear the public address now?
> KEITH JACKSON: I'm not sure that I would want to be shaking hands with some idiot that's just running out on the field in the course of a game. In the first place, how do you know how he's going to behave when he gets there?
> COSELL: You're just telling it like it is, Mr. Jackson.

But no one in right field was listening. First one, then three cherry bombs exploded around Reggie. He got the message, and the fearless slugger called time and ran toward the Yankee dugout for his batting helmet. In the brief interim a horde of steamed upper deck spectators went on a scavenger hunt for projectiles along the aisles of the high-priced field level boxes.

That started the fights, but they were just the preliminary bouts leading up to the main event. The bell sounded at the third out. The police were helpless. Fans dived, ran, leapfrogged, slithered, jumped, fell or were pushed onto the field, grabbing for players, uniforms, grass, bases, rosin bags and each other.

Reggie Jackson started jogging in from right field but when he saw what awaited him quickly shifted gears. The former high school halfback lowered his head, weaved and dodged, and then rammed into the zealots. He knocked one over, cut another down with a swift chop from his right hand. This wasn't O.J. running for his rent-a-car. This was R.J. running for his life.

So was Yankee Graig Nettles. At the precise moment pitcher Mike Torrez caught the game-ending pop-up, the third baseman was racing across the diamond, punching his way into the sanctuary of the dugout.

Out near the left field bleachers, an area sportswriters call Death Valley because few hitters have ever slammed a baseball there, the cops had their hands full. Helmeted police were being attacked with everything from a barrage of red delicious apples to a two-by-four hurled from the main level.

The bases had already been ripped off, home plate had been ripped up, and now the bottles were ripping away, hitting cops and fans. At least 50,000 onlookers remained in the stands to watch the bloody postgame show. "We're busy, and we're beating heads," yelled 21-year-old stadium cop John Cwikla. "These people are fuckin' crazy." He stopped momentarily to lead his partner to a first-aid station inside the stadium.

The action moved quickly from the reddish dirt warning track of center field, littered with the remains of blue plastic bleachers seats, to the pitcher's mound. Almost instinctively, a few hundred of the crazies ripped up the infield sod, turned to face the ABC booth and responded to Humble Howard's earlier fan diatribes. With fists raised, they chanted "CO-SELL SUCKS . . . COSELL SUCKS." There they were, the Bad News Bears in a Brave New World Series, destined to go down as one of the most violent in history.

Near third base, an injured fan was on the ground, bleeding from a head wound inflicted by a fast-moving bottle of Early Times. The cops had already handcuffffed one of his assailants, but some of the vicious Lilliputians just didn't like the guy. They surrounded him while a few of their number punched and kicked him. It lasted for a few minutes. One fan took particular pleasure in going for the man's kidneys. "C'mon, Larry, let's go home," begged his date, tugging unsuccessfully at his jacket. "No, let's stay," he smiled sadistically, digging the right toe of his hiking boot under the fan's rib cage. "This is history."

Fear and loathing in the stands is certainly not a new phenomenon, but mass recreational violence has never before been so rampant in the sports arenas of America.

On one hand, the attendance statistics are impressive. Thirty-one million fans—a regular season record—paid to see major league baseball games in 1977. Twelve million more will see National Football League contests during the next few weeks. And the National Hockey League expects more than nine million Americans at the rinks this winter.

But while America continues to celebrate the jock, an old sports maxim is sadly being rewritten for players, officials and even spectators. It's not whether you win or lose, it's whether you can survive the fans that counts.

Since the days of the Roman gladiators, spectators have reveled in the violence of the arena. But now, stadium violence has followed seasons of vicarious thrill-seeking and emotional identification with individual teams and players, and the fans are turning thumbs down on just about everybody. "We get rowdy," says Michael, a 19-year-old San Francisco Giants fan, "when we start losing. It's a frustration at the team's performance. So it's the only way you can contribute to the game, throwing bottles and stuff. I mean, your team's losing," he explains, "so what can you do?"

Well, you can always try to kill yourself. In 1973 a Colorado man put a gun to his head after his favorite team, the Denver Broncos, had just fumbled seven times in the course of losing badly to the Chicago Bears. "I have been a Broncos fan since the Broncos were first organized," he scribbled before pulling the trigger, "and I can't stand their fumbling any more."

Appropriately, he also fumbled, and lived to see the Broncos lose again.

Sometimes, the nature of the game itself is sufficient to provoke a rampage. In 1974, while shooting *Rollerball* at the Olympic basketball stadium in Munich, director Norman Jewison needed a few hundred extras to play fans for the filming of the futuristic game, a contest hypothetically designed to let society take out its aggressions in gory no-win, no-survive combat. Surprisingly, before they were able to finish the bloody championship battle of Houston versus Tokyo, real and unexpected fights broke out in the stands.

Many students of fan behavior believe that by identifying with a team the fan is afforded the chance to affirm his own worth and quality. But, as in the near-fatal Denver case, he often does it at some risk. If his team wins, he feels good about himself. But if defeat is snatched from the jaws of victory, he feels like a loser, and the resulting violence is channeled inward.

More often than not, however, the spectator directs his attack at players, officials or other fans. "Nobody abuses a fan like another fan," says N.Y.

Daily News sportswriter Dick Young. "The fan in the upper deck pours beer on the fan in the lower deck . . . The fan in the row behind shouts to Reggie Jackson 'You bleeping so and so . . .' and pretty soon there's a free-for-all."

The class warfare between the cheap and expensive ticket holders, and between fans and players cannot be underestimated. "The socioeconomic distance is so great between most fans and highly paid athletes," says behaviorist Dr. Arnold Beisser, a professor of psychiatry at UCLA, "that the athletes don't seem like real people. So the fans are more apt to be callous towards them."

Within the anonymity of a crowd of 50,000 people, callousness is often transformed into unprovoked retaliation for a host of real and imagined problems.

To be sure, we have entered into a new era of sports addiction. In the recent past, an athletic contest provided an often healthy, temporary escape into a world of heroics, a quasi-religion of physical combat and ritualized violence.

But for many fans, that ephemeral sporting sojourn has become an all too easily embraceable lifestyle. "In the old days," says Beisser, "the sports fan yelled 'Kill the umpire.' The new fan tries to do it."

In one game, a fan almost succeeded. On December 28, 1975, the Dallas Cowboys and Minnesota Vikings met for the NFC championship at Metropolitan Stadium in Bloomington, Minnesota. With only 20 seconds to go and the Cowboys trailing, Dallas quarterback Roger Staubach dropped back to pass. Downfield, Cowboy end Drew Pearson was tightly covered by Viking defensive back Nate Wright, but Staubach nevertheless lofted the ball toward Pearson. In what has gone down in football folklore as the "Immaculate Reception" play, Pearson pushed Wright aside, caught the ball, and raced into the end zone for the go-ahead touchdown. The Viking bench was outraged by the infraction—Fran Tarkenton screamed from the sidelines—but no offensive interference penalty was called. With that, an incensed Viking fan hurled a bottle at veteran official Armen Terzian. It struck him in the head, cutting him so badly that a bandaged Terzian had to leave the gridiron.

Refs are vulnerable to fans-turned-tigers outside the stadium as well. After a high school football game in Odessa, Texas, a few seasons ago, a hawk-eyed but tortoise-slow official was ambushed by indignant spectators and penalized four broken ribs and a concussion for his earlier flag throwing.

In many Central and South American countries sports officials are forced to live life in the fast lane as a matter of uncontrollable tradition. Fan violence toward referees and other fans there has added a terrifying dimension to most soccer games. The problem has been that some fans don't consider the contest decided until countless spectators have been injured and the referees have been either beaten unconscious or killed.

Five persons were hacked to death at a Guatemala City soccer match when hometown fans, bitter over their loss, advanced against the winning team with machetes.

In Lima, Peru, nearly 300 spectators were killed and another 500 injured in 1964 during a brawl following a disputed referee's call. In 1971, 66 fans were crushed to death in a Glasgow, Scotland, stadium stampede.

When players and spectators disagreed with a call made by a soccer official in Buenos Aires in 1948, they beat him to death, and after the 1964 Peru-Argentina game, referee Angel Pazos secured himself from angered fans in his steel-doored dressing room. Frustrated, the crowd next took on the police, then the scorekeeper, who locked himself in his booth.

And who could forget the 1969 Honduras-El Salvador "soccer war"? Riots accompanied all three World Cup soccer matches between the two countries that June. Following the last game and hundreds of serious fan injuries, diplomatic and commercial relations were severed, and the El Salvadorean army, aroused by rumors of "genocide" against their fans in Honduras, mobilized and moved across the border.

While many league officials and team owners deny the presence of a fan violence problem, many are quietly taking a hard look at the sale of alcohol at sporting events—the common denominator at almost every major fracas.

Many stadiums, like Cleveland's Municipal, now selectively ban the sale of alcohol. At Chavez Ravine, the Dodgers no longer sell beer in the notorious outfield pavilion area. And Schaefer Stadium has banned the hawking of suds in the stands. Fans there now must walk to concession stands for their brew.

There is also concern over the subtle but strong role the media plays in inciting fans to leave their seats. Television has allowed people to become professional fans, and some psychologists suggest that stadium rampages may actually be an indirect result of the "instant replay" syndrome. "Violence in sport is magnified by television," says sociologist Harry Edwards. "The [television] fan can identify with violence in terms of what he would like to do with the forces he cannot control."

Once at a game, however, fueled by previously televised instant replays of football cheap shots, hockey square-offs and basketbrawls, along with the hope of perhaps getting a little air time himself, the fan seeks his new identity.

Professional games are not the only events victimized by these lost souls. Many college football games have been transformed into an alcoholic Knute Rockne story directed by Sam Peckinpah.

"Our cameramen get hit with stuff at almost every game," says John Allen, an ABC technical director, who has worked every college game of the week since 1968. "The NCAA won't like hearing this," he says, "but it's almost becoming a controlled riot out there. The fans are getting worse and worse. Ten years ago, even during the antiwar days, it was never this bad. At LSU they throw Coke bottles, in Alabama they come to the game with bags of oranges. But Colorado is the worst. One of their favorite tricks is to make snowballs with rocks inside, and they throw them at us if they start losing. The problem," Allen charges, "is that they take this damn shit so personally. It's just a goddamn college game."

Nevertheless, "winning [one for the gipper] isn't everything . . . it's the only thing." Unfortunately, that famous Vince Lombardi quote, which the high priest of victory attempted to retract before he died, lives on. "There's been a progressive, paranoiac desire to win," says Arnold Mandell, former team psychiatrist for the San Diego Chargers, "and violence is a natural product of that. Win or be killed is where it's at."

In some cases of fan violence, the players on the field have responded in kind. Once, during a Yankee-Red Sox game, a fan persisted in shouting accusations about Ted Williams' sex life that could be heard throughout the entire lower level. When the legendary outfielder came to bat, Yankee catcher Yogi Berra asked him how he could take the verbal abuse. Williams simply asked Berra for a favor. "Tell him to pitch it inside," he said, and the pitcher obliged. The fan, sitting down the line in foul territory, had a half dozen line drives sprayed at him. He got the message and left.

On April 22, 1976, the fans' verbal barrage provoked four Philadelphia Flyers to charge into the stands at Toronto's Maple Leaf Gardens. Players Bob Kelly and Joe Watson were charged with assault and heavily fined.

It has reached the point where stadium architects and police have begun to experiment with new forms of crowd control. "They had five hundred policemen at Yankee Stadium," says Reggie Jackson. "If they couldn't do anything about the mob then, well I can't see how they're gonna do anything about it again."

But they're trying. At Minnesota's Metropolitan Stadium, ground crews coat the goal posts and stadium beams with STP. Detoxification vans stand just outside the stadium for fans who drink too much. At the new Meadowlands Stadium near Hackensack, New Jersey, the first row of seats is 12 feet above field level. The NHL has ordered that every penalty box be enclosed in thick shatterproof glass, and special coverings have also been erected over the player exits.

One soccer stadium in Brazil features a 9-foot-wide moat between the players and the fans, filled alternately with water, jagged glass and every conceivable hindrance short of crocodiles. At the center of the field, there's a trap door hidden under the turf to allow the referees to flee should the fans come equipped with, lets say, LSTs.

Even the use of German shepherds has been suggested. "Trained police dogs," Dodger pitcher Tommy John told reporters after the Series, "will back those guys right into a corner."

They would have needed an entire "K9" kennel at Yankee Stadium to achieve that goal. The fans took and held the 3.5-acre playing field for an incredible 35 minutes. "Thank God it went only six games," sighed Emil Ciccotelli, a tired police inspector standing at what used to be second base. "I don't think we could have handled another game here."

An hour later, the stadium lights were dimmed, and the score was almost official: 38 arrested, four dozen injured, including one who was admitted to a local hospital with a concussion and other injuries.

But up on the elevated platform of the 161st Street subway station there was still time for one final extra-innings attraction. A group of seven half-drunk Yankee fans were grouped around a small, frightened gray mouse. "Get him, get him," shouted their leader. "He's gonna escape!" They did, kicking the small station dweller against a sheet metal wall. Suddenly they were quiet, waiting for the stunned mouse to move. If fandom had its rewards that night, then certainly this unfortunate rodent was no small prize.

"C'mon, step on his head—he's still alive!" The mouse stirred just enough to be kicked again, this time under the tracks and to its death on the streets below. The young stomper looked up, faced his friends with extended index fingers and yelled "We're number one!"

Considerations

1. Is "Wild in the Stands" a traditional essay? Explain.
2. Give examples of your own which may apply to the following statement:

   Many students of fan behavior believe that by identifying with a team the fan is afforded a chance to affirm his own worth and quality.

   (See "The Match," by Alan Sillitoe.)
3. Does the fact that real fights broke out among the extras signed to portray fans for the movie, "Roller Ball," indicate that people are just as easily moved by an imitation of violence as they are by the real thing? Comment. (See "Roller Ball Murder.")
4. Exactly why don't athletic officials severely punish the offending fans?
5. List some possible remedies for unruly or violent fans.

LARRY McMURTRY
It's Always We Rambled:
An Essay on Rodeo

The only moment of surprise I experienced at the rodeo in Madison Square Garden a few weeks ago occurred on the escalator, as I was riding up to see it. Approaching Level Two I caught a whiff of old familiar vapors, and a second later, along with my fellow passengers, was almost overcome by the smell of cowshit—a substance with which I have had a long and bitter involvement. For years I scarcely set foot on anything else, and would have thought, consequently, that I would be prepared to expect it anywhere. But, what with time and the tide, one grows unwary. I had not expected to find myself being overcome by that odor on an escalator in New York.

Had I been stopped, I might have floated off into a Proustian reverie of sorts, back through decades of experience with various grades and classes of ordure to the time long ago on the plains (such as they are) of Archer County, when I toddled off the porch of the ancestral ranch-house into my first cowpile. But escalators are inimicable to reverie. There is the stop-off to consider, Level Three was on me in seconds—odorless as a bank vault—and before I had time to think about anything it was the next afternoon and I was in the middle of a large discount store in Denver, Colorado, trying to buy some tennis balls. A friend was with me. The signs to the left of us said LAWN NEEDS; the signs to the right said FEMININE HYGIENE NEEDS. PET NEEDS lay just ahead, but we were looking for TENNIS NEEDS. The store encompassed something like eighteen acres, all of them crammed with American needs. "I get depressed every time I come here," my friend said. "Look at all these Things!"

There seemed no getting around the fact that the American Dream had given rise to a lot of tacky products, but before I had time to think about *that* it was the next morning and I was in Hollywood. In the course of chatting with a producer I happened to notice, reminiscent of FEMININE HYGIENE NEEDS, that he had on his desk three flavored (scented ?) douches, the flavors (scents) being champagne, orange pekoe, and strawberry. His secretary happened to notice these, too, and stared at them with a wild surmise. As I was leaving I noticed that she seemed to have taken advantage of the fact that she wasn't on an escalator and had fallen into a reverie of her own—wondering, perhaps, what pleasures life might hold if her fundamental flavor was strawberry.

In Texas, the following day, I switched from flying to driving, which meant that at least I had time to give some thought to the Madison Square Garden Cowtown Rodeo. In fact, I had more time in which to think than I had rodeo to think about. Rodeo *qua* rodeo, the show in the Garden was the worst I had ever seen. The purse was tiny—$17,000 as compared to $50,000 or more at the larger shows in the west—and only a handful of the top touring pros showed up to compete for it. Most of the contestants were from New York, Pennsylvania, Connecticut, or New Jersey—nice places all, I'm told, but not necessarily the best places to hail from if one wants to be a rodeo hand. The result was a sad little dribble of a show, pathetic in its relation to its own history and more pathetic still in its constant obsequiousness toward the hostile culture which engulfed it. One might be tempted to ignore such a rodeo completely; but to ignore an event just because it is dull would be to insult the most sophisticated traditions of modern journalism. Not for nothing have these sophistications been developed: a dull rodeo can be made to seem as richly significant as anything else, provided one makes use of a few techniques taken over from novelists and keeps clearly in mind that it is best to frame the whole against a background of one's personal activities. If one has any ginger at all, these will be sure to be interestingly chaotic, and will make a good story in themselves.

With that tradition at my back it should be easy enough to relate the M.S.G. Cowtown Rodeo to the Judaeo-Christian tradition, and, more particularly, the current unrest. It was irksome to note, at the outset, that there was scarcely any way one could wander around behind the chutes, that being where the fun takes place at most rodeos. Behind these chutes were passages leading down into the concrete bowels of the Garden; to descend would have removed one completely from the scene of the action, and anyway the prospect seemed a little Dantesque. I wouldn't have cared to do it without a leopard. The cowboys seemed to feel the same way; they huddled as closely to the arena as possible. I noticed a number of them cleaning their fingernails, which is what cowboys do when they feel vulnerable and at a loss. They were cut off from their culture, and had neither sky above nor land below; the only honest soil around was under their fingernails. Cowboys shrink and become inhibited when they have to go indoors, and these kept their voices down, as if they were afraid they might make some rude remark and be overheard.

I should have engaged one or two in conversation and tried to secure a pithy quote, but I didn't. Years ago, for reasons having more to do with disorder and early sorrow than any deep interest in the subject, I set out to write a scholarly book about rodeo. In the course of my travels I tried many times to secure pithy quotes from leading cowboys, not a few of whom would brook comparison with the famous tackle Bolenciecwcz, in James Thurber's "University Days." It would not be fair to say that they were less communicative than fenceposts, but there were certainly those among them with whom a fence post could have held its own.

In the Garden, in any case, it would have been impossible to hear a pithy quote even if one had been uttered, thanks to the well-amplified efforts of the rodeo band. This group exhibited a musical eclecticism which was quite unprecedented in my experience of rodeos; for them to have emitted anything resembling a twang would have been unthinkable. "When the Saints Go Marchin' In" seemed to be a particular favorite, and before the evening was over we were even subjected to:

> Way down yonder in Louis-i-ana,
> Just about a mile from Tex-ar-kana,
> In them old cottonfields back home . . .,

a song so prevalent in our culture that I always seem to end up quoting it, no matter what I set out to report. Its presence in a rodeo repertoire was a rank insult, which in the west might well have resulted in the band leader getting stomped. No one, to my knowledge, has ever done anything except suffer, in cottonfields, and any cowboy worth his salt, given a choice between gangrene and picking cotton, would invariably and cheerfully incur gangrene.

The crowd, however, having lost touch with the homefolks sufficiently to have forgotten even this ancient wisdom, clapped along happily. It was a crowd that yielded next to nothing in the way of atmospherics. I had come on Rosh Hashanah, and the gathering was somberly gentile and suburban. There were many well-dressed couples with nice looking kids, none of whom seemed wildly excited at the prospect of broncs and bulls. In most cases, I suspect, either Momma or Poppa had grown up in the West, and wanted to show the rest of the family what it was like.

Unfortunately, it is impossible to convey anything of what the West is like by events, however inspired or authentic, that take place indoors. Both literally and mythically the West is a great *out-of-doors*, and, in contrast to the East, it is an out-of-doors in which the sky is more affecting than the land. Little towns, little people, long roads, flat land, all held beneath a vast and ever-varying sky: that is what the West is like.

If one looks for rodeo to inform one about that West, then it must be rodeo considered as community experience, not rodeo considered as sport. The very best place to see rodeo is in a small Western town; there, at least, one can be assured of a colorful occasion, and the show will have a summer evening and a long Western sundown setting it off. The stars will be just coming out, and one can sit in the grandstand and look across twenty or thirty miles of plain to the lights of the next little town. A sense of the distances around one is essential, for it is precisely the monotony and isolation those flat distances force upon people that the sport of rodeo was created to relieve. Below one, as the dusk deepens, horsemen will gather in scores and perhaps in hundreds, dressed in their vividest garb. A hillbilly band will have begun to warm up for the big dance later, to which the actual rodeo serves as excuse and genteel prelude. Riding clubs assemble, flags are unfurled, and the lights and the dust and the horses and the afterglow all merge into one richly-accented visual scene. Contestants with numbers pinned to their shirts sit on the fences around the stock pens, watching the animals on which they are about to risk their lives. The animals watch them back, and switch at flies. Lots of beer flows, women who scarcely get in off the ranches twice a year can visit with their neighbors, horses get traded, kids run amok, the menfolk look forward to a little excitement with the livestock, everyone feels slightly sexier than usual, the announcer and the clown keep up a patter of mildly scatological humor which strikes everyone as risque and hilarious—and so on. From the grandstand one can see beneath one a whole little local culture loosening itself up for an evening of sport and general fellowship, while around one, in the deepening darkness, stretch the miles and miles of lonely landscape that form the daily context of the individual lives.

That texture, that ambiance, cannot be had at an indoor rodeo, however large the purse or skilled the cowboys. Professional rodeo represents a merging of two distinct and conflicting traditions, the Wild West Show on the one hand, the ranch-contest on the other. The Wild West Show, out of Ned Buntline and Buffalo Bill, was always show business. It was designed to entertain people who have had little or no direct experience of the West, and the emphasis was on trick riding, trick roping, Indians, stagecoach races, and the like. The ranch-contest, on the other hand, was an intrinsically *local* thing, and was designed to entertain the cowboys themselves. It was a get-together, essentially, in which men from neighboring ranches came in from the isolation of line camps and competed with one another at riding and roping; the get-together being probably more important to them than the competition. Cowboys are not, by nature, very competitive men. Handling cattle on a large scale is of necessity a cooperative enterprise, in which over-achievers, more often than not, only get in the way. Individual brilliance is considered immodest and in most cases offensive, and the constant emphasis on ranches is on group work, not specialized show-offy expertise.

That tradition not withstanding, by the Twenties promoters had managed to merge the two lines of development and package rodeo for public consumption. Madison Square Garden has never been one of the classic stations of the sport—those being Pendleton, Calgary, and Cheyenne—but there was a time when it had a high prominence. From the late Twenties into the late Fifties, rodeo came to the New York Island in style. The purses were huge and the best of the West came with all the flair they could muster to show off to the best of the East. In 1947, in the Garden, a bullrider and steerwrestler named Todd Whatley carried off almost $9,000 in prize money—the most, to this day, that one man has ever won at a single show. In 1952, while at the Garden, the flamboyant saddlebronc rider Casey Tibbs had his picture on the cover of LIFE.

Casey Tibbs was perhaps the most charismatic performer the sport has ever known; after winning 6 saddlebronc titles and two All Round Championships he settled in Hollywood; he can be seen, I believe, for one second in *Junior Bonner*. The current superstar, Larry Mahan, is a distinctly less charismatic imitation, tie-dye chaps or no. The sport was dominated throughout the Fifties by the less flamboyant but highly persistent Jim Shoulders, who won 16 world titles before going home to Henrietta, Oklahoma, to become a promoter and start a rodeo school.

Since then a glory has definitely fallen from the air. Except in the small towns, and on a few of the classic stations, show business has had its way with the sport, and has done what could be done to make an essentially anachronistic spectacle amenable to people who, perhaps despite themselves, have become imbued with the modern temper. In a sophisticated time, with sophisticated media, the very brevity of the events of rodeo work against its popularity as a sport. The rides all last eight seconds or less, and it shouldn't take more than fifteen seconds to rope and tie a calf or dog a steer. It is a competition of a very interrupted sort, made more difficult to appreciate by the fact that it takes place at such a distance from the spectator that whatever fine skills it involves will be largely invisible. Only the riding judges are close enough to the action to appreciate points of style in a saddlebronc ride. Since nothing lasts more than a few seconds, rodeo cannot approach the sustained drama we may get from professional football, basketball, tennis, or golf. Even the bull-ride, in theory at least the most dangerous and most crowd-pleasing of the events, arouses only the crudest and most gladiatorial emotions, and those not very deeply. One is mildly curious as to whether the man will stay on the bull, or whether the bull will butt him or stomp him if he doesn't, but the emotion aroused is indeed mild if one compares it to the emotion generated by a bull-fight. The bull-ride has neither a moral nor an aesthetic resonance—the men are not cowards, or they wouldn't be on the bulls, but neither do we see them as artists, and it all takes place at such a distance that in a sense we never see *them* at all. The sport doesn't televise well and in consequence we never familiarize ourselves with the faces of the major competitors. Joe Namath, Jack Nicklaus, Bill Russell, Muhammed Ali—we may not know the men but we know the faces. Who knows what Phil Lyne, a recent All-Round Champion, looks like? Thanks to *Junior Bonner*, Steve McQueen is now the best known bull-rider in the world.

In that connection, one might observe that *Junior Bonner, J. W. Coop, The Honkers* and the two or three other examples of the film industry's recent and unfortunate little love affair with rodeo are so alike thematically as to lead one to believe that in rodeo there is one story and one story only. This is the story of Odysseus the Wanderer as hardup ageing small-town rodeo hand. In the course of his journeying he returns to his hometown to find to his joy that he is still beloved of his people, even though he has left them go to rack and ruin. Unfortunately, however, age is catching up with him, and times have changed. The suitors have been at Penelope, and the pastoral ideals which despite his restlessness he staunchly upholds have given way to a ticky-tacky world full of mobile homes, eighteen-acre department stores, and strawberry douches.

What we get in these movies, essentially, is a vision of the Hero as Lovable Fuckup, a man who truly loves his people and his land, even though he can't settle down to labor with either of them. To settle down would be to betray the true spirit of the Old West, which he alone, through the purity of his restlessness, continues to embody and uphold.

This view of the rodeo cowboy is, to put it crudely, horseturds. It is as phony as the Bull Durham tag that hangs out of Steve McQueen's shirt pocket all through *Junior Bonner*. That Bull Durham tag would have been an affectation in *The Lusty Men*, the Robert Mitchum-Susan Hayward rodeo number, made in 1951. Mr. Peckinpah might be nostalgic for Bull Durham, but I doubt that Phil Lyne and Larry Mahan even know what it is. Top rodeo hands today tend to have started in Junior Rodeo, when they were 10 years old. Very likely they compete in high school rodeo and go to college on rodeo scholarships; if their college coaching is not sufficient they can acquire their final polish at Jim Shoulders' rodeo school, or any of several others.

It might be argued that these movies aren't about the big winners, or the young pros who sharpen their skills in college, but about the little losers, the men who drag along from rodeo to rodeo, barely making their entry fees, because it's the only free way of life left open to them. They are, their apologists seem to say, men of such largeness of spirit that death beneath the horns of a bull would be preferable to the loss of their freedom. This is the view, naturally, that rodeo announcers stress in their constant little interpolations on frontier individualism.

A simpler, contrary view is that held by most cattlemen, which is that rodeo hands are lazy fuckups, men, essentially, who fear danger less than they hate work. It is perhaps worth pointing out here that in the mythology which movies and books have created for the American West the drifter has always been glorified at the direct expense of the settler. The drifter-figure has come to represent for us all that was romantic and free about the West, the settler all that is bourgeois, stable and dull.

There were, however, settlers who were men of spirit too, and men not necessarily inferior in their love of freedom to the drifters. The cattleman's not-so-latent contempt for the rodeo hand is based upon the knowledge that rodeo hands have been content to fiddle while the West burned. The rancher's view is the precise opposite of what one gets from the movies. As they see it, rodeo hands are pre-eminently the accommodationists, modern men who hold themselves responsible only to the demands of their egos, men who take no care of the land itself and have no respect for the labor or the traditions of the herdsman. They are men, so far as the cattlemen are concerned, who have little patience, no love of work, and essentially crude skills; they are not very useful in intricate cattle-work and are seldom willing to stay around and do the dull but necessary chores once the fun of the roundup is over.

This view of the rodeo cowboy has no mythic or aesthetic appeal, but it is not without accuracy. Rodeo hands are a sporting breed, which is fine, but they hardly deserve to be glorified as holdouts against a system which they use and cater to every day. Whether they like to admit it or not, they are in show business, and their work is in the towns, not on the land. They cheerfully charter the

System's planes, when they can afford it, in order to compete in two shows at once, and their talk, by and large, is of the Show, not of a place or of the problems of the agrarian life.

The true holdouts against the system are not the Junior Bonners and J. W. Coops, these Lonely-Are-The-Brave types, but the thousands of embittered small stockmen about the West and Mid-West, in whose lives there have been no quick cuts from horse to horse, woman to woman, town to town or state to state. These are men, for the most part, who have lived in one place, loved the West and its ideals, and increased only in despair—as the oil industry ruined their grass, as the air and water grew foul, as the land taxes rose so high they could not afford to stock their acreage, as their politics became meaningless, their life styles scorned and then parodied, their children drawn away to the cities and there subverted. In these men one finds a love of the Old and a hatred of the New so passionate and intense that it makes the beery rebelliousness of rodeo cowboys seem like half-hearted posturing, which is what it usually is; and such men lead lives of a moral and physical astringency compared to which the lives of rodeo hands are sybaritic and epicurean.

Real cattle people are sad now, with something of the sadness of gorillas. Like gorillas they may become truculent and make noises to scare interlopers away, but in reality they are a breed in retreat, with a deeply ingrained sense of their own doom. They would be glad just to get out of the way, if there was only some place that civilization didn't want, but there is no such place. Only when you see them on the remoteness of ranches, far from towns and crowds and hoopla, do they show themselves as men of wit and grace, playfulness and occasional nobility; though sad, it is not altogether to be lamented that so many of them have been kept from prosperity, for if one thing is evident about cowboys it is that they are men who show their best qualities only under the worst of natural conditions. It is poverty and drought, isolation and toil that bring out their richest humor and strongest loyalty, their deepest feeling for nature and their keenest joy in life. Give them money and creature comforts and everything that is lean, well-crafted, enduring and humanly beautiful in them disappears and they quickly degenerate into mindless and tasteless suburbanized slobs. And compared to the men of the ranches, the rodeo hands are—and have been—the suburbanites of the West.

When I set out to do my book on rodeo I was fresh out of graduate school and flushed with the headiest scholarly ambitions. I was willing to construct a metaphysic and a sociology for the sport, and I believe I succeeded in tracing its anthropological origins back to the Bull Dancers of Crete. Later, still under the delusion that I was serious about the book, I submitted an outline to the Rodeo Cowboy's Association, thinking they might want to make suggestions. The Rodeo Cowboy's Association was stunned, not because they resented being associated with the bull dancers of Crete but because I had planned a chapter called "Coitus on Horseback" in which I proposed to treat such matters as rodeo groupies and suggested, reasonably enough, I thought, that some rodeo hands were at times less than exemplary in their domestic lives.

Not so, I was told. Rodeo hands *are* exemplary in their domestic lives. They wouldn't fuck no groupies, nohow—I was told—and even if a few bad eggs could be found who might attempt such acts it would be very wrong of me to put such a thing in my book. Why, I wondered?

Because—I was told—rodeo is now a kid-oriented sport. The cleaner its image can be kept, the more little kiddies will get to come see it. This need to consider childish sensibilities and childish attention spans has resulted in the elimination of two of rodeo's most interesting events: single steer roping, because it is too brutal, and the cutting-horse contest because it is too ballet-like and refined for children to pay attention to.

As a sop to the women, however, there is still the Girl's Barrel Race. It is surprising to me that the militants of the women's movement haven't done something about the Cowgirl, there being in the whole of America's sexist culture no more glaring example of the complete stylistic violation of the female by the male. *Ms.* should by all means send Germaine Greer to the Miss Rodeo America contest when it's held this year in Las Vegas. The Girl's Barrel Race is only added evidence that the men of the West don't consider women good for anything but bedding down with. It is a strictly non-functional event in which the girls flog their horses around three barrels. Granted that sport needn't be functional—it is not often, in daily life, that one is required to hurl a javelin, or run 5000 meters—there is nonetheless, in the men's events, a pretense that we are seeing something that might be useful on a ranch. Nothing could be less useful than racing a horse around three barrels—all it does is ruin the horse for any other work. The event, however, is a steady crowd-pleaser, and leads one to speculate that perhaps rodeo's most basic appeal is simply kinetic: the appeal of the chase or the race—of seeing horses run.

The eminent French critic M. Roland Barthes, in his fine essay on wrestling, has taught us that there is an alternative to judging a sporting event on its literal level, as sport. Such things may also be judged as Spectacle. If one were to apply that standard, and judge the rodeo in The Garden for its mythological content, it's interesting and somewhat paradoxical to note that the culminating moment of the evening's performance was a moment from which men had been excluded completely. This was the performance of Miss Judy Lynn, the country singer from Idaho.

Miss Lynn came riding in on a snow white horse, astride an immensely heavy silver-mounted saddle. She wore a yellow suit, liberally sprinkled with sequins. The horse, we were three times told, was one she had trained herself, though what she had trained him to do, other than carry that saddle, was something of a mystery. If that horse had shown up in a cow camp someone would have summarily whacked him on the head with an axe, it being a well-known Western fact that cattle are deathly afraid of white horses and will instantly gather themselves and dash over the nearest precipice if exposed to one.

The climax of Miss Lynn's performance, as well as of the show, was a rendition of "America, the Beautiful" into which Miss Lynn appeared to be pouring her whole soul. Men were excluded by the simple expedient of turning off the lights. Miss Lynn sang under one spotlight, while across the arena, under another spotlight, stood a small boy in a cowboy hat, holding a small American flag. Super-patriotism has always been a part of rodeo—I normally pay it no mind, and was about to skip Miss Lynn's singing and go get a hot dog when it occurred to me that here was a new mythological wrinkle. An emblem was being formed in the arena—what we were getting was, in a modest way, a vision of history. Those possibly horny men, who were just about to try and ride those demonstrably well-hung bulls, were blacked out. Miss Lynn sang "America, the Beautiful" as voluptuously as it is possible to sing it—metaphorically, I believe, she stood for the fruited plain. While she was singing the little boy, in his spotlight, carried the American flag across the arena and stood at her side, looking up at her worshipfully. The white horse, for emphasis, came and stood on Miss Lynn's other side, and as she finished the song she put her arm around the child. With the snow white horse to help him, emblematically, the little boy with his flag, his cowboy hat, and his boots, managed to support the weight both of Frontier Individualism (the announcer was right there with it) and of American Purity, while Miss Lynn in her yellow and her sequins, as amber in the spotlight as many waves of grain, was Plenitude, an American madonna, at once our achievement and our reward: There's the Old West for you, folks!

Like the hot dog I eventually ate, it was a sight to gag a buzzard.

Most of my driving in Texas, this time, was done on a lovely, dewy morning. Somewhere near Waco I was forced to stop at one of those strange, inexplicably remote traffic lights that I am always encountering in Texas, miles from anywhere, just when I am enjoying going a hundred miles an hour. While I was waiting for the light to change I noticed two melancholy-looking young men in cowboy hats, standing on the shoulder of road watching steam come out from under the hood of their blue pickup. On the back window of the pickup was a bumper-sticker that read GOAT ROPERS NEED LOVE TOO. I thought it a wonderful sentiment. I have certainly never been much more in need of love than on those occasions in the past when it had been my unhappy fate to rope a goat. Naturally I offered to help the two young goat-ropers whose pickup was burning up, and just as naturally, because I didn't look native, they were suspicious of me. They would really have rather stood there until someone they knew came along, but after awhile the younger of them agreed to accept a lift to the nearest gas station. He was a thin teenager named Don, with something distinctly fatalistic in his melancholy. Also, the incident seemed to have given him hay fever. As he got out of the car he looked back up the road and shook his head.

"Ort not never to of tried to go nowhere this mornin', nohow," he said, in parting. It was his only remark, and most of the thirty or forty cowboys I saw perform in the Garden rodeo ought to have it engraved in tiny bloodstones on their big silver belt-buckles. They looked—to use that most accurate of Western Freudianisms—like good old boys, but most of them ort to have stayed home. One or two got stomped, several got drug, a number missed calves, a number bucked off, and most of the rest, judging from what I saw, probably wound up having pickup trouble, somewhere on the New Jersey Turnpike.

Considerations

1. How does McMurtry link the fragrances mentioned in the opening of the essay with the overall tone of the Madison Square Garden Rodeo?

2. Consider McMurtry's humor. Is it more akin to that of a television comedian or, say, Mark Twain? Support your answer.
3. Would you consider McMurtry a reporter of events, or an interpreter of them? If you had to categorize him as a sportswriter, would you place him with Jimmy Cannon or Jimmy Breslin? Explain.
4. What does he mean, "show business has had its way with the sport"? What, also, does he mean by Hollywood's "recent and unfortunate little love affair with rodeo"?
5. What does he say about the myth of the rodeo hand? Why do real cattlemen hold a "not-so-latent contempt" for them?
6. Why was the Rodeo Cowboy's Association opposed to McMurtry's book on rodeo? Does their stance remind you of the NCAA and the NFL? Explain.
7. Why does he refer to rodeo as a "sop to the women"?
8. Discuss his description of Judy Lynn's performance. In terms of myth or "illusion," can you connect it to the commercial fragrances mentioned in the beginning?

PAUL HOCH

Coliseums and Gladiators

A few years ago, on an otherwise quiet November afternoon, 6,000 citizens of Columbus, Ohio, poured out onto the streets for what was to be perhaps the longest and most violent demonstration that city had ever seen. It lasted more than nine hours before it was halted by rain. Traffic on the main street was stopped. Cars were walked on, painted on, overturned. "Store windows were broken," reported *The New Republic* (Dec. 7, 1968). "Police officers were manhandled by young rioters; by-standers were hit by flying bottles and bricks. And the mayor, who habitually responds to peaceful protests by sending in his club-swinging D-platoon, joined the festivities." Columbus newspaper reporters, who had exploded with rage after long-haired young people marched in Chicago, cheerfully reported property damage and pronounced the whole affair delightful. Police joyfully escorted the rioters about. And, according to *The New Republic,* Governor Rhodes, who had previously called out the National Guard at the slightest provocation, felt it had been "a great day for Ohio." It was a grand old riot. Clean-cut American sports fans were celebrating football victory of Ohio State over Michigan. The same thing happened in Pittsburgh when the 1971 Pirates won the World Series.

In the spring of 1970, with tear gas drifting in the window as he wrote, the *Daily Cal's* sports editor, Lewis Leader, felt compelled to say something about the Berkeley athletic department's use of sports to try to convince everyone that things were normal. "People are being gassed and clubbed," he wrote. "There have been perhaps 50 arrests in two days. Dozens of people have been injured. As I write this I can see police pushing a student into a window on the terrace. . . . Yet the athletic department has decided to continue on with its full schedule of athletic events." Similarly, he added, when President Kennedy was assassinated, the National Football League decided to go ahead with their full schedule of games just two days later. Commissioner Rozelle's reasoning at the time was that the country needed something in such a time of national tragedy. A fix? Another weekly pep pill? And when Martin Luther King was assassinated in 1968, Los Angeles Dodgers' owner, Walter O'Malley, insisted that his team's scheduled league opener with the Philadelphia Phillies go ahead regardless. (The game was canceled only when the Phillies insisted as a team that they would rather forfeit than play.) Leader concluded his article by explaining to those sport fans who might criticize him for not presenting "normal sports coverage" in the crisis that if we choose to adopt a business-as-usual attitude toward crises by "pretending nothing is wrong," then in effect "we work to perpetuate the problems."

Leader's comments have far broader significance than perhaps even he realized. Ours is, after all, a society in crisis. And in many ways organized spectator sports are constantly being used, with some success, as a smoke screen by all those who want us to believe that nothing is really wrong. Surveys have repeatedly shown that about one third of the newspaper-reading public reads only the sports news. What sort of a dream world are the sports editors creating for them? And with a year-round schedule of sports activity from football to basketball to hockey to baseball, packed with the bowl games, the world series, the basketball and hockey play-offs, it is extremely hard for many people to concentrate on the fact that we've been fighting a war in Vietnam for over ten years. After all, the war is over there, irregularly (and boringly) reported. Spectator sport is right here in every home town, consistently and colorfully reported, made immediate and exciting, made important. It is much easier to think about the "long bomb" that scored the winning touchdown than the one that killed fifty Vietnamese peasants.[1] It is much easier to get all worked up about the Big Game than about big unemployment, big grocery prices, and big military spending: "Were this excess energy not channeled in America's mania for sports, it might well be used in dangerously antisocial ways. The value of this safety valve function cannot be accurately estimated, but it may be of considerable social significance." (Gelfand and Heath, *Modern Sportswriting*, Ames, Iowa: Iowa St. U. Press, 1969.)

"I do not share in the common view that athletics as such is the curse of the American university," wrote former Columbia dean Jacques Barzun in 1954. "It is better than the dueling mania, the organized drunkenness, and the other *social and political substitutes current abroad.*" (*Teacher in America*, Garden City: Doubleday & Co., Inc., Anchor, 1954, p. 206, my italics.) "Sports and recreation," writes psychoanalyst Robert Moore in his book *Sports and Mental Health* (Springfield: C. C. Thomas, 1966, p. 74), "are particularly valuable as a means of partial outlet of aggressive and sexual impulses whether we are participant or observer." And Conrad Lorenz in his rather slick treatise *On Aggression* (New York: Bantam, 1966, p. 271) adds that, "the main function of sport

---

[1] Recent American administrations have been well aware of this, and in order to preserve an aura of "normalcy" during wartime, the military has collaborated in what amounts to mass "draft-dodging" by professional athletes: allowing them to enroll in the National Guard, rather than the regular Army, and handing out special weekend leaves so that the pro jocks won't miss the big games.

today lies in the cathartic discharge of aggressive urge. . . ." If, unlike Conrad Lorenz, we do not choose to regard "aggression" as some innate quality outside society and outside history, we might ask whether there might indeed be serious shortcomings in our present social order that give rise to widespread frustration and aggression. And if we conclude that this is so, would we not have to re-examine the role of mass spectator sports in providing an "outlet" or "cathartic discharge" for this frustration, without in any way touching its societal causes?

Five generations ago Karl Marx called religion the opiate of the masses. Today that role has been taken over by sports. In 1967 there were more than 228,000,-000 paid admissions to major sports events, including 67.8 million at the race tracks, 35.9 million for football, 34.7 million for baseball and 22 million for basketball. Perhaps "opiate" seems too strong for all this. But what else can we call it when a country in the midst of a savage war that has left millions dead or wounded professes more concern over whether Muhammed Ali will defeat Joe Frazier than over the widening of the Vietnam war into Laos? What else can you call it when hundreds of thousands of Americans protest the war by picketing the White House, only to find that millions more—including their President—are off watching football games? What else can you call it when industrial workers are so rabidly involved with the fates of their sports heroes that they are perfectly oblivious to the exploitative conditions in their own factories?

In this connection it is useful to recall to what extent our professional sports have traditionally been aimed at potentially restless minority or disadvantaged groups, whether as spectators or players. It is well known, for example, that a disproportion of American football players (and the first professional football fans) have come from the coal and steel towns of Pennsylvania. The same is true of English soccer and Canadian ice hockey. These sports, too, grew up in the shadows of the factories, and gave otherwise restless workers what their managers considered "something constructive" to do. American basketball has long been the sport of the big-city ghettos, with the sizable proportion of the top professional players now coming from the streets of New York's Harlem ghetto. The same holds for American boxing and professional wrestling. These sports have traditionally formed the spectator pastimes of newly arrived immigrant groups and lately of the racially oppressed black and Latin population.

What we mean by an "opiate" is anything that tends to frustrate the solution of social problems by providing individuals with either (1) a temporary high (or as Bill Bradley put it, a "fix") which takes their minds off the problem for a while but does nothing to deal with it; or (2) a distorted frame of reference or identification which encourages them to look for salvation through patently false channels. Things like sports spectacles, whiskey, and repressively desublimated sex provide examples of opiates of the first kind. If we believe that the solution to the problems of monopolization of wealth and power will come through working people getting together to build a more democratic and egalitarian world, then, clearly, things like nationalism, racism, and sexism provide opiate barriers of the second kind. In particular, these poisonous ideologies encourage workers to seek their salvation in their nation, race, or sex, and thus divide working people one from the other, even one *against* the other. Religion probably provides an example of an opiate in both senses. Church going, prayer, and hymn singing provide the temporary fixes. And Christian theology encourages people to look for salvation in the next world, even as their lives in this one go to hell.

These different opiates tend to reinforce one another. Sports, whiskey, and sexism come together in the cult of the hard-drinking, hard-loving, hard-fighting he-man. On the other hand, the Fellowship of Christian Athletes, an organization of around 20,000 coaches, athletes, and ordinary churchgoers, has been using clean-living sports heroes to sell religion. (In fact, today's team sports were originated in England in the last century by a movement led by such people as Thomas Hughes and Charles Kingsley, who were called the "muscular Christians" because they believed that sports was the best socializer for a Christian temperament.) ...

At a recent sports symposium held at Queens College, *New York Times* sportswriter Leonard Koppett remarked that if we are going to call sports the opiate of the people, we might as well say the same about all the other products of the mass media and all other forms of mass entertainment. Berkeley sociology professor Harry Edwards replied that, be that as it may, there is one thing that makes sports watching a more efficient opiate from the power elite's point of view than virtually any other—namely, the total sense of *identification* of the spectators with the values and personalities being communicated from the field. A man might watch a war movie on television, says Edwards, but he doesn't normally jump up and down in his seat, screaming, "kill the enemy," and cheering every time "his" army makes a breakthrough. But while watching a football game, he can be both drugged out of taking any action that might upset the present *status quo,* and also drugged in a most efficient way into accepting the values and world view of the present *status quo.*

A good example of the opiate-oriented pattern of thinking is the following "explanation" of why football has become America's most popular spectator sport. This argument was put forward by Dr. Ernest Dichter, head of the Institute of Motivational Research, one of America's top corporate consulting firms. Football's popularity, he says, can be explained by four factors. First, the illicit violence in today's society—riots, student uprisings, bombings, crime in the streets, and revolutionary deeds—are all frustrating to the (well-socialized) citizen because, says Dichter, they represent chaos without control and flaunting of law and rules. By contrast, the clean, hard violence of football is refreshing and reassuring, because it is done according to rules. The referee is obeyed. Lawbreakers are promptly penalized. And everything is "neatly and firmly controlled." This, then, is the *opiate* of officialized, rule-governed football violence (in which the referees and judges have the final say). This, in turn, provides powerful ideological support for the officialized, rule-governed violence in society, in which judges have the final say. In short, the fans are supposed to identify with the distorted framework of law and order, both on the football field and in society, irrespective of what that law and order is supposed to protect.

Dichter's second explanation for football watching is that it acts as an "encounter group" therapy. Even the television fan in his living room partakes in the strong in-group feeling of the spectator. He is a member of the fan group and, as a result, "his response to the progress of the game takes on an unconscious crowd behavior." If he actually attends the game, he can have an even more vivid encounter session with the other spectators, yelling at each other and at the players and patting each other on the back when "our" team scores, and in general purging his pent-up emotions. (Maybe even yelling, "Kill the ump"?) This is, in reality, a plug for various opiates—identification with the fan tribe (tribalism), identification with a team (team nationalism), or the temporary emotional purge or "fix." The demand for these opiates probably provides the most common explanation for the public rituals of mass-spectator sports watching. For example, wrestler "Whipper" Billy Watson once remarked that, for fans to watch live wrestling "is a good way to release their pent-up emotions. If they can't take it out on their boss, yelling for their favorite or giving the Bronx cheer to his opponent is good for them." But is this really so? Sports may be "good" for them (and particularly for their bosses) as a temporary fix, which enables them to function in an oppressive job environment, but it does nothing whatever to remove the causes of that oppression. In fact, it exhausts so much time, energy, conversation, and thought that it pretty well ensures that the real problems will never even be discussed, much less solved.

The third reason for football's popularity today, says Dichter, is that it provides a reassurance of masculinity in a society in which the ordinary male has fewer and fewer opportunities to "prove" he is a "man." By identifying with the he-men on the field, even just as a living-room TV watcher, the fan helps revive the drives of the strong, assertive male animal. Women, says our big business motivational researcher, should stay away at such times because men resent their horning in on this "male" activity. And to bolster this special right, men alone become the "experts," knowing all the ins and outs of every play, statistics, and fine points of the game.

This shows, as nothing else, how completely inane the celebration of masculinity has become. Instead of identifying with the people with whom he must solve his social problems or suffocate—including his own wife—the "fan" is supposed to identify with the beefsteaks on "his" team.[2] And just so he can conduct his own alienation in this way without women horning in, he memorizes reams of trivial fine points and statistics. Salvation supposedly lies in masculinity. The kind measured in touchdowns.

The fourth high that sports fans can get out of football is a crutch for their Spartan ethic. Dichter calls it the congeniality of hard working, clean living, disciplined young men. This is supposedly of special importance to fans who see the younger generation as having gone soft and fat with affluence, populated

---

[2] On September 19, 1971, the United Press reported that Eulalia Fuchs, a forty-four-year-old housewife, had been charged with the second-degree murder of her husband, following an argument over whether or not they would watch the Cincinnati Bengals-Philadelphia Eagles football game. She reportedly preferred to listen to the stereo. Chataway and Goodhart, in their book *War Without Weapons* (London: W. H. Allen, 1968), note that "Some wives apparently live in dread of Saturdays and wait apprehensively to see what mood their husbands will return home in after the football match. If the local side loses, a wife may fear her husband will return home the worse for drink and give her a thrashing to get rid of the anger he feels about the lost game." Apparently as an opiate for the other opiate?

with boys who look "like girls," and who would scoff at athletes as "tools" of professionalism. So the true football fan sees his heroes as respected, clean, fair-minded, team-spirited young men who typify the way they feel men should live and behave. In other words, "Good Guys versus Bad Guys." The situation is almost reminiscent of a cops-and-robbers soap opera. Unfortunately, most American sports fans have the same Manichean "Good versus Evil" view of the world, with this country on the side of Good. Here the opiates leading to salvation include clean living (clean language, religion, and sexual repression), hard work (irrespective of who or what the work is for), and discipline (which usually means obedience).

N. and H. Howell have noted that "during the depression years participation in sports greatly increased. [Many] turned to sports to boost their morale during those dark years." (*Sports and Games in Canadian Life*, Toronto: Macmillan, 1969.) Of course this was no accident. Governments were willing to put a good deal of money into sports as a way of keeping the restless masses quiet. In America, they suddenly discovered the heretofore peripheral sport of basketball and started building courts everywhere. More recently, Congressman Emanuel Celler has said that, "Pro football provides the circus for the hordes." Avery Brundage, President of the International Olympic Committee, has reportedly stated that, as investment in sports facilities increases, the amount necessary for police, prisons, and hospitals decreases. This may seem straightforward enough to the Establishment, but if we see police, prisons, and mental hospitals as part of the state apparatus by which one class imposes its rule on another, then clearly the opiate of sports must be classified as part of the ideological police force by which one class keeps another in line.

If one is going to supply the harmless outlets for pent-up frustrations and vicarious violence of a Roman amphitheater, it is a good idea to have some gladiators around. In professional boxing this is straightforward enough. And arranging the big shows so that each gladiator has a clear-cut (and harmless) social significance for fans to identify with is not that difficult, either. In a racist society, the main bouts are usually between "Big Bad Niggers" and either "Great White Hopes" or obvious "Uncle Toms." (In his day, Jack Johnson met one Great White Hope after another and, in our own, Muhammed Ali has been matched against a long series of Uncle Toms.) Even in the gladiatorial game of professional ice hockey—in which fighting is an integral part of playing—the same verbiage is often applied. A Toronto paper recently remarked that, "Hadfield, a resolute left wing (for the New York Rangers), would win any White Hope tournament that did not contain John Ferguson." So, too, for the black and white gladiators of professional football, with their helmets and face masks reminiscent of their predecessors of the Roman coliseum. The area between the two lines is even called "the pit." A recent biography of smashing pass-rusher Deacon Jones is called *Life in the Pit*. It strikes me as odd that even as firm a supporter of college football as Max Rafferty can casually call the participants "gridiron gladiators." What does this say about the society that encourages them to be gladiators? (It should also be pointed out that, as in Ancient Rome, the professional "gladiators" are drawn primarily from the lowest social classes—

including especially the most recently arrived immigrant groups and the largest oppressed racial group.)

The level of violence today far surpasses anything the Romans could offer. A recent article in the Toronto *Globe and Mail* estimated that 50,000 knee operations are being performed in the United States every year as a result of football injuries. The yearly death toll from the "game" runs around forty. "Any time you get a chance to put that head gear on 'em," highly respected Texas University football coach Darrell Royal told his players before the 1971 Cotton Bowl game (his instructions were later broadcast on national television by ABC), "any time you get a chance to take 'em out . . . I expect and I encourage you to do it." Or again, "We got a letter from Headquarters," begins one of the main cheers of the University of New Mexico Loboes football team. "What did 'e say? What did 'e say?" answers the crowd. Then everyone cheers, "He said, 'HIT TO KILL, BOYS!' "

An article in the Toronto *Star's Canadian Magazine* quoted NHL president Clarence Campbell as saying that the first fight in hockey is an inevitable part of the sport: "fighting is the emotional outlet in a game that is prone to violence." And a Toronto *Star* review of Brian Connacher's book on the National Hockey League wondered whether hockey "has become a game of dimwitted gladiators —whether, in fact, the game is fated to go the way of bull-baiting, lion-feeding, and similar sanguinary spectacles."

A sociology professor writing an article on the criminology of sports in the British journal *The New Society* notes that law and order on the playing fields is breaking down. Joe Namath says, "The name of the game [in football] is kill the quarterback!" There are hatchetmen (often called "policemen") in every sport whose only job is to put the opposition's best player in the hospital.

These are not "natural" phenomena, but reflections of the increasing preoccupation with officialized and controlled violence in society generally, as well as the system's ability to encourage people to displace their pent-up frustrations into demands for sacrificial thrashings. And if the fans can be encouraged by their society to demand higher and higher levels of gladiatorial violence, sports owners can easily supply it. Professional athletes are encouraged to maim one another, not only by the macho-minded sportswriters and fans cheering them on from the side lines, but by the knowledge that if they're not tough enough there are literally thousands of minor league and college players around to take their jobs. It's the old reserve army of labor breathing down their necks, making the competition for jobs on pro teams one of the most murderous dog-eat-dog struggles since the Roman amphitheater. The players simply cannot let down. They have to be aggressive, have to give out one better than they get, have to protect their jobs. In a militarized society, gladiatorial combat brings in profits at the box office. So it's all part of the game. But whose game?

An article in a March 1972 issue of the *Sporting News* by long-time hockey writer Stan Fischler notes that ". . . violence remains part of the woof and warp of the game, mostly because the men who run big league hockey want it that way." Fischler goes on to quote Conn Smythe, who for many years managed the Toronto Maple Leafs and is regarded as one of the "pioneers" of the NHL, and who set the official attitude that still applies today when he declared, "Yes, we've got to stamp out this sort of thing or people are going to keep buying tickets." Fischler also quotes former Eastern Hockey League player George Forgie, who said that fights, "preferably with blood," are "what they tell us to give them." The latter gladiator even recalls one pregame fight between himself and Bob Taylor that resulted in both being called to the league commissioner's office. "You know what the commissioner did?" Forgie asks. "He gave us hell for fighting during warm-up before all the fans could get to their seats to enjoy it." This is the kind of gladiatorial combat that owners can make money from. And that keeps the fans "happy."

Considerations

1. Discuss the difference in attitude toward riots, depending on whether they are football riots or anti-war riots.
2. The title of this essay suggests a well known aspect of ancient Roman life. The Roman Circuses were government-sponsored games designed to distract the Roman citizens from their problems. List the examples cited by Hoch that such is the intent of modern governments.
3. Assuming that sports have replaced religion, as Marx expressed it, as the "opiate of the masses," is that necessarily bad? Do societies need distractions from the frustrations of life and outlets for their aggression? Support your answer.
4. Discuss the four reasons, according to Hoch, that football is the most popular spectator sport.
5. Discuss the following quote:
   "Some wives apparently live in dread of Saturdays and wait apprehensively to see what mood their husbands will return home in after the football match. If the local side loses, a wife may fear her husband will return home the worse for drink and give her a thrashing to get rid of the anger he feels about the lost game."
   (See "The Match.")
6. Discuss Hoch's assertion that the use of "gladiators" to describe athletes is typical of a racist society. Who were the ancient gladiators?
7. Hoch says that "In a militarized society, gladiatorial combat brings in profit at the box office"; but in the years since the Vietnam War militarism seems to have waned in popularity. Does this tend to explain the current interest in non-violent sports, such as tennis, soccer, and jogging? Support your answer.

COMPETING WITH THE
MUSCULAR CHRISTIAN

Why should you be sitting there, where an M. Donald Grant wants you, flesh sodden, head filled with gibberish and numbers, past anger, past moving, past caring, when there is still light in the sky and time left in the day to hear the pounding of your heart and taste salt in your mouth and feel cool air caress the dampness of your skin?

—Robert Lipsyte

ROBERT LIPSYTE

Designated Heroes,
Ranking Gods,
All-Star Holy Persons

SportsWorld has always considered its traditional oppression of women as something of a locker-room joke: Sports is a male sanctuary, therefore any woman who tries to invade it is not really a woman. In the 1930s, the same male sportswriters who called Babe Didrikson the greatest all-round athlete in the country were also quick to describe the down on her upper lip, the prominence of her Adam's apple and the angular contours of her "boyish" body. When she turned professional and began to wear cosmetics, style her hair, and dress in a more conventionally "feminine" fashion, the sportswriters were divided; some thought she was merely "glamorizing" herself to attract more commercial endorsements, while other congratulated her on finally growing into womanhood. Innuendoes about her sexuality followed her into marriage with George Zaharias, a huge professional wrestler.

As a performing athlete and as a winner, Babe Zaharias was in a class with Jim Thorpe and Babe Ruth, but sports herstory has yet to be written in which her confidence, courage, and accomplishments are given the same exposure as those of hundreds of lesser men.

245

From the late nineteenth century until the 1920s, women's sports were on the increase, probably reflecting the burgeoning women's movement. ("Many a woman," wrote Elizabeth Cady Stanton, "is riding to suffrage on a bicycle.") Calisthenics, riding, boating, swimming, tennis, skating, and basketball were introduced at the women's colleges. In 1912, women began participating in the Olympic Games.

The gains were not only wiped out during the sports boom of the twenties, but regressive legislation was passed that eliminated most state basketball tournaments for high school girls and severely restricted the types and extent of competition available to women. The reactionary and male-dominated Amateur Athletic Union took over women's sports in 1922. A year later, the Equal Rights Amendment was brought before Congress and stifled in committee.

In those years, as the women's movement itself was checked, the vital separation was made: SportsWorld for the men, HouseWorld for the women; SportsWorld to prepare men for industrial production and warfare (draft officials had been shocked by the percentage of men physically unfit for World War I combat), and HouseWorld to contain the energies and progressive tendencies of women who had just won the right to vote; SportsWorld to provide a safety valve and a male sanctuary and a manipulative entertainment, HouseWorld to create stability and a breeding shed for capitalism.

Mildred Ella Didrikson was born in 1914 and raised in Beaumont, Texas, one of seven children. Her parents were Norwegian immigrants, her father a ship's carpenter, her mother a housewife who had been an outstanding skater and skier in Norway. They encouraged all their children in athletics, and built a gymnasium in the garage and backyard. Babe was an athletic prodigy. By 15 she was a schoolgirl basketball sensation, as well as a superior student, a harmonica player, a gold-medal typist, and a prize-winning dressmaker. In 1930 she was recruited out of high school to play on the employees' basketball team of a Dallas insurance company. She led them to a national championship, and was named all-America three years in a row.

Babe ran, swam, dove, and played softball on high competitive levels. The company sponsored her first real flyer at organized track and field events, the Olympic tryouts in Chicago. She won a place on the American team, and at the 1932 Games in Los Angeles, she won two gold medals, in the javelin throw and the hurdles. After breaking the world record in the high jump she was disqualified because her western roll technique had not yet been officially recognized.

In his 1938 *Farewell to Sport*, Paul Gallico wrote off her phenomenal athletic success as "simply because she would not or could not compete with women at their own best game—man-snatching. It was an escape, a compensation. She would beat them at everything else they tried to do."

In the early fifties, when I first read that, I believed it. Years later, my consciousness partially raised, I accepted it as routine sportswriter sexism. Only recently, rereading Grantland Rice's *The Tumult and the Shouting* and Babe Zaharias' own 1955 autobiography, *This Life I've Led*, did another explanation present itself. Once, during a round of social golf, Rice promoted a foot race between Babe and Gallico, who was a fine and vain athlete himself. Babe ran Gallico into the ground.

Between 1935, when Zaharias began playing golf seriously, and 1956, when she died, she won nearly every prize and title in the women's game. In a 1970 letter to me, her widower wrote, "She told me when things were tough, George, I hate to die. I said, why—she said, I'm just learning to play golf."

Of such stuff SportsWorld creates hymns and gospels for men. Zaharias was operated on for cancer of the lower intestine in 1953. A permanent colostomy was necessary. Three months later she was playing tournament golf, and in 1954 she won the National Womens Open. She talked about her operation publicly "because I believe the cancer problem should be out in the open. The more the public knows about it the better."

Also in his letter, George Zaharias wrote, "After she won the Womens British Open golf championship—1947 press party at Toots Shor's—with all the great sportswriters including Grantland Rice for openers. Fred Corcoran, who was 'Babe's manager asked her what her plans were. 'Babe' said Guess I'll play in the U.S. Open. No other question was asked. All the writers hit the door. All the papers had it 'Babe' to play in the U.S. Open. It didn't take Joe Dey long, the very first edition the name was changed to the U.S. Mens Open. Check it."

I never did. The story may be apocryphal, but it rings with a sad truth— nothing seems to panic the functionaries of SportsWorld faster than the threat of a woman athlete beating a man in fair combat. We are constantly assured that it can't happen, for biological, psychological, and sociological reasons, and that if it somehow should happen, then the woman would be more than a woman and the man less than a man. Babe Zaharias, being a woman, was obviously frustrated, abnormal, perhaps genetically confused, according to many of the commentators of her day, to display such toughness and competitive fire.

In *Rip Off the Big Game*, Marxist commentator Dr. Paul Hoch has equated America's sexual apartheid in sports with South Africa's racial apartheid—both were established in England's all-white, all-male public school training grounds for elitist rule.

Dr. Thomas Boslooper, a New Jersey clergyman and author of *The Feminity Game*, has said, "Men can keep women in a secondary position by keeping them weak, and the best way to keep them weak is to keep them physically inactive."

For all her talent, fierce ambition, and friendly press relations, Babe Zaharias had continual financial problems until her 1938 marriage. She turned pro, although the best golf was then in the amateur game. She was always going back to type for Employers Casualty Company. She even toured for a while with the otherwise all-male House of David basketball team.

The best advice she ever got in sports, she says, was Babe Ruth's "Get yourself an annuity," but until George Zaharias appeared to give her financial and emotional support, she had trouble surviving on a day-to-day basis. And it was only through George that she was able to quit pro golf long enough to reclaim her amateur standing and develop her game to its potential.

George Zaharias had been stimulated to write to me by a column of mine about a golf match between Doug Sanders, a touring pro best known for the size and variety of his wardrobe, and Carol Mann, the best female golfer. Their comparative statistics are noteworthy. At the time of their match, Sanders had won seventeen tournaments and his accumulated prize money, $550,000, placed him eighth among men, while Mann, the No. 1 woman, had won twenty-nine tournaments, but only $203,000. By SportsWorld logic, the discrepancy in their earnings was proof of the superiority of the men's game rather than the inequality of winners' purses.

By playing Sanders, Mann hoped to generate the favorable publicity that could lead women's golf into better television contracts, richer endorsements, and more serious press and fan attention. No one actually expected her to win. Maureen Orcutt, a famous amateur golfer who worked in *The Times'* sports department, expressed the conventional female line: "It would be wonderful if Carol won, but Doug just won't let her." Had Carol won, of course, the entire project would have been reinterpreted; after all, the male line would go, isn't there something queer about a man who travels with twenty-five pairs of shoes? And this 6-foot 3-inch Carol Mann—has anyone scraped the inside of her cheek for chromatins lately?

Sanders won the match by twelve strokes, but Mann made her point—a man and a woman can compete on equal terms without washing the greens in blood, tears, or excess hormones. For the summer of 1970, a watershed season in SportsWorld's version of the battle of the sexes, this was a rather new and important point.

A few weeks before the Sanders-Mann match, a 27-year-old schoolteacher, Pat Palinkas, became the first woman to play men's professional football. In a minor league exhibition game in Orlando, Florida, Palinkas was sent in to hold the ball for her husband to place kick. But the snap from center was off-target, and Palinkas bobbled the ball. Before she could recover and set for the kick, a 240-pound opposition linebacker, Wally Florence, crashed through and knocked her down. He said, "I tried to break her neck. I don't know what she's trying to prove. I'm out here trying to make a living and she's out here prancing around making folly with a man's game."

At first, my sympathies were with Palinkas, this doughty little 122-pounder who sprang up unhurt to inspire her Orlando Panthers to victory. Why shouldn't she be allowed to play, to find the limits of her skill and talent, to gain the fame and fortune that SportsWorld bestows upon its stars? Man's game, indeed. Florence (as symbolic a name as Mann) couldn't even knock her down for keeps.

Later I thought about Florence as victim. I called him a few days later at Project Cool, a ghetto vocational training agency in Bridgeport, Connecticut. He was a Big Brother in charge of keeping the Little Brothers off Downtown Whitey's back. Florence needed some cooling off himself. "I wanted to show her this is no soft touch," he told me. "I wanted to smash her back to the kitchen."

Florence had earned his scars and stripes. He had played at Purdue, he had been cut by the Giants and Jets, he had been dropped by several minor league teams before hooking on with the Bridgeport Jets. He was 27. This was his last chance to get his game together for a final shot at the big leagues, and now, before the regular season even opened, he was a national joke.

The wealthy businessmen who toyed with minor league football franchises were bush-leaguers ogling Wally Florence because they couldn't afford O. J. Simpson. But they weren't losers like Florence because they had the power to send in Pat Palinkas to hype the box office, and because they knew that the codes of SportsWorld, the locker-room slogans about manliness and discipline and integrity, were theirs to bend or change.

Only fools like Palinkas and Florence and me were expected to take the rules seriously because we had to make our ways in a system we neither created nor controlled. If Palinkas had to ridicule Florence's dreams, and if Florence had to mock-rape Palinkas, and if I had to turn them both into symbols, well, that's the way of the world. Unless the three of us could get together and take over the league. A tidy microcosm, this.

The Sanders-Mann and Florence-Palinkas match-ups were only two of the male-female skirmishes that summer. Women jockeys were riding at major race-tracks, threatening the pathetically macho male jockeys who had escaped into the one sport which gave a small man refuge from a world of bullies. Some male jockeys actually stoned and fire-bombed female jockeys' dressing quarters. Male reporters were less physical but no less threatened and hostile keeping accredited women reporters out of their press boxes. It was no victory at all when Elinor Kaine, denied a seat in the Yale Bowl press box, was eventually seated in an auxiliary area. She had been covering football for years with greater intelligence, energy, ingenuity, contacts, and background than most of the men who took their seats as a birthright.

II

"To me," wrote Billie Jean King in her 1974 autobiography, "Women's Libera-tion means that every woman ought to be able to pursue whatever career or personal lifestyle she chooses as a full and equal member of society without fear of sexual discrimination. That's a pretty basic and simple statement, but, golly, it sure is hard sometimes to get people to accept it. And because of the way other people think, it's even harder to reach the point in your own life where you can live by it."

As the Feminist Statement from a woman who has been promoted as Sports-World's model WOMAN to Vince Lombardi's FATHER and Joe Namath's SON, it seems mild, even stale, in the mid-seventies. But to Billie Jean's ever-lasting glory, she was saying pretty much the same thing back in the late six-ties when I first met her, long before it was considered fashionable or even acceptable.

"Almost every day for the last four years," she told me once, "someone comes up to me and says, 'Hey, when are you going to have children?'

"I say, 'I'm not ready yet.'

"They say, 'Why aren't you at home?'

"I say, 'Why don't you go ask Rod Laver why he isn't at home?'"

At the time it seemed revolutionary, a woman in sports actually equating herself with a man. Ask Rod Laver why he isn't home? The cheekiness of the broad. Rod Laver isn't at home because he doesn't have to be. Like male sports-writers.

"My husband's the one who thinks women's lib is really great," she said back then. "He feels everybody should be equal. He's loose and limber. I think he knows in his heart and mind he'll be a real big daddy some day. I still think you can be feminine and do your own thing. I agree with most of the women's lib things, but some of it seems far out. But that might be just for attention. Lord knows, you really have to exaggerate things these days to get attention."

Billie Jean always got attention because she was "good copy," the first requirement of celebrity. Sportswriters might call her "outspoken" or even "kooky," but they could count on her always to cooperate, to accommodate yet another interview in which she would answer questions frankly. Her reputation for being "controversial," however, did not come from an early feminist position but from an unselfconscious populism that was so exotic in tennis that those who weren't horrified found it "refreshing." She believed that fans should stomp and cheer at tennis matches, that players had the right to question referees and officials, that the game had to shuck its country-club image and plunge into the arena to survive. In this, she was ahead of her time. The following quote, delivered breathlessly while we watched a tennis match in Madison Square Garden, was advanced for 1968.

"If I was an announcer, I'd try to influence people. I'd tell them how grueling tennis is, I'd get away from this sissified image.

"I mean, after all, they stop the action because a player's got a blister. The fans have to laugh, they've seen hockey players get their teeth knocked out. And I'd go into poverty neighborhoods, middle-class neighborhoods, I'd get those kids out to play. And it doesn't matter what they're wearing.

"Do you know, for my first tournament, I was 11 or 12, my mother made me a pair of white shorts. We couldn't afford to go out and buy shorts then. It was a southern California junior tournament, and Perry T. Jones pushed me out of the group picture. He said I should be wearing a tennis dress. I felt bad for my mother."

Billie Jean has described her mother, Betty Moffitt, as "a creative person. She liked painting and ceramics, and made rugs for the den." She was a part-time Tupperware saleswoman, a sometime Avon Lady.

Bill Moffitt, for whom Billie Jean was named while he was away at war, "loved being a fireman and never even made a big effort for advancement, just so he could continue doing what he liked doing best—working as an engineer on all those trucks and pumping equipment." He could never afford to buy a new car during Billie Jean's childhood.

An active recreational athlete himself, Moffitt began coaching Billie Jean in ball sports at 4. By the time she was 10, in 1954, she was shortstop and youngest member of the girl's softball team that won the Long Beach, California, public parks championship. Billie Jean also played sandlot football. She remembers that most of her schoolmates played tennis and golf at their parents' country clubs, and some of them owned horses. She has always been keenly aware of people acting "snobby" toward her. She remembers carrying her lunch to tournaments as a junior player because of the "outrageous" $2 price of a sandwich at the Los Angeles Tennis Club. Her parents felt uncomfortable there, too.

She has characterized her family as middle-American, religious (Bob Richards, the pole-vault champion, was the minister of their Protestant church), and "pretty basic." She wrote, "Dad was the boss, the breadwinner, the one who made all the final decisions." He was against homosexuals, interracial marriage, unpatriotic expression. He believed in hard work, discipline, and traditional roles. Her younger brother, Randy, went on to become a major league baseball pitcher, but Billie Jean's baseball and football careers were aborted when she was 11. She agreed they were not "ladylike."

Her father suggested she choose from among tennis, golf, and swimming, and when none of them appealed to her he endorsed tennis. "Well, you run a lot and you hit a ball. I think you'd like it."

She began taking lessons at a municipal park from a city instructor, a man in his sixties who was delighted with this big—5 feet 4 inches, 125 pounds— enthusiastic, strong, and "hungry" girl. Within a year she began playing in tournaments, and entered the traditional, outrageous, snobby world of amateur tennis.

There had always been great women tennis players, cherished and honored by the sport even after their playing days. Billie Jean would break no new ground merely by being a female.

Despite her competitive drive—her scrambling style and fierce net play were said to be copied from "the men's game"—she has never been considered the equal of such past champions as Suzanne Lenglen and Helen Wills Moody.

And she was certainly no prole pioneer in the game. Althea Gibson, a Harlem black, and Pancho Gonzalez, a Los Angeles Chicano, were tolerated and exploited as young amateurs long before this self-styled "El Chubbo" in harlequin glasses appeared to cry "Nuts" and gamier expletives whenever she missed a shot.

What Billie Jean had, and may even still have, was a naive faith in the opportunity and justice of the American system. It came from being raised a lower-middle-class WASP in southern California after World War II. Billie Jean's people had always known they were true Americans, that the history books had been written for them, that the heroes and heroines of movies bore their names and that all they needed to do was work hard, be honest, God-fearing, and single-minded, and they could ride a big talent to the top of the heap. There was no question in Billie Jean's mind that if she could just hit enough backhands, concentrate hard enough, sacrifice enough candy bars, and get enough sleep, she could be, as she would say, Número Uno.

And when Billie Jean found out she was wrong, that in tennis at least, the officials were more interested in retaining control than in making money or turning on the nation to their sport, Billie Jean had the confidence, articulateness, assertiveness, and self-righteousness to take their sport away from them.

I am not suggesting that Billie Jean, all by herself, snatched the game from the Lawwwn Ten-Nis bureaucrats and served it into the Big Bucks. There was Texas money (once again, Lamar Hunt), and a community of interest that included television, sporting goods, clothing, construction, cigarettes, Las Vegas. The tracks of the pro tour had been laid by Jack Kramer and Pancho Gonzalez and a score of their Australian mates over thousands of one-night stands. New patterns of leisure hooked up the spectator boom with the participant boom, and they nourished each other.

But the animus/anima that gave soul to the trend was Billie Jean. She personalized this bringing of tennis—classiest of sports—to the people. And she was the only one who could have done it, male or female. Others grumbled about the hypocrisy of the United States Lawn Tennis Association, about the humiliation of having to accept secret payments from the very officials who had solemnly ruled them illegal, about having to dance attendance upon wealthy patrons, of playing under poor conditions, of slipping into a dependent life instead of being allowed to sweat and fight for independence and wealth. But nobody who had as much to lose from the old way and as much to gain from the new way stepped up and spoke as boldly as Billie Jean.

She said she wanted to turn pro so she could be an honest person. She said she wanted to hear the fans hoot and holler so she'd know they cared. She said she wanted to make lots and lots of money. The fact that she was a woman emboldened the other women and shamed the men.

Nowadays, with tennis crowds screaming, "Get it baby," and linesmen no longer as secure as Supreme Court justices and players' costumes as cheery as parfaits, it is hard to recall the stiff white formality of amateur tennis in the early sixties, the library hush around a final match, the awesome pomposity of the beribboned officials. Tennis seemed grim, except when it was hilariously fantastic.

Imagine Lipsyte, a cub reporter, stalking the corridors of the Mayflower Hotel in Washington, D.C., while the USLTA delegates he had been sent to cover moved from secret conclave to executive session, plotting counterattacks against Jack Kramer's pro raids, staging high-tea coups against each other, rewarding friends with sanctioned tournaments, and constructing intricate new legislation to further restrict their flighty young wards, the players.

I was covering because *The Times'* regular tennis writer, nay, its Ambassador to Racket Games, Allison Danzig, was gravely ill. Danzig, a fine, erudite, helpful man who wrote beautiful rolling 100-yard sentences, was missed—for years he had certified these conventions with his presence, and after matches players always approached him deferentially and asked for an analysis of their strokes— but politicians among the delegate were letting me know that if I became "the new Danzig" his perks and news sources would be mine. The Timesman is dead, long live the Timesman, an early lesson of inestimable value.

But stalking the corridors, most un-Danzigian, I noticed a mop-sink closet adjacent to one of the meeting rooms. I stepped in briefly, hoping to eavesdrop, but I could hear only the mumbling of voices through the wall, no distinct words. As I stepped out again, a USLTA regional vice-president saw me, and cried, "You heard it all?"

"Yeah, sure," I grumbled, and went upstairs to my room. I called the airline to reconfirm my flight home. As I replaced the phone, a national vice-president who also was a *Times* advertising executive burst into my room.

"You phoned in your story," he accused.

"What story?"

He brushed me aside, picked up my phone, and called *The Times* sports desk. He ordered my story killed. He must have interpreted the puzzled silence on the other end as abject surrender because he slammed down the receiver with a triumphant flourish and looked down at me with benign majesty.

"You're young. You'll understand someday." He was very tall, very thin, very old. He had great flapping arms. "There are some things far, far more important than a newspaper story. Tennis. Sports. The future of young people. Our country."

Much later, when I thought about it, I became furious, at his arrogance and my passivity. He was tampering with Freedom of the Press. I should have killed him for trespassing. Even later, when I found out the big story was an obscure, internecine dialogue of little significance or interest to *Times* readers, I could still get angry with a flashback. Today the USLTA, tomorrow the White House. But at the moment, I was simply dumbfounded. The national vice-president paused at the door on his way out.

"Naturally," he said, "I'll have to mention this to Allison."

Apparently he did because Danzig made what was considered a miraculous recovery and returned to reclaim his beat.

Imagine Billie Jean in such company.

"They love you when you're coming up," said Billie Jean of those ranks of vice-presidents. "But they don't like winners. And they especially don't like me because I talk about money all the time. I'm mercenary. I'm a rebel."

Yet her rebellion was not against society, or even against tennis. It was against the crumbling traditions of a game about to be refurbished, an ancient family business on the verge of a corporate take-over.

The rebel got married because it was obviously the thing to do in 1965 when a 21-year-old woman fell in love and wanted to establish herself as a person outside her mother's kitchen. She "stayed home all that fall and winter because I thought it was really important to be a good wife." It was her husband, Larry, then a law student, who was sensitive enough to send her back into the arena and encourage her to seek her salvation.

"Being a girl was not the only thing I had to fight," she told Frank Deford in a 1975 *Sports Illustrated* profile. "I was brought up to believe in the well-rounded concept, doing lotsa things a little, but not putting yourself on the line. It took me a while before I thought one day: who is it that says we have to be well-rounded? Who decided that? The people who aren't special at anything, that's who. When at last I understood that, I could really try to be special."

And she became special in the same ruthless way everyone else becomes special—she let her marriage slide into a sporadic relationship, she traveled continually for instruction and tournament experience, she underwent extensive knee surgery, she blotted out anything that might distract her from becoming No. 1.

And she became No. 1, justifying, in SportsWorld at least, the disruption, the sacrifice, the pain. And when President Nixon called her up it was to congratulate her on becoming the first woman athlete to earn $100,000 in a single year.

That was 1971, the year of the women's breakaway tournament circuit, sponsored by Virginia Slims (she tends to sneer at those who suggest she should not be associated, however indirectly, with cigarettes) and the year of her abortion, which she later made public ("I was only about a month pregnant; I didn't feel I was killing a life or anything like that. But the real reason for my decision was that I also felt it was absolutely the wrong time for me to bring a child into the world.").

But, of course, it took a man to finally authenticate Billie Jean. On September 20, 1973, in a grotesque extravaganza in the Houston Astrodome that brought tennis into the show-biz division of SportsWorld, Little Myth America beat Bobby Riggs, a male of comparable size, but considerably less championship experience, twenty-six years older, and far, far less admirable by any humanistic measure.

When it was all over, when this Rigged-up superstar was acclaimed the Joan of Ace, when this flat-chested, stubby girl in glasses (as she describes herself), whose father still called her "Sissy," was besieged by toothpaste, deodorant, suntan oil, and hair curler manufacturers, when it was implied that she had hung a pair of balls on every American woman who wanted them, only Billie Jean made sense. She said:

"This is the culmination of nineteen years of work. Since the time they wouldn't let me be in a picture because I didn't have on a tennis skirt, I've wanted to change the game around. Now it's here. But why should there be a rematch? Why any more sex tennis? Women have enough problems getting to compete against each other at the high school and college levels. Their programs are terribly weak. Why do we have to worry about men?"

Considerations

1. What is "SportsWorld"? What is a woman's place in it? (For a 1928 discussion of this idea, read "The Great Sports Myth.")
2. Lipsyte implies that sportswriter Paul Gallico failed to give Babe Didrikson her due as an athlete because she outran him in a foot race. Does this story indicate the need for legitimate female sportswriters?
3. According to Lipsyte, what would the SportsWorld line have been had Carol Mann beaten Doug Sanders?
4. Although Billie Jean King is "outspoken," why is she nevertheless acceptable to SportsWorld? How does Lipsyte view her defeat of Bobby Riggs?

ROBERT LIPSYTE

The Wheelchair Games

June 15, 1968. It's a very hot day in New York City, and I am standing, in my regulation jacket and tie, on a rutted asphalt parking lot behind the Joseph Bulova School of Watchmaking, in Astoria, Queens. I have been interviewing a buxom, red-haired young woman from Chicago, Linda Laury, who tells me she is 26 years old and works for the government in social security administration. She is nervous because in a few minutes she will compete in her very first athletic contest, a 60-yard dash.

She tries to be flip. "I didn't come to set records, I came to have fun."

"Sure," says a friend of hers, a blonde named Ella Cox, who won this event two years ago, setting a record, and lost it last year. "You going to race with your pocketbook? I'll hold it."

I watch Linda move out to the starting line, and my stomach tightens for her, my mouth is dry. I am 30 years old, eight months a columnist, and considerably tougher than I will be later on. I don't care if she wins or loses, only that she will be satisfied with her performance.

The starter's gun snaps, and Linda gets a good start. Her hands move rhythmically on the outer steel rims of the big back wheels in short, choppy strokes that bring the wheelchair to early speed. The eight-inch front casters of the chair have been tightened so the chair will not veer out of its lane during the race, and the brake has been removed so Linda will not inadvertently engage it during her follow-through. Half-way down the course Linda begins pumping steadily, long, coasting strokes that carry her into the lead. A young woman a lane away founders in a rut, two others lose strength, and Linda flashes across the finish line a winner. My eyes are wet, with perspiration, I hope.

Ella laughs and claps as Linda, flushed and feigning surprise, rolls back to where we are waiting for her. Her hands shake as she lights a cigarette. She takes her pocketbook back, and Ella's, too, as the slim young blonde woman rolls out for the next heat of the 60-yard dash. We watch her in silence.

The National Wheelchair Games were twelve years old at the time, and they rarely rated much more than a paragraph or two in most papers. I'm not sure what had brought me out that first time—curiosity, sentimentality, the drive to be different, or a reaction against all the gross spectacles I had been covering, the Indy 500, the Super Bowl, the Kentucky Derby, the America's Cup Yacht Races, those swollen carnivals that had made pimps of the best of us. And so I had driven out to this shoe-string two-day tournament to reclaim my soul and write some honest emotion and do the crips a favor.

I had wandered around for an hour or more before I found Ella and Linda and Hope Chafee, a 23-year-old chemist. The atmosphere of the Games had surprised me: The noisy, nervous, confident, intense, flirting athletes might have been warming up for any of a hundred track and field meets I had attended, except, of course, for the chairs and the crutches and the stumps. But such qualifications were mine, not theirs. Magnanimously, I was willing to accept them as athletes, *handicapped* athletes, to be sure, while they saw themselves as archers and weightlifters and swimmers and sprinters with opponents to psych out and titles to win. I knew these sports had been developed after World War II for therapeutic purposes—Ben Lipton, guiding spirit of American wheelchair games, told me to come back in a year or two when the Vietnam paraplegics would be leaving hospitals and rehabilitation centers—but the athletes insisted that the Games were now basically social and recreational. It was a way of meeting people and of earning trips to international events. The next Paralympic Games, for example, would be held later that year in Israel, and winners here would make the American team.

Ella wins her heat, and rolls back to us. My pencil and pad are out, I make notes, but my questioning somehow seems flabby to me, cautious, solicitous. It takes forever to find out that Linda and Ella and Hope all met as undergraduates at the University of Illinois, which has one of the country's finest rehabilitation centers. Now they all work, live in regular apartment buildings, bowl and square dance from their chairs, and drive cars, which is essential if a person in a chair is to travel with any measure of independence.

"If you're a good gimp you'll do all right," says the flip Linda. When I wince at the word, which somehow sounds like nigger or fag, she grins and says, "We like to use that word first, before an A.B. does."

"An A.B.?"

"Able-bodied." She makes it sound like whitey or straight, and liberates me. Confirmed as an outsider, I begin to relax and regain my technique. I ask them how they all got to be gimps, the question they were all waiting to answer and get out of the way.

Ella was stricken with polio at 5, Hope at 8. Both are now 23, and they think they had it easier than Linda. Suddenly and mysteriously one morning when she was 13 years old, Linda was unable to rise from the breakfast table.

"Small children make adjustments and friends," says Ella, "and adults, if they don't become embittered, work hard to get their independence back. But teen-agers are just at the age when everyone is running off for a pizza, and there's a great tendency to withdraw."

"I had depressions," says Linda, "but not so much over my handicap as over where to go to meet other people like me. I had to function the best I could in an A.B. world."

Hope nods. "You never really know what a wheelchair can do until you see other people doing it."

We talk some more, mostly about the events, about the classifications, which are according to the extent of disability, about records and titles and equipment and, as is also standard with amateur athletes, about the general lack of press coverage. Then they are called for their next heat, and wheel away. I start walking toward the finish line for a better view. A chair whirrs up beside me. It is Ella.

"You know, we consider this sport. We come here to win and have fun. But A.B.s don't really understand this. Even after you give them some big hairy explanation, it comes out sob-sister for most people. Please, one thing, don't go back and write a sob story about us."

I promise I won't.

Two years later, I went back to the Wheelchair Games and met Bob Wieland, a 24-year-old weightlifter. When he was 23, he had stood 5 feet 11½ inches and weighed 205 pounds. In Vietnam his legs were blown off by a booby-trapped 82-millimeter mortar round. He contracted malaria in the hospital and his weight dropped to 95 pounds. But the day I met him, June 12, 1970, he weighed 166 pounds and he had just bench-pressed 300 pounds to win the Games light-heavyweight championship.

"You think you'd really be charged up for the Nationals," he said over lunch. "I mean, this is the National Championships, wow. But I used to get much more turned on before a college football game. I guess it's because I don't really want to be here. This is a substitute, the best there is, but still a substitute. I'd rather have legs."

Wieland was one of only eight recent veterans among the more than 280 male and female competitors in those 14th Games. The waves of new athletes Ben Lipton had predicted never materialized. The World War II veterans had been older men, they had had a greater sense of purpose, and they had been treated as heroes on their return. Vietnam produced many more amputees and paraplegics than did World War II, but the Vietnam veterans were tucked away out of sight.

"A lot of guys I was in the hospital with refused to face reality," said Wieland. "They drank alcohol and smoked grass and waited for their legs to come back. In the hospital it was all right, you were accepted, but out in society, well, it's not that they don't like you, it's that they don't know what to say to you, and they really don't want to see you and hear about what happened."

Wieland was from Milwaukee. He had been an athlete at Wisconsin State University. He turned down a contract to pitch in the Phillies farm system. He was, he said, "doing well, real well" for himself when he was drafted, and now he was "making the most of living in a different world."

"There are times when you just lie in bed and cry, 'Oh, my legs,' but it's all up to the individual and most guys make it. A lot depends on how stable you were before, on your home life. I have an outgoing personality, and that helped.

"I keep reminding myself that I had twenty-three good years, that I can remember running along the beach and jumping into the water, dancing, going down the basketball court on legs. A lot of the kids here never had it to lose, and I think it's easier for them than the veterans."

Wieland was an only child, living at home, driving a Cadillac Eldorado and collecting about $800 a month in disability pay. Seven months before I met him he had begun lifting weights to build up his strength for artificial legs. An athlete, he had barely mounted the legs when he began thinking competition. The paralympic weightlifting technique requires more wrist snap and more explosive muscle action than the A.B. style because the weight bar is only two inches above the lifter's chest. Even after winning his championship that day, Wieland began planning his training schedule for the coming months. He was sure he could lift more than 300 pounds, and he wanted an international title.

"When I get down, I think about June 14, 1969," he said. He smiled faintly. "My first anniversary. Day after tomorrow. Those 82s can destroy a tank, so I'm lucky to be alive. I say, 'Every day's a holiday.' Well, you know what I mean.

"My stumps are short, the left one is five inches, the right is twelve inches. If they were longer I could walk much better. I'd really be dangerous. But there are guys with no stumps at all.

"I can go out and enjoy the weather. I can have a good time. I'm alive. People tend to let themselves down after an injury. What it all comes to is this: You've got to learn some new moves, and keep yourself together."

You've got to learn some new moves, and keep yourself together. Write that on your locker-room wall.

If Linda Laury and Bob Wieland were products of a broad-based government program of rehabilitation through sports, or even of recreational fitness, there might be some reason to have hope for the physical culture of America. But the wheelchair sports are basically supported by scattered institutions and a few corporations, most notably Bulova, which employs and trains many disabled persons. Despite overwhelming medical evidence of the enormous physical and psychological benefits of such programs, sports for the disabled, the blind, for old people and mentally retarded children, are erratically funded, usually by private agencies, and shamefully neglected by the media, which conserves its time and space for paying customers, and by the functionaries of SportsWorld, who have not been doing all that much for A.B.s, either.

Considerations

1. In this interview, the wheelchair athletes talk about the general lack of press coverage, but no explanation is given for such a lack. What is your explanation?
2. Why were the Vietnam amputees and paraplegics "tucked away out of sight"?
3. Discuss the last sentence of the essay.

PAUL WEISS

Women Athletes

Amateurs and professionals differ in prospect and objective, and usually in experience and skill. They are to be sharply distinguished, without being prevented from playing together or against one another under controlled conditions. Women are not always so readily distinguishable from men, particularly when they are clothed, or when sex differences are not determined by an examination of their sexual organs, but by a microscopic study of the composition of their cells. Normally, though, we have less difficulty in distinguishing them from men than we have in distinguishing professionals from amateurs. What is far more difficult is the settlement of the question: are women athletes to be viewed as radically and incomparably different from men or as comparable with them, both as amateurs and as professionals?

Whatever difficulty we may have in identifying an individual as a man or a woman, athletic bodies have shown no hesitation in laying down conditions and rules which apply to one and not the other.

> At the Olympic level, women are not permitted to lift heavy weights or to throw the hammer. They are, however, permitted to put the shot, hurl the discus, and throw the javelin. Similarly, they are barred from the pole vault, the high jump, the high hurdles, and the longer foot races, but they are permitted to compete in the long jump, the low hurdles, and the shorter races. They are also barred from the more strenuous team games, but in 1964 they were permitted to compete in the milder game of vollyball—the only team game in which there is no possibility of direct body contact between opponents.[1]

> There is no serious competition in which women are matched against men.

[1] Eleanor Metheny, *Connotations of Movement in Sport and Dance* (Dubuque, Iowa, 1965), p. 53.

Rather, in those sports in which men and women participate together, they play as partners, with women generally accepting the supporting rather than the dominant role.[2]

At the international level, some forms of competition appear to be categorically unacceptable, as indicated by the fact that women are excluded from Olympic Competition in ... wrestling, judo, boxing, weight lifting, hammer throw, pole vault, the longer foot races, high hurdles, and all forms of team games, with the recent exception of volleyball. These forms appear to be characterized by one or more of the following principles: an attempt to physically subdue the opponent by bodily contact; direct application of bodily force to some heavy object; attempt to project the body into or through space over long distances; cooperative face-to-face opposition in situations in which body contact may occur.[3]

Some forms of individual competition are generally acceptable to the college women of the United States ... swimming, diving, skiing, and figure skating ... golf, archery, and bowling ... characterized by one or more of the following principles: attempts to project the body into or through space in aesthetically pleasing patterns; utilization of a manufactured device to facilitate bodily movement; application of force through a light implement; overcoming the resistance of a light object. ... Some forms of face-to-face competition are also generally acceptable ... fencing, ... squash, badminton, tennis.[4]

There is considerable justification for these decisions in the results of tests and studies which have been made on women by themselves and in comparison with men. Women have comparatively less muscular strength and lighter arms, do not use their muscles as rapidly, have a longer reaction time, faster heart rates, and achieve a smaller arm strength in relation to their weight than men do. Their bones ossify sooner, they have a narrower and more flexible shoulder girdle, smaller chest girth, and smaller bones and thighs. They also have wider and more stable knee joints, a heavier and more tilted pelvis, longer index fingers, and a greater finger dexterity. They have shorter thumbs, legs, feet, and arm length, a smaller thoracic cavity, smaller lungs, smaller hearts, lower stroke volumes, a smaller average height, lower blood pressure, fatigue more readily, and are more prone to injury. Their bodies are less dense and contain more fat; they have less bone mass, and throw differently.

Some women are outstanding athletes and have better records than most of the men involved in the sport. Some women have made better records in the Olympic Games than were previously made by men. But it is also true that when women compete in the same years with men, the women's records are not better than the men's. Marjorie Jackson won the 100-meter race in 1952 at eleven and one-half seconds, but the best time made in 1896 by a man was twelve seconds. In 1896 the best time for the men's 100-meter free style swimming race was one minute and twenty-two seconds, but in 1932 Helene Madison made the distance in one minute and six-tenths second. More spectacular advances are reported of Russian women in the shot-put and discus. That these and other women can more than match the records made by men in other years is under-

---

[2] *Ibid.*, p. 55.
[3] *Ibid.*, p. 49.
[4] *Ibid.*, p. 50.

standable when we take account of the fact that women begin their athletic careers at an earlier age than they once did, that they are willing to practice for considerable periods, that they are benefiting from improved training methods, that they are using better equipment than they had previously, and that more of them are participating in contests and sports.

Women are unable to compete successfully with the best of men, except in sports which emphasize accuracy, skill, or grace—shooting, fancy skating, diving, and the like. Their bones, contours, musculature, growth rate, size, proportion, and reaction times do not allow them to do as well as men in sports which put a premium on speed or strength.

It is part of our cultural heritage to make an effort to avoid having women maimed, disfigured, or hurt. That is one reason why they do not usually engage in and are not officially allowed to compete in such contact sports as boxing, wrestling, football, and rugby, with inexplicable exceptions being made for ka-rate and lacrosse. In the United States women gymnasts do not compete on the long horse, and since 1957 they do not perform on the flying rings, apparently because they there overstrain and injure themselves. A woman's shoulder girdle is different from a man's.

One way of dealing with these disparities between the athletic promise and achievements of men and women is to view women as truncated males. As such they could be permitted to engage in the same sports that men do (except where these still invite unusual dangers for them), but in foreshortened versions. That approach may have dictated the different rules which men and women follow in basketball, fencing, and field hockey. Where men have five players on a basket-ball team, women have six, and are not permitted to run up and down the court. Men fence with foils, the target of which is the torso ending with the groin lines, with épées, the target of which is the entire body, and with the sabre the target of which is the region above the waist, including the head and arms, but women fence only with foils and then at a target of which the lower limit is at the hip bones. Women's field hockey, a most popular team sport, is played in two thirty-minute halves whereas the men play in two thirty-five minute halves.[5] The illustrations can be multiplied. But enough have been given to make the point that in a number of cases the performances of males can be treated as a norm, with the women given handicaps in the shape of smaller and sometimes less dangerous or difficult tasks.

Men and women can be significantly contrasted on the average and on the championship level as stronger and weaker, faster and slower. So far as the excellence of a performance depends mainly on the kind of muscles, bones, size, strength, that one has, women can be dealt with as fractional men. This approach has considerable appeal. It not only allows us to compare men and women, but to acknowledge that some women will be outstanding, and, given their handicaps, surpass the men. But we will then fail to do justice to the fact that there are men who are more like most women in relevant factors than they

---

[5] On these see Frank G. Menke, *Encyclopedia of Sports* (New York, 1963), and Parke Cummings, ed. *The Dictionary of Sports* (New York, 1949).

are like most men, and that there are women who are more like most men in these respects than they are like most women.

Simply scaling women in relation to men in terms only of their physical features and capacities, can lull us into passing over a number of important questions. Are women and men motivated in the same way? Do they have the same objectives? Is the team play of women comparable to that of men's? Negative answers to these questions need not blur the truth that men and women are of the same species, and that what is of the essence of human kind is therefore present in both. If it is of the nature of man to seek to become self-complete, both male and female will express this fact, but not necessarily in the same way. They may still face different problems and go along different routes. The very same prospects may be realized by both of them, but in diverse ways. Their characteristic desires give different expressions to a common drive; similar activities do not have the same import for both of them.

Comparatively few women make athletics a career, even for a short time, and fewer still devote themselves to it to a degree that men do. Many reasons for this fact have been offered. Social custom, until very recently, has not encouraged them to be athletes. Fear of losing their femininity plays some role. Also, the appeal of a social life quickly crowds out a desire to practice and train, particularly where this forces them to be alone and without much hope of being signally successful. Swimmers, champions at thirteen and fourteen, seem bored with competitive swimming as they move toward the twenties. But more important than any of these reasons seems to be the fact that a young woman's body does not challenge her in the way in which a young man's body challenges him. She does not have to face it as something to be conquered, since she has already conquered it in the course of her coming of age. Where a young man spends his time redirecting his mind and disciplining his body, she has only the problem of making it function more gracefully and harmoniously than it natively can and does.

Men are able to live in their bodies only if they are taught and trained to turn their minds into bodily vectors. And they can become excellent in and through their bodies, only if they learn to identify themselves with their bodies and what these do. Normal women do not have this problem, at least not in the acute form that it presents to the men. A women's biological growth is part of a larger process in which, without training or deliberation, she progressively becomes one with her body. What a man might accomplish through will and practice after he has entered on his last period of biological growth, she achieves through a process of bodily maturation. By the time she passes adolescence she is able to live her body somewhat the way in which a male athlete lives his.

A woman starts with an advantage over the man in that she masters her body more effortlessly and surely than he does his. If he is to be one with his body, he must prevent his mind from continuing to venture according to its bent, and must make it into a director of the body. He, but not she, has to deal with the body as though it were somewhat resistant to a drive toward its own perfection, and needs to be restructured, redirected, and controlled so that it becomes as excellent as it can be. With less effort she becomes better coordinated and more unified than he; she does not have to turn her mind away from its own concerns to make it function on behalf of the body. It never, despite her genuine interest in intellectual matters and her flights of fancy, is long occupied with the impersonal and nonbodily.

A women is less abstract than a man because her mind is persistently ordered toward bodily problems. Emotions, which are the mind and body interwoven intimately, are easily aroused in her as a consequence. There are times when she will give herself wholeheartedly to intellectual pursuits, and may then distinguish herself in competition with men. But easily, and not too reluctantly, she slips quite soon into a period when her mind functions on behalf of her body in somewhat the way in which a trained athlete's mind functions on behalf of his. A woman, therefore, will typically interest herself in sport only when she sees that it will enable her to polish what she had previously acquired without thought or effort.

The athlete becomes one with his body through practice. Competition in games continues his practice, and in addition offers him a means for measuring his achievements in comparison with those obtained by others, and by himself at a previous time. No less than he, a woman wants and deserves to be measured too. By competing in games, she can learn where she stands. There she will discover just what she can bodily do and therefore what she is as a unified being. Usually, though, it is easier for her to judge herself by her attractiveness, and measure this in terms of its social effects. Where a man might be proud of his body, she is proud in her body; where he uses it, she lives it as a lure.

This account raises some hard questions. Why do not more women become athletes? Is it because they find that the advantage that they have in their comparatively easy and satisfying union with their bodies, makes athletic exertion and competition of not much interest? Is that why women athletes are often so young and stop their careers so soon? Why are not men, who have become one with their bodies, content with the result? Why do they go on to use that body, to identify themselves with equipment, to test themselves in contests, and to make themselves into representatives in games? Do they think of their attractiveness as too adventitious and episodic to be able to give them the kind of satisfaction they need? Why is not a good physique enough for all men or even for a good number of those who embark on an athletic career?

An almost opposite set of questions arises when we assume that biologic urge and social pressure tend to make men use an impersonal and women a personal measure of the success they achieve as embodied humans. Why do some men avoid all athletics? Why is it that some women follow an athletic career? It is too easy an answer, and one not apparently supported by the facts, to say that neither is normal. Many a man appears well adjusted, healthy, happy, and admired, despite the fact that he participates in no sport. Many women athletes are attractive; some are married; some have children. We beg our question when we assume that women athletes are men *manqué*, females without femininity, a fact supposedly evidenced by their devotion to an athletic career; we beg it, too, when we assume that nonathletic men are emasculated males, a fact supposedly evidenced by their unconcern with athletic matters.

If perfection can be achieved through the use of a perfected body, one should expect that women would want to compete with their peers. The fact that most do not, cannot be altogether ascribed to the social demands that are made on their bodies and their time. They are not biologic and social puppets. If they were, must we not also say that men are puppets as well, and that they do not devote themselves, as women do, to the task of making themselves attractive, because this is not a socially respectable goal for them? And what should we say then of those who withstand the pressures? Do they alone have a free will enabling them to counter what the others are driven to do? But a free will is not an adventitious feature, like hair, or bow legs, or a snub nose, resident in only some humans; if some women and men have will enough to withstand natural forces, surely all the others have it too, and might be expected to exercise it.

It is sometimes said that women feel challenged by men and yet know that they are not strong enough to overcome them through force. Their best recourse is to try a different route. This is an old story, told again and again in song, play, and novel, and for that reason alone should give us pause. From this perspective, the woman athlete is seen to be at a disadvantage in comparison with men, and must try to become equal or to prove herself superior to them by deception or flattery, or by disorienting them or taking advantage of their weaknesses. But she can also be taken to suppose that she is suffering from an unfair disadvantage, and must strive first to put herself in the position where her biological and social status is on a footing with his. The first of these alternatives sees women as inescapably inferior beings who compensate through wiles for what they cannot obtain through open competition; the second takes her to be disadvantaged and the disadvantages are to be overcome by discipline and determination. Neither alternative is satisfactory; neither takes adequate account of the joy, the devotion, the dedication, and the independence of spirit exhibited by many woman athletes, their concentration on their own game, and their indifference to what men are doing.

Training and practice can be friendless and boring. A sport such as skiing leaves one much alone. Nevertheless, there are women who train and practice; others ski in competitions with great intensity. While making enormous efforts and sacrifices to become highly skilled, they refuse to obscure the fact that they are women. They emphasize their femininity. It would be obviously wrong to say that they reject their sex or that they are less feminine than non-athletic women. It is no less incorrect to say that they train, practice, and perform only in order to ensnare or to show themselves to be the equal of men.

A woman must train and practice if she is to become an athlete. This demands that she make an effort to stand away from her body. The result she obtained through biological maturation she must for a while defy.

Most women do not make the effort to train or to participate because they are not subject to the tensions that young men suffer—tensions resulting from the discrepancy in the ways in which their minds and bodies tend to be disposed; the women have already achieved a satisfying integration of mind and body. Nevertheless, women can improve the functioning of their bodies. This is best done through exercise. And it can be helped through a vital participation in games.

A woman who wants to be an athlete must, for the time being, stand away from her body in preparation for the achievement of a different kind of union than that which she naturally acquired, and then must work at reaching the stage at which a man normally is. He starts with a separated mind and body; she must produce this before she can enter on an athletic career. She has to make a sacrifice of a natural union before she begins her athletic career, while he must for a while sacrifice only the pursuit of merely intellectual matters.

A man, of course, has achieved some union of mind and body, but it is not as thorough as a woman's normally is; she, of course, has had her intellectual moments and has found them desirable, but they do not last as long nor come as frequently as his do. Embarked on their athletic careers, both must make similar sacrifices of time and interest in other tempting activities. But some of them—security, a family, and a home—appeal to the woman more strongly and at an earlier age than they appeal to the man, and as a consequence she is prone to end her athletic career sooner than he.

Comparatively few women interest themselves in sport, and when they do they rarely exhibit the absorption and concern that is characteristic of large numbers of men. They do not have as strong a need as men to see just what it is that bodies can do, in part because they are more firmly established in their roles as social beings, wives, and mothers, than the men are in their roles as workers, business men, husbands and fathers, or even as thinkers, leaders, and public figures.

The number of people who give themselves wholeheartedly to an athletic career is not large. More men do so than women, but not enough to make the women who do have the shape of aberrational beings who are to be accounted for by means of a distinct set of principles. Both women and men seek to be perfected. But a woman finds that her acceptance of her matured body, promoted by her carrying out biological and social functions, offers a readily available and promising route by which the perfection can be reached.

Team play does not have much of an appeal to most women. The contests women enter are usually those in which they function as individuals alongside one another. Women are evidently more individualistic in temper, more self-contained than men. They live their own bodies while men spend their time and energy on projects, some of which demand team work.

Like men, women inevitably represent something other than themselves, and in the last resort, like men, represent man as such and at his best, given such and such a nature and such and such rules determining how he is to perform. But despite their status as a member of some team, and as a representative of all of us, women do not normally assume a role which is carried out in the light of the way in which others carry out their roles. They do not readily function as teammates.

There are, of course, exceptions. Women make good partners in tennis, and good members of teams in field hockey, basketball, and lacrosse. These exceptions do not belie a general tendency of women to perform as individuals. That tendency is supported by the fact that team sports invite undesirable injuries, and the fact that a woman's acceptance of her body, gradually intensified as she develops, encourages an individualistic outlook. This persists even when she makes a strong effort to abstract from her natural bodily condition and tries to identify herself with her body in the way male athletes identify with theirs.

Considerations such as these make desirable a distinctive approach the problem of how to interest women in athletics. Apparently, they must be made to see that it is good to separate oneself from one's body for a while in order better to unite with it later. One must make evident to them that the later union is a better union but of the same kind as that which they natively acquired. Some young women have been able to see that this is a truth which gymnastics, swimming, diving, skating, and skiing sustains; other sports could be similarly supported.

Once women have decided to engage in athletic activities they must, like men, train and practice; otherwise they cannot hope to do well. Their training follows the same general procedures followed by men, with account, of course, being taken of their difference in musculature, strength, and attitudes toward exhaustion, injury, and public display. Since they do differ from men in these regards, there should be sports designed just for them, enabling them to make maximal use of their distinctive bodies. Thought should be given to the woman's lower center of gravity, her greater flexibility in the shoulders, girdle, and fingers, to her greater stability in the knee joints, and to her greater heat resistance, if we are to give her opportunities for attaining a degree of excellence comparable to that attained by men, and this without taking her to be a fractional male. Though basketball was not designed to take advantage of neglected muscles or organs, but merely to provide an opportunity for men to play in summer and winter, with a minimum amount of easily available equipment, etc., it testifies to the truth that a sport can be a fresh creation, made to satisfy definite purposes. Other new sports could be created; some of these should be built around the use of a woman's body. The rules that govern women's games, particularly those involving teams, today often pay attention to what women can do and what they wish to avoid. Still further rules could be introduced which promote the perfecting of women, by making it possible for them to use their distinctive ways.

The sports we have today are heterogeneous. They do not explore every side of the human body; they are not grounded in an understanding of the main bodily types. More often than not, they are accidental products of history, slowly modified to take advantage of various innovations and to avoid discovered limitations. It is not likely that they are now in the best possible form for men; foreshortened versions cannot be expected to be altogether appropriate to women.

Apart from softball and what is called women's lacrosse, thinking about women's athletics has tended to emphasize gracefulness, accuracy, and coordination, particularly in those sports where some attempt is made to avoid imitating the men. There is an inclination to treat their sports as developments and extensions of the dance. Part of the reason for this, undoubtedly, is our socially inherited view of women's capacity and function; another part is traceable to the fact that women have come into educational institutions and public activities in only comparatively recent times; a third reason is the firm conviction that women should be graceful rather than strong or swift. It is also true that thinking about women's athletics has been characterized by a singular lack of imagination, inventiveness, and concern.

Little choice has been given to women to do more than dance or to adapt the sports which men pursue. Rarely has there been an attempt made to observe and objectively measure what they do. Even in those educational institutions reserved for them, the needs of women are not given the attention they deserve. Women's high schools and colleges often yield to the temptation to become vocational schools preparing women for an eventual career as homemakers and mothers, as though it were the task of an educational institution to prepare students for the kind of lives previous generations led, or which most of the students will most likely lead. The institutions seem to have forgotten that it is their task to promote the self-discovery, the awakening of interests, the extending of the imagination, the civilizing of students, to set them on the way toward becoming enriched, matured beings.

Considerations

1. According to Weiss, how should women athletes be viewed with relation to men?
2. Discuss the following statement from the essay:
   Where a man might be proud of his body, she is proud in her body; where he uses it, she lives it as a lure.
3. How is the feminine attitude toward her body as stated above a disadvantage if she wishes to become an athlete?
4. Besides the physical differences, what are the other differences between men and women in sports?
5. Discuss the following statement from the essay:
   There is some inclination to treat their (women's) sports as developments and extensions of the dance.
6. Read "The Feminine Physique" and discuss the most important differences between the viewpoints of the authors.

THOMAS BOSLOOPER AND MARCIA HAYES

The Feminine Physique

So far as the excellence of a performance depends mainly on the kind of muscles, bones, size, and strength that one has, women can be dealt with as fractional men.

—Paul Weiss, *Sport: A Philosophic Inquiry*

Feminine strength and endurance have always been economic assets for men— a source of cheap labor for business and industry, of unpaid labor in the home. For centuries women have toiled on farms and in factories. Crawling on their hands and knees, stripped to the waist, they have pulled loads through coal mine tunnels too narrow to accommodate a horse. In Russia today, women build roads, lay bricks, and operate heavy equipment. Back in our own frontier days, every pioneer woman had to be able to do "a man's work."

But not long after paychecks entered the picture, the feminine physique became a liability. It was all right for women and girls to strain their backs and their eyes at looms and sewing machines twelves hours a day, seven days a week. Yet when the typewriter was invented, promising women better wages and working conditions, their capacity to stand the physical strain of operating such machines was questioned. As a result, until World War I, most secretaries were male.

Today, most people—certainly most men—invoke physical differences between the sexes as evidence of insurmountable barriers to athletic equality. Because of these differences, women are said to be more suited to some sports than others—and unfit to compete directly with men in *any* contact sport.

"One way of dealing with these disparities between the athletic promise and achievements of men and women," says Yale philosophy professor Paul Weiss, "is to view women as truncated males. As such they should be permitted to engage in such sports as men do (except where these still invite unusual dangers for them), but in foreshortened versions."

Aristotle referred to women as "misbegotten men"; Freud called them "castrated." Now Weiss comes up with "truncated men" who must be "permitted" to engage in sports.

If a man can enlist in the armed forces knowing he may not survive his tour of duty, it seems reasonable that a woman be allowed to decide whether she wants to risk losing a tooth or bruising a breast in athletic competition.

Professor Weiss, who, as the author of *Sport: A Philosophical Inquiry*, has quite a following among physical educators, disagrees. "It is part of our cultural heritage to make an effort to avoid having women maimed, disfigured, or hurt," he writes. "That is one reason why they do not usually engage in and are not physically allowed to compete in such contact sports as boxing, wrestling, football, and rugby, with inexplicable exceptions being made for karate and lacrosse."[1]

Ever since men assumed control of women's sports in the early nineteen-twenties, most physical educators have shared Weiss's views, bolstering their arguments with questionable facts about female physiognomy. These "facts" are worth reviewing, if only because so many women have been brainwashed into believing them.

The National Little League, for instance, bars girls from playing ball on the grounds that they have slower reaction times, less muscle fiber, and weaker bones.

As far as reaction time is concerned, the Little League's conclusions were drawn from a study of nine hundred women of all ages who were compared to men in similar age brackets. No attempt was made to carry out a controlled study of men and women with similar athletic backgrounds. Most boys play football and baseball throughout childhood. How many girls do?

As for muscle mass, women do indeed, according to some studies, have

[1] Paul Weiss, *Sport: A Philosophic Inquiry.*

roughly half the muscle mass of men. And men are, on the average, a third stronger than women. But as far back as 1918, the *Journal of the American Medical Association* attributed much of this disparity to male muscle-flexing.[2] Most women are in poor physical condition, sedentary, and often overweight. Were they given the opportunities men have to keep fit, the strength gap would narrow considerably.

Obviously, few women, even if they cared to, could attain the proportions of the six-foot-four, 290-pound defensive end drafted a couple of years ago by one pro football team. But size and strength aren't always indicative of physical power. In golf, for example, it's assumed that women, being smaller, can't drive the ball as far as a man. Some golf courses, like the one in Darien, Connecticut, even specify on their tournament programs that certain greens require fewer shots for men than for women. Men are expected to reach the four-hundred-yard fifth green in Darien in two shots; women in three. Well, Laura Baugh, who stands five two and weighs 110 pounds, made the fifth green at Darien in two strokes at the age of fifteen.

The petite build of many top women gymnasts belies their extraordinary strength. Muriel Davis Grossfeld, the 1960 U.S. Olympic gymnast, is just over five feet tall. Yet fitness tests at the University of Illinois revealed that she was as strong as the average male college athlete.

A few years ago, U.S. women's water ski champion Dicksie Ann Hoyt's slalom score was higher than any of the male competitors'. How had she done it? asked one of them. "Brute strength," said Dicksie. On an earlier occasion she'd taken on a string of linemen from the University of Florida football team in arm-wrestling and beat all but one. ("He was a skinny guy," she said later, "but he was real strong.")

So strength is relative, often deceptive, and frequently irrelevant in comparison to skill. But what about bones? It's true, as the Little League contends, that women's bones ossify sooner than men's. That's because girls reach puberty earlier. But this is a plus, not a minus. Adolescent boys run a greater risk of injury because their bones aren't fully ossified until their late teens. At the 1972 conference on women in sport at Penn State University, it was reported that girls and women have fewer orthopedic injuries than men—partly because of earlier ossification, partly because, at maturity, women's bones are harder than men's.

Other so-called disadvantages women have to put up with are smaller hearts, higher pulse rates, smaller lung capacity, lower aggressive instincts, bad spatial orientation, and more body fat—all of which supposedly combine to give them less endurance.

First of all, taking on this impressive list in order, women's smaller hearts can work relatively harder than men's without any ill effects. At the Penn State conference, medical researchers reported that a pulse of 200 could be attained

---

[2] Clelia D. Mosher, M.D., "The Muscular Strength of College Women," *Journal of the American Medical Association,* Vol. 70, No. 3, January 19, 1918. According to Dr. John Kane, who reported at the Penn State Conference on Women and Sport that he had been unable to find any such studies in the literature.

without risk in a fifteen-year-old girl, while adult women athletes can reach 180 easily during exertion—about 20 beats faster than a man.

Going on to the lungs, we find that the average adult male has a 30 per cent greater "aerobic capacity" or "vital capacity" (the volume of air that can be exhaled from the lungs after breathing in deeply) than the average woman. This is partly because men, being bigger, have bigger lungs partly because the statistics are stacked in favor of men. There have been no large-scale studies done on female respiration. Until there are, this difference must remain theoretical.[3]

As for aggression, men apparently do have a natural edge here. Studies of infant male primates and little boys indicate that males play rougher and show a greater preference for bruising physical contact than do female apes and little girls. On the other hand, little boys are encouraged from infancy to be aggressive and little girls are punished for displays of aggressiveness; so it's hard to know where to draw the line. An authority on aggression, Dr. John Scott, of the Bowling Green University Research Center, has demonstrated that both girls and boys have an aggressive drive; he feels the difference is merely one of degree.[4]

Any innate difference in aggressiveness is generally agreed to be hormonal. Androgen and estrogen, the male and female hormones that produce secondary sexual characteristics, have a profound influence on the physical appearance and the temperament of both men and women. Androgen, the male hormone, has been shown in rats to strike some chemical chord that increases aggressive behavior. Hormones also influence the size of bones and the character of the muscular system. Estrogen, the female hormone, inhibits muscle and bone growth; androgen encourages it.

Yet among members of each sex, a good deal of variation occurs in the amount of hormonal output—and, even, in the chemical concentration of the hormones. Women who secrete greater amounts of androgen are usually more aggressive than others. They also tend to have better-developed muscles and bigger bones.

Sex differences begin to show up in the fetus five to six weeks after conception, when the male embryo is given an "androgen bath." Until then the human embryo is essentially female. The male XY chromosome, the genetic unit that determines sex, is really an incomplete female XX chromosome with the leg of one X broken off. Because his smaller chromosome can't carry all the duplicate genetic information contained on the female unit, the male is more prone to hereditary disease. In a woman, defects on one gene can be corrected by automatic substitution of healthy components from the twin gene; but in men, many of these genetic alternatives are missing. (Aristotle, Freud, and Weiss, take note! If either sex deserves to be called "misbegotten," "castrated," or "truncated," it is the male, with his fractured sex chromosome.)

Chromosomes have recently become something of an international issue with the discovery of hermaphroditism at the Olympics. (Occasionally a biological

[3] From authors' notes, Penn State Conference on Women and Sport, August 1972.
[4] From Dr. Boslooper's notes on Conference on Women and Girls in Sport and Play at the American Association for the Advancement of Science annual meeting, December 1968, in Dallas, Texas.

short circuit occurs during fetal development, resulting in a hermaphrodite—a person who either possesses the sexual characteristics of one sex and the chromosomal pattern of the other, or who exhibits primary and secondary sexual characteristics of both sexes.) The few hermaphrodites who have turned up at the Olympics have gotten more than their share of publicity, and the public image of the female Olympic athlete is, as a result, that of a big, square-shouldered track and field star. Before being allowed to compete, all female Olympic athletes now must have their chromosomes analyzed—not in the privacy of a physician's office, but in a line up, with the male-or-female verdict rendered as each participant reaches the end of the queue. Until 1971, cells were collected from the inside of the athletes' cheeks and examined under a microscope. Today, strands of hair are tested instead; but women who have stood in the line up still describe the experience humiliating.

The chromosome tests have served to cast suspicion on the sexual identity of all ruggedly built women. Our current feminine body ideal is the thin, delicate build characteristic of most fashion models. In the past, the feminine body ideal was often pear-shaped—certainly heavier and more rounded than the ultra-thinness for which many women now starve. The muscular build typical of most men has never been the Western world's ideal for women. Muscular women have, in fact, been consistently discriminated against as unfeminine.

The burly woman athlete image has persuaded a lot of women that strenuous athletic activity leads to ungainly muscles. It isn't so. "Proper training is the answer," says Walter Kostric, trainer of Canadian track and field star Debbie Van Kiekebelt. "Some exercises can develop protruding muscles, but others don't. A good coach knows the difference."

"Contrary to lay opinion," exercise physiologists Carl E. Klafs and Daniel Druheim have written in *Psychology Today*,[5] "participation in sports does not masculinize women or build excess muscle." They added that women with muscular builds are often successful as athletes, but that athletics doesn't create heavy muscles.

Most women have more body fat than men. And where fat exists, muscle obviously doesn't. Conditioning has a lot to do with this, of course, but even physically active women do have more fat than men. In some areas of athletics—endurance swimming, for instance—a little extra fat can be an advantage, providing warmth and buoyancy. But when a woman is in top form, the extra fat doesn't affect her performance at all, in *any* sport.

Another much-touted difference between the sexes is spatial orientation. Men are supposedly better at orienting themselves in space—at "keeping their eye on the ball," using their own physical positions as a reference point to activity around them.

Women tend to use peripheral objects as points of reference and are easily distracted by visual stimuli. Men, for instance, can pick a figure out of a complex pattern more readily than women. Perhaps, it has been suggested, this is a throwback to prehistoric times when life depended on a man's ability to keep

[5] Daniel Druheim and Carl E. Klafs, "The Star Spangled Scramble," *Psychology Today*, September 1972.

his eye on a fleeting stag in the underbrush. More likely, it's a psychological difference, resulting from greater self-confidence on the part of men.

Joan Strati, physical education director at the Mamaroneck School in Mamaroneck, New York, found that girl athletes consistently underestimated their own physical measurements. Asked to guess the length of their arm span, for instance, thirty girls estimated the distance to be less than it actually was. A control group of nonathletes yielded identical answers—confirming the finding that women generally have an inferior body image, reflecting lack of self-confidence. They rely on their environment rather than themselves as reference points, and are consequently distracted by extrapersonal influences.[6]

Dr. Julia Sherman, associate scientist at the University of Wisconsin Psychiatric Institute, reported the preliminary results of a study on sex differences in spatial orientation. It was her hypothesis that education, especially in elementary and high schools, short-changes females by concentrating more on verbal than on spatial training. Although it has been believed for years that spatial ability could *not* be enhanced by training, Dr. Sherman found definite improvement of this ability in girls given special visual training before testing.[7]

Until now, this discussion of the feminine physique has been limited to Western culture. But in other parts of the world women are physically equal or superior to men. Robert Briffault has noted, for example, that among the Bushmen, women are an average of four centimeters taller than the men; and that Arab, Afghanistan, and Druse women are as tall as their men and as strongly developed. "Among the Adombies of the Congo, the women are often stronger than the men and more finely developed," he writes. "And among the Ashira, the men are not nearly so finely built as the women. A Kikuyu man is quite unequal to carrying a load that his women think nothing of. . . . A crew of Dayak women can beat a crew of Malay men."

Though many anthropologists have cited the prehistoric role of man as hunter to explain his athletic superiority today, Briffault (and, more recently, Yale's David Philbeam) contends that the primitive division of labor is not based on female physical inferiority.

"There are numerous reports of women hunters among uncultured peoples," says Briffault. "In West Africa the women formerly used to carry bows and arrows and go out hunting without the aid of men. Among the Hill Dayaks of Borneo, a spear is part of the equipment of every woman, and they go hunting with dogs. Of the women of Nicaragua, we are told that they could run and swim and shoot with bows and arrows as well as the men. . . ."[8]

It seems clear from these examples that differences in reaction time, muscle mass, bones, hearts, lungs, hormones, strength, spatial orientation, and body fat—when they exist—don't necessarily make much of a difference where relative performance is concerned. But what about menstruation, pregnancy, and endurance? Here, surely, are three clear-cut examples of inferiority.

[6] From authors' notes at the Penn State Conference on Women and Sport, August 1972.
[7] Dr. Julia Sherman, quoted in a press release from the University of Wisconsin at Madison, February 1973.
[8] Robert Briffault, *The Mothers: The Matriarchal Theory of Social Origins.*

Female students are still getting excused from gym classes at "that time of the month," it's often argued. How can a woman athlete compete on the same level with men if she's likely to be out of commission three days out of thirty?

Because she's not. At the 1964 Olympics in Melbourne, for example, six gold medal winners were menstruating at the time of their victories. A Hungarian physician, Dr. Gyula J. Erdelyi, has found that it is largely psychological rather than physical factors that effect performance during menstruation. One third of Erdelyi's study group of 729 women athletes showed *no* change in performance during menstruation, a third declined, and a third improved.[9]

Many women athletes believe that strenuous physical activity eliminates menstrual difficulties. Track and field star Debbie Van Kiekebelt says that menstruation improves her performance; in fact, two of her Canadian national championships were won on first days of menstrual periods. "For a woman in good condition, the period is a natural and emotionally rewarding release," says her coach, Walter Kostric.

"Most of women's fears about exercise and menstruation are unfounded," says Dr. Clayton Thomas, a member of the U.S. Olympic Team's medical staff and medical research director for Tampax. "Women athletes have much less difficulty in this area than those who are sedentary."

Drs. Franz Alexander and Boris B. Rubenstein concluded after extensive study that the production of estrogen during menstruation "stimulates the ego to higher integration and coordination."[10] And Dr. Ferguson Anderson of Glasgow University has only good news about hormonal effects on feminine endurance. "Women live longer than men because nature has equipped them with a six-cylinder engine compared with man's four-cylinder one," he says. "Women have a better heart and better system generally."[11]

Recently Dr. Grace Fischer, of the University of Pennsylvania, stated that women probably have fewer heart attacks than men because estrogen keeps their arteries more elastic, helping to offset arterial sclerosis and fat buildup.[12]

All the myths and distortions about hormones in general and menstruation in particular may be a carryover from the very ancient past. In *The First Sex,* Elizabeth Gould Davis notes that the old matriarchial calendar was based on the twenty-eight-day lunar and menstrual cycle—a thirteen-month calendar. Ever since the patriarchal takeover (circa 1000 B.C.), menstruation and the number 13 have been taboo.[13]

As for pregnancy, here's another interesting statistic: ten of the twenty-six Soviet women champions at the Melbourne Olympics were pregnant at the time of their victories.

---

[9] Gyula Erdelyi, M.D., "Gynecological Survey of Female Athletes," *Journal of Sports, Medicine and Physical Fitness,* Vol. 2, No. 3, September 1962, pp. 174–77.

[10] Drs. Franz Alexander and Boris B. Rubenstein, quoted in *Family Health,* November 1971.

[11] Dr. Ferguson Anderson, also quoted in above article.

[12] Grace Fischer in speech to the American Heart Association convention, May 6, 1972.

[13] Elizabeth Gould Davis mentions this theory in her book *The First Sex* ("Fetishes and Their Origins"). The unluckiness of the number has also been attributed to Judas's numerical rank. But if the number had not already borne a stigma it seems unlikely that anyone would have noticed he was the thirteenth disciple.

Contrary to popular belief and some medical opinion, there is plenty of evidence that pregnancy *enhances* physical performance during the first six months, and that exercise is seldom harmful to either the mother or the fetus. Two thirds of the 729 athletes interviewed by Dr. Erdelyi said they continued their sports during the first three months of pregnancy. And efficiency tests on another group of 33 pregnant women showed that during the twenty-fourth to thirty-third week after conception they were more efficient than their nonpregnant counterparts.

Still another study revealed that 70 per cent of a group of 207 women athletes continued their sports through the sixth month of pregnancy. One rower, who competed when three months pregnant, came in first in a field of 17 nonpregnant rivals. A discus thrower who was four and a half months pregnant won a national championship at the Compeorata de Athletismo de Europa.[14]

Dr. Erdelyi has concluded that pregnancy and sport are not only compatible but desirable, leading to easier labor and early resumption of normal activities after giving birth. Deliveries among female athletes, he found, were 87 per cent faster than among nonathletes; and the time athletes spent in the second stage of labor was half the norm. The figures were the same for top athletes and mediocre ones, which would suggest that general physical conditioning rather than prowess is the determinant.

All in all, it is far more natural for a woman to be active than sedentary during pregnancy. Years ago, when pregnancy was treated as an illness and women were "confined," the risk of complications during delivery was strikingly higher than it is now. Circulation, vital to the health of the child, and muscle tone, which speeds delivery, are improved by physical activity.

Bad falls are obviously to be avoided during pregnancy, but the female reproductive system is designed to protect the fetus against all but the most severe accidents. The uterus is surrounded by structures of almost the same specific gravity as itself, with no air space around it. It floats in a pool of pelvic viscera, much as an egg floats in a tightly sealed jar of water. When shaken, it simply can't fly violently through the fluid. (If you want to test this out, place a raw egg in an airtight jar full of water. No amount of shaking that doesn't smash the jar will injure the egg.)

When it comes to endurance, men, because of their greater strength and lung capacity, supposedly become exhausted less quickly than women. "Look at all the male long-distance runners that women haven't begun to catch up to," we're often told. But there are many more men than women running marathons, and in the Olympics women aren't allowed to run more than 1500 meters, so this evidence is only relative. Furthermore, women have greater *tolerance* for fatigue, which tends to even things out.

And let us not forget Diane Struble Rippon, a woman who in 1958 swam forty-two miles in New York's Lake George. Jack Dempsey had proposed the challenge in 1928, and the best swimmers in the world had tried—and failed—to meet it. Though greater distances have been conquered in other bodies of

[14] Study cited in "Sporting Activities During Pregnancy," *Journal of Obstetrics and Gynecology*, Vol. 32, No. 5, November 1968.

water, Lake George's turbulence and icy temperatures demand almost super-human endurance.

Rippon, who was pushing thirty at the time and in a condition which she described as a "physical and emotional wreck," decided to get back in shape by taking on Lake George. After a few months of training and careful preparation, she dived in. Toward the evening of her second day in the water, Diane stepped ashore at the southern tip of Lake George. "I wish the lake had been longer," she said. "I could have gone further."

A few years later a U.S. Marine set out to duplicate her feat—"to uphold manly valor." He did make it (in two and a half days), becoming the second person and first man to swim Lake George. But rumor has it that he was out of commission for several days afterward. Diane was feeling pretty normal, she said, ten minutes after drying off.

For an encore, Rippon swam around Manhattan Island, navigating both the East River and the Hudson, taking into account ocean tides to calculate the precise moment she would arrive at each location. Just off the Seventy-ninth Street boat basin, she had to tread water for three hours while the New York police checked out her credentials, then refused to let her go around again.

After that she crossed Boston Harbor with ease and later swam thirty-six miles in Lake Champlain. By this time she had built up quite a following, and scores of boats gathered to escort her across. A few hours out a storm came up, and all boats except the pilot boat streaked for cover. Her husband and three other men in the pilot boat tried to persuade her to turn back with them; she refused, then completed the crossing. When a reporter asked Rippon what was on her mind while she was on the lake in the middle of the night with a storm raging around her, she said, "I worried about what I'd do if that boat overturned and I had to save all those men."

In 1963, at age thirty-five, Rippon entered the sixty-mile Lake Michigan swim "just for fun. I only went thirty miles," she said. "My new baby was a few months old, and I couldn't risk being out of commission with five kids to dress and feed."

That particular contest was won by the thirty-four-year-old Egyptian Abdel Latif Abo Heif, who swam the sixty miles from Chicago, Illinois, to Benton Harbor, Michigan, in thirty-four hours and forty-five minutes, never going slower than sixty strokes per minute.

For the first fifteen hours, Latif was paced by Gretta Anderson at seventy-two strokes a minute. But a $15,000 winner-take-all prize was at stake, and Latif really poured it on ("I had to get that woman out of my wake," he told reporters). He broke Anderson's pace and went on to an incredible victory.

Diane Rippon was one of the first to congratulate Latif. Later she told a friend, "I didn't mind being out of the contest. It was a great experience just to be in the same water with such a remarkable athlete."

Most men are not as gracious when they lose to women. Nor are they at all eager to reexamine misconceptions about the feminine physique in light of all the new evidence. Dr. Eleanor Maccoby of Stanford University, a psychologist who has done extensive research on sex differentiation and has questioned for years the relevance of physical differences to women's participation in competitive sport, is not taken seriously by many of her colleagues. "In our circle we treat her with amusement," says the head of the Yale Physiology and Anatomy Department. "It's a well-known biological fact that the male is twice as strong as the female."

Ho hum. And more yawns for Paul Weiss, who not only persists with his re-actionary notions about physique but extends them to include athletic prowess as well. "Women are unable to compete successfully with the best of men," he says, "except in sports which emphasize accuracy, skill, or grace—shooting, fancy skating, diving, and the like. Their bones, contours, musculature, growth rate, size, proportion, and reaction times do not allow them to do as well as men in sports which put a premium on strength and speed."[15]

That red flag is worth exploring further.

Considerations

1. What do the authors point to as the chief reason for women being given secondary roles in athletics?
2. Discuss the following statement from the essay:
    (Aristotle, Freud, and Weiss, take note! If either sex deserves to be called "mis-begotten," "castrated," or "truncated," it is the male, with his fractured sex chromosome.)
3. Summarize the most important of the authors' refutations of the many traditional beliefs about the athletic inferiority of women.

JACK LONDON

The White Hope

Jeffries-Johnson Fight

Reno, Nev., July 4.—Once again has Johnson sent down to defeat the chosen representative of the white race, and this time the greatest of them all. And, as of old, it was play for Johnson. From the opening to the closing round he never ceased his witty sallies, his exchanges of repartee with his opponent's seconds and with the spectators. And, for that matter, Johnson had a funny thing or two to say to Jeffries in every round. The golden smile was as much in evidence as ever, and neither did it freeze on his face nor did it vanish. It came and went throughout the fight spontaneously, naturally.

It was not a great battle, after all, save in its setting and its significance. Little Tommy Burns down in far-off Australia put up a faster, quicker, livelier battle than did Jeff. The fight today, and again I repeat, was great only in its signifi-cance. In itself it was not great. The issue, after the fiddling of the open-ing rounds, was never in doubt. In the fiddling of those first rounds the honors

---

[15] Paul Weiss, *Sport: A Philosophic Inquiry.*

lay with Johnson, and for the rounds after the seventh or eighth it was more Johnson, while for the closing rounds it was all Johnson.

Johnson played, as usual. With his opponent not strong in the attack, Johnson, blocking and defending in masterly fashion, could afford to play. And he played and fought a white man in a white man's country, before a white man's crowd. And the crowd was a Jeffries crowd. When Jeffries sent in that awful rip of his the crowd would madly applaud, believing it had gone home to Johnson's stomach, and Johnson, deftly interposing his elbow, would smile in irony at the spectators, play-acting, making believe he thought the applause was for him—and never believing it at all.

The greatest battle of the century was a monologue delivered to twenty thousand spectators by a smiling negro who was never in doubt and who was never serious for more than a moment at a time.

As a fighter Johnson did not show himself a wonder. He did not have to. Never once was he extended. There was no need Jeff could not make him extend. Jeff never had him in trouble once. No blow Jeff ever landed hurt his dusky opponent. Johnson came out of the great fight practically undamaged. The blood on his lip was from a recent cut received in training which Jeff managed to reopen.

Jeff failed to lead and land. The quickness he brought into the fight quickly evaporated, and while Jeff was dead game to the end, he was not so badly punished. What he failed to bring into the ring with him was his stamina, which he lost somewhere in the last seven years. Jeff failed to come back. That is the whole story. His old-time vim and endurance were not there. Something has happened to him. He lost in retirement, outside of the ring, the stamina that the ring itself never robbed him of. As I have said, Jeff was not badly damaged. Every day boys take worse lacings in boxing bouts than Jeff took today.

Jeff today disposed of one question. He could not come back. Johnson in turn answered another question. He has not the yellow streak. But he only answered that question for to-day. The ferocity of the hairy-chested caveman and grizzly giant combined did not intimidate the cool-headed negro. Many thousands in the audience expected this intimidation and were correspondingly disappointed. Johnson was not scared, let it be said here and beyond the shadow of a doubt. Not for an instant did he show the flicker of fear that the Goliath against him might eat up.

But the question of the yellow streak is not answered for all time. Just as Johnson has never been extended, so has he never shown the yellow streak. Just as a man may rise up, heaven alone knows where, who will extend Johnson, just so may that man bring out the yellow streak, and then again, he may not. So far the burden of proof all rests on the conclusion that Johnson has no yellow streak.

And now to the battle and how it began. All praise to Tex Rickard, the gamest of sports, who pulled off the fight after countless difficulties, and who, cool, calm and quick with nervous aliveness, handled the vast crowd splendidly at the arena, and wound up by refereeing the fight.

Twenty thousand filled the great arena and waited patiently under the cloud-flecked wide Nevada sky. Of the many women present, some elected to sit in the screened boxed far back from the ring, for all the world like olden Spanish ladies at the theatre. But more, many more women, sat close to the ringside beside their husbands or brothers. They were the wiser far.

Merely to enumerate the celebrities at the ringside would be to write a sporting directory of America—at least a directory of the 400 of sportdom and of many more hundreds of near four hundreds. At 1:56, Billy Jordan cleared the ring amid cheers, and stood alone, the focal point of 20,000 pairs of eyes, until the great Muldoon climbed through the ropes to call tumultuous applause and ringing cheers from the 20,000 throats, for the State of Nevada, the people of Nevada and the Governor of Nevada.

Beginning with Tex Rickard, ovation after ovation was given to all the great ones, not forgetting Fitzsimmons, whom Billy Jordan introduced as "the greatest warrior of them all." And so they came, great one after great one, ceaselessly, endlessly, until they were swept away before the greatest of them all—the two men who were about to do battle.

It was 2:30 when Johnson entered. He came first, airy, happy and smiling, greeting friends and acquaintances here, there and everywhere in the audience, cool as ice, waving his hand in salute, smiling, smiling ever smiling, with eyes as well as lips, never missing a name nor a face, placid, plastic, nerveless, with never a signal flown of hesitancy nor timidity. Yet was he keyed up, keenly observant of all that was going on, even hearing much of the confused babble of tongues about him—hearing, ay, and understanding, too. There is nothing heavy nor primitive about this man Johnson. He is alive and quivering, every nerve fiber in his body and brain, withal that it is hidden, so artfully, or naturally, under that poise of facetious calm of his. He is a marvel of sensitiveness, sensibility and perceptibility. He has a perfect mechanism of mind and body. His mind works like chain lightning and his body obeys with equal swiftness.

But the great madness of applause went up when Jeffries entered the ring two minutes later. A quick superficial comparison between him and the negro would lead to a feeling of pity for the latter. For Jeff was all that has been said of him. When he stripped and his mighty body could be seen covered with mats of hair, all the primordial adjectives ever applied to him received their vindication. Nor did his face belie them. No facile emotion played on that face, no whims of the moment, no flutterings of a light-hearted temperament. Dark and somber and ominous was that face, solid and stolid and expressionless, with eyes that smouldered and looked savage.

The man of iron, grim with determination, sat down in his corner. And the care-free negro smiled and smiled. And that is the story of the fight. The man of iron, the grizzly giant was grim and serious. The man of summer temperament smiled and smiled. That is the story of the whole fight. It is the story of the fight by rounds.

At the opening of the first round they did not shake hands. Knowing the two men for what they are, it can be safely postulated that this neglect was due to Jeff or to the prompting of Jeff's corner. But it is not good that two boxers should not shake hands before a bout. I would suggest to these protagonists of a perishing game, if they wish to preserve the game, that they make the most of these little amenities that by custom grace their sport, and give it the veneer of civilization.

Both men went to work in that first round very easily, Johnson smiling, of course, and Jeff grim and determined. Johnson landed the first blow, a light one, and Jeff, in the clinches, gave a faint indication of his forthcoming tactics by roughing it, by crowding the negro around and by slightly bearing his weight upon him. It was a very easy round, with nothing of moment. Each was merely feeling the other out and both were exceedingly careful. At the conclusion of the round Johnson tapped Jeffries playfully on the shoulder, smiled good-naturedly and went to his corner. Jeff, in the first, showed flashes of cat-like quickness.

Second round, Jeff advanced with a momentary assumption of his famous crouch, to meet the broadly smiling Johnson. Jeff is really human and good-natured. He proved it right here. So friendly was that smile of Johnson, so irresistibly catching that Jeff, despite himself, smiled back. But Jeff's smiles were doomed to be very few in this fight.

And right here began a repetition of what took place down in Australia when Burns fought Johnson. Each time Burns said something harsh to Johnson, in the hope of making him lose his temper, Johnson responded by giving the white man a lacing. And so to-day, of course, Jeff did not talk to Johnson to amount to anything, but Corbett, in the corner, did it for Jeff. And each time Corbett cried out something particularly harsh, Johnson promptly administered a lacing to Jeff. It began in the second round. Corbett, in line with his plan of irritating the negro, called out loudly: "He wants to fight a little, Jim."

"You bet, I do," Johnson retorted, and with that he landed Jeff a stinging right uppercut.

Both men were tensely careful, Jeff trying to crowd and put his weight on in the clinches, Johnson striving more than the other to break out of the clinches. And at the end of the round, in his corner, Johnson was laughing gleefully. Certainly Jeff showed no signs of boring in, as had been promised by his enthusiastic supporters.

It was the same story in the third round, at the conclusion of which the irrepressible negro was guilty of waving his hands to friends in the audience.

In the fourth round Jeff showed up better, rushing and crowding and striking with more vim than hitherto shown. This seemed to have been caused by a sally of Johnson's and Jeff went at him in an angry sort of way. Promptly Jeff rushed, and even ere they came together, Johnson cried out:

"Don't rush me, Jim. You hear what I'm telling you?"

No sign there of being intimidated by Jeffries' first dynamic display of ferocity. All he managed to do was to reopen the training cut in Johnson's lip and to make Johnson playful. It was most anybody's round, and it was certainly more Jeff's than any preceding one.

Round five brought Jeff advancing with his crouch and showed that the blood from Johnson's lip had turned his smile to a gory one. But still he smiled and, to balance things off, he opened Jeff's lip until it bled more profusely than his own. From then until the end of the fight Jeff's face was never free from blood, a steady stream later flowing from his right nostril, added to by the opened cut on his left cheek. Corbett's running fire of irritation served but to make Johnson smile the merrier and to wink at him across Jeff's shoulder in the clinches.

So far no problems had been solved, no questions answered. The yellow streak had not appeared. Neither had Jeff bored in, ripped awfully, nor put it over Johnson in the clinches. Yet one thing had been shown. Jeff was not so fast as he had been. There was a shade of diminution in his speed.

Johnson signalized the opening of the sixth round by landing stinging blows to the face in one, two, three order. Johnson's quickness was startling. In response to an irritating remark from Corbett, Johnson replied suavely, "Too much on hand right now," and at the same instant he tore into Jeff. It was Johnson's first real, aggressive rush. It lasted but a second or two, but it was fierce and dandy, and at its conclusion it was manifest that Jeff's right eye was closing fast. The round ended with Johnson fighting and smiling strong, and with Jeff's nose, lip and cheek bleeding and his eye closed. Johnson's round by a smile all the way through.

The seventh round was a mild one, opening with Jeff grim and silent, and with Johnson leading and forcing. Both were careful and nothing happened, save that once they exchanged blows right niftily. So far, Jeff's roughing, and crowding and bearing on of weight had amounted to nothing. Also, he was doing less and less of it.

"It only takes one or two, Jim," Corbett encouraged his principal in the eighth round. Promptly Johnson landed two stingers. After a pause he landed another. "See that?" he chirped sweetly to Corbett in the corner. Jeff showed signs perceptibly of slowing down in this round, rushing and crowding less and less. Johnson was working harder and his speed was as flash light as ever. Jeff's slowing down was not due to the punishment he had received, but to poorness of condition. He was flying the first signals of fatigue. He was advertising, faintly, it is true, that he had not come back.

The ninth round was introduced by a suggestion from Corbett, heroically carrying out the policy that was bringing his principal to destruction. "Make that big stiff fight," was Corbett's suggestion. "That's right; that's what they all say," was Johnson's answer, delivered with true Chesterfieldian grace across his adversary's shoulder. In the previous rounds Johnson had not wreaked much damage with the forecasted punch, the right uppercut. In this round he demonstrated indisputably that he could drive the left hand in a way that was surprising. Be it remembered that it had been long denied that he had any sort of a punch in that left of his. Incidentally, in this round he landed a blow near to Jeff's heart that must have been discouraging.

The tenth round showed Johnson, with his deft, unexpected left, as quick as ever, and Jeff's going slower and slower.

The conclusion of the first ten rounds may be summed up as follows: The fight was all in the favor of Johnson, who had shown no yellow, who had shown condition, who had shown undiminished speed, who had not used his right uppercut much, who had developed a savage left, who held his own in the clinches, who had not the best of the infighting and the outfighting, who was unhurt and who was smiling all the way. Jeff was in bad shape; he was tired, slower than ever, his few rushes had been futile, and the sports who had placed their money against him were jubilant. There were men who proclaimed they saw the end.

I refused to see this end, for I had picked Jeff to win, and I was hoping hugely—for what, I did not know; but for something to happen, for anything, that would turn the tide of battle. And yet I could not hide from myself the truth that Jeff had slowed down.

The eleventh round looked better for Jeff. Stung by a remark of Corbett's, Johnson rushed and provoked one grand rally from Jeff. It was faster fighting, and more continuous than at any time in the preceding ten rounds, culminating in a fierce rally, in which Jeff landed hard.

Round twelve found Johnson, if anything, quicker and more aggressive than ever.

"Thought you were going to have me wild?" Johnson queried sweetly of Corbett.

As usual, every remark of Corbett's brought more punishment to Jeffries. And by the end of this round the second of two great questions was definitely answered. Jeff had not come back.

The thirteenth round was the beginning of the end. Beginning slowly enough, but stung by Corbett, Johnson put it all over him in the mouth fighting, and all over Jeff in the outfighting and infighting. From defense to attack, and back again, and back and forth. Johnson flashed like the amazing fighting mechanism he is. Jeff was silent and sick, while, as the round progressed, Corbett was noticeably silent.

A few entertained the fond hope that Jeff would recuperate. But it was futile. There was no come back to him. He was a fading, failing, heartsick, heartbroken man.

"Talk to him, Corbett," Jeff's friends appealed, in the fourteenth round. But Corbett could not talk. He had long since seen the end.

Yet through this round Johnson went in for one of his characteristic loafing spells. He took it easy, and played with the big gladiator, cool as a cucumber, smiling broadly as ever, yet as careful as ever.

"Right on the hip," he grinned once, as Jeff, in a desperate, dying flurry, managed to land a wild punch in that vicinity.

Corbett, likewise desperate, ventured a last sally. "Why don't you do something?" he cried to the loafing, laughing Johnson. "Too clever, too clever, like you," was the response.

Round fifteen, and the end. It was pitiful. There happened to Jeff the bitterness that he had so often made others taste, but which for the first time, perforce, he was made to taste himself. He who had never been knocked down was knocked down repeatedly. He who had never been knocked out was knocked out. Never mind the technical decision. Jeff was knocked out. That is all there is to it. An ignominy of ignominies, he was knocked out and through the ropes by the punch he never believed Johnson possessed—by the left, and not by the right.

As he lay across the lower rope while the seconds were told off, a cry that had in it tears and abject broken plea went up from many of the spectators.

"Don't let the negro knock him out, don't let the negro knock him out," was the oft-repeated cry.

There is little more to be said. Jeff did not come back. Johnson did not show the yellow streak, and it was Johnson's fight all the way through. Jeff was not old Jeff at all. Even so, it is to be doubted if the old Jeff could have put away this amazing negro from Texas, this black man with the unfailing smile, this king of fighters and monologists.

Corbett and Berger and the others were right. They wanted Jeff to do more boxing and fighting in his training. Nevertheless lacking the come back as he so potently did, this preliminary boxing and fighting would have profited him nothing. On the other hand, it would have saved his camp much of the money with which it backed him.

It was a slow fight. Faster, better fights may be seen every day of the year in any of the small clubs in the land. It is true these men were heavy-weights, yet for heavy-weights it was a slow fight. It must be granted that plucky Tommy Burns put up a much faster fight with Johnson a year and a half ago. Yet the American fight follower had to see this fight to-day in order to appreciate just what Burns did against this colored wonder.

Johnson is a wonder. No one understands him, this man who smiles. Well, the story of the fight is the story of a smile. If ever a man won by nothing more fatiguing than a smile, Johnson won to-day.

And where now is the champion who will make Johnson extend himself, who will glaze those bright eyes, remove that smile and silence that golden repartee?

Considerations

1. London, probably the most famous writer in the world at that time, went to Reno in 1910 to cover the boxing match between the first black heavyweight champion, Jack Johnson, and James J. Jeffries, the immensely popular former champion and current "white hope." Why does a heavyweight contest attract so many great writers, as well as artists of all kinds?
2. London is obviously biased in his support of Jeffries. Aside from his basic racial attitude, what are examples of this bias? (Consider his references to Johnson's "yellow streak.")
3. Racism was a way of life in Johnson's day. Does it still exist in boxing? Explain how Muhammad Ali capitalized on this "white hope" syndrome.
4. Compare Johnson's ring behavior with that of Muhammad Ali. What other points do they have in common? (Consider their harassment by law officials.)
5. Identify:
   (a) Tommy Burns
   (b) Tex Rickard
   (c) Fitzsimmons
   (d) Corbett

LIGHT FROM THE EAST

We can travel through life numbing our feelings, thus minimizing pain and minimizing joy. Or we can join the dance of existence with hearts open to pain, grief, tears, and the awareness of death, and thus realize those connections best described by a word which in the context of this culture is likely to both charm and discomfort us: ecstasy.

—George Leonard

GEORGE LEONARD

The Dance Within the Game

The March 1974 issue of *MS.* magazine has an article by Clayton Riley entitled "Did O. J. Dance?" Riley notes that the superb beauty and control of football's greatest running back, O. J. Simpson, has been largely lost on white fans because he has not yet played on a winning team. Riley quotes a black friend who has this to say: "White boys only want to know what the final score was; they're only interested in the results. Brothers want to know what happened *in* the game, like, 'Did O. J. *dance?*'"

Riley goes on to draw a sharp line between the way white and black males experience life. The whites, in their single-minded pursuit of victory, dehumanize their opponents and themselves and eventually lose touch with existence itself. The blacks, deprived of the corrupting effects of power "because we simply don't have any," focus on style, on the very essence of life.

There is truth in what he says. White Western culture at its worst and most extreme can be characterized in one simple phrase: It is anti-dance. The dance aspects of our religious rites have been relentlessly rooted out. Sacrament and movement have been split apart. We walk to get somewhere. We run to get in shape or to set records. We do everything *because of* something else. Dance is an activity that is performed on stage. Blacks, on the other hand, have somehow managed to remain aware of the dance that lies at the heart of every movement. By their very way of walking, they are likely to signal the fact that they are tuned into the rhythmic, pulsing, dancing nature of existence.

Riley is right, but I believe he draws too sharp a line. There is a desire in all of us—however veiled, however corrupted by lust for victory—to see O. J. dance. Out of a lifetime of sports spectating, the moments that live for us, whatever our race, are pure dance. We may forget league standings and final scores and even who won, but we can never forget certain dancelike moments: that supernatural Brodie to Washington pass in the 1971 playoff game with the Redskins, that classic, utterly pure blow with which Sugar Ray Robinson ended his 1957 bout with Gene Fullmer, that transcendent running catch by Willie Mays in the first game of the 1954 World Series in the Polo Grounds. Perhaps it is actually this desire for the transcendent rather than for mere victory that keeps us locked to our television sets on those sunny afternoons when we ourselves might be out playing. Perhaps even the most avid team supporter, dispirited and surly after a defeat of "his" team, has gained an unspoken understanding of the dance that will keep him coming back again and again, regardless of the final score.

Indeed, we could say that the whole complex structure of pro football was really created primarily so that O. J. (and others like him) can dance. To dance, O. J. needs worthy teammates and effective coaches. He also needs worthy opponents; it is, in fact, their excellence and their full commitment to stop him that forces his dance to higher levels. He needs a physical and psychological context for his dance—thus the stadium, the business organization, the public-relations and ticket-sales effort, the officials, the fans, and, finally, the collusion of all involved to make each game and each season into something dramatic and significant. In this context, we can read Coach Lombardi's "Winning isn't everything. It's the only thing" not as any kind of statement of fact, but as a part of the collusion to create a supercharged atmosphere. It would be more accurate to say: "Winning isn't everything. It's one element in the dance."

Aikido, one of the most dancelike of sports, forbids competition and lacks the familiar business and public-relations superstructure. Yet even here an attacker is required to create the dance. Every aikidoist faces the problem of finding a good practice partner, one who will attack with real intent. The greatest gift the aikidoist can receive from a partner is the clean, true attack, the blow that, unless blocked or avoided, will strike home with real effect. This gift of energy can be turned into a lovely dance in which neither partner is hurt and both are joined. The halfhearted, off-target attack is harder to deal with and more likely to lead to injury. There is, of course, an unspoken contract involved in what Master Morihei Uyeshiba called, "The loving attack and the peaceful reconciliation." The attack offered the beginner is gentle and slow but no less true. And the advanced student may ask for a "slow motion" or "medium speed" attack. But the all-out attack is implicit in every interaction.

One of my teachers, Frank Doran, never fails to stress this point. "Aikido, perhaps alone among the martial arts, takes responsibility for the safety and well-being of the attacker. We practice love and gentleness. We try with all our skill to use the gentle end of the spectrum of response. But we must be prepared to do whatever is necessary, and that includes turning an aggressor's harshest force back against him. We may practice the softest flowing techniques, but make no mistake, aikido is *budo,* a martial art." Indeed, without *budo* the art of

aikido would be incomplete and the dance within the art would finally degenerate into mere formalism.

The black-belt examination is the aikidoist's most significant rite of passage.
Aikido students from miles around gather to watch as the candidate is called
on the mat before a board of examiners consisting of five aikidoists of black-belt
rank. The candidate first demonstrates proficiency in a multiplicity of techniques
against a single attacker. Then three or four black belts (depending upon the
size of the mat) are chosen at random to provide an all-out, simultaneous attack.
Traditionally, the candidate is extremely well prepared before being allowed to
take the examination, so the occasion is expected to be one of validation and
celebration. But success is by no means automatic. The possibility of failure, of
symbolic death, adds poignancy to this ritual dance.

My teacher called me in one day and, reminding me that my own black-belt
exam would be coming up before too long, suggested that I attend every exam
I could over the next several months. Following his suggestion, I happened to
see one of those rare examinations that end in failure. Two candidates were there
at a carefully padded handball court on a university campus. I and other spectators watched from the balcony as the first candidate, a young man of Oriental
ancestry, glided through his techniques with a confidence and grace I coveted
for myself. His response to a three-man attack was no less impressive. He spun
and dodged and sent his attackers flying again and again. The gallery began
applauding before he finished, and he bowed to a fine ovation at the end.

When the second candidate performed his first basic techniques, it was obvious that something was wrong. His movements were forceful and harsh; rarely
did he blend fully with the incoming energy. I wondered how he had come to
be there. Later, I learned that he had arrived at the last moment. Although it is
the custom for a teacher to accompany a pupil, his teacher was not with him.
But he had invoked his teacher's name and insisted on being examined. The
board of examiners, bending over backwards not to offend the teacher, had reluctantly agreed. Watching his performance was actually painful for me. I was
tempted to turn away or walk outside for a breath of fresh air. Instead, calling
upon my own training, I centered myself and tried to open my entire being to
the present moment, to whatever might come.

The candidate was able to overpower his single attacker. (Later, one of the
examiners, a former police officer, told me he was "very strong, probably a good
street fighter.") But what he was doing did not look like a dance. I wondered
what would happen in the multiple attack. Would the black-belt attackers, fully
realizing his unpreparedness, moderate their attacks? Even though my sympathy was with the candidate, I found this thought disturbing.

The multiple attack began and my doubts disappeared. The three attackers
might have given less energy to the second candidate than to the first, if only
because his lack of skill made fewer good attacks possible. But their strikes were
hard and true. He was repeatedly nailed; twice he went down. At the end, he
was applauded for his gameness, and was invited by the examiners to come back
and try again after further preparation. But I had the feeling, watching the
failed candidate walking dazedly down the hall, that the episode was somehow
decisive. There was no way to deny or soften the failure.

For me, this experience has put a sharper edge on the art of aikido. The art is based on harmony, but harmony is not to be achieved through blandness. Actions have consequences. The highest moments often contain within them the risk of failure. This is true at every level of athletics. Sadly, the majority of present-day physical-education programs have little to offer Babcock, the fat boy, and others like him who start out lacking physical ability. Happily, many people in the field of physical education are now concerned with developing programs that will give Babcock his measure of success. If complete, however, these programs will not deny him the dignity of failure. The dance is not inconsequential. Even O. J. Simpson is sometimes—thank God!—thrown for a loss.

"But what of all this violence? Aren't you caught up in a contradiction—you an advocate of nonviolence and harmony, and yet talking about *attacks?*" A middle-aged woman threw me this challenge on the first night of an energy-awareness workshop. She had bristled when I had explained that aikido was a martial art. "If it's *martial,* that means *war,* and there's nothing *that* could possibly have for *me.*" I diffidently asked this woman, who threatened to walk out without further ado, just to stay for a while and see what the work might offer her. But I didn't deny the apparent contradiction. I've often questioned myself on this matter, and I'm not sure I have a satisfactory answer. In spite of Heraclitus's remark that opposites make the best harmony, I sometimes wonder how I can justify the thousands of hours I've spent engaged in attacks.

Yet I know that nonviolence is not the denial of violence but the refusal of violence. The only way to deny violence is to deny the world. Such a denial leads eventually to a kind of insanity, a death in life. The glorification of violence and evil, on the other hand, generally reflects mere romantic posturing. The worst that can be said about most Satanic cults is that they are trivial.

Neither denial nor glorification can set our minds to rest on the subject of violence. But violence can be danced, and perhaps in this way understood. The power of the Dancing Shiva is that it shows us the dancer of destruction and the dancer of creation joined in a single body, dancing together to sustain the world (spring flowers feeding on fallen heroes, new cultures rising from the ashes of the old). We are all joined in that larger dance, the dance of the body, the dance of the world. We may have been led to forget that we are dancers, to believe instead that we are plodding our way through life. But there are moments when the veil of forgetfulness is ripped away and we can hear the music, feel the rhythm, see the other dancers. In those rare moments we are secure within an uninterpreted world, dancing our life while customary definitions fall away. Summer and winter, daylight and dark dance together, and we understand at last how it has come to be that the veiled meaning of Death, the thirteenth card in the Major Arcana of the Tarot, is creation, renewal, transformation.

The dance within the Game of Games tends to move in a dialectical spiral. There is the Dance of Eros, of love, joining, merging. There is the Dance of Thanatos, of death, destruction, dissolution. And these dances, thesis and antithesis, come together in the Dance of Cosmos, of unity, harmony, perfection. We can see this process again and again in primitive dance. African tribal dancers often appear to Western eyes as savage and frightening. Yet all this brilliant savagery is joined with erotic urgency toward a highly moral function, the establishment of etiquette, justice, equilibrium. In the counterplay of good and evil, of individual desire and group good, of inaction and overreaching, the tribal dancers demonstrate the triumph of reconciliation and balance.

This preoccupation with balance, foreign to our off-balance expansionist culture, is seen in the Epa dance of the Ekiti Yoruba, in Nigeria. Carrying fifty pounds or more of carved wooden headdress, a young Yoruba dancer leaps to the top of a high mound of earth before the elders and chief of the tribe. The headdress, unveiled, reveals the figures of warrior, shaman, priestess, and king—the makers of Yoruba culture. By his very manner of carrying his headdress while moving to the rhythm of the drums, the dancer proves literally his ability to shoulder the weight of responsibility. For only if the individual body is balanced and centered can the social order achieve necessary balance.

The Kao gle ("hook spirit") dancers of the Dan, on the northwestern Ivory Coast, teach etiquette by the dialectical process, that is, by doing the wrong things. The dancers, who carry sharp wooden or metal hooks, dance around the village pretending to do mischief. Then they throw their hooks at the band of accompanying athlete-musicians, who leap above the flying missiles with practiced calm. The dance expresses a fundamental truth of tribal life: disruptive influences within the village are best compensated for by immediate, calm action, so the order of the village can be maintained.

All primitive art may be seen as addressing itself to the self-corrective nature of the social order. We may view primitive dance as celebration and sacrament; but it is also cautionary teaching. To a drumbeat that can strike fear in the hearts of those whose culture created the H-bomb, primitive dancers all over the world warn against the promiscuous use of power and give support to the implicit commandment that the security of the gifted must not be established upon the insecurity of the less fortunate.

A self-correcting equilibrium is necessary for any social order. Transformation is not a purely linear process but one which involves the creation of equilibrium on a higher level. Primitive peoples have always known what is only now becoming clear to ecologists and energy specialists. In the words of general energy systems theorist Howard Odum, "Disordering is a necessary part of the continuous cycle of order and disorder, since maintenance of complex structure is more cheaply done by redevelopment than repair." What Odum and others are telling us is that, as we attempt to create ever-higher states of order; we must learn to deal with an inevitable increase in disorder; we must also avoid overreaching ourselves by forcing excessive order on our social systems. The excessively neat individual, the too-orderly society may menace the world.

Apparant disorder can be part of a larger order. Floods and forest fires ultimately increase the energy yield of the land. Death is not only a connection with the eternal but is also a necessity in this world, requisite for social stability and for transformation as well. Thus, we dance violence as a part of the celebration of harmony. Our New Games, to provide a complete ecology of play, must include Slaughter and Circle Football along with the gentler Infinity Volleyball and Mating. The New Physical Education, to be truly humane, must continue to provide some games of hard contact along with new sports such as Orienteering.

As for aikido, I'm still not entirely sure that there's not some intractable contradiction between my practice and my espousal of nonviolence. But I do know how I feel after a good session, and it has nothing whatever to do with fighting or war. Viewed as a dance, aikido moves swiftly, again and again, toward harmony; each cycle of attack and defense contains all three elements of the dialectic. The attacker dances Thanatos. The defender, accepting and blending with the attack, dances Eros. And in the harmonious merging of the two, Cosmos may be achieved—two limited human bodies emulating the joining of mountain streams, the swing of distant stars.

"Did O. J. dance?" If that is a good question to ask of a football game, it is also a question we might ask about the larger game. Did you dance your summer? Am I dancing my autumn? Are we dancing our life? It is all a matter of awareness. The more deeply we see into life, the more clearly we perceive the dance. Pursuing reality down into the heart of the atom, we find nothing at all except vibration, music, dancing. And the world of our senses is also dancing. (Spider web shimmering in the sunrise, trees sweeping the wind, cars burning along the highway, blood pulsing behind our eyes.) We only have to become aware, and we find ourselves dancing too.

Walking to work can be an unavoidable waste of time. It can also be an adventure in movement and balance. Cleaning the kitchen can be a chore. It can also be an intricate dance. Numbed to everything except results, we are likely to miss the dance. But what are *results*? We get to work. The walk between home and work was a meaningless interval. The kitchen is clean. It will be dirty again tomorrow. We have built the tallest building, the longest expressway, the biggest cities. We have won the game. But how did we feel from the inside while we were doing it? Did we dance?

Doctors at the Institute of Sports Medicine and Trauma at the Lenox Hill Hospital, New York City, have made a study of the physical demands placed on individuals in various strenuous activities. As a part of the study, they have rated a number of these activities in terms of ten categories: strength, endurance, body type, flexibility, coordination, speed, agility, balance, intelligence, and creativity. The results will come as no surprise to aficionados of the dance. When the ratings were added up, ballet emerged as the most demanding—above basketball, soccer, and football, high above baseball. There are overweight baseball players. But when a ballet dancer gains too much weight? "Then he or she leaves," says ballet master George Balanchine.

If only one subject were to be required in school, it should be, in my opinion, some form of dance—from nursery school through a Ph.D. I can't say that a dancer is the Ultimate Athlete. I am quite certain, however, that the Ultimate Athlete is a dancer.

Sensing the Energy Body and practicing energy awareness is dancelike in its every particular—the concentration on breathing and balance, the openness to existence that comes from awareness of *hara,* or center, the Energy Body itself, constantly changing in size, shape, and density, and the ineffable but somehow festive energy streamers that seem to join all things. No formal study of the Energy Body, however, is needed for you to join the dance. It began a long time ago. It will never end. It tenders an invitation that is eternally renewable. It doesn't even require that you renounce results, but only that you put them in the proper perspective. All that is required is the slightest shift in consciousness, perhaps only a question asked of yourself not once (for we so easily forget our own existence) but again and again: Am I dancing?

If this small shift in consciousness can sometimes be easy, it can also be very hard, for it is likely to involve pain. When we refuse the dance by holding ourselves rigidly, there is a good reason for it: we are simply unwilling to endure the pain of full awareness. To create numbness we have unknowingly clenched the muscles and the viscera. In order to relax them, we must have some control over them. To control them, we must have awareness of them. Awareness brings pain. To avoid pain, we avoid awareness. Thus, we cannot relax and open ourselves to existence. We cannot truly dance our way through life. Consider the strategies we have devised to keep awareness at bay: the "I-work-hard-and-play-hard" syndrome, the use of tobacco and alcohol and other drugs, greedy consumption, somnambulism, aimless travel. We have gone as far as to idealize numbness, in the *macho*-cowboy-detective-spy, on one hand, and the caustic, ironic intellectual, on the other. All of it goes back to the avoidance of deep feelings, the unwillingness to endure pain.

This is no small matter, and I offer no personal model of enlightenment; many are the times I have declined a deeper engagement with existence in order to avoid pain. But I know that I have an existential choice, as we all do. We can travel through life numbing our feelings, thus minimizing pain and minimizing joy. Or we can join the dance of existence with hearts open to pain, grief, tears, and the awareness of death, and thus realize those connections best described by a word which in the context of this culture is likely both to charm and discomfort us: ecstasy.

But, there is no way for us to avoid the dance entirely. We have all danced Thanatos in every move to destroy the constraints of form, to sweep away old limiting structures. Deprived of the saving Dionysian revels of wiser cultures, we have still danced the liberating disorder that contains and is contained in order.

We have all danced Eros in every move to create, to join together, to find form where previously no form had seemed to exist. We have danced Eros in every attempt to merge with God or nature, or to get inside our lover's skin. (Only an aberrant desire to manipulate, to exploit, to "score," can deny us the dance of our own love-making.)

And we have all danced Cosmos, too—though it might be very hard to perceive harmony and unity in a culture that devotes so much energy to discontent and fragmentation. But there are undeniable moments of perfect flow and reconciliation which exist as the highest function of literature—mowing hay in perfect rhythm during a brief summer shower, standing on the deck of a sailing ship and sensing a perfect oneness with the sea, lying on a hillside that day of the apple tree, the singing and the gold with your first love. I believe we have all experienced those rare moments when there is no separation between the dancer and the dance.

It may be possible for us to conceptualize a whole game of football as having been created primarily so that O. J. could dance. Would it be unendurably difficult, then, for us to imagine that this larger game, the Game of Games, was created on this planet so that everyone, every living thing, could dance?

Considerations

1. How does the quest for power take the dance out of life, acccording to Leonard?
2. Does Leonard maintain that aikido is a way for whites, "corrupted by power," to learn to put the dance back into their lives? Explain.
3. How is the dance representative of balance and harmony? Incorporate the implications of the following statement into your discussion: "The excessively neat individual, the too-orderly society may menace the world."
4. Discuss the following statements from the essay:
    Pursuing reality down into the heart of the atom, we find nothing at all except vibration, music, dancing.
    Numbed to everything except results, we are likely to miss the dance.
5. Why, according to Leonard, is it better not to avoid pain? Why are we "unwilling to bear the pain of full awareness"?
6. Explain why Leonard believes that the ultimate athlete is a dancer.

MICHAEL MURPHY

Golf's Hidden but Accessible Meaning

Certain events may reflect the significant dimensions of all your life, mirroring your entire history in a passing moment. Have you ever had an experience like that? Have you been caught by an event that suddenly pulled the curtains back? Shivas Irons maintained that a round of golf sometimes took on that special power.

The archetypes of golf are amazingly varied, he said, that is the reason so many people gravitate to the game.

Golf as a Journey

"A round of golf," he said in his Journal notes, "partakes of the journey, and the journey is one of the central myths and signs of Western Man. It is built into his thoughts and dreams, into his genetic code. The Exodus, the Ascension, the Odyssey, the Crusades, the pilgrimages of Europe and the Voyage of Columbus, Magellan's Circumnavigation of the Globe, the Discovery of Evolution and the March of Time, getting ahead and the ladder of perfection, the exploration of space and the Inner Trip: from the beginning our Western World has been on the move. We tend to see everything as part of the journey. But other men have not been so concerned to get somewhere else—take the Hindus with their endless cycles of time or the Chinese Tao. Getting somewhere else is not necessarily central to the human condition."

Perhaps we are so restless because like Moses we can never make it to the promised land. We tell ourselves that It is just over the next hill: just a little more time or a little more money or a little more struggle will get us there; ". . . even our theology depends upon that Final Day, that Eschaton when the journey will finally arrive, to compel our belief in God."

The symbol of the journey reflects our state, for man is surely on the move toward something. Many of us sense that our human race is on a tightrope, that we must keep moving or fall into the abyss. "This world is for dyin'," he said that night. We must die to the old or pay more and more for remaining where we are.

Yes, there is no escaping the long march of our lives: that is part of the reason people re-enact it again and again on the golf course, my golfing teacher said. They are working out something built into their genes.

But there are other myths to govern our lives, other impulses lurking in our soul, "myths of arrival with our myths of the journey, something to tell us we are the target as well as the arrow."

So Shivas Irons would have us learn to enjoy what *is* while seeking our treasure of tomorrow. And—you might have guessed it—a round of golf is good for that, ". . . because if it is a journey, it is also a *round*: it always leads back to the place you started from . . . golf is always a trip back to the first tee, the more you play the more you realize you are staying where you are." By playing golf, he said, "you re-enact that secret of the journey. You may even get to enjoy it."[1]

The Whiteness of the Ball

What the golf ball was to Shivas has been hinted; what it has come to mean for me remains unsaid. And for a reason. Its power as a symbol is so complex and labyrinthine, so capable of lending itself to the psyche of each and every player, that once an attempt like this has begun to comprehend its "inner meaning," all bearings may be lost. For the golf ball is "an icon of Man the Multiple Amphibian, a smaller waffled version of the crystal ball, a mirror for the inner body; it is a lodestone, an old stone to polarize your psyche with." The more I ponder its ramifications the more I see that each and every bit of this world reflects the whole.

A friend of mine sees it as a satellite revolving around our higher self, thus forming a tiny universe for us to govern—a marvelous image really when you think about it, one I am sure Shivas Irons and Seamus MacDuff would have approved of. Our relation to the ball is like the Highest Self's relation to all its instruments and powers; the paths of its orbits reflect those of the planets and suns. The ball is then a symbol of all our revolving parts, be they mental or

---

[1] I have often thought that his sense of golf as the journey-round was deepened by his memory that the eighteenth green at Burningbush was built on a grave.

physical; for a while we re-enact the primal act of all creation: the One casting worlds in all directions for its extension and delight. Shivas anticipated the image in his notes: "For a while on the links we can lord it over our tiny solar system and pretend we are God: no wonder then that we suffer so deeply when our planet goes astray."

The ball is also a reflection, as Adam Greene said, of projectiles past and future, a reminder of our hunting history and our future powers of astral flight. We can then ponder the relation between projectile and planet, our being as hunter and our being as God; the hunter, the golfer, the astronaut, the yogi, and God all lined up in the symbol of the ball.

"The ball is ubiquitous," say the notes. "It is in flight at this very moment above every continent. Moreover, it is in flight every moment of the day and night. It may take flight one day on the moon, especially when you consider the potential prodigies of mile-long drives and the wonder they would bring to millions. Consider the symbolism inherent in that indubitable fact: a golf ball suspended in air at every moment!" There are so many golfers around the globe.

At rest, it is "like an egg, laid by man," for who can tell what prodigies the next shot will bring? In flight it brings that peculiar suspended pleasure which lies at the heart of the game; it is "a signal that we can fly—and the farther the better!"— it is a symbol of our spirit's flight to the goal. It is perfectly round, for centuries of human ingenuity and labor have made it so, and "the meanings of roundness are easy to see." (Parmenides and other Greek philosophers said that Being itself was a globe, that we must therefore "circulate" our words in order to tell a "round truth.")

So the symbols and meanings are endless. But when all these are said and done, there is a fact about the ball that overpowers all the rest. It is the whiteness of the ball that disturbs me more than anything else. "Though in many natural objects whiteness enhances beauty, as if imparting some special virtue of its own," said Herman Melville in a well-known passage, "and though certain nations have in some way recognized a certain pre-eminence to it, there yet lurks an elusive something in the color which strikes panic to the soul."

Only black so reminds us of the great unknown. Black and white, we throw them together in the old cliché, but somewhere deep in both there lies a hint of powers unforeseen. Do they remind us of the void, since they represent the absence of all ordinary hue?" Is it annihilation we fear when we encounter them? "All colors taken together congeal to whiteness, the greatest part of space is black," say the journal notes. "What would happen if someone introduced a golf ball painted black?"

The Mystery of the Hole

In no other game is the ratio of playing field to goal so large. (Think of soccer, American football, lacrosse, basketball, billiards, bowling.) We are spread wide as we play, then brought to a tiny place.

The target then leads into the ground, leads underground. I realized this once reaching into one of the exceptionally deep holes our Salinas greenkeeper was cutting in 1949 (he had procured a new hole-cutter). What a strange sensation reaching so far into the ground. What was down there, underneath the ball?

There was a section in his notes entitled "The Psychology of Passageways," which has a bearing on the hole's mystery. In it there was a list of "holes and doorways in our ordinary life," which included a long paragraph about the significance of looking through windows (something to the effect that windows have a function other than letting us look outside, that we build them to simulate our essentially imprisoned state), another on the subject of toilets and the draining away of our refuse (including some sentences about the need to examine our stool whenever we feel disjointed), an essay on picture frames and other boundaries on art objects, and a list of all the "significant openings" in his own apartment (apparently, he had taken a careful inventory of these). There was also a list of "Extraordinary Openings." This included a constellation in the new zodiac he had made (see "A Golfer's Zodiac," p. 153), various kinds of mystical experience—an entire catalogue in fact of transports and ecstasies; a list of historic figures (including Joan of Arc, Pythagoras, Sri Ramakrishna, Seamus Mac-Duff, the Egyptian Pharaoh Ikhnaton, and a Dundee cobbler named Typhus Magee); a list of historic events (including the outbreak of philosophy all over the world during the sixth century B.C., the first flights at Kitty Hawk, and a drive he had hit sometime during the summer of 1948); certain places in Burningbush and its environs (I think he compared these to the points on the body which are probed during treatments with acupuncture), a golf course in Peru (perhaps the Tuctu golf course, which he had mentioned during our conversation at the McNaughtons); certain phrases, philosophical terms, and lines of poetry (including the word *Atman*, the *Isha Upanishad*, and a limerick by one of his pupils); a list of coincidences in his life; and the unpublished manuscript of his teacher.

Our first passageways, he said, are the avenues of sense—our eyes, ears, nostrils, and mouth. We build our houses and churches to simulate these, we relate to the earth itself as if it were our body, for "we start as someone looking out, and as soon as we look we think of escape."

"Life is a long obsession with passageways," the notes go on, "we are ever breaking through to the other side—of ignorance, isolation, imprisonment. Memory, catharsis, travel, discovery, ecstasy are all ways of getting outside our original skin."

He thought it significant that an entire fairway, with its green, rough, hazards, and traps was called a "hole," that the tiny target was used to characterize all the rest of the playing field. " 'How many holes have you played?' is the way the question is asked, not 'how many fairways?' or 'how many tees?' " He thought it had something to do with the fact that after all our adventures, all our trials and triumphs on the journey-round we are left with that final passage through; that the hole and what it leads to is really what the game is all about.

As it turns out some of the most original thinking on the subject has been done by Jean-Paul Sartre, who ends Part Four of *Being and Nothingness* with a short essay on the hole and its implications. I don't recall Shivas quoting Sartre but their thinking on the subject has some extraordinary similarities. The French philosopher, admittedly, is not an accomplished golfer, but his apparent grasp of the hole's mystery suggests that he has had his problems and triumphs on the links. "Thus to plug up a hole," he says, "means originally to make a sacrifice of my body in order that the plenitude of being may exist." (How we golfers can sympathize with that.) "Here at its origin we grasp one of the most fundamental tendencies of human reality—the tendency to fill. . . . A good part of our life is passed in plugging up holes, in filling empty places, in realizing and symbolically establishing a plenitude." In establishing a plenitude? Perhaps this is the most fundamental clue. And the comprehension of that essential act of sacrifice involved in every disappearance of the ball into the hole (sacrifice and inevitable rebirth)! For the journal notes say, "In golf we throw ourselves away and find ourselves again and again. . . . A ball is in flight somewhere at every moment. . . ." What are all these but glimpses of plenitude! To fill the hole with our ball is to reaffirm that fullness.

Replacing the Divot

Our green-loving philosopher claimed there was no better way to deal with our existential guilt than replacing a divot or repairing a friendship. "We act on friendship every moment: with our fellows, our land, our tools, with the unseen spirits and the Lord whose world we are tending."

"Golf is a game of blows and weapons. In order that the game continue we must make amends for every single act of destruction. In a golf club everyone knows the player who does not replace his divot. One can guess how he leads the rest of his life."

Replacing the divot is "an exercise for the public good." It is also a reminder that "we are all one golfer." There would simply be no game if every golfer turned his back on the damage he did.

A Game for the Multiple Amphibian

Bobby Jones and other lovers of the game have attributed its widespread appeal to the fact that it reflects so much of the human situation: comedy, tragedy, hard work, and miracle; the agony and the ecstasy. There is something in it for almost everyone. Shivas liked to quote the *Religio Medici*, especially the passage that described man as ". . . that great and true Amphibian whose nature is disposed to live, not only like other creatures in divers elements, but in divided and distinguished worlds." He believed that golf was uniquely suited to our multiply amphibious nature. It gives us a chance to exercise so many physical skills and so many aspects of our mind and character.

I need not catalogue the game's complexity to make my point: you know about all the long and the short shots; all the nuance of weather, air, and grass; all the emotion and vast resolution; all the schemes for success and delusions of grandeur, and the tall tales unnumbered; the trials of patience and fiendish frustrations; all the suicidal thoughts and glimpses of the Millennium. We all have a golfing friend we have had to nurse past a possible breakdown or listen to patiently while he expounded his latest theory of the game. How often have we seen a round go from an episode out of the Three Stooges to the agonies of King Lear—perhaps in the space of one hole! I will never forget a friend who declared after his tee shot that he wanted to kill himself but when the hole was finished said with total sincerity that he had never been so happy in his entire life. No other game is more capable of evoking a person's total commitment.[2]

This immense complexity delighted Shivas. In fact, he would add more complexity to the game, perhaps to satisfy his endlessly adventurous spirit. Running, for example, has been left out, as well as jumping and shouting; so he advocated your exercising basic functions sometime during the golfing day if you wanted to balance your mind and nerves. We must give these large needs adequate expression, he said, otherwise golf would "imprint too much of its necessarily limited nature on us." For ". . . every game must have its limits, simply to exist, just as every form and every culture does, but our bodies and our spirits suffer." So somewhere and somehow we should run and jump and sing and shout. (I don't want to give you any advice about this, especially when I think about some of the trouble I have had on golf courses when I have tried to follow his advice. Perhaps you should confine these more strenuous activities to your local schoolyard or gym. But you might find it interesting to see how your game fares when you exercise those muscles and functions that golf neglects.)

This is true for much more than running, jumping, and shouting though. For our golfing teacher maintained in his inexorable way that our "emotional and mental body" needed as much exercise as our physical body did. So "poetry, music, drama, prayer, and love" were essential to the game too. "There is no end to it," he said, "once you begin to take golf seriously."

Of a Golf Shot on the Moon

It can now be argued that golf was the first human game played on another planetary body. Those two shots Alan Shepard hit with a six iron at the "Fra Mauro Country Club" have brought a certain stature and gleam of the eye to golfers the world over. Coming as they did while I was writing this book, they appeared to me as synchronicity: the game has a mighty destiny, the event said; Shivas Irons was right. In the shock I felt when the news appeared (I had not seen the television show) I thought that in some inexplicable way those shots had been engineered by Shivas (from his worldly hiding place) or by Seamus MacDuff (from his hiding place on the other side). But the subsequent news that Shepard and his golf pro, Jack Harden, had planned the thing ruled out Shivas and restored some perspective to my hopeful speculations. Still, the meaning of it continued to loom before me. Golf on the moon! And the command module named Kitty Hawk! (Shivas had called Kitty Hawk an "extraordinary opening" in this unfolding world and had worked with Seamus all those years on the possibilities of flight with "the luminous body.") The event was a tangle of synchronicities.

I wonder how many other golfers have felt the same way. So many of us are alive to the other edge of possibility (perhaps because the game has tried us so

[2] An insightful book in this regard is *The Mystery of Golf*, by Arnold Haultain, recently reprinted by The Serendipity Press, though out of print now (ca. 1971).

sorely) and ever alert for the cosmic meaning. This event confirms our sense of mighty things ahead.

There are other implications, however, some less promising. A trusted friend of mine, someone with a quick keen eye for injustice and intrigue, saw an ugly side to the whole affair. It was, he said, an imperial Wasp statement, however unconscious, that this here moon is our little old country club for whites, thank you, and here goes a golf shot to prove it. I hated to hear that, for I wanted to dwell on the hopeful meanings. And I hated to think what Seamus would do, being half-black, if he were fiddling around with it all from his powerful vantage point. The Kitty Hawk might not make it back to earth! But the heroes are back and so far so good. Still, I am left wondering what latent imperialism lay behind that six-iron shot.

And I am left with other thoughts about the character of Alan Shepard. What could have led the man to design that faulty club, smuggle it on board with those "heat-resistant" balls and risk some billion-dollar disaster from flying divots or tears in his space suit? What could have led him to such monumental triviality amind the terrors and marvels of the Moon? The madness of the game had suffered again, I thought, as I pondered his motives.

Had NASA put him up to it for public relations reasons? Maybe they wanted some humor in the enterprise or the backing of certain rich and powerful golfing senators. Perhaps he would collect on some stupendous bet (after all, he was interested in money and had made a pile in his astronaut years). Or could it simply be that all his golfer's passion to hit the ball a mile now had a chance to express itself, indeed the chance of a lifetime, the chance of history! Perhaps the collective unconscious of all the golfing world was delivering itself at last, seizing him as instrument for the release of a million foiled hopes for the shot that would never come down. And indeed the cry came down from space, ". . . it's sailing for miles and miles and miles," Alan Shepard was giving the mad cry of golfers the world over who want to put a ball in orbit and reassume their god-like power.

Yes, indeed, indeed, Shivas was right; the game keeps giving us glimpses.

Considerations

1. Exactly how does Shivas Irons connect East and West through golf?
2. Summarize the symbolism of the ball. Why *is* the ball white instead of black?
3. Explain the symbolism of the hole. How does plugging up a hole establish "the plenitude of being"? as Jean-Paul Sartre puts it.
4. Explain the symbolism of repairing the divot.
5. Does the fact that Astronaut Shepard played golf on the moon seem to point up the cosmic significance of the game? Is that lunar golf swing the embodiment of all the symbols set forth in this essay? Support your answer.

LOYAL RENEGADES

I've never been a good team man. I don't like partners.
I've gone my way by myself, and that's how it figures.
The games I was best at were casino and five-card stud.

—Jimmy Cannon

WILFRID SHEED

Muhammad Ali—King of the Picture Gods

We loved him as a martyr, but at current prices he's no martyr now. He turns off questions about his draft evasion with vague remarks about "doing what's right" that might apply to brushing his teeth, and he has not been a zealous supporter of amnesty. That was yesterday's hornet's-nest. Today the talk is about his accomplishments. He has done martyrdom; now, like his young followers, he is doing success.

And this has won him his strangest fan club of all. The squares love him now. He has become, by magic, their kind of nigger: self-reliant, keeps to his own kind, harmlessly entertaining. He also feeds their sense of black mystery, giving off emanations of a zestier world that delights them in small doses. In this sense his separatism has reproduced a Southern type of situation. We can truly love Negroes on those terms, and feel that a little contact with them enriches our own lives. The small-town businessmen who crowd around him so joyously are absolved of bigotry—"You see, I like Ali! He's so clean."

Thus the mantle of Joe Louis awaits him after all. And in his new Chamber of Commerce state of mind it seems to suit him. He can go on being a devil, because that's part of his charm—in fact, his naughtiness seems almost old-fashioned by now and ready for the nostalgia bank.

But squares get older and their love is fleeting. If Ali wants to hang on to the youth market, which makes and destroys celebrities, he will soon need something more than his current imitation of a mischievous Rotarian. In a period of exhaustion, it's fine. But who knows what the tots will be brewing up in a year or two?

Ali will undoubtedly think of something. Meanwhile he has his preaching. Unfortunately, Muslim doctrine, since Elijah's death, has become rather pale and may not be enough to feed the fire in his belly or the expectations in his audience. Already Wallace has declared the movement open to whites (there has so far been no great rush) and it has lost its defining racist trademark. He has also opened its books (revealing 42 million in assets), so there goes its secrecy. And Wallace, a rather neutral character, seems unlikely to brew up any more of Elijah's spectacular theology that so enthralled young Cassius. (Elijah's wonder stories were originally designed to wow blacks fresh off the farm and don't seem right for young businessmen on the way up.)

So all the reasons he had for joining so ardently have been shot down, one by one, leaving him with a real estate conglomerate and a vague allegiance to World Islam. Some of the other members who joined for racial identity will want to hang on to that for grim life, and they will try to use Ali as they appeared to use him in Cleveland. And a resurgence of race warfare, brought on by hard times, might find him listening. But right now there is just not enough box office in racism. The 25,000 crowd hollering for him at the Kuala Lumpur airport are a powerful persuader simply to go international and broaden his temple. And World Islam not only multiplies his ratings but, in a pinch, his wives. If the obliging Wallace were to go along with some *de facto* polygamy too, it would be a sizable step in Ali's moccasins. After all, seldom has a religion been so willing to tailor itself to its star.

Will he be a religious leader himself? I asked an insider, who said, "Are you kidding? He can't even lead himself. He *follows* himself." More specifically, my source added that Ali lacks the guile and diplomacy for religious leadership, and would be hopeless at the in-fighting on which religion thrives.

That would seem to be that for now. The Muslims were always threatening to fall apart even under the shrewd Elijah, so without him there could be a death struggle for identity. And Ali's talents for generalship have so far been totally absorbed by boxing. But he is only 33 and growing; and if he finds his face slipping out the back end of *People* magazine, he might find a religious title irresistible.

Could he be a real king outside of a story? As usual, half of him probably could and half of him couldn't. At one moment, he will tell you how he makes all his own decisions, and at the next he will say it isn't up to him who he fights next. Both statements are as true as he wants them to be, as he careens between active and passive, willfulness and total dependence. In the ring, he is God: Pacheco says the only cornerman he needs is a mirror; but outside he is now father, now son, now free spirit. If the three-part Christian God somehow images the human psyche, Ali is a classic rendering.

If he doesn't get his stuff together soon, he would be a high-risk leader. Worse, he would be bored. But celebrities are expected to do *something*, and Ali does have at least one peculiar advantage to the Muslims: his fame and charm serve to unify this frenzied group and give it personality. Even the puritan wing, which deplored Elijah's habit of snuggling with his secretaries, seems merely bemused by Ali's leering cupidity.

If he were to become a leader, in fact or by example, where would he lead? One problem with victim-figures is that they can turn nasty when on top. Ali's admirers are distressed and puzzled when he occasionally delays a kill in order to humiliate a well-beaten opponent, yet this is only the other side of masochist behavior. Don't ever let a masochist get the upper hand; his vengeance has been feeding a long time.

Fortunately, Ali seems to be growing more merciful—as a fighter at least—as if he had worked that particular poison out of his system. If he still humiliates Dundee by commanding him to fetch and carry, it is all in fun, an acting-out of a spent sadism. In Cleveland, where things got tense around him, he reverted to cruelty. But he had the wisdom to return to Miami from there and calm down. He *wants* to be nice.

So much the case for mellowing. On the other side lie the incalculable effects of aging. His virtues are such youthful ones, and they could wrinkle badly. When he no longer feels a funky joy at being alive, what will he feel instead? Relief that he's proved his point, or bitterness that it's all over?

Probably both, and a lot besides. Quitting boxing has to be a sickening wrench. For twenty years, time has stood still while he boxed. Now he must pick it up again where he left it at 13.

Will it be too late to retrain the lush brain cells that nature gave him, for peaceful purposes? Studies show that children who don't learn to read and write go on developing their instinctive intelligence long after the literates have quit. And Ali's intelligence is of this sort, a genuine animal wisdom like Marlon Brando's, that makes him perversely attractive to the inarticulate generation. For all his gabble, he is one of them.

Something tells me he won't settle for this. He has enormous respect for trained intelligence, and would like to add this to his repertoire. He would love to be a sage and will work on that. A lot depends now on who gets his ear. Malcolm X is long gone, and Bundini's wisdom isn't getting any younger, but Herbert and Wallace Muhammad seem at least shrewd and level-headed, and I see them sheltering him against the charms of fanaticism as long as they can. When he discovers how difficult real intelligence is, he may get sore all over again.

But reading this man's future beyond next week is a fool's errand. Right now he is improving visibly as a platform performer, sharpening his timing, as he does in the ring, by endless repetition. At a recent booksellers' convention he charmed the socks off the denizens with lines he's used a hundred times before. His ad libs are now so sharp that you can't tell the real ones from the retreads. His sparkle, in boxing and in life, comes from plodding dedication.

This may be the most interesting of all his contradictions. For an apparently flighty man, he is willing to endure bone-crushing boredom to produce just the right effect of carelessness. Like Fred Astaire, he labors long hours over his jauntiness. Which is not to say that his high spirits are faked, but only that they are harnessed to an iron discipline. The ebullient kid from Louisville has become a polished global entertainer by sheer hard work.

That is why his interviews and press conferences have such a curious air of irrelevance. They are simply rehearsals, and he uses them to run through his new material regardless of the questions. Like most comics, he needs fresh audiences constantly; and if the sports-writers sound jaded, remember, they have been sitting in the studio a long time.

Would his stuff seem funny if it wasn't Muhammad Ali's? Or would it wilt like the rope-a-dope? At the moment it doesn't matter because his meteor is up there and blazing. And as long as he can dredge more great fights out of his magnificent body and its seven crazy owners, his jokes will be the funniest you ever heard.

But what happens to the meteor when he loses? Even he doesn't know, which is why he keeps fighting, driving his body and spirit to the limit, and using every trick of self-preservation in his magic kit. He may still be recognized on every street ten years from now, but he can't be sure—Frankie Avalon, Fabian, the stars of his youth, who'd know them now? Warhol's Age of the 15-Minute Celebrity is a stiff challenge. So he stages another fight, and another.

The race is on between body and spirit and boredom. Imagination has kept him going in a dogged profession, but imagination requires fresh food every day, and you can almost hear it growling louder and louder. Is there a new way to train he hasn't thought of? Why not hold the next fight in an igloo? Who's the greatest thumb-wrestler? Some night a hungry fighter with nothing else on his mind will interrupt his thoughts and scatter them. Which would give him a chance for that last great comeback, and it would be at least as super-colossal as the *Third* Coming of course. But boxing stories wind down eventually and one thinks of the last days of Sugar Ray and Joe Louis himself—coming back, not coming back. Who cares? Ali the celebrity would be much better off retiring if he can keep the fighter away from the bright lights.

Here his interest in Marciano and Tunney, both white and undefeated, may come in handy. His first clumsy flirtation with retirement may not be altogether a hoax but more like dipping your toe in boiling water and yanking it out again. Until recently black athletes could not afford to retire (which has produced such prodigies of longevity as Satchel Paige and Archie Moore), and Ali has kept the habit. He is not a carefree man. But he can afford it now. Whatever anxieties he may have picked up around his father's house have been beaten senseless by payday after payday, and he is ready to enter the world of pure celebrity, where he doesn't need pantomime build-ups with Wepners and Foremans and other terrestrial characters, but can be himself. Alone. At last.

The only trouble now is the public, and divining what it wants. Ali became a hero by defying the government and sticking to his guns about it; yet when he talks about the beliefs that made him do it, we yawn, like the kids in Cleveland: "Do the shuffle, Ali. Make us laugh." We want our celebrities to stay the same forever, until they bore us—and then to come back on appointed feast-days and bore us again. (These are known as TV specials.) The death of God has left us in a fine mess celebrity-wise, but photography came along in time to give us new ones on the theory that if you show anybody's image often enough, even Walter Cronkite's, that person becomes a god by accumulation. The more you see the picture, the more likely you are to see the man; and once you see the man, you have to see more pictures—until bedrooms hang like shrines. Even Jesus Christ could only come back as a superstar.

Ali is now the king of these picture-gods, and as such he must be touched, verified, asked to identify himeslf: "Dance. Say something about Howard Cosell. Do something we *recognize*." People follow him with shining eyes, just to make sure he exists. "My God, it's Ali!"—such is our prayer.

But how can he ensure that his picture will go on being taken and circulated forever and ever, and not just on feast-days? Frantically, as he leaves boxing, he tries to diversify, and we get this flush of crazy headlines. We've gladly bought him as a model husband and father, but he also wants to be able to say to the students at Harvard, "I judge a school by how many sisters are around." Likewise we've bought him as an entertainer, but he calls that stuff "foolishness": we are to understand that he is also a preacher, a serious man. He tells the students, "I had to tell you that there are more sides in Muhammad Ali than you see on TV."

But we can't cope with all these personalities. We want the one he started with, *the funny one*. So, reluctantly, he interrupts his ministry to give us another burst of that. The response he gets from just being funny is so full-blooded, and the response to his preaching so numb and flat, that he falls back on clowning like an addict even at his most serious moments. The great man of Zaire and the laughing boys of Louisville still play the boards together, inextricably entwined.

The graduation day session at Harvard is a fine illustration of how he fights for his many faces against a public that only wants one. After giving his lecture, as warned, about the heart and its intoxications, he tells the graduates that "people don't pay for that, they pay for foolishness." But so, it turns out later, do graduates.

"Remember who you are today, because when you make it you have a tendency to forget what you were yesterday." Ali is poised classically between the motions of humility, which is his new game, and a real and rueful self-knowledge —except that with him the two are one: the act is real. "I'm from Louisville, Kentucky, a little black boy who made $18 a week (how?) and wanted to be Golden Gloves champion."

The sense of loss is genuine—he can conjure up a golden youth that is as real as a good poem—but at the same time he knows that a sense of loss is a terrific thing to have in itself, a kingly emotion. Did Keats really care that much about nightingales? He did for one night, and that's all that counts.

Considerations

1. Sheed says that the "squares" love Ali now. If so, why? Has he changed? Have they? Explain.
2. This essay deals with Ali's future. Cite some of Sheed's remarkably accurate predictions.
3. Discuss Sheed's curious statement about religious leaders. "One problem with victim-figures is that they can turn nasty when on top." How was Ali a victim?
4. What do Ali's fans expect of him? What does he think of their adulation of him as an entertainer?
5. Discuss the following statement in regard to Ali and other figures like him:

We want our celebrities to stay the same forever, until they bore us—and then to come back on appointed feast-days and bore us again. . . . The death of God has left us in a fine mess celebrity-wise, but photography came along in time to give us new ones on the theory that if you show anybody's image often enough, even Walter Cronkite's, that person becomes a god by accumulation.

JIMMY CANNON

A Self-Interview
From "No Cheering in the Press Box"

Today was a big day for me. For the first time I took a leak standing up. Maybe I shouldn't say that. People will think I'm feeling sorry for myself, playing for sympathy. But it was a big day. There are things that happen to you that make you realize that life is not a series of glorious experiences but a chain of small happenings.

Like today. It was the first time since I've been in bed, or in a wheelchair, that I've been out. I have a wonderful man who is taking care of me, named Charles Ford. He took me shopping, to Bloomingdale's. We looked around the town, and then he pushed me in my wheelchair over to Toots Shor's new restaurant. A couple of us sat around and cut up touches, and I was able to go to the men's room and stand and take a leak. And this was a moment of triumph for me, an elation.

You know what's a very important thing in your life but you don't realize it? Posture. I try to sit up straight, but you can't get comfortable in a wheelchair. You keep slipping down, and when you sit in one with your clothes on your fly tightens up. It's just one of those God damned uncomfortable things.

I'll tell you how I found out I was getting old. Or I was old. I was on the train one day with Mickey Mantle and Whitey Ford. I was telling some Lefty Gomez stories, and Mantle looked at me with amazement. It was his first year. He was about eighteen or nineteen, and he says, "Did you see Gomez pitch?"

"Did I see Gomez pitch? I traveled with the ball club when he was pitching. He was my running mate on the road."

Mantle looked at me with great astonishment, and the thing that hit me was that Gomez was about the same age as I am. And I realized he was being regarded by Mantle as I used to listen to Damon Runyon and Warren Brown talk about guys like Moose McCormick and Amos Rusie. They were some guys lost in the fog of time.

Time is a vandal and the young ball players should enjoy what's happening to them today, because a lot of times famous men quit baseball and it's like they fell off the rim of the world into some sort of obscurity.

When I was in the hospital, the greatest pitcher who ever lived came to see me, Waite Hoyt of the Yankees. He was big in New York, like Tom Seaver is today, except that he was pitching on the Babe Ruth ball clubs. And he came to see me in the hospital, still handsome and looking very young, and the only people who recognized his name were guys around seventy years old. And this guy was a legend, not only in New York, but all over the league. He was about sixteen years old when he broke in. He was called the Brooklyn Schoolboy.

I saw Carl Furillo come to Brooklyn. Until Clemente, I didn't know a better right fielder. He was very hard, a very tough guy. He was the working stiff in sports. He played baseball like guys who go to work on a job with a pick and shovel. But he did everything. I watched his career, saw him at the finish, and now Carl Furillo is considered an ancient by most of the young ball writers. Incredible!

Joe Louis was the greatest heavyweight I ever saw, and Ray Robinson the best all-around fighter. Most of the kids reading sports pages today never saw them fight. A sportswriter doesn't realize this. We have a tendency to write about the past, to let time telescope on us. We live through so many generations of ball players, they all get mixed up in our minds. We do not judge time at all. A sportswriter is entombed in a prolonged boyhood.

We were talking about cheering in the press box. It goes on all around the league. It's one of the great boasts of all journalists, and especially baseball writers, that they are not influenced by their relationships with people off the field. This is an absolute myth. I always considered myself a fair and neutral man, and yet how could I not be for Joe DiMaggio, who lived in the same hotel with me? We went on vacations together. We were great friends.

But I never cheered out loud. I've heard guys cheering. Most of them do. They're in every town. Most of the guys traveling with ball clubs are more publicists than reporters. A guy might be traveling with the Cincinnati Reds, though it could be any team, and he refers to the ball club as "we." I've seen sportswriters with World Series rings, and they wear them as though they had something to do with the winning of the World Series. Maybe they're entitled to them. Maybe their biased cheerfulness helped the club. I wouldn't know. I would not wear a World Series ring.

Sportswriting has survived because of the guys who don't cheer. They're the truth-tellers. Lies die. Go into any town where they have placid baseball writing, where they're all for the home team, and you'll find out that in that town baseball is not considered an exciting game. Telling the truth—and writing it with vigor and clarity—that's what makes it exciting.

A guy shouldn't hang out strictly with baseball writers. It gets incestuous. Baseball, that's all you talk about. You close the world out, and the world must be let in. The thing I try to do is get the world in over the bleacher walls. That was my whole idea in sportswriting.

The worst thing a sportswriter can be is a fan. I was never a fan, not since I was in short pants. My great hero in sports, when I was a kid, was Pie Traynor. He played a wonderful third base for the Pittsburgh Pirates and was particularly good against the Giants. I think the name fascinated me. I never heard of a guy called Pie before, except there was a homely girl in our neighborhood who we called Pie-face.

I don't want sportswriters being fans. I want them to be the guys who neither love nor hate the sport and whose life is not wrapped up in the sport and who remember they are working newspapermen and not baseball people. No more than a police reporter is a cop. You hear these guys in press boxes arguing whether it's good for baseball, or bad for baseball, as if they owned the thing. What I care about, what I hope I care about, is, "Is it good for the paper? Is it a good piece?"

We're not like police reporters because the police reporter has to scuffle. Every time a police reporter goes out on a story, it's a new deal. It's a new precinct, new detectives, certainly new criminals. There is no schedule on crime. A guy is hit in the head. There is no spring training for murderers. They don't go south with the club. The muggers don't take infield practice.

The sportswriter is given a reserved seat in the press box, and the ball clubs work to make it easy for him and it gets easier year by year. But as you grow a year older it doesn't seem easier. It gets tougher as you age.

A baseball writer's relationship with a ball player is a cop-and-crook relationship. You're not there as his buddy, as his fan, as his teammate. It's an adversary relationship. A lot of writers think that ball players love them. But ball players are amused by writers and consider them necessary evils. One thing I know about ball players: They never thank you for the praise. But they really complain if you rip them. They think they are entitled to good notices.

I don't agree with the delusion that a baseball writer is similar to a drama critic. The guys who cover the theater don't live with the actors and the actresses. They don't travel with them on the same trains and the same planes and stay in the same hotels. They're not on the road with their subjects. I know some guys, career baseball writers, say they've spent more time with ball players than their own kids.

The drama critic sits back and watches, like we do, but he never goes backstage, or very rarely, and says, "Why did you give a bad performance tonight?" The baseball writer goes to the losers after every game and demands that the athletes discuss their flaws. The baseball writer has it tough. He is many things: part psychiatrist, part stool pigeon, part house detective, part doctor, certainly part friend and enemy. And he is forced to take a game seriously, and you must take it seriously when you realize how much it affects the lives of the guys who are playing it. And it's not, as I've heard said, a children's game. Children play for fun and out of gladness. Professional ball players play for money and for fame. It's a tough hustle at the major league level.

I have never felt any envy toward the ball player. I had a normal childhood of baseball and football, a little basketball. But I never felt bad about not being a good athlete. I would much rather have been Ernest Hemingway than Babe Ruth or Red Grange. Anyway, I've never been a good team man. I don't like partners. I've gone my way by myself, and that's how it figures. The games I was best at were casino and five-card stud.

I remember when Louie Effrat, who is on the *Times*, a good sportswriter, was being interviewed on one of the talk shows here and he said what a great life he'd led and how fortunate he was that he had met all the great athletes of his time. I think the great athletes are fortunate that they met me.

I love the newspaper business. I can't imagine myself doing anything else. I love the pace. It's right now, the immediacy of it. You do it and it's out. You don't have to wait a long time to find out how it hangs together.

I once tried the advertising business. I was a copy writer for a couple of years. After a while I hated the work. I went back to the papers for less money because that was the kind of life I wanted. This was in the thirties, for Lord and Thomas. No, for Arthur Kudner. I think it's folded. I guess I contributed to the folding of it. I did signed ads. They sent me out with a detective to find a brand of car, where it was parked, who owned it. It was like covering a story, or pretending to. It was an advertisement for the sale of a car. I don't remember what car.

Writing is work for me. I hate it. I always hated it. It's a struggle. But I have stretches. Sometimes I'm going good and it flows easily, and sometimes there's a big block there. I can get a column done in two, two and a half hours, but I've labored eight hours on a column, too. Time doesn't seem to improve it, or disfigure it. I can write a story under the gun that is just as good as when I take a long time.

I like writing at home best, but I've written most of my stuff in press boxes. Even though I can ignore them, there are always more distractions in the press box. At home you can shut it all out. I like writing for a deadline, when the press box is good, and when I've got my own typewriter and the distractions aren't great. I like the feel I've got on my own typewriter. I think that the speed at which I write influences the quality, even the thought. The feel of a typewriter is important. A bad typewriter has given me many a bad story. I'll tell what can give me a bad story—stuck keys. It breaks your whole rhythm, your whole chain of thought.

I think the three greatest writers I ever read in newspapers were Ben Hecht, when he was doing a column in Chicago, Westbrook Pegler, and Damon Runyon. Maybe Percy Hammond, too. I didn't know his stuff when he was in Chicago, but I knew it when he was the drama critic on the old *Tribune*. The *Herald Tribune*.

Rebecca West was once quoted by ship-news reporters as saying that I was one of the writers in America she wanted to meet. She is a charming and graceful woman, as interesting as she is a writer. And incidentally, Truman Capote came out with *In Cold Blood* and announced that this was a new form of literature. Rebecca West had been doing that for years. Did you read her piece on Lord Haw Haw? When I named the people I thought wrote very well for newspapers I neglected Miss West because she wrote for English papers and I was talking about American papers. No one in the history of the world ever wrote better than Rebecca West. I'm always burned up at people who say, "That's too good for a newspaper." Nothing is too good for a newspaper.

I've tried. There was a piece the other day written by Jack Newfield. It was a serious piece in which he said that the New Journalism that all these guys are now claiming as their own was started by me thirty years ago. I'm perfectly willing to take the bow. But I've got to add something else—the so-called New Journalism was the iceberg that sank the *Herald Tribune*.

And if the New Journalists are my bastard children, I want to disown them. I prefer them not to bear my name. My main objection to some of them is that they make up quotes. They invent action. When I was a kid we used to call it faking and piping, smoking the pipe, opium smoking.

The Newfield piece and a lot of other pieces claim Jimmy Breslin is a pup out of me. I think Breslin is capable of writing good, authentic copy, but it's not enough for him.

I'm paid and so is he to report an event the way it is. But he writes the way he thinks it should be. He fakes it until it becomes fantasy. Then it stops being journalism with me. It's a betrayal of your readers.

We covered a fight together one night in Philadelphia, a Ray Robinson fight. Breslin was sitting alongside of me. We asked John Condon, who works for Madison Square Garden, to go back to the dressing room after the fight was over and Condon came out with a very, very shallow quote from one of the fighters. I followed the quote carefully, wrote it just the way Condon reported it to us.

But Breslin stretched it into a long, long quote. He also had a description of Robinson and his handlers as they got into the car that picked them up outside and how the night looked as they left the arena. And he wrote this while he was still sitting at ringside. Anyway, I don't want to savage him. He and I are not very friendly. We don't go to the same places, or hang out with the same people.

Most of the new guys on the baseball beat aren't so bad. I gave 'em their name—Chipmunks. You know how that happened? I was trying to write a piece in the Yankee Stadium press box and four guys are sitting next to me, jabbering away. I said, "You sound like small, furry animals. You're making that kind of noise." I said, "You sound like a God damn lot of chipmunks."

And the name hung on 'em. Some of them are now going bald, and have grey hair, but they're still known as Chipmunks. My definition of a Chipmunk is a guy who wears a corduroy jacket and stands in press boxes with other guys wearing corduroy jackets and they only discuss what they've written. They don't watch the game. They hate baseball. They hate the players. Except those ball players who fawn on them, who insult them. Like Bob Gibson. He's hostile, so they love him. They loved Bouton, too. They'd rather have Bouton than Mickey Mantle because Mantle has some class. The Chipmunks love the big-word guys, the guys with the small batting averages but who have the big vocabularies.

The Chipmunks refuse to follow the techniques of the interview. They go up and challenge guys with rude questions. They think they're very big if they walk up to an athlete and insult him with a question. They regard this as a sort of bravery. They risk the chance of ending interviews in the first few minutes.

The trick of interviewing is to start with the easy question. I usually start with a little small talk. You warm up slowly. Then you drop the bomb, and if the guy doesn't answer, the interview will be almost completed. I save the tough questions for last because I don't want an empty notebook.

Let's face it, the ball player, or the average ball player, considers the writer a spy. None of us like to have our skin peeled back. That's why the ball player would rather be interviewed on television or radio. It's a pleasant sit-down routine with the radio and television guys, who are usually shills for the club, asking routine questions that will make the ball player look good.

There isn't much left of the newspaper business in New York today, only three papers. They don't hire guys without college educations. I guess that's the way it is everywhere. Sometimes I wonder if Thomas Edison could get a job at IBM today.

These kids keep coming out of the journalism schools, and I say they should escape the schools of journalism. The people that come out of them all write like they were writing for the AP or *The New York Times* or the Washington *Post*. Originality of style—that's what's important. It's not encouraged by the journalism professors. Still, I think sportswriting today, as a general rule, is better than it was in my generation. At the top, maybe, we were better. But the general sportswriter is up. There are better sportswriters today. But we had a couple of flashier guys.

I grew up on the Lower West Side. My father's name, naturally, was Cannon. He's dead. My mother's name was Monahan. So, I'm an FBI—full blooded Irish. I had a Catholic education. I went to St. Anthony's down in the unfreaky part of Greenwich Village. Then I went to Regis Prep School, run by the Jesuits. I went there a year. I don't have what is considered a formal education.

Reading interested me. As long as I can remember I was reading books. My family didn't encourage me. It was my own idea. Some of the people in my family were worried I would ruin my eyes. I used to go to the public library on Leroy Street, in Manhattan. I read the usual things that everybody read in those days—Frank Merriwell, Horatio Alger, *Boys' Life*.

We lived in a cold-water flat, near the docks. My old man always had a good job, for that place. He worked for the city as a clerk. He was a Tammany politician, a minor one. He believed in what he did. He thought it was disgraceful to take money from a neighbor for doing them a favor. And he spent his whole life doing small favors for people in the neighborhood. He wound up without any money but there was enough insurance to take care of his family. He liked all of his kids. He was a very decent man.

I was about fourteen when I started as an office boy on the *Daily News*. I worked the lobster trick—from midnight to eight in the morning. One night, after I'd been there for about two years, there was a shortage of rewrite men. The whiskey must have been flowing pretty well, and for some reason a guy on the desk gave me a short story to write, about three hundred words. It was on Decoration Day, about a kid who ran away from a summer resort and came to Manhattan.

Harvey Duell, who was one of the great newspapermen, was the city editor of the *Daily News*. He read the story, and the next day there was a note in my box: "See Mr. Duell." Well, us boys didn't see the city editor unless we were in trouble. I thought I was in trouble. When I went to see him, he was very kind and said, "I understand you wrote this, young man."

He asked me where I learned to write. I said, "I don't know if I can write at all."

Then he told me, "This is the second thing you've done that's impressed me."

"What's the first?"

"I sent you out for coffee one night and you refused a tip."

I said, "I don't remember. I must have been crazy that night."

That's how I became a city-side reporter.

I covered the Lindbergh kidnapping trial. That's when I first met Damon Runyon. It's been written, many times, that I was his protégé. I suppose you could say that. I was about twenty-four or twenty-five then, and Damon came to me and said, "You shouldn't be doing this. You have a natural style. You should be a sportswriter." I was working then for the *Journal*, the Hearst afternoon paper, and Runyon was with the *American*. So he got me on the *American*.

Maybe subconsciously you could say Damon influenced my writing. But I'm not sure if that's true. I'm not being pompous when I say this, but my style just developed. It's the way I write. Damon never acted as an editor with me. He treated me like a kid brother. He was thirty years older than I was. I went out with him a lot. He took me to all the places. He was great for guys like me. He was a great listener. He'd put you on, get you to talk. He liked to listen. He listened to just about everybody, and he always picked up the tab with news-papermen but never with anyone else. I think he thought newspaper guys were entitled to a little freeloading. I don't think Damon was a champion freeloader, but I think he did his share.

The greatest freeloader I ever heard of is a guy who is now a boxing press agent. One time he was a boxing writer. One night, in a blizzard, he went from his home in Brooklyn to a party in Yonkers for a Swedish heavyweight, for a smorgasbord. This was back in Joe Louis's time. When you go through a blizzard for a meatball, you're a pretty good freeloader.

Runyon used to cover fights and did something you rarely see. He did the running on a fight on a typewriter. He wouldn't take notes after the round. He had an operator named Levitt, a postal telegraph guy who read over his shoulder all the time. And the big thing about Runyon in those days, he used to cover all the big murder trials that would bring the stars out. They would all use legmen. But he didn't. He did all his own work.

He covered the Judd Gray–Mrs. Snyder murder trial. A man and a woman beat up the woman's husband, killed him with a sashweight. The guy was sup-posed to have used the sashweight. And Runyon, in describing the scene as the guy reenacted it in the courtroom, said, "When he picked the sashweight up, his batting stance reminded me of Paul Waner."

Runyon loved heavyweights. I think he would rather have managed the heavy-weight champion of the world than anything else. His walk was boxing, beyond all other things, though he did own horses. His favorite athlete, I've always thought, was Dempsey, in a dead heat with Christy Mathewson. He thought Mathewson was a great pitcher, an intelligent guy, and a great card player. They played cards together a lot. Damon wasn't particularly a great card player. He was a gin rummy player, and once I complimented him on playing a good gin rummy. He said, "You can teach a monkey to play gin rummy."

A lot of people talk of Damon as a cold, remote man. But he was kind and generous to me. I lived in his house in Miami every winter. He'd spend a lot of time talking to me about writing. And one of the odd things about Damon was that he was a very cultured man. He pretended he wasn't. He concealed his culture and much of his knowledge. I have no idea why—but I think Damon wanted to get as close to the people he wanted to write about as he could. He wrote about mugs because they were interesting people.

Damon did things that were extraordinary for those times, and for these times. They talk about guys doing daring things. Well, Runyon's heroes were pimps and prostitutes and murderers. He treated them as human beings. This is now the style. He was one of the forerunners.

He'd take a stickup guy—that was the guy's business—and he'd write about the stickup guy as writers and novelists write about clergymen. I remember one of his lines. He mentioned a certain guy and he said, "He's out hustling, doing the best he can. It's a very over-crowded profession today." A hustler is a knock-around guy who'll take a piece of an illegitimate proposition.

He disguised most of the people he wrote about, but I can pick them out. I knew most of them. Some of them knew they were being written about, I guess. I never heard one complain. But they never knew how sophisticated Damon really was. Most of all, he was a fairytale teller. He liked writing the stuff he did. It was his choice and I think he made it early. That was his style. He made that choice because he was a sportswriter. Let's face it—sportswriters, well, we're not hanging around with brain surgeons.

Damon was a night guy. He was married, and once in a while his wife would go out with him. But mostly he was a single duke. He was a Western guy. His father was a tramp printer, out of the mining towns of the old West. Damon was closer to the frontier than most people realize. He worked in Denver, Trinidad—towns like that.

He had three flowers delivered to himself every day. Carnations—red, white, and blue, in a water glass on his dresser. He had special closets built for his suits. He had more suits than any man I've ever known. And he dressed Broadway style. He looked like a guy who might have managed a good shoe store, or had a very good job in a bank. When he'd go out in his Broadway clothes, and he knew how to wear them, he always suggested to me a city pigeon disguised as a peacock. And he was aware of everything about himself. He was one of the big celebrities in the country.

Damon was a cynical humorist. He was like Ring Lardner. I didn't think he thought very much of the human race. We've had three great original writers—Lardner, Mark Twain, and Ernest Hemingway. And I think Lardner has to be classified among the ten greatest serious writers produced by this country. He was ferociously accurate. He just didn't think much of people. I don't think he masked his humor. This was the way he saw life, and that was the way it came out. There was a bias against Lardner because he was a sportswriter. The critics thought he was a guy who just wrote funny little stories about ball players.

Hemingway was a sportswriter. Read him and you'll find out that he was concerned with losers—from Robert Jordan lying under a tree to die, to his bullfighters. They all lost. He was the only guy who could make fishing sound interesting to me. Fishing, with me, has always been an excuse to drink in the daytime.

I once wrote a piece saying he was a sportswriter, and he sent me a letter, thanking me for it. Ernest and I were very good friends. I liked him very much. But he could be very cruel. He was a tough, blustering guy, but I think as a novelist he is the greatest artist we've ever produced. He didn't dissipate his talent. He never let any of it trickle away into small jobs like other guys did. He never took a job in Hollywood to make a quick touch. He did his trade. I don't think he ever wrote a bad sentence.

Ernest was very physical, very proud of his strength. He might have been the heavyweight champion if he had gone up as a kid, through the amateurs, and decided to become a professional fighter. He boxed very well and he boxed all the time, in George Brown's gym here, and he could hold his own with a lot of tough guys, ex-fighters. He was still boxing when he was fifty.

I remember one night in the Stork Club. We were loaded. He was much younger then, and he invited me to come to watch him box at nine o'clock in the morning. It was then four o'clock. I never showed up. I just paid no attention—at four o'clock in the morning a drunken guy is saying he's going to box at nine o'clock. But he did.

And he called me up the next day, very indignant, and said, "We had a date this morning."

Incidentally, the most neglected writer in this country lives in Chicago. Nelson Algren. I've met him and I like him. I hope he reads this because I want him to know he's not the first guy who was born in a slum. He acts like he discovered poverty, put a flag on it, and claimed it for himself. But I thought *The Man with the Golden Arm* was one of the great novels of America. His descriptions of that neighborhood, that saloon, and those people. He wrote better about Chicago than anybody—including Carl Sandburg. What happened to Algren? Did he just get tired and peter out? I knew Ben Hecht, too. But he was a fiction writer.

Of all writers maybe I revere Mencken the most. He influenced my generation more than anybody influenced any generation since I've been alive. Mencken taught a whole generation how to think, and one of the reasons I adored him was because he was a newspaperman. He was like Runyon. No matter how well they did outside the newspaper business, they were still newspaper people. Mencken wrote awfully good stuff, and his best was in the Baltimore *Sun*. Newspaper people are special to me, probably because I'm a newspaperman. Maybe if I was a plumber I'd talk about plumbers.

I've covered everything there is to cover on a newspaper, but I like sports the best. To begin with, it's a better life. It's an easier life. In sports everything happens in front of you. The thing about politics is that it's happening in rooms. People don't see murders. They go to murder trials and hear people talk about it. But I write best about action, that's why they made me a war correspondent.

When I was a young guy they sent me to Washington to cover the White House. I did it for a while, but the town bored me and I left. I can't stand politicians. They lie more than football coaches. I had to be transferred out of there. I did a radio column, too, but I didn't like it. It was the loneliest kind of life. Sportswriting is best and that's what I am—a sportswriter. I can't think of myself as being anything else.

Some of the best and some of the worst writing in newspapers can be found on the sports page. And when sportswriting is bad, it's the worst in the paper. When it's good, it's the best. You always know when it's bad. You can feel the clink.

I've been the luckiest guy on earth. I've had a great life. I sat, most of my life, at glad events, as a sportswriter, amid friendly multitudes, gathered for the purpose of pleasure. And I've liked some of the people. My two favorite people in sports—and it's a dead heat— were Joe Louis and Joe DiMaggio. They were my friends, and I think explaining friendship is like explaining pain. It's impossible after it's subsided. I have terrible pain right now.

Considerations

1. Discuss Cannon's characterization of a sportswriter as one "entombed in a prolonged boyhood." Could that characterization apply to sports fans as well?
2. Summarize Cannon's remarks about truth in sportswriting. Is objectivity on the part of the reporter important to the average fan? Support your answer.
3. Consider the following statement:
   > You hear these guys in press boxes arguing whether it's good for baseball, or bad for baseball, as if they owned the thing. What I care about, what I hope I care about, is, "Is it good for the paper? Is it a good piece?"
   That sounds very good when applied to newspapers, but it takes on a different tenor when applied to network sports. Should a network sports journalist write his commentary so as to sell network time to sponsors? If so, is he or she consequently under the control of the corporations who sponsor the shows? Explain.
4. Discuss Cannon's remarks about the relationship between athlete and writer.
5. Is it surprising to hear a professional writer, and a good one, like Cannon, say that he hates writing? Are we often told that we should love to write, as if it were a hobby?
6. Who are the "Chipmunks"? Summarize Cannon's attitude toward them. Which athletes does he say they like? Why?
7. Cannon accuses the "Chipmunks" of writing "fantasy." They accuse him and his era (Runyon, Gallico, Rice, et al.) of writing myth. Which is right? Perhaps both are correct. Or neither. Discuss.
8. Discuss Cannon's remarks about schools of journalism for sportswriters. Is his background reflected in his attitude?
9. What does he think about Damon Runyon? Ring Lardner? Ernest Hemingway? H. L. Mencken?
10. Explain why the era of sportswriters like Cannon, Runyon, and Lardner is gone forever. What killed it?

AL STUMP

Fight to Live

Ever since sundown the Nevada intermountain radio had been crackling warnings: "Route 50 now highly dangerous. Motorists stay off. Repeat: AVOID ROUTE 50."

By 1 in the morning the 21-mile, steep-pitched passage from Lake Tahoe's 7,000 feet into Carson City, a snaky grade most of the way, was snow-struck, ice-sheeted, thick with rock slides and declared unfit for all transport vehicles by the State Highway Patrol.

Such news was right down Ty Cobb's alley. Anything that smacked of the impossible brought an unholy gleam to his eye. The gleam had been there in 1959 when a series of lawyers advised Cobb that he stood no chance against the Sovereign State of California in a dispute over income taxes, whereupon he bellowed defiance and sued the commonwealth for $60,000 and damages. It had been there more recently when doctors warned that liquor will kill him. From a pint of whisky per day he upped his consumption to a quart and more.

Sticking out his chin, he told me, "I think we'll take a little run into town tonight."

A blizzard rattled the windows of Cobb's luxurious hunting lodge on the crest of Lake Tahoe, but to forbid him anything—even at the age of 73—was to tell an ancient tiger not to snarl. Cobb was both the greatest of all ballplayers and a multimillionaire whose monthly income from stock dividends, rents and interests ran to $12,000. And he was a man contemptuous, all his life, of any law other than his own.

"We'll drive in," he announced, "and shoot some craps, see a show and say hello to Joe DiMaggio—he's in Reno at the Riverside Hotel."

I looked at him and felt a chill. Cobb, sitting there haggard and unshaven in his pajamas and a fuzzy old green bathrobe at 1 o'clock in the morning, wasn't fooling.

"Let's not," I said. "You shouldn't be anywhere tonight but in bed."

"Don't argue with me!" he barked. "There are fee-simple sonsofbitches all over the country who've tried it and wish they hadn't." He glared at me, flaring the whites of his eyes the way he'd done for 24 years to quaking pitchers, basemen, umpires and fans.

"If you and I are going to get along," he went on ominously, "*don't increase my tension*."

We were alone in his isolated 10-room $75,000 lodge, having arrived six days earlier, loaded with a large smoked ham, a 20-pound turkey, a case of Scotch and another of champagne, for purposes of collaborating on Ty's book-length autobiography—a book which he'd refused to write for 30 years, but then suddenly decided to place on record before he died. In almost a week's time we hadn't accomplished 30 minutes of work.

The reason: Cobb didn't need a risky auto trip into Reno, but immediate hospitalization, and by the emergency-door entrance. He was desperately ill and had been even before we'd left California.

We had traveled 250 miles to Tahoe in Cobb's black Imperial limousine, carrying with us a virtual drugstore of medicines. These included Digoxin (for his leaky heart), Darvon (for his aching back), Tace (for a recently-operated-upon malignancy for the pelvic area), Fleet's compound (for his infected bowels), Librium (for his "tension"—that is, his violent rages), codeine (for his pain) and an insulin needle-and-syringe kit (for his diabetes), among a dozen other panaceas which he'd substituted for doctors. Cobb despised the medical profession.

At the same time, his sense of balance was almost gone. He tottered about the lodge, moving from place to place by grasping the furniture. On any public street, he couldn't navigate 20 feet without clutching my shoulder, leaning most of his 208 pounds upon me and shuffling along at a spraddle-legged gait. His bowels wouldn't work: they impacted, repeatedly, an almost total stoppage which brought moans of agony from Cobb when he sought relief. He was feverish, with no one at his Tahoe hideaway but the two of us to treat this dangerous condition.

Everything that hurts had caught up with his big, gaunt body at once and he stuffed himself with pink, green, orange, yellow and purple pills—guessing at the amounts, often, since labels had peeled off many of the bottles. But he wouldn't hear of hospitalizing himself.

"The hacksaw artists have taken $50,000 from me," he said, "and they'll get no more." He spoke of "a quack" who'd treated him a few years earlier. "The joker got funny and said he found urine in my whisky. I fired him."

His diabetes required a precise food-insulin balance. Cobb's needle wouldn't work. He'd misplaced the directions for the needed daily insulin dosage and his hands shook uncontrollably when he went to plunge the needle into a stomach vein. He spilled more of the stuff than he injected.

He'd been warned by experts from Johns Hopkins to California's Scripps Clinic—that liquor was deadly. Tyrus snorted and began each day with several gin-and-orange-juices, then switched to Old Rarity Scotch, which held him until night hours, when sleep was impossible, and he tossed down cognac, champagne or "Cobb Cocktails"—Southern Comfort stirred into hot water and honey.

A careful diet was essential. Cobb wouldn't eat. The lodge was without a cook or manservant—since, in the previous six months, he had fired two cooks, a male nurse and a handyman in fits of anger—and any food I prepared for him he pushed away. As of the night of the blizzard, the failing, splenetic old king of ballplayers hadn't touched food in three days, existing solely on quarts of booze and booze mixtures.

My reluctance to prepare the car for the Reno trip burned him up. He beat his fists on the arms of his easy chair. "I'll go alone!" he threatened.

It was certain he'd try it. The storm had worsened, but once Cobb set his mind on an idea, nothing could change it. Beyond that I'd already found that to oppose or annoy him was to risk a violent explosion. An event of a week earlier had proved *that* point. It was then I discovered that he carried a loaded Luger wherever he went and looked for opportunities to use it.

En route to Lake Tahoe, we'd stopped overnight at a motel near Hangtown, California. During the night a party of drunks made a loud commotion in the parking lot. In my room next to Cobb's, I heard him cursing and then his voice, booming out the window.

"Get out of here, you —— heads!"

The drunks replied in kind. Then everyone in the motel had his teeth jolted.

Groping his way to the door, Tyrus the Terrible fired three shots into the dark that resounded like cannon claps. There were screams and yells. Reaching my door, I saw the drunks climbing each other's backs in their rush to flee. The frightened motel manager, and others, arrived. Before anyone could think of calling the police, the manager was cut down by the most caustic tongue ever heard in a baseball clubhouse.

"What kind of a pest house is this?" roared Cobb. "Who gave you a license, you mugwump? Get the hell out of here and see that I'm not disturbed! I'm a sick man and I want it quiet!"

"B-b-beg your pardon, Mr. Cobb," the manager said feebly. He apparently felt so honored to have baseball's greatest figure as a customer that no police were called. When we drove away the next morning, a crowd gathered and stood gawking with open mouths.

Down the highway, with me driving, Cobb checked the Luger and reloaded its nine-shell clip. "Two of those shots were in the air," he remarked. "The *third* kicked up gravel. I've got permits for this gun from governors of three states. I'm an honorary deputy sheriff of California and a Texas Ranger. So we won't be getting any complaints."

He saw nothing strange in his behavior. Ty Cobb's rest had been disturbed —therefore he had every right to shoot up the neighborhood.

About then I began to develop a twitch of the nerves, which grew worse with time. In past years, I'd heard reports of Cobb's weird and violent ways, without giving them much credence. But until early 1960 my own experience with the legendary Georgian had been slight, amounting only to meetings in Scottsdale, Arizona, and New York to discuss book-writing arrangements and to sign the contract.

Locker-room stories of Ty's eccentricities, wild temper, ego and miserliness sounded like the usual scandalmongering you get in sports. I'd heard that Cobb had flattened a heckler in San Francisco's Domino Club with one punch; had been sued by Elbie Felts, an ex-Coast League player, after assaulting Felts; that he booby-trapped his Spanish villa at Atherton, California, with high-voltage wires; that he'd walloped one of his ex-wives; that he'd been jailed in Placerville, California, at the age of 68 for speeding, abusing a traffic cop and then inviting the judge to return to law school at his, Cobb's, expense.

I passed these things off. The one and only Ty Cobb was to write his memoirs and I felt highly honored to be named his collaborator.

As the poet Cowper reflected, "The innocents are gay." I was eager to start. Then—a few weeks before book work began—I was taken aside and tipped off by an in-law of Cobb's and one of Cobb's former teammates with the Detroit Tigers that I hadn't heard the half of it. "Back out of this book deal," they urged. "You'll never finish it and you might get hurt."

They went on: "Nobody can live with Ty. Nobody ever has. That includes two wives who left him, butlers, housekeepers, chauffeurs, nurses and a few mistresses. He drove off all his friends long ago. Max Fleischmann, the yeast-cake heir, was a pal of Ty's until the night a houseguest of Fleischmann's made a remark about Cobb spiking other players when he ran the bases. The man only asked if it was true. Cobb knocked the guy into a fish pond and after that Max never spoke to him again. Another time, a member of Cobb's family crossed him —a woman, mind you. He broke her nose with a ball bat.

"Do you know about the butcher? Ty didn't like some meat he bought. In the fight, he broke up the butcher shop. Had to settle $1,500 on the butcher out of court."

"But I'm dealing with him strictly on business," I said.

"So was the butcher," replied my informants. "In baseball, a few of us who really knew him well realized that he was wrong in the head—unbalanced. He played like a demon and had everybody hating him because he *was* a demon. That's how he set all those records that nobody has come close to since 1928. It's why he was always in a brawl, on the field, in the clubhouse, behind the stands and in the stands. The public's never known it, but Cobb's always been off the beam where other people are concerned. Sure, he made millions in the stock market—but that's only cold business. He carried a gun in the big league and scared hell out of us. He's mean, tricky and dangerous. Look out that he doesn't blow up some night and clip you with a bottle. He specializes in throwing bottles.

"Now that he's sick he's worse than ever. And you've signed up to stay with him for months. You poor sap."

Taken aback, but still skeptical, I launched the job—with my first task to drive Cobb to his Lake Tahoe retreat, where, he declared, we could work uninterrupted.

As indicated, nothing went right from the start. The Hangtown gunplay incident was an eye-opener. Next came a series of events, such as Cobb's determination to set forth in a blizzard to Reno, which were too strange to explain away. Everything had to suit his pleasure or he had a tantrum. He prowled about the lodge at night, suspecting trespassers, with the Luger in hand. I slept with one eye open, ready to move fast if necessary.

At 1 o'clock of the morning of the storm, full of pain and 90-proof, he took out the Luger, letting it casually rest between his knees. I had continued to object to a Reno excursion in such weather.

He looked at me with tight fury and said, biting out the words:

"In 1912—and you can write this down—I killed a man in Detroit. He and two other hoodlums jumped me on the street early one morning with a knife. I was carrying something that came in handy in my early days—a Belgian-made pistol with a heavy raised sight at the barrel end.

"Well, the damned gun wouldn't fire and they cut me up the back."

Making notes as fast as he talked, I asked, "Where in the back?"

"WELL, DAMMIT ALL TO HELL, IF YOU DON'T BELIEVE ME, COME AND LOOK!" Cobb flared, jerking up his shirt. When I protested that I believed him implicitly, only wanted a story detail, he picked up a half–full whisky glass and smashed it against the brick fireplace. So I gingerly took a look. A faint whitish scar ran about five inches up the lower left back.

"Satisfied?" jeered Cobb.

He described how after a battle, the men fled before his fists.

"What with you wounded and the odds 3-1," I said, "that must have been a relief."

"Relief? Do you think they could pull that on *me*? I WENT AFTER THEM!"

Where anyone else would have felt lucky to be out of it, Cobb chased one of the mugs into a dead-end alley. "I used that gunsight to rip and slash and tear him for about 10 minutes until he had no face left," related Ty, with relish. "Left him there, not breathing, in his own rotten blood."

"What was the situation—where were you going when it happened?"

"To catch a train to a ball game."

"You saw a doctor, instead?"

"I DID NOTHING OF THE SORT, DAMMIT! I PLAYED THE NEXT DAY AND GOT TWO HITS IN THREE TIMES UP!"

Records I later inspected bore out every word of it: on June 3, 1912, in a bloodsoaked, makeshift bandage, Ty Cobb hit a double and triple for Detroit, and only then was treated for the knife wound. He was that kind of ballplayer through a record 3,033 games. No other player burned with Cobb's flame. Boze Bulger, a great oldtime baseball critic, said, "He was possessed by the Furies."

Finishing his tale, Cobb looked me straight in the eye.

"*You're driving me into Reno tonight,*" he said softly. The Luger was in his hand.

Even before I opened my mouth, Cobb knew he'd won. He had a sixth sense about the emotions he produced in others: in this case, fear. As far as I could see (lacking expert diagnosis and as a layman understands the symptoms), he wasn't merely erratic and trigger-tempered, but suffering from megalomania, or acute self-worship; delusions of persecution; and more than a touch of dipsomania.

Although I'm not proud of it, he scared hell out of me most of the time I was around him.

And now he gave me the first smile of our association. "As long as you don't aggravate my tension," he said, "we'll get along."

Before describing the Reno expedition, I would like to say in this frank view of a mighty man that the greatest, and strangest, of all American sport figures had his good side, which he tried to conceal. During the final ten months of his life I was his one constant companion. Eventually, I put him to bed, prepared his insulin, picked him up when he fell down, warded off irate taxi drivers, bartenders, waiters, clerks and private citizens whom Cobb was inclined to punch, cooked what food he could digest, drew his bath, got drunk with him and knelt with him in prayer on black nights when he knew death was near. I ducked a few bottles he threw, too.

I think, because he forced upon me a confession of his most private thoughts, that I know the answer to the central, overriding secret of his life: was Ty Cobb psychotic throughout his baseball career?

Kids, dogs and sick people flocked to him and he returned their instinctive liking. Money was his idol, but from his $4 million fortune he assigned large sums to create the Cobb Educational Foundation, which financed hundreds of needy youngsters through college. He built and endowed a first-class hospital for the poor of his backwater home town, Royston, Georgia. When Ty's spinster sister, Florence, was crippled, he tenderly cared for her until her last days. The widow of a onetime American League batting champion would have lived in want but for Ty's steady money support. A Hall of Fame member, beaned by a pitched ball and enfeebled, came under Cobb's wing for years. Regularly he mailed dozens of anonymous checks to indigent old ballplayers (relayed by a third party)—a rare act among retired tycoons in other lines of business.

If you believe such acts didn't come hard for Cobb, guess again: he was the world's champion pinchpenny.

Some 150 fan letters reached him each month, requesting his autograph. Many letters enclosed return-mail stamps. Cobb used the stamps for his own outgoing mail. The fan letters he burned.

"Saves on firewood," he'd mutter.

In December of 1960, Ty hired a one-armed "gentleman's gentleman" named Brownie. Although constantly criticized, poor Brownie worked hard as cook and butler. But when he mixed up the grocery order one day, he was fired with a check for a week's pay—$45—and sent packing.

Came the middle of that night and Cobb awakened me.

"We're driving into town *right now*," he stated, "to stop payment on Brownie's check. The bastard talked back to me when I discharged him. He'll get no more of my money."

All remonstrations were futile. There was no phone, so we had to drive the 20 miles from Cobb's Tahoe lodge into Carson City, where he woke up the president of the First National Bank of Nevada and arranged for a stop-pay on the piddling check. The president tried to conceal his anger—Cobb was a big depositor in his bank.

"Yes, sir, Ty," he said. "I'll take care of it first thing in the morning."

"You goddamn well better," snorted Cobb. And then we drove through the 3 a.m. darkness back to the lake.

But this trip was a light workout compared to that Reno trip.

Two cars were available at the lodge. Cobb's 1956 Imperial had no tire chains, but the other car did.

"We'll need both for this operation," he ordered. "One car might get stuck or break down. I'll drive mine and you take the one with chains. You go first. I'll follow your chain marks."

For Cobb to tackle precipitous Route 50 was unthinkable in every way. The Tahoe road, with 200 foot drop-offs, has killed a recorded 80 motorists. Along with his illness, his drunkenness, and no chains, he had bad eyes and was without a driver's license. California had turned him down at his last test; he hadn't bothered to apply in Nevada.

Urging him to ride with me was a waste of breath.

A howling wind hit my car a solid blow as we shoved off. Sleet stuck to the windshield faster than the wipers could work. For the first three miles, snow-plows had been active and at 15 mph, in second gear, I managed to hold the road. But then came Spooner's Summit, 7,000 feet high, and then a steep descent of nine miles. Behind me, headlamps blinking, Cobb honked his horn, demanding more speed. Chainless, he wasn't getting traction. *The hell with him,* I thought. Slowing to third gear, fighting to hold a roadbed I couldn't see even with my head stuck out the window, I skidded along. No other traffic moved as we did our crazy tandem around icy curves, at times brushing the guard rails. Cobb was blaring his horn steadily now.

And then here came Cobb.

Tiring of my creeping pace, he gunned the Imperial around me in one big skid. I caught a glimpse of an angry face under a big Stetson hat and a waving fist. He was doing a good 30 mph when he'd gained 25 yards on me, fishtailing right and left, but straightening as he slid out of sight in the thick sleet.

I let him go. Suicide wasn't in my contract.

The next six miles was a matter of feeling my way and praying. Near a curve, I saw tail lights to the left. Pulling up, I found Ty swung sideways and buried, nosedown, in a snow bank, his hind wheels two feet in the air. Twenty yards away was a sheer drop-off into a canyon.

"You hurt?" I asked.

"Bumped my——head," he muttered. He lit a cigar and gave four-letter regards to the Highway Department for not illuminating the "danger" spot. His forehead was bruised and he'd broken his glasses.

In my car, we groped our way down-mountain, a nightmare ride, with Cobb alternately taking in Scotch from a thermos jug and telling me to step on it. At 3 a.m. in Carson City, an all-night garageman used a broom to clean the car of snow and agreed to pick up the Imperial—"when the road's passable." With dawn breaking, we reached Reno. All I wanted was a bed and all Cobb wanted was a craps table.

He was rolling now, pretending he wasn't ill, and with the Scotch bracing him. Ty was able to walk into the Riverside Hotel casino with a hand on my shoulder and without staggering so obviously as usual. Everybody present wanted to meet him. Starlets from a film unit on location in Reno flocked around and comedian Joe E. Lewis had the band play *Sweet Georgia Brown*—Ty's favorite tune.

"Hope your dice are still honest," he told Riverside co-owner Bill Miller. "Last time I was here I won $12,000 in three hours."

"How I remember, Ty," said Miller. "How I remember."

A scientific craps player who'd won and lost huge sums in Nevada in the past, Cobb bet $100 chips, his eyes alert, not missing a play around the board. He soon decided that the table was "cold" and we moved to another casino, then a third. At this last stop, Cobb's legs began to grow shaky. Holding himself up by leaning on the table edge with his forearms, he dropped $300, then had a hot streak in which he won over $800. His voice was a croak as he told the other players, "Watch 'em and weep."

But then suddenly his voice came back. When the stickman raked the dice his way, Cobb loudly said, "You touched the dice with your hand."

"No sir," said the stickman. "I did *not*."

"I don't lie!" snarled Cobb.

"I don't lie either," insisted the stickman.

"Nobody touches my dice!" Cobb, swaying on his feet, eyes blazing, worked his way around the table toward the croupier. It was a weird tableau. In his crumpled Stetson and expensive camel's-hair coat, stained and charred with cigarette burns, a three-day beard grizzling his face, the gaunt old giant of baseball towered over the dapper gambler.

"You fouled the dice. I saw you," growled Cobb, and then he swung.

The blow missed, as the stickman dodged, but, cursing and almost falling, Cobb seized the wooden rake and smashed it over the table. I jumped in and caught him under the arms as he sagged.

And then, as quickly as possible, we were put into the street by two large uniformed guards. "Sorry, Mr. Cobb," they said, unhapply, "but we can't have this."

A crowd had gathered and as we started down the street, Cobb swearing and stumbling and clinging to me, I couldn't have felt more conspicuous if I'd been strung naked from the neon arch across Reno's main drag, Virginia Street. At the streetcorner, Ty was struck by an attack of breathlessness. "Got to stop," he gasped. Feeling him going limp on me, I turned his six-foot body against a lamppost, braced my legs and with an underarm grip held him there until he caught his breath. He panted and gulped for air.

His face gray, he murmured, "Reach into my left hand coat pocket." Thinking he wanted his bottle of heart pills, I did. But instead pulled out a six-inch-thick wad of currency, secured by a rubber band. "Couple of thousand there," he said weakly. "Don't let it out of sight."

At the nearest motel, where I hired a single, twin-bed room, he collapsed on the bed in his coat and hat and slept. After finding myself some breakfast, I turned in. Hours later I heard him stirring. "What's this place?" he muttered.

I told him the name of the motel—Travelodge.

"Where's the bankroll?"

"In your coat. You're wearing it."

Then he was quiet.

After a night's sleep, Cobb felt well enough to resume his gambling. In the next few days, he won more than $3,000 at the tables, and then we went sightseeing in historic Virginia City. There, as in all places, he stopped traffic. And had the usual altercation. This one was at the Bucket of Blood, where Cobb accused the bartender of serving watered Scotch. The bartender denied it. Crash! Another drink went flying.

Back at the lodge a week later, looking like the wrath of John Barleycorn and having refused medical aid in Reno, he began to suffer new and excruciating pains—in his hips and lower back. But between groans he forced himself to work an hour a day on his autobiography. He told inside baseball tales never published:

". . . Frank Navin, who owned the Detroit club for years, faked his turnstile count to cheat the visiting team and Uncle Sam. So did Big Bill Devery and Frank Farrell, who owned the New York Highlanders—later called the Yankees."

". . . Walter Johnson, the Big Train, tried to kill himself when his wife died."

". . . Grover Cleveland Alexander wasn't drunk out there on the mound, the way people thought—he was an epileptic. Old Pete would fall down with a seizure between innings, then go back and pitch another shutout."

". . . John McGraw hated me because I tweaked his nose in broad daylight in the lobby of the Oriental Hotel, in Dallas, after earlier beating the hell out of his second baseman, Buck Herzog, upstairs in my room."

But before we were well started, Cobb suddenly announced we'd go riding in his 23-foot Chris-Craft speedboat, tied up in a boathouse below the lodge. When I went down to warm it up, I found the boat sunk to the bottom of Lake Tahoe in 15 feet of water.

My host broke all records for blowing his stack when he heard the news. He saw in this a sinister plot. "I told you I've got enemies all around here! It's sabotage as sure as I'm alive!"

A sheriff's investigation turned up no clues. Cobb sat up all night for three nights with his Luger. "I'll salivate the first dirty skunk who steps foot around here after dark," he swore.

Parenthetically, Cobb had a vocabulary all his own. To "salivate" something meant to destroy it. Anything easy was "soft-boiled," to outsmart someone was to "slip him the oskafagus," and all doctors were "truss-fixers." People who displeased him—and this included almost everyone he met—were "fee-simple sons-ofbitches," "mugwumps" or (if female) "lousy slits."

Lake Tahoe friends of Cobb's had stopped visiting him long before, but one morning an attractive blonde of about 50 came calling. She was an old chum—in a romantic way, I was given to understand, of bygone years—but Ty greeted her coldly. "Lost my sexual powers when I was 69," he said, when she was out of the room. "What the hell use to me is a woman?"

The lady had brought along a three-section electric vibrator bed, which she claimed would relieve Ty's back pains. We helped him mount it. He took a 20-minute treatment. Attemping to dismount, he lost balance, fell backward, the contraption jackknifed and Cobb was pinned, yelling and swearing, under a pile of machinery.

When I freed him and helped him to a chair, he told the lady—in the choicest gutter language—where she could put her bed. She left, sobbing.

"That's no way to talk to an old friend, Ty," I said. "She was trying to do you a favor."

"And you're a hell of a poor guest around here, too!" he thundered. "You can leave any old time!" He quickly grabbed a bottle and heaved it in my direction.

"Thought you could throw straighter than that!" I yelled back.

Fed up with him, I started to pack my bags. Before I'd finished, Cobb broke out a bottle of vintage Scotch, said I was "damned sensitive," half-apologized, and the matter was forgotten.

While working one morning on an outside observation deck, I heard a thud inside. On his bedroom floor, sprawled on his back, lay Ty. He was unconscious, his eyes rolled back, breathing shallowly. I thought he was dying.

There was no telephone. "Eavesdropping on the line," Cobb had told me. "I had it cut off." I ran down the road to a neighboring lodge and phoned a Carson City doctor, who promised to come immediately.

Back at the lodge, Ty remained stiff and stark on the floor, little bubbles escaping his lips. His face was bluish-white. With much straining, I lifted him halfway to the bed and by shifting holds finally rolled him onto it, and covered him with a blanket. Twenty minutes passed. No doctor.

Ten minutes later, I was at the front door, watching for the doctor's car, when I heard a sound. There stood Ty, swaying on his feet. "You want to do some work on the book?" he said.

His recovery didn't seem possible. "But you were out cold a minute ago," I said.

"Just a dizzy spell. Have 'em all the time. Must have hit my head on the bed-post when I fell."

The doctor, arriving, found Cobb's blood pressure standing at a grim 210 on the gauge. His temperature was 101 degrees and, from gross neglect of his diabetes, he was in a state of insulin shock, often fatal if not quickly treated. "I'll have to hospitalize you, Mr. Cobb," said the doctor.

Weaving his way to a chair, Cobb angrily waved him away. "Just send me your bill," he grunted. "I'm going home."

"Home" was the multimillionaire's main residence at Atherton, California, on the San Francisco Peninsula, 250 miles away, and it was there he headed later that night. With some hot soup and insulin in him, Cobb recovered with the same unbelievable speed he'd shown in baseball. In his heyday, trainers often sewed up deep spike cuts in his knees, shins and thighs, on a clubhouse bench, without anesthetic, and he didn't lose an inning. Grantland Rice one 1920 day sat beside a bedridden, feverish Cobb, whose thighs, from sliding, were a mass of raw flesh. Sixteen hours later, he hit a triple, double, three singles and stole two bases to beat the Yankees. On the Atherton ride, he yelled insults at several motorists who moved too slowly to suit him. Reaching Atherton, Ty said he felt ready for another drink.

My latest surprise was Cobb's 18-room, two-story, richly landscaped Spanish-California villa at 48 Spencer Lane, an exclusive neighborhood. You could have held a ball game on the grounds.

But the $90,000 mansion had no lights, no heat, no hot water.

"I'm suing the Pacific Gas & Electric Company," he explained, "for over-charging me on the service. Those rinky-dinks tacked an extra $16 on my bill. Bunch of crooks. When I wouldn't pay, they cut off my utilities. Okay—I'll see them in court."

For months previously, Ty Cobb had lived in a totally dark house. The only illumination was candlelight. The only cooking facility was a portable Coleman stove, such as campers use. Bathing was impossible, unless you could take it cold. The electric refrigerator, stove, deep-freeze, radio and television, of course, didn't work. Cobb had vowed to "hold the fort" until his trial of the P.G.&E. was settled. Simultaneously, he had filed a $60,000 suit in San Francisco Superior Court against the State of California to recover state income taxes already col-lected—on the argument that he wasn't a permanent resident of California, but of Nevada, Georgia, Arizona and other waypoints. State's attorneys claimed he spent at least six months per year in Atherton, thus had no case.

"I'm gone so much from here," he claimed, "that I'll win hands down." All legal opinion, I later learned, held just the opposite view, but Cobb ignored their advice.

Next morning, I arranged with Ty's gardener, Hank, to turn on the lawn sprinklers. In the outdoor sunshine, a cold-water shower was easier to take. From then on, the back yard became my regular washroom.

The problem of lighting a desk so that we could work on the book was solved by stringing 200 feet of cord, plugged into an outlet of a neighboring house, through hedges and flower gardens and into the window of Cobb's study, where a single naked bulb, hung over the chandelier, provided illumination.

The flickering shadows cast by the single light made the vast old house seem haunted. No "ghost" writer ever had more ironical surroundings.

At various points around the premises, Ty showed me where he'd once installed high-voltage wires to stop trespassers. "Curiosity-seekers?" I asked.

"Hell, no" he said. "Detectives broke in here once looking for evidence against me in a divorce suit. After a couple of them got burned, they stopped coming."

To reach our bedrooms, Cobb and I groped our way down long, black corridors. Twice he fell in the dark. And then, collapsing completely, he became so ill that he was forced to check in at Stanford Hospital in nearby Palo Alto. Here another shock was in store.

One of the physicians treating Ty's case, a Dr. E. R. Brown, said, "Do you mean to say that this man has traveled 700 miles in the last month without medical care?"

"Doctor," I said "I've hauled him in and out of saloons, motels, gambling joints, steam baths and snowbanks. There's no holding him."

"It's a miracle he's alive. He has almost every major ailment I know about."

Dr. Brown didn't reveal to me Ty's main ailment, which news Cobb, himself, broke late one night from his hospital bed. "It's cancer," he said, bluntly. "About a year ago I had most of my prostate gland removed when they found it was malignant. Now it's spread up into the back bones. These pill-peddlers here won't admit it, but I haven't got a chance."

Cobb made me swear I'd never divulge the fact before he died. "If it gets in the papers, the sob sisters will have a field day. I don't want sympathy from anybody."

At Stanford, where he absorbed seven massive doses of cobalt radiation, the ultimate cancer treatment, he didn't act like a man on his last legs. Even before his strength returned, he was in the usual form.

"They won't let me have a drink," he said, indignantly. "I want you to get me a bottle. Smuggle it in in your tape-recorder case."

I tried, telling myself that no man with terminal cancer deserves to be dried up, but sharp-eyed nurses and orderlies were watching. They searched Ty's closet, found the bottle and over his roars of protest appropriated it.

"We'll have to slip them the oskefagus," said Ty.

Thereafter, a drink of Scotch-and-water sat in plain view in his room, on his bedside table, under the very noses of his physicians—and nobody suspected a thing. The whisky was in an ordinary water glass, and in the liquid reposed Ty's false teeth.

There were no dull moments while Cobb was at the hospital. He was critical of everything. He told one doctor that he was not even qualified to be an intern, and told the hospital dietician—at the top of his voice—that she and the kitchen workers were in a conspiracy to poison him with their "foul" dishes. To a nurse he snapped, "If Florence Nightingale knew about you, she'd spin in her grave."

(Stanford Hospital, incidentally, is one of the largest and top-rated medical plants in the United States.)

But between blasts he did manage to buckle down to work on the book, dictating long into the night into a microphone suspended over his bed. Slowly the stormy details of his professional life came out. He spoke often of having "forgiven" his many baseball enemies, then lashed out at them with such passionate phrases that it was clear he'd done no such thing. High on his "hate" list were McGraw; New York sportswriters; Hub Leonard, a pitcher who in 1926 accused Cobb and Tris Speaker of "fixing" a Detroit-Cleveland game; American

League President Ban Johnson; onetime Detroit owner Frank Navin; former Baseball Commissioner Kenesaw Mountain Landis; and all those who intimated that Cobb ever used his spikes on another player without justification.

After a night when he slipped out of the hospital, against all orders, and we drove to a San Francisco Giants-Cincinnati Reds game at Candlestick Park, 30 miles away, Stanford Hospital decided it couldn't help Tyrus R. Cobb, and he was discharged. For extensive treatment his bill ran to more than $1,200.

"That's a nice racket you boys have here," he told the discharging doctors. "You clip the customers and then every time you pass an undertaker, you wink at him."

"Goodbye, Mr. Cobb," snapped the medical men.

Soon after this Ty caught a plane to his native Georgia and I went along. "I want to see some of the old places again before I die," he said.

It now was Christmas eve of 1960 and I'd been with him for three months and completed but four chapters. The project had begun to look hopeless. In Royston, a village of 1,200, Cobb headed for the town cemetery. I drove him there, we parked, and I helped him climb a wind-swept hill through the growing dusk. Light snow fell. Faintly, yule chimes could be heard.

Amongst the many headstones, Ty looked for the plot he'd reserved for himself while in California and couldn't locate it. His temper began to boil. "Dammit, I ordered the biggest damn mausoleum in the graveyard! I know it's around here somewhere." On the next hill, we found it: a large, marble, walk-in-size structure with "Cobb" engraved over the entrance.

"You want to pray with me?" he said, gruffly. We knelt and tears came to his eyes.

Within the tomb, he pointed to crypts occupied by the bodies of his father, Prof. William Herschel Cobb, his mother, Amanda (Chitwood) Cobb, and his sister, Florence, whom he'd had disinterred and placed here. "My father," he said reverently, "was the greatest man I ever knew. He was a scholar, state senator, editor and philosopher. I worshipped him. So did all the people around here. He was the only man who ever made me do his bidding."

Arising painfully, Ty braced himself against the marble crypt that soon would hold his body. There was an eerie silence in the tomb. He said deliberately:

"My father had his head blown off with a shotgun when I was 18 years old— *by a member of my own family.* I didn't get over that. I've never gotten over it."

We went back down the hill to the car. I asked no questions that day.

Later, from family sources and old Georgia friends of the baseball idol, I learned about the killing. One night in August of 1905, they related, Professor Cobb announced that he was driving from Royston to a neighboring village and left home by buggy. But, later that night, he doubled back and crept into his wife's bedroom by way of the window. "He suspected her of being unfaithful to him," said these sources. "He thought he'd catch her in the act. But Amanda Cobb was a good woman. She was all alone when she saw a menacing figure climb through her window and approach her bed. In the dark, she assumed it to be a robber. She kept a shotgun handy by her bed and she used it. Everybody around here knew the story, but it was hushed up when Ty became famous."

News of the killing reached Ty in Augusta, where he was playing minor league ball, on August 9. A few days later he was told that he'd been purchased by the Detroit Tigers, and was to report immediately. "In my grief," Cobb says in the book, "it didn't matter much. . . ."

Came March of 1961 and I remained stuck to the Georgia Peach like court plaster. He'd decided that we were born pals, meant for each other, that we'd complete a baseball book beating anything ever published. He had astonished doctors by rallying from the spreading cancer and, between bouts of transmitting his life and times to a tape-recorder, was raising more whoopee than he had at Lake Tahoe and Reno.

Spring-training time for the big leagues had arrived and we were ensconced in a $30-a-day suite at the Ramada Inn at Scottsdale, Arizona, close by the practice parks of the Red Sox, Indians, Giants and Cubs. Here, each year, Cobb held court. He didn't go to see anybody; Ford Frick, Joe Cronin, Ted Williams, and other diamond notables came to him. While explaining to sportswriters why modern stars couldn't compare to the Wagners, Lajoies, Speakers, Jacksons, Mathewsons and Planks of his day, Ty did other things.

For one, he commissioned a noted Arizona artist to paint him in oils. He was emaciated, having dropped from 208 pounds to 176. The preliminary sketches showed up his sagging cheeks and thin neck.

"I wouldn't let you kalsomine my toilet," ripped out Ty, and fired the artist.

But at analyzing the Dow-Jones averages and playing the stock market, he was anything but eccentric. Twice a week he phoned experts around the country, determined good buys and bought in blocks of 500 to 1,500 shares. He made money consistently, even when bedridden, with a mind that read behind the fluctuations of a dozen different issues. "The State of Georgia," Ty remarked, "will realize about one million dollars from inheritance taxes when I'm dead. But there isn't a man alive who knows what I'm worth." According to the *Sporting News*, there was evidence upon Cobb's death that his worth approximated $12 million. Whatever the true figure, he did not confide the amount to me— or, most probably, to anyone except attorneys who drafted his last will and testament. And Cobb fought off making his will until the last moment.

His fortune began in 1908, when he bought into United (later General) Motors; as of 1961, he was "Mr. Coca Cola," holding more than 20,000 shares of that stock, valued at $85 per share. Wherever we traveled, he carried with him, stuffed into an old brown bag, more than $1 million in stock certificates and negotiable government bonds. The bag never was locked up. Cobb assumed nobody would dare rob him. He tossed the bag into any handy corner of a room, inviting theft. And in Scottsdale it turned up missing.

Playing Sherlock, he narrowed the suspects to a room maid and a man he'd hired to cook meals. When questioned, the maid broke into tears and the cook quit (fired, said Cobb). Hours later, I discovered the bag under a pile of dirty laundry.

Major league owners and league officials hated to see him coming, for he thought their product was putrid and said so, incessantly. "Today they hit for ridiculous averages, can't bunt, can't steal, can't hit-and-run, can't place-hit to the opposite field and you can't call them ballplayers." He told sportswriters,

"I blame Frick, Cronin, Bill Harridge, Horace Stoneham, Dan Topping and others for wrecking baseball's traditional league lines. These days, any tax-dodging mugwump with a bankroll can buy a franchise, field some semi-pros and get away with it. Where's our integrity? Where's *baseball?*"

No one could quiet Cobb. Who else had a lifetime average of .367, made 4,191 hits, scored 2,244 runs, won 12 batting titles, stole 892 bases, repeatedly beat whole teams single-handedly? Who was first into the Hall of Fame? Not Babe Ruth—but Cobb, by a landslide vote.

By early April, he could barely make it up the ramp of the Scottsdale Stadium, even hanging onto me. He had to stop, gasping for breath, every few steps. But he kept coming to games—loving the sounds of the ball park. His courage was tremendous. "Always be ready to catch me if I start to fall," he said. "I'd hate to go down in front of the fans."

People of all ages were overcome with emotion upon meeting him; no sports figure I've known produced such an effect upon the public.

We went to buy a cane. At a surgical supply house, Cobb inspected a dozen $25 malacca sticks, bought the cheapest, $4, white-ash cane they had. "I'm a plain man," he informed the clerk, the $7,500 diamond ring on his finger glittering.

But pride kept the old tiger from ever using the cane, any more than he'd wear the $600 hearing aid built into the bow of his glasses.

One day a Mexican taxi-driver aggravated Cobb with his driving. Throwing the fare on the ground, he waited until the cabbie had bent to retrieve it, then tried to punt him like a football.

"What's your sideline," he inquired, "selling opium?"

It was all I could do to keep the driver from swinging on him. Later, a lawyer called on Cobb, threatening a damage suit. "Get in line, there's 500 ahead of you," said Tyrus, waving him away.

Every day was a new adventure. He was fighting back against the pain that engulfed him again—cobalt treatments no longer helped—and I could count on trouble anywhere we went. He threw a salt-shaker at a Phoenix waiter, narrowly missing. One of his most treasured friendships—with Ted Williams—came to an end.

From the early 1940's, Williams had sat at Ty Cobb's feet. They often met, exchanged long letters on the art of batting. At Scottsdale one day, Williams dropped by Ty's rooms. He hugged Ty, fondly rumpled his hair and accepted a drink. Presently the two greatest hitters of past and present fell into an argument over what players should comprise the all-time, all-star team. Williams declared, "I want DiMaggio and Hornsby on my team over anybody you can mention."

Cobb's face grew dark. "Don't give me that! Hornsby couldn't go back for a pop fly and he lacked smartness. DiMaggio couldn't hit with Speaker or Joe Jackson."

"The hell you say!" came back Williams, jauntily. "Hornsby out-hit *you* a couple of years."

Almost leaping from his chair, Cobb shook a fist. He'd been given the insult supreme—for Cobb always resented, and finally hated, Rogers Hornsby. Not until Cobb was in his 16th season did Hornsby top him in the batting averages. "Get . . . away from me!" choked Cobb. "Don't come back!"

Williams left with a quizzical expression, not sure how much Cobb meant it. The old man meant it all the way. He never invited Williams back, nor talked to him, nor spoke his name again. "I cross him off," he told me.

We left Arizona shortly thereafter for my home in Santa Barbara, California. Now failing fast, Tyrus had accepted my invitation to be my guest. Two doctors inspected him at my beach house by the Pacific and gave their opinions: he had a few months of life left, no more. The cancer had invaded the bones of his skull. His pain was intense, unrelenting—requiring heavy sedation—yet with teeth bared and sweat pouring down his face, he fought off medical science. "They'll never get me on their damned hypnotics," he swore. "I'll never die an addict . . . an idiot. . . ."

He shouted, "Where's anybody who cares about me? Where are they? The world's lousy . . . no good."

One night later, on May 1, Cobb sat propped up in bed, overlooking a starlit ocean. He had a habit, each night, of rolling up his trousers and placing them under his pillows—an early-century ballplayer's trick, dating from the time when Ty slept in strange places and might be robbed. I knew that his ever-present Luger was tucked into that pants-roll.

I'd never seen him so sunk in despair. At last the fire was going out. "Do we die a little at a time, or all at once?" he wondered aloud. "I think Max had the right idea."

The reference was to his onetime friend, multimillionaire Max Fleischmann, who'd cheated lingering death by cancer some years earlier by putting a bullet through his brain. Ty spoke of Babe Ruth, another cancer victim. "If Babe had been told what he had in time, he could've got it over with."

Had I left Ty that night, I believe he would have pulled the trigger. His three living children (two were dead) had withdrawn from him. In the wide world that had sung his fame, he had not one intimate friend remaining.

But we talked, and prayed, until dawn, and then sleep came; in the morning, aided by friends, I put him into a car and drove him home, to the big, gloomy house in Atherton. He spoke only twice during the six-hour drive.

"Have you got enough to finish the book?" he asked.

"More than enough."

"Give 'em the word then. I had to fight all my life to survive. They all were against me . . . tried every dirty trick to cut me down. But I beat the bastards and left them in the ditch. Make sure the book says that. . . ."

I was leaving him now, permanently, and I had to ask one question I'd never put to him before.

"Why did you fight so hard in baseball, Ty?"

He'd never looked fiercer than then, when he answered. "I did it for my father, who was an exalted man. They killed him when he was still young. They blew his head off the same week I became a major leaguer. He never got to see me play. But I knew he was watching me and I never let him down."

You can make what you want of that. Keep in mind what Casey Stengel said, later: "I never saw anyone like Cobb. No one even close to him. When he wiggled those wild eyes at a pitcher, you knew you were looking at the one bird nobody could beat. It was like he was superhuman."

To me it seems that the violent death of a father whom a sensitive, highly-talented boy loved deeply, and feared, engendered, through some strangely supreme desire to vindicate that father, the most violent, successful, thoroughly maladjusted personality ever to pass across American sports. The shock tipped the 18-year-old mind, making him capable of incredible feats.

Off the field, he was still at war with the world. For the emotionally disturbed individual, in most cases, does not change his pattern. To reinforce that pattern, he was viciously hazed by Detroit Tiger veterans when he was a rookie. He was bullied, ostracized and beaten up—in one instance, a 210-pound catcher named Charlie Schmidt broke the 165-pound Ty Cobb's nose. It was persecution immediately heaped upon the deepest desolation a young man can experience.

Yes, Ty Cobb was a badly disturbed personality. It is not hard to understand why he spent his entire life in deep conflict. Nor why a member of his family, in the winter of 1960, told me, "I've spent a lot of time terrified of him . . . I think he was psychotic from the time that he left Georgia to play in the big league."

"Psychotic" is not a word I'd care to use. I believe that he was far more than the fiercest of all competitors. He was a vindicator who believed that "father was watching" and who could not put that father's terrible fate out of his mind. The memory of it threatened his sanity.

The fact that he recognized and feared this is revealed in a tape-recording he made, in which he describes his own view of himself: "I was like a steel spring with a growing and dangerous flaw in it. If it is wound too tight or has the slightest weak point, the spring will fly apart and then it is done for. . . ."

The last time I saw him, he was sitting in his armchair in the Atherton mansion. The place still was without lights or heat. I shook his hand in farewell, and he held it a moment longer.

"What about it? Do you think they'll remember me?" He tried to say it as if it didn't matter.

"They'll always remember you," I said.

On July 8, I received in the mail a photograph of Ty's mausoleum on the hillside in the Royston cemetery with the words scribbled on the back: "*Any time now.*" Nine days later he died in an Atlanta hospital. Before going, he opened the brown bag, piled $1 million in negotiable securities beside his bed and placed the Luger atop them.

From all of major league baseball, three men and three only appeared for his funeral.

Considerations

1. Ty Cobb was probably the most valuable baseball player in history, but his unusual escapades on the diamond are legendary. Would you say that he mellowed in his old age?
2. It was said that Cobb was "possessed by the Furies." Look up the Furies in Greek mythology. What real incident in Cobb's life may explain his anti-social behavior?

3. Freud might have diagnosed Cobb as an almost total Id. Look up this word and point out its characteristics in his behavior.
4. What are some examples of his benevolent side?
5. What was his attitude toward doctors? About women? Try to speculate as to the source of his hatred for them.
6. Judging from the odd behavior of his father, is it worthwhile to consider the possibility that Cobb may have inherited his "disorder"?
7. What is suggested about mind over body in light of his longevity despite all his ailments, any one of which might have killed an "ordinary" person?
8. Why do you think he says that "they" killed his father? Does this incident shed any light on his attitude toward women? Explain.

POETRY

Poetry is the least cherished of all the arts. Sculptures and paintings may be displayed in homes and galleries, and when they grace the walls and hallways of the home they bring great prestige to their owners. Sculpture engages the added sense of touch. Instrumental music can awaken the emotions and stir the listener to dance. Prose informs, directs, persuades, and entertains—but in less unusual language. Although poetry is the universal language of love and of all the great religions of the world, it plays but little part in the conscious, daily lives of even the most intelligent people. And it has been the student's bane.

"I, too, dislike it," says Marianne Moore, one of the finest poets of this century. But if it is sometimes "unintelligible," she adds, "the same thing may be said for all of us." Tolstoy confessed that if poetry were not written in verses he could not distinguish it from prose. To Wordsworth, it is the "spontaneous overflow of powerful feelings, recollected in tranquility." It is "news that stays news," proclaims Ezra Pound; "yet men die miserably every day," adds William Carlos Williams, "for lack of what is found there." James Dickey says it is "telling what it means to be alive on the planet." It is "the mediation of life," says Kenneth Koch. That it "should be fine is not enough," writes Horace, it must have "Charm." It should be something that "succeeding generations will not willingly let die," says Milton. Wallace Stevens views it as the embodiment of truths more appropriate to the modern world than those of all the outdated religions. "It has to find what will suffice," he says. It should "make people happy temporarily," says Koch, at least "pleasantly surprised." This kind of surprise, says E. E. Cummings, is best illustrated by the old vaudeville routine in which the straight man says, "Would you hit a woman with a baby?" and his partner says, "No. I would hit her with a brick."

Poets write their poetry for various reasons, but most would perhaps agree with Robert Lowell, who compares it with the privacy of growing a garden—"It is something you do for yourself and wouldn't want it to be televised." William Barney agrees: "A book of poetry is like an illegitimate child—you may have to defend it in court, but you wouldn't want to brag about it in public." Waiting for acclaim for it, says Don Marquis, is "like dropping a rose-petal down the Grand Canyon and waiting for the echo."

Marquis has no doubt put his finger on one of the reasons why more young people are interested in sports than in poetry: societies almost always reward aggressive rather than passive behavior, especially among males. However, it is not altogether true that sports and poetry, and athletes and poets have little in common. Dating from Homer, ("Nestor," "Wrestling to a Draw," "The Boastful Boxer"), poets have been fascinated with the precision and beauty of athletic performance. The boxing poems of Lucilius ("Boxer Loses Face and Fortune," "Advice to a Prizefighter," "The Retired Boxer"); Euripides' scathing attack on athletes ("The Greek Athlete"); and the great Roman poets, Virgil ("Entellus") and Ovid ("Atalanta"), represent only a few of the poets writing on sports in the classical era. Contemporary poets are still writing poems about sports on much the same themes—Youth, Love, The Aging Athlete, and Death. Some of them have been athletes themselves, including Robert Frost and James Dickey. Not only poets, but all of us have marveled at the beauty of the athlete in performance, and it has become a cliché to refer to it as "poetry in motion." Marianne Moore has written of such a comparison in "Baseball and Writing," as have Robert Francis in "Catch," and Robert Wallace in "Double Play."

The following poems are meant to be enjoyed, as are most poems—and most art for that matter. However, to broaden the perimeters of pleasure, a brief summary of some of the more important analytical terms will be helpful, as will a concise review of the dynamics, or inner workings, of poetry. First, poems may be enjoyed on the **literal** level. This is the manifest, or surface, meaning of the poem, the poem's "story" or "plot." Not all poems contain anything resembling an actual story, but except for a few, they all contain some literal occurrences or concrete details. Except for the final three lines, "Ball Game" by Richard Eberhart seems to be a simple description of a baserunner getting caught off first base. Yet the reader feels all along that there is something deeper here than that, the **symbolic** level. This is the area in which concrete, material things, or situations in this case, represent a higher, intangible something that is more difficult to express, or even impossible to express, otherwise. The baseball game in this poem is a symbol of life, and the runner's decision to try to make it to second base, then scrambling back to first to avert failure is loaded with various possible symbols of the many risks which occur in every normal life. The final three lines contain the poem's **analogy**. Closely resembling symbol, the analogy is a comparison of two things or situations, usually considered dissimilar, in order to extend their meaning. In this instance, childhood, in most ways the logical opposite of old age, is used as its analogy in terms of the *security* associated with both.

Another level on which poetry may be enjoyed is simply the **euphonic** level, the way a poem sounds when read. The importance of this aspect is sometimes underrated, but in fact reading poetry aloud is an old tradition, as poetry is older than writing. The best poets will say that a word's sound ranks with its meaning(s) in importance. A poem's euphony is sometimes its outstanding element, or reason for being ("Cheers"). Others in which the poet has attempted more philosophical revelations will also contain the best or most appropriate sounds the poet can achieve. The poet does this in various ways. Everyone knows there are some words that just sound better than others—"seeing the rain" in Robert Wallace's "Swimmer in the Rain," sounds better than "observing the precipitation." When poets put words together whose sounds vary dramatically they are said to be using **inflection**. Dave Smith begins "Night Fishing for Blues" with "The big-jawed Bluefish . . .," capitalizing on the euphonic effect of the five different vowel sounds of those three words.

It is said that English is no longer rich in inflection, so poets have found it necessary to use **rhyme** to compensate. Developed by the French Provencals, roving minstrels, in the fourteenth century, rhyme has provided poets with an effective euphonic tool, creating an "illusion" of inflection. Although there are many kinds, rhyme is generally the repetition of similar sounds at the ends of lines, either successively, or in varying patterns. Since Walt Whitman, however, poets have relied on rhyme less and less, despite the opinion of Robert Frost (who had an uncanny talent for it) that "writing poetry without rhyme is like playing tennis without a net"; in other words, it is too easy. But many poets feel that it is more difficult to make a poem sound good by relying only on the natural inflectional beauty of the language. And we are all painfully familiar with the excesses of poor doggerel in which the aspiring poet inverts syntax and throws in a second, needless thought, just to make a rhyme.

Sometimes, the way a poem *looks* can be an important factor. Most poets strive to make their poems pleasing to the eye, usually by arranging them in lines of more or less even lengths; but sometimes poets shape poems to create a visual representation of the poem's theme or subject. Maxine Kumin's "400-Meter Freestyle," for example, is shaped like the laps of a swimming race.

A final level on which poetry may be enjoyed and one which incorporates the symbolic is the **mythical** level, the verbal imitation of ritual. The myth is the timeless world of imagination, of dreams, of a world not in which things have happened but one in which things *can* happen. Originating in this vaporous world, myths are fanciful stories that give meaning to a mysterious and often forbidding universe. An unfortunate misconception of "myth" that has developed over the years is that it is a "lie," when, if anything, the opposite is the case. Although we now know, through science, that many old stories attempting to explain certain occurrences in nature—such as earthquakes, lightning, and the sun "rising"—are not literally true, they nevertheless contain many symbolic truths. Joseph Campbell, perhaps today's greatest authority on myths, says we tend to be more honest in our dreams than when awake, and that myths are but "public dreams." (For an example of the importance of myth in poetry, see the dialogue on James Dickey's "The Lifeguard" at the end of this introduction.)

In addition to these areas which may enhance the appreciation of poetry, there is also the special language of poetry, often called **figurative** language —the rich and heightened technique of saying one thing in terms of something else. However, just as we are painfully aware of the excesses associated with rhyme, so have we seen the often humorous attempts by some "poets" to achieve immortality by using such expressions as "finny tribe" for "fish," and "mud's thirsty sister" for "dust." Furthermore, there is for some reason an irresistible temptation among some to overemphasize the *terminology* associated with this technique. Those who would never consider it necessary to learn the names of the musical notes and techniques of a piece of music in order to enjoy listening to it, may see nothing unusual about overemphasizing the terminology of poetic technique. An understanding of a poem's *meaning*, however, can be greatly beneficial.

The most frequently used figures of speech in poetry are **metaphor** and **simile.** A simile is an obvious comparison between two ordinarily different things, connected with "like," "as," "than," or a similar word. In "The Base Stealer," Francis refers to the baserunner as "taut like a tightrope-walker." A metaphor is a similar comparison but without the connecting words: "—Why, life's a carnival!" says Elder Olson in "Ice-Skaters," and "His eyes / Were gun barrels," says Jon Stallworthy in "First Blood." In "On The College Archery Range," Wallace refers to the girls as "death's small deer."

Then, there is **personification,** the attributing of human qualities to inanimate things. In "The Skaters" Wordsworth refers to "a star / That fled" and "shadowy banks" that "came sweeping through the darkness. . . ." Closely akin to personification is **apostrophe,** a technique in which something is addressed: in "For the Last Wolverine," Dickey addresses the "Dear God of the wildness of poetry . . ." An **oxymoron** is the use together of two words of opposite meaning, such as "bloodthirsty / Non-survivor" in that same poem. **Hyperbole** is the exaggeration of the characteristics of someone or something, as in John Updike's parody, "Superman." Other terms are included in the Glossary.

After the following poem is an example of a dialogue that could occur between a teacher and a student. Notice how the student slowly becomes aware of meanings he has seen in the poem, especially in the realm of myth.

JAMES DICKEY

The Lifeguard

In a stable of boats I lie still,
From all sleeping children hidden.
The leap of a fish from its shadow
Makes the whole lake instantly tremble.
With my foot on the water, I feel
The moon outside

Take on the utmost of its power.
I rise and go out through the boats.
I set my broad sole upon silver,
On the skin of the sky, on the moonlight,
Stepping outward from earth onto water
In quest of the miracle

This village of children believed
That I could perform as I dived
For one who had sunk from my sight.
I saw his cropped haircut go under.
I leapt, and my steep body flashed
Once, in the sun.

Dark drew all the light from my eyes.
Like a man who explores his death
By the pull of his slow-moving shoulders,
I hung head down in the cold,
Wide-eyed, contained, and alone
Among the weeds.

And my fingertips turned into stone
From clutching immovable blackness.
Time after time I leapt upward
Exploding in breath, and fell back
From the change in the children's faces
At my defeat.

Beneath them I swam to the boathouse
With only my life in my arms
To wait for the lake to shine back
At the risen moon with such power
That my steps on the light of the ripples
Might be sustained.

Beneath me is nothing but brightness
Like the ghost of a snowfield in summer.
As I move toward the center of the lake,
Which is also the center of the moon,
I am thinking of how I may be
The savior of one

Who has already died in my care.
The dark trees fade from around me.
The moon's dust hovers together.
I call softly out, and the child's
Voice answers through blinding water.
Patiently, slowly,

He rises, dilating to break
The surface of stone with his forehead.
He is one I do not remember
Having ever seen in his life.
The ground I stand on is trembling
Upon his smile.

I wash the black mud from my hands.
On a light given off by the grave
I kneel in the quick of the moon
At the heart of a distant forest
And hold in my arms a child
Of water, water, water.

A Dialogue on James
Dickey's "The Lifeguard"

Professor: What are the literal events in this poem?
Student: A child has drowned and the lifeguard is hiding in the boathouse in shame.
Professor: Is that all?
Student: I think he finds the child later on that night.
Professor: Why do you say that?
Student: Because the lifeguard walks out across the water and calls the boy's name and he rises up from the bottom. Then, the lifeguard carries him to shore in his arms.
Professor: Is this part to be taken literally?
Student: What do you mean?
Professor: Well, can a person actually walk on water? Can someone be raised from the dead?

Student:	I wondered about that. Is the lifeguard supposed to be a god or something like that?
Professor:	Earlier I asked you about the literal events in this poem. What other kinds of events are there?
Student:	Well, is it something like religion?
Professor:	I think you are on to something there, but we will get back to that question later. Aside from the literal level, what other level is there?
Student:	The figurative? I get it. The lifeguard is only imagining that he walks across the lake and raises the dead boy up. It is nice to imagine something like that.
Professor:	I think you are right. But why does the lifeguard swim under water to the boathouse and hide, instead of helping with the search until the boy is found?
Student:	I think the poem states clearly that he dived into the water "time after time," I think it says. And, as I said before, he is ashamed.
Professor:	Yes, you did say that, didn't you. But why is he ashamed?
Student:	For several reasons, I guess. He is young, right? He is probably in some kind of trance because the boy "died in his care," as the poem says. He feels responsible. And guilty. I guess he is crazy with guilt. And he just can't face the boy's friends. He can't stand to see their faces after failing them again. And the prospect of seeing the boy's body may have been too much for him. So he slipped away and hid in the boathouse till it got dark. In shame.
Professor:	I would say you are right on target. Now, let's get back to that religious element you mentioned earlier. Man's helplessness in the face of death has inspired countless myths. Do you see evidence of such a myth in this poem?
Student:	I'm not sure what you mean. Do you mean religion?
Professor:	It is in the realm of what some call religion. Death is too ominous to face unarmed. So we arm ourselves—comfort ourselves—with imaginative stories of people being raised from the dead. Many myths have been superseded by scientific explanation, such as those attempting to explain volcano eruptions, earthquakes, tidal waves, the movement of heavenly bodies, lightning. But science has not yet come close to explaining death. So these myths persist. The young lifeguard calls on this myth to sustain him in his trauma. I think you are absolutely right in calling it that. It is always a tragedy when a child dies, but it would be magnified a thousand times if you felt responsible. He wants the child to be alive so much that he has a vision in which he sees himself, radiating with the moon's magical light, walk out across the water and raise that child up from the dead.
Student:	It's a beautiful vision.
Professor:	Of course it is. And it sustains the lifeguard, for a while, anyway. Perhaps until he can accept what has happened.
Student:	I guess myths are pretty important, then.
Professor:	They are very important. And we all need them. Those who say they don't may need them most of all.

INITIATION, FATHERS AND CHILDREN

Before I am old
I shall have written him one
Poem maybe as cold
And passionate as the dawn.

—**W. B. Yeats**

PHILIP BOOTH

First Lesson

Lie back, daughter, let your head
be tipped back in the cup of my hand.
Gently, and I will hold you. Spread
your arms wide, lie out on the stream
and look high at the gulls. A dead-
man's float is face down. You will dive
and swim soon enough where this tidewater
ebbs to the sea. Daughter, believe
me, when you tire on the long thrash
to your island, lie up, and survive.
As you float now, where I held you
and let go, remember when fear
cramps your heart what I told you:
lie gently and wide to the light-year
stars, lie back, and the sea will hold you.

Considerations

1. Does the advice given in this poem apply to more than swimming? Explain.
2. Contrast the attitude and advice of the father in this poem with that of Clifford Hill in "First Practice."

GARY GILDNER

First Practice

After the doctor checked to see
we weren't ruptured,
the man with the short cigar took us
under the grade school,
where we went in case of attack
or storm, and said
he was Clifford Hill, he was
a man who believed dogs
ate dogs, he had once killed
for his country, and if
there were any girls present
for them to leave now.
                              No one
left. OK, he said, he said I take
that to mean you are hungry
men who hate to lose as much
as I do. OK. Then
he made two lines of us
facing each other,
and across the way, he said,
is the man you hate most
in the world,
and if we are to win
that title I want to see how.
But I don't want to see
any marks when you're dressed,
he said. He said, *Now.*

Considerations

1. From whose point of view do we get this poem? Exactly how does this particular
   point of view make the poem so effective?
2. Discuss Clifford Hill. Are the Clifford Hills of the world a positive or negative force?
3. Explain the football-warfare connection in this poem.
4. Is Hill "overdone" in this poem? Or is he a realistic characterization?

JON STALLWORTHY

First Blood

It was. The breech smelling of oil,
The stock of resin—buried snug
In the shoulder. Not too much recoil
At the firing of the first slug

(Jubilantly into the air)
Not yet too little. Targets pinned
Against a tree: shot down; and there
Abandoned to the sniping wind.

My turn first to carry the gun.
Indian file and camouflaged
With contours of green shade and sun
We ghosted between larch and larch.

A movement between branches—thump
Of a fallen cone. The barrel
Jumps, making branches jump
Higher, dislodging the squirrel

To the next tree. Your turn, my turn.
The silhouette retracts its head.
A hit. "Let's go back to the lawn."
"We can't leave it carrying lead

"For the rest of its life. Reload.
Finish him off. Reload again."
It was now *him*, and when he showed
The sky cracked like a window pane.

He broke away: traversed a full
Half dozen trees: vanished. Had found
A hole? We watched that terrible
Slow spiral to the clubbing ground.

His back was to the tree. His eyes
Were gun barrels. He was dumb,
And we could not see past the size
Of his hands or hear for the drum

In his side. Four shots point-blank
To dull his eyes, a fifth to stop
The shiver in his clotted flank.
A fling of earth. As we stood up

The larches closed their ranks. And when
Earth would not muffle the drumming blood
We, like dishonored soldiers, ran
The gauntlet of a darkening wood.

Considerations

1. This poem describes the horror that almost every boy has suffered. Why does the reference to the squirrel switch from "it" to "him"?
2. Explain, "when he showed / The sky cracked like a window pane."
3. Discuss the final stanza.

WILLIAM D. BARNEY

A Post Card
Out of Panama

The young man at the plate, bat bristling,
studies us in a hazel calm.
Whatever world and wind serve up,
he'll meet it. Just the right aplomb,
none of that sneering, Casey-like,
how he'll unseam the white horsehide.
He knows his muscle and his eye
feed on a fast one, high, inside.

It turns out he's not up to hit;
the thing is history: on the back
in a bold script tough as his swing
he writes, and you can hear it crack:
"After I'd hit the longest drive
ever seen on the Isthmus." He is proud.
I hear that jungle-bordered park,
the roar going up from a wild crowd.

He had a thin time growing up,
but once filled out, he made a man;
tasted some triumphs, and more losses,
he lived clean as the strongest can.
Look at him, come to his high hour,
leaning his body toward the pitch
with every sinew, bone and cell alive—
my father was exceedingly rich.

Considerations

1. What does the title tell the reader about this poem?
2. Discuss the easy, subtle, natural rhyme.
3. Discuss the meaning of the baseball metaphor of the third stanza.

STEPHEN VINCENT

Basketball

I never let you come to the games. I never
invited you. You never asked. You never
saw me on the court handle the round skin
of the basketball. You never came to see me
spread my warm fingers like the edges of stars
around the ball as I went like a smooth fox
down the court my tennis shoes squeaking faster
than a grasshopper through clover. At sixteen
I travelled fast
father. Lay in, set shot, jump shot, bounce pass,
chest pass, bucking, elbowing as high as I could,
reacher for what was never given, the smooth flow
of the ball arching high towards the rim, its high arc
lifting subtly down, a smooth swish through
the star shapes of the unbroken
white net. Let me play that game again. I was on the court
with Willie, Leroy, Hobo & Sam. I the only white
with four blacks. Don't get me wrong. I was scared of them
as you of me or I of you. But it began. Somebody
poked me in the eye, it stung, and I released everything
traveling up and down the court a young man
with a quick gun and a sharp elbow. For the first time
we held together like a rapid running loom weaving
up and down between the other players who held together
stiff as strings as we broke through all their empty
edges. Suddenly it was no game. Perfect harmony
of movement and song. The referee could blow no whistle.
In victory I always refused you
entry. This time
I am going to win.

Considerations

1. What father-son relationship is suggested in the last two lines?
2. Does the poem suggest a sense of regret on the part of the speaker? Support your answer.
3. Discuss the effectiveness of the vivid similes.

DABNEY STUART
Ties

When I faded back to pass
Late in the game, as one
Who has been away some time
Fades back into memory,
My father who had been nodding
At home by the radio,
Would wake asking
My mother, who had not
Been listening, "What's the score?"
And she would answer, "Tied."
While the pass I threw
Hung high in the brilliant air
Beneath the dark, like a star.

Considerations

1. Explain the double meaning of the title.
2. Does the speaker imply any regret that his parents do not come to watch him play? Support your answer.
3. Why does the mother answer "Tied" when the father asks the score?

WILLIAM BUTLER YEATS
The Fisherman

Although I can see him still,
The freckled man who goes
To a grey place on a hill
In Grey Connemara clothes
At dawn to cast his flies,
It's long since I began
To call up to the eyes
This wise and simple man.
All day I'd looked in the face
What I had hoped 'twould be
To write for my own race
And the reality;
The living men that I hate,

The dead man that I loved,
The craven man in his seat,
The insolent unreproved,
And no knaves brought to book
Who has won a drunken cheer,
The witty man and his joke
Aimed at the commonest ear,
The clever man who cries
The catch-cries of the clown,
The beating down of the wise
And great Art beaten down.

Maybe a twelvemonth since
Suddenly I began,
In scorn of this audience,
Imagining a man,
And his sun-freckled face,
And grey Connemara cloth,
Climbing up to a place
Where stone is dark under froth,
And the down-turn of his twist
When the flies drop in the stream;
A man who does not exist,
A man who is but a dream;
And cried, 'Before I am old
I shall have written him one
Poem maybe as cold
And passionate as the dawn.'

Considerations

1. To whom is this poem a tribute? How do you know?
2. Is this poem "cold / And passionate as the dawn"? Explain.

BETTY ADCOCK

The Sixth Day

Here where the river is naming itself
in heat that clings like a history,
two men are walking through wildgrape,
over seasons of pine.
They walk with their knowledge of snakes,
the old dance of the hunter, though the step
is arthritic now, altered.

One is my father. He has come
to fish with his oldest companion.
And this is not the place, but near to it,
near the deep woods, the thick net of beasts
these men have lived in as one might
stay on in a treacherous house
because it is home.

Now they sit out an afternoon's sweat,
salting the river with stories
of hounds with the gift of speech,
of guns with second sight, of deaths
that struck back.

It is like the way they run fingers
over the sharp dust of antlers
and boar's jaws and the head of a wildcat
my father has nailed in his barn.

They talk, and the thickets tangle
around them, move closer. Their compasses
break. They come again upon phosphorous
in the deadwood of midnight, brighter than foxes.

The two men have drawn up a few fish.
The day runs them down, a dragonfly
dimming on water. They rise
for their homes in that light.
And the red wolf is not here,
nor the bear nor the wildcat
whose head on the wall is not magic enough
to call up a mate in the pinewoods,
to raise the dead.

The two go home to the structures
of their children. There are no eyes
in the backs of their lives
to see what I imagine: two images
of red clay, two rough
thumbed-on faces, and not gleaming
not holy, but a simple color of place,
an absolute love without knowledge, dark
with the absence of pity.

I have guessed for my father an innocence
pale as water. He moves through it,
away from me. Breaking that surface,

he strides in his sleep the deep land
empty of animals, empty
except for the quick coil of memory
under the foot of his sleeping,
the sure, small dream that kills,
that keeps.

Considerations

1. What is the significance of the title. Does it have biblical overtones?
2. What is the "sure, small dream that kills, / that keeps"?
3. What is the speaker's vision of her father?

ANONYMOUS

Cynisca

(Trans. by Tom Dodge)

I, Cynisca, who descend from Spartan kings,
    Place this stone myself to mark
The race I won with my quick-footed steeds,
    The only woman in all of Greece to win.

Considerations

1. Although Cynisca's victory could not have occurred in the Olympic Games, as women were excluded from competition, it was nevertheless a rare and momentous one. It may have happened in Sparta, where women enjoyed more freedom than in any other part of Greece.
2. This victory obviously occurred in a men's event (four-horse chariot racing). If women can qualify for men's competition today, should they be allowed to enter? Support your answer.

NANCY JONES

Running Blind

Slender man in jogging duds
And glasses dim,
You fall in step with me, you think,
And run along beside
Until I tire of you and turn aside.
Translucent, you offer beer at my door
To ransom words or chancing smile;
Squinting in the noonday sun,
"My wife doesn't know me,"
As you blink and polish your lenses
With the handkerchief that wiped
The sweat from your brow.
It just won't work, my friend;
Take your Coors and go away.
Go home to your clouded lady
Opaque non-communicant.
Unstop her ears, unstitch her eyes
And leave me
To run my life
Alone.

Considerations

1. In these automated days, jogging has become a substitute for work. What other activities has it become a substitute for, according to the implications of this poem?
2. List the characteristics of popular culture mentioned in this poem.

345

ANACREON
The Thracian Filly
(Trans. by Tom Dodge)

Thracian filly, why glance at me indifferently,
then prance away sidelong as if I were a fool?

I could bridle you and straddle you with ease,
reins in hand, for a turn around the track.

But you frolic in the meadow, still in clover,
never having had a master ride astride you.

Considerations

1. The famous steeds from Thrace were known for their grace and fine mettle. Translators differ but this one suggests that the poem is not really about a horse at all. Explain.
2. What is the idiomatic meaning of "still in clover"?

ROBERT WALLACE
On the College Archery Range

Girls, at bows, string concentric blooms
on the distances of aim,
these leafy afternoons;
huntresses, in a game.

The arrows as often lodge in trees or grass
as in the rings. They practice
only grace
that pierces lovers—for the fact is

they are themselves (beautifully)
death's small deer.
The beauty is, how wholly
they attend their huntings here.

Considerations

1. Would devotees of the women's movement take exception with certain implications of this poem? Explain.
2. Why are the "girls" called "death's small deer"?

CALLIMACHUS

The One Who
Runs Away

(Trans. by Tom Dodge)

Hunters search out every mountain hollow, Epicydes,
    Even in the snow, to trace the scent of some gazelle
And satisfy their lust. But if someone tell them, "Shoot!
    A sleeping beast!" they'll pass it by. Love's like that—
The trollop's swollen lips are nice, but she's just another lay.
    I prefer the nether-treasure of the one who runs away.

Considerations

1. Discuss the analogy in this poem. Although it was written over 2,000 years ago, is it still applicable today?
2. Just exactly how universal is it? Are there those who are perfectly willing to shoot a "sleeping beast"? Explain.

LUCILIUS

The Retired Boxer

(Trans. by Tom Dodge)

Cleombrotus retired from the ring
    and married some female bruiser
with a repertoire of punches to equal
    any he absorbed in his Olympian bouts.
Now, home is worse than the ring
    because she never lets up,
even in bed—and she beats him there, too.

Considerations

1. What familiar theme does this poem employ?
2. Is the satire intended to be taken seriously? Explain.

OVID

Atalanta

(Trans. by Rolfe Humphries)

You may have heard (she said) about a girl
Who could outrun the swiftest men. The story
Is very true: she really could outrun them.
It would be hard to say, though, whether her speed
Or beauty earned more praise. She was very lovely.
She asked the oracle, one day, to give her
Advice on marriage. "You don't need a husband,"
The god replied, "Avoid that habit! Still,
I know you will not: you will keep your life,
And lose yourself." So Atalanta, frightened,
Lived in the shadowy woods, a single woman,
Harshly rejecting urgent throngs of suitors.
"No one gets me who cannot beat me running,
Race me!" she told them, "Wife and marriage-chamber
Go to the winner, but the slow ones get
The booby-prize of death. Those are my terms."
The terms were harsh, but beauty has such power
That those harsh terms were met by many suitors,
Foolhardy fellows. Watching the cruel race,
Hippomenes had some remarks to make:
"Is any woman worth it? These young men
Strike me as very silly." But when he saw her,
Her face, her body naked, with such beauty
As mine is, or as yours would be, Adonis,
If you were woman, he was struck with wonder,
Threw up his hands and cried: "I beg your pardon,
Young men, I judged you wrongly; I did not know
The value of the prize!" And he caught fire
From his own praising, hoped that no younger runner
Would beat her, feared they might, was worried, jealous.
"Why don't I try?" he thought, "God helps the bold."
And, swifter than his thought, the girl sped by
On winged feet, swifter than Scythian arrow,
Yet not too swift for a young man's admiration,
And running made her livelier: the breeze
Bore back the streaming pinions of her sandals,
Her hair was tossed back over ivory shoulders,
The colored ribbons fluttered at her knees,
And a light flush came over her girlish body
The way a crimson awning, over marble,

Tints it in pastel color. As he watched her,
She crossed the finish line, received the crown
Of victory, and the beaten suitors, groaning,
Were lead away to death.
                                    'Hippomenes,
Undaunted, came from the crowd; he fixed his eyes
On Atalanta, and he made his challenge:
"This is too easy, beating all these turtles!
Race against me!" he said, "If you are beaten
It will be no disgrace. Megareus is my father,
Whose grandfather was Neptune, and that makes me
Great-grandson of the king of all the oceans.
Nor is my worth inferior to my race.
Beat me, and you will have something to boast of!"
Listening, looking almost tenderly
At that young man, she wondered, in confusion,
Which would be better, to win or lose. "What god"
She thought, "So hates the young and handsome
He wants to ruin this one, tempting him
To risk his precious life to marry me?
I do not think I'm worth it. I am not moved
By his beauty (though I could be); I am moved
Because he seems so young: he does not move me,
Only his age. What of his manly courage,
His nerve, his claim to proud descent, his love
For me, so great a love that death, he claims,
Is an advantage if he cannot have me?
Go while you may, O stranger, flee this marriage,
There is too much blood upon it. Any girl
Would marry you, and wisely. Why do I care,
Why worry for him, when I have slain so many?
Let him look out for himself, or let him die
Since the death of all those others has not warned him,
Since life is such a bore! Is he to die
Because he wants to live with me? Is death
To be the price of love? I shall be hated
In victory. It is not my fault. Poor fellow,
I wish you would forget it but, since you are crazy,
I wish at least you could run a little faster!
He looks like a girl, almost. I wish he had never
Laid eyes on me. He should have lived. If I
Were luckier, if the fates allowed me marriage,
He was the only one I would have taken
To bed with any pleasure." Atalanta
Was green in love, untutored—she did not know
What she was doing, and loved, and did not know it.

Meanwhile the people and her father, restless,
Were clamoring for the race. Hippomenes
Called me in supplication: "O, may Venus
Be near, I pray, assist my daring, favor
The love she gave me!" And a gentle breeze
Bore this soft prayer my way; it moved my heart,
I own, and there was little time to aid him.
There is a field the natives call Tamasus,
The richest part of Cyprus, which the ancients
Hallowed for me, and built my temples there,
And in a field there stands a golden tree,
Shining with golden leaves and branches rustling
With the soft click of gold, and golden apples
Are the fruit of that golden tree. I came from there
With three such apples in my hand, and no one
Saw me except Hippomenes, and I
Told him how he should use them.
                            'The trumpets sounded
The start: the pair, each crouching low, shot forward,
Skimming the sand with flying feet, so lightly
They could run on waves and never wet their sandals,
They could run on fields of grain and never bend them.
He heard them cheering: "Go, Hippomenes,
Lean to the work, use all your strength: go, go,
You are sure to win!" I could not tell you whether
The cheering pleased him more, or Atalanta.
How many times, when she could have passed, she lingered,
Slowed down to see his face, and, most unwilling,
Sprinted ahead! And now his breathing labored,
Came in great sobbing gasps, and the finish line
Was a long way off, and he tossed one golden apple,
The first one, down. She looked at it with wonder,
Eager to have the shining fruit, she darted
Out of the course, and picked it up, still rolling,
The golden thing. He gained the lead again
As all the people roared applause. She passed him
Again, and once again lost ground to follow
The toss of the second apple, and once more
Caught up and sprinted past him. "O be near me,
Gift-bringing Goddess, help me now!" he cried,
And this time threw the last third apple farther,
Angling it off the course, way to one side.
She hesitated, only for a moment,
Whether to chase it, but I made her do it,
And made the fruit weigh more, so she was hindered
Both by the burden and her own delay.

To run my story quickly, as the race
Was run, the girl was beaten, and the winner
Led off his prize.

Considerations

1. In this poem, Venus is telling Adonis the story of Atalanta, the princess who vowed to marry the man who could outrun her. How does this myth invert the traditional story of the woman chasing and winning the man?
2. What help does Hippomenes have? Is there symbolic meaning in the role Venus (Goddess of Love) plays in his victory?

JOHN BETJEMAN

A Subaltern's Love Song

Miss J. Hunter Dunn, Miss J. Hunter Dunn,
Furnish'd and burnish'd by Aldershot sun,
What strenuous singles we played after tea,
We in the tournament—you against me!

Love-thirty, love-forty, oh! weakness of joy,
The speed of a swallow, the grace of a boy,
With carefullest carelessness, gaily you won,
I am weak from your loveliness, Joan Hunter Dunn.

Miss Joan Hunter Dunn, Miss Joan Hunter Dunn,
How mad I am, sad I am, glad that you won.
The warm-handled racket is back in its press,
But my shock-headed victor, she loves me no less.

Her father's euonymus shines as we walk,
And swing past the summer-house, buried in talk,
And cool the verandah that welcomes us in
To the six-o'clock news and a lime-juice and gin.

The scent of the conifers, sound of the bath,
The view from my bedroom of moss-dappled path,
As I struggle with double-end evening tie,
For we dance at the Golf Club, my victor and I.

On the floor of her bedroom lie blazer and shorts
And the cream-colored walls are be-trophied with sports,
And westering, questioning settles the sun
On your low-leaded Window, Miss Joan Hunter Dunn.

The Hillman is waiting, the light's in the hall,
The pictures of Egypt are bright on the wall,
My sweet, I am standing beside the oak stair
And there on the landing's the light on your hair.

By roads "not adopted," by woodlanded ways,
She drove to the club in the late summer haze,
Into nine-o'clock Camberly, heavy with bells
And mushroomy, pine-woody, evergreen smells.

Miss Joan Hunter Dunn, Miss Joan Hunter Dunn,
I can hear from the car-park the dance has begun.
Oh! full Surrey twilight! importunate band!
Oh! strongly adorable tennis-girl's hand!

Around us are Rovers and Austins afar,
Above us, the intimate roof of the car,
And here on my right is the girl of my choice,
With the tilt of her nose and the chime of her voice.

And the scent of her wrap, and the words never said,
And the ominous, ominous dancing ahead.
We sat in the car-park till twenty to one
And now I'm engaged to Miss Joan Hunter Dunn.

Considerations

1. This poem is marked by the subdued exhilaration of its romance. Are we to infer that the speaker loses the tennis match because Miss J. Hunter Dunn is a better player or because he is merely weak with love? What is the significance of the word "love" in tennis?
2. What is a subaltern? Do you think the speaker is overly awed by her "class"? How important is social class in this poem? Speculate as to its place and time.

MABEL M. KUYKENDALL

Baseball Pitcher

Strange that we should sit here like this
and I be telling you the story of my life . . .
on our first date.

At five I was the star of tin-can shinny
on our street.
At ten I found that I could put a ball
anywhere I wanted it.
In grammar school I was pitching
for the big boy's club.

By the time I reached fifteen,
during every recess at school,
every afternoon till dark,
and every Saturday and Sunday
I practiced and I practiced;
and the ball was obedient.
I learned direction. I learned control.
I learned speed. I mastered slowdown.

When I was twenty I knew what I could do.
I analyzed every move I made. I found
that where I fixed my eye, the ball would go.
I set my goals. I was the highest paid
player in our league.
I won what my eye was set on.

My eye is fixed on you.

Considerations

1. What is "tin-can shinny"?
2. What does this poem suggest about the ability of girls to play a "boy's" sport?
3. Discuss the possibility of a double meaning in the third stanza.

W. H. AUDEN

Hunting Season

A shot: from crag to crag
    The tell-tale echoes trundle;
Some feathered he-or-she
    Is now a lifeless bundle
And, proud into a kitchen, some
Example of our tribe will come.

Down in the startled valley
    Two lovers break apart;
He hears the roaring oven
    Of a witch's heart;
Behind his murmurs of her name
She sees a marksman taking aim.

Reminded of the hour
And that his chair is hard
A deathless verse half done
One interrupted bard
Postpones his dying with a dish
Of several suffocated fish.

Considerations

1. Explain how, in these brief verses, Auden manages to poke considerable jest at hunters, lovers, and a poet.
2. Explain the double meaning of the second verse.

ROGER McGOUGH

40———Love

middle	aged
couple	playing
ten	nis
when	the
game	ends
and	they
go	home
the	net
will	still
be	be
tween	them

Considerations

1. Explain the significance of the title.
2. Explain the visual analogy in this poem. Is the content more important than its shape, or the other way about? Explain.
3. Is there a "net" between middle-aged couples only, or does it exist between every two people?

EDNA ST. VINCENT MILLAY

Huntsman,
What Quarry?

"Huntsman, what quarry
On the dry hill
Do your hounds harry?

When the red oak is bare
And the white oak still
Rattles its leaves
In the cold air:
What fox runs there?"

"Girl, gathering acorns
In the cold autumn,
I hunt the hot pads
That ever run before,
I hunt the pointed mask
That makes no reply,
I hunt the red brush
Of remembered joy."

"To tame or to destroy?"
"To destroy."

"Huntsman, hard by
In a wood of grey beeches
Whose leaves are on the ground,
Is a house with a fire;
You can see the smoke from here.
There's supper and a soft bed
And not a soul around.
Come with me there;
Bide there with me;
And let the fox run free."

The horse that he rode on
Reached down its neck,
Blew upon the acorns,
Nuzzled them aside;
The sun was near setting;
He thought, "Shall I heed her?"
He thought, "Shall I take her
For a one-night's bride?"

He smelled the sweet smoke,
He looked the lady over;
Her hand was on his knee;
But like a flame from cover
The red fox broke—
And "Hoick! Hoick!" cried he.

Considerations

1. What are the "hot pads," the "pointed mask," and the "red brush / Of remembered joy"?
2. Why does the hunter refuse the lady's offer? Would you call him a true sportsman?

ITS OWN REWARD

The body too can be
Spirit, when set free
By pure delight of motion
Without destination.

—Elder Olson

WILLIAM WORDSWORTH

The Skaters

From *The Prelude*

And in the frosty season, when the sun
Was set, and visible for many a mile
The cottage windows blazed through twilight gloom,
I heeded not their summons: happy time
It was indeed for all of us—for me
It was a time of rapture! Clear and loud
The village clock tolled six,—I wheeled about
Proud and exulting like an untired horse
That cares not for his home. All shod with steel,
We hissed along the polished ice in game
Confederate, imitative of the chase
And woodland pleasures,—the resounding horn,
The pack loud chiming, and the hunted hare.
So through the darkness and the cold we flew,
And not a voice was idle; with the din
Smitten, the precipices rang aloud;
The leafless trees and every icy crag
Tinkled like iron; while far distant hills
Into the tumult sent on alien sound
Of melancholy not unnoticed, while the stars
Eastward were sparkling clear, and in the west
The orange sky of evening died away.
Not seldom from the uproar I retired
Into a silent bay, or sportively

Glanced sideway, leaving the tumultuous throng
To cut across the reflex of a star
That fled, and, flying still before me, gleamed
Upon the glassy plain; and oftentimes,
When we had given our bodies to the wind,
And all the shadowy banks on either side
Came sweeping through the darkness, spinning still
The rapid line of motion, then at once
Have I, reclining back upon my heels,
Stopped short; yet still the solitary cliffs
Wheeled by me—even as if the earth had rolled
With visible motion her diurnal round!
Behind me did they stretch in solemn train,
Feebler and feebler, and I stood and watched
Till all was tranquil as a dreamless sleep.

Considerations

1. Although fine, Wordsworth's poetry has been the inspiration for countless sentimental Christmas card verses. Explain how Wordsworth's poem, while romantic,
   rises above sentimentality.
2. Explain the motif of mysticism in this poem.
3. Discuss the emphasis on motion. On oneness.

EDMUND BLUNDEN

Winter: East Anglia

In a frosty sunset
       So fiery red with cold
The footballers' onset
       Rings out glad and bold;
Then boys from daily tether
       with famous dogs at heel
In starlight meet together
       And to farther hedges steal;
Where the rats are pattering
       In and out the stacks,
Owls with hatred chattering
       Swoop at the terriers' backs
And, frost forgot, the chase grows hot
       Till a rat's a foolish prize,

But the cornered weasel stands his ground,
Shrieks at the dogs and boys set round,
Shrieks as he knows they stand all round,
And hard as winter dies.

Considerations

1. "Winter: East Anglia" is a rustic poem that recalls a time when life was simpler. In what period do you think it is set? Why?
2. The last line is a counterpoint to the charming mood created by Blunden in the previous lines. What does it literally say? What does it suggest?

ELDER OLSON

Ice-Skaters

Snow-hills all about,
And snowy woods; and snow
Falling: a full moon's out;

The river's frozen; across
Its avenue of ice
Vivid skaters swirl

In the cold, in the moon's light.
Look, look: the young, the old,
Set moving by delight.

—The whole town's on the ice!
Whirling in a gay
Preposterous ballet.

Look, the strides, the glides,
Cossack-leaps, dervish-twirls,
Clown-tumblings, clown-falls!

Racers, rapt in speed
As in an ecstasy,
Swerving in a flash of sleet;

Lovers, hand in hand,
Enchanted by their own
Music without sound,

And the older pairs,
A little clumsy now,
But merry as waltzing bears,

And children, intently
Scuffing foot by foot,
Stiffly rocking in and out,

All intricately winding in a Christmas-colored maze
With Lord, what a racket! till the hills
Go wild with echoes, bellows like mad bulls

And in the dark ravines
Beneath the crystal floor
Fish quiver, and wave their fins.

The town clock chimes the hour
Unheeded: let it chime,
Time has lost its power.

What monkey-shines, what fun!
Flesh is no burden now,
It never lay so lightly on the bone.

The body too can be
Spirit, when set free
By pure delight of motion

Without destination;
Shows its own fantasy,
Wit, and imagination.

Is this the being Lear could call
A poor, bare,
Forked animal?

Strike that out; say this,
That in a harsh season,
Above a dark abyss,

The mortal creature
Rejoiced in its own nature;
Revelled, itself the reason.

—Why, life's a carnival! Snow
Falls like confetti now;
The moon, in comic mood,

Turns to a grotesque
Snowball; hides in cloud;
Comes back in a clown's mask.

The skaters swirl and swirl;
All their motions cry
It is joy, sheer joy,

That makes the atoms dance
And wings the flying stars
And speeds the sun upon his golden course.

Considerations

1. Discuss the mood of this poem. What is the narrator's view of man as opposed to Lear's?
2. What is the "dark abyss" used by Olson as a counterpoint?
3. Compare this poem with Wordsworth's "The Skaters." How is the idea of motion significant in both?

ROBERT WALLACE

Swimmer in the Rain

No one but him
seeing the rain
start—a fine scrim
far down the bay,
smoking, advancing
between two grays
till the salt-grass rustles
and the creek's mirror
in which he stands
to his neck, like clothing
cold, green, supple,
begins to ripple.

The drops bounce up,
little fountains
all around him,
swift, momentary—
every drop tossed back
in air atop
its tiny column—

glass balls balancing
upon glass nipples,
lace of dimples,
a stubble of silver
stars, eye-level,
incessant, wild.

White, dripping, tall,
ignoring the rain,
an egret fishes
in the creek's margin,
dips to the minnows'
sky, under which,
undisturbed, steady
as faith the tide pulls.
Mussels hang
like grapes on a piling.
Wet is wet.

The swimmer settles
to the hissing din—
a glass bombardment,
parade of diamonds,
blinks, jacks of light,
wee Brancusi's, chromes
like grease-beads sizzling,
myriad—and swims
slowly, elegantly,
climbing tide's ladder
hand over hand
toward the distant bay.

Hair and eye-brows
streaming, sleek crystal
scarving his throat—
no one but him.

Considerations

1. Many poems have a controlling characteristic—the imagery in this one is almost
   overwhelming. Make a list of this poem's images and discuss the ones that impress
   you most.
2. Discuss the implication of this poem that it is more exhilarating to be a participant
   than a spectator. How does this poem celebrate the ecstasy of being alive?

ROBERT WALLACE

After the Swimmer

Clear, the shaken water
busies in its claws
clouds, light,
from which he climbed.

Considerations

1. This poem has seventeen syllables. Why isn't it a haiku?
2. Why is the water busy? What are its "claws," its "clouds," its "light"?

IZAAK WALTON

The Angler's Song

As inward love breeds outward talk,
The hound some praise, and some the hawk,
Some, better pleas'd with private sport,
Use tennis, some a mistress court:
    But these delights I neither wish,
    Nor envy, while I freely fish.

Who hunts doth oft in danger ride;
Who hawks, lures oft both far and wide
Who uses games shall often prove
A loser; but who falls in love,
    Is fetter'd in fond Cupid's snare:
    My angle breeds me no such care.

Of recreation there is none
So free as fishing is alone;
All other pastimes do no less
Than mind and body both possess:
    My hand alone my work can do,
    So I can fish and study too.

I care not, I, to fish in seas,
Fresh rivers best my mind do please,
Whose sweet calm course I contemplate,
And seek in life to imitate:
    In civil bounds I fain would keep,
    And for my past offences weep.

And when the timorous Trout I wait
To take, and he devours my bait,
How poor a thing, sometimes I find,
Will captivate a greedy mind:
      And when none bite, I praise the wise
      Whom vain allurements ne'er surprise.

But yet, though while I fish, I fast,
I make good fortune my repast;
And thereunto my friend invite,
In whom I more than that delight:
      Who is more welcome to my dish
      Than to my angle was my fish.

Considerations

1. Modern physicians sometimes recommend fishing as therapy for stress. How does this poem articulate the wisdom of that prescription?
2. Explain the narrator's admiration for the river. Why is it something to imitate?

WILLIAM CULLEN BRYANT

The Hunter of the Prairies

Ay, this is freedom!—these pure skies
      Were never stained with village smoke:
The fragrant wind, that through them flies,
      Is breathed from wastes by plough unbroke.
Here, with my rifle and my steed,
      And her who left the world for me,
I plant me, where the red deer feed
      In the green desert—and am free.

For here the fair savannas know
      No barriers in the bloomy grass;
Wherever breeze of heaven may blow,
      Or beam of heaven may glance, I pass.
In pastures, measureless as air,
      The bison is my noble game;
The bounding elk, whose antlers tear
      The branches, falls before my aim.

Mine are the river-fowl that scream
      From the long stripe of waving sedge;
The bear that marks my weapon's gleam,
      Hides vainly in the forest's edge;

In vain the she-wolf stands at bay;
    The brinded catamount, that lies
High in the boughs to watch his prey,
    Even in the act of springing, dies.

With what free growth the elm and plane
    Fling their huge arms across my way,
Gray, old, and cumbered with a train
    Of vines, as huge, and old, and gray!
Free stray the lucid streams, and find
    No taint in these fresh lawns and shades;
Free spring the flowers that scent the wind
    Where never scythe has swept the glades.

Alone the Fire, when frost-winds sere
    The heavy herbage of the ground,
Gathers his annual harvest here,
    With roaring like the battle's sound,
And hurrying flames that sweep the plain,
    And smoke-streams gushing up the sky:
I meet the flames with flames again,
    And at my door they cower and die.

Here, from dim woods, the aged past
    Speaks solemnly; and I behold
The boundless future in the vast
    And lonely river, seaward rolled.
Who feeds its founts with rain and dew?
    Who moves, I ask, its gliding mass,
And trains the bordering vines, whose blue
    Bright clusters tempt me as I pass?

Broad are these streams—my steed obeys,
    Plunges, and bears me through the tide.
Wide are these woods—I tread the maze
    Of giant stems, nor ask a guide.
I hunt till day's last glimmer dies
    O'er woody vale and glassy height;
And kind the voice and glad the eyes
    That welcome my return at night.

Considerations

1. Bryant was a romantic but lacked the poetic powers of his English models, namely
   Wordsworth (see "The Skaters"). From a conservationist's point of view, what is
   repugnant about the attempt at the sublimity of hunting in this poem?
2. The Bible was an important influence on most early American writers, including
   Bryant. What biblical tradition probably influenced the common attitude, articu-
   lated in this poem, toward animals? (For a different view, see "First Blood," "Landscape, Deer Season," "In Autumn," and "Revenge of the Hunted.")

JOHN CLARE

Badger

When midnight comes a host of dogs and men
Go out and track the badger to his den,
And put a sack within the hole, and lie
Till the old grunting badger passes by.
He comes and hears—they let the strongest loose.
The old fox hears the noise and drops the goose.
The poacher shoots and hurries from the cry,
And the old hare half wounded buzzes by.
They get a forkèd stick to bear him down
And clap the dogs and take him to the town,
And bait him all the way with many dogs,
And laugh and shout and fright the scampering hogs.
He runs along and bites at all he meets:
They shout and hollo down the noisy streets.

He turns about to face the loud uproar
And drives the rebels to their very door.
The frequent stone is hurled where'er they go;
When badgers fight, then everyone's a foe.
The dogs are clapt and urged to join the fray;
The badger turns and drives them all away.
Though scarcely half as big, demure and small,
He fights with dogs for hours and beats them all
The heavy mastiff, savage in the fray,
Lies down and licks his feet and turns away.
The bulldog knows his match and waxes cold,
The badger grins and never leaves his hold.
He drives the crowd and follows at their heels
And bites them through—the drunkard swears and reels.

The frighted women take the boys away,
The blackguard laughs and hurries on the fray.
He tries to reach the woods, an awkward race,
But sticks and cudgels quickly stop the chase.
He turns agen and drives the noisy crowd
And beats the many dogs in noises loud.
He drives away and beats them every one,
And then they loose them all and set them on.
He falls as dead and kicked by boys and men,
Then starts and grins and drives the crowd agen;
Till kicked and torn and beaten out he lies
And leaves his hold and cackles, groans, and dies.

Considerations

1. This poem deals with a sport similar to coon hunting. Does the poet attempt to justify the activity by attributing to it a higher purpose? Is it a better, or worse, poem for it? Explain.
2. Is the rhyme pattern appropriate to the subject? Why or why not?

DAVE SMITH

Night Fishing for Blues

Fortress Monroe, Virginia

The big-jawed Bluefish, ravenous, sleek muscle slamming
into banked histories of rock
    pile, hair-shaggy pier legs, drives
    each year to black Bay shallows, churns,

      fin-wheels, convoys, a black army, blue

stained sequins rank after rank, fluting bloodshot
gill-flowers, sucking bitter land water, great Ocean
Blues with belly-bones ringing like gongs.

      Tonight, not far from where Jefferson Davis

hunched in a harrowing cell, gray eyes quick
as crabs' nubs, I come back over planks
deep drummed under boots, tufts of hair

floating at my ears, everything finally right
    to pitch through tideturn and mudslur
    for fish with teeth like snapped sabers.

      In blue crescents of base lights, I cast hooks

baited with Smithfield ham: they reel, zing,
plummet, coil in corrosive swirls, bump on
scum-skinned rocks. No skin divers prowl here,

      visibility an arm's length, my visions

hand-to-hand in the line's warp. A meat-
baited lure limps through limbs nippling the muck,
silhouettes, shoots forward, catches a cruising Blue

      sentry's eye, snags and sets

case-hardened barbs. Suddenly, I am not alone:
   three Negroes plump down in lawn chairs, shudder-
   casting into the black pod plodding under us. One

      ripples with age, a grandmotherly obelisk,

her breath puffing like a coal stove. She swivels
heavily, chewing her dark nut, spits thick juice
like a careful chum.
         When I yank the first Blue
   she mumbles, her eyes roll far out on the black-
   blue billowing sea-screen. I hear her canting

      to Africa, a cluck in her throat, a chain

song from the fisherman's house. I cannot
understand. Bluefish are pouring at me in squads.
I haul two, three at a time, torpedoes, moon-shiners,
jamming my feet into the splintered floor, battling
whatever comes. I know I have waited
a whole life for this minute. Like purple dreams

      graven on cold cell walls, Blues walk over

our heads, ground on back-wings, grind their teeth.
They splash rings of blues and silver around us, tiaras
of lost battalions. I can smell the salt of ocean
runners as she hollers *I ain't doing so bad
for an old queen.* No time to answer. Two

      car-hoods down her descendants swing sinewy arms

in Superfly shirts, exotic butterflies: I hear them
pop beer cans, the whoosh released like stale breath
through a noose no one remembers. We hang

      fast flat casts, artless, no teasing fishermen,

beyond the book-bred lures of the pristine streams,
speeded-up, centrifugal, movie machines rewound
too far, belts slipped, gears gone, momentum

      hauling us back, slinging lines, winging wildly

as howitzers. Incredibly it happens: I feel
the hook hammer and shake and throw my entire weight
to dragging, as if I have caught the goddamndest

Blue in the Atlantic. She screams: *Oh my God!*

Four of us fumbling in beamed headlight and blue
arclight cut the hook from her face. Gnats butterfly,
nag us: I put it in deep and it must be gouged out
like a cyst. When it is free, I hear Blues not yet

dead flopping softly. I tell her it is a lucky
thing she can see. She mops blood blued over
gold-lined teeth and opens her arms so her dress

billows like a caftan. She wants

nothing but to fish. I hand her her pole, then cast
as far as I can. She pumps, wings a sinker and hooks
into flashing slop and reels hard. In one instant both

our lines leap rigid as daguerreotypes; we have

caught each other but we go on for the blue blood of
ghosts that thrash in the brain's empty room.
We pull at shadows until we see there is nothing, then
sit on the shaky pier like prisoners. Coil after coil
we trace the path of Bluefish-knots backward.

unlooping, feeling for holes, giving, testing,

slapping the gnats from our skins. Harried, unbound,
we leap to be fishers. But now a gray glow
shreds with the cloud curtain, an old belly-fire

guts the night. Already the tide humps around

on itself. Lights flicker like campfires in duty windows
at Ft. Monroe. She hooks up, saying *Sons they done
let us go.* I cast once more but nothing bites. Everywhere

a circle of Blues bleaches, stiffens

in flecks of blood. We kneel, stuff styrofoam
boxes with blankets of ice, break their backs
to keep them cold and sweet, the woman gravely
showing us what to do. By dawn the stink has passed

out of our noses. We drink beer like family.

All the way home thousands of Blues fall from my head,
falling with the gray Atlantic, and a pale veiny light
fills the road with sea-shadows that drift in figure

eights, knot and snarl and draw me forward.

Considerations

1. It is not unlikely that Dave Smith has been influenced, consciously or unconsciously, by the poetry of James Dickey. Read "Trout Fishing" and discuss such a possibility.
2. Which poem displays the broader vision? Which has more depth? Support your answer.
3. Discuss the richness of this poem's language.

JOHN BETJEMAN

Seaside Golf

How straight it flew, how long it flew,
It cleared the rutty track
And soaring, disappeared from view
Beyond the bunker's back—
A glorious, sailing, bounding drive
That made me glad I was alive.

And down the fairway, far along
It glowed a lovely white;
I played an iron sure and strong
And clipp'd it out of sight,
And spite of grassy banks between
I knew I'd find it on the green.

And so I did. It lay content
Two paces from the pin;
A steady putt and then it went
Oh, most securely in.
The very turf rejoiced to see
That quite unprecedented three.

Ah! seaweed smells from sandy caves
And thyme and mist in whiffs,
In-coming tide, Atlantic waves
Slapping the sunny cliffs,

Lark song and sea sounds in the air
And splendor, splendor everywhere.

Considerations

1. The tone is this poem's outstanding element. Would you call it restrained exhilaration? What does it communicate except mood? Is that alone enough to make
the poem worthwhile? Explain.
2. The rhyme pattern is *ab ab cc*. Why is that a particularly effective pattern for
this poem?

THE SONG OF MOVEMENT

What
is too swift for deception
is final, lost, among the loosened figures

jogging off the field
(the pitcher walks), casual
in the space where the poem has happened.

—Robert Wallace

ROBERT FRANCIS

Pitcher

His art is eccentricity, his aim
How not to hit the mark he seems to aim at,

His passion how to avoid the obvious,
His technique how to vary the avoidance.

The others throw to be comprehended. He
Throws to be a moment misunderstood.

Yet not too much. Not errant, arrant, wild,
But every seeming aberration willed.

Not to, yet still, still to communicate
Making the batter understand too late.

Considerations

1. Except for the last line, could this poem be titled "Poet"? Why or why not?
2. For a similar view of baseball as poetry, read Robert Wallace's "The Double Play."

ROBERT FRANCIS

Catch

Two boys uncoached are tossing a poem together,
Overhand, underhand, backhand, sleight of hand, every hand,
Teasing with attitudes, latitudes, interludes, altitudes,
High, make him fly off the ground for it, low, make him stoop,
Make him scoop it up, make him as-almost-as-possible miss it,
Fast, let him sting from it, now, now fool him slowly,
Anything, everything tricky, risky, nonchalant,
Anything under the sun to outwit the prosy,
Over the tree and the long sweet cadence down,
Over his head, make him scramble to pick up the meaning,
And now, like a posy, a pretty one plump in his hands.

Considerations

1. Is Francis attempting to shed light on the nature of a poem, or of catch? Explain.
2. Who are the "prosy" that it is important to "outwit"?
3. Have you ever wondered why poems are "difficult"? How does Francis explain it?

ROBERT WALLACE

The Double Play

In his sea lit
distance, the pitcher winding
like a clock about to chime comes down with

the ball, hit
sharply, under the artificial
banks of arc-lights, bounds like a vanishing string

over the green
to the shortstop magically
scoops to his right whirling above his invisible

shadows
in the dust redirects
its flight to the running poised second baseman

pirouettes
leaping, above the slide, to throw
from mid-air, across the colored tightened interval,

to the leaning-
out first baseman ends the dance
drawing it disappearing into his long brown glove

stretches. What
is too swift for deception
is final, lost, among the loosened figures

jogging off the field
(the pitcher walks), casual
in the space where the poem has happened.

Considerations

1. What is suggested by the last line?
2. Literally speaking, can a double play be a poem? (In Greek "poem" is *poieio*—"I make").
3. Discuss Wallace's talent for transforming action into words.

FRED CHAPPELL

Spitballer

A poet because his hand goes first
to his head & then to his heart.

The catcher accepts the pitch
as a pool receives a dripping diver;
soaks up the curve like
cornflakes in milk.

The batter makes great
show of wringing out his bat.

On the mound he grins, tiger
in a tree, when the umpire
turns round & round the ball
magically dry as alum.

He draws a second salary as maintenance man.
Since while he pitches he waters the lawn.

Considerations

1. In the first stanza, Chappell establishes the spitball pitcher as poet. Does he subtlely continue the metaphor throughout the poem? Support your answer.
2. Discuss this poem as an examination of the metaphorical properties of deception.
3. "Spitballer" has a definite classical quality about it. For a comparison, read the Greek and Roman selections.

MARIANNE MOORE

Baseball and Writing

Fanaticism? No. Writing is exciting
and baseball is like writing.
    You can never tell with either
        how it will go
        or what you will do;
    generating excitement—
    a fever in the victim—
    pitcher, catcher, fielder, batter.
            Victim in what category?
Owlman watching from the press box?
            to whom does it apply?
        Who is excited? Might it be I?

It's a pitcher's battle all the way—a duel—
a catcher's, as, with cruel
        puma paw, Elston Howard lumbers lightly
            back to plate. (His spring
            de-winged a bat swing.)
    They have that killer instinct;
    yet Elston—whose catching
    arm has hurt them all with the bat—
            when questioned, says, unenviously,
        "I'm very satisfied. We won."
            Shorn of the batting crown, says, "We";
            robbed by a technicality.

When three players on a side play three positions
and modify conditions,
        the massive run need not be everything.

"Going, going . . ." Is
  it? Roger Maris
has it, running fast. You will
never see a finer catch. Well . . .
"Mickey, leaping like the devil"—why
          gild it, although deer sounds better—
snares what was speeding towards its treetop nest,
      one-handing the souvenir-to-be
      meant to be caught by you or me.

Assign Yogi Berra to Cape Canaveral;
he could handle any missile.
    He is no feather. "Strike! . . . Strike *two!*"
    Fouled back. A blur.
    It's gone. You would infer
  that the bat had eyes.
  He put the wood to that one.
Praised Skowron says, "Thanks, Mel.
  I think I helped a *little* bit."
      All business, each, and modesty.
    Blanchard, Richardson, Kubek, Boyer.
    In that galaxy of nine, say which
    won the pennant? *Each.* It was he.

Those two magnificent saves from the knee—throws
by Boyer, finesses in twos—
    like Whitey's three kinds of pitch and pre-
      diagnosis
    with pick-off psychosis.
  Pitching is a large subject.
  Your arm, too true at first, can learn to
  catch the corners—even trouble
    Mickey Mantle. ("Grazed a Yankee!
My baby pitcher, Montejo!"
    With some pedagogy,
    you'll be tough, premature prodigy.)

They crowd him and curve him and aim for the knees.
              Trying
indeed! The secret implying:
  "I can stand here, bat held steady."
    One may suit him;
    none has hit him.
  Imponderables smite him.
  Muscle kinks, infections, spike wounds
  require food, rest, respite from ruffians. (Drat it!
    Celebrity costs privacy!)

Cow's milk, "tiger's milk," soy milk, carrot juice,
   brewer's yeast (high-potency)—
  concentrates presage victory

sped by Luis Arroyo, Hector Lopez—
deadly in a pinch. And "Yes,
  it's work; I want you to bear down,
   but enjoy it
   while you're doing it."
  Mr. Houk and Mr. Sain,
if you have a rummage sale,
don't sell Roland Sheldon or Tom Tresh.
   Studded with stars in belt and crown,
the Stadium is an adastrium.
   O flashing Orion,
  your stars are muscled like the lion.

Considerations

1. What is "stream of consciousness"? In "Baseball and Writing" does Marianne Moore employ this mode? How so?
2. What was the inspiration for the poem? How do you know?
3. Does Moore extend her comparison throughout the poem? Cite examples.
4. Identify as many of the baseball players mentioned in the poem as you can. On what famous team did they play? When?
5. Contrast the style and form of this poem with that of "Ballad of Dead Yankees."

PETER MEINKE

Byron vs. DiMaggio

Yesterday I was told
the trouble with America is that
these kids here
would rather be DiMaggio
than Byron: this shows our decadence.
But I don't know,
there's not that much difference.
Byron also would have married Monroe
or at least been in there trying;
he too covered a lot of territory,
even with that bum foot,
and make the All-European swimming team
in the Hellespont League.

And, on the other hand, you
have to admit that DiMag played
sweet music
out there in the magic grass
of centerfield.

Considerations

1. This poem is one of the many connecting sport and art. What is the poet's central theme? Why is Byron now a model for children when, during his life, he was considered the very worst of influences?
2. Explain: (a) Monroe; (b) "bum foot"; and (c) "Hellespont League." (See "Written After Swimming From Sestos to Abydos.")

MORRIS BISHOP

Settling Some Old Football Scores

This is the football hero's moment of fame.
    Glory is his, though erstwhile he may have shunned
        it.
In hall and street he hears the crying of his name
    By youth and maiden, alumnus and radio pundit.

Fierce on the newspaper pages his features show
    He smites his foe in the innumerable cinema
And in a myriad maidens' dreams. But oh,
    In literature his fame has reached its minima!

See, in the Broadway drama, what he has become, he
    Who was triply-threatening All-American!
He is a lubberly fellow, a downright dummy!
    And serious fiction is what he is frankly barbaric in.

We read of him telling victories won of yore,
    We see him vainly pursue fame's fleeting bubble;
The maid he adores is certain to leave him for
    A small dark wiry person, the author's double!

O football hero! Now while a million throats
    Acclaim thy glorious deeds, just set this much down:
A small dark wiry person is taking notes.
    Literature will make the ultimate touchdown.

Considerations

1. What one word, suggested by the title, defines the theme of this poem?
2. Is it quite possible that the football hero could not be less concerned by his literary image? Explain.

How flower-light they toss themselves, how light
They toss and fall
    And flower-light, precise, and arabesque
    Let their praise be.

                                        —Robert Francis

ROBERT FRANCIS

Watching Gymnasts

(for P. T.)

Competing not so much with one another
As with perfection
    They follow follow as voices in a fugue
    A severe music.

Something difficult they are making clear
Like the crack teacher
    Demonstrating their paradigms until
    The dumb see.

How flower-light they toss themselves, how light
They toss and fall
    And flower-light, precise, and arabesque
    Let their praise be.

Considerations

1. Discuss the possibility that the last verse could very well serve as a statement about Robert Francis' poetry.
2. Define: (a) fugue; (b) paradigms; and (c) arabesque.

ROBERT FRANCIS

The Base Stealer

Poised between going on and back, pulled
Both ways taut like a tightrope-walker,
Fingertips pointing the opposites,
Now bouncing tiptoe like a dropped ball
Or a kid skipping rope, come on, come on,
Running a scattering of steps sidewise,
How he teeters, skitters, tingles, teases,
Taunts them, hovers like an ecstatic bird,
He's only flirting, crowd him, crowd him,
Delicate, delicate, delicate, delicate—now!

Considerations

1. Discuss Francis' choice of words and rhythm. What effect does he achieve?
2. Francis uses four similes. How effective are they? Why do you think he chooses not
   to use rhyme?
3. Compare this poem with Richard Eberhart's "Ball Game." What element does
   Eberhart add?

ROBERT FRANCIS

Two Wrestlers

Two bronzes, but they were passing bronze before
The sculptor

All glint, all gleaming, face to face and grace
To grace

Balanced almost beyond their balance, tingling
To spring—

Who ever saw so point-by-point, so perfect
A pair

That either one—or both—or neither one—
Could win?

If this is trickery, the trick is smooth
In truth

One wrestler challenging—oh how unsafe—
Himself.

Considerations

1. What is the controlling idea in this poem?
2. Does the final stanza suggest a kind of self-destruction? Is that why it is unsafe? Discuss.

ROBERT FRANCIS

Skier

He swings down like the flourish of a pen
Signing a signature in white on white.

The silence of his skis reciprocates
The silence of the world around him.

Wind is his one competitor
In the cool winding and unwinding down.

On incandescent feet he falls
Unfalling, trailing white foam, white fire.

Considerations

1. How is it that the skier "falls / Unfalling"?
2. Compare this poem with "The Skiers" by Robert Penn Warren. Discuss the added element in Warren's poem.

ROBERT FRANCIS

High Diver

How deep is his duplicity who in a flash
Passes from resting bird to flying bird to fish,

Who momentarily is sculpture, then all motion,
Speed and splash, then climbs again to contemplation.

He is the archer who himself is bow and arrow.
He is the upper-under-world-commuting hero.

His downward going has the air of sacrifice
To some dark seaweed-bearded seagod face to face.

Or goddess. Rippling and responsive lies the water
For him to contemplate, then powerfully to enter.

Considerations

1. How important is the title to this poem? Could you have identified the subject without it? How?
2. Explain the importance of "contemplation" in this poem. Is it different from the popular sports term, "concentration"? Explain.
3. Discuss the economy and precision of the diction in this poem.

ANONYMOUS

The Pole-Vaulter

Balancing 'twixt earth and sky
Unto you an instant's given
Shared with birds that soar and fly
In and from the vaulting heaven.

With a grace deliberate
That firm wand in hand retain you:
As a ladder starward set,
Yet a bond on earth to chain you.

Then: an agile twist and weave
Onward, upward, and you hover
Hawklike, as the rod you leave
Instantly, and down—you're over!

Considerations

1. In both the first and last verses, there is the hint of a momentary suspension as the pole-vaulter begins his descent. Is there such a point in the process? Does the poem adequately express the feeling?
2. What is the "bond on earth to chain you"?

ANONYMOUS

The High Jump

He slowly paced his distance off, and turned,
    Took poise, and darted forward at full speed;
Before the bar the heavy earth he spurned,
    Himself an arrow. They who saw his deed
Tensed muscles, poised and ran and leaped, and
        burned
    With close-drawn breath, helping him to succeed:
Now he is over, they are over, too;
Foeman and friend were flying when he flew.

Considerations

1. This poem has two important elements? What are they? Which takes precedence?
2. How does this poem point out one of the most important aspects of spectator sports?

ANDREI VOZNESENSKY

Soccer

(Trans. by Anselm Hollo)

Left
    Forward! He's the leanest in the shower,
a record-holder in the way of penalties—
breaks all that crockery, my God!
mind the geraniums, will you?

He's like a bullet among aces
a gleaming parrot set apart from cowards,
he runs, and shoots, and runs:
the Stadium is a magnifying glass to focus
on the smoking ball—

Hissing hoarsely like a hundred syphons
the man who plays right forward toils to cover him
—a hundred medals jingle on his chest,
that is the number of men whose feet
he has undone—

But you
>   know, left forward, my lover, how
to use your head!
Good luck to your foes—"Come on, make it *go!*"
Left forward, all your toes!

A thousand eyes
>   and a small Latvian girl
shapely and sweet, a piece
of sun, somewhere among them; O
she hardly dares
>   to breathe. . . .

Attacks, attacks, come, ecstasy! The dizzy joys
of kicking it—the ball, the ball
yet what is in a ball?—but no, go,
>   go
"Us—Them—God Heaven help us!
What has he done! what has he done!"
The ball,
>   in his own goal. . . . He made it, yes
the sun is a black frying pan.

You walk away,
hunching your shoulders
in the great hush.

Dreams don't come true, the ball
deceives the foot.
The sweet-curved
chick. . . . Oh, her.

You let
the tap splash
water on your head
so full of
blues. . . . And yet,
a murmur:
>   "Well, so what—
it *was* a shot! A shot—
>   that's all that matters."

Considerations

1. Would you say that Voznesensky captures the exhilaration of the game? Is there a subtle analogy in this poem?
2. From whose point of view does this poem unfold? A player's? A fan's?

DAMAGETUS

The Spartan Wrestler

(Trans. by Tom Dodge)

It's not from Argos or Messene that I hail
But from Sparta, man-ennobling Sparta.
Unlike Spartan boys, they are skilled in the wrestling art
But it's with strength alone that I prevail.

Considerations

1. Does this poem give a brief insight into the Spartan culture? What would you say were its prime virtues?
2. Identify: (a) Argos and (b) Messene.

ADRIEN STOUTENBURG

Sky Diver

Grotesque, jumping out
like a clothed frog, helmet and glasses,
arms and legs wading the sky,
feet flapping before the cloth flower opens;
then suspended, poised,
an exclamation point upside-down,
and going down, swaying over corn and creeks
and highways scribbled
over the bones of fish and eagles.

There is the interim between air and earth,
time to study steeples
and the underwings of birds going over,
before the unseen chasm,
the sudden jaw open and hissing.

Lying here after the last jump
I see how fanatic roots are,
how moles breathe through darkness,
how deep the earth can be.

Considerations

1. Discuss the sense of perspective in this poem.
2. What is "the unseen chasm, / the sudden jaw open and hissing"?
3. Compare this poem with Richmond Lattimore's "Sky Diving."

R. P. DEXTER

Shadow Dirge

Cautious yet unafraid, twirling lightly
Between the tree rows which line his flight,
Marking each quiet eddy and ruddy water rock,
Softly whistling, the shadow skims along;
Now steeply banking, then sliding easily through
The crisp clear morning, just above
The water's icy silent movement. Whistling and soft.
A lean blue glint flashes sharply against
The richest reds and yellows along the reedy shore.
Eternity, captured in an autumn movement
As the fleeting form flares upward into airy thinness,
Searching, reaching, straining as for life itself,
Explodes in a searing acrid flash.
The winging shape shudders and falls tumbling,
Easy, soft and silent down the echoing sounds.
Far along the bank the quiet mourning dove
Leaps into whirring startled flight.
The squirrel, hidden in his oaken bower,
Ceases his searching and stares,
Frozen, like the ice beside the bank,
As the shadow, turning slowly in the current,
Slips silently down the river's winding way.

Considerations

1. This poem is a rich synchrony of form, language, and content. Discuss each of these elements.
2. Explain the significance of the title. What is a dirge?
3. What is the attitude of the controlling consciousness toward the occurrence? Compare it in this regard with Barbara Howes's "Landscape, Deer Season."

MAY SWENSON

Bronco Busting, Event #1

The stall so tight he can't raise heels or knees
when the cowboy, coccyx to bareback, touches down

tender as a deerfly, forks him, gripping the rope-
handle over the withers, testing the cinch,

as if hired to lift a cumbersome piece of brown
luggage, while assistants perched on the rails arrange

the kicker, a foam-rubber band around the narrowest,
most ticklish part of the loins, leaning full weight

on neck and rump to keep him throttled, this horse,
"Firecracker," jacked out of the box through the sprung

gate, in the same second raked both sides of the belly
by ratchets on booted heels, bursts into five-way

motion: bucks, pitches, swivels, humps, and twists,
an all-over-body-sneeze that must repeat

until the flapping bony lump attached to his spine is gone.
A horn squawks. From the dust gets up a buster named Tucson.

Considerations

1. Is this a better, or worse, poem for its having no central analogy? Explain.
2. Identify the similes in stanzas 2 and 3. Also, identify the metaphor in the eighth stanza.

DANIEL HALPERN

The Hunt

Setters mark the turf and run
For quail, spring to a point where wings
Fold and flying stops. Water on branches,
In beads—the sun explodes, sparks
The eyes of the setters, of the quail.
The hunters sweat on steel, taut jerkins
Stiff, and eye the bush for game—
Their dogs have eyed it to the ground.
Slowly they move in, stealthy and clever,
Guns in air. The scene tightens.
The quail feel the stare of the setters,
Of the hunters—the smell of their metal
And jerkins—of life in the morning
When light is still low. The men drop
To their knees in a familiar pose,

Eyeing the V, lining up life
In their blind sights. A finger squeezes
Action into the cold morning,
And the quail jump from sound
Into air.

Considerations

1. Does the point of view in this poem more closely resemble that in R. P. Dexter's "Shadow Dirge" or Barbara Howes's "In Autumn"? Explain.
2. Why does Halpern say "The quail feel the stare. . ."? Explain.

RICHMOND LATTIMORE

Sky Diving

They step from the high plane and begin to tumble
down. Below is the painted ground, above
is bare sky. They do not fumble
with the catch, but only fall; drop sheer; begin to move

in the breakless void; stretch and turn, freed
from pressure; stand in weightless air
and softly walk across their own speed;
gather and group, these dropping bundles, where

the neighbor in the sky stands, reach touch
and clasp hands, separate and swim
back to station (did swimmer ever shear such
thin water?) falling still. Now at last pull the slim

cord. Parasols bloom in the air, slow
the swift sky-fall. Collapsed tents cover
the ground. They rise up, plain people now.
Their little sky-time is over.

Considerations

1. Lattimore says the sky divers "walk" and "swim" in air. Compare with Stoutenburg's "Sky Diver," whom he describes as "wading" and "an exclamation point upside-down."
2. Compare Lattimore's parachute ("Parasols bloom") with Stoutenburg's "cloth flower opens."
3. Is part of the appeal of sky diving that, while engaged in it, the divers are not "plain people"? Explain.

GEORGE ABBE

The Passer

Dropping back with the ball ripe in my palm,
grained and firm as the flesh of a living charm,
I taper and coil myself down, raise arm to fake,
running a little, seeing my targets emerge
like quail above a wheat field's golden lake.

In boyhood I saw my mother knit my warmth
with needles that were straight. I learned to feel
the passage of the bullet through the bore,
its vein of flight between my heart and deer
whose terror took the pulse of my hot will.

I learned how wild geese slice arcs from hanging pear
of autumn noon; how the thought of love cleaves home,
and fists, with fury's ray, can lay a weakness bare,
and instinct's eye can mine fish under foam.

So as I run and weigh, measure and test,
the light kindles on helmets, the angry leap;
but secretly, coolly, as though stretching a hand to his chest,
I lay the ball in the arms of my planing end,
as true as metal, as deftly as surgeon's wrist.

Considerations

1. What sensory experiences from childhood have prepared the passer for his duty?
2. Compare this poem with James Dickey's "In the Pocket." Which is more immediate and intense? More reflective and philosophical?
3. What would be the reaction of the interviewing sports announcer if a quarterback answered with this poem when he was asked how he executed that touchdown pass?

JAMES DICKEY

In the Pocket

NFL

Going backward
All of me and some
Of my friends are forming a shell   my arm is looking

Everywhere and some are breaking
In   breaking down
And out   breaking
Across, and one is going deep   deeper
Than my arm. Where is Number One hooking
Into the violent green alive
With linebackers? I cannot find him he cannot beat
His man   I fall back more
Into the pocket   it is raging and breaking
Number Two has disappeared into the chalk
Of the sideline   Number Three is cutting with half
A step of grace   my friends are crumbling
Around me the wrong color
Is looming   hands are coming
Up and over between
My arm and Number Three: throw it hit him in the middle
Of his enemies   hit move scramble
Before death and the ground
Come up   LEAP STAND KILL DIE STRIKE

Now.

Considerations

1. Football is often compared with warfare. Discuss this poem's martial overtones.
2. Is the execution of the pass from the pocket actually this charged with intensity, even panic? How would you rate this poem in terms of realism?

WALT WHITMAN

The Runner

On a flat road runs the well-train'd runner,
He is lean and sinewy with muscular legs,
He is thinly clothed, he leans forward as he runs,
With lightly closed fists and arms partially rais'd.

Consideration

1. This description of a runner was written over a hundred years ago. Would a modern runner agree with the wisdom of the last two lines? Why or why not?

EDWARD CRACROFT LEFROY

A Football-Player

If I could paint you, friend, as you stand there,
Guard of the goal, defensive, open-eyed,
Watching the tortured bladder slide and glide
Under the twinkling feet; arms bare, head bare,
The breeze a-tremble through crow-tufts of hair;
Red-brown in face, and ruddier having spied
A wily foeman breaking from the side,
Aware of him,—of all else unaware:
If I could limn you, as you leap and fling
Your weight against his passage, like a wall;
Clutch him, and collar him, and rudely cling
For one brief moment till he falls—you fall:
My sketch would have what Art can never give—
Sinew and breath and body; it would live.

Considerations

1. What special form does this poem employ? How does it differ in rhyme pattern
   from a poem of similar form, such as "The Sportsman."
2. What else is unusual about the structure of this poem?

HOMER

The Funeral Games for Patroclus:
Wrestling to a Draw

From *The Iliad*, Book XXIII

(Trans. by Ennis Rees)

Then Achilles,
Before all the Danaans, put up rewards for the painful
And toilsome wrestling, the third event in the games—
For the winner, a truly tremendous three-legged cauldron
To straddle the fire, one valued as worth twelve oxen
Among the Achaeans, and for the loser he brought out
Among them a woman of many skills, whom they valued
As worth four oxen. Then Peleus' son arose
Mid the Argives and said:
    "Up now, whichever two men
Among you intend to compete in this contest."
    He spoke,

And up got huge Telamonian Ajax and with him
Resourceful Odysseus, skilled at tricks and contriving.
Then, having girded themselves, the two men strode out
To the midst of the place of assembly and immediately locked
Their powerful arms, reminding one of the sloping
Beams some famous builder connects at the roof
Of a high-gabled house to keep out the blustering winds.
And their backs fairly creaked as they gripped each other hard
With their hands and grappled for all they were worth, streaming
With sweat and raising many a blood-livid welt
On each other's ribs and shoulders, as both of them strained
Every muscle to win the fair-fashioned tripod. Odysseus,
However, could no more win a fall over Ajax
Than Ajax could over him, so firm was his stance.
But when they had grappled so long that the strong-greaved
        Achaeans
Began to get bored and restless, gigantic Ajax,
Telamon's son, grunted thus to Odysseus:
    "O god-sprung
Son of Laertes, resourceful Odysseus, either you
Lift me or let me lift you, and the outcome we'll leave
To Zeus."
    So saying, he lifted Odysseus, but that
Wily man was alertly on guard, and kicking the bend
Of Ajax's knee with his heel, he caused his legs
To buckle at once, so that backward he fell with Odysseus
Riding his chest. Next it was much-bearing, noble
Odysseus' turn to lift, and though he could raise him
From earth a few inches only, he crooked his knee
Behind that of Ajax and down the two went again,
Side by side in the man-clinging dust. And now
The two men would have sprung up again to try a third fall,
If Achilles had not stood up and restrained them, saying:
    "Struggle no further, nor wear yourselves out with agonized
Effort. Both of you win. Take equal prizes
And go, that other Achaeans may also compete."
    To this they willingly listened, then did as he said,
Wiping the dust from their bodies and putting their tunics
Back on.

Considerations

1. One of the least exciting of the funeral games for Patroclus proved to be the wrestling competition. Why? (For a modern equivalent read "The Wrestlers" by Robert Francis.)
2. What does the loser's prize say about the Greeks' attitude toward women? What was first prize?
3. How is the match finally decided? Why does it prove to be so boring to the audience?

HOMER

The Funeral Games for Patroclus:
The Boastful Boxer

From *The Iliad,* Book XXIII

(Trans. by Ennis Rees)

Achilles spoke thus:
"Atrides, and all
You other hard-greaved Achaeans, we now invite
The best pair of boxers here to square off and throw punches
Like fury for these two prizes. Let him whom Apollo
Gives strength to outlast the other, as witnessed by all
The Achaeans, go off to his lodge with the work-hardy mule,
While he who loses shall take the two-handled cup."
        He spoke, and at once a huge man, courageous and skilled
As a boxer, stood up, one Panopeus' son Epeus,
And laying a hand on the work-hardy mule, he vaunted:
"Now let him come out and fight, whoever covets
This two-handled cup. For the mule, I think, will not
Be won by any Achaean who first of all has to
Beat me with his fists, since I claim to be the best boxer
Here. So I'm not so good in battle—one can't be
Expert in every endeavor! But this I say now,
And believe me I'll do what I say—namely, crush
Every bone in my crazy opponent's carcass and pound
His flesh to a pulp! So let his nearest and dearest
Of kin stand by in a body, that they may carry
Him off unconscious when I have finished with him."
        Such was his challenge, and all for a time sat utterly
Silent. At last one man stood up to face him,
A godlike man, Euryalus, son of the son
Of Talaus, Mecisteus the King, who had journeyed to Thebes
For the funeral and games that followed great Oedipus' downfall,
And in those games had defeated all the Cadmeans.
Quickly, Euryalus' spear-famous kinsman, Tydeus'
Son Diomedes, girded his cousin's loins
With a cloth and bound his knuckles with thongs well cut
From the hide of a range-roaming ox, warmly encouraging
Him with words, for greatly he wished him to win.
When the two had been girded, they strode to the midst of the
        place
Of assembly and, squaring off, began to throw powerful
Punches, awesomely grinding their teeth and streaming
All over with sweat. Then able Epeus brought one

Up from the ground, as it were, as Euryalus peered
For an opening, and caught him crashingly under the jaw.
Nor did he remain after that in an upright position
For long, since there on the spot his splendid limbs
Were unstrung. And as when a fish darts up from beneath
The North Wind's ripple and leaps up out of the water
And onto the sea-weedy sand of a shallow, then quickly
Is hidden again beneath a dark wave, so now
Euryalus arched through the air and flopped on his back,
So great was the force of the blow. But gallant Epeus
Took him and set him once more on his feet, and his cherished
Companions crowded about him and helped him off
Through the place of assembly, his feet dragging trails in the dust
As he went, dangling his head to one side and spitting out
Clots of blood. And they set him down—still
None too sure where he was—in the midst of his fellows, while
        they
Went out and claimed the two-handled cup.

Considerations

1. One of the athletic events in the funeral games for Achilles' friend Patroclus was the boxing competition. How were the boxers prepared for the match?
2. We may expect our modern athletes to be more modest than was Epeus, but in his tradition, an athlete who did not boast was considered not to have much mettle. What famous modern boxer would have fit very well in this tradition?
3. What is a "Homeric simile"? Can you locate one in this selection?
4. A tradition in epic literature is the *litotes,* understatement. Can you find an example?

BABETTE DEUTSCH

Morning Workout

The sky unfolding its blankets to free
The morning
Chill on the air. Clean odor of stables.
The grandstand green as the turf,
The pavilion flaunting its brilliance
For no one.
Beyond hurdles and hedges, swans, circling, cast
A contemplative radiance over the willow's shadows.
Day pales the toteboard lights.
Gilds the balls, heightens the stripes of the poles.
Dirt shines. White glisten of rails.

The track is bright as brine.
Their motion a flowing,
From prick of the ear to thick tail's shimmering drift.
The horses file forth.
Pink nostrils quiver, as who know they are showing their colors.
Ankles lift, as who hear without listening.
The bay, the brown, the chestnut, the roan have loaned
Their grace to the riders who rise in the stirrups, or hunch
Over the withers, gentling with mumbled song.
A mare ambles past, liquid eye askance.
Three, then four, canter by: voluptuous power
Pours through their muscles,
Dancing in pulse and nerve.
They glide in the stretch as on skis.
Two
Are put to a drive:
Centaur energy bounding as the dirt shudders, flies
Under the wuthering pace,
Hushes the hooves' thunders,
The body's unsyllabled eloquence rapidly
Dying away.
Dark-skinned stable-boys, as proud as kin
Of their display of vivacity, elegance,
Walk the racers back.
Foam laces the girths, sweaty haunches glow.
Slowly returning from the track, the horse is
Animal paradigm of innocence, discipline, force.
Blanketed, they go in.
Odor of earth
Enriches azuring air.

Considerations

1. How do the short phrases at the beginning suit the action being described? Why do they lengthen as the poem develops?
2. Discuss the sensual richness of the final six lines.

JOHN BUNYAN

Neither Hook nor Line

You see the ways the fisherman doth take
To catch the fish; what engines doth he make!
Behold! how he engageth all his wits;
Also his snares, lines, angles, hooks and nets;
Yet fish there be, that neither hook nor line,
Nor snare, nor net, nor engine, can make thine:
They must be groped for, and be tickled too,
Or they will not be catch'd, whate'er you do.

Considerations

1. What is Bunyan's analogy in this poem?
2. Look up "engine" in the *Oxford English Dictionary*. What did it originally mean?

MAXINE KUMIN

400-Meter Freestyle

THE GUN full swing the swimmer catapults and cracks

                                                              s
                                                                i
                                                              x
feet away onto that perfect glass he catches at
     a
  n
     d
throws behind him scoop after scoop cunningly moving

                                                        t
                                                          h
                                                            e
water back to move him forward. Thrift is his wonderful
  s
 e
  c
ret; he has schooled out all extravagance. No muscle

                                                            r
                                                              i
                                                            p
ples without compensation wrist cock to heel snap to

h

i

s

mobile mouth that siphons in the air that nurtures

h

i

m

at half an inch above sea level so to speak.

T

h

e

astonishing whites of the soles of his feet rise

a

n

d

salute us on the turns. He flips, converts, and is gone

a

l

l

in one. We watch him for signs. His arms are steady at

t

h

e

catch, his cadent feet tick in the stretch, they know

t

h

e

lesson well. Lungs know, too; he does not list for

a

i

r

he drives along on little sips carefully expended

b

u

t

that plum red heart pumps hard cries hurt how soon

i

t

s

near one more and makes its final surge   TIME: 4:25:9

Considerations

1. What is the controlling element of this poem? What is this form of poetry called?
2. Why does perfect execution depend on "thrift"?
3. Would you say that the poet has more than layman's familiarity with swimming? (See "Morning Swim.")

THOSE WATCHING

. . . the crowd, forever small in
its distance
has applauded again and again like wind rattling the
dry trees
of a hill beyond.

—John Ciardi

WILLIAM CARLOS WILLIAMS

At the Ball Game

The crowd at the ball game
is moved uniformly

by a spirit of uselessness
which delights them—

all the exciting detail
of the chase

and the escape, the error
the flash of genius—

all to no end save beauty
the eternal—

So in detail they, the crowd,
are beautiful

for this
to be warned against

saluted and defied—
It is alive, venomous

it smiles grimly
its words cut—

The flashy female with her
mother, gets it—

The Jew gets it straight—it
is deadly, terrifying—

It is the Inquisition, the
Revolution

It is beauty itself
that lives

day by day in them
idly—

This is
the power of their faces

It is summer, it is the solstice
the crowd is

cheering, the crowd is laughing
in detail

permanently, seriously
without thought

Considerations

1. Why is the crowd at the ball game delighted "by a spirit of uselessness?"
2. Why is it beautiful "in detail," but "alive, venomous"?
3. Critics of modern sports have called it the new "opiate for the masses." Discuss the last stanza from that point of view.

LAURENCE LIEBERMAN

My Father Dreams of Baseball

On hot September nights, when sleep is scarce,
in place of sheep Dad counts home runs that carry
the left-field fence and fly clean out of the ball park.

Father snaps off the twi-night doubleheader;
Behind his back, the screen door loosens a hinge
He escapes to the backyard retreat to rant at the ump.
Hopped-up in the Porsche, he's off for an all-night binge.

By morning, Mother's throat has a telltale lump.
He takes his losses hard, a heavy bettor.

In his dreams, white dashing figures circle the bases.
Their caps dazzle in the sun like lights on a scoreboard.
The diamond is worn a foot deep under hammering cleats.

He attends home games. Through Dad's binoculars
the power hitters charge home plate like bulls,
and make the picador pitcher's heart stand still.
(A curve ball is a lance that bull's-eyes skulls.)
My father in the stands directs the kill
like a black matador in Madrid spectaculars.

Just inches inside the foul line, a figure is poised
three feet in the air, his arm outstretched for the catch.
His mouth is pinched with the pain of a near-miss.
The features are fixed with the dull metallic glow
of an ancient face, cast in bronze or brass.

Considerations

1. On the surface, this seems to be a poetic characterization of a loyal baseball fan by his child, but its unorthodox mixture of images and liberties taken with point of view (the narrator relates the father's dreams and what he sees through the binoculars) defies conventional interpretation. One clue, perhaps, lies in its structure—what is the significance of the indention of stanzas 2 and 5?
2. Stanzas 1, 4, and 6 seem to deal with the father's dream. What may be symbolized in stanza 6 by the figure's near-miss? Is this a common fear of most middle-aged men?

ST. JOHN EMILE CLAVERING HANKIN

De Gustibus

I am an unadventurous man,
And always go upon the plan
Of shunning danger where I can.

And so I fail to understand
Why every year a stalwart band
Of tourists go to Switzerland,

And spend their time for several weeks.
With quaking hearts and pallid cheeks,
Scaling abrupt and windy peaks.

In fact, I'm old enough to find
Climbing of almost any kind
Is very little to my mind.

A mountain summit white with snow
Is an attractive sight, I know,
But why not see it *from below?*

Why leave the hospitable plain
And scale Mont Blanc with toil and pain
Merely to scramble down again?

Some men pretend they think it bliss
To clamber up a precipice
Or dangle over an abyss,

To crawl along a mountain side,
Supported by a rope that's tied
—Not too securely—to a guide;

But such pretences, it is clear,
In the aspiring mountaineer
Are usually insincere.

And many a climber, I'll be bound,
Whom scarped and icy crags surround,
Wishes himself on level ground.

So I, for one, do not propose
To cool my comfortable toes
In regions of perpetual snows.

As long as I can take my ease,
Fanned by a soothing southern breeze
Under the shade of English trees.

And anyone who leaves my share
Of English fields and English air
May take the Alps for aught I care!

Considerations

1. This poem could serve as a testament for millions of confirmed spectators. Do you think it is honest, or a rationalization? Explain.
2. The title is Latin for "taste." Does such a "scholarly" title imply more substance than the poem actually possesses?
3. What benefit does the poem express for such a sedentary life, other than that it is easy and comfortable?
4. Discuss the possibility that the poet is having his fun with us—that the poem is not to be taken seriously. Support your answer.

ANONYMOUS

To a Baseball

You're going into play? An instant more
        And yours the eyes of thousands. There's
            for you
Huge plaudits welcoming the needed score,
        Deep disapprovals at misplays they view,
And, best of all, the eager silence there
When, swift from bat or hand, you hang in air.

Considerations

1. What does "you" refer to in the poem?
2. Why is the "eager silence" the best response of all from the crowd?

WILLIAM D. BARNEY

The Rasslers

This is all flummery, a feast of sham,
pure unspontaneous skullduggery;
pay it no heed, that hairy straining ham,
that shriek of pain, the murderous vis-à-vis.
Neither mud nor cayenne in a writhing eye
played catalyst to set off this grotesque
ballet. And this is not (who seems to die)
a swan, his knotted rump an arabesque.

No one is next to death in this fierce scene:
they who enact the all-but-bloody brawl
tomorrow have contracted to convene
in this selfsame embrace, to keel and haul.
Even the muscles rippling are mere blobs
of gentlemanly flab, averse to pang.
The Duke and the Wild Bull, can they be slobs
who squeak threats out in a high girlish twang?

Mishmash of pantomime and ribald props—
who has arranged to swoon, and who gets stuck
is merely mentionable to the cops
who sometimes are annoyed by impure muck.
Only one thing is genuine in all
the sweat—the Watching Faces who have willed
one hope, one prayer.
           Please God, don't let them stall.
Let someone get hurt good. Maybe get killed.

Considerations

1. Until the last three or four lines this seems to be an amiable and lighthearted poem about the theatrical antics of wrestlers. Discuss the sudden shift of focus and mood at the end.
2. Do you consider this poem a comment on just wrestling fans or of fans in general?
3. What is "impure muck" as opposed to "pure muck"? Would "legitimate" sports be "pure muck"? Explain.

JOHN CIARDI

Polo Match

Helmeted, booted, numbered, horsed, and always at
    a distance,
the polo players mill, fumble, jostle, and one at last
    clicks
the white ball far on its high arc while six knot up
    behind
and one in an epic lunge chases the white curve to hit
    or miss
the nothing between two uprights. He is, of course,
    pursued

by the giant that is always there to oppose giants, and
  who means
to deflect the diagram his way, spinning the arc back
  through
the pack, and beyond, and to click it home to his own
  nothing
between the uprights at the other end of the world.
                                                      So
from pole to pole they go, Greeks and Trojans,
  identical
to the end and great in their distances, their seven-
  and-a-half
minutes at a time and six times over till the last
  diagram
has been risked, the falls taken, the horses lathered,
  replaced,
and lathered again, and the crowd, forever small in
  its distance,
has applauded again and again like wind rattling the
  dry trees
of a hill beyond.
              Then, breathing hard, they walk their
              horses
to the grooms, station wagons, and trailers that wait
to pack distances close and take them expensively to
  rest
between glories; and the players, dismounted, with
  towels
around their necks and their hair sweat-curled, light
  cigarettes
and are no longer giants in the dusty world the cars
  leave
for their home beyond heroes; till only the field is left,
like an emptied world, its grasses charged by great
  shadows.

Considerations

1. Discuss the way Ciardi contrasts the illusion of sports with the reality. What is the purpose of referring to the players as "giants" and as Greeks and Trojans?
2. Why is it necessary for the events to occur "always at / a distance"?
3. Does the poem place a moral judgment on the demand for illusion and myth in sports?

ROBERT PENN WARREN

Skiers

With the motion of angels, out of
Snow-spume and swirl of gold mist, they
Emerge to the positive sun. At
That great height, small on that whiteness,
With the color of birds or of angels,
They swoop, sway, descend, and descending,
Cry their bright bird-cries, pure
In the sweet desolation of distance.
They slowly enlarge to our eyes. Now

On the flat where the whiteness is
Trodden and mud-streaked, not birds now,
Nor angels even, they stand. They

Are awkward, not yet well adjusted
To this world, new and strange, of Time and
Contingency, who now are only
Human. They smile. The human

Face has its own beauty.

Considerations

1. The controlling element of this poem is counterpoint. It is also a study in illusion. How does Warren play off illusion and reality against one another? What is to be gained by such a contrast?
2. The beauty of fantasy and illusion is often stated and obvious, but what does Warren say in behalf of reality?
3. What is "the sweet desolation of distance"?

GEORGE GORDON, LORD BYRON

The Bull Fight

From *Childe Harold's Pilgrimage*

Canto the First

LXXIV

In costly sheen and gaudy cloak array'd,
But all afoot, the light-limb'd Matadore
Stands in the centre, eager to invade
The lord of lowing herds; but not before

The ground with cautious tread is traversed o'er,
Lest aught unseen should lurk to thwart his speed:
His arms a dart, he fights aloof, nor more
Can man achieve without the friendly steed—
Alas! too oft condemn'd for him to bear and bleed.

LXXV

Thrice sounds the clarion; lo! the signal falls,
The den expands, and Expectation mute
Gapes round the silent circle's peopled walls.
Bounds with one lashing spring the mighty brute,
And, wildly staring, spurns with sounding foot
The sand, nor blindly rushes on his foe:
Here, there, he points his threatening front, to suit
His first attack, wide waving to and fro
His angry tail; red rolls his eye's dilated glow.

LXXVI

Sudden he stops; his eye is fix'd: away,
Away, thou heedless boy! prepare the spear:
Now is thy time, to perish, or display
The skill that yet may check his mad career.
With well-timed croupe the nimble coursers veer;
On foams the bull, but not unscathed he goes;
Streams from his flank the crimson torrent clear:
He flies, he wheels, distracted with his throes;
Dart follows dart; lance, lance; loud bellowings speak his woes.

LXXVII

Again he comes; nor dart nor lance avail,
Nor the wild plunging of the tortured horse;
Though man and man's avenging arms assail,
Vain are his weapons, vainer is his force.
One gallant steed is stretch'd a mangled corse;
Another, hideous sight! unseam'd appears,
His gory chest unveils life's panting source;
Though death-struck, still his feeble frame he rears;
Staggering, but stemming all, his lord unharm'd he bears.

LXXVIII

Foil'd bleeding, breathless, furious to the last,
Full in the centre stands the bull at bay,
Mid wounds, and clinging darts, and lances brast,
And foes disabled in the brutal fray:
And now the Matadores around him play,

Shake the red cloak, and poise the ready brand:
Once more through all he bursts his thundering way—
Vain rage! the mantle quits the conynge hand,
Wraps his fierce eye—'tis past—he sinks upon the sand!

LXXIX

Where his vast neck just mingles with the spine,
Sheathed in his form the deadly weapon lies.
He stops, he starts, disdaining to decline;
Slowly he falls amidst triumphant cries,
Without a groan, without a struggle dies.
The decorated car appears, on high
The corse is piled—sweet sight for vulgar eyes;
Four steeds that spurn the rein, as swift as shy,
Hurl the dark bulk along, scarce seen in dashing by.

LXXX

Such the ungentle sport that oft invites
The Spanish maid, and cheers the Spanish swain;
Nurtured in blood betimes, his heart delights
In vengeance, gloating on another's pain.
What private feuds the troubled village stain!
Though now one phalanx'd host should meet the foe,
Enough, alas, in humble homes remain
To meditate 'gainst friends the secret blow,
For some slight cause of wrath, whence life's warm stream must flow.

Considerations

1. Byron says the bullfight "invites / The Spanish maid, and cheers the Spanish swain." (lover) Why are Americans, supposedly so violent, not attracted to the sport?
2. The Spanish bullfight fan, says Byron, "delights / In vengeance, gloating on another's pain." Is this a universal characteristic? Explain.

OGDEN NASH

Confessions of a Born Spectator

One infant grows up and becomes a jockey,
Another plays basketball or hockey.
This one the prize ring hastes to enter,
That one becomes a tackle or center.
I'm just as glad as glad can be
That I'm not them, that they're not me.

With all my heart do I admire
Athletes who sweat for fun or hire,
Who take the field in gaudy pomp
And maim each other as they romp;
My limp and bashful spirit feeds
On other people's heroic deeds.

Now A runs ninety yards to score;
B knocks the champion to the floor;
C, risking vertebrae and spine,
Lashes his steed across the line.
You'd think my ego it would please
To swap positions with one of these.

Well, ego might be pleased enough,
But zealous athletes play so rough;
They do not ever, in their dealings,
Consider one another's feelings.
I'm glad that when my struggle begins
Twixt prudence and ego, prudence wins.

When swollen eye meets gnarlèd fist,
When snaps the knee, and cracks the wrist,
When calm officialdom demands,
Is there a doctor in the stands?
My soul in true thanksgiving speaks
For this most modest of physiques.

Athletes, I'll drink to you or eat with you,
Or anything except compete with you;
Buy tickets worth their weight in radium
To watch you gambol in a stadium,
And reassure myself anew
That you're not me and I'm not you.

Considerations

1. Would you say that Nash speaks for the majority of fans in this poem? Why or
   why not?
2. Do the following lines speak for more spectators than would admit it?
       My limp and bashful spirit feeds
       On other people's heroic deeds.

BABETTE DEUTSCH

A Bull

His sad brown bulk rears patient as the hills
Hunched like dark herders at the pasture's back,
Swaying, he will not topple like those clouds
Heavy with throttled thunders. Lust that thrills
The crowd, to see such power pricked and teased
Through hot blind plunges to a sandy death
While they breathe blood, rage flowering in their veins,
His poor tame suffering will not have appeased,
Who takes the sun's barbs in a sullen drowse.
The ritual of his fertility
Is simple; he was bred only to breed,
The homely husband to a score of cows.
Yet monstrous as a myth, his front denies
His humbled horns, as, hugely male, he stands
Hung with endurance as with iron weights.
Clustering flies mate round his red-rimmed eyes.

Considerations

1. Would you consider this an "earthy" poem? If so, cite examples.
2. Why does Deutsch say that bullfight crowds are thrilled with "lust"?
3. Why doesn't the death of the bull "appease" their "rage"?
4. Why is the bull a traditional fertility symbol?

W. R. MOSES

Little-League Baseball Fan

No closer the glove clings to the sweaty hand
Than clings my drybones heart
To the being of greenbones there where he jumps and hollers
For a batter to get a hit;
Then comes himself to the proof, the plate, holding
The long bat heavy
And strong to reverse the flight of the whirling, humming
Pitch: sock it like hell.

Lord knows what kind of mystery puts together
Into one flesh the two
Of drybones and greenbones. Yet his every twitch,
Every glint of triumph
At having mastered the ball's trajectory
Is mine, mine too.
I am warm, thoughtless, grinning in the twilight;
My flesh glows, and I thrill.

So be it. For maybe a glow of flesh will cancel
A cold vision clutched
Under the flesh, in my long bones' cells:
Every-man Me confronting
(Unwilling batter) in a game that will not continue
Many more outs, the crossfire
Of the daily sun. And my God, who could connect
With those impossible curves?

Considerations

1. What is the central analogy (metaphor) in this poem? (Read the last stanza closely.)
2. Is this poem more in keeping with the emotions and dreams of the average spectator than Ogden Nash's "Confessions of a Born Spectator"? Why or why not?

MAY SWENSON

Watching the Jets Lose
to Buffalo at Shea

The feel of that leather baby
solid against your sternum,
you hug its skull and bottom
between huge huddled shoulders.
It's wrapped in your arms and wedged
under the hard muzzle
of your stuck-out faceguard.

Your thighs pumping, you run
to deliver the baby
to a cradle of grass at the goalposts.
But it's bumped from your arms,
and you're mounted
as if your back were leather.
Your legs cut away, you fold,

you tumble like a treetrunk.
Your brain's for the ground to split
like a leather egg, but it doesn't.
Your helmet takes the concussion.
Sent aloft by a leather toe,
a rugged leather baby
dropped from the sky and slammed

into the sling of your arms.
Oh, the feel of that leather bundle.
Oh, what a blooper and fumbler
you are, that you couldn't nest it,
that you lost and couldn't nurse it ,
long enough to lay it
in a cradle of grass at the goalposts.

Considerations

1. What is the repeated metaphor in this poem? How does it signal that the poem is written from a woman's point of view?
2. Explain how the entire poem seems to be a metaphor of a mother who has lost a child.

I entered
The ancient halls of visionary grace,
Bird-call sounded, sky
Appeared miraculous along,
And evil thickets held red histories.

—**Richard Eberhart**

JOHN UPDIKE

Tao in the Yankee Stadium Bleachers

Distance brings proportion. From here
the populated tiers
as much as players seem part of the show:
a constructed stage beast, three folds of Dante's rose,
or a Chinese military hat
cunningly chased with bodies.
"Falling from his chariot, a drunk man is unhurt
because his soul is intact. Not knowing his fall,
he is unastonished, he is invulnerable."
So, too, the "pure man"—"pure"
in the sense of undisturbed water.

"It is not necessary to seek out
a wasteland, swamp, or thicket."
The old men who saw Hans Wagner
scoop them up in lobster-hands,
the opposing pitcher's pertinent hesitations,
the sky, this meadow, Mantle's thick baked neck,
the old men who in the changing rosters see

a personal mutability,
green slats, wet stone are all to me
as when an emperor commands
a performance with a gesture of his eyes.

"No king on his throne has the joy of the dead,"
the skull told Chuang-tzu.
The thought of death is peppermint to you
when games begin with patriotic song
and a democratic sun beats broadly down.
The Inner Journey seems unjudgeably long
when small boys purchase cups of ice
and, distant as a paradise,
experts, passionate and deft,
wait while Berra flies to left.

Considerations

1. Tao means "The Way." It is a religion that teaches harmony through the oneness of opposites. Is this idea present in the first stanza? In the second?
2. The quotations are from the Tao of Lao Tze. How do the lines that follow them serve as examples?

MAXINE KUMIN

Morning Swim

Into my empty head there come
A cotton beach, a dock wherefrom

I set out, oily and nude
Through mist, in chilly solitude.

There was no line, no roof or floor
To tell the water from the air.

Night fog thick as terry cloth
Closed me in its fuzzy growth.

I hung my bathrobe on two pegs.
I took the lake between my legs.

Invaded and invader, I
Went overhand on that flat sky.

Fish twitched beneath me, quick and tame.
In their green zone they sang my name

And in the rhythm of the swim
I hummed a two-four-time slow hymn.

I hummed *Abide With Me*. The beat
Rose in the fine thrash of my feet,

Rose in the bubbles I put out
Slantwise, trailing through my mouth.

My bones drank water; water fell
Through all my doors. I was the well

That fed the lake that met my sea
In which I sang *Abide With Me*.

Considerations

1. How does the reader know immediately that this poem is a fantasy?
2. What purpose does the fantasy serve?
3. Do the couplets suggest any idea that might coincide with any element of the action? Explain.

JOHN BERRYMAN

The Ball Poem

What is the boy now, who has lost his ball,
What, what is he to do? I saw it go
Merrily bouncing, down the street, and then
Merrily over—there it is in the water!
No use to say "Oh there are other balls":
An ultimate shaking grief fixes the boy
As he stands rigid, trembling, staring down
All his young days into the harbor where
His ball went. I would not intrude on him,
A dime, another ball, is worthless. Now
He senses first responsibility
In a world of possessions. People will take balls,
Balls will be lost always, little boy,
And no one buys a ball back. Money is external.
He is learning, well behind his desperate eyes,

The epistemology of loss, how to stand up
Knowing what every man must one day know
And most know many days, how to stand up.
And gradually light returns to the street,
A whistle blows, the ball is out of sight,
Soon part of me will explore the deep and dark
Floor of the harbor . . . I am everywhere,
I suffer and move, my mind and my heart move
With all that move me, under the water
Or whistling, I am not a little boy.

Considerations

1. The critics identify Berryman as a member of the "confessionalist" school of poets—
   simply speaking, one who writes to "bare his chest" or "cleanse his soul." Discuss
   these characteristics in "Ball Poem."
2. What does the ball represent in this poem? The boy?
3. There are many definitions of poetry, but one quality that is generally accepted is
   that it should be written in a heightened form of the language, distinguishable from
   prose by its intensity, exactness, and compression. Discuss this poem from that
   point of view.

ROBERT FRANCIS

Diver

Diver go down
Down through the green
Inverted dawn
To the dark unseen
To the never day
The under night
Starless and steep
Deep beneath deep
Diver fall
And falling fight
Your weed-dense way
Until you crawl
Until you touch
Weird water land
And stand.

Diver come up
Up through the green

Into the light
The sun   the seen
But in the clutch
Of your dripping hand
Diver bring
Some uncouth thing
That we could swear
And would have sworn
Was never born
Or could ever be
Anywhere
Blaze on our sight
Make us see.

Considerations

1. Discuss the diver as metaphor.
2. Why does the narrator ask that the diver bring back "Some uncouth thing"? What usually happens to someone who tries to "Make us see"? Support your answer.
3. Discuss the structure of the poem: the first line of each stanza, its shape.

ROBERT FRANCIS

Swimmer

Observe how he negotiates his way
With trust and the least violence, making
The stranger friend, the enemy ally.
The depth that could destroy gently supports him.
With water he defends himself from water.
Danger he leans on, rests in. The drowning sea
Is all he has between himself and drowning.

Considerations

1. In the religion of Zen, one is taught the harmony of opposites. Does this poem contain the teachings of Zen? Support your answer.
2. What is meant by "The drowning sea / Is all he has between himself and drowning"?

JAMES DICKEY
Listening to Foxhounds

When in that gold
Of fires, quietly sitting
With the men whose brothers are hounds,

You hear the first tone
Of a dog on scent, you look from face
To face, to see whose will light up.

When that light comes
Inside the dark light of the fire,
You know which chosen man has heard

A thing like his own dead
Speak out in a marvelous, helpless voice
That he has been straining to hear.

Miles away in the dark,
His enchanted dog can sense
How his features glow like a savior's,

And begins to hunt
In a frenzy of desperate pride.
Among us, no one's eyes give off a light

For the red fox
Playing in and out of his scent,
Leaping stones, doubling back over water.

Who runs with the fox
Must sit here like his own image,
Giving nothing of himself

To the sensitive flames,
With no human joy rising up,
Coming out of his face to be seen.

And it is hard,
When the fox leaps into his burrow,
To keep that singing down,

To sit with the fire
Drawn into one's secret features,
And all eyes turning around

From the dark wood
Until they come, amazed, upon
A face that does not shine

Back from itself,
That holds its own light and takes more,
Like the face of the dead, sitting still,

Giving no sign,
Making no outcry, no matter
Who may be straining to hear.

Considerations

1. This is a poem about fox hunting as it is done in the South, with the hunters sitting by the fire drinking whiskey while their dogs chase the fox. Why is the speaker different from the others?
2. Dickey has described this poem as being maybe "a little obvious or too pat." Why do you agree or not with his assessment?

JAMES DICKEY

The Summons

For something out of sight,
I cup a grass-blade in my hands,
Tasting the root, and blow.
I speak to the wind, and it lives.
No hunter has taught me this call;
It comes out of childhood and playgrounds.
I hang my longbow on a branch.
The wind at my feet extends

Quickly out, across the lake,
Containing the sound I have made.
The water below me becomes
Bright ploughland in its body.
I breathe on my thumbs, and am blowing
A horn that encircles the forest.
Across the lake, a tree
Now thrums in tremendous cadence.

Beneath it, some being stumbles,
And answers me slowly and greatly
With a tongue as rasping as sawgrass.
I lower my hands, and I listen
To the beast that shall die of its love.
I sound my green trumpet again,
And the whole wood sings in my palms.
The vast trees are tuned to my bowstring

And the deep-rooted voice I have summoned.
I have carried it here from a playground
Where I rolled in the grass with my brothers.
Nothing moves, but something intends to.
The water that puffed like a wing
Is one flattened blaze through the branches.
Something falls from the bank, and is swimming.
My voice turns around me like foliage,

And I pluck my longbow off the limb
Where it shines with a musical light,
And crouch within death, awaiting
The beast in the water, in love
With the palest and gentlest of children,
Whom the years have turned deadly with knowledge:
Who summons him forth, and now
Pulls wide the great, thoughtful arrow.

Considerations

1. This is a poem about a hunter who uses a childhood technique of whistling to summon an animal so that he can kill it. Why does the hunter say he has "grown deadly with knowledge"?
2. Why will the beast "die of its love"?
3. Discuss the heightened language of this poem.

JAMES DICKEY

Winter Trout

In the concrete cells of the hatchery
He nourished a dream of living
Under the ice, the long preparations
For the strange heat of feeling slowly

Roofs melt to a rhythmic green,
But now, in the first cold of freedom,
Riding motionless under the road
Of ice, shaping the heart

Of the buried stream with his tail,
He knows that his powers come
From the fire and stillness of freezing.
With the small tremors of his form

The banks shift imperceptibly,
Shift back, tremble, settle,
Shift, all within utter stillness.
I keep in my quiver now

An arrow whose head is half-missing.
It is useless, but I will not change
The pulled, broken tooth of its head
For I have walked upon banks

Shaken with the watchfulness of trout
Like walking barefoot in sleep
On the swaying tips of grainfield,
On the long, just-bending stems,

Almost weightless, able to leap
Great distances, yet not leaping
Because each step on that ground
Gave a new sense of limitless hope.

Under the ice the trout rode,
Trembling, in the mastered heart
Of the creek, with what he could do.
I set myself up as a statue

With a bow, my red woolen back
Climbed slowly by thoughtful brambles
And dead beggar-lice, to shoot
At an angle down through the shadow

Of ice, and spear the trout
With a shot like Ulysses'
Through the ax heads, with the great weapon.
I shot, and the trout did not move

But was gone, and the banks
Went rigid under my feet
As the arrow floated away
Under the paving of ice.

I froze my right hand to retrieve it
As a blessing or warning,
As a sign of the penalties
For breaking into closed worlds

Where the wary controllers lie
At heart of their power,
A pure void of shadowy purpose
Where the gods live, attuning the world,

Laying plans for the first green
They ever have lived, to melt
The ice from their great crowns.
Their secret enemies break

Like statues, as the king rises slowly,
Keeping only the thinnest film
Of his element—imagination—
Before his eyes as he lifts

Into spring, with the wood upside down
Balanced perfectly in all its leaves
And roots as he deeply has
All winter made provisions for,

The surface full of gold flakes
Of the raw undersides of leaves,
And the thing seen right,
For once, that winter bought.

Consideration

1. Difficult poems like this one demand diligent, line-by-line study. Discuss each of the
   capsulated statements, then try to connect and unify them. For example, in the first
   two stanzas, the young troutling in the hatchery has only a vague, cellular notion of
   destiny, but as he slowly develops the "strange heat of feeling" he becomes dimly
   aware of the concrete of the hatchery melting "to a rhythmic green" (the foliage
   that rises above the stream). Continue this process and the poem will slowly yield.

BARBARA HOWES
Out Fishing

We went out, early one morning,
Over the loud marches of the sea,
In our walnut-shell boat,
Tip-tilting over that blue vacancy.

Combering, coming in,
The waves shellacked us, left us breathless, ill;
Hour on hour, out
Of this emptiness no fish rose, until

The great one struck that twine-
Wrapped flying-fish hard, turned and bolted
Off through the swelling sea
By a twist of his shoulder, with me tied fast; my rod

Held him, his hook held me,
In tug-of-war—sidesaddle on the ocean
I rode out the flaring waves,
Rode till the great fish sounded; by his submersion

He snapped the line, we lost
All contact; north, south, west, my adversary
Storms on through his world
Of water: I do not know him: he does not know me.

Considerations

1. What is the existential question implied in this poem?
2. Discuss Howes' rich poetic diction, especially her imaginative verbs.

TOM CLARK
Baseball

One day when I was studying with Stan Musial, he pointed out
that one end of the bat was fatter than the other. "This end is
more important than the other," he said. After twenty years I
learned to hold the bat by the handle. Recently, when Willie
Mays returned from Europe, he brought me a German bat of

modern make. It can hit any kind of ball. Pressure on the shaft at the end near the handle frees the weight so that it can be retracted or extended in any direction. A pitcher came with the bat. The pitcher offers not one but several possibilities. That is, one may choose the kind of pitch one wants. There is no ball.

Considerations

1. This is a prose poem and it has a surrealistic (look up this term) quality. What is the purpose behind Clark's juxtaposition of absurd details with matter-of-fact and understated "small talk"?
2. Discuss the possibility that this poem may be the result of a dream.
3. Why would there be no ball? Isn't the ball the most important and substantial element of the game? If baseball represents something else in this poem—art, for example—what would the absence of a ball symbolize?

TOM CLARK

Baseball and Classicism

Every day I peruse the box scores for hours
Sometimes I wonder why I do it
Since I am not going to take a test on it
And no one is going to give me money

The pleasure's something like that of codes
Of deciphering an ancient alphabet say
So as brightly to picturize Eurydice
In the Elysian Fields on her perfect day

The day she went 5 for 5 against Vic Raschi

Considerations

1. Many modern critics insist there is too much emphasis on sports statistics. Explain how this poem defends the reading of statistics as a kind of communion.
2. Identify:
    (a) Eurydice
    (b) Elysian Fields
    (c) Vic Raschi

DABNEY STUART

The Fisherman

Alcemon, a pupil of Pythagoras, thought that men die
*   because*
they cannot join their beginning and their end.

—**W. B. Yeats**

Thick water laps
The seawall's edge as the tide ebbs,
Leaving its stain
On the shelved, gray stone.
Out past the shallows where crabs
Eke trails nobody maps

My sinker nudges the ooze.
Above it two barbed hooks
Wave in the current like weeds.
On this end of the line I practice tricks
To convince some sucker fish he needs
To play this game of what we've got to lose.

All day on the stone wall
And nothing's worked. The same cheap shrimp
I started with slog beyond the shoals,
Going nowhere. Long past cramps
Numb to my nape, in the ebbing light
I'm caught. How does a hooked man fight?

The thick dark flows around me half asleep:
Sparrows peck dung in a green street.
Gulls, hung above a liner's stern like kites,
Scrounge garbage. Vultures, who know their rights,
Pluck out a dead man's eyes. A winding sheet
Unrolls a sailor's body, lets it drop.

I wake. Though bottom-blind, afraid
These waters might yield
A catch so rich and strange that I could wield
It no better than my dreams, I wait
For whatever spawn or breed
Will take my bait.

Considerations

1. What is the significance of the epigraph by Yeats?
2. Is Stuart's subtle rhyme effective?
3. Explain the dream symbols of the fourth stanza. What are the symbolic implications of the final stanza?

JUDITH WRIGHT
Sports Field

Naked all night the field
breathed its dew until
the great gold ball of day
sprang up from the dark hill.

Now as the children come
the field and they are met.
Their day is measured and marked,
its lanes and tapes are set;

and the children gilt by the sun
shoulder one another;
crouch at the marks to run,
and spring, and run together—

the children pledged and matched,
and built to win or lose,
who grow, while no one watches,
the selves in their sidelong eyes.

The watchers love them in vain.
What's real here is the field,
the starter's gun, the lane,
the ball dropped or held;

and set towards the future
they run like running water,
for only the pride of winning,
the pain the losers suffer,

till the day's great golden ball
that no one ever catches,
drops; and at its fall
runners and watchers

pick up their pride and pain
won out of the measured field
and turn away again
while the star-dewed night comes cold.

So pride and pain are fastened
into the heart's future,
while naked and perilous
the night and the field glitter.

Considerations

1. Discuss the quality of mutability, change, in this poem.
2. Why do the "watchers" love the children "in vain"? Does it have to do with their constant change, as opposed to the status of the field, the gun, the ball? Why do children "run like running water"?

RICHARD EBERHART

Spring Mountain Climb

Till thinking had worn out my enterprise,
I felt, and felt the flesh
Salt-swart, blood-sweet,
To which bird-song stung mysterious
And the white trillium mysterious in the wood;

I saw the mountain and the lake,
I followed where the source sounded,
Over boulders, crossed logs,
Up rugged reaches, where
The gates of mystery increased;

Sacred justice moved me, I entered
The ancient halls of visionary grace,
Bird-call sounded, sky
Appeared miraculous along,
And evil thickets held red histories;

Here divine justice made me sweat;
While an eye nebulous and profound
Partook of a huge nature, endless
Sufferings redeemed in rushwater,
Song falling, searching the world.

Such were the signatures I saw
Written by the hand of God
In knotted density, mysteries
Of incontestable day, while I
Passed the singing brook, so

Controlled by its eternal sound
As to be a living witness
To spirit, and to spirit reaching,
And to the sound falling back,
And man fallen to his endless burden.

Considerations

1. This poem is about the mysticism to be sensed by walking in the woods. Discuss:
   (a) "The gates of mystery"
   (b) "Sacred justice"
   (c) "ancient halls of visionary grace"
   (d) "evil thickets held red histories"
   (e) "Sufferings redeemed in rushwater"
2. Explain the sense of loss implied in the beginning of the poem. Can thinking displace feeling? Explain.

RICHARD EBERHART

Ball Game

Caught off first, he leaped to run to second, but
Then struggled back to first.
He left first because of a natural desire
To leap, to get on with the game.
When you jerk to run to second
You do not necessarily think of a home run.
You want to go on. You want to get to the next stage,
The entire soul is bent on second base.
The fact is that the mind flashes
Faster in action than the muscles can move.
Dramatic! Off first, taut, heading for second,
In a split second, total realization,
Heading for first. Head first! Legs follow fast.
You struggle back to first with victor effort
As, even, after a life of effort and chill,
One flashes back to the safety of childhood,
To that strange place where one had first begun.

Considerations

1. On the surface this is a poem about a baserunner caught off first base, but it goes deeper than that. Discuss Eberhart's analogy in detail.
2. When the experience is over, why is it that "One flashes back to the safety of childhood"?
3. What is the significance of the title?

ROBERT HAYDEN

The Diver

Sank through easeful
azure. Flower
creatures flashed and
shimmered there—
lost images
fadingly remembered.
Swiftly descended
into canyon of cold
nightgreen emptiness.
Freefalling, weightless
as in dreams of
wingless flight,
plunged through infra-
space and came to
the dead ship,
carcass that swarmed with
voracious life.
Angelfish, their
lively blue and
yellow prised from
darkness by the
flashlight's beam,
thronged her portholes.
Moss of bryozoans
blurred, obscured her
metal. Snappers,
gold groupers explored her,
fearless of bubbling
manfish. I entered
the wreck, awed by her silence,
feeling more keenly
the iron cold.
With flashlight probing
fogs of water
saw the sad slow
dance of gilded
chairs, the ectoplasmic
swirl of garments,
of buoyancy,
drunken shoes. Then
livid gesturings,
eldritch hide and

seek of laughing
faces. I yearned to
find those hidden
ones, to fling aside
the mask to call to them,
yield to rapturous
whisperings, have
done with self and
every dinning
vain complexity.
Yet in languid
frenzy strove, as
one freezing fights off
sleep desiring sleep;
strove against the
cancelling arms that
suddenly surrounded
me, fled the numbing
kisses that I craved.
Reflex of life-wish?
Respirator's brittle
belling? Swam from
the ship somehow;
somehow began the
measured rise.

Considerations

1. Describe the form of this poem. What does it suggest?
2. Why does the diver want to "yield to rapturous / whisperings"? Why doesn't he? Does the deep diver experience an exhilaration caused by the nitrogenized air? What are the symptoms of such an exhilaration?

DONALD JUSTICE

Here in Katmandu

We have climbed the mountain,
There's nothing more to do.
It is terrible to come down
To the valley
Where, amidst many flowers,
One thinks of snow,

As, formerly, amidst snow,
Climbing the mountain,
One thought of flowers,
Tremulous, ruddy with dew,
In the valley.
One caught their scent coming down.

It is difficult to adjust, once down,
To the absence of snow.
Clear days, from the valley,
One looks up at the mountain.
What else is there to do?
Prayerwheels, flowers!

Let the flowers
Fade, the prayerwheels run down.
What have these to do
With us who have stood atop the snow
Atop the mountain,
Flags seen from the valley?

It might be possible to live in the valley,
To bury oneself among flowers,
If one could forget the mountain,
How, setting out before dawn,
Blinded with snow,
One knew what to do.

Meanwhile it is not easy here in Katmandu,
Especially when to the valley
That wind which means snow
Elsewhere, but here means flowers,
Comes down,
As soon it must, from the mountain.

Considerations

1. This is not the first poem to suggest the overwhelming attraction the high mountain
   holds for one who has stood atop it. Does this poem explain what that attraction is?
   What do you think it is?
2. Why is it "not easy" when the wind begins to blow down "from the mountain"?
3. Compare this exhilaration with that of "The Diver" by Robert Hayden.

R. S. THOMAS

Alpine

About mountains it is useless to argue,
You have either been up or you haven't;

The view from half-way is nobody's view.
The best flowers are mostly at the top

Under a ledge, nourished by wind.
A sense of smell is of less importance

Than a sense of balance, walking on clouds
Through holes in which you can see the earth

Like a rich man through the eye of a needle.
The mind has its own level to find.

Considerations

1. Compare this poem with "Here in Katmandu." How do they differ regarding flowers?
2. Explain the allusion of line 9.

JON ANDERSON

The Parachutist

Then the air was perfect. And his descent
to the white earth slowed.
                              Falling
became an ability to rest—as

the released breath
believes in life. Further down it snowed,

a confusion of slow novas
which his shoes touched upon, which seemed,
as he fell by,

to be rising. From every
small college and rural town,
      the clearest, iced blossoms of thought,

but gentle.
                Then the housetops
of friends, who
he thought had been speaking of his arrival,
withdrew, each from another.

He saw that his friends
lived in a solitude they had not ever said aloud.

Strangely he thought this good.

        The world, in fact,
which in these moments he came toward,
seemed casual.

                Though not new.
Had he been thinking this all along?
        A life
where he belonged—having lived with himself

always—as a secret friend?

A few may have seen him then. In evidence:
the stopped dots
of children and dogs, sudden weave

        of a car—
acquaintances circling up
into the adventure they imagined. They saw him drop

through the line breaks
and preciousness of art

down to the lake
which openly awaited him.
                Here the thin
        green ice allowed him in.

Some ran, and were late.
These would
forever imagine tragedy

(endless descent,
his face floating among the reeds, by the fish
unrecognized), as those

who imagine the silence of a guest
to be mysterious, or wrong.

Considerations

1. Discuss the different perspective achieved by the parachutist.
2. But does he feel that a part of him may have had this perspective all along? Why
   does he have to jump out of a plane to realize it?

ROBERT FROST

The Rabbit-Hunter

Careless and still
The hunter lurks
With gun depressed,
Facing alone
The alder swamps
Ghastly snow-white.
And his hound works
In the offing there
Like one possessed,
And yelps delight
And sings and romps,
Bringing him on
The shadowy hare
For him to rend
And deal a death
That he nor it
(Nor I) have wit
To comprehend.

Considerations

1. What is Frost's attitude toward his subject? (Compare with "In Autumn.")
2. Frost was the master of the art of faint rhyme. What is the rhyme pattern in this
   poem? Is it regular?

WALKER GIBSON
Billiards

Late of the jungle, wild and dim,
Sliced from the elephant's ivory limb,
Painted, polished, here these spheres
Rehearse their civilized careers—
Trapped in a geometric toil,
Exhibit impact and recoil
Politely, in a farce of force.
For this, I utter no remorse
But praise the complicated plan
That organizes beast and man
In patterns so superbly styled,
Late of the jungle, dim and wild.

Considerations

1. Without the title would the subject of this poem be recognizable? Explain.
2. What attitude does the speaker exhibit toward the harvesting of tusks for man's entertainment?

ROLFE HUMPHRIES
Polo Grounds

Time is of the essence. This is a highly skilled
And beautiful mystery. Three or four seconds only
From the time that Riggs connects till he reaches first,
And in those seconds Jurges goes to his right,
Comes up with the ball, tosses to Witek at second
For the force on Reese, Witek to Mize at first,
In time for the out—a double play.

(Red Barber crescendo. Crowd noises, obbligato;
Scattered staccatos from the peanut boys,
Loud in the lull, as the teams are changing sides) ...

Hubbell takes the sign, nods, pumps, delivers—
A foul into the stands. Dunn takes a new ball out,
Hands it to Danning, who throws it down to Werber;
Werber takes off his glove, rubs the ball briefly,

Tosses it over to Hub, who goes to the rosin bag,
Takes the sign from Danning, pumps, delivers—
Low, outside, ball three. Danning goes to the mound,
Says something to Hub. Dunn brushes off the plate,
Adams starts throwing in the Giant bull pen,
Hub takes the sign from Danning, pumps, delivers,
Camilli gets hold of it, a *long* fly to the outfield,
Ott goes back, back, back, against the wall, gets under it,
Pounds his glove, and takes it for the out.
That's all for the Dodgers. . . .

Time is of the essence. The rhythms break,
More varied and subtle than any kind of dance;
Movement speeds up or lags. The ball goes out
In sharp and angular drives, or long, slow arcs,
Comes in again controlled and under aim;
The players wheel or spurt, race, stoop, slide, halt,
Shift imperceptibly to new positions,
Watching the signs, according to the batter,
The score, the inning. Time is of the essence.

Time is of the essence. Remember Terry?
Remember Stonewall Jackson, Lindstrom, Frisch,
When they were good? Remember Long George Kelly?
Remember John McGraw and Benny Kauff?
Remember Bridwell, Tenney, Merkle, Youngs,
Chief Myers, Big Jeff Tesreau, Shufflin' Phil?
Remember Matthewson, and Ames, and Donlin,
Buck Ewing, Rusie, Smiling Mickey Welch?
Remember a left-handed catcher named Jack Humphries,
Who sometimes played the outfield, in '83?

Time is of the essence. The shadow moves
From the plate to the box, from the box to second base,
From second to the outfield, to the bleachers.

Time is of the essence. The crowd and players
Are the same age always, but the man in the crowd
Is older every season. Come on, play ball!

Considerations

1. The mutability of life is a frequently used theme in poetry. How does Humphries use the baseball commentary to add another dimension to the essence of time flying?
2. Why is it that "The crowd and players / Are the same age always, but the man in the crowd / Is older every season"?

DAVE SMITH

Running Back

Much of what is seen is best avoided.
I squint sometimes, sometimes I go slant.
In the nature of things, inevitably,
the tackle looms, second zero
to left and right in the black and white
skull sessions. These are human dreams,
our best approximations of reality,
becoming facts we know, or will know.

When I collide with them I often think
how the sportscasters will write it up,
a day of carnage, the red claw of fate,
defeat in the fourth stanza, a joke
whose ending is 'You had to be there.'
I've seen lips squeezed grape-like,
my own teeth litter the turf,
a string of pearls like years
cast at the feet of shrieking cheerleaders.

My history is that blurred chalk I see
badly after each performance. The caged
face remains, sighted over the rear
of the pigskin where I squint.
Squint or not, that's what ahead.
Coaches with theories, from Ivy League
to Mid-West Renaissance will swear
the heart's given, it's all in the feet,

like John Keats, say, cutting at the ode.
Some are blunter. *This is a football,*
you don't have have no idea but it! Hold
on tight, don't think! I don't think
lips and teeth mean the same to them,
who see the field sideways and scream
for zig-ins, zag-outs and executions
in a jargon remote and perfect as code.
I'm paid to crack a rock that growls.

Knuckles on what used to be soothing dirt,
I stare into a line of butts and see,
beyond, that face. It talks and hurts,
therefore I try to run artfully
behind the abstract backs of blockers,
direct, disguised, at the zero's middle.
I don't have to look for what will be
there, dark, pure, calling incomprehensibly.

Considerations

1. Does this poem contain a single analogy, or more? If so, what?
2. Explain the first line within the context of this poem, and also in its more general applications.
3. In the final stanza, why are the "backs of the blockers" described as "abstract"?
4. In the analogy at the end, who are the "blockers"? Who is it that is "direct, disguised," the speaker (the running back) or the blockers? How do you know? What is in the "zero's middle"? Explain.

JOHN WILLIAMS

The Skaters

Graceful and sure with youth, the skaters glide
Upon the frozen pond. Unending rings
Expand upon the ice, contract, divide,
Till motion seems the shape that movement brings,

And shape is constant in the moving blade.
Ignorant of the beauty they invent,
Confirmed in their hard strength, the youths evade
Their frail suspension on an element,

This frozen pond that glisters in the cold.
Through all the warming air they turn and spin,
And do not feel that they grow old
Above the fragile ice they scrape and thin.

Considerations

1. What is the controlling analogy in this poem?
2. Discuss the tone. Exactly how does it differ from Wordsworth's "The Skaters"? How are they similar?

EASY TARGETS, TO WIT:

Who would dare to supersede me,
Super-super-superwho?

—John Updike

JOHN UPDIKE

Superman

I drive my car to supermarket
    The way I take is superhigh,
A superlot is where I park it,
    And Super Suds are what I buy.

Supersalesmen sell me tonic—
    Super-Tone-O, for relief.
The planes I ride are supersonic
    In trains I like the Super Chief.

Supercilious men and women
    Call me superficial—*me*.
Who so superbly learned to swim in
    Supercolossality.

Superphosphate-fed foods feed me;
    Superservice keeps me new.
Who would dare to supersede me,
    Super-super-superwho?

Considerations

1. What is hyperbole? Is that what this poem is about? Explain.
2. Explain how this poem relates to sports. Who is responsible for such inflation of the language? How is *de*flation caused by *in*flation?

EVE MERRIAM

Cheers

The frogs and the serpents each had a football team,
and I heard their cheer leaders in my dream:

"Bilgewater, bilgewater," called the frog,
"Bilgewater, bilgewater,
Sis, boom, bog!
Roll 'em off the log,
Slog 'em in the sog,
Swamp'em, swamp'em,
Muck mire quash!"

"Sisyphus, Sisyphus," hissed the snake,
"Sibilant, syllabub,
Syllable-loo-ba-lay.
Scylla and Charybdis,
Sumac, asphodel,
How do you spell Success?
With an S-S-S!"

Considerations

1. If this poem is intended as satire, what is being satirized, cheerleaders or poetry?
2. Who were Sisyphus, Scylla, and Charybdis? Does it matter in this poem?

ROBERT LOUIS STEVENSON

The Careful Angler

The careful angler chose his nook
At morning by the lilied brook,
And all the noon his rod he plied
By that romantic riverside.
Soon as the evening hours decline
Tranquilly he'll return to dine,
And, breathing forth a pious wish,
Will cram his belly full of fish.

Considerations

1. The humor of this poem lies in the counterpoint of lines 2 and 4 with 8. How does line 8 change the tone?
2. Why is "cram his belly full" superior to "fill his stomach"?

RICHARD ARMOUR

Fish Story

Count this among my heartfelt wishes:
To hear a fish tale told by fishes
And stand among the fish who doubt
The honor of a fellow trout,
And watch the bulging of their eyes
To hear of imitation flies
And worms with rather droopy looks
Stuck through with hateful, horrid hooks,
And fishermen they fled all day from
(As big as this) and got away from.

Consideration

1. What popular joke does this poem invert?

REGINALD ARKELL

A Public Nuisance

You know the fellow,
I have no doubt,
Who stands and waggles
His club about.

Empires crumble
And crowns decay;
Kings and Communists
Pass away.

Dictators rise
And dictators fall—
But *still* he stands
Addressing his ball.

Considerations

1. Usually a poem's title has a definite connection with the poem's subject. Discuss the possible connections of this title. Does the poem characterize the golfer as a public nuisance?
2. Is the poem satirizing golfers or political ideologies, or both? Explain.

CONRAD DIEKMANN
Winter Trees [1]

I think that I shall never ski
Again against so stout a tree.

A tree whose rugged bark is pressed
In bas-relief upon my chest.

A tree that with bacchantic air
Wears ski poles in its tangled hair.

. . . . .

I've learned my lesson: Fools like me
Should never try to shave a tree.

Considerations

1. This verse is a parody of what popular American poem?
2. What is "bacchantic air"? Who is Bacchus?

DAVID McCORD
The Sportsman

Partridge and quail, of course. Occasional woodcock,
Snipe, odd rabbits, squirrels, crows, coot—in fact,
All superficial life in range; lock, stock
And double barrel. Acquainted mallards quacked,
Considerable geese veered, and the gun's impact
Was pleasant to his shoulder. What a flock
Of startling memories rose to re-enact
Each death in feathers falling like a rock!
Decembers in red flannel, cold but game,
He pioneered through bullet-spattered wood.
The generous heart cried *kill.* If poor of aim,
He used the knife to comfort when he could.
Then suddenly, for no conspicuous reason,
He up and shot himself—well out of season.

Considerations

1. Compare the point of this poem with that of "In Autumn," by Barbara Howes. Discuss the effectiveness of both.
2. Read "First Blood." Which death affects you more—the sportsman's or the squirrel's. Explain.
3. What special form does this poem employ?

[1] From *Sports Illustrated.*

WILLIAM D. BARNEY

Caught in the Pocket

Here lies Sprawlings, a quarterback,
Victim of one too many a sack.
The hour was late, the hour was prime;
He passed away before his time.

Under this rug of astro-clover
He waits the ultimate turnover.
Five words of scripture tell, alas,
His tale of woe: And it came to pass.

Considerations

1. The humor in this poem depends heavily on the reader's appreciation of the poet's clever use of double entendres. Explain the double meaning of the following words:
   (a) Sprawlings
   (b) Prime
   (c) Passed
   (d) Astro-clover
   (e) Turnover
2. Do you detect a bit of good-natured satire in this little verse? Explain.

OGDEN NASH

The Hunter

The hunter crouches in his blind
'Neath camouflage of every kind,
And conjures up a quacking noise
To lend allure to his decoys.
This grown-up man, with pluck and luck,
Is hoping to outwit a duck.

Considerations

1. Although the tone of this poem is humorous, is the reader to take its point lightly? Why or why not?
2. Compare the attitude of Nash to his subject to that of R. P. Dexter in "Shadow Dirge."

OGDEN NASH

Who Taught Caddies to Count?
or
A Burnt Golfer Fears the Child

I have never beheld you, O pawky Scot,
And I only guess your name,
Who first propounded the popular rot
That golf is a humbling game.
You putted perhaps with a mutton bone,
And hammered a gutty ball;
But I think that you sat in the bar alone,
And never played at all.

Ye hae spoken a braw bricht mouthfu', Jamie,
Ye didna ken ye erred;
Ye're richt that golf is a something gamie,
But humble is not the word.
Try arrogant, insolent, supercilious,
And if invention fades,
Add uppitty, hoity-toity, bilious,
And double them all in spades.

Oh pride of rank is a fearsome thing,
And pride of riches a bore;
But both of them bow on lea and ling
To the Prussian pride of score.
Better the beggar with fleas to scratch
Than the unassuming dub
Trying to pick up a Saturday match
In the locker room of the club.

The Hollywood snob will look you through
And stalk back into his clique,
For he knows that he is better than you
By so many grand a week;
And the high-caste Hindu's fangs are bared
If a low-caste Hindu blinks;
But they're just like one of the boys, compared
To the nabobs of the links.

Oh where this side of the River Styx
Will you find an equal mate
To the scorn of a man with a seventy-six
For a man with a seventy-eight?
I will tell you a scorn that mates it fine
As the welkin mates the sun:
The scorn of him with a ninety-nine
For him with a hundred and one.

And that is why I wander alone
From tee to green to tee,
For every golfer I've ever known
Is too good or too bad for me.
Indeed I have often wondered, Jamie,
Hooking into the heather,
In such an unhumble, contemptful gamie
How anyone plays together.

Considerations

1. What is the serious point behind this humorous poem?
2. To whom is the speaker addressing the poem?

MEANINGS QUESTIONED, AIMS IN DOUBT

Does not that car bear
Sorry insignia: brown,
On a field of pastel,
A stag dormant, antlered?

—Barbara Howes

JAMES DICKEY

For the Last Wolverine

They will soon be down

To one, but he still will be
For a little while   still will be stopping

The flakes in the air with a look,
Surrounding himself with the silence
Of whitening snarls. Let him eat
The last red meal of the condemned

To extinction, tearing the guts

From an elk. Yet that is not enough
For me. I would have him eat

The heart, and, from it, have an idea
Stream into his gnawing head
That he no longer has a thing
To lose, and so can walk

Out into the open, in the full

Pale of the sub-Arctic sun
Where a single spruce tree is dying

Higher and higher. Let him climb it
With all his meanness and strength.
Lord, we have come to the end
Of this kind of vision of heaven

As the sky breaks open

Its fans around him and shimmers
And into its northern gates he rises

Snarling   complete   in the joy of a weasel
With an elk's horned heart in his stomach
Looking straight into the eternal

Blue, where he hauls his kind. I would have it all

My way: at the top of that tree I place

The New World's last eagle
Hunched in mangy feathers   giving

Up on the theory of flight.
Dear God of the wildness of poetry, let them mate
To the death in the rotten branches,
Let the tree sway and burst into flame

And mingle them, crackling with feathers,

In crownfire. Let something come
Of it   something gigantic   legendary

Rise beyond reason over hills
Of ice   SCREAMING   that it cannot die,
That it has come back, this time
On wings, and will spare no earthly thing:

That it will hover, made purely of northern

Lights, at dusk   and fall
On men building roads: will perch

On the moose's horn like a falcon
Riding into battle   into holy war against
Screaming railroad crews: will pull
Whole traplines like fibres from the snow

In the long-jawed night of fur trappers.

But, small, filthy, unwinged,
You will soon be crouching

Alone, with maybe some dim racial notion
Of being the last, but none of how much
Your unnoticed going will mean.

How much the timid poem needs

The mindless explosion of your rage,

The glutton's internal fire   the elk's
Heart in the belly, sprouting wings,

The pact of the "blind swallowing
Thing," with himself, to eat
The world, and not to be driven off it
Until it is gone, even if it takes

Forever. I take you as you are

And make of you what I will,
Skunk-bear, carcajou, bloodthirsty

Non-survivor.
           Lord, let me die   *but not die*
Out.

Considerations

1. Discuss this poem's combination of mysticism (beast mythology), reality (threat of extinction) and moral concept (revenge).
2. Discuss this poem's hyper-intense diction.
3. Discuss the philosophical implications of the italicized prayer at the end.

BARBARA HOWES

In Autumn

Redmen come
Lounging in pale sedans and
Then, at some entrance to the wilderness,
Dismount. Storming
Hill after hill,

Redcoated irregulars march,
Holding their guns like flagpoles;
Flannel men, pocketing small game,
Stamp through our threadbare wood . . .

Then head for home,
Guns at half-mast
For the carcass roped to the hood
Of the pale sedan.
Horns hook out over a headlight,
Nostrils drip
Blood on the fender, eyeballs bulge
At death. The male emblem is red.
Does that car not bear
Sorry insignia: brown,
On a field of pastel,
A stag dormant, antlered?

Considerations

1. Compare this poem about hunting to "The Hunter of the Prairies" by William Cullen Bryant. Discuss their difference in tone.
2. Also compare it with James Dickey's "The Summons." What is each poet's attitude toward hunting?
3. What is Howes' analogy in the first stanza?

BARBARA HOWES

Landscape, Deer Season

Snorting his pleasure in the dying sun,
The buck surveys his commodious estate,
Not sighting the red nostrils of the gun
Until too late.

He is alone. His body holds stock-still,
Then like a monument it falls to earth;
While the blood-red target-sun, over our hill,
Topples to death.

Considerations

1. Discuss the tone of this poem.
2. Why does Howes switch pronouns, from "he" to "it" in line 6?
3. Point out the rich figures of speech. What is their function? There are two examples of personification (look up this term). What are they?

WILLIAM HEYEN

The Stadium

The stadium is filled,
for this is the third night the moon
has not appeared as even a thin sickle.

We light the candles we were told to bring.
The diamond is lit red with torches.
Children run the bases.

A voice, as though from a tomb,
leads us to the last amen of a hymn.
Whole sections of the bleachers begin to moan.

The clergy files from the dugouts
to the makeshift communion rails
that line the infield grass.

We've known, all our lives,
that we would gather here in the stadium
on just such a night,

that even the bravest among us
would weep softly in the dark aisles,
catching their difficult breath.

Considerations

1. Critics of organized sports since John R. Tunis have been speaking of its evolution
   into a religion. In this poem, Heyen carries that idea to its final point. When would
   you say is the time setting? Do you think that baseball is still played there?
2. Why is it a sad occasion? Why are the people "catching their difficult breath"?
3. Discuss the tone of the poem. What historical period does it remind you of?

JAMES WRIGHT

A Mad Fight Song for
William S. Carpenter, 1966[1]

Varus, varus, gib mir meine Legionen wieder[2]

Quick on my feet in those Novembers of my loneliness,
I tossed a short pass,
Almost the instant I got the ball, right over the head
Of Barrel Terry before he knocked me cold.

When I woke, I found myself crying out
Latin conjugations, and the new snow falling
At the edge of a green field.

Lemoyne Crone had caught the pass, while I lay
Unconscious and raging
Alone with the fire ghost of Catullus, the contemptuous graces
    tossing
Garlands and hendecasyllabics over the head
Of Cornelius Nepos the mastodon,
The huge volume.

At the edges of southeast Asia this afternoon
The quarterbacks and the lines are beginning to fall,
A spring snow,

And terrified young men
Quick on their feet
Lob one another's skulls across
Wings of strange birds that are burning
Themselves alive.

Considerations

1. The subject of this poem is a combination of football, art, and war. Cite examples
   of each.
2. Discuss the analogies of the final stanza.

[1] Captain Carpenter, a graduate of West Point, called for his own troops to be napalmed
rather than have them surrender. General Westmoreland called him a "hero" and made him
his aide, and President Johnson awarded him a silver star for courage.
[2] Varus, Varus, give me back my legions.

PAUL GOODMAN

Don Larsen's Perfect Game

Everybody went to bat three times
except their pitcher (twice) and his pinch hitter,
but nobody got anything at all.
Don Larsen in the eighth and ninth looked pale
and afterwards he did not want to talk.
This is a fellow who will have bad dreams.
His catcher Berra jumped for joy and hugged him
like a bear, legs and arms, and all the Yankees
crowded around him thick to make him be
not lonely, and in fact in fact in fact
nothing went wrong. But that was yesterday.

Considerations

1. Why is Larsen "a fellow who will have bad dreams"? Is not perfection the goal of almost everyone? Does it have its drawbacks? Explain.
2. What happened to Don Larsen after that?

PAUL GOODMAN

Surfers at Santa Cruz

They have come by carloads
with Styrofoam surfboards
in the black wetsuits
of the affluent sixties,
the young Americans

kneeling paddle with their palms
and stand through the breakers
One World Polynesians
lying offshore
as if they were fishing for the village.

They are waiting for the ninth wave
when each lone boy falling downhill
ahead of the cresting hundreds of yards
balancing communicates
with the ocean on the Way

how beautiful they are
their youth and human skill
and communion with the nature of things,
how ugly they are
already sleek with narrow eyes.

Considerations

1. Why is *Way* capitalized?
2. Discuss the final stanza. How can something be both beautiful and ugly?

KENNETH PATCHEN

The Origin of Baseball

Someone had been walking in and out
Of the world without coming
To much decision about anything.
The sun seemed too hot most of the time.
There weren't enough birds around
And the hills had a silly look
When he got on top of one.
The girls in heaven, however, thought
Nothing of asking to see his watch
Like you would want someone to tell
A joke—"Time," they'd say, "what's
That mean—time?" laughing with the edges
Of their white mouths, like a flutter of paper
In a madhouse. And he'd stumble over
General Sherman or Elizabeth B.
Browning, muttering, "Can't you keep
Your big wings out of the aisle?" But down
Again, there'd be millions of people without
Enough to eat and men with guns just
Standing there shooting each other.

So he wanted to throw something
And he picked up a baseball.

Considerations

1. Like most of Patchen's poems, this one does not deal with the realm of ordinary
   reality; it combines myth, baseball, and politics. Cite the elements of each.
2. What are the implications of the wings on General Sherman and Elizabeth B.
   Browning?
3. How does Patchen satirize our devotion to mythical origins?

J. V. CUNNINGHAM

The Chase

The rabbit crossed and dodged and turned
I'd swear she neither saw nor heard
But ran for pleasure, unconcerned,
Erratic as a garden bird,

Timid and shy, but not afraid.
Say that her life was in the chase,
Yet it was nothing that God made
But wild blood glorying in a race

Through the cornfields of the lower Kaw.
My horse was tired before she fell.
Love does not work by natural law,
But as it is it's just as well,

For when the dogs retreated, fought,
And circled the embarrassed doe,
The doe moved only to be caught,
Quite pleased to be encircled so,

And I sat still, gun at my side.
Esteem and wonder stayed desire.
The kill is down. Time will abide.
Time to remember and inquire.

Considerations

1. What is the fundamental point of this poem?
2. If you have ever seen rabbits or deer caught by dogs, would you agree or disagree with the speaker's description of their deaths? Explain.
3. Rhyme in poetry is a rarity nowadays. Do you think it improves a poem or detracts from it? Or does it depend on the subject of the poem? Explain.

PHILIP BOOTH

Fisherman

Under hawk-watch
over the river
quick-schooled minnows
riffle the shallow
where I wade.

Fingerlings rise
in the pooled jade
at amber flies,
but only
fish-hawk hover
or kingfisher eye
can see below
the current-run
and river-race
to the legend
lying dark
in slow-finned grace.

And I, who lost
the rainbow risen
in the torrent
of my need,
cast and cast
again where he
lies deep while
his torn gills bleed.

And the dreamer hawk
high over that pool
in the streaming air
cries high and cool.

Considerations

1. This poem is not so important for what is says as for the atmosphere it creates. Is there a unity or oneness to this ambience?
2. Is there a rhyme pattern to the poem? What about the second stanza?

JOHN MASEFIELD

Partridges

Here they lie mottled to the ground unseen,
This covey linked together from the nest.
The nosing pointers put them from their rest,
The wings whirr, the guns flash and all has been.

The lucky crumple to the clod, shot clean,
The wounded drop and hurry and lie close;
The sportsmen praise the pointer and his nose,
Until he scents the hiders and is keen.

Tumbled in bag with rabbits, pigeons, hares,
The crumpled corpses have forgotten all
The covey's joy of strong or gliding flight.

But when the planet lamps the coming night,
The few survivors seek those friends of theirs;
The twilight hears and darkness hears them call.

Considerations

1. What is Masefield's attitude toward his subject in this poem? Compare it with that of Robert Frost in "The Rabbit-Hunter."
2. How does this poem differ in tone from "Shadow Dirge"? Explain.

MAY SWENSON

Death Invited

Death invited to break his horns
on the spread
cloth. To drop his head
on the dragged flag on the sand.
Death's hooves slipping
in blood, and a band
of blood down the black side.
Death's tongue, curved in the open mouth
like a gray horn, dripping
blood. And
six colored agonies decking the summit
of his muscled pride.
Death invited to die.

The head
of death, with bewildered raging eye,
flagged down,
dragged down to the red
cloth on the sand.
Death invited to stand,
legs spread,
on the spot of the cape.
To buckle stubborn knees and lie
down in blood on the silken shape.
Beg blindness come to the sun-pierced eye.

The sword, sunk at the top of the shoulder's pride—
its hilt a silver cross—drawn forth now lets
hot radiant blood slide
from bubbling nostrils
through cloth to thirsty ground.

Yearning horns found
fleeing cloth and bloodless pillow,
substance none. Arrogant thighs,
that swiped and turned death by,
now, close as love, above lean lunging,
filling the pain-hot eye.
That stares till it turns to blood.
With the short knife dug
quick!
to the nape.
And the thick
neck drops on the spot of the cape.

Chains are drawn
round the horns, whose points are clean.
Trumpets shout.
New sand is thrown
where death's blood streamed.
Four stout,
jingling horses with gilded hooves
tug death out.

Life is awarded ears and flowers.
Pelted with hats and shoes, and praise,
glittering life, in tight pink thighs,
swaggers around a rotunda of screams and *Oles*

Death is dragged from the ring,
a clumsy hide,
a finished thing—
back to his pen.
The gate swings shut.

The gate swings wide.
Here comes trotting, snorting death
let loose again.

Considerations

1. What sport does this poem describe? Discuss the poet's attitude toward her subject.
2. If violence is so important to American sports fans, as critics say, why is this sport illegal in the United States? Do we prefer our violence to be less conspicuous? Explain.

R. A. D. FORD

Revenge of the Hunted

The gun, the trap, the axe are borne
head high at dusk in triumph home—
the tramp of hunting boots,
the bloody mantle thrown
down, these challenge to the soul
the flagrant horn, and send
to the far bounds of the green
hills the trumpeting of death in shame.

There will be a beating out some day,
from bush to field to stone
farm; then, lugged in the mud,
spattered with wings torn and unclean
ugly parts of snake and lame
beasts, will with crude
arms barbarously destroy,
with fierce voices savagely proclaim:
Here lies the broken gun alone,
the green weeds sweeping it away,
and here the judgment of the wood.

Considerations

1. What does this poem have in common with James Dickey's "For the Last Wolverine"? There is one considerable difference in theme. What is it?
2. What single element does it have in common with David McCord's "The Sportsman"?

JOHN BRUCE

The Pike

I take it he doesn't think at all,
But muscles his slippery fight, an engine
Green deep, powering his belly flash
In his water mother, his horizonless well;
The hooked gill the fault in the world
Of his will, his preying paradise.

Near enough to net I have him,
And the murk of his body is my fear
Of our meeting somehow equally.
He pauses on the strain of my line;
I have him netted, sluicing the air,
How pure brave my wet thrasher, my enemy.

Considerations

1. Compare "The Pike" with "Out Fishing" by Barbara Howes. What are the similarities? The differences?
2. Why is "The hooked gill the fault in the world / Of his will"?

BINK NOLL

The Picador Bit

Inside that figure rides opaque malice
who by drilling makes the great heart lift
its fountain and waste the lake of blood.
His lance strikes, holds. Longer, the don's full weight.

Men for this circumstance of sport have made
laws that order place, gear, conduct and four tries
but the bull learns rage instead. He erupts
through headlong pain and strikes wrath back again.

Today's malice, part horse by blindfold
and morphine from panic at horns, stands,
its legal right side out, and standing so
tempts this, the next enlargement of the hole

—and part brawny don, mechanic who finds
and fits his point to drain the immense will.
Again the spot. The centaur shocks sideward
till the hole is important, like a whale's spout.

The crowd feels the lance in its own ripe hole,
in its hump knows the monster with two heads,
the blackness of its law, this letting of force
and the pump emptying the tongue of red.

Blood foams down. The head is dropped forever now.
Justice is satisfied. Its constable trots
darkly off. Left to his killers, the bull—
danger's substance, lure, huge hate itself—

thrills every male groin while he swings there
and, helpless, spills the fire of his urine.

Considerations

1. This is a highly crafted poem, compressed to its limit. Render into prose the following poetic delicasies:
   (a) "opaque malice"
   (b) "drain the immense will"
   (c) "the monster with two heads"
   (d) "the tongue of red"
   (e) "spills the fire of his urine"
2. Like Babette Deutsch in "A Bull," Noll emphasizes the bull's male symbolism. Why does the killing of the bull thrill "every male groin"?

EURIPIDES

The Greek Athlete

(Trans. by Tom Dodge)

Of the many ills afflicting Greece,
The worst is this species called athletes.
Bondsmen to their jaws and guts,
They seldom lay by and store.
Bad times always find them unprepared
And, benighted as they are of providence,
They can never deal with being poor.
In the prime of youth they strut about,
To be admired like gleaming sculpture;
But then comes harsh old age
And they are useless as threadbare garments.
What a shameful Greek tradition,
Exalting these men at official assemblies—
Using them as sops to people a feast.
So what if a man be crowned as greatest grappler?
As fleetest on his feet?
As discus-pitcher extraordinaire?
Or as jaw-breaker beyond compare?

Will such abilities repel an enemy attack?
Would these sportsters sail a discus at the foe?
Bob and spar with a wall of shields?
Jab the invaders from their land?
A blade is seldom parried by such monkeyshines.
Laurels should go to the good and the wise,
To the leader best suited to serve;
To him whose learned words impede corruption,
Thwart petty contention, bond feuding factions.
Such would be the greatest good for every Greek.

Considerations

1. With his typical intemperance, Euripides characterizes the athlete as being somewhat undeserving of his reputation. By implication, what is another target of Euripides' considerable disapproval?
2. Cite elements from this selection that are astoundingly modern. Which elements give away the fact that it was written nearly 2,500 years ago?
3. Euripides, now considered one of the half-dozen or so greatest playwrights of all time, was comparatively unappreciated in his lifetime, and was finally exiled. Does this selection suggest why? Explain. What is an iconoclast?

LOSERS

Eighth notes and fluttering cue balls
And Tibetan gongs in the side pockets
Those are what Charley Johnson heard
When he got his bell rung

—Tom Clark

TOM CLARK

The X of the Unknown

Sweet notes in dimensionless clusters
Eighth notes and fluttering cue balls
And Tibetan gongs in the side pockets
Those are what Charley Johnson heard
When he got his bell rung

He could stand but he could not see
He could hear but he could not talk
He could think but he could not walk
And over his head in the thought balloon
Little birds tweeted

So he continued to stand there
Until they came out and got him
And even then it was hard to head him off
For he seemed like a man leaving his mind behind him
Somewhere there on the ground

Considerations

1. Charley Johnson was a boxer in the fifties whose face was no stranger to the canvas. Besides describing one of Johnson's losing performances, what is Clark's purpose in this poem?
2. Discuss the possible meanings of the title?
3. Compare line 4 of the second stanza with line 6 of "On Hurricane Jackson."

WALKER GIBSON
Athletes

The groggy fighter on his knees
Sways up at nine, postpones the count;
The jockey, forty-to-one shot, sees
Them all go by, yet whips his mount;
The losing pitcher, arm gone lame,
Still drops that last one in, a strike—
So you and I play a stubborn game,
Disaster prodding us alike.
So you and I, ignoring odds,
Tug caps, clutch ropes, and flail our whips,
Make sacrifices to the gods,
Breed children and build battleships,
Though ours is not an athlete's doom,
Nor death like any shower room.

Considerations

1. Explain the analogy in this poem. In which line does the comparison begin?
2. Are we to infer from this analogy that every defeat is a death? What symbolizes death to the athlete?
3. Explain the last two lines: Is death worse, or less, than the shower room?

ROBERT WALLACE
A Snapshot for Miss Bricka
Who Lost in the Semifinal Round of the
Pennsylvania Lawn Tennis Tournament
at Haverford, July, 1960

Applause flutters onto the open air
like starlings bursting from a frightened elm,
and swings away across the lawns
in the sun's green continuous calm

of far July. Coming off the court,
you drop your racket by the judge's tower
and towel your face, alone, looking off,
while someone whispers to the giggling winner,

and the crowd rustles, awning'd in tiers
or under umbrellas at court-end tables,

glittering like a carnival
against the mute distance of maples

along their strumming street beyond
the walls of afternoon. Bluely, loss
hurts in your eyes—not loss merely,
but seeing how everything is less

that seemed so much, how life moves on
past either defeat or victory,
how, too old to cry, you shall find steps
to turn away. Now others volley

behind you in the steady glare;
the crowd waits in its lazy revel,
holding whiskey sours, talking, pointing,
whose lives (like yours) will not unravel

to a backhand, a poem, or a sunrise,
though they may wish for it. The sun
brandishes softly his swords of light
on faces, grass, and sky. You'll win

hereafter, other days, when time
is kinder than this worn July
that keeps you like a snapshot; losing,
your eyes, once, made you beautiful.

Considerations

1. Why does Wallace call this poem a "snapshot"?
2. Explain how this poem makes losing more beautiful than winning.

ERNEST LAWRENCE THAYER

Casey at the Bat

The outlook wasn't brilliant for the Mudville nine that day;
The score stood four to two with but one inning more to play.
And then, when Cooney died at first, and Barrows did the same,
A sickly silence fell upon the patrons of the game.

A straggling few got up to go in deep despair. The rest
Clung to that hope which springs eternal in the human breast;
They thought, If only Casey could but get a whack at that
We'd put up even money now, with Casey at the bat.

But Flynn preceded Casey, as did also Jimmy Blake,
And the former was a lulu and the latter was a cake;
So upon that striken multitude grim melancholy sat,
For there seemed but little chance of Casey's getting to the bat.

But Flynn let drive a single, to the wonderment of all,
And Blake, the much despisèd, tore the cover off the ball;
And when the dust had lifted, and men saw what had occurred,
There was Jimmy safe at second, and Flynn a-hugging third.

Then from five thousand throats and more there rose a lusty yell;
It rumbled through the valley, it rattled in the dell;
It knocked upon the mountain and recoiled upon the flat,
For Casey, mighty Casey, was advancing to the bat.

There was ease in Casey's manner as he stepped into his place;
There was pride in Casey's bearing and a smile on Casey's face.
And when, responding to the cheers, he lightly doffed his hat,
No stranger in the crowd could doubt 'twas Casey at the bat.

Ten thousand eyes were on him as he rubbed his hands with dirt,
Five thousand tongues applauded when he wiped them on his shirt;
Then while the writhing pitcher ground the ball into his hip,
Defiance gleamed from Casey's eye, a sneer curled Casey's lip.

And now the leather-covered sphere came hurtling through the air,
And Casey stood a-watching it in haughty grandeur there.
Close by the sturdy batsman the ball unheeded sped;
"That ain't my style," said Casey. "Strike one," the umpire said.

From the benches, black with people, there went up a muffled roar,
Like the beating of the storm waves on a stern and distant shore.
"Kill him! Kill the umpire!" shouted someone on the stand;
And it's likely they'd have killed him had not Casey raised his hand.

With a smile of Christian charity great Casey's visage shone;
He stilled the rising tumult, he bade the game go on;
He signaled to the pitcher, and once more the spheroid flew;
But Casey still ignored it, and the umpire said, "Strike two."

"Fraud!" cried the maddened thousands, and echo answered "Fraud!"
But one scornful look from Casey and the audience was awed;
They saw his face grow stern and cold, they saw his muscles strain,
And they knew that Casey wouldn't let that ball go by again.

The sneer is gone from Casey's lip, his teeth are clenched in hate,
He pounds with cruel violence his bat upon the plate;
And now the pitcher holds the ball, and now he lets it go,
And now the air is shattered by the force of Casey's blow.

Oh, somewhere in this favored land the sun is shining bright,
The band is playing somewhere, and somewhere hearts are light;
And somewhere men are laughing, and somewhere children shout,
But there is no joy in Mudville—mighty Casey has struck out.

Considerations

1. The reason for this poem's renown probably cannot be attributed to the art of its composition. Why does it represent a source of identification for almost everyone who reads it?
2. What happened in a game in 1932 between Chicago and the New York Yankees that proved to be a bit more successful for a real-life "Casey"?

LUCILIUS

First in the Pentathlon

(Trans. by Tom Dodge)

In wrestling I was pinned first,
    The race I ran dead last.
My discus tumbled far behind the rest.
    At the jump, my feet stayed on the ground
And a cripple could have beaten my javelin throw.
    Yet, in something I was first—first to lose all five.

Considerations

1. Could this athlete be suffering from the Charlie Brown Syndrome? Would his face ever adorn a box of classical Wheaties?
2. For a modern treatment of this theme, see "A Mighty Runner (Variation of a Greek Theme)."

LUCILIUS

Monument to a Boxer

(Trans. by Tom Dodge)

With this stone his foes honor Apis the fighter,
For making their work one hell of a lot lighter.

Considerations

1. Literally, this poem translates, "We, the combatants of Apis the pugilist, erect this stone in honor of him who caused us to suffer but little pain." In your opinion,

which is more important, literalness or poetry (assuming that both cannot be attained)? Support your answer.
2. Also, should a translator add rhyme and a title although Greek poets saw no need for either? Support your answer.

LUCILIUS

Boxer Loses Face and Fortune

(Trans. by Tom Dodge)

This Olympian pug you see now, Sir, once possessed
    A nose, a brow, eyelids, ears and chin,
all of which he lost in the ring; and he lost
    his birthright to his brother when their old man
took one look at this bozo's ragged mug
    and swore he belonged to somebody else.

Considerations

1. Explain the pun (look up this work) on "face" in the title.
2. Judging from this poem, could you speculate on the status of boxers in ancient Greece? How would you compare it with that of today?

LUCILIUS

Advice to a Prizefighter

(Trans. by Tom Dodge)

Odysseus, twenty years gone, was recognized
    by Argos, his dog, when he came home.
But you, Stratophon, box four hours
    and your friends don't know you,
let alone the dogs. Take a look at yourself
    and you'll say, "I'm not Stratophon."

Considerations

1. Explain the reference to Odysseus.
2. Look up the ancient Greeks' style of boxing. Judging from this poem how would you compare it with today's sport? (See "On Hurricane Jackson.")

EDWIN ARLINGTON ROBINSON

A Mighty Runner
(Variation of a Greek Theme)

The day when Charmus ran with five
In Arcady, as I'm alive,
He came in seventh.—"Five and one
Make seven, you say? It can't be done."—
Well, if you think it needs a note,
A friend in a fur overcoat
Ran with him, crying all the while,
"You'll beat 'em, Charmus, by a mile!"
And so he came in seventh.
Therefore, good Zoilus, you see
The thing is plain as plain can be;
And with four more for company,
He would have been eleventh.

Considerations

1. Why does Robinson subtitle his poem "Variation of a Greek Theme"? (See "First in the Pentathlon.")
2. This poem is arranged in couplets except for one deviation? What is it?

ANDREW YOUNG

Climbing in Glencoe

The sun became a small round moon
And the scared rocks grew pale and weak
As mist surged up the col, and soon
So thickly everywhere it tossed
That though I reached the peak
With height and depth both lost
It might as well have been a plain;
Yet when, groping my way again,
On to the scree I stept
It went with me, and as I swept
Down its loose rumbling course
Balanced I rode it like a circus horse.

Considerations

1. What caused the climber to lose sense of perspective at the peak?

2. Explain how the climber's agility would not exactly qualify him for Edmund Hillary's Everest crew.
3. Define:
    (a) col
    (b) scree

RICHARD ARMOUR

Good Sportsmanship

Good sportsmanship we hail, we sing,
    It's always pleasant when you spot it.
There's only one unhappy thing:
    You have to lose to prove you've got it.

Considerations

1. In this poem, Richard Armour shows us the dark side of the silver lining. In a system in which so much emphasis is placed on winning, is it *really* possible to reward the loser? Explain.
2. Is this poem accurate? Can't winners exhibit good sportsmanship? Why or why not?

EDWARD FIELD

The Sleeper

When I was the sissy of the block who nobody wanted
    on their team
Sonny Hugg persisted in believing that my small size
    was an asset
Not the liability and curse I felt it was
And he saw a use for my swift feet with which I ran
    away from fights.

He kept putting me into complicated football plays
Which would have been spectacular if they worked:
For instance, me getting clear in front and him
    shooting the ball over—
Or the sensation of the block, the Sleeper Play
In which I would lie down on the sidelines near the
    goal

As though resting and out of action, until the
      scrimmage began
And I would step onto the field, receive the long
      throw
And to the astonishment of all the tough guys in the
      world
Step over the goal line for a touchdown.

That was the theory anyway. In practice
I had the fatal flaw of not being able to catch
And usually had my fingers bent back and the
      breath knocked out of me
So the plays always failed, but Sonny kept on trying
Until he grew up out of my world into the glamorous
Varsity crowd, the popular kids of Lynbrook High.

But I will always have this to thank him for:
That when I look back on childhood
(That four psychiatrists haven't been able to help me
      bear the thought of)
There is not much to be glad for
Besides his foolish and delicious faith
That, with all my oddities, there was a place in the
      world for me
If only he could find the special role.

Considerations

1. This poem is a tribute to the Sonny Huggs of the world. Why don't they ever become psychiatrists? What usually happens to them? What is the "glamorous / Varsity crowd"?
2. Does our system make enough allowances for non-athletic boys? If not, what changes might be made?

IN MY DAY

...What does Charlie Gates see in his eye burning
With the goal line? Does he see a middle-aged man from
the Book
Of the Dead looking for him in magic shoes
From Tyree's disappeared pool hall?

—James Dickey

WILLIAM BUTLER YEATS

At Galway Races

There where the course is,
Delight makes all of the one mind,
The riders upon the galloping horses,
The crowd that closes in behind:
We, too, had good attendance once,
Hearers and hearteners of the work;
Aye, horsemen for companions,
Before the merchant and the clerk
Breathed on the world with timid breath.
Sing on: somewhere at some new moon,
We'll learn that sleeping is not death,
Hearing the whole earth change its tune,
Its flesh being wild, and it again
Crying aloud as the racecourse is,
And we find hearteners among men
That ride upon horses.

Considerations

1. The speaker is recalling an earlier, better time and predicting a time when "the whole earth" will "change its tune." Discuss.
2. What is it that is sleeping but not dead? How is whatever it is symbolized by the racecourse?

470

FRANCIS THOMPSON

At Lord's

It is little I repair to the matches of the Southron
    folk,
Though my own red roses there may blow;
It is little I repair to the matches of the Southron
    folk,
Though the red roses crest the caps, I know.
For the field is full of shades as I near the shadowy
    coast,
And a ghostly batsman plays to the bowling of a
    ghost,
And I look through my tears on a soundless-clapping
    host
As the run-stealers flicker to and fro,
To and fro:——
O my Hornby and my Barlow long ago!

Considerations

1. Why does the former athlete, returning to the place of his former glory "look through my tears"?
2. What are the "shades" that the field is full of? Explain the "soundless-clapping host." What does *repair* mean, in the first line?

ROBERT WALLACE

Driving By

On August nights,
in little towns you sometimes see
from the throughways
bloom

the ball field lights—
domes
of smoky brilliance:
brighter than daylight colors,

figures through wire-mesh on the green,
figures in the plank stands,
a tiny moon
dropping out toward left.

They stay
much as we left them—
lichen of the blue American nights
from which we come.

Considerations

1. Identify the analogy in this poem.
2. What is lichen and how is it used in this poem?
3. Why are ball fields important as symbols?

DONALD PETERSEN

The Ballad of
Dead Yankees

Where's Babe Ruth, the King of Swat,
Who rocked the heavens with his blows?
Grabowski, Pennock, and Malone—
Mother of mercy, where are those?

Where's Tony (Poosh 'em up) Lazzeri,
The quickest man that ever played?
Where's the gang that raised the roof
In the house that Colonel Ruppert made?

Where's Lou Gehrig, strong and shy,
Who never missed a single game?
Where's Tiny Bonham, where's Jake Powell
And many another peerless name?

Where's Steve Sundra, good but late,
Who for a season had his fling?
Where are the traded, faded ones?
Lord, can they tell us anything?

Where's the withered nameless dwarf
Who sold us pencils at the gate?
Hurled past the clamor of our cheers?
Gone to rest with the good and great?

Where's the swagger, where's the strut,
Where's the style that was the hitter?
Where's the pitcher's swanlike motion?
What in God's name turned life bitter?

For strong-armed Steve, who lost control
And weighed no more than eighty pounds,
No sooner benched than in his grave,
Where's the cleverness that confounds?

For Lou the man, erect and clean,
Wracked with a cruel paralysis,
Gone in his thirty-seventh year,
Where's the virtue that was his?

For nimble Tony, cramped in death,
God knows why and God knows how,
Shut in a dark and silent house,
Where's the squirrel quickness now?

For big brash Babe in an outsize suit,
Himself grown thin and hoarse with cancer,
Still autographing balls for boys,
Mother of mercy, what's the answer?

Is there a heaven with rainbow flags,
Silver trophies hung on walls,
A horseshoe grandstand, mobs of fans,
Webbed gloves and official balls?

Is there a power in judgment there
To stand behind the body's laws,
A stern-faced czar whose slightest word
Is righteous as Judge Kenesaw's?

And if there be no turnstile gate
At that green park, can we get in?
Is the game suspended or postponed,
And do the players play to win?

Mother of mercy, if you're there,
Pray to the high celestial czar
For all of these, the early dead,
Who've gone where no ovations are.

Considerations

1. Identify as many of the former Yankees as you can. Are they *really* better players than those of today? Why is the past often considered the "good old days"?
2. Is the mythologizing of sports a good or bad thing? Support your answer.

MILTON BRACKER
Where, O Where?

Where are the heroes of yesteryear?
Has ever their like been seen?
  Terry and Gehrig and Melvin Ott
  Lining another one out of the lot—
And Harry (The Cat) Brecheen.

Where are the stars of my misspent youth—
Like Meusel and Frisch, I mean?
  Tony Lazzeri (before Di Mag)
  Leading the Yanks to a runaway flag—
And Harry (The Cat) Brecheen.

Where are the players I loved so well—
Art Nehf, and the Brothers Dean?
  Who in the multitude does not miss
  Walter and Alex and Tyrus and Tris—
And Harry (The Cat) Brecheen?

Considerations

1. Identify as many of the names as you can. Who is Harry (The Cat) Brecheen? Why is he emphasized? Is it because of his greatness, or his name?
2. What is a refrain? Explain why it is the most important element of this poem.

JAMES DICKEY
Looking for the Buckhead Boys

Some of the time, going home, I go
Blind and can't find it.
The house I lived in growing up and out
The doors of high school is torn
Down and cleared
Away for further development, but that does not stop me.
First in the heart
Of my blind spot are
The Buckhead Boys. If I can find them, even one,
I'm home. And if I can find him   catch him in or around
Buckhead, I'll never die: it's likely my youth will walk
Inside me like a king.

First of all, going home, I must go
To Wender and Roberts' Drug Store, for driving through I saw it
Shining   renewed   renewed
In chromium, but still there.
It's one of the places the Buckhead Boys use to be, before
Beer turned teen-ager.
                              Tommy Nichols
Is not there. The Drug Store is full of women
Made of cosmetics. Tommy Nichols has never been
in such a place: he was the Number Two Man on the Mile
Relay Team in his day.
                              What day?

My day. Where was I?
                              Number Three, and there are some sunlit pictures
In the Book of the Dead to prove it: the 1939
North Fulton High School Annual. Go down,
              Go down

To Tyree's Pool Hall, for there was more
Concentration of the spirit
Of the Buckhead Boys
In there, than anywhere else in the world.
                              Do I want some shoes
To walk all over Buckhead like a king

Nobody knows? Well, I can get them at Tyree's;
It's a shoe store now. I could tell you where every spittoon
Ought to be standing. Charlie Gates used to say one of these days
I'm gonna get myself the reputation of being
The bravest man in Buckhead. I'm going in Tyree's toilet
And pull down my pants and take a shit.
                              Maybe
Charlie's the key: the man who would say that would never leave
Buckhead. Where is he? Maybe I ought to look up
Some Old Merchants. Why didn't I think of that
Before?
              Lord, Lord! Like a king!

Hardware. Hardware and Hardware Merchants
Never die, and they have everything on hand
There is to know. Somewhere in the wood-screws Mr. Hamby may have
My Prodigal's Crown on sale. He showed up
For every football game at home
Or away, in the hills of North Georgia. There he is, as old
As ever.
      Mr. Hamby, remember me?
                              God A'Mighty! Ain't you the one

Who fumbled the punt and lost the Russell game?

That's right.

How're them butterfingers?

Still butter, I say,
Still fumbling. But what about the rest of the team? What about Charlie Gates?
He the boy that got lime in his eye from the goal line
When y'all played Gainesville?

Right.

I don't know. Seems to me I see . . .

See? See? What does Charlie Gates see in his eye burning
With the goal line? Does he see a middle-aged man from the Book
Of the Dead looking for him in magic shoes
From Tyree's disappeared pool hall?

Mr. Hamby, Mr. Hamby,

Where? Where is Mont Black?

Paralyzed. Doctors can't do nothing.

Where is Dick Shea?

Assistant Sales Manager
Of Kraft Cheese.

How about Punchy Henderson?

Died of a heart attack
Watching high school football
In South Carolina.

Old Punchy, the last
Of the windsprinters, and now for no reason the first
Of the heart attacks.

Harmon Quigley?
He's up at County Work Farm
Sixteen. Doing all right up there; be out next year.

Didn't anybody get to be a doctor
Or lawyer?

Sure. Bobby Laster's a chiropractor. He's right out here
At Bolton; got a real good business.
Jack Siple?

Moved away.

Gordon Hamm?

Dead
In the war.

O the Book
Of the Dead, and the dead bright sun on the page
Where the team stands ready to explode
In all directions with Time. Did you say you see Charlie
Gates every now and then?

Seems to me.

Where?
> He may be out yonder at the Gulf Station between here and Sandy
> Springs.

Let me go pull my car out
Of the parking lot in back
Of Wender and Roberts'. Do I need gas? No; let me drive around the block
Let me drive around Buckhead
A few dozen times   turning   turning in my foreign
Car till the town spins   Whirls till the chrome vanishes
From Wender and Roberts'   the spittoons are remade
From the sun itself   the dead pages flutter the hearts rise up, that lie
In the ground, and Bobby Laster's backbreaking fingers
Pick up a cue-stick   Tommy Nichols and I rack the balls
And Charlie Gates walks into Tyree's un-
imaginable toilet.
I go north
Now, and I can use fifty
Cents' worth of gas.
It is Gulf. I pull in and praise the Lord Charlie
Gates comes out. His blue shirt dazzles
Like a baton-pass. He squints he looks at me
Through the goal line. Charlie, Charlie, we have won away from
We have won at home
In the last minute. Can you see me? You say
What I say: where in God
Almightly have you been all this time? I don't know,
Charlie. I don't know. But I've come to tell you a secret
That has to be put into code. Understand what I mean when I say
To the one man who came back alive
From the Book of the Dead   to the bravest man
In Buckhead   to the lime-eyed ghost
Blue-wavering in the fumes
Of good Gulf gas, "Fill 'er up."
With wine? Light? Heart-attack blood? The contents of Tyree's toilet?
The beer
Of teen-age sons? No; just
"Fill 'er up. Fill 'er up, Charlie."

Considerations

1. This may be the definitive poem about going home. Is it a happy, or sad, one?
2. Extinction is the theme of a number of Dickey's poems (see "For the Last Wolverine"). Is it an important element in this one? Why is it so essential that one of the Buckhead Boys be found?
3. This poem is a rare fusion of the poetry of fancy speech (in italics), common speech, and nostalgic narrative, climaxing in the whirling transformation of new into old, of the dead to life. Discuss the religious overtones of these elements.

J. A. R. McKELLAR
Football Field: Evening

Cross-bars and posts, the echo of distant bells,
The cool and friendly scent of whispering turf;
And in the air a little wind that tells
Of moonlit waves beyond a murmuring surf.

The glittering blue and verdant afternoon
Has locked up all its colours, leaving dearth,
Deserted, underneath a careless moon,
The glory has departed from this earth.

The goals stand up on their appointed lines,
But all their worth has faded with the sun;
Unchallenged now I cross their strict confines;
The ball is gone, the game is lost and won.

I walk again where once I came to grief,
Crashing to earth, yet holding fast the ball,
Symbol of yet another True Belief,
The last but surely not the least of all:

To strain and struggle to the end of strength;
To lean on skill, not ask a gift of chance,
To win, or lose, and recognize at length
The game the thing; the rest, a circumstance.

And now the teams are vanished from the field,
But still an echo of their presence clings;
The moon discovers what the day concealed,
The gracefulness and grief of passing things.

Quick as the ball is thrown from hand to hand
And fleetly as the wing three-quarters run,
Swifter shall Time to his defences stand
And bring the fastest falling one by one,

Until the moon, that looked on Stonehenge ground
Before the stones, will rise and sink and set
Above this field, where also will be found
The relics of a mystery men forget.

Considerations

1. Why is a football stadium so important a symbol?
2. Is the athlete more acutely aware of the passage of time than the rest of us? Is it more painful? Why or why not?
3. Would you consider the final verse a hopeful, or hopeless, resolution? Explain.

INTO THE VALE OF YEARS

Each year, the court expands,
the net moves back, the ball
hums by—with more spin.

—**Paul Petrie**

JOHN UPDIKE

Ex-Basketball Player

Pearl Avenue runs past the high-school lot,
Bends with the trolley tracks, and stops, cut off
Before it has a chance to go two blocks,
At Colonel McComsky Plaza. Berth's Garage
Is on the corner facing west, and there,
Most days, you'll find Flick Webb, who helps Berth out.

Flick stands tall among the idiot pumps—
Five on a side, the old bubble-head style,
Their rubber elbows hanging loose and low.
One's nostrils are two S's, and his eyes
An E and O. And one is squat, without
A head at all—more of a football type.

Once Flick played for the high-school team, the Wizards.
He was good: in fact, the best. In '46,
He bucketed three hundred ninety points,
A county record still. The ball loved Flick.
I saw him rack up thirty-eight of forty
In one home game. His hands were like wild birds.

He never learned a trade, he just sells gas,
Checks oil, and changes flats. Once in a while,
As a gag, he dribbles an inner tube,
But most of us remember anyway.
His hands are fine and nervous on the lug wrench.
It makes no difference to the lug wrench, though.

479

Off work, he hangs around Mae's Luncheonette.
Grease-grey and kind of coiled, he plays pinball,
Sips lemon cokes, and smokes those thin cigars;
Flick seldom speaks to Mae, just sits and nods
Beyond her face towards bright applauding tiers
Of Necco Wafers, Nibs, and Juju Beads.

Considerations

1. On the surface this is merely a poem about a filling-station attendant who was once a good basketball player. But the unasked question in the poem is: Why do so many former "star" athletes end up this way?
2. What constitutes Flick's only cheering section now?

LEONTIUS SCHOLASTICUS

To an Aging Charioteer

(Trans. by Tom Dodge)

As a boy you outdrove the masters.
    Sixty now, you still defeat the young
To earn the emperor's special award
    That marks your fame in stone
For generations evermore.
    If only you were immortal as your fame.

Considerations

1. This driver was a latter-day Satchel Paige (see "To Satch" by Samuel Allen). How is this poem different in tone from the usual poem about aging athletes?
2. How does the last line sum up the Greek attitude toward death? Achilles spoke for all Greeks when he told Odysseus in the Underworld:
    Better, I say, to break sod as a farm hand for some poor country man, on iron rations, than lord it over all the exhausted dead.
                                    (Trans. by Robert Fitzgerald)

GWENDOLYN BROOKS

Old Tennis Player

Refuses
To refuse the racket, to mutter No to the net.
He leans to life, conspires to give and get
Other serving yet.

Considerations

1. What is symbolized by the net? By "serving"?
2. Is this poem an extended metaphor? Explain.

JOHN UPDIKE

Golfers

One-gloved beasts in cleats, they come clattering
down to the locker room in bogus triumph, bulls
with the *pics* of their pars still noisy in them,
breathing false fire of stride, strike, stride, and putt.
We dread them, their brown arms and rasp of money,
their slacks the colors of ice cream, their shoes
whiter than bones that stipple the downtrodden green,
that take an open stance on the backs of the poor.
Breathing of bourbon, crowing, they strip:
the hair of their chests is grizzled, their genitals
hang dead as practice balls, their blue legs twist;
where, now, are their pars and their furor?
Emerging from the shower shrunken, they are men,
mere men, old boys, lost, the last hole a horror.

Considerations

1. "Golfers" is a good example of how lethal a weapon a poem can be. For a similar view of golfers, read "A Caddy's Diary" by Ring Lardner.
2. Are these professional golfers or country club golfers? How do you know?
3. How do they "take an open stance on the backs of the poor"?

ELDON RAY FOX

The Bumper Sticker on His Pickup Said, "I'm a Lover, I'm a Fighter, I'm a Wild Bull Rider"

From the rodeo's mazy stalls
He had come molded, rope and hand,
And they had seen that he was child's head
And his body, beast hard, erect and young,
As the gate sprung his wide bull's bawl and lunge;
And for years he had ridden easy
With all the buck and thigh he could.

But then his rig unraveled
(fit the loop and rope about the hand
and so hold on, hold on, the measurement
of a certain form, one hand breast high,
the feet no higher than a bed, he told his fans
and grinned with chaw and middle age) as the crowds
Had roared on and the clowns had barreled in

Even as he was thrown, impotent and well-hung:
Dangling, he held on by a thread
As his rope played out
(they had always told him
to go flaccid into his fall, he said,
just relax, just relax:
but he had to perform, to flank and spur,

he told the sportscaster as he held his arm:
it's hard to keep it up, he said).

Considerations

1. This poem is about an over-the-hill bull rider. The humor depends heavily on double entendre. Why are rodeo performers especially likely targets for such satire?
2. Explain the special significance of the title.

JAMES DICKEY

The Bee

To the football coaches of Clemson College, 1942

One dot
Grainly shifting   we at roadside and
The smallest wings coming   along the rail fence out
Of the woods   one dot   of all that green. It now
Becomes flesh-crawling   then the quite still
Of stinging. I must live faster for my terrified
Small son   it is on him. Has come. Clings.

Old wingback, come
To life. If your knee action is high
Enough, the fat may fall in time   God damn
You Dicky, *dig*   this is your last time to cut
And run   but you must give it everything you have
Left, for screaming near your screaming child is the sheer
Murder of California traffic: some bee hangs driving

Your child
Blindly onto the highway. Get there however
Is still possible. Long live what I badly did
At Clemson   and all of my clumsiest drives
For the ball   all of my trying to turn
The corner downfield   and my spindling explosions
Through the five-hole over tackle. O backfield

Coach Shag Norton,
Tell me as you never yet have told me
To get the lead out   scream whatever will get
The slow-motion of middle age off me   I cannot
Make it this way   I will have to leave
My feet   they are gone   I have him where
He lives   and down we go singing with screams into

The dirt,
Son-screams of fathers   screams of dead coaches turning
To approval   and from between us the bee rises screaming
With flight   grainily shifting   riding the rail fence
Back into the woods   traffic blasting past us
Unchanged, nothing heard through the air-
conditioning glass   we lying at roadside full

Of the forearm prints
Of roadrocks   strawberries on our elbows as from
Scrimmage with the varsity   now we can get
Up   stand   turn away from the highway   look straight
Into trees. See, there is nothing coming out   no
Smallest wing   no shift of a flight-grain   nothing
Nothing. Let us go in, son, and listen

For some tobacco-
mumbling voice in the branches   to say "That's
a little better,"   to our lives still hanging
By a hair. There is nothing to stop us   we can go
Deep   deeper   into elms, and listen to traffic die
Roaring, like a football crowd from which we have
Vanished. Dead coaches live in the air, son   live

In the ear
Like fathers, and *urge*   and *urge*. They want you better
Then you are. When needed, they rise and curse you   they scream
When something must be saved. Here, under this tree,
We can sit down. You can sleep, and I can try
To give back what I have earned by keeping us
Alive, and safe from bees: the smile of some kind

Of savior—
Of touchdowns, of fumbles, battles,
Lives. Let me sit here with you, son
As on the bench, while the first string takes back
Over, far away   and say with my silentest tongue, with the man-
creating bruises of my arms   with a live leaf a quick
Dead hand on my shoulder,—"Coach Norton, I am your boy."

Considerations

1. "Among intellectuals," Dickey has said, "I realize that football players are looked
   on as proto-fascist figures. But I have never had anything but the more extreme
   gratitude for my football coaches." Discuss "The Bee" in the light of this statement.
2. This poem, Dickey has said, is literally true. Does this fact really matter? Support
   your answer.

CHRISTOPHER MORLEY

The Old Swimmer

I often wander on the beach
Where once, so brown of limb,
The biting air, the soaring surf
Summoned me to swim.

I see my old abundant youth
Where combers lean and spill,
And though I kiss the salt no more
Other swimmers will.

Oh, good exultant strength to meet
The arching wall of green,
To break the crystal, swirl, emerge
Dripping, taut, and clean.

To climb the moving hilly blue,
To dive in ecstasy
And feel the salty chill embrace
Arm and rib and knee.

What brave and vanished laughter then
And tingling thighs to run,
What warm and comfortable sands
Dreaming in the sun.

The crumbling water spreads in snow,
The turf is hissing still,
And though I taste the foam no more
Other swimmers will.

Considerations

1. Does the rhyme add to or detract from the quality of this poem?
2. Does the poem's language adequately support the sentiment inherent in its central idea? Support your answer.

PAUL PETRIE

The Old Pro's Lament

Each year, the court expands,
the net moves back, the ball
hums by—with more spin.

I use my second serve,
lob deeper, slice more,
stay away from the net, and fail
to win.

As any fool can tell,
it is time
to play the game purely
for the game's sake—to applaud
the puff of white chalk,
shake hands,
and grin.

Others retire
into the warm corners of memory,
invent new rules, new games,
and win.
Under the hot lances
of the shower, I play each point over,
and over,
and over
again.

Wisdom is the natural business
of old men—
to let the body go,
the rafters, moth-eaten and decayed,
cave in.

But nightly in dreams I see
an old man
playing in an empty court
under the dim floodlights
of the moon
with a racket gone in the strings—
no net, no ball, no game—
and still playing
to win.

Considerations

1. What options does the old pro have? Which does he choose?
2. What is the fear that expresses itself in the dream? Is this a universal fear?
3. Is the subtle rhyme effective? Explain.

STEPHEN DUNN

Day and Night Handball

I think of corner shots, the ball
hitting and dying like a butterfly
on a windshield, shots so fine
and perverse they begin to live

alongside weekends of sex
in your memory. I think of serves
delivered deep to the left hand,
the ball sliding off the side wall

into the blindnesses of one's body,
and diving returns that are impossible
except on days when your body is all
rubber bands and dreams

unfulfilled since childhood.
I think of a hand slicing the face
of a ball, so much english
that it comes back drunk
to your opponent who doesn't have
enough hands to hit it,
who hits it anyway, who makes you think
of "God!" and Goddamn!", the pleasure

of falling to your knees
for what is superb, better than you.
But it's position I think of most,
the easy slam and victory

because you have a sense of yourself
and the court, the sense that old men
gone in the knees have,
one step in place of five,

finesse in place of power,
and all the time
the four walls around you
creating the hardship, the infinite variety.

Considerations

1. Why is the technique of handball so important to the narrator?
2. What are the compensations of age to the athlete? Are they really compensation enough? Discuss.
3. Discuss the title's significance.

NEIL WEISS

The Aging Athlete

You're through—now walking up and down,
you think of speed and dig your heels,
testing this soil and that for a start,
but it's no go . . . Practicing for leaps,
you start forward, but exhaust the push
and end up with a damaging rush,
arms hanging, hands twitching at your sides,
chin bobbing on your chest: no pride
that once sustained you as you leapt
the next hurdle, hair up then down,
the wind in your ears, the crowd beside
itself, shouting, Come on! Come on!
and you smashed the tape with your chest
and sank into the arms of many lovers.

Considerations

1. In terms of hope, how does this aging athlete contrast with the one in "The Old Pro's Lament," "Day and Night Handball," and "Game Resumed"?
2. There quite possibly may be no harsher two words than the first two words of this poem. Discuss the possible reasons for Weiss' choosing to begin his poem with them.

RICHMOND LATTIMORE

Game Resumed

My locker, green steel,
hung on its hooks a row
of old shorts and T-
shirts, sneakers down at the heel
I wore eight years ago,
still there waiting for me.

Rectangular pit, white
walls flooded in light
are still and always the same.
Why did I ever let go?
Old men can play this game.
Legs slow,
eyes unsharpen, but the wrist
still drives the shape of play,
where the antagonist
is partner. Fadeaway
backhand to front wall
drops softly into place,
as turn by turn we chase
the black sinewy ball,
and, by twos and fours, our deep
drives and corner slants
weave the pattern we keep
turn by turn like a dance.

So, after half an hour,
and after eight years or more
elapsed, after the shower,
we are what we have been,
back where we were before
on the bench at the green
and steel locker, on whose wall
the shorts and the outworn ball
on the corner of the shelf
held, these years between
(forgotten and unseen),
my self.

Considerations

1. The locker, the uniform, and the court are still the same after eight years. What does the narrator decide about himself?
2. Is it significant that winning is not mentioned in the poem? Discuss.

GEORGE GORDON, LORD BYRON

Written After Swimming
From Sestos to Abydos

If, in the month of dark December,
  Leander, who was nightly wont
(What maid will not the tale remember?)
  To cross thy stream, broad Hellespont!

If, when the wintry tempest roar'd,
  He sped to Hero, nothing loth,
And thus of old thy current pour'd,
  Fair Venus! how I pity both!

For *me*, degenerate modern wretch,
  Though in the genial month of May,
My dripping limbs I faintly stretch,
  And think I've done a feat to-day.

But since he cross'd the rapid tide,
  According to the doubtful story,
To woo,—and—Lord knows what beside,
  And swam for Love, as I for Glory;

'T were hard to say who fared the best:
  Sad mortals! thus the Gods still plague
    you!
He lost his labour, I my jest;
  For he was drown'd, and I've the ague.

Considerations

1. Look up the story of Hero and Leander in Greek myth.
2. Although Byron duplicated Leander's feat (once), he was still not satisfied. What self-recriminations are expressed in the poem?
3. What could possibly motivate a world-famous poet to attempt such a feat?

HOMER

Nestor

From *The Iliad*, Book XXIII
(Trans. by Ennis Rees)

. . . My feet and limbs, young friend, are no longer
Steady and strong, nor do my fists any more
Lash lightly out from the shoulder. If only I were

Young again and as sure of my brawn as I was on that day
At Buprasium when the Epeans were holding last rites
For King Amarynceus and his sons put prizes up
For games in his honor. That day no man was my peer,
Neither mid the Epeans, nor mid my own people the Pylians,
Nor mid the great-souled Aetolians. In boxing I won
Over the Enops' son Clytomedes, and in wrestling over
Ancaeus of Pleuron, who pitted his strength against me.
Iphiclus, fast though he was, I beat in the foot-race,
And in the javelin-throw I defeated Phyleus
And Polydorus. I lost but one event,
The chariot-race, in which the two sons of Actor
Outstripped me, since they were two against one, fiercely
Begrudging me victory and forcing their horses ahead,
For the best prize of all was still in the lists. They were twins,
And one of them drove with sure hand, a very sure hand,
While the other laid on the lash. Even such was the man
I once was, but now I leave these endeavors to men
Who are younger, since now I must yield to irksome old age,
But go, and finish these funeral rites and games
For your comrade too. This gift I gladly receive,
And my heart rejoices that always you think of me
As a friend, nor do you neglect to honor me duly
Among the Achaeans. May the gods in return give you
Abundant grace to fulfill each desire of your heart.

Considerations

1. Athletic games were held in honor of the dead in Ancient Greece. At Achilles'
   funeral games for his friend Patroclus, Nestor has declined to participate due to
   advanced age. As is the case for most aging athlete-warriors he must be content with
   re-living his triumphs. Do athletes always know when to "yield to irksome old age"?
2. Nestor was known as the wisest and most eloquent of the Achaeans. Does this
   speech bear out this reputation?

HOMER

Odysseus and the
Phaeacian Games

From *The Odyssey*, Book VIII

(Trans. by Ennis Rees)

"O leaders and counselors
Of the Phaeacians, your attention please. Now
That we have regaled ourselves with fine food and its
Companion the lyre, let us go out and try

Our skill in the various athletic events, that our guest,
When he returns home, may tell his friends how superior
We are at boxing, wrestling, jumping, and running."
    He led and they followed, while the herald
        hung the clear-toned lyre
On its peg, took the hand of Demodocus, and led him
        from the hall
In the same direction the Phaeacian nobles had taken
On their way to the games. They all set out for the place
Of assembly, accompanied by a countless throng. There
To take part in the games were many splendid young men—
Acroneus, Ocyalus, Elatreus, Nauteus, and Prymneus,
Anchialus, Eretmeus, Ponteus, Proreus, Thoön,
And Anabesineus, and Amphialus, son of Polyneus
And grandson of Tecton. And Naubolus' son Euryalus
Arose, the equal of man-slaughtering Ares. He,
In looks and physique, surpassed all the Phaeacians but one,
Matchless Laodamas, who was also there to compete,
Along with his brothers, Halius and godlike Clytoneus,
All three the sons of royal Alcinous. The first
Event was a race. A course was laid out for them
And they all ran swiftly, beating up dust from the plain,
But the able Clytoneus was so far the swiftest that he
Outran them all by the length of a furrow such as mules
Plow in the fallow, and so was first to arrive
At the crowd about the finish. Next they strove
At hard wrestling, and in this Euryalus defeated all comers.
Amphialus beat everyone else at jumping, and Elatreus
Was much the best with the discus, as the skillful son
Of Alcinous, Laodamas, was in the boxing. When all
Had had their fill of delightful competition, Laodamas,
Son of Alcinous, spoke thus among them:
    "Come on,
My friends, let us ask our guest over there what games
He's good in. He's built like a man indeed, what with
Those legs and arms and that powerful neck of his.
He's bound to be strong, and surely he's still young enough,
Though broken by many misfortunes. In my opinion
There's nothing worse than the sea to confound a man,
No matter how strong he may be."
    And Euryalus said:
"Laodamas, I quite agree with what you say.
Go over and speak with the stranger and deliver our challenge."
    At this the fine son of Alcinous took his stand in the midst
Of the crowd and spoke to Odysseus: "Come, good sir,
Take part in the games, if you have any athletic skill,
And have it you must, for there's no greater glory in life

Than that which a man may win with his feet and hands.
So come, throw your worries away and do what you can.
You'll soon be on your way home. Already your ship
Has been launched and the crew is waiting."
    Then resourceful Odysseus
Replied: "Laodamas, why do you mock me this way?
My mind is far more full of grief than games.
I have suffered and toiled a great deal, and now I am interested
Only in my return home, as I sit in this gathering
Of yours and make my plea to the King and all
Of his people."
    Euryalus answered with an obvious insult:
"Truly, stranger, I wouldn't take you for an athlete
Anyway, though many men have such skill. To me
You look far more like a captain of seagoing merchants,
One who goes back and forth in his many-oared ship
With a mind full of freight and the greedy profit he'll make
By his trip. No, you surely don't look like an athlete!"
    At this the quick-witted Odysseus scowled, and replied:
"That, sir, was not well spoken, the speech of a fool,
But then the gods aren't accustomed to give their good gifts
Of physique and mind and eloquence to all alike.
Sometimes a man is not handsome at all, but God
Bestows on his words such form and grace that men
Look on in delight as he speaks in a way that combines
Unfaltering technique with an obvious lack of conceit.
He alone stands out among them, and whenever he goes
Through the city, he is gazed upon like a god. But another
Is like the immortals themselves in appearance, but no crown
Of grace is bestowed on his words. Even such are you,
For in looks you stand out from the rest—no god could
        improve them—
But you're sadly lacking in brains. And now your bad manners
Upset me. I'm not, despite what you say, at all poor
In sports, but was, I believe, among the first
So long as I could rely on my youth and my hands.
But now I'm oppressed by all that I've suffered in war
And the weltering waves. But in spite of all that sorrow,
I will compete in your games, for your words bite deep
In my heart and provoke me."
    With this he sprang up, and not even
Removing his mantle he seized a large discus, thick
And a good deal more weighty than those the Phaeacians used
In their competition. He spun and let it fly
From his powerful hand, and the stone went whizzing away
As the long-oared, ship-famous Phaeacians ducked down

    beneath it.
Swiftly it left his hand and whirred through the air
Beyond all the other marks, and Athena, in the form
Of a man, set a mark for it and called back to him:
   "Even a blind man, sir, would know your mark
Just groping around with his hands, for it's not even close
To the others, but first by far. You may rest easy
About this event at least. No Phaeacian will equal
This throw, much less surpass it!"
   So spoke the goddess,
Delighting the patient Odysseus, who was glad to see
A true friend in the crowd, and now he addressed the Phaeacians
In a much lighter mood: "Now let's see you youngsters
    match that!
Pretty soon, I think, I'll toss out another as far
Or farther. As for you others, if any man feels
His heart and soul so moved, let him come forth
And compete with me—for you have offended me deeply—
At boxing, wrestling, or for that matter running. I don't
Really care. I'll take on all comers except Laodamas,
For who would quarrel with his host? Both stupid and worthless
Is he who would challenge the man who befriends him abroad.
He would but spoil his own chances. But as for the rest,
I'll neither back down nor belittle. I'm eager indeed
To take on all comers and try my strength against theirs.
For I am not half bad in any event
Performed among men. I do very well, for instance,
With the polished bow, and I would always be first
To pick off my man in the thronging enemy ranks,
No matter how many stood with me and shot at the foe.
At Troy, Philoctetes alone did better than I
When we Achaeans shot. But I claim to be best
By far of all other bread-eating mortals now living
On earth. With men of old, however—with Heracles
Or Oechalian Eurytus—I would not wish to compete.
With the bow those two strove even with gods, and so
The great Eurytus met sudden death, nor did he live
To be old in his palace. For when he challenged Apollo
To shoot with the bow, the god grew angry and killed him.
But I can throw the spear farther than any
Other mortal can shoot an arrow. At running, however,
I have my doubts about winning, for there was in my ship
No exhaustless supply of provisions, and I was badly battered
Mid many waves. So my legs are in very poor shape."
   Then they all remained silent till Alcinous answered
    him thus:

"Stranger, since not without grace and charm you have spoken
These things, wishing to show the fine abilities
You obviously have and angry at him who came up
To you in the crowd and made light of your prowess, as no
Well-mannered mortal would do—but come now, hear
What I have to say, that when you are home in your halls
And feasting once more with your wife and your children, you
May remember us and tell your peers of those feats
In which Zeus has given us skill from our forefathers' time
Until now. In boxing and wrestling, it's true we're not perfect,
But we're fast on our feet and the best of all sea-going men,
And always we love the feast, the lyre, and the dance,
Fresh clothes, hot baths, and the bed. But come, let all
The best dancers among the Phaeacians show us their art,
That when our guest gets home he may tell his friends
How far we surpass all others in seamanship and running
And dancing and singing. Someone go quickly and bring
The sweet lyre to Demodocus. It's back there somewhere
    in the palace."

Considerations

1. Odysseus was a good athlete in his prime, but he is well past it now. How does he use his wits to bluff the Phaeacians down? What does King Alcinous say after Odysseus's throw of the discus and hearing his speech?
2. Athletic games usually followed religious ceremonies in Greece but they could be held at any occasion. What activity had just preceded these events?
3. Although Odysseus must be approaching fifty, he lays his bad legs to being at sea. Is this a typical explanation for a proud warrior-athlete?

VIRGIL

The Funeral Games for Anchises: Entellus

From *The Aeneid*, Book V
(*Trans. by Rolfe Humphries*)

    ... "Whoever has courage
And fighting spirit in his heart, step forward
And put the gloves on!" There are double prizes,
For the winner a bullock, decked with gold and ribbons,
A sword and shining helmet for the loser.
Without delay, Dares gets up; a murmur
Runs through the crowd as this big man comes forward.

They know that he was Paris' sparring-partner,
And they recall his famous match with Butes
At Hector's tomb, where he knocked out that champion
And stretched him dying on the yellow sand.
Now Dares holds his head up for the battle,
Shakes his broad shoulders loose, warms up a little,
A left, a right, a left, in shadow-boxing.
Who will oppose him? No on puts the gloves on,
No one, from all that throng, is in a hurry
To take on Dares. So, exultant, thinking
Himself a winner by default, he grabs
The bullock by one horn, says to Aeneas:—
"If no man, goddess-born, is taking chances,
How long must I keep standing here? How long
Hang around waiting? Give the order, let me
Lead home my prize!" The Trojans all applaud him.
But king Acestes, sprawling on the greensward
Beside Entellus, nudges him a little:—
"What was the use, Entellus, of being a hero,
Of having been our bravest, under Eryx?
Where is that old Sicilian reputation,
And all those prizes, and you sit here tamely?"
Does Dares get away with this, no contest,
And all those prizes, and you sit here tamely?"
Entellus answers, "Oh, I still love glory
And praise; there's nothing the matter with my courage,
But I'm too old, the blood is slow and colder,
The strength not what it used to be. That bragger
Has one thing, youth, and how he revels in it!
If I had what he has, I'd not need prizes,
Bullocks or helmets either, to get me fighting."
From somewhere he produced the gloves of Eryx
And tossed them into the ring, all stiff and heavy,
Seven layers of hide, and insewn lead and iron.
The people stand amazed, and Dares shudders,
Wanting no part of gloves like these; Aeneas
Inspects them, turning them slowly, over and over,
And old Entellus adds a word of comment:—
"Why, these are nothing! What if you had seen
The gloves of Hercules? He used to fight here.
These are the gloves that Eryx wore against him.
You still can see the blood and a splash of brains
That stained them long ago. I used to wear them
Myself when I was younger, and unchallenged
By Time, that envious rival. But if Dares
Declines these arms, all right, make matters equal,

Don't be afraid; I waive the gloves of Eryx,
You put the Trojan gloves aside; Aeneas
Will see fair play, Acestes be my second."
He throws the double cloak from off his shoulders,
Strips down to the great limbs, great bones, great muscles.
A giant in the ring. Aeneas brings them
Matched pairs of gloves.
They take their stand, each
     rising
On the balls of his feet, their arms upraised, and rolling
Their heads back from the punch. They spar, they lead,
They watched for openings. Dares, much the younger,
Is much the better in footwork; old Entellus
Has to rely on strength; his knees are shaky,
His wind not what it was. They throw their punches,
And many miss; and some, with a solid thump,
Land on the ribs or chest; temples and ears
Feel the wind of a miss, or the jaws rattle
When a punch lands. Entellus stands flat-footed,
Wasting no motion, just a slip of the body,
The watchful eyes alert. And Dares, feinting,
Like one who artfully attacks a city,
Tries this approach, then that, dancing around him
In varied vain attack. Entellus, rising,
Draws back his right (in fact, he telegraphs it),
And Dares, seeing it coming, slips aside;
Entellus lands on nothing but the wind
And, thrown off balance, heavily comes down
Flat on his face, as falls on Erymanthus
A thunder-smitten oak, and so on, and so on.
Roaring, the Trojans and Sicilians both
Rise to their feet; the noise goes up to heaven;
Acestes rushes in, to raise his comrade
In pity and sorrow. But that old-time fighter
Is not slowed down a bit, nor made more wary;
His rage is terrible, and his shame awakens
A consciousness of strength. He chases Dares
All over the ring, left, right, left, right, the punches
Rattle like hailstones on a roof; he batters Dares,
Spins him halfway around with one hand, clouts him
Straight with the other again. At last Aeneas
Steps in and stops it, with a word of comfort
For the exhausted Dares:—"Luckless fellow,
Yield to the god! What madness blinds your vision
To strength beyond your own?" They rescue Dares,
And drag him to the ships, with his knees caving,

Head rolling side to side, spitting out blood
And teeth; he hardly sees the sword and helmet.
They leave the palm and bullock for Entellus,
Who, in the pride of victory, cries aloud:
"Look, goddess-born! Watch, Trojans, and discover
Two things—how strong I was when I was younger,
And what a death you've kept away from Dares!"
And, with the word, he faced his prize, the bullock,
Drew back his right hand, poised it, sent it smashing
Between the horns, shattering the skull, and splashing
Brains on the bones, as the great beast came down, lifeless.
"This life, a better one than Dares', Eryx,
I vow as sacrifice, and so, victorious,
Retire, and lay aside the gloves forever."

Considerations

1. Virgil, the most gifted poet of his age, wrote these lines nineteen hundred years ago. Compare the theme (the aging athlete) with the poems of today that deal with the same subject.
2. Is Entellus' victory a rarity among athletes who try to regain their former glory? What occurrence contributes probably more than anything else to his victory?
3. How does this victory display "how strong I was when I was younger"?

DON JOHNSON

Ripper Collins' Legacy

On the blue corner's top rope
the rumored missing link,
Pampero Firpo, looms gigantic.
Launched, the "pampas bull"
balloons in mid-flight, shutting
the crowd's shouts like a clamped
hatch, blotting the ring lights
out before becoming Whitewolf,
who can fly, and does. Rising
only to descend and rise
again, the grinning Indian's
face distends and shrinks
the long night long. His knee hangs
fixed three feet above the mat,
about to float abruptly
through the Ripper's kidneys.

"This is me in Pittsburgh
as the Crusher, the year
I won the Tri-State tag
team belt with Yukon Ike.
In the beginning
I had hopes,
but by then I only played
at playing roles.
You can't do that."

Winter nights the knife
wound suffered when some fan
forgot himself in Carolina
aches, keeps him awake,
and, fortunately, dreamless.
In the dark he picks
through scattered lies
he'd lied about for ages
hoping to choose the one
best suited for the match
upcoming with the Masked Executioner.

Considerations

1. Which "sport" does Ripper Collins participate in? How do you know?
2. What are the "scattered lies / he'd lied about for ages"?
3. Explain the significance of the title.

DENNIS TRUDELL

The Jump Shooter

The way the ball
hung there
against the blue or purple

one night last week
across town
at the playground where

I had gone to spare
my wife
from the mood I'd swallowed

and saw in the dusk
a stranger
shooting baskets a few

years older maybe
thirty-five
and overweight a little

beer belly saw him
shooting there
and joined him didn't

ask or anything simply
went over
picked off a rebound

and hooked it back up
while he
smiled I nodded and for

ten minutes or so we
took turns
taking shots and the thing

is neither of us said
a word
and this fellow who's

too heavy now and slow
to play
for any team still had

the old touch seldom
ever missed
kept moving further out

and finally his t-shirt
a gray
and fuzzy blur I stood

under the rim could
almost hear
a high school cheer

begin and fill a gym
while wooden
bleachers rocked he made

three in a row from
twenty feet
moved back two steps

faked out a patch
of darkness
arched another one and

the way the ball
hung there
against the blue or purple

then suddenly filled
the net
made me wave goodbye

breathe deeply and begin
to whistle
as I walked back home.

Considerations

1. How does Trudell return to his opening lines? What is "the blue or purple"?
2. What is "the mood I'd swallowed"?

PETER MEINKE

To an Athlete Turned Poet

(for James Dickey)

Fifteen years ago   and twenty
he'd crouch   line-backer   gang-tackler
steel stomach flexing for
contact   contact   cracking
through man after man   weekend hero
washing the cheers down
with unbought beer

and now his stomach's soft   his books
press out his veins as he walks
and no one looks

but deep in his bone stadium
the roar of the crowd wells
as he shows them again

crossing line after line
on cracking fingers   heart red-
dogging with rage and joy over the broken backs
of words   words   words

Considerations

1. In what specific way is Meinke imitating Dickey's style? What well known Dickey poem does the last line parody?
2. Explain "deep in his bone stadium / the roar of the crowd wells."

DAVID HILTON

The Poet Tries to Turn in His Jock

*The way I see it, is that when
I step out on that court and feel
inside that I can't make the plays,
it'll be time to call it quits.*

—Elgin Baylor

Going up for the jump shot,
Giving the kid the head-fakes and all
'Til he's jocked right out the door of the gym
And I'm free at the top with the ball and my touch,
Lofting the arc off my fingertips,
I feel my left calf turn to stone
And my ankle warp inward to form when I land
A neat right angle with my leg,
And I'm on the floor,
A pile of sweat and sick muscles,
Saying,
Hilton,
You're 29, getting fat,
Can't drive to your right anymore,
You can think of better things to do
On Saturday afternoons than be a chump
For a bunch of sophomore third-stringers;
Join the Y, steam and martinis and muscletone.
But, shit,
The shot goes in.

Considerations

1. How does the Elgin Baylor epigraph fit in with the last line?
2. What does the last line seem to indicate about all aging athletes trying to find a reason to keep playing?

WILLIAM D. BARNEY

Nearly Everybody Loves
Harvey Martin

That's not any old six-foot rabbit
nor a half-Brahma bull, half-grizzly bear stampeding—
it's only loveable Harvey coming round the corner
distributing people, dividing them left and right
just like it was, and it is, Dooms Day.

Six foot-and-a-half Harvey is the Artist:
when he paints pictures you can always tell;
when you read his terrible lines you know what he means.
None of that toying around with ambiguous,
no metaphysical junk. He does business.
Always straightforward, round-the-bend, whatever
it takes to amass a one-man massacre.

And that hapless soul back there with the ball,
that's not Fran. Or Bert. Or Jim. Or Billy.
It's poor little Davey with his slingshot
getting ready to throw the bomb.
You'd better look out is all we say—
the center cannot hold, the scripture's fractured,
the Philistines are upon you.
It's not that we don't like underdogs;
we're just fed up with shifty dwarves

scrambling around, eluding the ultimate end.
Old Harvey has got out his lobster claws,
he's going to give you the *abrazo.*

So maybe they double-team him all day long;
they sit on Vesuvius for three quarters—
when he erupts (and he will) it's going to be a sight
when the whole stadium, twenty millions dens,
rise up and scream for Harvey Rampant
coming like judgment through the clouds
and the battle rages almost five seconds—
till the quarterback's sacked and spread on the ground,
sprawled on the slopes of astro turf.

Whether it's Terry or Ken or Craig,
there's only one dirge to go tell in Gath:
How are the mighty fallen
and the weapons of war, are they perished!

Considerations

1. How does Barney combine elements of the Bible, Hollywood, Yeats, and football in this poem? Identify each.
2. Gene (Big Daddy) Lipscomb was another friendly giant in the N.F.L. Read Randall Jarrell's "Say Goodbye to Big Daddy" and contrast the moods of the two poems.
3. Identify the allusion in the last two lines. (It is in the Old Testament.)
4. Make a list of the references to warfare in this poem. Is football a "substitute for war"?

ALAN ROSS

Stanley Matthews

Not often *con brio,* but *andante, andante,*
        horseless, though jockey-like and jaunty,
Straddling the touchline, live margin
        not out of the game, nor quite in,
Made by him green and magnetic, stroller
Indifferent as a cat dissembling, rolling
A little as on deck, till the mouse, the ball,
        slides palely to him,
And shyly, almost with deprecatory cough, he is off.

Head of a Perugino, with faint flare
Of the nostrils, as though Lipizzaner-like,
     he sniffed at the air,
Finding it good beneath him, he draws
Defenders towards him, the ball a bait
They refuse like a poisoned chocolate,
     retreating, till he slows his gait
To a walk, inviting the tackle, inciting it.

At last, unrefusable, dangling the ball at the instep
He is charged—and stiffening so slowly
It is rarely perceptible, he executes with a squirm
Of the hips, a twist more suggestive than apparent,
     that lazily disdainful move *toreros* term
        a Veronica—it's enough.
Only emptiness following him, pursuing some scent
Of his own, he weaves in towards,
     not away from, fresh tacklers,
Who, turning about to gain time, are by him
     harried, pursued not pursuers.

Now gathers speed, nursing the ball as he cruises,
Eyes judging distance, noting the gaps, the spaces
Vital for colleagues to move to, slowing a trace,
As from Vivaldi to Dibdin, pausing,
     and leisurely, leisurely, swings
To the left upright his centre, on hips
His hands, observing the goalkeeper spring,
     heads rising vainly to the ball's curve
Just as it's plucked from them; and dispassionately
Back to his mark he trots, whistling through closed lips.

Trim as a yacht, with similar lightness
     —of keel, of reaction to surface—with salt air
Tanned, this incomparable player, in decline fair
     to look at, nor in decline either,
Improving like wine with age, has come far—
     born to one, a barber, who boxed
Not with such filial magnificence, but well.
'The greatest of all time,' *meraviglioso*, Matthews—
     Stoke City, Blackpool and England.
Expressionless enchanter, weaving as on strings
Conceptual patterns to a private music, heard
Only by him, to whose slowly emerging theme
He rehearses steps, soloist in compulsions of a dream.

Considerations

1. According to this poem, what single characteristic would you say sets Stanley Matthews apart from other excellent players?
2. List the similes and metaphors Ross uses to describe Matthews.
3. Does Ross exhibit an understanding of the fine points of the game? Explain.

TOM CLARK

The Ty Cobb Story

Ty Cobb never went to a movie or read a newspaper, afraid it would ruin his perfect hitter's eyes. He spent his sparetime in Georgia, drinking peach brandy. He never knew he was a media-moron.

When Daddy Warbucks first met Ty Cobb, he said to himself, "here is a man starved for images." He sprayed Ty's eyes with negative image-junk of Orphan Annie's bare ass. That year Cobb hit .396 for the Tigers. After the season he looked up Daddy Warbucks and begged him for another hit.

As for Annie, she knew a good thing when it was addicted to her. The next step was to cut image lines and go in on the natural. She was in furs and sapphires before spring training rolled around.

Ty hung around the officer's club a lot in those days. He was heard to say: "I don't care if I see another xerox as long as I live."

Considerations

1. What is poetry of the "Absurd"? (For a story using a similar style, read "The Wound," by Donald Barthelme.)
2. Should the reader look for conventional meaning in this poem? If not, then what is its purpose?

TOM CLARK

To Bert Campaneris

You've had your problems
over the years but when
the money's on the table
you come out smokin', Campy

You didn't have to go through all this atavism, you know

You could have stayed home and made lariats in the rope factory like your father
but you went away to the big leagues
for $500
and on your first time up even though your English was bad
you hit a home run
and that made Charley Finley happy
and after he made you play all nine positions in one game for a joke
he made you his shortstop for life
meaning until your legs start to go
which I hope isn't soon
since I love the way you play the field
with a cool mechanical glide
and intensely run the bases
so diminutive and severe

We're both 35
and you're earning 100 grand now
and looking for a five year contract
and I'm getting a hundred bucks
for doing this poetry reading

Which I guess just goes to show
how good you know English
don't count for everything

Considerations

1. What philosophical question is asked in the fourth stanza? Does Clark answer it satisfactorily? Why or why not?
2. What would happen to art if it were rewarded by money, as baseball is?
3. Is money, then, only a substitute for a higher reward? Explain.

TOM CLARK

And You Are There

Wearing the familiar Yankee pinstripes
With the heraldic 🅽🆈 elegantly covering the heart
over a longsleeve white sweatshirt
Babe Ruth sits on a hardback chair in front of his locker
It is locker No. 3

The photographer has caught him in the act of
Reaching across his body with his large and powerful right hand
To untie his left shoe

His long slim legs in black knee socks are crossed
And his body hunches forward over them
With his left hand dangling in his lap

His head is moon-shaped and seems much too big for his body

He cocks his head up to the left as if someone there is speaking
His eyes are intelligent and wary
His nose is broad
His ears are enormous
They are pinned back flat against the side of his head

In its cowish amplitude his face
Slightly resembles Severn Darden's

The Babe is saying something we can't hear
To a person whom we do not see
Probably a reporter since the whole scene looks strictly posed

Three doors down the row of lockers
On a Persian strip rug
Which covers the board floor of the clubhouse
There is a pair
Of two-tone Oxfords—brown and white?—
The kind golfers used to wear

Maybe they're Wally Pipp's

Considerations

1. This poem seems to offer some kind of unauthorized glimpse behind the "strictly posed" scene. Is it a description of a photograph?
2. Compare the language of this poem with that of "Baseball" (p. 422). Could this one just as easily be a prose poem? What benefit is derived in arranging it into lines? Support your answer.

ALAN DUGAN

On Hurricane Jackson

Now his nose's bridge is broken, one eye
will not focus and the other is astray;
trainers whisper in his mouth while one ear
listens to itself, clenched like a fist;
generally shadow-boxing in a smoky room,
his mind hides like the aching boys
who lost a contest in the Pan-Hellenic games
and had to take the back roads home,
but someone else, his perfect youth,
laureled in newsprint and dollar bills,
triumphs forever on the great white way
to the statistical Sparta of the champs.

Considerations

1. This poem is a before-and-after view of a once up-and-coming young heavyweight. Does its statement focus on boxing, society, or Jackson? Explain.
2. What is the "statistical Sparta of the champs"? For what quality is Sparta most famous?

SAMUEL ALLEN

To Satch
(or American Gothic)

Sometimes I feel like I will *never* stop
Just go on forever
Till one fine mornin
I'm gonna reach up and grab me a handfulla stars
Swing out my long lean leg
And whip three hot strikes burnin down the heavens
And look over at God and say
How about that!

Considerations

1. Look up Satchel Paige. What is particularly remarkable about his career?
2. Although death is not mentioned here, isn't this poem a romanticized view of it? Explain.

FALLEN STARS

The world won't be the same without Big Daddy.
Or else it will be.

—Randall Jarrell

RANDALL JARRELL

Say Goodbye to Big Daddy

Big Daddy Lipscomb, who used to help them up
After he'd pulled them down, so that "the children
Won't think Big Daddy's mean"; Big Daddy Lipscomb,
Who stood unmoved among the blockers, like the Rock
Of Gibraltar in a life insurance ad,
Until the ball carrier came, and Daddy got him;
Big Daddy Lipscomb, being carried down an aisle
Of women by Night Train Lane, John Henry Johnson,
And Lenny Moore; Big Daddy, his three ex-wives,
His fiancee, and the grandfather who raised him
Going to his grave in five big Cadillacs;
Big Daddy, who found football easy enough, life hard enough
To—after his last night cruising Baltimore
In his yellow Cadillac—to die of heroin;
Big Daddy, who was scared, he said: "I've been scared
Most of my life. You wouldn't think so to look at me.
It gets so bad I cry myself to sleep—" his size
Embarrassed him, so that he was helped by smaller men
And hurt by smaller men; Big Daddy Lipscomb
Has helped to his feet the last ball carrier, Death.

The big black man in the television set
Whom the viewers stared at—sometimes, almost were—
Is a blur now; when we get up to adjust the set,
It's not the set, but a NETWORK DIFFICULTY.
The world won't be the same without Big Daddy.
Or else it will be.

Considerations

1. Does this poem attempt to perpetuate the myth of organized football? Explain.
2. Explain the second line of the second stanza. Does it touch on the most basic appeal that football has for spectators?
3. The final two lines are among the most profound in all of Jarrell's poetry. What do they say to society as a whole?
4. James Dickey says this ending is prophetic of Jarrell's own death and its consequences—or lack of consequences. What do you think he means?

JAMES DICKEY

For the Death of
Vince Lombardi

I never played for you. You'd have thrown
Me off the team on my best day—
No guts, maybe   not enough speed.
Yet running in my mind
As Paul Hornung, I made it here
With the others, sprinting down railroad tracks,
Hurdling bushes and backyard Cyclone
Fences, through city after city, to stand, at last, around you,
Exhausted, exalted, pale
As though you'd said "Nice going": pale
As a hospital wall. You are holding us
Millions together: those who played for you,
And those who entered the bodies
Of Bart Starr, Donny Anderson, Ray Nitschke, Jerry Kramer
Through the snowing tube on Sunday afternoon.
Warm, playing painlessly,
In the snows of Green Bay Stadium, some of us drunk
On much-advertised beer   some old   some in other
Hospitals—most, middle-aged
And at home. Here you summon us, lying under
The surgical snows. Coach, look up: we are here
We are held in this room
Like cancer.
The Crab has you, and to him
And to us you whisper
Drive, *Drive*. Jerry Kramer's face floats near—real, pale—
We others dream ourselves
Around you, and far away in the mountains, driving hard
Through the drifts, Marshall of the Vikings, plunging, burning

Twenty-dollar bills to stay alive, says, still
Alive, "I wouldn't be here
If it weren't for the lessons of football." Vince, they've told us;
When the surgeons got themselves
Together and cut loose
Two feet of your large intestine,
The Crab whirled up,   whirled out
Of the lost gut and caught you again
Higher up. Everyone's helpless
But cancer. Around your bed
The knocked out teeth like hail pebbles
Rattle down miles of adhesive tape from hands and ankles
Writhe in the room like vines   gallons of sweat
Blaze in buckets
In the corners   the blue and yellow of bruises
Make one vast sunset around you. No one understands you.
Coach, don't you know that some of us were ruined
For life? Everybody can't win. What of almost all
Of us, Vince? We lost.
And our greatest loss was that we could not survive
Football. Paul Hornung has withdrawn
From me, and I am middle-aged and grey like these others.
What holds us here?
It is that you are dying by the code you made us
What we are by? Yes, Coach, it is true: love-hate is stronger
Than either love or hate. Into the weekly, inescapable dance
Of speed, deception, and pain
You led us, and brought us here weeping,
But as men. Or, you who created us as George
Patton created armies, did you discover the worst
In us; aggression, meanness, deception, delight in giving
Pain to others, for money? Did you make of us, indeed.
Figments   overspecialized, brutal ghosts
Who could have been real
Men in a better sense? Have you driven us mad
Over nothing? Does your death set us free?

Too late. We stand here among
Discarded TV commercials
Among beer cans and razor blades and hair tonic bottles,
Stinking with male deodorants: we stand here
Among teeth and filthy miles
Of unwound tapes, novocaine needles, contracts, champagne
Mixed with shower water,
Unraveling elastic, bloody face guards,
And the Crab, in his new, high position

Works soundlessly. In dying
You give us no choice, Coach,
Either. We've got to believe there's such a thing
As winning. The Sunday spirit screen
Comes on   the bruise colors brighten   deepen
On the wall   the last tooth spits itself free
Of a linebacker's aging head   knee cartilage cracks,
A boy wraps his face in a red jersey and crams it into
A rusty locker to sob, and we're with you
We're with you all the way
You're going forever, Vince.

Considerations

1. Is this poem an idealized view of Lombardi, or does it include negative elements of his influence? Can you cite examples of both?
2. Does the speaker in the poem satisfactorily answer the questions raised at the end of the first segment? Support your answer.
3. The second segment mentions the less-mythical aspects of organized football? Is the poem judgmental? Explain.
4. Explain how the poem subtlely examines Lombardi's famous statement, "Winning isn't everything. It's the only thing." What conclusion is reached?

LOU LIPSITZ

To a Fighter Killed
in the Ring

In a gym in Spanish Harlem
boys with the eyes of starved leopards
flick jabs at your ghost
chained to a sandbag.

They smell in the air the brief truth of poverty
just as you once did:
                    "The weak don't get rich."

You made good.
Probably you were a bastard,
dreaming of running men down in a Cadillac
and tearing blouses off women.

And maybe in your dreams great black teeth
ran after you down dead-end alleyways
and the walls of your room
seemed about to collapse,
bringing with them a sky of garbage
and your father's leather strap.
And you sat up afraid you were dying
just as you had so many nights as a child.

Small bruises to the brain.
An accumulation
of years of being hit.

I will not forget that picture of you
hanging over the ropes, eyes closed,
completely wiped out.
Like a voice
lost in the racket of a subway train
roaring on under the tenements of Harlem.

Considerations

1. Is the "brief truth of poverty" really true? Why or why not? Did this fighter die for a Cadillac?
2. What fighter was beaten to death on national television by Emile Griffith? Could he have been the subject of this poem?

ROBERT FRANCIS

That Dark Other Mountain

My father could go down a mountain faster than I
Though I was first one up.
Legs braced or with quick steps he slid the gravel slopes
Where I picked cautious footholds.

Black, Iron, Eagle, Doublehead, Chocorua,
Wildcat and Carter Dome—
He beat me down them all. And that last other mountain
And that dark other mountain.

Considerations

1. How does Francis achieve the best possible metrical effect in lines 5 and 6?
2. Explain the significance of the title.

ROBERT PENN WARREN
He Was Formidable

He was formidable, he was, the little booger,
As he spat in his hands and picked up the Louisville Slugger,
And at that bat-crack
Around those bases he could sure ball the jack,
And if from the outfield the peg had beat him home,
He would slide in slick, like a knife in a nigger.
So we dreamed of an afternoon to come,
In the Series, the ninth-inning hush, in the Yankee Stadium,
Sun low, score tied, bases full, two out, and he'd waltz to the plate with
                                                             his grin—

But no, oh no, not now, not ever! for in
That umpireless rhubarb and steel-heeled hugger-mugger,
    He got spiked sliding home, got spiked between the boxcars.

Oh, his hair was brown-bright as a chestnut, sun-glinting and curly,
And that lip that smiled boy-sweet could go, of a sudden, man-surly,
And the way he was built
Made the girls in his grade stare in darkness, and finger the quilt.
Yes, he was the kind you know born to give many delight,
And entering on such life-labor early,
Would have moved, bemused, in that rhythm and rite,
Through blood-throbbing blackness and moon-gleam
                                    and pearly thigh-glimmer of night,
To the exquisite glut: *Woman Slays Self for Love,* as the tabloids would
                                                             tell—

But no, never now! Like a kid in his first brothel,
In that hot clasp and loveless hurly-burly,
    He spilled, as boys may, too soon, between the boxcars.

Or, he might have managed the best supermarket in town,
Bright with banners and chrome, where housewives push carts up and
                                                             down,
And morning and night
Walked the street with his credit A-rated and blood pressure right,
His boy a dentist in Nashville, his girl at State Normal;
Or a scientist flushed with *Time*-cover renown
For vaccine, or bomb, or smog removal;
Or a hero with phiz like hewn cedar, though young for the stars of a
                                                             general,
Descending the steps of his personal plane to view the home-town
                                                             unveiling.
But no, never now!—battle-cunning, the test tube, retailing,

All, all, in a helter-skeltering mishmash thrown
    To that clobber and grind, too soon, between the boxcars.

But what is success, or failure, at the last?
The newspaper whirled down the track when the through freight has
                                    passed
Will sink from that gust
To be of such value as it intrinsically must,
And why should we grieve for the name that boy might have made
To be printed on newsprint like that, for that blast
To whirl with the wheels' fanfaronade,
When we cannot even remember his name, nor humbly have prayed
That when that blunt grossness, slam-banging, bang-slamming, blots black
                            the last blue flash of sky,
And our own lips utter the crazed organism's cry,
We may know the poor self not alone, but with all who are cast
    To that clobber, and slobber, and scream, between the boxcars?

Considerations

1. The boy in this poem was killed before he had a chance to prove himself. Aside from baseball, in what other fields could he possibly have excelled?
2. What important question is asked toward the end of the poem? Is it satisfactorily answered?
3. Is there a hint of sarcasm in the description of the possible fields the boy may have entered had he lived? Explain.

EZRA POUND

For E. McC.

THAT WAS MY COUNTER-BLADE UNDER
LEONARDO TERRONE, MASTER OF FENCE

Gone while your tastes were keen to you,
Gone where the grey winds call to you,
By that high fencer, even Death,
Struck of the blade that no man parrieth;
Such is your fence, one saith,
    One that hath known you.
Drew you your sword most gallantly
Made you your pass most valiantly
    'Gainst that grey fencer, even Death.

Gone as a gust of breath
Faith! no man tarrieth,
'Se il cor ti manca,' but it failed thee not!
'Non ti fidar,' it is the sword that speaks
'In me.'[1]
Thou trusted'st in thyself and met the blade
'Thout mask or gauntlet, and art laid
As memorable broken blades that he
Kept as bold trophies of old pageantry.

As old Toledos past their days of war
Are kept mnemonic of the strokes they bore,
So art thou with us, being good to keep
In our heart's sword-rack, though thy sword-arm sleep.

ENVOI

Struck of the blade that no man parrieth,
Pierced of the point that toucheth lastly all,
'Gainst that grey fencer, even Death,
Behold the shield; He shall not take thee all.

Considerations

1. Pound uses an extended metaphor in this eulogy. What is "the blade that no man parrieth"?
2. Define: (a) gauntlet; (b) old Toledos; (c) mnemonic; and (d) ENVOI

WILLIAM CARLOS WILLIAMS

The Yachts

contend in a sea which the land partly encloses
shielding them from the too-heavy blows
of an ungoverned ocean which when it chooses

tortures the biggest hulls, the best man knows
to pit against its beatings, and sinks them pitilessly.
Mothlike in mists, scintillant in the minute

brilliance of cloudless days, with broad bellying sails
they glide to the wind tossing green water
from their sharp prows while over them the crew crawls

---

[1] 'Se il cor ti manca, non ti fidar in me.' 'If thy heart fail thee, trust not in me.' (Sword-rune)

ant-like, solicitously grooming them, releasing,
making fast as they turn, lean far over and having
caught the wind again, side by side, head for the mark.

In a well guarded arena of open water surrounded by
lesser and greater craft which, sycophant, lumbering
and flittering follow them, they appear youthful, rare

as the light of a happy eye, live with the grace
of all that in the mind is fleckless, free and
naturally to be desired. Now the sea which holds them

is moody, lapping their glossy sides, as if feeling
for some slightest flaw but fails completely.
Today no race. Then the wind comes again. The yachts

move, jockeying for a start, the signal is set and they
are off. Now the waves strike at them but they are too
well made, they slip through, though they take in canvas.

Arms with hands grasping seek to clutch at the prows.
Bodies thrown recklessly in the way are cut aside.
It is a sea of faces about them in agony, in despair

until the horror of the race dawns staggering the mind,
the whole sea become an entanglement of watery bodies
lost to the world bearing what they cannot hold. Broken,

beaten, desolate, reaching from the dead to be taken up
they cry out, failing, failing! their cries rising
in waves still as the skillful yachts pass over.

Considerations

1. How is the horrible fate of the yachtsmen foreshadowed in the first stanza?
2. How does Williams use counterpoint to heighten the horror of sudden death?

A. E. HOUSMAN

Twice a week
the winter thorough

Twice a week the winter thorough
   Here I stood to keep the goal:
Football then was fighting sorrow
   For the young man's soul.

Now in Maytime to the wicket
    Out I march with bat and pad:
See the son of grief at cricket
    Trying to be glad.

Try I will; no harm in trying:
    Wonder 'tis how little mirth
Keeps the bones of man from lying
    On the bed of earth.

Considerations

1. In this poem football and cricket are used as therapy to allay the grief for a dead lover. Is this a hopeful poem? Compare it with "Is my team ploughing." How are these poems alike? How are they different?
2. Discuss the possible meanings of the last three lines. Do they imply that it is the sports that keep the speaker from committing suicide? Or is the meaning more general than that? Explain.

A. E. HOUSMAN

To an Athlete Dying Young

The time you won your town the race
We chaired you through the market-place;
Man and boy stood cheering by,
And home we brought you shoulder-high.

Today, the road all runners come,
Shoulder-high we bring you home,
And set you at your threshold down,
Townsman of a stiller town.

Smart lad, to slip betimes away
From fields where glory does not stay
And early though the laurel grows
It withers quicker than the rose.

Eyes the shady night has shut
Cannot see the record cut,
And silence sounds no worse than cheers
After earth has stopped the ears;

Now you will not swell the rout
Of lads that wore their honour out,
Runners whom renown outran
And the name died before the man.

So set, before its echoes fade,
The fleet foot on the sill of shade,
And hold to the low lintel up
The still defended challenge-cup.

And round that early-laurelled head
Will flock to gaze the strengthless dead
And find unwithered on its curls
The garland briefer than a girl's.

Considerations

1. Exactly what does the fifth stanza say about the making of sports heroes? Why is an early death important in this hero-making process?
2. Can you think of athletes who died at the height of their glory? Also, those "whom renown outran / And the name died before the man"?

A. E. HOUSMAN

Is my team ploughing

"Is my team ploughing,
    That I was used to drive
And hear the harness jingle
    When I was man alive?"

Aye, the horses trample,
    The harness jingles now;
No change though you lie under
    The land you used to plough.

"Is football playing
    Along the river shore,
With lads to chase the leather,
    Now I stand up no more?"

Aye, the ball is flying,
    The lads play heart and soul;
The goal stands up, the keeper
    Stands up to keep the goal.

"Is my girl happy,
　　That I thought hard to leave,
And has she tired of weeping
　　As she lies down at eve?"

Aye, she lies down lightly,
　　She lies not down to weep:
Your girl is well contented.
　　Be still, my lad, and sleep.

"Is my friend hearty,
　　Now I am thin and pine;
And has he found to sleep in
　　A better bed than mine?"

Yes, lad, I lie easy,
　　I lie as lads would choose;
I cheer a dead man's sweetheart,
　　Never ask me whose.

Considerations

1. Is this a religious poem? Why or why not?
2. Why must we "suspend disbelief" for this poem to work? What is the nature of the dialogue?
3. What does the poem imply about the significance of life and death? Would you call it an optimistic poem? Why or why not?
4. Is it a romantic poem? What does it say about the nature of love? Of friendship?

LOUISE GLÜCK

The Racer's Widow

The elements have merged into solicitude.
Spasms of violets rise above the mud
And weed, and soon the birds and ancients
Will be starting to arrive, bereaving points
South. But never mind. It is not painful to discuss
His death. I have been primed for this—
For separation—for so long. But still his face assaults
Me; I can hear that car careen again, the crowd coagulate on asphalt
In my sleep. And watching him, I feel my legs like snow
That let him finally let him go
As he lies draining there. And see
How even he did not get to keep that lovely body.

Considerations

1. Why should the racer's widow be especially reminiscent of his death at this particular time of year?
2. Explain her choice of "draining" instead of "bleeding." Also, explain the use of "coagulate." What ironic meaning does it have?

PHILIP BOOTH

Elegy for a Diver

Hawk free of jess,
the diver springs
toward fire no son can bear,
arcs instantly,
and forms his highdive fall
against the incandescent air
still stressed with his lost wings.

His nerve-ends guess
grave distances
of space, but his sunstruck
timing fails:
he overreaches, swans,
and bellyflops in luck
gone bad in all grave instances.

New Aegeans press
their welcome over him:
his deepening flight
downs him
in green spectra where the sun
is drowned; phosphorescence lights
the treasurer of his oceanic whim,

but in a wilderness
of eelgrass, kelp
and shell, his breath is spent
imagining
that lanternfish are stars.
Unfounded in this third element,
he fathoms down beyond all help

while every Daedalus
schemes on to soar.
Where discovery is to drown
he sounds
the whaling sea—this son
with sculpin, coin, and bone,
become the dark he must explore.

Considerations

1. This is a poem based on the famous Greek myth of Daedalus and Icarus, which may be found in any dictionary of Greek mythology. What is the "fire no son can bear"? Explain the pun on the word, "son."
2. Define: (a) jess; and (b) sculpin.

ADRIENNE RICH

Phantasia for
Elvira Shatayev [1]

The cold felt cold until our blood
grew colder   then the wind
died down and we slept

If in this sleep I speak
it's with a voice no longer personal
(I want to say   *with voices*)
When the wind tore   our breath from us at last
we had no need of words
For months   for years   each one of us
had felt her own *yes*   growing in her
slowly forming   as she stood at windows   waited
for trains   mended her rucksack   combed her hair
What we were to learn   was simply   what we had
up here   as out of all words   that *yes*   gathered
its forces   fused itself   and only just in time
to meet a *No* of no degrees
the black hole   sucking the world in

[1] Leader of a women's climbing team, all of whom died in a storm on Lenin Peak, August 1974. Later, Shatayev's husband found and buried the bodies.

I feel you climbing toward me
your cleated bootsoles leaving   their geometric bite
colossally embossed   on microscopic crystals
as when I trailed you in the Caucasus
Now I am further
ahead   than either of us dreamed   anyone would be
I have become
the white snow packed like asphalt by the wind
the women I love   lightly flung   against the mountain
that blue sky
our frozen eyes unribboned   through the storm
we could have stitched that blueness   together   like a quilt

You come (I know this)   with your love   your loss
strapped to your body   with your tape-recorder   camera
ice-pick   against advisement
to give us burial in the snow   and in your mind
While my body lies out here
flashing like a prism   into your eyes
how could you sleep   You climbed here for yourself
we climbed for ourselves

When you have buried us   told your story
ours does not end   we stream
into the unfinished   the unbegun
the possible
Every cell's core of heat   pulsed out of us
into the thin air   of the universe
the armature of rock beneath these snows
this mountain   which has taken   the imprint of our minds
through changes elemental and minute
as those we underwent
to bring each other here
choosing ourselves   each other   and this life
whose every breath   and grasp   and further foothold
is somewhere   still enacted   and continuing

In the diary I wrote: *Now we are ready*
and each of us knows it   I have never loved
like this   I have never seen
my own forces so taken up and shared
and given back
After the long training   the early sieges
we are moving almost effortlessly in our love

In the diary as the wind   began to tear
at the tents over us   I wrote:
We know now we have always been in danger
down in our separateness
and now up here together   but till now
we had not touched our strength

In the diary torn from my fingers I had written:
What does love mean
what does it mean   "to survive"
A cable of blue fire ropes our bodies
burning together in the snow   We will not live
to settle for less   We have dreamed of this
all of our lives

Considerations

1. A "phantasia" is a mirage or illusion. It could possibly be brought on by snow blindness. What does it mean in this poem?
2. How important is the footnote? Is it important to know that this poem is based on an actual incident? Why or why not?
3. Erica Jong has said that Adrienne Rich's poetry deals with "the problems of women in a patriarchal society." Another admirer, author Wendy Martin, calls her "mid-wife to a new age," and quotes her as saying, "Any woman's death diminishes me." Discuss this poem with these statements in mind.
4. In light of Rich's position as voice of a new "community of women," discuss the various suggestions of the final three lines.

DAVE SMITH

The Roundhouse Voices

In full glare of sunlight I came here, man-tall but thin
as a pinstripe, and stood outside the rusted fence
with its crown of iron thorns while
the soot cut into their lungs with tiny diamonds.
I walked through houses with my grain-lovely slugger
from Louisville that my uncle bought, and stood
in the sun which made its glove soft on my hand
until I saw my chance to crawl under and get past
anyone who would demand a badge and a name.

The guard hollered that I could get the hell from
    there quick
when I popped in his face like a thief. All I ever wanted
to steal was life and you can't get that easy
in the grind of a railyard. *You can't catch me,*
lard-ass, I can go left or right good as the Mick
I hummed to him, holding my slugger by the neck
for a bunt laid smooth where the coal cars
jerked and let me pass between tracks
until, in a slide on ash, I fell safe and heard
the wheeze of his words: *Who the hell are you, kid?*

I hear them again tonight, Uncle, hard as big brakeshoes,
when I lean over your face in the box of silk. The years
you spent hobbling from room to room alone crawl
up my legs and turn this house to another
house, round and black as defeat, where slugging
comes easy when you whip the gray softball over
the glass diesel globe. Footsteps thump on the stairs
like that fat ball against bricks and, when I miss,
I hear you warn me to watch the timing, to keep
my eyes on your hand and forget the fence,

hearing also that other voice that keeps me out and away
from you on a day worth playing good ball. Hearing
Who the hell . . . I see myself, like a burning speck
of cinder, come down the hill and through a tunnel
of porches like stands, running on deep ash,
and I give him the finger, whose face still gleams
clear as a B & O headlight, just to make him get up
and chase me into a dream of scoring at your feet.
At Christmas that guard staggered home sobbing,
the thing in his chest tight as a torque-wrench.
In the summer I did not have to run and now

who is the one who dreams of a drink as he leans over
tools you kept bright as a first girl's promise? I
have no one to run from or to, nobody to give
my finger to as I steal his peace. Uncle, the light
bleeds on your gray face like the high barbed-wire
shadows I had to get through and maybe you don't
    remember
you said to come back, to wait and you'd show me
the right way to take a hard pitch
in the sun that shudders on the ready man. I'm here

though this is a day I did not want to see. In the
    roundhouse
the rasp and heel-click of compressors is still,
soot lies deep in every greasy fingerprint.
I called you from the pits and you did not come up
and I felt the fear when I stood on the tracks
that are like a star which never makes it
into any kind of light and I don't know who'll
tell me now when the guard sticks his blind snoot
between us to take off and beat the bastard out.
Can you hear him over the yard, grabbing his chest,
cry out *Who the goddam hell are you, kid?*

I gave him every name in the book, Uncle, but he
    caught us,
and what good did all those hours of coaching do?
You lie on your back, eyeless forever, and I think
how once I climbed to the top of a diesel and stared
into that gray roundhouse glass where, in anger,
you threw up the ball and made a star
to swear at greater than the Mick ever dreamed.
It has been years but now I know what flowed there
every morning the sun came up, not light
but the puffing bad-bellied light of words.

All day I have held your hand, trying to say back
    that life,
to get under that fence with words I lined
and linked up and steamed into a cold room
where the illusion of hope means skin torn in boxes
of tools. The footsteps come pounding into words
and even the finger I give death is words
that won't let us be what we wanted, each one
chasing and being chased by dreams in a dark place.
Words are all we ever were and they did us
no damn good. Do you hear that?

Do you hear the words that, in oiled gravel, you
    gave me
when you set my feet in the right stance to swing?
They are coal-hard and they come in wings
and loops like despair not even the Mick
could knock out of this room, words softer
than the centers of hearts in guards or uncles,
words skinned and numbed by too many bricks.

I have had enough of them and bring them back here
where the tick and creak of everything dies
in your tiny starlight and I stand down
on my knees to cry *Who the hell are you, kid?*

Consideration

1. The difficulty of this poem does not lie with its subject: it is the recollections of a man at his uncle's funeral of how his uncle had helped him learn baseball in the rail yard. The difficulty lies rather in the stream of consciousness narration. The answers to the following questions may unravel the thread of the narrative:
   (a) Why did he break into the rail yard?
   (b) What is the thematic significance of the refrain, "Who the hell are you, kid"?
   (c) Does the guard hold any symbolic significance? If so, what?
   (d) What leads the reader to believe that the uncle could have been a star like, "the Mick"? Who is "the Mick"?
   (e) Why does the narrator say, "Words are all we ever were and they did us no damn good"? Is this like saying, "Talk's cheap"?
   (f) What is the mood of this poem? Does it convey a sense of victory or defeat? Explain.

DAVE SMITH

Blues for Benny Kid Paret

For years I've watched the corners for signs.
A hook, a jab, a feint, the peekaboo prayer of forearms,
anything for the opening, the rematch I go on dreaming.
What moves can say your life is saved?

As I backpedaled in a field the wasp's nest waited,
playing another game: a child is peeping out of
my eyes now, confused by the madness of stinging,
wave after wave rising as I tell my fists punish me,
counter the pain. I take my own beating and God help

me it hurts. Everything hurts, every punch
jolts, rips my ears, my cheeks, my temples. Who hurts
a man faster than himself? There was a wall to bounce
on, better than ropes. I was eleven years old.

Eleven years age I saw the fog
turn away and rise from the welts you were
to run away with its cousin the moon. They smacked

your chest and crossed your arms because you fell down
while the aisles filled with gorgeous women, high heels
pounding like Emile, the Champion, who planted his
good two feet and stuck, stuck, stuck, stuck
until your brain tied up your tongue and sighed.

> Somebody please, please I cried
> make them go away, but the ball in my hand had turned
> feverish with its crackling light. I could not let go
> as I broke against the wall. I was eleven years old.

Benny Paret, this night in a car ferrying
my load of darkness like a ring no one escapes,
I am bobbing and weaving in fog split only by a radio
whose harsh gargle is eleven years old, a voice in the air

telling the night you are down, counting time,
and I hear other voices from corners with bad moves say
Get up, you son of a bitch, get up! But you will not
get up again in my life where the only sign you give me

is a moon I remember sailing down on your heart
and blood growing wings to fly up in your eyes.
And there, there the punches no one feels grow weak,
as the wall looms, break through the best prayer you had
to dump you dizzied and dreaming in the green grass.

Considerations

1. On the night of March 24, 1962, at Madison Square Garden, Bennie Paret was beaten to death on national television by Emile Griffith. Officially, he wasn't pronounced dead until ten days later, but novelist Norman Mailer, who was at ringside, says, in *The Presidential Papers,* that "he died on his feet . . . with some little half-smile of regret, as if he were saying, 'I didn't know I was going to die just yet. . . .'" In this poem by Dave Smith, the narrator is listening to the fight on the radio and the terrible punishment Paret is receiving reminds him of a painful incident with a swarm of bees when he was eleven. Explain how the first four lines serve to define the analogy of the entire poem.
2. Smith uses "fog" three times in this poem. Does it mean the same thing each time? Why or why not?

APPENDIXES

SUGGESTED WRITING TOPICS

The following topics are recommended for papers of 400-1,000 words.

1. Jonathan E. as a Threat to Corporate Power in Harrison's "Roller Ball Murder"
2. Public and Private Morals in Lardner's "A Caddy's Diary"
3. Wodehouse's View of Women in "The Clicking of Cuthbert"
4. Harrison's Attitude Toward Competition in Sports in "Nirvana, Götterdämmerung and the Shot Put"
5. A Comparison of Harrison's "Roller Ball Murder" and Greenberg's "Wild in the Stands"
6. Factors Leading to Roller Ball as a Popular Sport in Harrison's "Roller Ball Murder"
7. The Nature of Morality in Connell's "The Most Dangerous Game"
8. Sillitoe's "The Loneliness of the Long-Distance Runner" as an Indictment of Western Society
9. Midge, in Lardner's "Champion," as an Example of a Media-Made Hero
10. The Effect of Violent Sports on the Viewer in Sillitoe's "The Match"
11. Damon Runyon's Romantic View of His Material in "Undertaker Song" and "Bred for Battle"
12. The Principles of Murphy's "Golf's Hidden But Accessible Meaning" Exemplified in Lardner's "A Caddy's Diary" and Wodehouse's "The Clicking of Cuthbert"
13. The Political Philosophy of Smith in Sillitoe's "The Loneliness of the Long-Distance Runner"
14. Lardner's Attitude Toward Women in "Champion" and "A Caddy's Diary"
15. Meaning in the Absurdity in Barthelme's "The Wound"
16. Characteristics of Naturalism in London's "A Piece of Steak" and Crane's "Lynx-Hunting"
17. A Comparison of Thurber's "You Could Look It Up" and Bill Veeck's Real-Life Counterpart
18. Housman's "To an Athlete Dying Young" and the Aging-Athlete Syndrome
19. A Contrast of John R. Tunis ("The Great Sports Myth") and Max Rafferty ("Interscholastic Athletics: The Gathering Storm") as Sports Analysts
20. Athletics as Seen from the Perspective of Children in Gildner's "First Practice" and King's "Getting 'em Ready for Darrell"
21. Similarity of Theme in "Nirvana, Götterdämmerung and the Shot Put," "Golf's Hidden But Accessible Meaning," Updike's "Tao in the Yankee Stadium Bleachers," and Leonard's "The Dance Within the Game"
22. The Importance of Mood in Connell's "The Most Dangerous Game"
23. The Nature of Love in Renault's "The Athenian Runner"
24. Tom King, in London's "A Piece of Steak," as Prototype (Model) for Butler in Hemingway's "My Old Man"
25. Max Rafferty's "Interscholastic Athletics: The Gathering Storm"—Ten Years Later
26. Possible Solutions to the Problem of Spectator Violence as Seen in "Wild in the Stands" by Peter Greenberg
27. The Motif of Fragrances in McMurtry's "It's Always We Rambled: An Essay on Rodeo"

28. Contrast of Views on Women Athletes in Weiss' "Women Athletes" and Boslooper and Hayes' "The Feminine Physique"
29. The Eastern Attitude Toward Sports as Seen in Leonard's "The Dance Within the Game"
30. The Accuracy of E. B. White's Predictions in "The Decline of Sport"
31. Contrast of Tone in Stallworthy's "First Blood" and Crane's "Lynx-Hunting"
32. The Father-Child Relationship in Selected Poems and Prose
33. The Love Analogy in Greek Sports Poems
34. A Comparison of Euripides' "The Greek Athlete" with Updike's "Golfers"
35. A Freudian Interpretation of Ovid's "Atalanta"
36. A Comparison and Contrast of Wordsworth's "The Skaters," Olson's "Ice-Skaters," and Williams' "The Skaters"
37. The Ecstasy of Athletic Participation in the Sports Poems of Robert Wallace
38. A Contrast of Tone in Bryant's "The Hunter of the Prairies," Howes' "Landscape, Deer Season" and "In Autumn," and Dexter's "Shadow Dirge"
39. A Comparison and Contrast of the Poetry of James Dickey and Dave Smith
40. A Comparison and Contrast of Stoutenburg's "Sky Diver," Lattimore's "Sky Diving," and Anderson's "The Parachutist"
41. Contrast of Tone and Imagery in Dickey's "In the Pocket" and Abbe's "The Passer"
42. Contrast of Tone in Barney's "Caught in the Pocket" and Dickey's "In the Pocket"
43. The Dream as Controlling Element in Lieberman's "My Father Dreams of Baseball" and Patchen's "The Origin of Baseball"
44. Wrestling as a Sport in Johnson's "Ripper Collins' Legacy," Francis' "Two Wrestlers," and Barney's "The Rasslers"
45. The Significance of Illusion in Ciardi's "Polo Match" and Warren's "The Skiers"
46. Views of Spectators in Williams' "At the Ball Game," Ciardi's "Polo Match," Barney's "The Rasslers," and Byron's "The Bull Fight"
47. A Feminine Spectator's View of Sports in Swenson's "Watching the Jets Lose to Buffalo at Shea" and "Bronco-Busting, Event #1"
48. A Comparison of the Poetry of Tom Clark and Barthelme's "The Wound"
49. A Comparison and Contrast of Eberhart's "Ball Game" and Francis' "The Base Stealer"
50. The Bullring as Metaphor in Swenson's "Death Invited" and Noll's "The Picador Bit"
51. Football as Extended Metaphor in Smith's "Running Back"
52. Smith's Use of Memory in "Roundhouse Voices" and "Blues for Benny Kid Paret"
53. The Poets' Attitudes Toward Their Subjects in Frost's "The Rabbit-Hunter," Dexter's "Shadow Dirge," and Cunningham's "The Chase"
54. The Idea of Chain of Being in Gibson's "Billiards"
55. A Glossary of Names for Moore's "Baseball and Writing," Petersen's "Ballad of Dead Yankees," Humphries' "Polo Grounds," and Bracker's "Where, O Where?"
56. The View of Golfers in Arkell's "A Public Nuisance" and Updike's "Golfers"
57. The Revenge Motif in Dickey's "For the Last Wolverine" and Ford's "Revenge of the Hunted"
58. Analogy in the Sports Poems of Robert Francis
59. The Correlation of Football, Art, and War in Wright's "A Mad Fight Song for William S. Carpenter, 1966"

60. The Idea of the Loser in Sports as a Subject of Derision
61. The Extinction Motif in Dickey's "Looking for the Buckhead Boys"
62. Updike's "Ex-Basketball Player" as Extension of Housman's "To An Athlete Dying Young"
63. A Freudian Interpretation of Fox's "The Bumper Sticker on His Pickup Said, 'I'm a Lover, I'm a Fighter, I'm a Wild Bull Rider'"
64. A Comparison of Virgil's "Entellus" with Muhammad Ali
65. The Differing Views of Hope for the Aging Athlete in Petrie's "The Old Pro's Lament," Dunn's "Day and Night Handball," Lattimore's "Game Resumed," and Weiss' "The Aging Athlete"
66. The Contrast of Moods in Barney's "Nearly Everybody Loves Harvey Martin" and Jarrell's "Say Goodbye to Big Daddy"
67. Variance of Tone within Dickey's "For the Death of Vince Lombardi"
68. A Comparison and Contrast of Housman's "To an Athlete Dying Young" and Warren's "He Was Formidable"
69. Housman's Views of Life and Love in "Is my team ploughing" and "Twice a week the winter thorough"
70. A Contrast of Perspectives in Gildner's "First Practice" with Smith's "Running Back"
71. A Modern Conservationist's View of Bryant's "The Hunter of the Prairies"
72. A Freudian Interpretation of Kumin's "Morning Swim"
73. Updike's "Superman"—A Reaction Against Hyperbolized Advertising
74. The Greek View of Athletes and Athletics in Selected Greek Poems
75. A Comparison and Contrast of Fox's "The Bumper Sticker on His Pickup Said, 'I'm a Lover, I'm a Fighter, I'm a Wild Bull Rider'" and Swenson's "Bronco Busting, Event #1"

The following topics are recommended for longer papers, possibly requiring research from sources cited in the Selected Bibliography.

76. The Athlete as Archetypal Hero
77. The Aging-Athlete Syndrome as a Theme in Fiction and Poetry
78. The Tradition of Religious Ritual in Athletics
79. The Importance of Sports in the Literary Works of Hemingway, London, and Irwin Shaw
80. The Importance of Myth in Sports Literature, Past and Present
81. Organized Athletics as a Political Institution
82. The "Gee Whiz!" and the "Aw Nuts" Schools of Sportswriting and Broadcasting
83. The Importance of Religion, Politics, and Sex in Organized Sports
84. Violent Sports—Healthy Outlet, or Dangerous Example?
85. The Prejudice Against Women Athletes among Male Sportswriters
86. The Longstanding Bias Against Handicapped Athletes in the Media
87. The Attitude of Organized Sports Promoters Toward Female Sportswriters
88. Thorstein Veblen's Views on Athletics in *Theory of the Leisure Class* and Its Modern Applications
89. The Importance of Illusion in Spectator Sports
90. The Influence of Jack London on American Sportswriting
91. Ernest Hemingway as a Sportswriter
92. Organized Sports—Government's Opiate for the People?

93. Organized Athletics as the Modern Equivalent of the Roman Circuses
94. The Mythologizing of Sports and Athletes
95. Women Athletes in Literature
96. The Religious (Mystical) Element in the Sports Poetry of James Dickey
97. Muhammed Ali—A Latter-Day Jack Johnson
98. A Collection of the Views in Poetry and Prose of the Death of Benny Paret
99. Why Bullfighting is Illegal in the United States
100. The Origin of Sports—In Religious Ritual or in Training for War?

GLOSSARY OF TERMS

Allegory A story in which abstract ideas of accepted truths (beauty, evil, honor) are represented by human beings or animals. Allegory may also be called extended metaphor or analogy.

Alliteration The repetition of the same sounds in the beginnings of words ("purple-plumed priest").

Allusion Reference to literary or historical persons, places, things, incidents, or other entities to promote clarity.

Ambiguity Multiple meaning used to enhance a literary work.

Anachronism A chronological error in literature, such as Shakespeare's reference to Aristotle in "Troilus and Cressida." Also anachronism can now refer to anyone or anything which has outlived its time.

Analogy An extended comparison of the similar properties of two otherwise different things.

Anticlimax A continuation of events after the major climax in order to relieve tension or introduce new complications.

Archetype A basic model for human ambition, fears, or values.

Ballad A simple narrative poem, usually springing from the folk culture and closely associated with music: "ball," "ballet."

Bathos Trite, insincere, or commonplace emotion, sometimes called sentimentality and used in an attempt to evoke an emotional response from a reader when no such response is warranted.

Blank verse Unrhymed iambic pentameter in poetry.

Characterization The process of giving life-like traits to persons in a literary work.

Cliché A wornout phrase, such as "hard as nails," "higher than a kite."

Conflict The discordant elements at the center of the plot.

Connotation A word's meaning suggested either by context or usage that goes beyond its manifest, or apparent, meaning.

Dactyl A metrical foot consisting of one accented syllable followed by two unaccented ones, used by Homer in *The Illiad* and *The Odyssey*.

Denotation The manifest, or literal, meaning of a word, the "dictionary definition."

Dialogue Conversation in literature between two or more persons.

Diction Choice of words in a literary work.

Doggerel Mediocre rhymed verse.

Double entendre Double meaning, usually risqué.

Dramatic irony Allowing the reader to know something important before the character is aware of it to promote tension.

Dramatic monologue A character addressing another character in an extended manner.

Elegy A poem written in tribute to the dead, named for a complex poetic form called elegiac meter.

Epic A long narrative poem written in lofty and elegant language about a character with larger-than-life qualities who represents the values and ambitions of a particular race or culture.

Episode A single event within a plot narrative.

Eulogy A formal and usually solemn expression of praise.

Euphemism A socially acceptable word for one not socially acceptable.

Euphony A pleasant and harmonious sound.

Figurative language The non-literal uses of words that promote insight through comparisons, understatements, or exaggerations. They attempt to reveal the abstract in terms of the concrete.

Flashback Reverting to a time past in a story.

Foreshadowing   A hint to the reader of an important event to come later in the story.

Free Verse   Verse that follows the natural rhythms of speech rather than a conventional metrical pattern.

Genre   A classification of literature, such as the essay, the short story, or poetry.

Haiku   A form of Japanese verse consisting of three lines of poetry with five, seven, and five syllables per line, seventeen syllables in all.

Homeric simile   A long comparison that parallels many similarities. Sometimes called epic simile.

Hyperbole   A figure of speech using exaggeration for special effect or irony or humor. Commonly called "hype" in advertising promotion.

Idiom   A common expression the literal meaning of which cannot be attained from its combination of words, i.e., "Cool it!"

Imagery   The re-creation of sensory experience by means of language.

Irony   A subtle switch of meanings in which the opposite occurs from what is intended.

Lament   A poem that expresses deep sorrow.

Literal meaning   The manifest, apparent meaning.

Local color   The highlighting in a story of the particular characteristics of a certain region.

Lyric poetry   Stanzaic poetry with a highly personal tone. Originally, lyric poetry comprised the choral ode and the monody.

Metaphor   A comparison of two things for the purpose of clarifying or universalizing: "He was a creeping sepulchre."

Metonymy   A figure of speech using a related idea for the thing itself: "The crown speaks for divine providence."

Metre   The rhythmic pattern within lines of poetry determined by stressed and unstressed syllables.

Minstrel   A wandering bard, or singer, who brought entertainment to isolated towns and villages in the Middle Ages.

The minstrel originated in Provence in Southern France and spread throughout Europe.

Mixed metaphor   A faulty figure of speech combining two valid (though often clichéd) metaphors into a single unmatched one: "The President is trying to keep the lid on it till he can get it all ironed out."

Monody   A highly personal lyric poem or song recited by a single poet.

Mood   The pervading atmosphere or tone of a literary work.

Motif   A pervading idea or theme that serves as the basis for literary work.

Muses   The nine Greek goddesses of literature and the arts.

Mysticism   The belief that universal or providential knowledge is attained through an unexplained human faculty that supersedes intellect.

Myth   A fanciful story which attempts, through symbols, to explain the unknowable, thereby giving meaning to life. Like a dream, it springs from the unconscious mind and is, in fact, "a public dream," says Joseph Campbell.

Narrative   The story related by a narrator.

Naturalism   The philosophy that things can be explained in terms of natural causes and laws without attributing moral, spiritual, or supernatural significance to them.

Ode   A lyric poem of complex stanzaic verse pattern with an exalted theme and elevated language.

Onomatopoeia   The poetic use of words whose sounds suggest their meanings: "bang," "hiss," "crackle."

Oxymoron   An ironic contradiction in which two words with opposite meanings used in combination suggest a startling meaning: "The fat man ate with a ferocious delicacy."

Paradox   A figure of speech involving an apparent contradiction which serves to suggest a new truth: "My life closed twice before its close."

Parody   An exaggerated imitation which seeks to ridicule.

Pathos   A quality in literature that evokes feeling in the reader.

Persona   The character through which an author tells a story.

Personification   A figure of speech in which human qualities are attributed to objects, animals, or abstractions: "The walls have ears."

Plot   The sequence of events within a story.

Point of view   The consciousness through which an author tells a story.

Portmanteau word   A word made by combining two words: "smog," from "smoke" and "fog."

Prosody   The analytical study of verse form and technique.

Pun   A playful interchange of sounds with two words to form an often absurd meaning: "I'd rather have a bottle in front of me than a frontal lobotomy."

Realism   An attempt in art to present things as they are rather than as they should be; accuracy of realistic details in literature.

Renaissance   The period between the Middle Ages and the modern era marked by a new reliance on humanism and an emphasis on the individual.

Rhyme   The similarity of sounds in corresponding position in lines of poetry.

Romanticism   A nineteenth-century reaction to formality in literature, which emphasizes individualism, nature, and freedom of the spirit.

Satire   A literary technique used to mock or ridicule in order to effect a change.

Sentimentality   The excessive reliance on emotion in literature.

Simile   A figure of speech comparing two different things by linking them with "like," "as," "than," or some other connective.

Sonnet   A lyric poem of fourteen lines with a definite pattern of rhyme.

Stanza   The basic division of lines in a poem unified by theme, rhythm, or rhyme.

Stream of consciousness   The often random thoughts of a character used by an author in an attempt to duplicate the interior monologue continually occurring in the mind.

Style   The unique characteristics that distinguish every author's work.

Surrealism   An imaginative technique using dreams, visions, hallucinations, and the like to depict the world in language unrestrained by "conscious reality."

Symbol   A specific or concrete sign, figure, or emblem that represents another abstract entity, in order to add connotative meaning.

Synecdoche   A figure of speech that uses a part of something to represent the whole: a "brain," for "brilliant person."

Theme   The pervading idea that serves as the basis for the other elements in a story.

Tone   The emotional atmosphere of a literary work.

Universality   The quality in literature that extends its appeal to all people in all places.

SELECTED BIBLIOGRAPHY

1. Algren, Nelson. *Never Come Morning*. New York: Harper & Row Perennial Library, 1965.
2. Ali, Muhammad, with Richard Durham. *The Greatest*. New York: Random House, 1975.
3. Allen, Woody. "A Fan's Notes on Earl Monroe," *Sport*, vol. 65, no. 5 (Nov. 1977), pp. 20–21+.
4. Anderson, Dave. "Ali's Radar Waves," *New York Times* (Jan. 11, 1976).
5. Andretti, Mario. *What's It Like Out There?* Chicago: Regnery, 1970.
6. Angell, Roger. "The Sporting Scene: Down the Drain," *New Yorker*, vol. 51, no. 18 (June 23, 1975), pp. 42–59.
7. _____. "Still Getting the Ink," *New York Times Book Review* (Oct. 13, 1974), pp. 6–8.
8. Arens, William. "Great American Football Ritual," *Natural History*, vol. 84, no. 8 (Oct. 1975), pp. 72–81.
9. Ashe, Arthur, with Frank DeFord. *Arthur Ashe: Portrait in Motion*. Boston: Houghton Mifflin, 1975.
10. Asinof, Eliot. *Seven Days to Sunday*. New York: Simon and Schuster, 1968.
11. Auguet, Roland. *Cruelty and Civilization: The Roman Games*. London: Allen and Unwin, 1972.
12. Avedon, Elliott, and Brian Sutton-Smith. *The Study of Games*. New York: Wiley, 1971.
13. Axthelm, Pete. *The City Game: Basketball in New York*. New York: Harper's Magazine Press, 1970.
14. Bannister, Roger. *The Four-Minute Mile*. New York: Dodd, Mead, 1955.
15. Barbieri, Ralph. "A Visit with Bill Walton . . . and from FBI," *Sport*, vol. 61, no. 2 (Aug. 1975), pp. 74–76+.
16. Baumbach, Jonathan. "Aesthetics of Basketball," *Esquire*, vol. 73 (Jan. 1970), pp. 140–146.
17. Bellow, Saul. *Dangling Man*. New York: New American Library Signet Books, 1965.
18. Belmonte, Juan. "The Making of a Bullfighter," *Atlantic*, vol. 159 (Feb. 1937), pp. 129–148.
19. Bent, Silas. *Ballyhoo: The Voice of the Press*. New York: Boni and Liverwright, 1927.
20. Bodo, Peter, and David Hirshey. *Pele's New World*. New York: Norton, 1977.
21. Bongartz, Roy. "The $100,000 Bowling Machine," *Sports Illustrated*, vol. 46, no. 11 (Mar. 7, 1977), pp. 66–76.
22. Bradley, Bill. *Life on the Run*. New York: Quadrangle/New York Times Book Co., 1976.
23. Butt, Dorcas Susan. *The Psychology of Sport*. New York: Van Nostrand Reinhold, 1976.
24. Cady, Edwin H. *The Big Game*. Knoxville: The University of Tennessee Press, 1978.
25. Campbell, Gail. *Marathon: The World of Long-Distance Athletes*. New York: Sterling, 1977.
26. Cohen, Marvin. "Baseball and Religion," *Dial*, vol. 67 (July 26, 1919), pp. 57–59.
27. _____. *Baseball the Beautiful*. New York: Link Books, 1974.
28. Colletto, Jerry, with Hack L. Sloan. *Yoga Conditioning and Football*. Millbrae, Calif.: Celestial Arts, 1975.
29. Columbo, Franco, and George Fels. *Winning Bodybuilding*. Chicago: Regnery, 1977.
30. Coover, Robert. *The Universal Baseball Association, Inc.: J. Henry Waugh, Prop*. New York: Random House, 1968.
31. Cratty, Bernard J. *Psychology in*

Contemporary Sport. Englewood Cliffs, N.J.: Prentice-Hall, 1973.

32. Crompton, Paul H. *Kung Fu: Theory and Practice.* Toronto: Pagurian Press, 1975.

33. Danzig, Allison. *The History of American Football.* Englewood Cliffs, N.J.: Prentice-Hall, 1956.

34. Davidson, Art. *Minus 148: The Winter Ascent of Mt. McKinley.* New York: Norton, 1969.

35. Denlinger, Kenneth, and Leonard Shapiro. *Athletes for Sale.* New York: Crowell and Co., 1975.

36. Diaz-Canabate, Antonio. *The Magic World of the Bullfighter.* London: Burke, 1956.

37. Doust, Dudley. "Opening the Mystical Door of Perception in Sport," *The Sunday Times* (Nov. 4, 1973).

38. Draeger, Donn F., and Robert W. Smith. *Asian Fighting Arts.* New York: Berkley, 1974 (1969).

39. Dulles, Foster R. *America Learns to Play.* New York: Dutton, 1940.

40. Dunning, Eric, ed. *Sport: Readings from a Sociological Perspective.* Toronto: University of Toronto Press, 1972.

41. Durso, Joseph. *The All American Dollar: The Big Business of Sports.* Boston: Houghton Mifflin, 1971.

42. Edwards, Harry. *Sociology of Sport.* Homewood, Ill.: Dorsey, 1973.

43. Exley, Frederick. *A Fan's Notes.* New York: Harper & Row, 1968.

44. Fairfax, John. *Britannia: Rowing Alone Across the Atlantic.* New York: Simon and Schuster, 1971.

45. Falls, Joe. *The Boston Marathon.* New York: Macmillan, 1977.

46. Faulkner, William. "The Bear," *Go Down, Moses.* New York: Modern Library, 1942.

47. Fessier, Michael, Jr. "Transcendental Running," *Human Behavior,* vol. 5, no. 7 (July 1976), pp. 17–20.

48. Fitzgerald, F. Scott. *The Great Gatsby.* New York: Charles Scribner's Sons, 1953.

49. Fixx, James. *The Complete Book of Running.* New York: Random House, 1977.

50. Flath, Arnold, ed. *Athletics in America.* Corvallis: Oregon State University Press, 1972.

51. Fluegelman, Andrew. *The New Games Book.* Garden City, N.Y.: Doubleday, 1976.

52. Frager, Robert, "Psychology of the Samurai," *Psychology Today,* vol. 2 (Jan. 1969), pp. 48–53+.

53. Gaines, Charles, and George Butler. *Pumping Iron.* New York: Simon and Schuster, 1974.

54. Gallwey, Timothy. *The Inner Game of Tennis.* New York: Random House, 1974.

55. Gallwey, Timothy and Bob Kriegel. *Inner Skiing.* New York: Random House, 1977.

56. Gardiner, E. Norman. *Greek Athletic Sports and Festivals.* London: Macmillan, 1910.

57. Gardner, Leonard. *Fat City.* New York: Dell Books, 1972.

58. Gaskins, G., and D. W. Masterson. "The Work of Art in Sport," vol. 1 (Sept. 1974), pp. 36–66.

59. Genasci, James E., and Vasillis Klissouras. "The Delphic Spirit in Sports," *Journal of Health, Physical Education, and Recreation,* vol. 37, no. 2 (Feb. 1966), pp. 43–45.

60. Gerber, Dan. "The Way It Feels: Sailfishing off Key West," *Outside,* vol. 1 (May 1978), pp. 53–54.

61. Gerber, Ellen W., ed. *Sport and the Body.* Philadelphia: Lea and Febiger, 1972.

62. Gilbey, John. *Secret Fighting Arts of the World.* Rutland: Tuttle, 1963.

63. Gluck, Jay. *Zen Combat.* New York: Ballantine Books, 1962.

64. Gordon, Caroline. *Aleck Maury, Sportsman.* New York: Charles Scribner's Sons, 1934.

65. Harris, Dorothy V. *Involvement in Sport.* Philadelphia: Lea and Febiger, 1973.

66. _____. "Sports Science: The Happy Addict," *Women Sports,* vol. 5, no. 1

(Jan. 1978), p. 53.

67. Harris, H. A. *Greek Athletes and Athletics*. Bloomington: Indiana University Press, 1966.

68. Hart, M. Marie, ed. *Sport in the Socio-Cultural Process*. Dubuque: Brown, 1972.

69. Heller, Peter. *"In This Corner."* New York: Simon and Schuster, 1973.

70. Hellison, Donald. *Humanistic Physical Education*. Englewood Cliffs, N.J.: Prentice-Hall, 1973.

71. Hemingway, Ernest. *Death in the Afternoon*. New York: Scribner's, 1932.

72. _____. *Islands in the Stream*. New York: Charles Scribner's Sons, 1970.

73. _____. *The Old Man and the Sea*. New York: Scribner Library, 1952.

74. _____. *The Short Stories of Ernest Hemingway*. Charles Scribner's Sons, 1953.

75. _____. *The Sun Also Rises*. New York: Charles Scribner's Sons, 1926.

76. Herrigel, Eugen. *Zen in the Art of Archery*. New York: Pantheon, 1953.

77. Hoch, Paul. *Rip Off the Big Game*. Garden City, N.Y.: Doubleday, 1972.

78. Huizinga, Johan. *Homo Ludens*. Boston: Beacon Press, 1950.

79. Irving, Washington. "The Legend of Sleepy Hollow," *The Sketch Book*. New York: Dodd, Mead & Co., 1954.

80. Isaacs, Neil D. "The Laurel and the Ivy," Chapter III of *Jock Culture USA*. New York: W. W. Norton, 1978.

81. Izenberg, Jerry. *How Many Miles to Camelot*. Garden City, N.Y.: Doubleday, 1977.

82. Jackson, Ian. *Yoga and the Athlete*. Mountain View, Calif.: World Publications, 1975.

83. Jackson, Marni. "Wheeling for Distance," *Outside*, vol. 1, no. 7 (Mar. 1978), pp. 49–54.

84. Jenkins, Dan. *Semi-Tough*. New York: Atheneum, 1972.

85. _____. *Saturday's America*. Boston: Little, Brown, 1970.

86. Johnson, William O. *Super Spectator and the Electric Lilliputians*. Boston: Little, Brown, 1971.

87. Jones, James. *From Here to Eternity*. New York: New American Library Signet Books, 1964.

88. Jones, Robert Tyre, Jr. *Golf Is My Game*. Garden City, N.Y.: Doubleday, 1960.

89. Kahn, Roger. *The Boys of Summer*. New York: Harper and Row, 1971.

90. Kerley, M. R. "Kitty O'Neil: A Deaf Stunt Woman Races the Speed of Sound," *Women Sports*, vol. 4, no. 4 (April 1977), pp. 17–19.

91. King, Billie Jean, with Kim Chapin. *Billie Jean*. New York: Harper and Row, 1974.

92. Knowles, John. *A Separate Peace*. New York: Bantam Books, 1966.

93. Lance, Kathryn. *Running for Health and Beauty*. Indianapolis: Bobbs-Merrill, 1977.

94. Lardner, Ring. "*Sport and Play*," in *Civilization in the United States*, ed. Harold Stearns. New York: Harcourt, 1922.

95. Larner, Jeremy. *Drive, He Said*. New York: Bantam Books, 1971.

96. Leonard, George. *The Silent Pulse: A Search for the Perfect Rhythm That Exists in Each of Us*. New York: Dutton, 1978.

97. _____. *The Ultimate Athlete*. New York: Viking, 1975.

98. Leuchs, Arne, and Patricia Skulka. *Ski with Yoga*. Matteson, Ill.: Greatlakes Living Press, 1976.

99. Lewis, Sinclair. *Babbitt*. New York: Harcourt, Brace & World, 1922.

100. Lipsyte, Robert. *Sportsworld*. New York: Quadrangle/New York Times Book Co., 1975.

101. Ludwig, Jack. *Games of Fear and Winning*. Garden City, N.Y.: Doubleday, 1976.

102. Malamud, Bernard. *The Natural*. New York: Dell Books, 1965.

103. Manry, Robert. *Tinkerbelle*. New York: Harper and Row, 1966.

104. Marquand, J. P. *H. M. Pulham, Esquire.* Boston: Little, Brown, 1941.

105. Michener, James A. *Sports in America.* New York: Random House, 1976.

106. Miller, David L. *Gods and Games: Toward a Theology of Play.* New York: World, 1970.

107. Minick, Michael. *The Wisdom of Kung Fu.* New York: Morrow, 1974.

108. Morley, David C. *The Missing Links: Golf and the Mind.* New York: Atheneum/SMI, 1976.

109. Morris, Wright. *The Huge Season.* New York: Viking Press, 1954.

110. Murphy, Michael. *Golf in the Kingdom.* New York: Viking, 1972.

111. Nemerov, Howard. *The Homecoming Game.* New York: Simon and Schuster, 1957.

112. Neugeboren, Jam. *Big Man.* Boston: Houghton Mifflin, 1966.

113. Nideffer, Robert M. *The Inner Athlete.* New York: Crowell, 1976.

114. Nieporte, Tom, and Don Sauers. *Mind Over Golf.* Garden City, N.Y.: Doubleday, 1968.

115. Nyad, Dianna. "Mind Over Water," *Esquire,* vol. 84, no. 4 (Oct. 1975), pp. 132–139.

116. Peterson, Robert. *Only the Ball Was White.* Englewood Cliffs, N.J.: Prentice-Hall, 1970.

117. Plimpton, George. *The Paper Lion.* New York: Harper and Row, 1966.

118. Powers, J. F. *Morte D'Urban.* Garden City, N.Y.: Doubleday, 1962.

119. Proxmire, William. *You Can Do It.* New York: Simon and Schuster, 1973.

120. Rice, Grantland. *The Tumult and the Shouting.* New York: A. S. Barnes, 1954.

121. Richard, Colette. *Climbing Blind.* New York: Dutton, 1967.

122. Roth, Philip. *Goodbye Columbus.* New York: Bantam Books, 1963.

123. Ruth, Babe, as told to Bob Considine. *The Babe Ruth Story.* New York: Dutton, 1948.

124. Santayana, George. *George Santayana's America: Essays on Literature and Culture,* ed. James Ballome. Urbana: University of Illinois Press, 1967.

125. Schaap, Dick. *The Perfect Jump.* New York: New American Library, 1976.

126. Schulberg, Budd. *The Harder They Fall.* New York: Random House, 1947.

127. Schwarzenegger, Arnold, and Douglas Kent Hall. *Arnold: The Education of a Bodybuilder.* New York: Simon and Schuster, 1977.

128. Scott, Jack. *The Athletic Revolution.* New York: Free Press, 1971.

129. Shaw, Gary. *Meat on the Hoof.* New York: St. Martin's, 1972.

130. Sheed, Wilfrid. *Muhammad Ali.* New York: Thomas Y. Crowell, 1975.

131. Sheehan, George. *Running and Being: The Total Experience.* New York: Simon and Schuster, 1978.

132. Silverman, Al, ed. *The Best of Sport 1946–71.* New York: Viking, 1971.

133. Singer, Robert R. *Myths and Truths in Sports Psychology.* New York: Harper and Row, 1975.

134. Slocum, Joshua. *Sailing Alone Around the World.* New York: Sheridan House, 1963.

135. Slovenko, Ralph, and James Knight, eds. *Motivation in Play, Games and Sports.* Springfield, Ill.: Charles C. Thomas, 1967.

136. Slusher, Howard. *Man, Sport and Existence.* Philadelphia: Lea and Febiger, 1967.

137. Summers, Montague. *The Physical Phenomena of Mysticism.* New York: Barnes and Noble, 1950.

138. Tarshis, Barry. *Tennis and the Mind.* New York: Atheneum, 1977.

139. Telander, Rick. *Joe Namath and the Other Guys.* New York: Holt, Rinehart and Winston, 1976.

140. Thomas, Vaughn. *Science and Sport.* Boston: Little, Brown, 1979.

141. Updike, John. *Rabbit Redux.* New

York: Alfred A. Knopf, 1971.

142. _____. *Rabbit, Run.* New York: Crest Books, 1962.

143. Vanderzwang, H. J. *Toward a Philosophy of Sport.* Reading, Mass.: Addison-Wesley, 1972.

144. Vanek, M., and B. Cratty. *Psychology and the Superior Athlete.* New York: Macmillan, 1970.

145. Veblen, Thorstein. *The Theory of the Leisure Class.* New York: 1899.

146. Weiss, Paul. *Sport: A Philosophic Inquiry.* Carbondale: Southern Illinois University Press, 1969.

147. Whiting, H. T. A. *Readings in Sports Psychology.* London: Kimpton, 1972.

148. Williams, Ted, and John Underwood. *My Turn at Bat.* New York: Simon and Schuster, 1969.

149. Willis, William. *Whom the Sea Has Taken.* New York: Meredith, 1967.

150. Wind, Herbert Warren, ed. *The Gilded Age of Sport.* New York: Simon and Schuster, 1961.

151. _____. *The Realm of Sport.* New York: Simon and Schuster, 1966.

152. Wolf, David. *Foul! The Connie Hawkins Story.* New York: Holt, Rinehart and Winston, 1972.

153. Wolters, Richard A. *The Art and Technique of Soaring.* New York: McGraw-Hill, 1971.

154. Worsley, F. A. *Shackkton's Boat Journey.* New York: Norton, 1977.

155. Zimmerman, Paul. *A Thinking Man's Guide to Pro Football.* New York: Dutton, 1970.

INDEX OF AUTHORS AND TITLES

INDEX OF FIRST LINES

547